The wick
not agair

The Gospel
of Matthew

The Gospel of Matthew

A Homiletical Commentary

by
David Thomas

KREGEL PUBLICATIONS
Grand Rapids, MI 49501

Gospel of Matthew by David Thomas.
Published 1979 by Kregel Publications,
a division of Kregel, Inc. All rights reserved.

Library of Congress Cataloging in Publication Data

Thomas, David, 1813-1894.
    Gospel of Matthew.
    (Kregel Bible Study Classics)

    Reprint of the 1873 ed. published byDickinson &
Higham, London, under title: *The
Genius of the Gospel,* a homiletical commentary
on the Gospel of Matthew.
    1. Bible. N.T. Matthew—Commentaries. I. Title.
GS2575.T5   1979   226'.2'07   78-11502
ISBN 0-8254-3812-8

Printed in the United States of America

Contents

vi / Contents

Preface

ALTHOUGH several thousand copies of this work have already been sold, most urgent demands have for some time been made for another edition. In yielding to the general request, the author has neither felt the necessity nor possessed the time for making any alterations; this edition, therefore, being identical with the last, the original preface is reproduced :—

"Able expositions of the Gospel, describing the manners, customs, and localities alluded to by the inspired writers, also interpreting their words and harmonizing their formal discrepancies, are happily not wanting amongst us; and many valuable additions, ripe in scholarship, far-reaching in thought, have recently been made to this affluent stock of sacred literature. But works on the Gospels, aiming to bring out their widest truths and highest suggestions for ethical and homiletical purposes, are confessedly few and much required, to enable the pulpit to meet the demands of an age, not only of rationalistic speculation, but of theological dogmatism and religious routine. My work has had this aim throughout, though polemics have been carefully eschewed, and the names of assailants are seldom mentioned, nor have their views been controversially stated. My belief is, that the best method for chasing away the clouds of scepticism that hang over the Book of God is, not to employ our powers in describing and denouncing them, but to bring forth, by an honest interpretation and philosophic analysis, the Divine beams of light that lie in the sacred text. It is not our little logic or learning, but God's own light, that must sweep the soul's firmament of its clouds of erroneous thought.

This work is made up, for the most part, of the substance of discourses first spoken from the pulpit and afterwards published in the "Homilist" from month to month, extending over a period of well-nigh fourteen years. This will account for, and I hope justify, the popular mould in which they are cast—their freedom from philological criticism, and the degrees of merit by which they

ix

are distinguished.   They are full or sketchy, discursive or condensed, according to the time at my disposal when I wrote—elaborate or analystic, vivacious or otherwise, according to my mood at the hour in which the thoughts took their rise, shaped their form, and gave their expression.

To have given the work a greater show of learning by a free use of Greek type, verbal criticisms, quotations from the Fathers, and references to the rare thinkers of olden times and the ripest scholars of my own age, would have been easy ; but this, whilst it might have given the glitter of scholarship to my efforts, would, at the same time, have added to the work, already too bulky, a weight to sink it into the ever-widening grave of verbose productions.

The assurance of the distinguished scholar who kindly undertook the editorship of this work, and under whose critical eye the whole edition has passed, that my interpretations of the sacred texts are justified by the best hermeneutical authorities, relieves, to some extent, the trembling hesitancy with which I allow a work to go forth to the world of whose many defects I am painfully conscious.

In conclusion, I acknowledge my special obligations to the following authors :—J. A. Bengel, Stier, Olshausen, Tholuck, Livermore, Ebrard, Jacobus, Brown, Lange, Andrews, Kitto, Archer, Butler, Robertson, Alford, Arnold, Blomfield, Trench, Webster and Wilkinson in their Greek Testament.   May this work enable many a preacher of the Gospel to enrich himself with the treasures of the Divine Book, and wisely to distribute those treasures to the people of his charge."

DAVID THOMAS

Introduction

THESE discourses remind me of the saying of our Lord, "The kingdom of heaven is like unto a householder who brings out of his storehouse things new and old!" In them will be found the truths which the Church universal has held from the beginning; the teaching of our Lord and Saviour, as it is delivered to us by the Apostles and Evangelists; the golden thread which runs through the writings of Augustine, Calvin, and Luther; of Pearson, Hooker, Beveridge; of Baxter, Howe, Charnock; of Matthew Henry, Philip Doddridge, and Thomas Scott. While these pages contain that which is old, they present also that which is new; they show that the Bible is no less a living Book in our own time than it was in the age in which it was written, that it meets the ever-varying wants and changing aspects of the Church in the present, as well as in any preceding century. Few can read this volume without discovering the justice of the remark made by a Pilgrim Father; "God has yet more light to break forth from His Holy Word." The well is deep, there is still a rich mine of pure gold in the inexhaustible treasure of Holy Writ.

I cannot better express my own opinion of the work, than by adopting the language in which Archdeacon Hare has described the expositions of Luther: "His strong good sense, and his familiarity with the Bible often enabled him to discern the truth by a kind of divination, even in difficult critical questions. . . . Well did Luther know the power of God's Word, the power which goes along with it when it is truly the word of the Spirit. He knew it from what he himself had felt; in fact, he could not have spoken of it as he does, except from personal experience. He knew it also from the effect which he had seen it produce, when it issued with the force of the Spirit from his own lips." ("Mission of the Comforter," Note H, p. 248; Note W, p. 427).

The critical and philological notes which the author requested me to add have been anticipated to a great extent by the results of his own reading, or by a kind of divination. My part, as editor, has been generally to confirm or elucidate what the author had already advanced; in a few cases only have I seen reason to express any difference or disagreement. A work like the present is fully entitled to the benefit of the canon which is generally conceded to the poet :—

> Verum ubi plura nitent, in carmine, non ego paucis
> Offendar maculis, quas aut circuria fudit,
> Aut humana parum cavit natura.

Here, again, I would commend to the reader's attention the discriminating language which Archdeacon Hare has applied to one of whom Dr. Thomas may be deemed a cautious and judicious follower.

" Calvin's Commentaries, though they take little note of critical and philological questions, keep much closer to the text, and make it their one business to bring out the meaning with fulness and precision. This they do with the excellence of a master richly endowed with the word of wisdom and with the word of knowledge : and, from the exemplary union of a *severe masculine understanding* with a profound insight into the spiritual depths of the Scriptures, are especially calculated to be useful in counteracting the erroneous tendencies of our age, when we are inundated with all that is fantastical and irrational in the evangelical mysticism of the Fathers, and are bid to see Divine power in allegorical cobwebs, and heavenly life in artificial flowers. . . . We may haply owe much gratitude and love, and the deepest intellectual obligations, to those whom, at the same time, we may deem to be mistaken on certain points. Perhaps it may be better for our frail human nature that there is no one who is not so mistaken, else I know not how we should be able to repress that proneness to idolatry, which led men to the worship of heroes in the heathen world, and to the worship of saints in the corrupt ages of the Christian." (Note H, p. 249.)

Preaching is that ordinance in the Church of later times which answers to the prophesying of the Apostolic age. The pulpit will never lose its power while sermons are delivered which, for freshness and terseness, for originality of thought, vigour of style, and catholicity of sentiment, culminating in heart-stirring application to men's minds and bosoms, can be compared with those in the present volume. Such qualities, which are valuable at all times, shine with greater lustre when they are sustained throughout one hundred and twenty homilies on a distinct portion of Scripture, as this expository mode tends much more to the edification of the hearer than to the popularity of the preacher. The superiority of this volume, and its adaptation to the present age, will at once appear if it is compared with works somewhat similar, such as Chrysostom's Homilies,

Simeon's or Dr. Lange's Homiletical Commentary. I cannot doubt
but that it will contribute valuable help to all who wish to meet
the 'exigencies of the times in their pulpit administrations, especially as it furnishes a successful example of the way in which
those who watch for souls may engraft fresh slips from the tree of
knowledge.

There are three striking features in these discourses upon
which I would make a few remarks, viz., Reality, Common Sense,
Fidelity.

There is a reality in this volume equally remote from that sacra-
mentalism and that sentimentalism which have nothing in common
save their want of reality and their blighting influence on pure and
undefiled religion. We may say of the author, *Nil falsi audet, nil
veri non audet dicere.* On every topic he says neither more nor less
than what he feels. Much of the preaching of the present day is
ineffectual because it is unreal. The preacher represents the hopes
and fears of a Christian, the joys and sorrows of religion, not in
language drawn from his own experience or his own convictions,
but in terms which he has borrowed from other men. That which
was perfectly just, natural, and real when originally indited, is
strange, simulated, and unnatural when retailed. Nothing of this
kind can be found in this volume; the author speaks only what he
knows, and testifies that only of which he is assured.

Another feature in these discourses is, the good common sense
which they evince in a remarkable freedom from the morbid dread
of legality. Many of those who are attached to the doctrines of
grace—and I can hardly think it possible for a man to be really a
minister of Christ Jesus who is not so attached—betray such a
jealousy for evangelical teaching, that they pay small attention to
what is practical. They consider spirituality to rise so far above
morality, that they throw into the shade the didactic and perceptive
teaching of Scripture. He who would make full proof of his
ministry must make up his mind to be accounted a moralist and a
legalist. It has recently been said that there are in every congregation four classes who need special admonitions, which they do not
receive—the dishonest, the unclean, the covetous, the assenters—
those who hang about the doors of the ark, but who never enter
in.* It is nearly forty years ago since Isaac Taylor, in his Natural

* See the *Christian Observer* for April, 1864, "On certain Omissions per-
ceptible in the Preaching now current among us." By One of the Congregation.

History of Enthusiasm, called attention to those who lived on better terms with angels and seraphs than with their children, servants, and neighbours. How are we to account for this state of things? My answer is, a morbid dread of legality, and a mistaken jealousy for the doctrines of grace.

A third feature in these discourses is their fidelity, the high-souled indifference to human censure or human applause. We may trace in the writer the features of an Ezekiel, "Thou shalt speak my words unto them whether they will hear or whether they will forbear;" or the lineaments of an Isaiah, "Cry out, spare not. Show my people their transgressions, and the house of Jacob their sin." Many popular preachers see no iniquity in those to whom they minister; they discern no transgression in the people of their charge. How miserable the minister who purchases popularity by dwelling on the faults of the absent, by delivering eloquent harangues against all the errors and heresies which can be found in Christendom, while he deals tenderly with the faults of his hearers, and treats slightly the sore of his own congregation.

In reading over these discourses as they passed through the press, there are many passages upon which I paused with the view of drawing attention to their peculiar merits. These became so numerous that I altogether forbear, lest I should extend this introduction to an inconvenient length. I shall heartily rejoice if this volume finds its way into the hands of those who usually restrict their reading to writers of their own branch of the Church Universal, believing that its perusal will assist the growth of truth and peace. I can heartily recommend it to all my clerical brethren who would adapt their preaching to meet the errors of the present day; to all, whether ministers or laymen, who wish to add to their store of knowledge. May they go forward in their toil, giving similar proof, with the author, that they are workmen who need not be ashamed; speaking out with all boldness, under the guidance of the Spirit of power and of love and of a sound mind.

W. WEBSTER

Homiletical Commentary on Matthew

Matthew 1:1-17

The Genealogical Table*—Its Moral Suggestions

THIS long catalogue of names is fraught with salutary suggestions. It suggests :—I. THE SOLEMN SUCCESSION OF THE RACE. The representatives of forty generations appear before us, and pass away. One generation is buried in the dust of another; and future generations will be entombed in our ashes. But though men depart, *man* remains. Generations, like waves, rise and break on the eternal shore; but humanity, like the ocean, rolls in undiminished plenitude and power. *The world can do without us.* This fact serves to *reprove worldliness*, and to *inculcate humility.* Death is the law and lot of all.

> " Not to thy eternal resting-place
> Shalt thou retire alone. * * *
> Thou shalt lie down
> With patriarchs of the ancient world, with kings,
> The powerful of the earth, the wise and good,
> Fair forms and hoary seers of ages past,
> All in one mighty sepulchre. The hills,
> Rock-ribbed and ancient as the sun ; the vales,
> Stretching in pensive quietness between ;
> The venerable woods, rivers that move
> In majesty, and the complaining brooks,
> That make the meadows green ; and, poured round all,
> Old ocean's gray and melancholy waste,—
> Are but the solemn decorations all
> Of the great tomb of man."

* For an explanation of the difference between the genealogies of Matthew and Luke, see Alford's Greek Testament ; Davidson on " Sacred Hermeneutics," p. 589 ; also Davidson on " Biblical Criticism," p. 371. The remarks of Jacobus, Dr. David Brown, and Dr. Lange, on the subject, deserve special attention. Dr. Mill and Lord Arthur Hervey may also be consulted on this subject. It is the general opinion that Matthew gives the *legal,* Luke the *natural,* pedigree of our Lord. The generations are arranged into three portions, each containing fourteen. In the first period the people of Israel were under prophets, in the second under kings, in the third under the Asmonean priests. The *first* begins with Abraham, who received the promise, and ends with David, to whom it was renewed with greater clearness. The *second* begins with the building of the temple, and ends with its destruction. The *third* opens with a temporal and terminates in a spiritual deliverance.

It suggests :—II. THE PHYSICAL CONNEXION OF THE RACE. Each of these generations springs from the other, as grain from grain. Humanity, however numerous its generations, is one : it may have a myriad branches, but it is one tree, rising from one germ and ruled by one law. This unity, 1st, demands the spirit of brotherhood. How monstrous does the belligerent element appear in its presence ! 2nd. It helps to explain the transmission of moral character. The tie of physical relationship which links men together is a stupendous instrument of moral influence—a vehicle through which moral ideas, dispositions, and habits are transmitted from sire to son. 3rd. It enables each generation to help its successors. Because of this unity, we can understand the thoughts and reasonings of men who lived thousands of years ago ; we can derive good from the writings of Moses, and David, and Paul. Though we have only a few years to live, we can work to bless posterity. *The heart of humanity is in us all, and to the heart of the last man we can speak.*

It suggests :—III. THE MORAL DIFFERENCES OF THE RACE. In this roll of names we recognise some men of distinguished goodness, some pre-eminent for wickedness. This shows that, however potent the influence which generations can exert on each other, it is not *resistless* and absolute. There is a power lodged in every man's bosom to prevent the combined influence of all past generations from moulding his character. This power is the glory of his nature—connects him with moral government—makes him a responsible agent.

It suggests :—IV. THE PARTIAL HISTORY OF THE RACE. Of these forty generations we have little more than the mention of the name of one individual of each. We talk of " the history of the world," but who knows the history of one of a generation ? What a biography has each ! What hopes, fears, sorrows, joys, battles, anarchies, epochs, revolutions, are connected with one soul ! Vast cycles in the great eternity will be absorbed in fathoming the history of mankind.

We have here—V. THE COMMON REDEEMER OF THE RACE. Down through all these generations, JESUS came. "*Forasmuch as the children are partakers of flesh and blood, He also Himself likewise took part of the same, that, through death, He might destroy him that had the power of death—that is, the devil ; and deliver them.*" God redeems man by man.

> " Who is this we must learn, for man He seems
> In all His lineaments, though in His face
> The glimpses of His Father's glory shine."—*Milton.*

Matthew 1:18-25

The Mental Difficulties of Joseph—Their Lessons

Learn, I. THAT GOD KNOWS THE MENTAL DIFFICULTIES OF GOOD
MEN. Mary's position was a trying one : her virtue was under a
cloud, and the eye of suspicion was turned at her ; but the inner
energy of conscious rectitude then, as ever, would nobly bear up her
spirit. Events soon cleared the mist, and brought her forth as the
spotless and honoured heroine of ages. *Suspected virtue can afford to
wait.* But Joseph's trial seems greater. Strong attachment and
high principles of honour and piety were battling within him ; for a
time, high hopes were blighted, and long-cherished purposes were
broken up. What soul-stirring thoughts would start in that breast
of his ! There was ONE who observed the workings of his anxious
mind—who understood his " thoughts afar off."

Learn, II. THAT GOD REMOVES MENTAL DIFFICULTIES IN CONNEXION
WITH CONSCIENTIOUS THOUGHTFULNESS. While he "thought on these
things," * the angel of the Lord appeared unto him in a dream. He
did not act from impulse ; he paused in the use of his reason, inquired for the right course, and the Almighty Spirit came to his help.
Thus He always guides man. He directs the planets by force,
brutes by instinct, man by reason. He controls all men, but guides
none save the *thoughtful.* He who would " follow Providence " must
become an earnest thinker—must "inquire in His temple."

Learn, III. THAT GOD REMOVES MENTAL DIFFICULTIES BY DISCLOS-
ING HIS REDEMPTIVE PLAN. " And she shall bring forth a Son," etc.
In the disclosure made to Joseph, the birth of Jesus is represented as
supernatural, the mission of Jesus as remedial, and the nature of
Jesus as divine. This disclosure was quite satisfactory. " *Then
Joseph, being raised from sleep,*" etc. A knowledge of God's redemp-
tive plan will solve all moral problems : it reveals the human and
divine, and sheds a clear light both on our duty and destiny—

> " As the great sun, when he his influence
> Sheds on the frost-bound waters, the glad stream
> Flows to the ray, and warbles as it flows."—*Coleridge.*

In all the intellectual difficulties of spiritual life, amidst inter-
winding paths, and under skies cold and dark with doubts, when
forced by urgent questionings and conflicting sentiments well-nigh
to a fearful crisis—let us, with Joseph-like thoughtfulness, pause,
even on the margin ; turn devoutly the eye and ear of reason up to
the ALL-KNOWING : " *He shall send from heaven,*" and help. Some
kind angel shall course his downward way, and inbreathe to the dis-
tracted bosom a thought that shall dispel the soul-clouds, and leave
the scene in all the serenity, beauty, and promise of a summer's day.
The source of Joseph's distress gave birth to the greatest blessing of

---

* Ταῦτα δὲ αὐτοῦ ἐνθυμηθέντος. Now while he had this in his mind.

his being : even so, out of the mental difficulties of the devout thinker, as from parturient chaos of old, shall come forth a system that shall encircle him with brightness, and emparadise him with bliss.

Matthew 2

Christ's Birth in Bethlehem.—Old Types of Modern Classes

The Bible is full of human nature: man, in some aspect of his being, appears on every page, and speaks in every verse. The *particular* men it presents to our notice, though living in remote ages, acting their part in a small and far-distant portion of the globe, and chiefly descendants of Abraham, represent the varied classes of men of every age, zone, and tribe. All modern men, whether chief of sinners or chief of saints, or of whatever stage in the development of virtue or vice, have their counterparts and representatives in this old, holy book. The Bible is a gallery of man-pictures, true to nature—nothing overdrawn—where each may find a portrait of his moral self. This *humanity* of the Bible, in its multiform aspects, is one of its chief characteristics and primal attractions, makes it the world's book—a book for all persons, in all places, and through all periods. The Eternal One speaks the most fully, and acts the most gloriously, through the *humanity* of this volume.

In the historic facts of this chapter we have types of four classes of men which have ever existed, and which exist still, namely— *those who earnestly seek the truth; those who rest in the letter of the truth; those who are fearfully alarmed at the truth;* and *those who are affectionate guardians of the truth.* The *Magi* represent the first, the Scribes and Pharisees the second, Herod the third, and Joseph and Mary the fourth.

With the utmost brevity, we shall merely intimate some of the points in which the historic personages of this chapter symbolize the aforementioned classes :—

I. THOSE WHO EARNESTLY SEEK THE TRUTH. These the "wise men from the East" represent.* There are several points in the visit of these philosophic disciples of Zoroaster and priests of the Zend religion to Bethlehem, strikingly illustrative of the conduct of every earnest seeker after truth :—1. *They sought truth under the impression of its reality.* Ere they left their eastern home they had an impression of the fact that *a King for the Jews* was born. This was the spring of their mission. How they obtained this impression— whether from the tradition of their fathers, or from the writings of

---

* For an account of the Magi, see Enfield's " History of Philosophy ;" also an interesting article in Kitto's " Cyclopædia of Biblical Literature." On the time of their visit, see Webster and Wilkinson.

Hebrew seers, or through one of those *presentiments* which frequently herald great events—it is neither possible nor necessary to
determine. They had it, and it moved and inspired them. Thus
it is ever with the earnest truth-seeker: the *native sentiment* that
there is *objective* truth somewhere is quickened into an impulse, and
the soul, like the Magi, leaves its own little home, enters other
regions of thought, and asks, " *Where shall wisdom be found, and
where is the place of understanding ?*" 2. *They sought truth at the
right source.* They were in quest of Him who was *born King of the
Jews;* and to Jerusalem, the metropolis of the country, and the
home of the Rabbis, they resorted. The earnest truth-seeker will
have respect to the right source. Is it *physical, psychological,
ethical,* or *redemptive* truth he is searching after? For the first he
appeals to *nature,* for the second to *mind,* for the third to the *moral
history of man and the Bible of God,* for the fourth to the *Gospel of
Christ.* 3. *They sought truth under divine direction.* They saw a
star in the East, which "went before them, till it came and stood
over where the young child was." What was this star? In this
question, biblical speculators have found ample scope for the play
of their imagination. Hence some have given us a comet, some
a planet, some a meteor, some a constellation, and some a flaming
seraph speeding his flight through the blue air. Some, indeed,
conjecture—and, if we have a choice, we prefer their hypothesis—
that the mystic light, the well-known symbol of Deity that flamed
on the sword of the cherubims "at the east of the garden of Eden,"
burnt in the bush of Moses, irradiated the guiding pillar of Israel,
gleamed for ages over the mercy-seat, shone around Christ in the
baptism, and spread over Him a lustrous canopy on the Mount of
Transfiguration,—now appeared in the starry realm, signalized itself
amongst the bright "orbs," and thus arrested the attention and
guided the feet of these men of astrologic notions in their wondrous
march to Bethlehem. But, somehow, we feel no great interest in
this question. The *what* here proves nothing—suggests nothing;
the *why* is everything, and the *why* we know. That "star" was
God's guide to these eastern inquirers. Thus it is ever with spirits
that are in earnest quest after truth. The "Great Jehovah" will
guide them. It is a law "settled in heaven," that he who seeks
shall find: to him there is promised ONE that "shall lead into all
truth." Let those vigorous spirits of this age, who have out-thought
old human systems of belief, and are leaving them, many as these
"wise men" left their homes, in search of something else, be fervent
and faithful, be diligent and devout, and on their intellect shall rise,
ere long, some divine idea that, like the "star," shall guide them to
Bethlehem, where dwells the LOGOS. 4. *They sought it to render it
homage.* "*And when they were come into the house, they saw the young
child with Mary His mother, and fell down and worshipped Him; and
when they had opened their treasures, they presented unto Him gifts;
gold, and frankincense, and myrrh.*" These symbols of respect they
carried with them. They left not their home from idle curiosity,

nor did they come to Bethlehem to dispute the claims of the Babe-King, but to "worship." *Reverence* mingled with their inquisitiveness, and inspired them in their discovery; they bore its fragrant symbols in their every step upon the road, and they expressed it in "the treasures" they adoringly presented to that *Majesty* they discovered in the *humble* home of Mary. He who would search successfully for truth must do likewise. Many now-a-day, under the garb of *truth-seekers*, seek rather their own intellectual aggrandisement and popularity. They have no idea of rendering homage to *objective* truth; everything must bow to their *imperial intuitions*. On their intellectual march they are ambitious and self-confident, not "meek and lowly." Their spirit is not fragrant with reverence; they carry not, as these Magi did, the "frankincense and myrrh" of loyal devotion, for they are in search of a kingdom, not a king. Truth can never be obtained thus; it must be sought with a reverent spirit, and for reverent ends, to be found. "*The secret of the Lord is with them that fear* [reverence] *Him, and He will show them His covenant.*"

Wouldst thou get truth, my brother?—understand something of those everlasting principles which light up the universe, as the shekinah of old illumined the bush in Midian? Be *reverent;* first feel that all about thee is sacred—awfully sacred. "Put off thy shoes from off thy feet, for the place whereon thou standest is holy ground." Then listen, and thou shalt hear something sublimer than ever fell on the ear of Moses.

We proceed now to another class here represented.

II. THOSE WHO REST IN THE LETTER OF THE TRUTH. These are represented in the conduct of the Scribes and Pharisees. "*And when he* [Herod] *had gathered all the chief priests and scribes of the people together, he demanded of them where Christ should be born. And they said unto him, In Bethlehem, of Judea; for thus it is written by the prophet, And thou, Bethlehem, in the land of Juda, art not least among the princes of Juda; for out of thee shall come a Governor, that shall rule my people Israel.*" There are three very remarkable things discoverable here:—1st. The *general expectation of the Messiah's coming*. The demand of Herod, and the conduct of this "full session of the Sanhedrim," proceed on a common and understood *pre-notion* of the fact. Whence this concurrent sentiment in the world's heart relating to an event perfectly unique?* 2nd. *A literal fulfilment of an old prophecy*. Although these letter religionists did not quote *verbatim* the passages, their words convey the essential meaning; and the meaning is, that obscure Bethlehem should be celebrated and honoured as the birth-place of the Messiah. This prediction of Micah, uttered upwards of seven centuries before, now met with its complete accomplishment. How is this to be explained? I ask the impugners of inspiration *how?* 3rd. *An accurate scriptural knowledge where there was no spiritual life*. These men

---

* See the testimony from pagan writers in Paley, Horne, etc.

were familiar with the writings of Moses and the prophets; the rubric of the Temple was ever on their lips. They had their own interpretations of the law, and crossed seas and land to spread them. But notwithstanding all this knowledge of the letter—yes, and their interest in it too—notoriously wanting were they in that spirit of universal love, truth, and right, for the inworking of which, to human hearts, "God spoke unto the fathers by the prophets." Sacred VERBALITY was their religion. They lived in *words*—their whole moral being, that should have winged through the wide realms of truth, shrank into the cold and narrow shell of words— they looked at God, humanity, and the universe, through *words;* and through this misty medium, the sublime Logos appeared to them a *heretic* unworthy of their country—unworthy of life.

Have these no antitypes in other places and times? Are such characters extinct? Were they confined to Judea, or did they die out with the last breath of the Jewish commonwealth? No; on every subsequent page of ecclesiastical history they appear, and often play a prominent part. We have them amongst us now—not their lingering shadow, but their living substance. In politics, they contend far more for "constitutions" and "precedents" than for the eternal principles of justice, equity, and order—more for that which man has written on parchment or paper, than that which God has written on the moral soul of society—" the common law." In churches, far more solicitous are they for "catechism" and "creeds," orders, and the technicalities of truth, than for the *spirit* that was in Christ Jesus. They will labour more to defend a Greek particle, or expound a Hebrew point, than to reclaim a wandering soul. When will this miserable, blighting spirit of *Jewish verbality* depart? Ah! when? Another class represented in this chapter are—

III. THOSE WHO ARE FEARFULLY ALARMED AT THE TRUTH. HEROD typified this class. "*When Herod the king had heard these things, he was troubled, and all Jerusalem with him.*" " It was," says Neander, "that Herod whose crimes were committed in violation of every natural feeling; which ever urged him on to new deeds of cruelty; whose path to the throne and whose throne itself were stained with human blood; whose vengeance against conspirators, not satiated with their own destruction, demanded that of their whole families; whose rage was hot, up to the very hour of his death, against his nearest kindred ; whose wife, Marianne, and three sons, Alexander, Aristobulus, and Antipater, fell victims to his suspicion, the last just before his own death; who, in a word, certainly deserved that the Emperor Augustus should have said of him,—"*Herodis mallem porcus esse, quam filius.*" On the page of human wickedness, few have figured in darker hues and in greater prominence than this Herod. Vice had extracted all virtuous sentiment from his breast ; he was a veteran in sin, and a tyrant to the inmost core; but he was, nevertheless, a coward. There are four things very remarkable here :—1st. *A king in trouble.* Popular sentiment ever associates happiness with the idea of a king. 2nd. A king in trouble about the *birth of a babe*. How strange that, before the idea of Bethlehem's Babe, the heart of this man, whose name struck terror into the people of Judea, should quail with alarm. 3rd. A king in trouble about that *in which the good rejoiced*. All the pious were in ecstasies, and angels carolled the event in rapturous music through the skies. 4th. A king in trouble about that which was designed *to bless him and the world*. Surely, trouble about such circumstances argues something miserably wrong in the man's soul. Now, we shall take this man as a type of an ever-living class of men—the *truth-dreaders*. In circles—political, mercantile, and religious— there are men ever "troubled" at the birth of a popular truth.

There is a suggestive analogy between Herod's fear and the fear of such men. First. *Herod dreaded the event of Christ's birth, because of its supposed opposition to him.* He had no faith in the rectitude of his position, and, therefore, no settled confidence in his security. He knew that his throne was reared on falsehood, injustice, and blood-shed. Everywhere amongst his subjects he discovered high political hopes associated with this event. The wondrous star seen by the wise men, the marvellous tale of the shepherds, the mysterious excitement that pervaded all classes, and the extraordinary reports which we may suppose such excitement would set in wide and rapid circulation, would tend also to touch his conscience into a sense of guilt, and thus heighten his ideas of danger. Conscious guilt unmans our nature, and converts the bravest into cowards. It was the imaginary bearing of the event upon Herod, in over-throwing his throne and crushing his power, that terrified him. Had he discovered in it no antagonistic aspect to himself, he would not have feared. Thus it is ever with the *truth-dreaders*. It is because the truth is seen to bear against their selfish interest that they dread it. Announce the doctrine of *human rights* amongst political tyrants whose pomp and power are derived and sustained by their violation; proclaim the doctrine of *spiritual equality* to the robed, titled, and plethoric ecclesiastics, who owe their all to the lordship they exercise over God's heritage; preach the doctrine of *universal peace* amongst those who owe their heraldry and their bread to the bayonet and the sword,—and in all such cases you may expect to see your audience "troubled," as Herod was at the birth of Christ. History teems with examples. The birth of a new truth has ever terrified the men who have discovered in it an opposi-tion to their principles and their position. Secondly. *Herod's dread stimulated him to the most reprehensible conduct.* To escape his gloomy apprehensions, he proposed the destruction of Jesus. The men who dread truth have ever acted in a similar way. They have sought to put pown the press, seal the tongue, and paralyse free-thought. But mark Herod's conduct in this attempt. 1st. It was *deceptive*. "*And he sent them to Bethlehem, and said, Go and search diligently for the young child; and when ye have found Him, bring me word again, that I may come and worship Him also.*"

Here he plays the hypocrite with consummate art. He moves in the dark, "privily" consults the Magi, puts on the mask of devotion, and intimates a reverence for Him he sought to murder. Men who dread truth have ever sought to put it down by cunning and deception: they conceal their hate under the profession of love; like Judas, they kiss to betray. 2nd. His conduct was *cruel*. "*Then Herod, when he saw that he was mocked of the wise men, was exceeding wroth, and sent forth, and slew all the children that were in Bethlehem, and in all the coasts thereof, from two years old and under, according to the time which he had diligently inquired of the wise men.*" You have abundant counterparts to this in the history of persecution, from the days of Stephen to this hour. Finally, his conduct was *futile*. An angel appeared "in a dream," both to the wise men and to Mary and Joseph, and frustrated the monarch's impious aim. Herod fulfilled his iniquitous course— died, and left a name of infamy for the execration of mankind; but the Babe he sought to murder, under the fostering care of Providence, grew to manhood, leavened His age with His regenerative doctrine, and bequeathed to humanity a system and an influence that shall one day secure for Him the "many crowns" of the world, "the heathen for His inheritance, and the uttermost parts of the earth for His possession." Thus it must ever be with the TRUTH. Men may seek to crush it as it is born into their domains, but there is a God watching over its cradle; there is a quenchless immortality in its infant struggles. My reader, there may be a truth rising in thy circle antagonistic to thy prejudices, position, and influence, and it may *trouble* thee. If thou wouldst get true peace, strip thyself forthwith of everything opposed to it, take it into thy heart, and mould thy character after its holy spirit; but seek not to crush it, for the effort must prove futile—yes, *futile*. Thou mightst as well try to dry up the Atlantic, or quench the everlasting stars, as to destroy a truth. Surrender to it, and it will save thee—battle with it, and it will be thy infamy and ruin. The others represented in this chapter are—

IV. THOSE WHO ARE THE AFFECTIONATE GUARDIANS OF THE TRUTH. Joseph and Mary are the types of this class—a class who have ever been the brightest ornaments and the greatest benefactors of the race. This class is here represented in two of its primary features: —1. The parents sought the protection of Jesus from impulses of genuine affection: He was dear to them parentally and religiously; their hearts were on Him both as their offspring and Messiah. This urged them to bear Him in their bosom down to Egypt, and back from Egypt to Nazareth. Christianity has ever had *professed* guardians of truth. But those who, like Joseph and Mary, have been stimulated by pure affection, are the only true ones. Many— the majority, alas !—have manifested more affection for the honours and immunities of the office than for the truth. 2. In seeking the protection of Jesus, they followed a divine direction: they moved as the "angel of the Lord" had counselled them. All the true guardians of truth ever act thus. They contend for it in God's way. *Fraud, uncharitableness, oppression, dogmatism, persecution, violence,* have too often been developed under the profession of guarding truth; but these are in opposition to the direction of God, and flagrant sins are they against *man, truth, and Heaven.*

Matthew 3:1-12

The Ministry of John

There are two classes of men—those that are made *by* the times, and those that are made *for* them. The former have ever constituted the great bulk, and still are the "millions." They are the moral products and portraits of their age; they reflect its spirit, they echo its sentiments. They are to it as straws on the current —as clay in the hands of the potter, moulded by its plastic force. The other and smaller class have but little in common with the prevalent disposition of things; they do not flow with the stream. On the contrary, they breast the billows. They have an individual energy: they have their own thoughts, and work them out in their own way, for their own end. Thus they stamp their own impress on the age, often work revolutions and create eras. To this class John the Baptist belonged. He was, emphatically, made *for* the times. He was consecrated from his birth to the work of a reformer. His youth he spent in ascetic devotions. In the lonely desert, communing with nature and with God, studying the law and the prophets, he trained his great faculties for the great work to which he was called. Here he appears in public for the first time; and from the banks of the Jordan, surrounded by multitudes of his countrymen, he calls, in thunder, for REFORMATION.* There are three great truths which this passage develops:—First. *That the system of Jesus is a system of divine rule.* "It is the kingdom of God." Christianity is not a subject for mere intellectual study or belief, nor is it merely a *ruling* power. All false religions are ruling powers. It is *the ruling power of God*—God reigning, by His truth, over the reason, heart, and conscience of man. Secondly. *That reformation is indispensable to the enjoyment of this system.* "Reform, for the kingdom of God is at hand." Thirdly. *That the*

---

* By μετανοεῖτε John repeated the summons of Isaiah, "Cease to do evil; learn to do well." The word implies, not merely a change of feeling, but a change of purpose, of object, of intention. Μετανοία denotes the repentance by which we forsake sin; the sanctified effect of μεταμέλεια, change of feeling, or λύπη, pain (2 Cor. vii. 10). Coleridge proposed *transmentation* as an equivalent for μετανοία. Lactantius and some of the fathers expressed the sense very happily by *resipiscentia*, return to one's senses, the recovery of a right understanding. On the phrase "kingdom of heaven," see Webster and Wilkinson, Matt. iii. 2 and vi. 10; Rom. xiv. 16–18.

effecting of this reformation is one of the greatest ministries of man.
This mission was John's. He had an insight into the heart of his
age : he discerned the sensuousness of soul, the hollowness of profession, the formality of worship, the spirit of Pharisaism, that
everywhere prevailed. He knew that, with all this, they would
never receive the spiritual doctrines that were about to be proclaimed by Him of whom he was the humble servant and the
honoured herald. Hence his cry for reformation—a cry whose
blast rang through the heart of his country, and drew forth its
thousands to the banks of the Jordan. Reformation became his
master-thought, and the prayer and purpose of his life. We are
much mistaken if there be not now, in our country, an amount of
sensuousness and formality, in relation to Christianity, if not equal,
nearly approximating to that which existed in connexion with
Judaism, when the Baptist came forth to public life from the solitudes of the desert. *Reformation seems to me as truly necessary to*
prepare our age for the true spiritual teacher, as it was to prepare
Judea for the ministry of Christ. We want, confessedly, teachers
that will present Christianity in its purest forms of thought and
widest aspects; that will bring it forth, not in the technicalities of
theology, but in the free language of common life—not from human
schools, but from the mountains of Capernaum and the shores of
Galilee; that will rather breathe it in gales of life-thought than
enunciate it in the stiff forms of logic. Verily, we want men now
to do a work like that which the Baptist did—thunder reformation
in the ear of a sensuous and formal people, and prepare the way for
a class of Christian teachers that shall more fairly represent the
system of Jesus, unfold its doctrines as congruous with the laws of
reason, present its provisions as commensurate with the wants of
the soul, and proclaim its promises as equal to the loftiest aspirations of mankind.

Let us now look at John's ministry as *a type of that ministry which*
is required for an age of religious sensuousness and form.

Several of the characteristics of John's ministry stand out in
these verses in bold outline and suggestive significance.

I. HIS MINISTRY WAS MORAL IN ITS AIM. His grand purpose, as
we have seen, was *reformation.* But what kind of reformation did
he seek ? Was it an *intellectual* one ? Did he preach to settle
metaphysical disputes in theology, or to establish the theoretical
accuracy of his own beliefs ? Did he labour to buttress an old
school, or to form a new one ? No ; he had a sublimer end than
this. His object was more with the heart than with the understanding; more with vital motives than with speculative beliefs ;
more with souls than with systems. Was it an *institutional* reformation that he sought ? a thing of parchment rather than of principle—of form rather than of spirit ? No ; such was not the
reformation that our reformer sought—he aimed at the reformation
of Judea's *heart.* " *Bring forth fruits meet for repentance.*"—Let
your outward actions be not something put on, but something

produced—"fruits;" and fruits springing from inward repentance. He wished to see his country change its conduct, systems, and institutions—as the landscape its dress, and as birds their plumage —by the infusion of new life. This feature of John's ministry I hold to be of transcendent importance. No ministry, whatever its pretensions, is valid or worth having that strives not supremely for this moral reformation. There are three facts that show this:— First. *That all systems of religion, erroneous either in idea or practice, spring from wrong moral principles.* Take, for instance, Popery as the masterpiece of the false in religion : its every absurd dogma and impious act can be traced to such moral principles as *pride, selfishness,* and *materialism.* These are the roots : they are the very spirits, not only of the Antichrist of Rome, but of all the "many Antichrists that are in the world." Secondly. *Systems thus erroneous may be destroyed in form, and the moral principles from which they spring remain as vigorous as ever.* In politics, we find the spirit of despotism growing after the throne of the despot has been burnt ; and in religion we find the spirit of Popery rampant after the authority of Rome has been renounced. Indeed, the spirit of a thing often gets new vigour by the manner in which its form has been assailed, and perhaps destroyed. Thirdly. *That the great mission of Christianity is to combat and crush the moral principles of wrong.* It has to do with errors as they exist in the *heart* rather than in the *head*—in men, rather than in systems ; in living impulses, rather than in logical propositions—with the germs of the upas, rather than with the branches. Worldliness, pride, dishonesty, carnality, and impiety, are the forces against which it directs its weapons. It is to bruise the head of the serpent. It seeks to save by "*teaching us that*—*denying ungodliness and worldly lusts*—*we should live soberly, righteously, and godly, in this present world.*"

In all this, let me not be understood as undervaluing an accurate and extensive knowledge of biblical truth, nor a systematic method of presenting it to the minds of men. Firmly, indeed, do I believe that the great truths, connected with the atonement of Christ as their central point, are essential to the effecting of the moral change of which I speak ; and equally strong is my conviction that they will only tell successfully upon the heart, as in teaching they are made to square, in some measure, with the native philosophy and logic of the human mind. But what I insist upon is, *that the grand end of the ministry should not be theological, but moral;* not to battle for the spread of its own opinions, but for the prevalence of Christ's spirit ; not to declaim against intellectual heretics, but to appeal calmly and effectually to the hearts of moral delinquents ; not to deal with sects divided by opinions, but with souls which are one in sin ; not to speak oracularly, as a dogmatist, to men's intellects, but plaintively, as a suppliant, to men's hearts, " beseeching them in Christ's stead, to be reconciled to God."

II. His MINISTRY WAS FAITHFUL IN ITS APPEAL. Two things here show his faithfulness :—First. His declaration of their character.

Deep and solemn was his impression of the evil principles that worked in the hearts of the men around him. As a great man he had strong convictions, and as an honest man he spoke them out in terms correspondingly strong; and hence he addresses them not as " dear brethren," but as " *a generation of vipers* "—men of specious manner, but of poisonous principles; and this he speaks not behind their back, but to their face, with his honest eyes flashing into theirs. Secondly. His faithfulness is seen in destroying the chief object of their glory. He knew that their relationship to Abraham was the foundation of their confidence, the theme of their constant boasting, that which elated them with all the arrogance of a heartless bigotry ; and, with an unflinching fidelity, he says, " *Think not to say within yourselves, We have Abraham to our father ; for I say unto you, that God is able of these stones to raise up children unto Abraham ;* "—as if he had said, You pride yourselves in your hereditary descent, but that confers no virtue on you. Personal piety is the indispensable need and duty of all. " Every tree which bringeth not forth good fruit is hewn down and cast into the fire." All men pride themselves in some object or other—some in their birth, some in scholarship, some in talent, some in money; and it requires no little faithfulness in a minister to demolish all these, as having no moral merit whatever—to say, right in the face of the unrighteous, though a millionaire, a scholar, a man of noble birth and high office,—" You are nothing, worse than nothing—a miserable compound of vile spirit and corrupt dust, without *personal moral goodness.*

III. HIS MINISTRY WAS CONNECTED WITH SYMBOLICAL RITUALISM. The religion of heaven has ever been associated with certain ceremonies or rites. In the Jewish church they were numerous, and often gorgeous; in the Christian they are few, and very simple. We take it that the grand end, both of the Jewish and Christian, was the same—namely, to *teach,* to portray, truth to the senses. They were adumbrations—the emblematic expression of ideas—and nothing more. Thus, we think, John regarded *baptism.* He did not regard it as a *regenerating* ordinance, the dream of a superstitious populace, and the fraud of a selfish priesthood ; nor as a *professional* ordinance, as many have regarded it; for he evidently administered it to thousands who had no true faith, else why did they persecute and crucify " the Lord of life and glory" ? nor as an *initiational* ordinance, of which there has been so much said ;—but his idea was *teaching.* So profound were his convictions of the moral defilement of his country, and of its need of spiritual cleansing, that he came forth from his desert-home, determined that what he could not express in words he would in things—that symbols should supplement his sayings. Nor can we conceive of a more impressive symbol than that which he selected. As he stood upon the banks of the mightiest river in their country, baptizing all who came to him with its waters, he gave to its calm and majestic flow a moral meaning; made its very wavelets speak to the assembled multitude—*Cleanse your hands, ye sinners, and purify your hearts.*

John, in baptizing, did what all teachers might do, and what all earnest teachers ever have done and ever will do—press nature into their service, make its mute objects speak, and symbolize thoughts which abstract language cannot express. Indeed, so *unutterably* strong were his convictions of the importance of spiritual reformation, that he not only made the Jordan help him to speak them, but his labouring soul made both his dress and diet *symbolic.* That rustic "raiment of camel's hair," so coarse, so roughly bound together with the "leathern girdle," those locusts and wild honey on which he daily fared, were all sermons—mute, but mighty, homilies were they on reformation; proclaiming to his countrymen—who prided themselves in their dress, and sought for sumptuous fare, as multitudes have ever done, and are doing still—his conviction that men's high interest and true greatness are independent of both; *that there is something transcendently more important for humanity than either food or raiment.*

IV. His MINISTRY WAS SELF-ABNEGATING IN ITS SPIRIT. Humility, unaffected and profound, pervaded the mind and ministry of this great man. "*He that cometh after me is mightier than I; whose shoes I am not worthy to bear.*" "*I am the voice of one crying in the wilderness.*" I am not truth, but merely its *voice.* The Speaker is coming. I am only the channel—the original fountain will soon outpour among you its own living streams. My ministry is but *water;* it touches the outward surface, and that is all. The ministry that is coming is *fire;* it will burn to the inmost core, and transmute all into its own pure essence. John's humility might be referred to the fact that he was suitably penetrated with the sense of his position. *Physically*, he stood where the high hills that overshadowed him, and the stream, fraught with historic associations, that rolled at his feet, would tend to overawe his spirit. Majestic scenery has ever a power to destroy our egotism. *Historically*, he stood between two wonderful economies. The magnificent theocracy with which the hopes and sympathies of his fathers through long ages had been identified, was an orb now drawing its last ray from man's horizon, and the bright day of grace was dawning "over the gloomy hills of darkness." *Spiritually*, he stood where he was touching springs in man's destiny that would propagate an influence through endless ages. All this would serve to produce the humility here displayed.

I have briefly mentioned the more salient features in the ministry of this great man—a ministry moral, not theological, in its aim; faithful, not temporizing, in its appeal; symbolic, not superstitious, in its ritualism; humble, not haughty, in its spirit. Such a ministry this age pre-eminently demands. We want men who have neither the vanity to suppose that they have fully sounded the depths of theological truth, nor the arrogance to pronounce those heretic who neither adopt their notions nor use their nomenclature; but who, on the contrary, have grace to believe in their own fallibility, and, like

John, in a teaching higher than their own. We want men who, instead of regarding themselves as the depositories of truth, and speaking with the authority of oracles, modestly, like John, think of themselves as a *voice*. We want men who, in passing off "life's narrow stage," will not so intimate their theological superiority over their successors as if they sought to throw the church into a premature sorrow for its anticipated loss, and to close its ears against the ministry that is to come; but who, like the noble Baptist, will withdraw from public life with a cheerful trust, pointing their contemporaries to better men; and as they sink to the tomb, proclaim, in good faith—*there are ministers coming after us whose shoe's latchet we are not worthy to unloose.*

Matthew 3:13-17

The Baptism of Christ; or, a Divine Inauguration to the Mission of Life

If we looked upon this wonderful narrative with the mere eye of criticism and speculation, there are five points which we would raise and canvass:—First. Was there any acquaintance between John and Christ prior to the baptism, or did the Baptist's knowledge of the Messiah now begin on the banks of the Jordan? Secondly. What object could the baptism of Christ have answered?—it being, as we take it, a mere symbol of the *necessity of cleansing*, and He being perfectly immaculate—what was its precise intent? Thirdly. Were the extraordinary phenomena, such as the appearance of the "dove," the opening of the heavens, and the articulate voice, things which came within the range of physical vision, or were they objects of entire spiritual perception? Did they occur without or within? —were they *objective* or *subjective*? Fourthly. What was the manner of Christ's life up to this period? He was now thirty years of age. Only once before He has appeared before us since His infancy. How has He lived, and what has been His occupation, during this long period? I confess to a strong curiosity on this point. Would that some hand could draw the curtain which veils this interesting portion of His history, that we might see Him passing on, from stage to stage, to the maturity which He now develops! Fifthly. What was the particular mode of Christ's baptism? Was it sprinkling or dipping? Was water applied to Him, or He to the water? To some, the attraction and sublimity of this wonderful event in our Lord's history is found in the expression—" Went up straightway out of the water." This to them is the *text* of the passage: there is a talismanic power in it to kindle inspiration, produce impassioned sermons, and create learned books. Though we have an opinion on this subject, it gives us no enthusiasm. We are not over-anxious either to sustain or state it. The prepositions " into," "from," " out of," etc., interpret them as you may in relation to baptism—bring out of them submersion, sprinkling, pouring, or any other conceivable *mode* of putting man's body in connection with water—and what, after all, have you done ? Show us, as the result of your labour, the great *moral* truth suited to touch the spiritual consciousness of humanity—to convert the sinner or sanctify the saint, and we will honour you for your critical toil and baptismal zeal; but, until then, you must excuse us if we feel no great interest in your intellectual evolutions. So long as there are vast fields, and even continents, of spiritual truth yet unexplored, we shall not waste our energy in digging on such little stony spots, that have vegetated with little else than a miserable sectarianism.

Such are some of the critical and speculative questions which this interesting event suggests, and which our purpose will only allow us thus briefly to mention.*

After thirty years of life, somewhere and somehow, amidst the solitudes of Nazareth, Jesus now appears in public for the first time. It is a momentous period in His history. He is to enter on new scenes ; He is to engage in new services. Stupendous issues depend upon that mission, into which He is now publicly inaugurated by that baptism which He receives at the hand of John. Now, although the mission of Jesus was *sui generis*, every man has as truly a mission as He had. No one is here by accident : there are a meaning and a message in the life of each ; and there is not one possessing a rational nature who has not some portion of divine work, which he is both fitted and required to do. Upon the right fulfilment of our individual missions depend our own true greatness and well-being, as well as our utility to the universe and our acceptance with God. Now, there are two things which Christ possessed at His inauguration, as here recorded, which every man must have if he would rightly " fulfil his course "—*a spirit of self-renunciation, and a special connexion with the Spirit of God.*

I. A SPIRIT OF SELF-RENUNCIATION. When Jesus made application for baptism, John, conscious of his personal inferiority, modestly " forbade Him, saying, I have need to be baptized of Thee, and comest Thou to me ?" To this Jesus replied, " Suffer it to be so now, for thus it becometh us to fulfil all righteousness ;" as if he had said, Baptism is a divine institution ; and although it is a ritual enactment, and not a moral principle, as it is not yet abrogated, and as I am " made under the law," it is binding on me. Whatever is duty, positive or moral—however apparently trivial or momentous—I shall obey. "It becometh us to fulfil ALL righteousness." This is the spirit with which our great Master here begins His public life. But what, in truth, is this spirit of duty ? It

* For a discussion of them, see Neander's " Life of Christ," " Olshausen on the Gospel," and an able article in the " Cyclopædia of Biblical Literature " on " the Baptism of Jesus by John."

is not a *calculating prudence*, that which concerns itself with " gains and losses," which attends to precepts for the sake of promises, and struggles for holiness for the sake of heaven ; but a sympathy with the *right*, so all-absorbing as to exclude all solicitude about results. It is not a *blind impulse*—that which is evoked by appeals which reason has never searched, and often stimulates to deeds which the calm judgment does not approve—a state of mind resembling the foaming billow in the tempest, raised for a moment by a foreign force above the level of its own nature, and which soon falls flat and tame again—but such an *enlightened* affection for God as draws, in calm, constant, and concurrent flow, the whole soul after Him. It is not a *timid servility*, urging men to work in religion with a trembling nerve and a quailing heart, as slaves under the curse and lash of a tyrant, but such a filial attachment as makes obedience to the will of God esteemed as the "meat and drink" of the soul. It is not a *fettering constraint*, by which one is impelled to a course by certain considerations, which he dares not oppose, but does not cordially approve—a coercion of some of the powers without the free acquiescence of others—but a vital inspiration, bringing out every faculty of the soul with a freedom joyous and elastic, like unto the "glorious liberty of the sons of God."

This is the spirit of duty—the spirit that now penetrated Christ in entering on His public mission ; and which was the inspiration of His life and the soul of His history. And, my friend, wouldst thou be initiated into the grand business and blessedness of being ? Wouldst thou start rightly on the course of an interminable existence ? Wouldst thou be divinely inaugurated into the high offices of God's spiritual universe ? If so, thou must have that spirit which Jesus now expressed to John on the banks of the Jordan, when He said, "It becometh us to fulfil all righteousness."

The other thing which Jesus had on commencing His public mission—as developed in this narrative, and which is indispensable to all who would answer the grand purpose of life—was

II. A special connexion with the Spirit of God. There are three things in this wonderful scene which indicated Christ's special connexion with God at this time :—First, the *vision* of the opening heavens. "Lo! the heavens were opened unto Him." An impressive expression this of the fact mankind have ever overlooked —namely, that behind the veil of matter there is a spiritual universe which is deeply interested in the doings and destinies of a holy man. How would this vision strengthen the heart of Christ for the stupendous mission He had undertaken! He would feel, as His trials multiplied, and the nation grew in wrath against Him, that up in those heavens—where the vulgar could discern nothing but the quiet seas of blue, the swimming clouds, and the twinkling lights of night—there were spirits bent in earnest affection over Him, and ready at any moment to throw open their glorious pavilion, and welcome Him to their home. Secondly. The *visit* of the holy dove. In the symbolization of the Bible, certain animals—such as the lamb, the lion, the eagle, the bull—are frequently employed as the representatives of character. In this hieroglyphical system the dove is the emblem of purity; and its descending and abiding upon Christ now, indicated that He was the temple of the Spirit of Holiness. This Spirit with Christ was not a transient visitant, as in the case of Saul, Samson, and others, but a permanent resident. The " dove abode " abode on Christ. Thirdly. The *voice* of the everlasting Father, "This is my beloved Son, in whom I am well pleased." This approving voice was the greatest blessing of all.

Now, all these things, indicating a special connexion with God, are as necessary for every man who would happily realise the great purpose of being as they were for Christ. Yes ; every man must have this divine *vision, visitant,* and *voice. The heavens must open ;* the thick veil of matter must be drawn aside ; the sensuous firmament of the soul must be rent asunder, and a deep and imperishable impression of a spiritual universe must be made upon the heart, and the whole man must be brought under the powers of the world to come. *The heavenly dove* must descend as the spirit of *purity,* not to pay a transient visit, and wing its way again, but as a permanent resident, consecrating the entire nature as its everlasting temple ; and the *approving voice* of Heaven must verberate in the depths of conscience, that we may go forth, not with "doubts and fears," but with a cheerful spirit and a courageous heart. "Oh, that thou wouldst rend the heavens "—unveil to us the spiritual world ; "that thou wouldst come down "—descend on us as the permanent visitant of purity, and as a VOICE, "bearing witness with our spirits that we are the children of God !"

Matthew 4:1-11

Temptation of Christ; or, the Ideal Battle

Assuming that this is not allegory, but narrative—not a mythical representation, but a veritable history*—there are three different hypotheses as to the *mode* in which Satan did now, in the solitude of the wilderness, assail the Son of God. One is, that it was in VISION—a mere imagination ; another, that it was in SUGGESTION— the same way as Christian men are ever tempted ; and the other, that it was in PALPABLE FORM—that Satan did actually appear to the bodily eye of Christ, and speak, as here recorded. We adopt the second hypothesis.

The first could scarcely be called a temptation : it would only have

---

* The character of the narrative as veritable history is confirmed by the words which denote a change of place, ἀνήχθη (Matt. i. 1); παραλαμβάνει (Matt. v. 8); ἐκβάλλει (Mark i. 12); ἤγετο, ὑπέστρεψεν (Luke iv. 1, 14); and by the additional feature presented in Mark i. 14, ἦν μετὰ τῶν θηρίων.

been a kind of dream; the third would have been altogether so extraordinary as to have put it out of the category of human temptations; the second justifies the statement that Christ was " tempted like as we are." Adopting this view, we shall regard His spiritual conflict in the wilderness as a divine illustration of that warfare in which every earnest and good man is engaged; and there are four points of similarity:—*It was a battle in the soul, a battle for dominion, a battle won by faith, and a battle resulting in glory.*

I. THAT IT WAS A BATTLE IN THE SOUL.—Whatever notion is adopted concerning the *mode* of Satan's attack, the fact must be admitted, that the *essence* of the temptation was in the influence exerted upon the heart of the Saviour. Had the seductive statements addressed to Him by the great moral adversary fallen merely on His external ear, and then died away with the echo, without entering the soul; or if they had entered merely the understanding, and made no impression upon the impulses of action; in either case they could not be considered as temptation. *Temptation implies moral excitement.* Nothing can be a temptation to any man that does not enter the soul, and touch certain susceptibilities there. Hence it is that what is a temptation to one man is not so to another; and even to the same man, what is a temptation at one period of his history is frequently never so again. We say, therefore, that these Satanic thoughts must have entered the very *heart* of Jesus, and made some impression there; that the real conflict was on the arena of His soul, between certain impulses which the tempter had awakened. All this is perfectly compatible with the *impeccability* of Christ's nature, and is indeed essential to give *virtue* to His triumph. There is no sin in the mere *possession* of any thought, but in the *entertainment* that is given to it. There are thoughts that come into the mind involuntarily: these are foreigners, not offspring; we are their thoroughfare, not their home. If we cherish them they corrupt, and may ruin us; but if we expel them as foes they taint us not. They may, indeed, rather benefit than harm us, for they increase the strength of our virtue by exercise. It seems to me, indeed, that the *susceptibility* not only of receiving but of feeling improper thoughts is essential alike to moral freedom and to moral *praiseworthiness.* Apostate angels and Adam had it in their innocence, or they would not have fallen. Jesus had it, or His temptation would have no meaning, and His unswerving rectitude no merit.

It may serve to give a deeper and more practical meaning to our Saviour's temptation, to remember that there are two very distinct elements, or forces, in the constitution of man. There is an instinct which stimulates thoughts and purposes about our own *personal* gratification and well-being, and an instinct which awakens deep thoughts and solicitudes concerning the transcendent claims of the ETERNAL. The instinct of *selfhood* and the instinct of *religion.* Everywhere these twofold forces are seen. They work in every breast. All the doings and institutions of the world may be resolved into one of these. The normal and proper relation of these to each other is that of a *subject* to a *sovereign*. The idea of God should be the governing idea. It should control all the sentiments, notions, and desires, ever generated by the *self-consciousness*. The Bible teaches this; and true philosophy declares that the only way to please self is to please God. Now, to disturb the order of these primitive impulses, to bring them into opposition, and to reverse their relative position, is the aim and work of Satan. Any circumstance so brought to bear upon the self-sense as to excite it to an undue influence in the soul is a temptation, and nothing else.

Now, this is truly what Satan here attempts with Christ. He appeals respectively to three impulses in our *selfhood*, in order to dethrone and prostrate the sovereign idea of duty and God. These instincts are *appetite, ambition,* and *avarice.* Perhaps the apostle referred to these three self-impulses under the terms "lust of the flesh, lust of the eyes, and the pride of life."

The first impulse—*appetite,* or desire for food—although seated in our mere animal nature, is the most powerful of all. It is a craving of the physical nature, not merely for gratification, but for life. Our mortal existence depends upon it. Hunger moves the world. It not only forces the body to toil and sweat "from morn to dewy eve," but presses intellect into its service, and makes even genius a drudge. Far am I from regarding this appetite as an evil; it is a necessary stimulus to intellectual development and moral culture. Without it the world would go to sleep, and souls would remain embryons for ever. Now, it was through this appetite that Satan first assailed Christ. He was "*an hungered.*" He felt those painful and gnawing cravings of nature which have often induced men to break through restrictions the most sacred, trample upon rights the most divine, and commit crimes the most enormous. His case seems to stand thus:—He had the *power* to convert stones into bread, but not the *right.* There was some reason—I know not what, nor is it of practical importance to determine—which would make it wrong for Him thus to use His miraculous might. He wanted bread, and He could get it at once, get it by a volition. There was nothing in the way but a *moral idea;* and the suggestion of the tempter was, in effect, to give up that *idea* for *bread.* The conflict in the Saviour's mind was between the pinching sense of hunger and the high sense of right.

The second impulse—namely, *ambition*—is equally universal, if not as powerful, as the former. This principle is really a desire for display, and it is native. It is seen in the first dawnings of intellect; it appears without disguise in the boasting lisp of infancy, and those little vainglorious feats which childhood often performs to win the applauding smile of the playfellow or the nurse. The adult world abounds with its developments. A love of self-exhibition can be often detected by a keen eye under the garb of apparently the most *genuine* humility. Plebeians as well as princes have their stage for self-manifestation; and those who lack nerve or talent to appear before the great public, will be found endeavouring to spread out for the best *effect* their powers or circumstances in their own little sphere. Each seeks a circle, however small, where he can play the hero. This principle, indeed, like every other power of our nature, has been sadly abused, and has ever been the *occasion* of serious evils. It puts a false face on society, tacks a polished veneer over rotten wood, spreads gold tinsel over common brass, robes falsehood and selfishness in the attire of truth and grace, and induces men to labour and lie, scheme and cheat, in order " to keep up appearances." Most of the horrors of war may be traced to it. Still, in itself, and in its intention, it is a great good. It was intended to induce men to show forth the glory of God, as do the heavens and the earth, by showing forth the noble nature that He has given ; and to promote social concord and peace, by prompting men to cultivate those attributes which they are made to love and admire.

> " Thirst for applause calls public judgment in
> To praise our own."

Now, Christ, having humanity, had this principle, and this principle Satan next appeals to. He was now entering on His public mission, and, in the lonely desert, dwelling unquestionably in thought upon the probabilities of His treatment by the Jews. As a man, it was perfectly natural for Him to desire to make a favourable impression of Himself upon the minds of those amongst whom He had to live and labour. Were He to enter their metropolis, go to their holy sanctuary, ascend the highest roof and cast Himself down into the midst of them, the probability would be that they would be impressed with His greatness, and receive Him as their Messiah, whom their prophets represented as " coming in the clouds." This was the suggestion. " *Then the devil taketh Him into the holy city, and setteth Him on a pinnacle of the temple, and saith unto Him, If thou be the Son of God, cast thyself down from hence : for it is written, He shall give His angels charge over thee to keep thee ; and in their hands they shall bear thee up, lest at any time thou dash thy foot against a stone.*" The conflicting question, it seems to me, was this :—" Shall I go amongst the Jews in my present humble appearance, which will expose me to their contempt and ridicule ; or shall I, by a miracle, which I can easily perform, at the outset manifest my greatness before them, and so gain their favour ? " Here, again, the battle in the Saviour's mind is between a native impulse in selfhood, and an *idea* of duty starting from the *sense* of God.

The third impulse—namely, *avarice*, or desire for possession—is no feeble instinct of our nature. It is seen as truly in the child that seeks to add to its stock of toys, as in the merchant who navigates oceans and traverses continents in search of gain. Civilization has nursed this instinct into a passion—an autocratic passion, pressing every power into its service, and bowing every agent to its iron will. It has thus become a serious evil amongst us. It supplies weights and measures for everything. It determines the worth of man and of truth. The purseless saint, however great his soul, is nothing.

The sublimest truths are visionary speculations unless they are promotive of wealth. It has permeated all things. The heart of the civilized world points to the golden mountains. Still, as an instinct, it is good and useful : it serves to develop the treasures both of earth and soul. Now, this instinct for *possession* was appealed to in Christ. All *the kingdoms of the world* were offered to Him if He would but surrender to evil. Christ could have taken possession of Palestine —yes, and the world—but there was some reason or *idea of duty* to prevent.

Through these impulses, then, belonging to the selfhood of our nature, Satan assailed Christ, and endeavoured to subvert His high sense of duty and God; and thus he acts now. Hence, in *all points, He was tempted as we are ;* for is it not through *appetite, ambition,* and *avarice,* that the arch-enemy assaults us ? Is it not through one of these gates he enters the spiritual dominion, dethrones the rightful sovereign, and rifles us of our moral possessions ? Does he not now enter the soul through *hunger ?* Verily, the experience of ages teaches the lessons we are slow to learn, that so close is the connexion between poverty and vice, that he who would improve the moral condition of the lower classes must carry bread with him as well as the Bible. Diabolus is never more potent than when he appears in the grim and ghastly form of hunger. The bitter gnawings of want often destroy the strongest citadels of virtue. How often, too, does he captivate the aspiring when he appeals to their *ambition,* by suggesting means of glory and distinction which will arrest the attention and command the plaudits of the vulgar ? His form is fascinating, and his wand is mighty, as he stands before them, and points to scenes where they can "make a show," and play a conspicuous part. He is the God of fashion. Nor is he less potent when he appeals to *avarice,* by pointing men to large possessions. Here, without exaggeration, he commands the energies, and wields a sovereignty over a large portion of the mercantile world. He stimulates the all-consecrating labour, suggests the falsehoods, and coins the tricks, of business.

But there is one circumstance which seems to me to have given a *peculiar* force to the temptation of Christ :—*He had the power to do and to get all that was suggested to Him through these impulses.* The motive to any effort is always weak in proportion to the *doubt* that may exist as to success. In most cases, when any sinful course is suggested to men, there comes this counteracting doubt. Is the man "an hungered," and is theft suggested to meet the cravings of nature ? The motive will be weak in proportion to the improbability of success. The same is true in relation to the other impulse. Whilst all men may desire power and wealth, all do not venture on the same course of falsehood and chicanery in order to realise them ; because of the *doubt* of success. We thank God for this doubt. It is a check to sin, it weakens temptation, it is a bridle on the demon passions of humanity. Give all men the power of getting their wishes, and our world becomes forthwith a pandemonium. Now,

Jesus had this power; He had no doubt about success. He could turn stones into bread by a volition; He could fall from the balustrade of the temple, and rise unhurt, amid the shouts of the multitude; He could take possession of all the kingdoms of the world in a moment. Oh, this capacity of certain success must have given a fearful and unparalleled power to His temptation! But He stood; the *idea* of duty and God triumphed over the meaner impulses of gratification and self.

We remark, again—

II. THAT IT WAS A BATTLE FOR DOMINION.—"*All these things will I give thee, if thou wilt fall down and worship me.*" The great end Diabolus sought in each attack, was the prostration of Christ's soul to the sway of his principles—the achieving of his infernal sovereignty over His inner being. This dominion meant at least two things: first, *the subordinating the spiritual to the material*—the getting of food, wealth, and power, at the sacrifice of great spiritual rights; and, secondly, *the subordinating of the divine to the self-seeking* —having the sense of God and duty swamped by personal considerations. God's will renounced, and personal will adopted as the sovereign principle. If this be the meaning, it follows that what was fruitlessly attempted with Christ, has succeeded in the case of humanity. Satan holds almost an absolute dominion. Everywhere the *material* is in the ascendency—the body with its five senses is on the throne—*intellect, genius,* and even *conscience,* are its serfs. And everywhere is the Divine will subordinated to the human. Alas, alas! the world has fallen down, and is now on its knees before Satan.

It is certainly here suggested *that this submission to Satan is the way to worldly possessions.* I will give Thee the world, says the EVIL ONE, "*if Thou wilt fall down and worship me.*" Is it not a general truth, that man must prostrate all that is divine in his soul to material and selfish impulses if he would gain much of the world?— that the highest prizes of Mammon are awarded to souls on their knees in the dust before Diabolus? Wouldst thou get worldly wealth and greatness, my friend? Then remember that *moral prostration of soul* is the condition. "ALL THESE THINGS WILL I GIVE THEE, IF THOU WILT FALL DOWN AND WORSHIP ME."

III. THAT IT WAS A BATTLE WON BY FAITH.—What was it that enabled Jesus to stand triumphantly against the powerful assaults of the arch-enemy of souls? Power not miraculous, but moral— power of faith. But faith in what? First. *Faith in the true Source of existence.* "It is written" (Deut. viii. 3), "Man doth not live by bread only, but by every word that proceedeth out of the Lord;" or, as the Hebrew has it, by "everything which proceedeth from the mouth of Jehovah." The language may mean either that man requires something more from God than bread in order to live, or that God's "word" or volition is the source of life. The former is true. Were we nothing but flesh and blood, bread might support us; but we are intellect, imagination, heart, conscience, and we crave for truth, beauty, goodness, God, as well as bread. Souls cannot feed on bread. But although this is a truth, the latter, we think, is the truth here taught. God's "word," or will, is the source of life. He can sustain us without bread, and starve us with it. The words of His mouth are the springs of created being. This is a deep truth, and Christ grasped it with an earnest faith. Second. *Faith in the true meaning of Scripture.* When the tempter quoted the passage from the 91st Psalm, Christ saw, at once, its misapplication, and said, " *It is written again, Thou shalt not tempt the Lord thy God;* " as if He had said, "Every attempt to force Scripture to wrong applications is to tempt—provoke—God ; and this, it is written, thou shalt not do." True faith in the Bible is not a faith in its words or forms, or mere human interpretations, but in its own spiritual meaning and true use. Third. *Faith in the true object of worship.* " *For it is written, Thou shalt worship the Lord thy God, and Him only shalt thou serve;* " as if He had said, "There is but one Being in the universe before whom I can prostrate my soul, and that is God." Now, it was by faith in these things that He stood ; and it is only by earnest, manly faith in these things that we can stand. Let these things be "WRITTEN," not merely on paper, on memory, on intellect, but on the broad and sunny tablet of every-day consciousness, and we shall stand against the wiles of the devil.

IV. THAT IT WAS A BATTLE RESULTING IN GLORY.—" *Then the devil leaveth Him, and, behold, angels came and ministered unto Him.*" His repulsion of the wicked was the attraction of the good. His high moral rectitude kept hell at bay and heaven in waiting. The coming of these angels to Christ suggests—(1) *that they are deeply interested in this moral conflict ;* and (2) *that their society is given only to the conqueror.* Angels came and ministered to Christ, because He crushed the great antagonist of virtue, God, and the universe.

> " So Satan fell; and straight a fiery globe
> Of angels, on full sail of wing, flew nigh,
> Who, on their plumy vans, received him soft
> From his uneasy station, and upbore,
> As on a floating couch, through the blithe air."

Matthew 4:12-25*

The Dawn of the Model Ministry

John "was cast into prison."† "The voice" which rose in the wilderness, rang its piercing tones through the heart of Jerusalem,

---

* Mark i. 14–20 ; Luke iv. 14, etc.

† For a detailed account of John's incarceration, see Matt. xiv. 3–12 ; Mark vi. 17–29 ; Luke iii. 19, 20.

and all Judea, and all the region round about Jordan, is now hushed in the oppressive silence of a cell; the ministry that was "a burning and shining light" has gone down amidst the dense gloom of a prison. But the world, though it incarcerates virtue, and seeks to quench the light of its great teacher, shall not be left in darkness. John's light has set, but with its last fading beams there mingles the dawn of another and a higher ministry. As the stars of all preliminary dispensations go down with John's imprisonment, the "GREAT LIGHT" from which they all derived their lustre arises "upon the people that sat in darkness."

This passage does not follow the preceding in immediate chronological relation; nor is there an immediate chronological relation even between the events which these verses bring together. But, notwithstanding this, they teach truths, in relation to the ministry of the Son of God—*the model ministry*—which are of universal application and of vital importance to all ages.

They teach us three grand truths about Christ's ministry, the practical development of which by the church is indispensable to the diffusion of Christianity and the spiritual progress of the world.

I. THAT ITS ASPECT WAS BOTH SPIRITUAL AND SECULAR.—In its *spiritual* aspect, the narrative suggests that it was *enlightening*. (1) It tells us that Jesus, according to an old prophecy, "*came and dwelt in Capernaum, which is upon the sea coast, in the borders of Zabulon and Nephthalim : that it might be fulfilled which was spoken by Esaias the prophet, saying,** *The land of Zabulon, and the land of Nephthalim, by the way of the sea, beyond Jordan, Galilee of the Gentiles; the people which sat in darkness saw great light; and to them which sat in the region and shadow of death light is sprung up.*" Christ was a *luminous* teacher : the truths He enunciated were all-revealing. They opened up a new world to the eye of the soul; they exposed time in the light of eternity, humanity in the light of God. And the way He presented them was most lucid. It was not in abstruse reasonings, nor incoherent declamation. He did not cloud His audiences with wordy redundances ; He did not perplex them with the dry formalities of logic, or the erudite references of criticism. His words were radiant. His hearers required neither the speculum of syntax nor science to see what He meant, for He spoke not so much to the critical, reasoning, or any other faculty, as to the *soul*. All the subjects He touched stood out in broad daylight to the common eye. Hence "the people who sat in darkness," when He appeared amongst them, saw a "great light" throwing its beams on those spiritual domains of existence which sin, for ages, had enwrapped in gloom. (2) The narrative suggests further, in relation to the spiritual aspect of Christ's ministry, that it was *reformative*. "*From that time Jesus began to preach, and to say,*

* The evangelist sees nothing accidental in the choice of this very locality, but, on the contrary, he sees in it the fulfilment of a prophecy of Isaiah (ix. 1, 2). The passage quoted means, that the light of the Messiah would reveal itself in the most brilliant manner, in the most despised localities of Palestine.—*Olshausen.*

Repent: for the kingdom of heaven is at hand." The reformation He sought was not a mere revolution in intellectual ideas, or in external habits. It would require the former as a means, and ensure the latter as a result. It was a thorough change in the *presiding* disposition of the soul that He sought. It is fully expressed in the two words, "Follow me," which He now addressed to those fishermen on the shores of Galilee, who forthwith became His disciples. True reformation of soul consists in *following* Him who is the divine embodiment and minister of that disinterested benevolence which is the one sovereign law of all holy mind, and the one necessary condition of all moral order and true joy.

But His ministry had a *secular* as well as spiritual aspect. He was not merely engaged in preaching to souls, but in "*healing all manner of sickness and all manner of disease among the people. And His fame went throughout all Syria: and they brought unto Him all sick people that were taken with divers diseases and torments, and those which were possessed with devils, and those which were lunatic, and those that had the palsy; and He healed them.*" What a catalogue of physical woes is this! and yet it is but a specimen of the bodily sufferings which He thus removed at the outset of His public life. Jesus did not overlook the claims and the woes of the body in His endeavours to enlighten and reform the soul. He fed those who were hungry and healed those who were sick; and thus He "*took our infirmities, and bore our sickness.*"

That the ministry of Christ had this twofold aspect is not only an unquestionable, but a significant, fact. It indicates the method in which His system should ever have been presented to mankind; that it should have been made to appear the friend of humanity in all its varied sufferings—the divine instrumentality to remove all evils, natural and moral, from the world. But how lamentably has the church failed in this matter! It has almost *entirely* neglected the secular aspect. Attempts to remove political wrongs, and promote measures for the physical well-being of society, have generally been considered as beneath her high calling, and a work too worldly for her holy hands. Had the church exhibited Christianity in the spirit of its Lord—made it appear to men more as a secular benefactor, and less as a theological belligerent; had the world seen it more in the acts of a genial messenger of deep and genuine philanthropy, penetrating the darkest scenes of trial, with a word to cheer and a hand to bless; and less in pompous ceremonies, conflicting creeds, and affected pietisms,—the secularly depressed, the great bulk of the race, would then have had their sympathies in warm and living connexion with it, instead of, as now, having their hearts loofed away in antipathy, and setting up a system of "secularism" to oppose and crush it. Moreover, the church has not only neglected the presentation of the secular aspect of Christianity, but it has often failed in the spiritual. Has it presented it as Christ did—to *enlighten* and *reform;* or to bewilder with party controversies, and to win over to little sects?

Has the reformation it has sought been an endeavour to turn men to the one true and living God, or to turn them to its own dogmas and politics? Let history answer.

II. THAT ITS SYMPATHIES ARE THOROUGH AND PRACTICAL.—The verses suggest three thoughts illustrative of the thoroughness of Christ's sympathies :—First. *They had respect to man in the lowest condition.* The tract of country here described as the scene on which Christ now entered, where he henceforth takes up His residence, and which He makes the special field of His ministry and miracles, was populated by the obscurest classes of the "Holy Land." The dwellers in those northern frontiers of the country were, for the most part, poor, ignorant, and despised. Living at such a remote distance from Jerusalem, the centre of religious light, and so near to the pagan world, they were truly a *"people which sat in darkness."* Yet these obscure and benighted men seem to excite the special sympathies of the Son of God. As a divine teacher, He could have selected the most aristocratic and enlightened portion of Palestine as the scene of His residence, and the sphere of His labour, but *" He descended into the lowest parts of the earth."* Does not this show the thoroughness of His interest in man? Does it not show that humanity, stripped of every vestige of adventitious worth, the creature of indigence and the child of woe, is an object of deep interest to Him? But these verses suggest another thought illustrative of the thoroughness of Christ's sympathies, and that is, secondly, *That they had respect to man in the entirety of his nature.* He did not, as we have already seen, overlook either part of man's nature, body or soul. He was neither of that class of semi-philanthropists who ignore the soul, and look at man as a mere bundle of corporeal interests; nor of that who weep sentimental tears over the unfelt woes of the soul, but are cold and callous in relation to the physical sufferings of mankind. His sympathies encompassed the whole man in all the elements of his being, the variety of his circumstances, and the vastness and variety of his relations. The verses suggest yet another thought illustrative of the thoroughness of Christ's sympathies, and that is, thirdly, *That they had respect to man in the influence of his social relation.* *" Follow me, and I will make you fishers of men."* An apt figure, taken from the daily calling of the men whom he addressed, intended to express the truth, that if they followed Him, He would employ them to collect men into His blessed empire of truth and love. *Christ seeks to make men useful in their influence.* The social influence of a man is the most serious item in his existence. No one can measure the influence of a solitary individual : it is a stream which, although insignificant at first, gets new volume every hour, works a channel through the soul of ages, imparts vitality or diffuses death as it wends its ever-swelling course ; and thus operates on posterity, either for good or ill, long after the name of its originator has sunk in oblivion. If the influence is not good, posterity is injured ;— yes, and the very person, too, who has exerted it will be made to suffer, both by a necessary reaction and a righteous retribution. Now, the thoroughness of Christ's sympathy for man is seen in the regard which He manifested for this *mighty power*. He sought to convert it into a power to bless posterity. " *I will make you fishers of men.*" Christ blesses men that they may bless their race. His heart was not confined to the men he saw, or to His contemporaries : distant empires and unborn generations were the objects of His love.

But all this thorough sympathy here displayed was *practical*. It was not a thing that expended itself in words, or tears, or prayers ; it took the form of earnest, persevering, all-consecrating labour. " *And Jesus went about all Galilee,*" etc. It were superfluous to ask whether the followers of Jesus have copied this feature of this *model* ministry. Where, in what post-apostolic age, and in what section of the church, do you find sympathies like these—sympathies so genuine and deep, so all embracing and practical ? These sympathies are the warm life-blood of the church ; and because they scarcely circulate in her veins, her appearance has the repulsive ghastliness of disease rather than the fascinating bloom of health. She is too languid : her voice is too feeble to pierce the ear of the age, and her hand too palsied for her work.

We infer again, from this passage, in relation to the ministry of Christ,—

III. THAT ITS USEFULNESS WAS BOTH DIRECT AND INDIRECT.— There are two kinds of influence which moral beings are capable of exerting—that which arises from an *intentional* effort, and that which arises *incidentally* as the social consequence of our conduct. If I reason with a man for any purpose, the influence I produce upon his mind is by intention ; but if others, through the report of my reasoning, are influenced by it, the influence is incidental ; it never entered into my purpose. Every man, perhaps, exerts more of the incidental than the intentional. Our direct efforts to influence men are only occasional. Incidentally, however, the whole of our life, which comes within the cognizance of others, produces an influence. The usefulness which springs from the two sources is the highest : and this was the usefulness of Christ's ministry. *Here is the direct or intentional.* To Peter and his brother Andrew, James and his brother John, Christ now makes a *personal* appeal, and the effect produced was what he designed. His merciful behest went at once to their hearts, and forthwith they left their craft and their nets, and followed Him. It is true that we have not the power over moral mind which Christ possessed, and therefore cannot calculate with certainty upon results, but we ought undoubtedly to imitate Him in the direct personalness of His appeals. We should ponder the fact, that our great Example dealt with men *individually* as well as collectively, in the unit as well as in the mass. But here, too, we have the *indirect* or incidental usefulness of Christ. " *His fame went throughout all Syria.*" " *And there followed Him great multitudes of people from Galilee, and from Decapolis, and from*

Jerusalem, and from Judea, and from beyond Jordan." The *indirect* influence which thus drew within the glance of Christ's eye, and the reach of His voice, these vast throngs from the different parts of the country, must have been highly useful. Many of them, undoubtedly, would go back to their homes, not only with new and stirring ideas, but with noble impulses and higher aims.

Here, again, the disparity between the ministry of Christ and that of the church painfully recurs to memory. How little, in the ministry of the church, has been the *personal* dealing with men— the bringing of soul into individual contact with soul. Has not Christianity been spoken more in the official than in the individual voice—more to the promiscuous assemblage than to the unit man? Has not its ministry been more that of a formal church to a vague world, than of person to person, soul to soul? How little, too, has been the indirect usefulness of the church! The multitudes have not gathered around her for many ages now; she has no attraction for them; and how to bring the millions within her precincts is the present all-absorbing problem of the good. My solution is this:— Let the church minister Christianity after the fashion of its model, and the people will flock to it as doves to the windows yet.

Matthew 5:1-12

The Beatitudes; or, the Elements of Well-being

It is obvious, both from this passage and the preceding one, that the biographers of Jesus have given us but brief specimens of the wonderful things which He did and said. We have but the outlines of His history, the texts of His sermons. Thanks to a merciful Providence for gathering up these precious fragments, and, from distant lands and remote centuries, conveying them safely into our hands this day. Jesus is now surrounded by "multitudes," who had followed Him from the different parts of Galilee through which He had passed; for it would seem that, at every stage He reached, His audience increased in numbers, like rivers by the inflowing of new streams. His *popularity* is full of significance. Although the fame of public teachers does not always reflect honour on themselves—proves, in too many cases, the *thoughtlessness* of their followers, rather than the superior power of their minds, greatness of their characters, or accuracy of their doctrines— still, in the case of Jesus, it illustrates the superiority of His *spiritual* power. There is no other way to account for it. He was known as the carpenter's son. He was the despised Nazarene, without friend or home; scowled at by the authorities of the country; and the doctrines He taught, too, clashed with all the prejudices of the men He addressed—men who were characterized by a blind and violent attachment to old dogmas and customs. His low pedigree, His known poverty, His humble appearance, His fearless honesty, and His doctrines, striking directly and obviously against the public sentiment of His times, leave the phenomena of His popularity to be explained only on the ground of His transcendent spiritual force.

"Seeing the multitudes" which now surround Him, "He went up into a mountain," and there—with the vast assemblage and His chosen disciples—He sat down, "and opened His mouth." There, on the open mountain, in the great amphitheatre of nature, He opened His mouth to teach. The expansiveness of the natural scenery around accorded with, and helped to express, the illimitable love which He breathed, and the universal truths which He taught. Neither the light that gladdened the scene, nor the breezes that swept over the mountain, were more free than the sentiments and spirit of His teaching. Indeed He made the natural objects which were spread about Him—the "lily of the field," the "birds of the air," the "city upon the hill," the "house upon the rock"—symbols to express His ideas. He made nature a mirror to reflect His mind. "*He opened His mouth.*" This was the dawn of a new era in the mental history of the world: it was as the rising of a new sun upon the spiritual firmament; or as the cleaving of another rock in our Horeb, to supply us with the refreshing streams of life. From those "blessed lips" proceeded ideas which the world had never heard before—ideas which, although repugnant to the general spirit of mankind, have been gaining ground ever since, and will one day be the imperial thoughts of cabinets and kingdoms.

At the very opening of His discourse, He brings at once under their notice the great subject of *happiness*—a subject which has ever been the master-theme of human thought, and the primal end of human purpose and action. Lived there ever a man, however learned, or however rude, through whose mind the question has not often revolved, as the most impulsive sentiment of the heart, "Who will show us any good?" It is the deep and unceasing cry of humanity, and He now responds to it who only could. The Teacher of the World took up the world-wide theme, and expressed in brief, but clear, language the *great elements of well-being.*

In looking closely at these *elements* of blessedness, we discover two things which are worthy of our attention—*a general correspondence between the whole, and a fundamental difference between some.* The examination of these two points will, we trust, develop the moral meaning and spirit of the passage. Here is—

I. A GENERAL CORRESPONDENCE BETWEEN THE WHOLE.—As sources of happiness, they agree in three things—they are all *spiritual, unpopular,* and *present.* First. They are all *spiritual*: they are states of *heart.* They are not something *out* of man, after which he has to reach, nor something that is put into him as an *entity* distinct from his being; they are states into which his heart is to pass—they are *habits of the soul.* This is a feature of Christ's theory of happiness that gives it a universal application, that puts blessedness within the reach of every man. Had Christ represented the elements of happiness as consisting in any particular condition of life, then it is clear that, whatever condition that might have been, it would have come not only not *partially* without the reach of all, but *wholly* without the reach of many; or had He represented them as connected with a certain order of intellectual talent, or a certain amount of intellectual acquirement, it is perfectly obvious that a large portion of every successive generation, from the diversity of capacity and opportunity, would be excluded from the blessedness of being. But when He makes them to consist in states of the heart, then he puts them within the reach of all. *Humility, meekness, mercifulness, desire for rectitude,* etc.—are they not states as attainable by the child as the adult, the poor as the rich, the untutored as the sage ? "*Keep thy heart with all diligence, for out of it are the issues of life.*" The river of life takes its rise in the heart, and the germs of paradise are imbedded there.

> Let its rock be smitten, that the river may flow ;
> Let its soil be tilled, that the germs may grow.

Another point of correspondence between them all is, secondly, that they are all *unpopular*. The general mind of mankind has looked for happiness everywhere rather than to the *heart*. It has never attached the idea of blessedness to the dispositions mentioned by Christ. It has ever said, Blessed are the men high in office, and robed in magnificence ; blessed are the opulent and the gay ; blessed are the victorious and the valiant ; and, sometimes, blessed are the intelligent and the wise ;—but public sentiment has never yet said blessed are the *poor in spirit* and the *meek in heart*. But whilst Christ's idea has *generally* been unpopular in the world, it was *especially* so with the men he addressed. They were Jews : all their notions of religion, greatness, and happiness, were pre-eminently material ; and it would seem that the minds of the "multitudes" who surrounded Jesus were filled and fired, at this moment, with gross ideas of well-being. Their hearts beat high with the hope that He whom they had followed up the mountain would assure them of the speedy conquest of Rome, and the reinstating of their country in more than the wealth and grandeur of ancient times. But how directly did the ideas of Jesus clash with all these notions and hopes ! What sublime indifference to popularity, what unconquerable integrity of soul did He display, who now—in the face of assembled thousands, whose excited minds were raging with ocean fury for conquest and dominion—stated, at the very outset of His discourse, views that would strike at the strongest prejudices, and dissipate the most eager and brilliant hopes ! The fact that Christ's views of happiness—which are undeniably true both in philosophy and experience—are thus so unpopular, argues (1) *the divinity of His mission,* and (2) *the moral darkness of man.*

But another point of correspondence between them all is, thirdly, they are all *present*. "Blessed *are*," says Christ; not blessed shall be. He who has these dispositions *is* blessed. The dispositions are blessedness, and as the dispositions increase in purity and strength, the blessedness will heighten and expand. We are not to look to any *distant* locality or onward period to get happiness, but to the state of the heart. The true heaven is in the soul. Unless glory is revealed within, there will be no glory without. A soul clouded with guilt, and turbulent with conflicting passions, will darken the brightest suns, and turn the sweetest music into discord.

II. A CIRCUMSTANTIAL DIFFERENCE BETWEEN SOME.—The elements of happiness here propounded by Christ divide themselves into two grand classes—the NECESSARY and the CONTINGENT—those which are indispensable to the happiness of a moral being in all worlds, and for ever, and those which depend upon the circumstances in which moral mind is found existing in this world of sin and suffering. Let us thoughtfully attend to each of these classes :—

First. *The necessary, or those which are indispensable to the well-being of moral souls in all worlds, for ever.* There are four of these in this passage—*humility, meekness, holy aspirations,* and *purity of heart.* Jesus refers to the first in the expression "poor in spirit." The word " poor " implies *destitution.* What, then, is the destitution here meant? It is not the destitution of *temporal good ;* for although physical poverty may be overruled for spiritual good, it is nevertheless an evil in itself. It is not the destitution of *intellectual knowledge.* This is a greater evil still. " *For the soul to be without knowledge is not good.*" Better be without food for the body than without ideas for the mind. Great ideas are the pinions of the soul : by them we soar, with eagle swiftness, from the earth, cleave the clouds, and bask high up in the bright day-beams of truth. Nor is it the destitution of *mental independency* that is here meant. That fawning spirit, the brand-mark of little souls, which sacrifices the rights of manhood for the smiles of power, has ever been, and still is, one of the greatest obstructions in the path of human progress. It is the broad base in society on which all despotisms, political and religious, rear their crushing iron thrones. But the destitution Jesus means is that of SELF-IMPORTANCE—the entire absence of all pride and egotistic thought and feeling. Where this humility is not, where there is pride in any mind, there can be no blessedness. By pride the pure spirits of heaven sank to hell; by humility the imperfect spirits of earth ascend to heaven. He that humbleth himself is exalted. Of these humble souls Jesus says, " *theirs is the kingdom.*" All the privileges and immunities of the good are *theirs* in experience now. How happy is a truly humble soul !—how free from all those painful emotions which ever start from restless ambitions, empty vanity, and foolish pride ! How acquiescent in Heaven's arrangements, and how sensible of every heavenly gift ! The smallest mercy touches the heart-chords into music, and, along the darkest path, the spirit sings, "I am not worthy of the least of all thy favours." Verily, "theirs is the kingdom of heaven."

Another of these elements of well-being, which are indispensable to the happiness of moral souls in all worlds, and for ever, is *meekness*. "*Blessed are the meek : for they shall inherit the earth.*" What is meekness? It is not *stoical insensibility*. Jesus was meek, and yet no nature was more sensitive than His : the softest zephyr rippled the deep crystal current of His heart. Nor is it *cowardice*—the opposite of the intrepid and the brave in feeling—but it is calm energy of soul. It is power blended with gentleness—boldness with humility—the harmlessness of the dove with the prowess of the lion. It is the soul in the majesty of self-possession, elevated above the precipitant, the irascible, the boisterous, and the revengeful. It is the soul throwing its benignant smiles on the furious face of the foe, and penetrating his heart and paralyzing his arm with the look of love. This is, indeed, an element of blessedness : they who have it, says Christ, "*shall inherit the earth.*" The allusion here may be to Canaan; and as the Jews in the wilderness looked forward to the inheriting of Palestine as the highest good, probably Jesus uses the expression to convey to their minds the idea, that the meek in spirit shall receive the best of blessings. Still the language need not be regarded as thus figurative. It is *literally* true that the men of holy meekness "*inherit the earth.*" Who is the man that most truly inherits the earth? Not the man of an ambitious and restless spirit, though he may call a million acres his own. Such a man has no spirit-home : his soul roams through his estates, like the unclean spirit in the desert, seeking rest, but finding none. It is the man of holy meekness that *inherits* the earth. Though, on legal grounds, he has no claim to a foot of soil, he feels a vital interest and a spiritual property in all. He is the master of himself; he can sit upon the throne of his own being, bid his intellect turn the phenomena of the universe into joyous realms of thought; his heart, the wide earth into a temple of devotion; and his faith, the fiercest roar of the elements into music. He *inherits* the earth—feels at home in all—appropriates all—makes all serve the high ends of his being.

Another of these elements of well-being, which are indispensable to the happiness of moral souls in all worlds, and for ever, is *holy aspiration*. "*Blessed are they which do hunger and thirst after righteousness, for they shall be filled.*" There are centering in our complicated nature a variety of appetites. These appetites are ever the springs of action. There are the animal for food, the intellectual for truth, the moral for rectitude. The power of the first is seen in all : it keeps the world in action. The power of the second is seen mainly in the thinker : it is the impulse of the philosopher. The power of the last is seen in the church : it is the spring of religion. The second is not so generally felt as the first, nor is the third so generally felt as the second, and yet the third far transcends the other two in importance. Man's deepest want is *righteousness*, and to hunger and thirst for it is therefore natural and right. Appetite implies two things :—(1) *Health.* The body without appetite for food is diseased, the intellect without an appetite for truth is diseased, and the soul without an appetite for righteousness is diseased; and the reason, therefore, why men do not hunger and thirst more after righteousness, is because the soul *is* diseased. Appetite implies (2) *Provision.* The existence of any native desire —physical, intellectual, or moral—implies a corresponding object. They that hunger and thirst after "righteousness"—moral excellence—"*shall* be filled." There is no obstacle to prevent the poorest man from becoming good. Goodness, like the air we breathe, is ever at hand; it encompasses our path. If we really *desire* it, we shall have it. This holy aspiration is indispensable to the happiness of all finite intelligences; without it, even angelic natures would have no stimulus, and would make no progress. Their energies would wane into weakness for the want of exercise. Under its craving force the world of happy spirits ever press "towards the mark" for a still higher "prize;" and, as they press, they rise to brighter scenes, and feel the ecstacies of sublimer joys. Truly blessed, then, are they that "*hunger and thirst after righteousness.*"

Another of these elements of well-being, which are indispensable to the happiness of moral souls in all worlds, and for ever, is *purity of heart.* "*Blessed are the pure in heart; for they shall see God.*" The Jews attended well to ceremonial cleanness, but sadly neglected cleanness of heart. A pure heart is a heart where divine love, like a celestial fire, flames on, burning up all that is sensual and false, illuminating every chamber of the soul, and making God visible in its beams. Under the Law, none but those who were ceremonially pure were admitted to the presence of God in His temple. This was an arrangement only to symbolize the truth before us, that without purity of heart—moral holiness—no man can *see the Lord.* God cannot be seen by the bodily eye, for He has no form; nor by the intellectual eye, for, beyond the utmost limits of all ratiocination, He "*dwells in light which no man can approach*" intellectually. He can be seen with the eye of the *heart,* and only with that eye when the heart is pure. The atmosphere around these hearts must be cleared of all the mists and fogs of evil, if we would see the Eternal Sun in His glory. The moral mirror of the soul must be burnished well before it can reflect the glorious image of its God. "Without holiness no man shall see the Lord."

Secondly. *The other class of the elements of well-being here mentioned are the contingent, or those which are indispensable to the happiness of a moral being in this world of sin and suffering.* These are *penitential sorrow, mercy, peace-making,* and *righteous endurance.* The first is referred to in the fourth verse :—"*Blessed are they that mourn : for they shall be comforted.*" Mourning arises from various causes. Disappointments, bereavements, diseases, poverty, social slander, oppression, moral contrition, are some of the sources from which proceed those manifold streams of sorrow which roll their turbulent billows over human souls. But it is, we think, to *moral mourning*—mourning on account of sin—that Jesus here refers. This penitential sorrow does not arise merely from the fear of the *consequences* of sin, either temporal or eternal, but from a deep sense of its enormity as rebellion against the God of infinite holiness and love. This "godly sorrow, which worketh repentance to salvation not to be repented of," is truly a "blessed" sorrow. Though painful, it is only the Great Physician probing the moral wound before He applies the "sovereign balm;" it is but the passing tempest, whose frowning fury is clearing the air, watering the earth, making bright the sky, and unveiling in fairer beauties the face of the world. This element of well-being is not necessary in heaven, because there is no sin there; but it is indispensable to the happiness of every depraved soul on earth. Christ announces an irrevocable law in this beatitude, and that is, that *penitential sorrow must precede human happiness.* "Except ye repent, ye shall likewise perish."

> E'er since the fall man's penitence his blessedness precedes ;
> 'Tis grief that tunes his heart to music,
> 'Tis tribulation fits him for the skies.

Mercy is another element indispensable to the happiness of a moral being in this world of sin and suffering. Mercy is a modification of benevolence: it is benevolence called out in a certain direction, and feeling for a certain class, and that class the suffering. Mercy is benevolence commiserating the sufferer. Nature, in her ten thousand modes, expresses God's benevolence. Christ, in His sympathies and prayers, His doctrines and doings, His sufferings and death; expresses God's mercy. He is benevolence in contact with suffering. So long as we are in a world of suffering, it is required of us that our benevolence should go out in the form of *mercy.* Mercifulness beseems our situation, and is essential to our spiritual culture. This form of love is not required in heaven, because of the absence of suffering from that happy scene. "The merciful," says Christ, "shall *obtain* mercy." We all here, as children of woe, *need* mercy. No law is more certain than this, both in relation to society and God. With what measure we mete, it shall be measured to us again. "Inasmuch as ye did it unto the least of these my brethren, ye did it unto me." Mercy is its own reward:—

> " It is twice blessed ;
> It blesses him that gives, and him that takes.
> 'Tis mightiest in the mightiest: it becomes
> The thronèd monarch better than his crown."

Another element here mentioned as belonging to the happiness of a moral being in this world of sin and suffering is, *peacemaking.* "Blessed are the peacemakers : for they shall be called the children of God." The disposition of a peacemaker is a blessed one: it implies *self-control—a generous sympathy with the conflicting parties—a calm, moral, mediating power, equal to the subjugation of antagonistic souls.* The peacemaker has far higher attributes than the warrior. A man has only to have the low cunning of the fox and the savage daring of the lion to become famous on the battle-field; but he must have the philosophy of a sage and the love of a saint to act effectively the "days-man"—put his hand upon contending parties, and of "twain make one." Such "shall be called"—*shall be*—"the children of God." The peacemaker is like the "God of peace;" and filiation to that God consists in *moral assimilation* to His character.

There is yet another element mentioned as belonging to the blessedness of moral being in this world of sin and suffering, and that is, *righteous endurance.* "*Blessed are they which are persecuted for righteousness' sake: for theirs is the kingdom of heaven. Blessed are ye when men shall revile you, and persecute you, and shall say all manner of evil against you falsely, for my sake. Rejoice, and be exceedingly glad : for great is your reward in heaven: for so persecuted they the prophets which were before you.*" Jesus does not say that all who suffer and are persecuted are blessed. This would not be true. He therefore states two attributes of the persecution to which He attaches these blessings: First. *It must be undeserved.* It must be evil said or done against you FALSELY. There could be no blessing in merited suffering. Secondly. *This undeserved persecution must be for "righteousness' sake."* It must be inflicted on account of your faithful attachment to right and Christ. "*For my sake.*" When persecution comes thus—when it is undeserved, and for Christ's sake—its endurance is, indeed, a great blessing. 1. It connects us with the highest system. "*Theirs is the kingdom of heaven.*" 2. It ensures for us the highest reward. "*Great is your reward in heaven.*" 3. It identifies us with the greatest men of all ages. "*For so persecuted they the prophets which were before you.*" Elijah, Elisha, Jeremiah, and Daniel, are a few of the great examples. Their sufferings lifted them to a world-wide and lasting renown.

Such are the elements of well-being here propounded by Christ. One class is indispensable to the happiness of moral mind everywhere, and for ever; and the other class is indispensable to the happiness of moral mind in this world, where there is sin and suffering, and war and persecution. Let us learn to seek our happiness, not in outward wealth and power, but in the cultivation of these moral elements. Philosophy and experience unite with Christ in declaring that such states of the heart are the only sources of true joy. The well-cultivated soul is man's only paradise. There are the "living fountains of waters;" there grows every tree that is pleasant to the sight and good for food. The "tree of life" springs from within : the soul is its own heaven.

Matthew 5:13-16

The Valuable Influence of Embodied Christianity

There are three great facts contained in this passage which claim our attention :—

I. THAT MAN'S SOCIAL HISTORY IS PRE-EMINENTLY THAT OF INFLUENCE. —Christ here refers to a physical fact—the influence of one kind of matter upon another—in order to express the power that man puts forth upon man. Science gives us to understand that the principle of influence pervades every part of the material universe; that the fluttering of an insect's wing sends its vibrations to the remotest orb in the great field of space. Be this as it may, man influences man. *"No man liveth unto himself."* Each influences, and is influenced. No one is either above or beneath the modifying touch of this subtle, all-penetrating, and ever-flowing element of power. By it man multiplies his moral self, gives immortality and universality to the ideas that spring from his intellect, and the principles that shape his life. The words that drop from his lips fall as pebbles into the centre of a placid lake, creating a series of undulating and ever-widening circles over the whole expanse. Thus the spirit of past generations throbs in us; and down through posterity it shall flow, and be the moral life-blood of the men that are to be.

There are two things which account, in some measure, for this wonderful fact in our history :—First. *The bond of physical relationship.* We have descended from one stock; we are branches of one primal root. The blood of Adam circulates through the veins of all. We are all of *one nature,* members of one organic whole. This relationship gives to the parent an almost absolute power over the mind and character of the child : the one feels that he has a *right* to wield the power, and the other that it is his *duty* and happiness to yield. I can conceive of beings existing together where there is no such physical bond; who are not produced through any secondary instrumentalities; who have no parent but One, and that is God; between whom and the ETERNAL, in the order of relationship, there stands no one. Such beings would, to a great extent, stand distinct from, and independent of, each other. Such is not man. Every man derives his existence from a line of ancestry which lengthens with every age; a link in the long chain is he, and the motion of all past links moves him. The other thing which serves to account for this fact in our history is, secondly, *the bond of universal interdependence.* The principle of mutual dependence is one of the most absolute to which we are subject. No man is independent of another; and, as a rule, those who pride themselves in their imaginary independence, are the most dependent. The diversities which exist in *the intelligent powers, mental attainments, the secular positions, the ages,* and *general capa-*

bilities of men, give universal sweep and resistless energy to this principle of interdependence. Man is dependent upon man for his education, his support, his protection, his comfort, and his religion. Who does not see that this law necessitates influence? There may be beings living together who are entirely independent of each other. There may be such a perfect *equality* between their *being* and *circumstances*, that one has no power either to help or injure another. They may derive their blessings *direct* from the Fountain, and not through the channel of mutual operation. If such creatures there be, we see not how they *could* influence each other. Such, however, is not man's case: he is ever *giving* to, and *receiving* from, his brother: he cannot live without it.

Such conditions may help to explain, and perhaps to impress the solemn fact, that *man's social history is pre-eminently that of influence.* The other fact contained in this passage is—

II. That embodied Christianity renders this influence incalculably valuable.—A power so gigantic as this power of influence— a power which may be said to be the *totality* of all other human powers —cannot but suggest and enforce the question, What must man become in order that his influence may be a blessing rather than a curse to the race? This question our great Instructor virtually answers in the passage before us, when He says, "*that they may see your good works, and glorify your Father which is in heaven.*" It is the GOOD WORKS that will induce others to "glorify our Father which is in heaven." But what are good works? Not occasional acts of goodness, but the uniform habits of a life inspired with supreme love to God; they are the natural branches of a soul whose affections are rooted in God and truth; they are the developments of Christ's life, embodied Christianity, the soul of our souls. If we have not these, then, however accurate our theology, unexceptionable our external conduct, and holy our professions, our character will be but as salt that has "*lost its savour*," "*thenceforth good for nothing but to be cast out and trodden under foot of men.*" It was thus with the Jewish nation; they were an orthodox people and regular in religious observances, but they had no *spiritual life;* their salt had "lost its savour"—lost its pungent spiritedness and anti-corrupting power: they had become a nation of insipid and soulless hypocrites, and were fit for nothing but the fate which awaited them,—but to be cast out, and to be trodden under the crushing foot of pagan Rome. This embodied Christianity does three things in its influence:— First. *It conserves the good.* "Herein," says Olshausen, "lies the point of comparison between the disciples and the salt: it is contained in that power which prevents corruption and imparts life." There is a tendency in animal matter to putrefaction, and the peculiar property of salt is, that it counteracts this tendency; it is a *preservative.* Here is the resemblance. There is a sad disposedness in humanity to degeneracy. Although the human soul has instinctive aspirations and powers to rise, although it is designed and in every way fitted to move upward for ever, it has somehow received a

strong bias downward, and external circumstances are ever bearing
it in that direction. History abounds with examples of moral de-
clination, and all hearts are conscious of this gravitating force. What
is the counteractive? *The life of Christ in man.* That life flashes a
light upon the corrupt heart of society, and makes it blush. But
few will dare to sin in the presence of living holiness. Night cannot
retain its empire in the presence of the sun. Vice cowers under the
radiant eye of virtue. Had not England been salted to some extent
with true Christian influence, what would have been the description of
her literature, the character of her laws, and the morals of her people?
Verily, unless "the Lord of hosts had left unto us a very small rem-
nant, we should have been as Sodom, and like unto Gomorrah."
Secondly. *It reveals the good.* "*Ye are the light of the world.*" A
true disciple is a light—an orb reflecting the rays of the Father of
lights. There is more of God seen in a good man than the whole
material universe can unfold: he is a partaker of the divine nature;
God shines *in* him and *through* him. Light brings distant things
near: scenes far away are brought into immediate contact with the
eye, and paint their image on the soul, through light. Even distant
stars are brought close home to our hearts through the pale and
gentle beams they shed on our path. Even so it is with the character
of a *true* disciple: his conversation, his conduct, his spirit, his life,
throw such a light upon the moral eye of men as to bring God, duty,
and eternity, very near. Thirdly. *It propagates the good.* It leads
men to "*glorify your Father which is in heaven.*" The language of
Christ implies, that if men really see good works in others, they will
be induced to glorify God; and to glorify God is the highest good
of man. "It is a good thing to give praise unto God;" it involves
all else. In it our powers alone receive their true development, our
deepest wants their supply, our highest aspirations their end.
Philosophically, man cannot rise in real power and blessedness without the true worship of the true God. The religious nature is the
spring and soul of our being, and this must be put right, or all else
will be wrong. Now, *embodied Christianity* is the highest appeal to
the religious in man: it is the voice of God in its most touching and
intelligible accents. There is a *causative* connexion between *seeing*
"good works" in others and glorifying God.

III. THAT THIS VALUABLE INFLUENCE OF EMBODIED CHRISTIANITY
IS DESTINED TO SPREAD. The passage shows that its diffusion is
guaranteed by three things—*inherent fitness, divine intention, moral
obligation.*

First. *Here is inherent fitness.* It is compared to "*salt.*" There
is a tendency in salt to penetrate the mass into which it is put—to
work its way through every particle, and to impart its character to
the whole. It is compared to "*light.*" There is a tendency in light
to throw its radiance over all the objects within its reach. It is
compared to "*a city that is set on a hill.*" There is a tendency in
that to attract the attention of the surrounding neighbourhood, and
to send its spirit down through all the suburban districts. Even so

there is a tendency, a fitness, in embodied Christianity to permeate the circles in which it lives and moves.

Secondly. *Here is a divine intention.* " *Neither do men light a candle, and put it under a bushel, but on a candlestick ; and it giveth light unto all that are in the house.*" Who kindled the lamp of moral goodness in the soul ? Who lighted up the bright and holy flame in the sin-darkened spirit ? HE who of old commanded the light to shine out of darkness. Why did He do it ? Not that it might be concealed, but exposed. He gives light to the sun, that it may fling its beams on the dark orbs that roll far away ; and these orbs catch the rays, and send them farther on. Even so it is in *morals :* God kindles a new light in a soul, that that soul may give light to all that are in the house—all within the sweep of its influence.

Thirdly. *Here is moral obligation.* "*Let your light so shine before men.*" Here is a divine command urging it. In connexion with the natural tendency of embodied Christianity to spread itself, its subject feels *bound,* by the same solemn obligations, to make its diffusion the grand end of being.

This *embodied* Christianity is the great desideratum, but it is, confessedly, a rare thing amongst us. Barren creeds, conventional formalities, and zeal far more denominational than divine, make up, to a great extent, the Christianity of this age. The Christianity which the Church is holding out to the world in these days is something like the sham beast that Prometheus is said to have offered to the God of thunder, without flesh or blood—a mere hide stuffed with bones ! — dry bones ! The *salt* has lost its savour : our religion has become tasteless. It has no pungent spiritedness. To induce people to contribute to the spread of the Gospel, missionary platforms often quote the good old aphorism, "Great is the truth, and it will prevail." But we are only deceiving ourselves, and others too, if we do not remember another aphorism equally true and profound—namely, that *Moral truth can only prevail over moral error by meeting it in its own form.* If the errors of the world existed only in abstract theories and fine speeches, then your truth, by abstract arguments and eloquent harangues, could put it down. But errors are *concrete* things : they are not merely in the brain, on the tongue, or in the folio, but they are in the life—they are *embodied.* Your infidelity, your paganism, your irreligions and wrong religions, are all *incarnations ;* they are realities in men, wrought into the very texture of their experience. If, therefore, your truth is ever to prevail over these errors, *its word must become flesh, and dwell amongst them.* Let "the Church's mind move in charity, rest in providence, and turn upon the poles of truth," and then its light shall so shine before men that others will see its "good works, and glorify our Father which is in heaven."

Matthew 5:17-48

The Mission of a True Reformer Constructive, not Destructive

The cautionary expression, "think not," with which our passage opens, implies, on the part of the Speaker, a fear lest His hearers should draw a wrong conclusion, either from what He had said, or was about to say. The wrong conclusion against which He guards them is that of regarding Him as aiming to destroy that grand system of religious truth and law which the Eternal had revealed to their forefathers, and which had been handed down to them from remotest antiquity.

There are four general truths running through this passage :—

First. *That the old revelation was of divine authority.* Had "the law and the prophets"—the writings of the Old Testament collectively—not been of God, Christ would not have spoken of them as He does here. The New Testament everywhere recognizes and teaches the divinity of the Old. The utterances of Moses and the prophets are as truly divine as those of Christ and His apostles.

Secondly. *That the Old and the New constitute but one system of truth.* The Law and the Gospel are not opposite, or even separate, systems ; they are one organic whole. Christ came " to fulfil "—to carry out into full and perfect development—the Old. The "law and the prophets*"* are *proto-plastic Christianity.* They are the architectural plan which the Gospel has carried into a superstructure ; the germ which it has ripened into fruit ; the dawn it has brightened into noon.

Thirdly. *That this one system of truth is indestructible.* " For verily I say unto you, *Till heaven and earth pass, one jot or one tittle shall in no wise pass from the law, till all be fulfilled.*" The idea is, that the whole creation shall sink into primeval nothingness before the smallest fraction of divine truth shall be destroyed. Those heavens seem very permanent: they are our most palpable and impressive emblems of eternity. Their " terrible crystal " is as firm and bright now as when Adam first lifted up his eyes on its rolling wonders, and felt his spirit glow with seraphic fires under its effulgent rays. But sooner shall these immutable heavens pass away than the smallest alphabet, or the tiniest point in the great volume of God's truth, be destroyed.

Fourthly. *That man's relation to this system of truth determines his true state.* " *Whosoever therefore shall break one of these least commandments, and shall teach men so, he shall be called the least in the kingdom of heaven; but whosoever shall do and teach them, the same shall be called great in the kingdom of heaven. For I say unto you, That except your righteousness shall exceed the righteousness of the Scribes and Pharisees, ye shall in no case enter the kingdom of heaven.*" This passage shows that men's relation to this great system of truth throws them into two grand classes :—First, *those that are in the kingdom of heaven,* and, secondly, *those that are excluded from it.* The former is divided into two classes, the "least" and the "greatest." The least are those of Christ's disciples, who, while they attend to some of the great points of truth, are regardless of *apparently* inferior points, and teach men also to neglect them. This sub-class includes those that are *one-sided* in doctrine, such as the *Arminian* and the *Calvinist.* These hold up a few theological points to the exclusion of many, and to the denial of some. In truth, all *doctrinalists* who do not implicitly hold the *whole* counsel of God, belong to this division. It includes also the *one-sided practicalists;* those who attend too much to ceremony, and those who repudiate all ceremonies ; those who magnify the duties of piety to the prejudice of social virtue, who pay much attention to prayer, and praise, and worship, but overlook the claims of truthfulness, honesty, and charity. All these *one-sided* doctrinalists and practicalists must be regarded as belonging to the former class in the text —those that are *least* in the kingdom. They are in the kingdom of heaven, subjects of Christ's moral empire, but they are almost contemptibly small. Perhaps the mass of Christians in this age belong to this class. The second class belonging to those who are in the kingdom of heaven, are the "great"—those who *do* and *teach* the "least" commandments as well as the greatest. They regard all the truths that God hath revealed as sacred ; they look at the whole law ; they do not draw their creed from isolated texts, but search the entire Scriptures ; they regard every day as holy, every act as religious. They do justice, they love mercy, they walk humbly. They are "*great in the kingdom of heaven.*"

The other general class are *those that are excluded from it.* They are "the Scribes and the Pharisees." "*Except,*" says Christ, "*your righteousness shall exceed the righteousness of the Scribes and Pharisees, ye shall in no case enter into the kingdom of heaven.*" These were persons who were intellectually acquainted with the truth, and who mechanically adhered even to the smallest points of duty, but who had no real and practical sympathy of soul with it. For the want of this *spirit* they were shut out of the kingdom.

Let us now direct our attention to those points in the passage in which the conduct of Christ appears as *a model for all true reformers.* We infer—

I. THAT, AS A REFORMER, CHRIST RECOGNIZED THE IMPERISHABLE-NESS OF THE DIVINE TRUTHS EXISTING AMONGST MEN. The law and the prophets contained truths which Christ here affirms could not pass away. What were those truths ? We may mention one or two as examples. There is the doctrine of *theism :* the existence of one God, the Creator and Sustainer of the universe, almighty in power, unsearchable in wisdom, sovereign in purpose, and spiritual in essence. There is the doctrine of *providence :* the superintendence of God, not only over the universe in general, but over the events, doings, and destinies of individual men. There is the doctrine of *human responsibility*: the obligation of mankind to love the Creator with supreme affection, and their amenableness to Him, not only for overt acts, but for hidden purposes, thoughts, and desires. There is the doctrine of *moral deliverance* : the raising of humanity from its conscious guilt, corruptions, and woes, to pardon, purity, and peace, through the intervention of another. There is the doctrine of *future retribution*: the existence of man, after his bodily dissolution, in woe or rapture, according to his earthly conduct. All these are truths running through "the law and the prophets." These truths Christ found in the world ; He did not bring them. Nor did He ignore them, or attempt to destroy them ; He recognized them as *imperishable* realities.

The man who would reform society must imitate Christ in this respect. There are certain truths everywhere in the world that he must bow to as *immutable things.* Indeed, I may say that the very truths I have specified as running through the law and the prophets, you may find, in some form or other, mixed up oftentimes with an immense amount of error in every part of the world. I stay not to inquire how the world has come into their possession ; I only state the fact. They pervade all religions ; they mingle with the general consciousness of souls ; they are dim, but quenchless, lights in the great firmament of human thought. There have been those who have set themselves up as reformers who have not only overlooked these truths, but opposed them. Such were the Atheists in France before the Revolution, such was Owen in England a few years ago, and such are the Secularists now. But their schemes *can* never succeed. The primitive beliefs of humanity are the great forces of the world. As lightnings rend the thunder-cloud, as volcanic fires rive the mountain, the primitive beliefs of humanity have ever destroyed all opposing systems and institutions. We infer—

II. THAT, AS A REFORMER, CHRIST SOUGHT THE DEVELOPMENT, AND NOT THE DESTRUCTION, OF THE DIVINE TRUTHS EXISTING AMONGST MEN. "*I am not come to destroy, but to fulfil.*" He made these truths radiate with a new brightness. He took them, as it were, from the law and the prophets, breathed into them new life, and clothed them with new forms of beauty. In His life, teaching, and death, the truths we have noticed were brought out as the most sublime and moving realities. See the doctrine of *theism* in the teaching of Christ ! He was the brightness of His Father's glory ; the express image of His person. See the doctrine of *providence* in the history of Christ ! He shows the Father clothing the lilies of the field, and feeding the birds of heaven, in order to assure man of the interest He feels in him, for whom all nature was made. See the doctrine of *human responsibility* in the history of Christ ! He shows the great Arbiter of our destiny as the lord who distributes to His servants various talents, and then calls them to an account for their use. See the doctrine of *moral deliverance* in the history of Christ ! He reveals Himself as the One sent of God to heal the diseased, ransom the captive, quicken the dead, and save the lost. See the doctrine of *future retribution* in the history of Christ! Examine the picture He has given of the day of judgment: Himself on the throne, angels His attendants, assembled nations before Him, and He dividing them as a shepherd divideth the sheep from the goats. How true it is, then, that He did not destroy these truths of the law and the prophets, but *fulfilled them*—brought them out to the eye of human consciousness in all their magnificent proportions, impressive solemnity, and profound suggestiveness.

All who would be true reformers must imitate Christ in this point also. The would-be reformers of whom we have spoken seek to destroy these truths; their banter, ridicule, and sophistry, are all directed against them. But theirs is at once a hopeless and wicked task. Hopeless, because you may as well endeavour to pluck a planet from its orbit as to eradicate any primitive belief from the human soul; and wicked, because it is hostility to the will of God and to the highest prerogatives of man. If you would improve mankind, you must appeal to their beliefs; you must bring out these truths in all the light which Christ has shed upon them. The world, I believe, can only advance as we appeal, through Christianity, to those intuitions of *God, providence, responsibility, moral deliverance,* and *future retribution,* which flit and flash through every man's soul. We infer—

III. THAT, AS A REFORMER, CHRIST REGARDED MEN ACCORDING TO THEIR RELATION TO THE DIVINE TRUTHS EXISTING AMONGST THEM. There are three classes of men here brought under our notice:—First. *Those whose relation to divine truth was such as to constitute them very inferior subjects of the spiritual empire of Christ;* they were in it, and that was all. They were little, *one-sided* men—moral dwarfs. Secondly. *Those whose relation to divine truth was such as to make them great in the spiritual empire of Christ*—broad-minded and world-loving men. And thirdly, *those whose relation to divine truth was such as to exclude them altogether from the spiritual empire of Christ.* These are the Scribes and the Pharisees. They *could not* enter in. "Except your righteousness," etc.

The true reformer must adopt Christ's classification of men. *He must respect them according to their relation to Christ's kingdom.*

Matthew 5:21-48

Jesus, the World-Legislator

The celebrated Neander considers this passage to be a general contrast between the judicial and the moral stand-points of theocratic law. Writing on this passage he says; "In these illustrations He (Christ) contrasts the *eternal* theocratic law with the *political* theocratic law; the absolute law with he particular law of

Moses. Although the former lay at the foundation of the latter, it could not, in that limited and contracted system, unfold and display itself, and it could not be fully developed until the shell, the restraining power, which had cribbed and confined the spirit, was broken and destroyed." Jesus here stands before us in the aspect of an illustrious legislator: the political forms which law had assumed under the Mosaic economy, with all the dogmatic interpretations which formalistic rabbis had. attached to it, He now repeals, and brings out into sunlight those eternal principles of rectitude, which are the foundation of all order and the law of all mind. The *political* heavens of the old Hebrews had grown very dark: tradition had well-nigh clouded every star, the heavens had "waxed old as doth a garment: and as a vesture," Christ now folds them up and lays them by; and forthwith spreads out "new heavens" to encircle all lands, and to radiate with those stars of *absolute* rectitude that shall burn for ever in their spheres.

We proceed to draw a few general truths from this passage concerning the *legislation of Christ*. We observe:—

I. That Christ's legislation recognizes the existence of moral evil. He refers to no less than five evils in this passage. There is Murder. "*Ye have heard that it was said by them of old time, Thou shalt not kill, and whosoever shall kill shall be in danger of the judgment.*" In this world men kill their fellow-men, they cut short their days, they take away the life of their brothers. Thousands die by the hands of their fellows every day. Now, this is a moral crime; it is contrary to the eternal principles of rectitude, as enforced both by Moses and Christ. The prohibition is most absolute and unqualified in its form: "*Thou shalt not kill.*" It does not say, thou shalt not kill *privately*, from any personal feeling, leaving room for the inference that man may kill in his official capacity, and from public considerations. The language meets man as man, in every capacity and position—it meets him as the judge upon the bench, as the executioner upon the scaffold, as the soldier upon the field. With this passage before us, we are bound to regard intentional killing, by whomsoever effected, however effected, and wherever effected, as a violation of God's eternal law.

There is matrimonial depravity. This includes "adultery" and "divorce." The former, in the scriptural sense, means not only unfaithfulness in the marriage relationship, but all lewdness and unchastity; and the latter, the breaking of those vows which are the most sacred, and the dissolution of those ties which should become stronger with years. The vitiation of the conjugal relationship is a tremendous social calamity, and it is right that Jesus, as the great reformer of the world, should thus enter the domestic circle, the birth-place of the race, and the font of social influence, and lay down some distinct principle for its government. He knew that the connubial relation involves the most tender, close, and lasting ties that unite human beings together in this life: that whilst it involves the interest, fortunes, and happiness of the parties conjoined, it also influences the eternal destinies of many. He knew that the welfare of coming generations, the triumph of truth over the world's mind, and the upward progress of humanity, depended upon the nuptial bond. Hence He clothed this relationship with solemn grandeur. To His holy eye it was a holy thing, He guarded its obligations, He expounded its unity, He graced its celebration with His presence ; the first miracle that His holy hand performed was at a bridal feast.

There is PROFANITY, an irreverent appeal to God. "*Swear not at all.*" I am inclined to take this expression in its widest sense, comprehending oaths in courts of justice, as well as in general conversation. Do not "swear" *to* anything, true or false ; the true does not require to be backed by an oath, and the sin of the false is increased by it : "swear" not *by* anything. It had become customary with the Hebrews to divide oaths into two classes, the lighter and the weightier; the former were those which did not contain the name of God, and which they considered might be used and broken with impunity. These had become prevalent in common conversation. Jesus strikes directly at this error, by affirming that whatever they swore *by* had a reference to God ; if by the earth, that was His "footstool:" if by heaven, that was His "throne :" if by Jerusalem, that was His "city:" if even by the hair of their own head, that was entirely at His disposal, for they could not make "one hair white or black." Every oath is an appeal to something, and everything is of God. Therefore, "swear not at all." Profanity is a mighty evil—If the soul has not *reverence*, what has it ? It has no depth of feeling, no balance of faculties, no true idea of life, no substratum of goodness. It has no virility. It is volatile and weak. It has no sympathetic connexion with the great Fountain of energy and peace. It moves through life, not like the imperial bird in the atmosphere, pursuing its aërial path however the winds may blow, and soaring sunward though massive clouds may roll between ; but like the loose feather, it is the sport of every wind ; it gyrates, but cannot fly.

REVENGE is another evil here referred to. *Ye have heard that it hath been said, an "eye for an eye, and a tooth for a tooth."* The principle of *jus talionis*, which has been acted upon by the Jews, had also become the common dictate of humanity. To return evil for evil was a general practice, which was even regarded as justifiable. Jesus here proscribes it. When he says, "*resist not evil,*" He does not mean that we are not to defend ourselves when threatened with danger. The principle of self-defence is innate, and an innate principle is divine ; and divine principles Christ came not "to destroy, but to fulfil." He means that we are never to do it in a spirit of *revenge*. It is revenge which He proscribes, and revenge is another of the primary evils of the world. It is an all-consuming fire in the soul. It burns up all kindly feelings of our nature. The man under its influence has no mercy on himself, and may truly say, *The pains of hell have got hold upon me.*

There is yet another evil referred to in these verses, and that is NATIONAL EXCLUSIVENESS. *" Ye have heard that it hath been said, Thou shalt love thy neighbour and hate thine enemy."* The Jews regarded none as *neighbours*, but those who belonged to their nation, and therefore regarded themselves as authorized, if not bound, to regard all others as enemies. This narrow *nationality* is an immense evil, an evil not confined to the Jews, but pervading all countries ; an evil which, under the dignified name of patriotism, has filled almost every page of earth's voluminous history with narratives of injustice, rapine, and bloodshed. Conventional patriotism means little more than hatred of all that dwell beyond the narrow boundaries of our own country. Christ requires *philanthropy*, not patriotism, to be the rallying point of empires, and all petty nationalities to be lost in the great sentiments of a world-wide brotherhood.

Such, then, are the evils which Christ recognizes in this short but significant piece of legislation. He saw these evils at work in the heart of the world ; every sentence of their terrible history He had read. He knew that they were the malaria in earth's moral atmosphere, and the head-springs of those poisonous streams that flowed through every channel of human life. It is a consoling thought that our Great Legislator knows the sinfulness of the world He has taken under His care. He has explored its remotest regions, sounded its deepest depths, and fully gauged it in all its huge and dark proportions.

We infer from this passage :—

II. THAT CHRIST'S LEGISLATION REGARDS ALL CRIMES AS PERPETRATED IN THE HEART. Who is the murderer ? *" Whosoever is angry with his brother without a cause."* Who is the adulterer ? *"Whosoever looketh on a woman to lust after her ; "*—such a man hath committed adultery in his heart. Who is the swearer ? He who appeals to anything with an irreverent spirit, whether he pronounces the Divine name or not. The soul is the theatre where moral actions, both good and bad, are performed. *" As a man thinketh in his heart, so is he."* What we *will*, that we *morally* do. This doctrine suggests, *that the world is really worse than it appears.* It appears bad enough ; its outward features and procedures are most repulsive to the eye of reflective virtue ; but not a tithe of the *heart's* dispositions does the body represent. The soul has a world of sentiment that neither tongue nor pen expresses ; it is conscious of hosts of volitions that the muscles and limbs never carry into effect. We thank God that the body is too frail, fully to work out the latent wishes of a depraved world. Where circumstances have been pre-eminently favourable for the play of the soul's propensities, we have had terrible exhibitions ; we have had Herods, Judases, Neros, and Napoleons, to tell us what depths of iniquity there are in the human heart. This doctrine also suggests *the necessity of heart introspection.* In estimating our character, we must do more than catalogue our outward acts, we must take account of our wishes and willings ; we must endeavour to ascertain, not merely what we have done, but what we *would* have done. And it suggests, moreover, *the kind of instrumentality required to reform the world*. A system to correct the outward conduct, however effective, if it did not touch the heart, would be of no essential service. Let a man externally stand before the world blameless, let every outward act and expression harmonize with the strictest rules of morality : if his inner sentiments and dispositions are not in thorough and vital sympathy with God, what is he ? A " whited sepulchre." What we want, therefore, to reform and elevate humanity, is some instrumentality that will go at once to the heart, that will strike at the root of evil, crush sin in its germ, and implant the seeds of truth and religion. There is one, and but *one*, system in the world that can do this, and that is Christianity. This is the power which casteth down imaginations and every high thing that exalteth itself against the knowledge of God, and bringeth into captivity every thought to the obedience of Christ.

We see in this passage :—

III. That Christ's legislation indicates a necessary connexion between heart-sins and sufferings. Two things are taught here concerning this connexion :—

First. *That the existence of heart-sin insures the existence of suffering.* The *spirit* of murder or *anger* is here represented as exposing its subject to sufferings, of which the "judgment," the "council," "hell-fire," and the "prison," are employed as emblems. The most terrible ideas of anguish were associated in the Jewish mind with the things here alluded to by Christ. The *spirit* of *matrimonial depravity*, "lust," is here represented as exposing its subject to the awful fires of Gehenna. This one "lust" is spoken of as sufficient to insure the destruction of the whole man. "*If thy right eye offend thee, pluck it out and cast it from thee : for it is profitable for thee that one of thy members should perish, and not that thy whole body should be cast into hell.*" Thus strongly does the world's legislator express the point which true philosophy and all experience confirm, namely, *that sensuality is necessarily injurious to the soul.* It is a fire that cauterizes the conscience, a hell-blast that scathes the moral powers. I read everywhere, in every law and faculty of the soul, on every page of history, as well as in every part of Christ's teaching, that if ye live after the flesh, ye shall die.

Profanity is here represented as evil. "*But let your conversation be Yea, yea ; nay, nay : for whatsoever is more than these, cometh of evil.*" All profanity leads to evil. In courts of justice I regard oaths as leading to evil. The conduct of the courts in the system of " cross-questioning " the witness shows, that for the purpose of public justice, they are not considered sufficient to settle the truth of an affirmation. But whilst they do no good they do evil : they insult the moral sense of the truthful, and they harden the false; they break down the distinction between the man of truth and the man of falsehood by the application of the same test. *Profanity*, everywhere, must lead to evil. *Irreverence* shuts out the soul from all that is great, glorious, and truly happy in the universe. Thus through the whole of this passage Jesus teaches that *he that sinneth wrongeth his own soul.* The other part which is here taught concerning the necessary connexion of sin and suffering is :—

Secondly. *That the measure of sin determines the measure of suffering.* There are gradations in sin. Not only are there some sinners worse than others, and some sinful passions worse than others, but the very same sinful passion admits of degrees of turpitude. Here is sinful anger, that is, anger " without a cause." Three stages— first, *unexpressed,* not quite impulsive enough for utterance : there it lies like a dormant germ, or smouldering fire without air to fan it into flame ; secondly, *expressed in contempt for the intellect of a brother.* " Raca," a Syriac word, meaning fool, dolt, senseless fellow, one beneath talking to ; and thirdly, *expressed in contempt for the man himself.* " Thou fool," meaning worthless wretch. Thus we have degrees of turpitude, even in the same passion. Now, according to these very degrees will be their suffering. There are the horrors of the " *judgment*" for the first, the greater horrors of the " *council* " for the second, and the still greater horrors of " *hell-fire* "* for the third. The sinner is to reap, not merely the same *kind* that he has sown, but the same *amount.* Man's hells are the " spontaneous combustion " of their own character ; and the fierceness of the flames is determined by the elements on which they are fed.

We see in this passage :—

IV. THAT CHRIST'S LEGISLATION INCULCATES THE OBLIGATION OF THE SINNER TO ABANDON HIS SINS. The man who is at enmity with another, is *required* to put an end to that enmity. " *Agree. with thine adversary quickly, whilst thou art in the way with him.*" Do it " *quickly,*" do it before even you attend to the ordinances of religion ; " *if thou bring thy gift to the altar, and there rememberest that thy brother hath aught against thee : leave there thy gift before the altar, and go thy way : first be reconciled to thy brother, and then come and offer thy gift.*" IF YOU ARE NOT RIGHT WITH MAN, YOU ARE NOT RIGHT WITH GOD. Do it before the enmity work out still worse results : " *lest at any time the adversary deliver thee to the judge, and the judge deliver thee to the officer, and thou be cast into prison. Verily, I say unto thee, thou shalt by no means come out thence till thou hast paid the uttermost farthing.*" The man who is the subject of sensual " lust," is *required* to free himself from it, though it be as painful as the plucking out of a right eye, or the cutting off of a right hand. The man who has formed the habit of swearing, who is

* The " Gehenna of fire " was a known visible object to the mind of the Jew as much as the judgment or the council. The word in Hebrew is the valley of Hinnom (Josh. xv. 8), the narrow valley skirting Jerusalem on the south, running westward from the valley of Jehoshaphat under Mount Zion. This valley was rendered odious by the idolatrous worship of Moloch (1 Kings xi. 7), and by the desecration which Josiah effected (2 Kings xxiii. 10–13). Afterwards it became a receptacle for the filth of the city : fires were kept to consume the carcases of animals which were thrown there.

habitually profane, is *required* to " swear not at all; " and the man
who is insulted and *injured* by another, is *required* not to return the
evil, but to love his enemy, and to return *good* for the evil. All this
is here inculcated as an obligation. The obligations, of course, imply
the *power* on man's part to attend to them. We are sometimes told
that the sinner can do nothing: but see the mighty work which is
here imposed upon him. Would infinite goodness enjoin duties we
had not the power to fulfil ? Sinners though we be, we *can* obtain
reconciliation with our foes if we try: we *can* repress sensual lust
if we try; habitual meditation upon the great themes of divine
thought, would soon quench the fires of the carnal man. We *can*
return good for evil, we have the power to possess our souls in
patience, to throw our smiles upon the frowning face of a foe, and
to break him down by our kindness. One might have thought that
no one who professed to teach Christ's system would have been
either so blind or so presumptuous * as to insist upon the *inability*
of man as a doctrine of the Gospel.

We infer from this passage :—

V. THAT CHRIST'S LEGISLATION PRESENTS THE HIGHEST MOTIVE FOR
OBEDIENCE. What is the motive? Affiliation to God. "*That ye
may be the children of your Father which is in heaven : for He maketh
His sun to rise on the evil and on the good, and sendeth rain on the just
and on the unjust.*" There are four facts here which will bring out
the force of the motive here presented.

First. *That all the operations of nature are the result of God's
agency.* "He maketh His sun to rise." "He sendeth rain." What
is called *science* refers these operations to "laws." It refers all the
stupendous phenomena of nature to "laws "—"laws " do everything. We are sick of this cant. What are these "laws "? Science
cannot answer. I call not that philosophy which cannot give me
an *intelligible and adequate* cause for events ; I see the rivers flow,
and the ocean roll, and the stars of heaven wheel along the dome of
night : I mark the revolutions of the sun, see the clouds laden with
oceans coursing through the upper fields of air, and the showers
descending on the earth, and the lands bursting into new forms of
life: and I feel that there must be some *mighty power* at work in the
universe. What is it ? I am told "*law.*" I do not understand the

---

* Many of the passages which are repeatedly quoted as proofs of man's inability
are unhappily rendered in our version. Thus John xv. 5 would be more correctly
rendered, " Apart from me ye are able to produce no fruit." 2 Cor. iii. 5 : " Not
that we are competent to form any conclusion of ourselves, as if from ourselves,
but our competency is from God." It should be remembered, too, that the
Bible is a book of *facts*, and not of *tenets*. We may speak of the doctrinal tenet,
" God is love," but the proof of this depends on the *fact* recorded (John iii. 16 ;
1 John iv. 9). The depravity of human nature is an inference from the undoubted
fact, which is taught by history, experience, and consciousness, that the wickedness of man is great in the earth. We ought, too, carefully to distinguish between
moral and physical inability. We have need to be humbled under the sense of
moral inability (Rom. vii. 23), and to be thankful for the influence of prævenient
grace (John vi. 44) ; but to assume the existence of physical inability is to represent God as the author of sin (James i. 13).—*Webster.*

answer, I am not satisfied. The Bible tells me God, and I bow; my philosophy and my deepest instincts acquiesce in the response. " He maketh His sun," &c. (Psalm civ.)

Secondly. *That God's agency towards our world is characterized by mercy.* He operates in nature for " *the just and the unjust, the evil and the good.*" It is not mere justice that presides over our world : otherwise, nature would bless the good and destroy the evil. It is mercy. Nature, in her bounteousness, makes no distinction between the just and the unjust, and that because God is dealing with man on the principle of *mercy.*

Thirdly. *That assimilation to the merciful character of God will constitute us His children.* " That ye may be the children of your Father." It is not *creation,* nor *baptism,* nor *profession,* that constitutes us the children of God, but *moral resemblance.* In what does moral resemblance consist ? In likeness of disposition ; God's disposition is *love,* and he that is ruled by love is like God, and is His child. Morally, all *may* and all *ought* to be like God, for all can love—the child as well as the seraph can love.

Fourthly. *That to be the children of God is the highest privilege of intelligent creatures.* Christ holds this out as the great motive. If we are the children of God, then He, as a Father, *protects* us, *educates* us, and *provides* for us through all the future. · "*If children, then heirs, heirs of God and joint-heirs with Christ.*"

I have thus gone through this passage. I have not taken the verses consecutively, nor entered into minute explanations of all the particular terms and allusions. With the numerous critical expositions now extant this would have been superfluous. I have looked at this passage as a *whole* in its broad moral outlines, and endeavoured to develop that spirit which characterizes Christ's legislation as " the King of Kings." In philosophic insight, in spiritual suggestiveness, in living congruity with our inmost consciousness, in moral majesty, how does this little piece of legislation throw into obscurity the sublimest codes of earth's wisest Solons ! How does it unmask the world, and expose its moral hideousness ! How does it impress us with the need of that *redemptive* help which He came amongst us to render !

> See thou thy peril in the effulgence of His *law,*
> And to His *love* flee thou for help without delay.

Matthew 6:1-18

The Religion of Semblance and the Religion of Substance

In these verses Christ draws a broad and palpable line of distinction between the *seeming* and the *real* in religion. The portraits of the mere pretenders, and the genuinely good, are here sketched by the hand of *infallibility* itself; every line, feature, and hue is true to life.

Let us endeavour to mark their points of agreement, and their points of contrast.

I. THEIR POINTS OF AGREEMENT. Wherein do they agree? Not, of course, in motive or spirit, but exclusively in features of external conduct.

First. *Christ intimates that both give.* Although the word "alms" in the first verse is supposed by some not to agree with the original text,* its correctness in the second verse is not disputed; and there it means *acts* of kindness to the poor : and these are attended to by both characters. Alms-giving was practised by the false, and Christ assumes that the *true*, as a matter of course, would practise it also. It is implied that the action itself is right and binding, and to some extent, at any rate, common. The great diversity in the secular circumstances of mankind, extending from the most abject destitution to almost unbounded opulence, affords an ample scope for the full play of the benevolent instincts in the form of alms-giving; and, perhaps, there are but few men who have the power, whatever their characters may be, who do not render at times some relief to the poor, although it may be very disproportionate to their means, and very disconnected from the highest motives. But whilst men generally do something *occasionally* in alms-giving, the *truly* pious do so *regularly;* it is a *moral necessity* with them—a law. He who befriends not the poor loves not God. Whilst you cannot argue the *genuineness* of a man's religion from the fact of his alms-giving, because the hypocrite gives "alms," you can argue the worthlessness of a man's religion from the *neglect* of his alms-giving; for "*whoso hath this world's good, and seeth his brother have need, and shutteth up his bowels from him, how dwelleth the love of God in him ?*"

Secondly. *Christ intimates that both pray.* "*And when thou prayest thou shalt not be as the hypocrites are,*" etc. Men of no religion and all religions pray. It would, we think, be difficult to find a sane man anywhere who has not, some time or other, called upon his God. Prayer is an instinct of the soul. Some pray from *fear :* they forbode peril, and call to the Supreme for deliverance : some pray from *acquisitiveness;* they earnestly desire some good which seems difficult to attain, and they ask the Almighty to interpose on their behalf: some pray from *fashion;* they have been brought up and trained amongst those who call upon God : and some pray from a mere *sense of duty ;* to quiet conscience they attend to the form. Though all these prayers are confessedly destitute of any *moral virtue*, still, inasmuch as there is an appeal

---

* Some editors—as Lachmann and Tischendorf—maintain that the original text reads "*righteousness*" instead of "*alms;*" if this be correct, the first verse would be the general text to the remarks which follow upon "alms," "fasting," and "prayer." These acts are then to be regarded as branches of this *righteousness.*

to God, they may be called prayers. Christ here speaks of the "hypocrites" and the "heathens" as *praying*. So far, therefore, as the mere act of prayer is concerned, there is an agreement between the false and the true; in their prayers they may bend at the same throne, sustain the same attitude, and adopt the same language.

Thirdly. *Christ intimates that both fast.* "*Moreover, when ye fast, be not, as the hypocrites, of a sad countenance,*" etc. There are two views of fasting in connexion with religion; one is, that it is a *positive duty;* and the other is, that it is a *natural necessity.* The former view seems to me inadmissible for three reasons : first, its incompatibility with divine goodness ; it is based upon the superstitious notion, which has prevailed in all ages, that the Deity is propitiated by the sufferings which His creatures voluntarily inflict upon themselves—that He is more pleased with their sufferings than their enjoyments. This is a pagan idea of the Deity. Through the whole system of heathen mythology there runs the idea that the gods are jealous of man's happiness. I cannot believe that Infinite Benevolence requires man to inflict mortifications and pains upon the physical nature He has given him. Secondly, it is incompatible with the general tenor of the Bible. "There is but one fast," says a modern writer, "enjoined by the great Hebrew lawgiver. And this injunction we are disposed to place amongst those things which Moses allowed, rather than originated ; bore with, rather than approved ; in consideration of the force of established custom, and from a wise fear of defeating his own good ends by attempting too much." Nor did *Christ* enjoin fasting as a *duty*. The people were rather astonished at this, and the disciples of John asked, "Why do we and the Pharisees fast oft, and thy disciples fast not ?" The answer disclaims all fasting as an *ordinance* in connection with the Christian Church : "*Can the children of the bride-chamber fast ?*" Thirdly, this idea is incompatible with the true view of spiritual improvement. Amongst ignorant and superstitious people the idea has ever been held, that fastings are means of grace, that to starve the body is to strengthen the soul; but the thoughtful student of the philosophy of his nature, and the doctrine of Him who "*came eating and drinking,*" repudiates the notion, as a perversion of religion, and an insult to the human understanding.

The other view of fasting is, that it is a *natural necessity, i.e.*, that it is a physical effect, springing naturally from certain deep and strong emotions in connexion with religion. Let some great emotion, especially of a painful character, seize and fill the soul, and the appetite is gone : under the influence of this feeling, for the time being, the man loathes food. Hence it is, that we read of so much fasting in the Old Testament, in connexion with individuals and communities under some great calamity or deep penitence, as in the case of Nineveh. This is the fasting we desiderate. We would have the world wrought into such deep feelings of contrition for sin, as would check, not only its love of money and pleasure, but even, for a while, its desire for food.

Now, these "hypocrites" fasted, and Christ intimates that the true disciple will fast too; but the former will do it as a matter of ceremonial observance, and the latter, because of the powerful emotions that swell and rise within him, deadening for a time all desire for food. From this it follows, that national fasting, where there is not national penitence, is national hypocrisy.

Fourthly. *Christ intimates that both are rewarded.* He says of the hypocrites, "*they have their reward.*" They sought public notice and praise, and they obtained it. Men looked at them and pronounced their praise, and they were pleased. The true, also, shall be rewarded; they sought truth, purity, spiritual freedom, vigour, and usefulness, and their Father shall reward them openly; they shall have what they sought under the open eye of the universe.

Herein, then, these characters agree—they both give alms, they both pray, they both fast, and they both "have their reward." Let us now notice—

II. THEIR POINTS OF DISSIMILARITY. In all that is inward and fundamental, we find them as widely distant as the poles.

First. *The religion of the one derives its motives from man, that of the other from God.* The hypocrites sought "*to be seen of men,*" they sounded a "*trumpet,*"—used means to attract the attention of their neighbours. In their alms-giving they blazoned their deeds abroad; in their prayers they stood in the synagogue, or at the corner of the street; in their fasting they disfigured their countenance; and all this that they "*might have glory of men.*" Now, their wrong was not in manifesting religion. Heaven kindles virtue in the breast that it may blaze forth upon the eyes of man. The "candle" is not to be "put under a bushel." But it was that they did it for the sake of applause. In contrast to this, the religion of the true derives its motives from God. It has no ostentation. It does not require its gifts to be announced at public meetings, or to be emblazoned in Reports; it does not let its "*left hand know what its right hand doeth.*" Genuine goodness, like real genius, is always modest; it shrinks from the platforms of display, it dislikes parade. Its motive is derived from the unseen Father, who "*seeth in secret.*" And what a motive is this! What a reality and force does it give to character! Moses endured as seeing Him who is invisible; and David set the Lord always before him, and was not afraid. How does it raise the spirit above the fear or favour of men, and instead of leaving it the mere creature of public sentiment, gives it a power to modify, mould, and master the current views and sympathies of mankind! How constant is the influence which it exerts! HE, whose love is its inspiring motive, *seeth in secret,* and therefore its conduct will be the same at all times, in midnight as in open day; ever independent of men, always full of God. Mark well this point of difference between the false and the true: the one derives all his incentives to acts of goodness from men; were there no human eyes to witness and no human tongue to laud his gifts, he would not be charitable: the other gets all his motives from God, and were there no human spectator of his deeds, he would not be the less pure, generous, or devout.

Secondly. *The religion of the one attaches importance to words, that of the other to sentiments.* The false think they "*shall be heard for their much speaking.*" We have two striking examples of tautological prayers in the Bible. The one in the worshippers of Baal, who, notwithstanding the bitter irony of the prophet, stood from morning till noon and cried to their god, "O Baal, hear us." The other in the inhabitants of Ephesus, who cried out with one voice for two hours, "Great is Diana of the Ephesians." The false, indeed, always use "*vain repetitions*"—babblings. Amongst the Jews, such maxims as these were common:—"Every one that multiplies prayers shall be heard;" "The prayer which is long shall not return empty." The formal and the false in religion have always attached undue importance to words. Words are everything to them in their prayers and their creeds. If you adopt not their nomenclature, you are irreverent and even heretical. They live in words; they are the mere creatures of the "letter." In opposition to all this, the true think but little of words, and much of sentiments. The spirit is everything to them.

There are two things in this passage which show that the *spirit* is everything in prayer, and that words profit nothing: first, *the character of the object of prayer.* "Your Father *knoweth* what things ye have need of before ye ask Him." In petitioning favours of our fellow-men we use words for a twofold purpose, to *inform* them of our wants and reasons, and to *induce* them to attend to our appeal. But words have neither of these functions in prayer. "*He knoweth*" more about the suppliant than he knows himself—knows all about him; knows all that he is, all that he has been, all that he ever will be. Nor are words necessary to *induce* any more than inform: "*He is your Father,*" ever filled with a love for you, and an interest in you, which no words can heighten.

The other thing here which shows that the spirit is everything in prayer, and that words profit nothing, is, secondly, *the character oj the model of prayer.* We say model, for it was evidently never intended to be a form; it was given to help us to avoid, not to encourage, "*vain repetitions.*" It is short, but comprehensive. Its words are few, but it teems with sentiments. It is suited for all times, ranks, and conditions. It contains four great general sentiments which constitute the very soul of religion—sentiments which are the germs of all holy deeds in all worlds. First. *Filial reverence.* "Our Father which art in heaven, hallowed be thy name." The object of prayer the good man addresses, not as the great unknown, not as the unsearchable governor, not as a mysterious power working everywhere in the universe but eluding our vision; but as a Father, the most *intelligible, attractive, and transforming name.* A name which he desires to *hallow* everywhere, in his heart, his family,

his business, and throughout the world. It contains, secondly:
Divine loyalty. "Thy kingdom come, thy will be done on earth as
it is in heaven." This implies that God has a will, that that will is
done in heaven, that on earth it is neglected, and that the fulfilment
of it on earth is supremely desirable. God's will is the expression
of His benevolence; to obey it, is to be happy; to rebel against it,
is hell—self-created hell. It contains, thirdly : *Conscious dependence.*
"Give us this day our daily bread, and forgive us our debts as we
forgive our debtors, and lead us not into temptation, but deliver us
from evil." Here is the expression of dependence, (1) for bodily
supplies—"daily bread;" (2) for absolution, "forgive us our
debts." The term "*debt*" must be regarded as highly figurative.
There are many points which distinguish a *debt* from a *sin.* A sin
is always a crime, debt is not so; debt is always transferable, sin is
not so; the discharge of a debt sets the debtor free from all obligation to his creditor, but the pardon of sin does not; the contracting
of a debt·implies the free consent of the creditor, but the commission
of a sin does not imply the consent of God. Although there are
these points of distinction, sin is a debt, inasmuch as it implies an
unfulfilled obligation. (3) Here is dependence for deliverance from
evil—all evils, moral and natural; God alone can deliver a man
from these. It contains, fourthly : *Unbounded confidence.* "For
thine is the kingdom, the power, and the glory." This implies the
most absolute confidence in God's power to grant whatever we
require.

This short model of prayer shows "that much speaking" is not
required in true worship.

If I am asked what religion is, I refer to no human formularies,
nor do I presume to give a definition of my own; but I point to this
model prayer and say, that the man who has the sentiments of *filial
reverence, divine loyalty, conscious dependence, unbounded confidence in
God,* couched in these few simple but sublime words of Jesus, is a religious man; that he whose inner heart these words express, is moving
in the right path—is one with all holy spirits in all worlds, is a child
of God. Infidels argue against *human* representations of religion in
the creeds, polities, and histories of churches; but against these sentiments, I defy them to argue, and they only are religion; the only
thing worth contending for. These sentiments are the fundamentals
of my *creed;* may they be my *life!*

Thirdly. *The religion of the one is artificial in its manifestation,
that of the other is natural.* The seemingly good are of a "*sad
countenance,*" and "*they disfigure their faces.*" These Pharisees
assumed on the fast-day a morose and melancholy expression ; they
neglected their usual dress, and endeavoured to depict feelings in
their looks which were not in their hearts; they *disfigured* their
countenances. But not so with the true : when they fasted, they
were to appear as usual; "*anoint thy head and wash thy face*"—do
on that day as on every other day, that "*thou appear not unto men
to fast.*" The generic idea is, Be *natural.*

The conduct of those who are but the *mere* professors of religion —alas! how numerous—has led the world to imagine that religion does violence to human nature. They have a face in the church, which is not seen in the market or at their own fireside; they have a voice in talking of religion, which is not heard on any ordinary topic of conversation. These grimaces and contortions in the church disgust and repel the world. The world, however, should remember that all this hypocrisy is *a necessity of sin and a tribute to goodness.* Worldly men, who denounce all Christians as hypocrites, should remember that *real* Christians are the only men that are *not* hypocrites, and that can *afford* to be natural. *The mere worldling is necessarily a hypocrite.* Were he to show to the eye of society all the dark thoughts, wicked schemes, and passions, which pass through his mind, his existence would not be tolerated, the world would not bear with him. In proportion to the sinfulness of a man's heart, is the force of his motive to hypocrisy. The *true* Christian alone can afford to be natural, and to appear what he is, let his full heart come out in all his outward life. This physical frame seems to me intended and admirably fitted, in its various gestures, looks, and tones, to express the entire soul. It is as natural for the body to express the heart, as it is for the plant to express the seed, the river the fountain, or the ray the orb of noon. Let a man, therefore, have true religion, be true, and his outward deportment will be perfectly natural, and being natural, it will be attractive and winsome; for nature in her loveliest forms is beauty, and in her wildest tones is music.

Fourthly. *The religion of the one receives its rewards from man, that of the other from God.* All the reward that the false have, is from men, the empty praise of the sycophant and the thoughtless; but the true receive their reward from the Father that "*seeth in secret.*" Hence, in the first place, *the reward of the one is satisfactory, that of the other is not.* Let society, through all its classes, enthusiastically unite in our praise, let the civilized world ring with our fame; can it satisfy us, if we have not the *consciousness* that our virtues entitle us to it? The "well done" of society only tends to our happiness, as it blends harmoniously with the "well done" of our own souls. But the reward which comes from the Father, is the "peace of God which passeth all understanding." Hence, secondly, *the reward of the one is uncertain, that of the other is not.* Human applause is very capricious. Society will cry "Hosanna" to-day, and "Crucify" to-morrow. But the reward which comes from the Father, springs from within, and is independent of all outward things. Hence, again, thirdly, *the reward of the one is transient, that of the other is not.* A false man, in this hazy scene of probation, may pass through the world, honoured on all hands as an illustrious saint; but amid the cloudless sun of eternity, the men who applauded him here, will recoil from him with ineffable disgust. But the reward which comes from the Father is for ever. "*He that seeth in secret will reward thee openly.*"

Matthew 6:19-34

The Secular and the Spiritual

There are two kinds of "*treasures*" mentioned in this paragraph; the one is spoken of as belonging to earth, the other to heaven; the one is exposed to destruction, the other is beyond the reach of any contingency. There is no difficulty in determining the exact nature of these treasures. The one, unquestionably, includes all worldly possessions, and the other all spiritual excellences; the one includes whatever enriches man in his narrow and transient *material* relations, as the passing tenant of this earth, and the other whatever enriches him in his immeasurable and permanent *spiritual* relations as the undying citizen of the universe.

Men have ever felt a greater interest in the "*earthly*" than the "*heavenly*." This interest has been the swaying passion of most men in all ages. Verily, *secularism* needs no propagandists; it is everywhere the main impulse—producing and controlling most phenomena of human activities. Practically, worldly wealth has been, and still is, with but few exceptions, the *summum bonum* of the race. It will buy everything else—time, intellect, justice, truth, conscience: the most sacred rights of humanity are bartered for this. The question of Judas, "What will ye give me?" has ever been the popular query; and, like Judas, the people will sell the most sacred thing for "silver."

Against this base and soul-destroying passion, it was to be expected that the World's Reformer would lift up His voice; that He would make some effort to stem the over-swelling torrent—present some motives, sufficiently potent, to turn the energies and enterprises of the world into another and a higher direction. This He does in this passage, as well as in many others. Indeed, His whole life and mysterious death were the mightiest conceivable protest against this reigning secularism.

We shall endeavour to develop the spirit of these words, by a few observations upon that *resemblance and dissimilarity* between these two "*treasures*"—the secular and the spiritual, which are here suggested:—

I. The resemblance subsisting between these treasures.

First. *Both are capable of accumulation.* The expression "*lay up*," or amass, applied to each, suggests this. So abundant and palpable are the illustrations around us that secular wealth can be accumulated, that it would be idle to dwell a moment upon the point. On all hands we see paupers becoming princes. I do not think that Jesus intended to denounce the *principle* of secular accumulation. Indeed, reason dictates, human existence demands, and Christianity inculcates, a provision for the future; and this implies amassing to some extent at least. The prohibition refers rather to the *avaricious* spirit of the act, than to the act itself; although it is obvious that great accumulation, inasmuch as it generally implies a wrong state of heart, has not the sanction of the Gospel. I have no faith in that man's religion who "*lays up*" large "*treasures upon earth*," whilst there are indigence and squalor in his neighbourhood, and souls are everywhere dying for the lack of knowledge.

But *spiritual* "treasures" can be accumulated too. What are those treasures? This question is not left to our speculation; Jesus teaches us that they consist in *practical love*. To the young man who inquired the way to eternal life, Christ said, "Go and sell all that thou hast, and thou shalt have TREASURE IN HEAVEN;" and Paul calls upon Timothy to exhort the rich "*that they do good, that they be rich in good works, ready to distribute, willing to communicate; laying up in store for themselves a good foundation against the time to come, that they may lay hold on eternal life.*" All spiritual "treasures," then, consist in *practical love*. And how much is involved in this! Love implies *knowledge*—knowledge of God and universal being. And here is work for the intellect! for love must be regulated by our ideas. *Practical* love implies *habits* of piety and benevolence, and here is work for all the activities of our nature. All the intellectual and moral treasures of the holiest and loftiest creature in the universe, are summed up in *practical love*.

In further illustration of this accumulation of spiritual treasure, we submit two remarks:—First, *That every man is daily increasing his spiritual stock.* It is a solemn fact, that accessions are made to our moral history with every new impression, thought, purpose, and act. We are not like channels, through which the waters of circumstance flow, and which never become more full; but rather like reservoirs into which all events, feelings, and acts of life flow as contributing streams, and there remain and augment. As a healthy tree gathers every moment a something from the external system, transmutes it into its own nature and makes it part of itself, so every moment we incorporate into our own moral being something that passes over our consciousness. Our moral stock is greater to-day than yesterday, and to-morrow will be greater still, and thus on for ever. Our whole life is a treasuring up; moral accumulation is the great law of our being. Secondly, *That the value of this ever-accumulating stock will depend on the moral state of the heart.* The presiding disposition gives its colour and character to every idea and event of our lives. It transforms everything into its own image. If the disposition be unholy, the whole knowledge and experience which a man accumulates, are not only worthless, but ruinous to him. "*He is treasuring up wrath against the day of wrath.*" But if the heart is pure and right, everything turns to moral value. From the same ray of heaven one plant drinks in poison and another nourishment; so from the same subject of consciousness the one man will get a blessing and the other a bane, and that according to his presiding disposition. Another point of analogy is—

Secondly. *Both may be attractive for the heart.* " *Where your treasure is, there will your heart be also.*" Christ thoroughly understood human nature; He throws out truths concerning it in the most free and unstudied way, to which the observation and inner consciousness of the world respond. Here is a specimen. Our hearts point to the treasure as the needle to the pole; our affections flow after it as the tides flow after the moon. Each of the treasures of which we speak has its attraction for the heart. The worldly man's heart is in his earthly possessions. He lives in them, they are the centre and the home of his sympathies. The spiritual man's heart is also in his treasure. His sympathies are absorbed in the great truths, laws, and purposes of Infinite Benevolence. " *How precious are thy thoughts unto me, O God !*" He glories in the cross of Christ—the grandest expression of eternal love, and counts all things but loss, for the excellency of the knowledge of Christ Jesus, his Lord.

Jesus here intimates, *that the position of a man's heart is a serious thing to him.* In this implied idea, indeed, lies the whole force of His argument. And is it not true ? Why, wherever the heart is, the *man* is : he lives in the object on which his affections are set ; it is his sphere, his world ; it binds his energies and being ; beyond it he cannot take a step. What a small soul-world, therefore, has the man whose treasures are *earthly !* It has no scope for the play of the spiritual powers ; it lacks the elements and influences necessary to his growth and health. The soil is sterile, the air is insalubrious, the little encircling firmament is dark with dust and smoke. The air of mammon infuses poison into the spiritual powers. The man who lives in this world must, from the necessity of the case, *lose his soul.* On the other hand, what a magnificent world does *his* spirit live in whose treasures are in heaven! Here are an immeasurable scope and an exhaustless nourishment for every faculty : it stretches into the infinite,—

" Its air is charged with ever-renewing life,
Its heavens are lit with ever-brightening suns."

Thirdly. *Both may be dominant forces.* " *No man can serve two masters : for either he will hate the one and love the other ; or else he will hold to the one, and despise the other ; ye cannot serve God and mammon.*" Mammon, here, is the same as the earthly treasure which, when it gets the heart, becomes the *sovereign* of the man. It is a fact, that whatever object we love *most,* is our monarch; it governs our thoughts, feelings, and purposes. If we love worldly wealth most, mammon is our master; if moral goodness most, God is our master. And as both these are loved supremely, both are *dominant* forces. But mark, they are never in the same mind at the same time. So essentially different is the world-loving spirit from that of the God-loving, that they cannot both rule in the same breast at the same time. "To find," says Neander, " one's true good in mammon, and to serve God as master, these things are incompatible." "Ye *cannot* serve God and mammon." One or other must be the dominant power. All men are swayed either by secular or spiritual interests. Let us now notice—

II. THE DISSIMILARITY WHICH EXISTS BETWEEN THESE TREASURES.

First. *The one refers to heaven, the other does not.* Jesus speaks of spiritual wealth as laid up in heaven, and secular as laid up on earth. Two ideas are suggested by this distinction :—First, That the one is more *universal* in its worth than the other. Earth is but an insignificant portion of the universe. Its wealth, therefore, is very limited in its value. Its worth is purely *relative.* Even on its own little domain, what would make a man rich in one land, would scarcely support him in another. It will be of no service to him in other worlds. We brought nothing into this world, and it is certain that we can carry nothing out. But "heaven" is immeasurable. Where is it? Wherever rectitude reigns ; and where does it not reign, except in hell and on this little planet, which are but as two small withered leaves in that forest of worlds of which the universe is composed? Hence, spiritual wealth is valuable, wherever truth, righteousness, and benevolence are appreciated. The value of gold is limited to earth : the value of moral goodness is co-extensive with the whole creation. The distinction suggests : —Secondly, That the one is more *future* in its worth than the other. Wealth is only valuable to us, so long as we continue here. To the longest liver, life is only a few years at most. But the good man's connexion with "heaven" stretches on through all future ages. A million centuries will leave it as far from the end as the first day of its existence. And hence, after countless cycles have rolled away, he will be able still to say, "*Henceforth,* there is laid up for me a crown of righteousness."

Secondly. *The one is certain in its continuance, the other is not.* Secular "treasures" are exposed to the "*moth,*" and "*rust,*" and "*thieves.*"* The rich man in the morning rejoices in the abundance of his possessions, but at night his soul is required of him. Belshazzar is this moment revelling in the splendour of empire, and the next aghast with horror at the departure of his kingdom. Herod is to-day worshipped by an idolatrous multitude, and to-morrow the prey of worms. How uncertain is all earthly good !

How precarious is the tenure on which all earthly wealth is held ! A commercial failure, a fire, a flood, a storm, may reduce one from a palace to a workhouse. "*Wilt thou set thine eye upon that which is not? for riches certainly make themselves wings; they fly away as an eagle towards heaven.*" But *spiritual* wealth is *imperishable.* It can be eaten by no moth, corrupted by no canker, stolen by no thief. It is not something *out* of man, or something merely added to him ; it becomes more a part of him than his own blood, it is incorporated

---

* In the East, the most valuable possessions often consisted of the productions of the earth, the precious metals, and numerous suits of clothing, which, as fashions are not there fluctuating as here, retained their full value for years."— Gen. xlii. 22 ; Judges xiv. 12 ; 2 Kings v. 5.

in his own soul; it is not merely the subject but the spirit of his consciousness, not the mere field but the faculty of his vision. It is as imperishable as the soul. "*Knowing that you have in heaven a better and enduring substance, cast not away your confidence, which hath a great recompence of reward.*"

Thirdly. *The one is conducive to the spiritual illumination, the other is not.* "*The light of the body is the eye: if, therefore, thine eye be single, thy whole body shall be full of light; but if thine eye be evil, thy whole body shall be full of darkness.*" There are three thoughts implied in these words, a brief statement of which will serve to show the opposite effect of the secular and the spiritual *disposition* upon the soul's vision:—First, *That there is an organ for divine sight in man.* There is an " eye " in the soul for the divine. This " eye " is something different from that faculty which discovers causes, adaptations, and logical proprieties—the *intellect;* and something different, too, from the faculty which discovers beauty in the exquisite forms of life, and the imitative forms of art—the *imagination;* it is that which sees *moral* truth, perfection, order, God—it is CONSCIENCE. Without this faculty, there could no more be an idea of God and moral truth, than there could be an idea of the forms and hues of this material universe without the eye of the body. Nor can there be a true and happy idea, unless the organ in both cases be in a *healthy* state. GOETHE says, "Had thine eye not been sunny, how could it ever have looked upon the sun?" Secondly, *That this optical faculty of the soul may become so diseased as to enjoy no moral light.* It may become " evil." The bodily eye may become so diseased as only to mislead, confound, and give pain. It may make creation hazy, grotesque, or hideous. Ay, and its tender nerves may convey agony to the brain with every ray of light. It may so happen with the soul's moral " eye." Nay, it *is* so in the case of the vast majorities of all lands. *Morally*, they see nothing clearly, they grope in darkness. On nearly every *ethical* question they are lost in the mists of speculation, worldliness, and doubt; and scarcely a solitary star gleams from the moral firmament: volumes of dense and ever-blackening clouds roll between the human spirit and its God. No catastrophe can befall a soul so terrible as this disease of its optical organ. "*If thine eye be evil, thy whole body shall be full of darkness!*" Let the bodily eye be incapacitated for its function, and all stars and suns shall shine in vain. A faint symbol this of spiritual blindness. *If the light that is in thee*—mark, IN thee—*be darkness, how great is that darkness!* Nothing can give vision if there be no eye. Sweep every luminary from the heavens, still, perhaps, we may kindle artificial lights and *see*, if the eye remain unimpaired. But if the eye be gone, there is no substitute; under a blazing firmament we are enfolded in thickest midnight. "*How great is that darkness!*" Thirdly, *That the secular disposition tends to produce this sad catastrophe.* There is nothing that impairs this spiritual organ so much as self-interest, or worldliness. It covers it with a film that shuts out the clear light of moral principles. To convince men of the *wrongness* of any dogma or measure that their *interest* is concerned in sustaining, is one of the most difficult achievements. As you flash your luminous arguments upon them, you are met by the common reply, " *We cannot see it.*" The fact is, truth, to be clearly seen, must be looked at in its most abstract relations ; but a selfish soul looks at it in its bearing upon its own little interests. Christ saw things as they really were : and why ? Because He was not selfish. " *My judgment is just, because I do not mine own will.*"

But whilst the worldly disposition thus darkens the soul, spiritual disinterestedness illuminates it : under its influence the man becomes "full of light." The man who looks at truth under the influence of the secular, is like an individual looking at nature down a valley on a misty day. He is shut in by the hills and trees, so that his prospect is but very limited, and the few things he sees seem very dim and confused. But he who looks at truth under the influence of the spiritual, is like one standing under the brightest sky, high up on the loftiest hill—his prospect is immense, and every object which comes within the sweep of his vision is distinctly seen.

It is *self* that obscures our moral vision. The smallest coin, held close to the eye's orb, shall shut out the landscape and hide the sun and stars. It is ever so with the vision of the soul : if you keep the world close to the heart, both the spiritual universe and the infinite God are excluded from your view. " *Blessed are the pure in heart, for they shall see God.*"

> " Thou celestial light
> Shine inward, and the mind through all her powers
> Irradiate ; there plant eyes, all mist from thence
> Purge and disperse."

We have already indicated three of those points of dissimilarity between the secular and the spiritual, which the passage under notice suggests. We now go on to notice the last.

Fourthly. *That the one claims supreme attention, the other does not.* This is the gist of the last ten verses. We are commanded to " *seek first the kingdom of heaven,*" &c. ; to " *take no thought, saying, what shall we eat ? or what shall we drink ? or, wherewithal shall we be clothed ?*"

What does the expression, " *Take no thought for the morrow,*" mean ? Is man to be regardless of futurity ? Is he, who is to live through all coming ages, to give no onward look ? This would be contrary alike to our instincts and interests. We are made to look forward. As the traveller looks on upon the road through which he intends directing his steps, the soul wistfully looks to the probable futurity which awaits it. The streamlets issuing from the distant hills do not more naturally hurry to their ocean home, than the sympathies of the soul flow into the morrow. More than half our life is in the morrow ; from it we derive most of our motives and our joys. Our ideal heaven is there. It does not mean, therefore, that we are to be absolutely indifferent to the future, for we *cannot;* and Christ requires no impossibilities. Nor does it mean that we are to exercise "no thought" for the *temporal* supplies of the future. Self-preservation and the Bible bind us to this. Were humanity to neglect this, one short year would terminate its *earthly* existence. We must sow in spring that we may reap in autumn.

The idea manifestly is, take no *anxious* "thought for the morrow." Do not distress yourselves. "The passage in Phil. iv. 6," says Olshausen, "forms a commentary on these words. There the Apostle places the command, μηδὲν μεριμνᾶτε—literally, be not anxious, *i.e.*, '*be careful for nothing*' in connexion with the charge to pray to God for things necessary. *Prayer*, then, is the opposite of care, because man engaged in prayer commends his care to God. The *natural* man cares without praying; the brute and the human being who has become brutal, care as little as they pray." *Over-anxious* thoughts for the *temporal* "things of the morrow," are all but universally prevalent. We see their brandmarks in the saddened expression and the furrowed cheeks of the thousands we meet in every walk of life. They agitate and distract the heart of society, they break the repose of night, they cloud the activities of day, they paralyze the heaven-soaring pinions of the soul and tie it down to earth, they undermine health and abbreviate the short span of life.*

Christ here condescends to do what is certainly not His custom, as an ethical teacher;—gives a *reason* for His injunctions. He does not generally reason, but authoritatively asserts. He speaks "*as one having authority*." But here He deigns to enforce His commands by arguments. And there are five facts upon which He bases His arguments against SECULAR SOLICITUDE.

First. *That man's existence is superior to all the secular blessings he requires.* "*Is not the life more than meat, and the body than raiment?*" The "body," σῶμα means the corporeal framework, which is fearfully and wonderfully made—a world of wonder in itself ; and the "life," ψυχὴ, the principle which animates this body, feels in the nerves, moves in the muscles, flows through the veins, propels and regulates every organ. The two terms designate man's *being;* and this being is greater than any of the secular blessings which it requires, "*Is not the life more than meat ?*" &c. The interrogation is an emphatic expression of the affirmative. Yes, man is more precious than the productions of all lands, or the wardrobes of all kings. He is the steward, representative, and priest of God on this earth—steward, for all earthly things are committed to his trust —representative, for he is the highest manifestation of God—priest, for on this earth he only can enter into the holy of holies in the great temple of the universe. One man is greater than this terraqueous globe, or the sidereal worlds above. He can inquire into the history of the creation, he can rise in thought to his Maker and hold communion with Him, and he will survive the dissolution of all.

---

* 'Ημέριμνα is the anxiety which draws the mind different ways (μέρις, division). Such an one is the double-minded man, James i. 8. Their heart is divided, Hosea x. 2.

Now, there are two thoughts which will show the force of the argument against secular solicitude, which Christ founds upon the superiority of man's existence. First. *That man's being, which thus transcends in value all secular good, is the gift of God.* Were we the mere products of chance, or did we merely spring out of the elements by the blind and resistless workings of nature, or were we even he *forced* workmanship of God, our existence, however great, would constitute no reason for expecting that God would supply that existence with all necessary good. But as our existence is not merely the creation of God, but His GIFT, that which he *might* have withheld, but that which He bestowed in the exercise of the infinite *freedom* of His love; there is a strong *à fortiori* argument that He who freely gave this, the greatest gift of existence, will bestow the minor gifts of supply.

The other thought, which shows the force of the argument which Christ built upon the superiority of our nature, is, secondly, *That this greatest gift of existence requires for its value the other minor supplies.* What would human existence be without "food" and "raiment?" Existence is only *valuable* to me as my native desires are gratified, and native powers developed, and native proprieties observed. Its value is in its complete maturity. *Infantile* existence is only potentially and prospectively valuable. The *à fortiori* argument here, therefore, is strengthened by the second thought, the certainty of the minor blessing following the greater. This appears more certain from the fact that the minor is indispensable to the worth of the greater.

Another fact, here, upon which Christ bases His argument against secular solicitude is :—

Secondly. *That this over-anxiety is utterly ineffective.* " *Which of you by taking thought can add one cubit unto his stature ?* " This is figurative language, and it evidently means, Who, by the utmost anxiety, can add the smallest period to his age ? * Who can add one moment to his years—one sand to the glass of his life ? Who would not prolong his life ? What youth would not live to old age ? What old man would not add to the number of his years ? But to extend, by a *fraction*, the short " hand-breadth " of life, is beyond the power of all. We spring up from infancy to manhood, we pass through the various stages independent of any volition or effort of our own, and we are borne on by a power we cannot resist. Man may glory in his might, and by heaven's permission he may perform some wondrous feats. He may subdue cities, overcome kingdoms, and build up stupendous empires on the ashes of the brave : yes, and still greater works than these he may effect ; he may originate thoughts that may move the intellect, thrill the

---

* That this is the meaning will be evident by considering that the addition of a cubit, or eighteen inches, to a man's height would relatively be very great. In Luke xix. 3, ἡλικία means stature; but in John ix. 21, 23, Heb. xi. 11, means age. Here it means duration of life, regarded as a course or stadium. Compare Ps. xxxix. 5, " Behold, thou hast made my days as a hand-breadth."

heart, reform the institutions, and change the destiny of mankind; but, notwithstanding all, can he either slacken or quicken his speed to eternity ? Can he hinder himself from growing old ? Can he hinder time from whitening his locks, wrinkling his brow, or stealing energy from his limb ? Can he bring back to the withered cheek one faint tint of youthful bloom, or can he brighten his dim eye with the lustre of his younger days ? No, no. Here he is powerless. He is borne on to eternity by a power which he can no more resist than he can check the flowing or the ebbing tides. We cannot add one cubit to our stature.

The argument is :—If, with all our anxious efforts, we cannot add aught to our allotted years, why should we be so solicitous about mere temporal things, and why should we not cheerfully trust that "tender providence which takes no advantage of our weakness, but ministers as the gentlest nurse to our need"?

Another fact, here, upon which Christ bases His argument against secular solicitude is :—

Thirdly. *That the divine attention is exercised over the inferior orders of existence.* (Verses 26, 28, and 30.) There are three facts included in the argument of Christ in these verses.

First. That God's providing agency is over every part of the creation. Christ selects two departments of nature as illustrations. " *Behold the fowls of the air,*" &c. As if He had said, See, how happy they are ! No anxious thoughts distract their little breasts about future supplies; " for they sow not, neither do they reap." Whether perched on the trees, or bounding on the wing, their brisk movements and blithsome notes indicate their freedom from all care about the future; yet they are fed, and fed by whom ? " *Your heavenly Father feedeth them.*" He provides for them suitable food, and by a necessary instinct directs them to the spot where it is to be found. And as to " raiment," " consider the lilies of the field." Behold the lilies of the valley beneath you, how beautiful their fragrance, how lovely their attire, how exquisitely splendid their expanding blossoms ! You have heard of Solomon, the greatest sage and sovereign of your country ; he sat on the throne of ivory and gold, and sovereigns came from a distance to behold his far-famed magnificence ; " *And yet I say unto you, that even Solomon in all his glory was not arrayed like one of these.*" How foolish is the pride of dress ! Your habiliments, however splendid, are outshone by the garments with which God clothes the frail flower, which springs up in the morning and is withered at noon.

The second thought included in this argument of Christ's is, that God's interest in His creatures is proportioned to the greatness of their nature. Though we feel a kind of philosophical impropriety in applying any *comparative* terms to the *regard* of one who is INFINITE, the analogy of human feeling—and we can only form an idea of God's feeling from our own—as well as providence and the Bible, indicate that He does not feel the same amount of interest in all created existences. We feel a greater interest in life than in dead matter, a greater interest in sentient than mere plantal life, in rational than sentient, and a greater interest still in spiritual life, in moral excellence than in rational. We instinctively do this, and we infer that He, whose offspring we are, and who gave us an instinct thus to feel, feels in some measure the same. We can only see God through our instincts. Anyhow, the force of Christ's argument here rests upon this idea. This, indeed, is the essence of His *à fortiori* reasoning.

The third thought included in Christ's argument here is, that man is greater than any other terrestrial existence. This is a fact so universally admitted that illustrations would be superfluous. One point of superiority is here indicated, and that is *perpetuity.* Human nature is contrasted with the " *grass of the field which to-day is, and to-morrow is cast into the oven.*" Man is to survive all terrestrial existence,

" The wreck of matter and the crash of worlds."

Taking these three thoughts together; with what force does the appeal of Christ come, " *Therefore I say unto you, take no thought for your life*"!

Another fact upon which Christ bases His argument against solicitude is :—

Fourthly. *That the anxious seeking after these temporal blessings is a characteristic of Pagan life.* " *For after all these things do the Gentiles seek.*" The force of this argument will appear from two considerations.

First. That the advantages of Christ's hearers were superior to those of the heathen. *They were acquainted with higher blessings, the heathens were not.* The supply of physical wants, the decoration of the person, and the gratification of the senses, the heathen regarded, for the most part, as the chief good. But the disciples of Jesus were informed concerning higher blessings—the blessings of an enlightened intellect, a pure heart, an approving conscience, and a fellowship with the eternal fountain of all good. *They were acquainted with a future state, the heathens were not.* The Pagans, though some of them had vague and shadowy dreams about a future existence, really viewed this life as the totality of their being, its dawn and night. This world was their all, the only sphere for action, the circumference of all their plans and hopes ; all was a blank, starless, midnight beyond. But the disciples of Jesus were taught to regard it as the infancy to a future manhood, ever young and hale ; the spring to a future harvest, joyous and exhaustless ; the morning to a future day, ever brightening into now effulgence, *They were acquainted with a God on whom to depend, the heathens were not.* The gods of the Pagans were local, heartless, dead ; they could not expect anything from them, and therefore they must take their keeping and destiny into their own hands. But the disciples of Jesus were taught to believe in a *parental* God, all-present, all-wise, all-powerful, and all-kind. On the ground, therefore, of their superior privieges they had not the same excuse for being anxious for the future, which the heathens had. But not only were their advantages superior to those of the heathen, but, secondly, they regarded *themselves* as superior to the heathen. This *conscious* superiority is, perhaps, the point upon which Christ founds this argument. As if He had said, you, as Jews, loathe the religion of the heathen, and shrink with horror from their practices; and you, *especially, as my disciples*, hate intensely the abominations both of their creed and conduct; you would not on any account become like them. But remember, if you are over-anxious about temporal things, you will be imitators of their conduct.

Another fact, upon which Christ bases His argument against secular solicitude is :—

Fifthly. *That anxious efforts for the temporal supplies of the future, in the case of Christ's disciples, are entirely unnecessary.* There are three things here suggested in support of this fact :—

First. The character of God. He is our FATHER, and knoweth our need. If our wants are not supplied by Him, it must be for one of three reasons; either that He has not the capacity, or that He has not the disposition, or that He is not aware of them. The first, no one *can* question in the presence of this mighty universe, which was produced and is upheld by His power. And as to the second, Jesus, by representing Him under the tenderly affectionate appellation of our "Father," assures us of His disposition to supply our wants. For "*like as a father pitieth his children, so the Lord pitieth them that fear Him.*" And as to the third, Christ declares that "*He knoweth that ye have need of these things.*" Our almighty and loving Father knows all that these frail natures require.

Secondly. The character of religion. "*Seek ye first the kingdom of God and His righteousness, and all these things shall be added unto you.*" The idea is, that if a man has real religion, he will have all necessary good.* Necessary temporal blessings will come to a *truly* religious man, not in a miraculous, but in a natural way.

---

* This passage gives us one of the most complete views of personal religion that can be found anywhere in the Scriptures. It teaches : I. *That personal religion is a great power over man.* 1. It is an *authoritative* power, a "kingdom ;" it is not a sentiment, or an idea, but a *regal* force swaying everything. 2. It is a *divine power,* a "kingdom of God." There are other religions which are *ruling* powers —Heathenism, Mahommedanism, and even Mormonism. But Christianity is the *ruling power of God.* 3. It is a *righteous* power—"His righteousness." God has a *right* to rule the soul. II. *That personal religion is to be sought as the supreme good.* 1. It is to be sought; "seek :" implying, first, that man at first is not in possession of it ; secondly, that it does not come to him irrespective of choice and effort. This kingdom, unlike human kingdoms, does not extend by force. "It cometh not with observation." It is man's prerogative to choose his own *mental sovereign,* and this, after all, is his only *real* sovereign. *The object we love most, is our mental monarch ;* to "seek" God's kingdom is to seek to love Him supremely. 2. It is to be sought supremely, "first." III. *That personal religion involves all necessary good.* "All these things shall be added unto you." The man who is rightly ruled, will *study* all the laws of being, physical, organic, mental, and moral, and obey the same ; and by *obedience* will get all he wants.

His spiritual ideas, sympathies, and habits, will deliver him from ignorance of the laws of his being; from that indolence, extravagance, and intemperance, which are the principal sources of secular poverty and destitution. Were men to attend to the laws of their being, there could be no poverty; and religion ensures attention to them because they are the holy institutions of God. " Let religion," says a modern expositor, " be the first thing in our affections and in our labours, and providence will be our mighty partner and helper in business." " *Godliness is profitable unto all things,*" &c. " *I have been young and now am old,*" said David, "*yet have I not seen the righteous forsaken, nor his seed begging bread.*"

Thirdly. The character of the future. *The future has its provisions.* "*To-morrow shall take thought for the things of itself.*" To-morrow will bring its own blessings; the sun will rise and shine, the air will breathe its life, the refreshing streams will flow, the earth will bud and bloom, and all nature will work beneath its God to-morrow, to supply the wants of man and beast. To-morrow will have a God as yesterday and to-day, opening His liberal hand and supplying the wants of every living thing.

The future has its trials. "*Sufficient unto the day is the evil thereof.*" To-morrow will have its trials as well as blessings: afflictions, pains, sorrows, vexations, disappointments, are in the morrow. Our morrow will not dawn as the morrow of heaven upon a sinless world, and therefore will have its trials. The expression " sufficient unto the day is the evil thereof," implies that not only every day has its trials, but that anxieties for the future augment the trials of the present. There is a tendency in man to *antedate* his sorrows as well as his joys. Antedated trials are imaginary, and such trials are often the worst. First, they may never actually occur. Imagination is a busy prophet, it is ever speaking " of things to come," but its auguries are seldom fulfilled. It has not only promised us joys that have never come, but threatened us with evils that happily have never come to pass. How often have men looked on to some day in the future which they expected would be most disastrous to them; they have seen the looming clouds gather and blacken, and felt the most terrible foreboding. The day came, and there was no storm. Secondly, when imaginary trials occur, they are seldom so severe as was expected. Imagination exaggerates everything, it magnifies and colours all it touches. Thirdly, there is no consolation promised under imaginary trials. They are not calamities, they are crimes. Fourthly, they augment the real trials of life. Every day has its own trials. Providence has mercifully spread our trials over the whole period of life, to every day its own. By over anxiety we bring them together, and thus impose burdens on ourselves which often bar us from the pleasures, and incapacitate us for the duties of the present. " Let us not," says an old writer, " pull that upon ourselves all together at once, which Providence has wisely ordered to be borne by parcels."

Be it ours to walk the changing path of life, identifying a loving God with every object along the road, and ever cherishing a child-like confidence in the parental providence which is over us, yes, and *before* us too. Let our steps be free and firm, let us bear the passing storms of the day, ever anticipating the sunshine of to-morrow.

Matthew 7:1-6

Christ's Lesson to the Censorious

The prohibition, μὴ κρίνετε—Judge not—does not, of course, mean either of the two following things :—

First. *It does not mean that we are not to judge ourselves.* Self-judgment is a solemn duty which we owe to ourselves, society, and God. It behoves each man to strive earnestly after an accurate estimate of himself. He should know his *intellectual* self—the general laws, the personal peculiarities, and the relative force, of his mental powers. This he should know, in order to ascertain the nature of his mission, and the best way to fulfil it. He should also know his *moral* self—the state of his heart before God, the feelings that possess his soul, and the principles that rule his life. He should search his inner nature, decipher its hieroglyphics, gauge its forces, fathom its depths, feel its moral pulse, and watch its heaving tides of feeling, to see whether they flow Godward or not. All true authorities command us to commune with our own hearts, to prove our own selves, and to see whether we are in the faith or not.

Secondly. *It does not mean that we are not to form a judgment on the characters of others.* There is something in our nature that leads us to inquire into the character of men : something which both induces and qualifies us to recognize the moral differences in society. By an instinct we interpret the looks of men, and read their disposition in the structure and expression of their face. Moreover this is *necessary.* If we are not to form our judgment of men, how are we to know on whom to rely, and with whom to associate ? How can social intercourse and order be maintained if you proscribe this prerogative ? Are the moral differences in society to be overlooked ? Are we to mingle together in a pro-miscuous mass, and treat the demon and the saint alike ? No. Reason and Christianity unite in calling upon us to *withdraw our-selves from every brother that walketh disorderly;* and does not this imply the necessity of judging another's character.

The prohibition evidently refers to the rash and rigorous judgment of the uncharitable and censorious. The allusion is to the Scribes and Pharisees, who were notorious for the hasty and ungenerous judgments which they formed of their fellow-men. " They," says Neander, " judged others severely, but were quite indulgent to themselves, and, indeed, never rightly examined themselves. He that knows what true righteousness is, and feels his own want of it, will be a rigid censor of his own life, but a mild and gentle judge of others."

The censorious spirit these Scribes and Pharisees so signally displayed, was not confined either to themselves, their age, or country. It circulates through all ages, and is world-wide in its influence. Nation passes censorious judgments on nation, church on church, class on class, family on family, man on man, the world over. It is an evil rife and rampant in all circles ; and the great spiritual Reformer of the world, as was highly meet, slays it with the sword of His mouth.

The passage contains four corrective lessons for the censorious.

I. That man's judgment will meet with due retribution. "*For with what judgment ye judge, ye shall be judged : and with what measure ye mete, it shall be measured to you again.*" This verse seems to have been a Jewish proverb. Proverbs are well-tested truths ; they have been tried in the crucible of the world's experience, and received the endorsement of the world's heart. Hence they pass from age to age as current coin of the mental realm, and few, if any, question their genuineness. They have become independent of argument. Mankind, by common consent, have placed them in the region of the undebatable and the certain. They are, themselves, imperial arguments ; their laconic testimony seldom fails to close discussion, and to carry conviction. Hence, Jesus frequently quotes them in order to give intelligibility and convincing force to His own great thoughts.

The *retribution* enunciated in this proverb refers to the *kind* and *amount ;* it means that the man shall have back *what* he gives, good or bad ; and *so much* as he gives, whatever the quantity may be. In Luke, the idea is expressed with greater amplitude :—" *Give, and it shall be given unto you ; good measure, pressed down, and shaken together, and running over, shall men give into your bosom.* For with what measure ye mete withal it shall be measured unto you again.*" Now in what way will this retribution be administered ?

First. *There is a retribution that comes from society to man.* It is a fact in morals as well as physics, that like begets like. Kindness begets kindness, cruelty begets cruelty, falsehood begets falsehood, flattery begets flattery, censoriousness begets censoriousness. A man generally receives back from society that which he gives out to it, and that too, oftentimes, with considerable interest. The suspicious man is suspected, the dishonest man is robbed, the

---

* " The use of the long flowing garment here alluded to, seems to have been common to all the nations of the East ; and, probably, among the Jews, Arabs, and others, who wore their long dresses belted round the waist with a sash, or girdle, the actual bosom, or upper portion of the dress, was pretty generally made use of as a receptacle for provisions or other necessary articles, as it would be allowed to fall in copious folds out over the belt, so as to form à large pocket-like receptacle, capable of containing a considerable quantity of anything."

misanthropic man is hated. Ishmael's hand is against every man, and hence every man's hand is against him. He that leadeth into captivity is in his turn led into captivity. The history of the world abounds with examples. The men who have played the malicious, and been tyrannical toward their race, have often had the demon passions they manifested flashed back upon themselves from the indignant face of society in an all-consuming fire. Society is to man what he makes it ; it is generally a reflection of himself : the merciful finds mercy in it, and the malicious, malice. " *With what measure ye mete to it, it measures to you again.*"

Secondly. *Retribution will be administered by God in a more direct way.* Indeed, the retribution that comes from society is, in a sense, from God. He is the author of those mental laws that insure it. But the Bible reveals a retribution altogether apart from this, and one more just, adequate, and terrible, too. It is written, " *With the merciful thou wilt show thyself merciful ; with an upright man, thou wilt show thyself upright; with the pure thou wilt show thyself pure ; with the froward thou wilt show thyself froward.*" It is a philosophical fact, that according to man's presiding disposition of soul, God will ever be to *his* consciousness. According to the state of our atmosphere, so are the bright orbs of heaven to us ; at times its murky vapours turn our very "sun into darkness," and our "moon into blood." And it is according to the moral atmosphere around our souls—the master sentiments—that the ABSOLUTE ONE will ever appear to the inner eye of our being. To the revengeful He will be robed in vengeance, and to the merciful He will be a God of love. Thus our own characters, whether good or bad, will be thrown back upon ourselves, with the conscious force of divinity. What is hell but sin's *reflections* of the Divine character—the rays of the Eternal falling upon the soul through the combustible medium of the moral corruption, and thus setting all on fire ? Let us remember, then, that there is to be a divine reflection of ourselves, and that exactly with *what measure we mete it, will it be measured to us again.* Then, "Why dost thou judge thy brother ? or, why dost thou set at naught thy brother ? for we shall all stand before the judgment-seat of Christ."

Another lesson here to the censorious is—

II. THAT A DISPOSITION TO PRONOUNCE A RASH JUDGMENT UPON OTHERS, IS INDICATIVE OF GREATER EVIL IN OURSELVES. " *And why beholdest thou the mote that is in thy brother's eye, but considerest not the beam that is in thine own eye ?* " &c. The comparison between the evil of the censurer and the censured is here likened to a little splinter of wood—a mere "mote," and a large log of timber—a "beam." The fact which Jesus here intimates, namely, *that the greatest sinner is the greatest censor,* must be obvious to every student of history, and to every thoughtful observer of society. How severe was the judgment which David pronounced upon the man whose portrait Nathan drew ! How rigorous and hasty was the judgment which the proud Pharisee in the temple passed upon the penitential

Publican! How ready were the Scribes and Pharisees ever to pronounce the severest judgment upon the conduct of Christ and His disciples! The greatest sinners adjudged to death the holiest being that ever trod this earth, even the blessed Son of God. There is no difficulty in accounting for this remarkable, but patent, fact.

First. *There is the self-blinding influence of sin.* The greater the sinner the more ignorant he is of himself. He becomes, at last, unconscious of the "*beam*" that is in his own eye. He fancies himself spiritually *rich and increased in goods, and needing nothing.*

Secondly. *There is the self-hardening influence of sin.* The more a man sins the less he cares for others. He respects neither the claims of society nor of God. He does not care for the feelings nor the reputation of others; fault-finding and slander become his most pleasing work.

Thirdly. *There is the self-dissatisfying influence of sin.* Sin makes his spirit restless as the "troubled sea." It is ever characteristic of a dissatisfied soul to envy the happiness of others and to seek to destroy it.

These considerations may serve to account for the fact under consideration. Let us remember that censoriousness grows with sin, and every desire to pass rash judgments upon others is an indication of some great wrong in ourselves. "*Charity hopeth all things.*"

Another lesson here to the censorious is—

III. THAT IT IS ONLY AS WE ARE FREE FROM OFFENCE THAT WE ARE COMPETENT TO PRONOUNCE A JUDGMENT UPON OTHERS. "*Thou hypocrite, first cast out the beam out of thine own eye, and then shalt thou see clearly to cast out the mote out of thy brother's eye.*" Such a man has neither the *moral* nor *intellectual* competence; neither the right nor the capacity to judge others. What *right* has he? Put a man, whose moral nature is steeped in sin—whose hands are warm and red with the blood of his fellow, into the seat of the judge, to decide upon some trivial charge brought against another, and heaven and earth will cry out against your outrage of justice. But is not justice equally outraged when one sinner sits in judgment upon the character of another less guilty than himself? "*Thou art inexcusable, O man, whosoever thou art that judgest; for whereas thou judgest another, thou condemnest thyself; for thou that judgest doest the same things.*"

There are three facts contained in the fifth verse which, although some of them have been referred to already, are so important as to require a full and distinct expression.

First. *That sin may exist in man to an enormous extent, and yet he be unconscious of it.* There may be a "beam" in the eye of the soul which hinders the light of heaven from illuminating the inner chambers, and the man may not know it. This is one of the darkest facts in connexion with depravity. There are several things that tend to produce this unconsciousness: 1. *There is habit.* Man begins his moral history in sin. He has no period of virtuous experience. All is one unbroken course of evil, until the hour of moral conviction come. Sin, therefore, by habit, becomes so much like a part of his nature, that he is unconscious of it. 2. *There is association.* If, in every-day life, he was called to mingle with the pure and the good, he would be painfully reminded, by contrast, of his spiritual error and delinquencies; but, instead of this, all are of the same depraved class as himself. They breathe the same air, adopt the same maxims, and follow out the same principles. And then, 3. *There is Satanic agency.* The god of this world is employed in blinding the eyes of men.

Another fact contained in this verse is—

Secondly. *That however unconscious of our own sins, we may be alive to the sins of others.* The Scribes and Pharisees, though they could not see the " beam " in their own eye, discovered the " mote " in the eye of others. This fact, which we have before alluded to, shows (1), that sin does not destroy the faculty for discerning moral distinctions; this faculty is preserved in hell. And (2) it shows the importance of Christians being circumspect in their conduct. The world has an eye to see your defects.

Thirdly. *That self-improvement is a necessary qualification for the improvement of others.* " *First cast out the beam out of thine own eye, and then thou shalt see clearly to cast out the mote out of thy brother's eye.*" David expresses this idea in one of his penitential psalms. " Restore unto me the joy of thy salvation, and uphold me with thy free spirit. Then will I teach transgressors thy ways, and sinners shall be converted unto thee." A man must *be* good, in order to *do* good. " *Thou, therefore, which teachest another, teachest thou not thyself? thou that preachest, a man should not steal, dost thou steal? thou that sayest, a man should not commit adultery, dost thou commit adultery? thou that abhorrest idols, dost thou commit sacrilege?* "

Another lesson here for the censorious is—

IV. THAT EVEN THE BEST JUDGMENT OF THE MOST QUALIFIED SHOULD BE MOST CAUTIOUSLY EXPRESSED. " *Give not that which is holy unto the dogs, neither cast ye your pearls before swine, lest they trample them under their feet, and turn again and rend you.*" Although the connexion of these words with the preceding is not very obvious, it is, nevertheless, more natural to suppose such a connexion, than to imagine the abrupt introduction of an entirely new topic. Viewed in this light, moreover, they express the idea stated in this our fourth general lesson, and which beautifully accords with the grand design of Christ in the foregoing verses, which is manifestly the correcting of censoriousness. Most of the best expositions adopt this view of the verse. Associating the passage, then, with the preceding ones, they present to us two thoughts:—

First. *That the holy thoughts of the good are very precious.* They are "*pearls.*" " A word fitly spoken is like apples of gold in pictures of silver." " As an ear-ring of gold, and an ornament of fine gold, so is a wise reprover upon an obedient ear." Who shall tell the value of one true thought? It is a quenchless ray from the infinite sun, an ever-multiplying bread-seed for millions, a fountain of vital influences which no time shall exhaust. Such thoughts mould and fashion the world anew into the moral image of its God. Man's strength lies in the trueness of his thoughts; the truest thinker is the prince and benefactor of men.

Secondly. *That there are characters to whom the administering of such thoughts would be injudicious.* They are "*dogs*" and "*swine*." The former represent men of a sour, malignant, and snarlish spirit, who, instead of listening to your counsels, will bark at you with the rage of a virulent depravity. The latter represent men of the grossest materialism, immersed in sensuality, whose hearts are made fat, who are moral swine. All your arguments will fall on them as flakes of snow on the flinty rock—they will make no impression. Such characters are to be found, undoubtedly, within the circle of every man's observation. Who does not know of some character whom he feels it would be foolish, if not perilous, to counsel about religion? There is not only a time for the good to speak, but a *class* to speak to. Jesus would not speak to some, not even in answer to their appeals. It is a solemn thought that there are men on earth who have passed the reach of moral influence, and whose day of probation is already past.

Matthew 7:7-12

True Prayer

True prayer is the subject of these five verses, and they teach the following things concerning it:—

I. THAT IT IS AN EARNEST APPLICATION OF SOUL TO GOD. "*Ask and it shall be given you, seek and ye shall find, knock and it shall be opened,*" &c. Here are three words expressive of three different acts used to designate *true* prayer. The one idea conveyed by the whole seems to be, *earnest application to God.* True prayer is not a mere sentiment, nor an emotion, nor a form of words, however scriptural. It is an *importunate* appeal to heaven, not merely occasional and verbal, but habitual and spiritual; it is an all-pervading and ever-ruling state of soul.

There are four things always implied in true prayer:—

First. *An undoubting faith in the existence of God.* To appeal earnestly and habitually to a being in whose *personal* existence we have no faith, is a mental impossibility. "*He that cometh to God must believe that He is.*" Can an *Atheist* pray? No. He owns no supernatural intellect to take cognizance of him, no supernatural heart to feel for him, and no supernatural hand to help him. To him there is nothing higher than blind, resistless, iron-hearted *nature.* Would it not be brainless fanaticism to invoke the orbs of heaven, call to the surging waves, or ask the mystic winds for help? Another thing implied in true prayer is—

Secondly. *An undoubting conviction of the personality of God.* It seems to me as mentally impossible to pray to an infinite *something* destitute of all *personal* attributes, as it is to pray to *nothing*. If I believe that there is nothing but God, that He is *Everything*, the All, the sum-total of being, and that I myself am a part of Him, how can I pray? An appeal to the INFINITE IT may be poetry, but cannot be prayer. The Pantheist can no more pray than the Atheist. Vagueness and vacuity are alike unsuited to evoke a praying state of soul.

Another thing implied in true prayer is—

Thirdly. *An undoubting belief in the susceptibility of God to human appeals.* Paul tells us that "*He that cometh to God must not only believe that He is, but that He is a rewarder of all those who diligently seek Him.*" It is manifest that unless a man believe that God attends to prayer, and that he can attain by it what he cannot without, he will never truly pray. The man who regards God as too great to attend to the individual concerns of His creatures, and as having established such a system of laws for the government of the universe as to admit of no such interpositions as are involved in the doctrine of "answers to prayer," can never pray. The *Deist*, therefore, can no more pray than either the Atheist or Pantheist.

Another thing implied in true prayer is—

Fourthly. *An undoubting consciousness of our dependence upon God.* Unless a man *feels* his need, he can never be in earnest for the necessary supply. A profound and ever-prevailing sense of our need of Divine help must ever lie at the foundation of all true prayer. Dependence upon God, as a doctrine, is common; no one who believes in a God could question it for a moment; but as a conscious, practical feeling, how very rare! And hence true prayer is rare, even where true theology prevails.

But there is one more thing implied in true prayer, and that is—

Fifthly. *An undoubting faith in the mediation of Christ.* Christ is man's medium of approach to God. "*No man can come unto the Father,*" says He, "*but by me.*" Now, we say, that these five things must be *deep-settled convictions* before there can be true prayer. Where they are still the subjects of debate and discussion—mere ideas of the intellect rather than vital impulses in the heart—you cannot have true prayer. Alas! they are generally nothing more than ideas in churches still, and hence we have but little real prayer.

Another thing in this passage concerning true prayer is—

II. THAT IT IS THE DIVINE CONDITION OF GOOD THINGS. What does prayer obtain? "*Good things.*" LUKE puts for the "good things," "The Holy Spirit:" and do not the fertile suggestions, the directing and disciplinary influences, and the safe guardianship of the Holy Spirit, comprehend all "good things"? All men agree in desiring *good things,* but they differ widely in their opinion of what things *are* good. Some, indeed, " call evil good," and strive for it as an end. What, then, are the good things obtained through prayer ?

First. *They are things of a spiritual character.* Prayer is a means of obtaining *a sense of God's favour.* On all prayerless spirits there rests, at times, the sense of Divine disapprobation. This hangs like a dark thunder-cloud over the soul, shutting out the warm life-giving beams of heavenly light. Prayer sweeps that cloud from the horizon, and brings the spirit into contact with the eternal sun. Prayer is a means of *spiritual development.* Our perfect well-being requires the full and harmonious unfolding of our spiritual sympathies and powers. The fruits of the celestial paradise grow out of the hidden germs of our being. Prayer is the necessary condition of this development. Physical exercise is necessary to develop our physical powers ; intellectual exercise is necessary to develop our intellectual powers; and religious exercise, the exercise of prayer and praise, is *indispensable* to develop our spiritual powers. As the earth can only send out her germs of life into blade, and flower, and fruit, as she turns her face to the sun; so the soul can only send out its spiritual energies into perfection, as it turns itself in prayer to the eternal fountain of life and light. Prayer is the power that *raises us above the world.* Prayerless souls are the creatures of the world ; they are as clay in its plastic hands ; as feathers amidst its shifting winds—as straws upon its flowing streams. Prayer lifts them from this degradation ; gives them the pinions of an eagle to battle with tempests, penetrate clouds, and bask in calm and sunny scenes above. The spirits of holy martyrs have risen from beneath all the antagonistic forces of the world, and sung triumphantly as they soared heavenward on the wing of prayer. In prayer, man fills his mind with the idea of God, and in the idea of God all earthly glories pale their light; and the universe itself seems to fade into a shadow. We link ourselves to omnipotence, and grow defiant of all other forces in prayer. The good things here spoken of are—

Secondly. *Things of a temporal character.* The Bible warrants us to pray for temporal blessings; *in everything by prayer and sup-plication, with thanksgiving, to make known our requests to God.* We do not feel so ready to acknowledge, that God now gives *temporal* good in answer to prayer, as we are to acknowledge that He gives spiritual. There are, perhaps, two reasons for this : one is, that multitudes enjoy temporal good, who never pray at all ; whereas, it is not obvious that any enjoy spiritual good who do not pray ; and the other is, that no temporal good seems to come to any man, how-ever devout or prayerful, but through ordinary and established laws.

Now, I think it would be easy to show, would space permit, that the fact that temporal good comes, *invariably,* through the ordinary constitution of things, is no valid objection to the fact that it comes, sometimes, as the effect of prayer. This we could show, not by the very imaginary hypothesis of Dr. Chalmers, namely, that there may be a mighty chain of causes extending from our immediate sphere of observation up to the throne of the Eternal, and that the Almighty may strike any one of the links which are beyond our view, and thereby work out His purpose through all the succeeding links downward : and thus the result come to us, apparently, in the ordinary course of nature. This, however beautiful and plausible, is but a conjecture, and, therefore, will not have much weight with a philosophic objector. But we would show the worthlessness of the objection we have stated, by three undoubted FACTS—

(1) *That man's temporal good, as a rule, depends upon his physical conduct ; (2) that his physical conduct is determined by the state of his mind ; and (3) that the state of his mind is influenced by prayer.*

God could change your temporal condition to-morrow without any show of miracle, by imparting to your mind to-day some new idea, or impulse. He could change the temporal condition of England, aye, and of the world, by changing the ideas and impulses of a few men. Your child is ill; he is to all appearance about to end his days; what is to be done? You approach your Maker in earnest prayer, and you entreat Him to restore the health and prolong the life of the dear one. But your physician says, restoration is impossible, and would involve a miracle; and perhaps, as is too often the case, ridicules the idea of praying for such an end. But still, that prayer may succeed, and yet there be no miracle. How ? An idea of a certain medicine may come to your mind, or to the mind of your physician, the application of which stays the disease, in perfect keeping with all the laws of his constitution. Or, a pestilence rages around you, hundreds are dying on the right hand and on the left; you approach your Maker in earnest prayer, you entreat Him to stay the plague, and "in wrath to remember mercy;" but you are ridiculed by the scientific materialists, and you are told, that God governs the universe by certain laws, and that one of of those laws is, that certain gases floating in the atmosphere destroy life, and that it is no use to pray, until you remove the causes of this poison. Still, plausible as all this is, your prayer for the staying of the plague may be answered. Through it God may give to you, or others, a correct idea of *what* that pestilential poison is, and *how* it may be destroyed, and also an *impulse* to apply the adapted means. And thus, by your prayer, you may terminate pestilence without the show of a miracle.

The other thing contained in these words concerning true prayer is—

III. THAT IT IS EVER EFFECTIVE WHEN RIGHTLY EMPLOYED. "*Or what man is there of you, whom if his son ask bread, will he give him a stone, or if he ask a fish, will he give him a serpent ?*" "*If ye then, being evil,*" &c., 9–11. All expositors agree in regarding the ἄνθρωπος—man, here, as emphatical. What *man* is there, to whatever country he may belong, whatever the colour of his skin, the nature of his creed, the measure of his civilisation, if he possess the common attributes of our nature, will he, "*if his son ask bread, give him a stone ?*" &c. The argument for the effectiveness of true prayer is most simple and telling; it is a *minori ad majus*, ascending from the affection of an imperfect earthly father towards his imploring child, to the love of the heavenly Father towards His praying children. The position implied in these words is, *that there is far greater reason to expect that God will answer the prayer of the true suppliant, than that an earthly father will attend to the earnest entreaties of his child.* Let us seek, by two or three remarks, to illustrate this argument.

First. *That there is no comparison between the amount of affection and ability of an earthly father, and that of the " heavenly" one.* The *affection* possessed by a human father towards his indigent and suppliant offspring, however strong, is limited, and liable to extinction. Children often wear it out. And then, the *ability* to help is very measured. Some parents, alas! have not to the power to help their children, even to bread. But, neither the affection nor the ability of the heavenly Father admits of any degrees; both are infinite. Redemption proves the infinitude of His love, and nature the infinitude both of His love and His power.

Secondly. *That this little affection and ability of the earthly father are both derived from the heavenly one.* Whence came the love that glows in our hearts for our children? It is but a spark emitted from that infinite flame which lights upon the universe. All the love in all creature hearts is but a little stream rising from the immeasurable depths of Divine affection. Whence, too, came the power to help? *" The earth is the Lord's, and the fulness thereof."*

Thirdly. *That in the earthly parent, this little and derived affection and ability are associated with " evil;" in the " heavenly Father," infinite love and ability are associated with absolute goodness.* The earthly parent, sometimes, gets his heart hardened against his child by selfishness, intemperance, worldliness, misinterpretation, &c. But the heart of this infinite Father is eternally unsusceptible of any evil influences. *" For the mountains shall depart, and the hills be removed, but my kindness shall not depart from thee,"* saith God.

These thoughts serve, we think, to illustrate the force of the argument contained in the passage, " If ye, then, being evil," &c.

Matthew 7:13

Social Morality

This subject you have in the twelfth verse, *" Therefore, all things whatsoever ye would that men should do to you, do ye even so to them; for this is the law and the prophets."* Here is the normal law, the golden rule, one which for ages has been trodden beneath the feet of mankind, but whose enthronement is necessary to the world's weal.

The words suggest two remarks concerning social morality.

I. That its normal principle is intelligible, reasonable, and

WHOLESOME. Is it not *intelligible?* The most simple and illiterate can understand it; it requires no exposition, no study; a wayfaring man, though a fool, cannot err therein. Is it not *reasonable?* Have not others the same fundamental relations and rights as ourselves? Are we not all the offspring of the same Father, subjects of the same Divine administration, co-sojourners on the same earth, and candidates for the same eternity? Therefore, ought we to do anything to them, that we would not they should do to us? Is it not *wholesome?* This law condemns *falsehood, dishonesty, cruelty, craft, bloodshed, and war,* and all the social evils under which humanity has been groaning for ages. Men's departure from this law is their social ruin; their return to it is their only social salvation.

II. THAT ITS INCULCATION AND ENFORCEMENT ARE ONE OF THE CHIEF ENDS OF REVELATION. *"For this is the law and the prophets."* The meaning is, that it involves the moral essence of the Old Testament.* One great aim of the Bible is, to make man right with his fellows, as well as right with God; and this can only be done by obedience to this golden law. The moral aspect of the Bible has been fearfully overlooked, even by the Christian Church. The Church has regarded the Bible rather as a creed than a code; and hence it has preached the theory of reconciliation with God, and sanctioned war with men; nay, it has sought to maintain its theology by the most flagrant violations of God's normal principle of morality. It will brand the man as a heretic who does not believe in its doctrine of original sin; and canonize him as a sainted hero, who, in some victorious engagement, has outraged every principle of that morality which pervades "the law and the prophets." When will the Church reverence the *ethics* as well as the *theology* of the Bible?

Matthew 7:13-14

The Divine View of Life

Christ's view of life you have expressed in these verses: *"Enter ye in at the strait gate: for wide is the gate and broad is the way that leadeth to destruction, and many there be which go in thereat. Because strait is the gate and narrow is the way which leadeth unto life, and few there be that find it."*

I. THAT HUMAN LIFE HAS TWO, AND BUT TWO MORAL PATHWAYS, the *"broad and the narrow way."* The diversities which obtain amongst mankind, in their circumstances, constitution, attainments, forms, spheres of action, and lines of pursuit, are well-nigh endless. On certain classifying principles it would be easy to arrange them into very numerous and distinct divisions. To the eye of Jesus, however, all appeared in two great journeying classes. He saw all souls flowing in one of two directions. In the moral march of mind, there

---

* Vide Olshausen in loco.

are but two lines—THE RIGHT and THE WRONG—there is no *middle* way for souls. Everything felt, thought, done, endured, or enjoyed, by a moral being, is moral, and is morally good or bad. This fact (1) makes human life very solemn ; and (2) renders the ascertainment of our true character very easy.

From this passage it appears—

II. THAT ALL ON BOTH THESE PATHWAYS ARE PROGRESSING TO APPROPRIATE ENDS.

First. *All are progressing.* In neither the broad nor the narrow way did Christ see any standing or sitting—all were *going.* There is nothing stationary ; the whole universe, mental and material, like an ever-moving machine, has every wheel in action, even the smallest dust is in motion. Nor is anything stationary about moral character ; it is ever passing from stage to stage. There are two features in the progress of moral character, whether in goodness or evil, worthy of note. First, *It is individually optional.* The stars, the winds, the waves, can neither modify nor stop their progress. They have no control over the forces which urge them on. Nor can we stay or modify the progress of our bodies to dissolution. We cannot pause a moment in our march to the grave ; both asleep and awake we are going. But, morally, the progress of the soul is with us, we move or stop it as we please. We can pause in our moral pathway, or retrace our steps, or go faster on. The other feature in the progress of the soul, worthy of note, is, secondly, *That it is ever accelerative.* By this I mean, that the longer it continues to move in the line, either of goodness or evil, the more momentum it gathers, and the faster it proceeds. Its progress is not like the progress of the planets or the ocean. The stars do not seem to move quicker now than they did in the days of Adam, nor does the ocean ebb or flow with greater speed. But the progress of the soul in character, is something like the progress of the cascade, it gathers fresh momentum every moment. Hence, a bad man will perpetrate deeds of iniquity to-day, the bare idea of which would have overwhelmed him a short time ago ; and hence, too, a good man will perform now, with ease and happiness, deeds of self-sacrifice, which at the outset of his religious life he would not venture to attempt.

Secondly. *All are progressing to appropriate ends.* The broad way " *leadeth to destruction.*" The word destruction does not mean *annihilation,* but perdition ; not the termination of existence, but the termination of the blessings of existence ; the loss of everything which makes existence worth having, or even tolerable. The narrow way " *leadeth unto life.*" Life, here, is the antithesis of destruction. It means, not mere existence, but *blessed* existence. The one course, therefore, leads to *ill*-being, and the other course to *well*-being. Now both these ends, though so *diverse,* are *appropriate* to the course. A life of sin leads, naturally, to this destruction. In every sin there is a throwing away of some portion of the blessings of existence, and man has only to keep on sinning in order to strip himself of everything but *sheer* being. And so of holiness ; holiness leads to life—is life. " *To be carnally-minded is death, but to be spiritually-minded is life and peace.*" "*Be not deceived, God is not mocked; whatsoever a man soweth, that shall he also reap; he that soweth to the flesh, shall of the flesh reap corruption; he that soweth to the spirit, shall reap everlasting life.*"

From this passage it appears—

III. THAT THE AVOIDANCE OF THE ONE PATHWAY, AND THE ADOPTION OF THE OTHER, ARE THE IMPERATIVE OBLIGATION OF ALL. Here is the command, "ENTER ye in at the strait gate."

Two things are here suggested :—

First. *That the duty involves great difficulty.* It is a "*strait gate.*" There is no difficulty in entering on the broad road. The gate is wide, you can step easily through. One cause of the difficulty we have here suggested is the difference in the *number* pursuing each course; there were *many* entering the "wide gate," and walking the "broad road," but only a "*few*" passed through the "strait gate" into the narrow way. Man, as a social being, is wondrously influenced by *numbers*. He will follow the multitudes, as the tides follow the moon. The social force of numbers has ever been against holiness in the world. It was especially so in the days of Christ. All the classes in Judea were against the new religion of rectitude and love. He, therefore, who would adopt a religious life, has to extricate himself from the ten thousand ties with which society binds him to itself. He must be *singular*—he must leave the multitude, and walk with the *few*.

But, however difficult, it *must* be done. God commands it, and our eternal well-being depends on it. No man has a right to be in the broad road ; every moment he is trampling on the eternal principles of law and order, battling with the moral influences of heaven —and with the intuitions, laws, and interests of his own nature.

Matthew 7:15-20

The Underlying Element of Moral Character

There is one thing of primary importance to every man ; and that is, moral CHARACTER. There are four things which show this.

First. *Moral character is man's only real property.* Man has nothing that he can call, in strict truth, his own, but this. His land, houses, money, are his only in a very inferior sense. Nor is his existence his. His being, with all its powers of body and mind, is the property of the eternal Creator. "All souls are mine," says the ABSOLUTE ONE. But moral character is the product of man's free and independent agency. It is his creation ; it never would have been, had he not existed. God claims man's existence, but not his character ; if the character is evil, He holds man to blame ; if good, He allows man the praise. Your character is *yours*, though parents, friends, society, heaven, and hell, have contributed to its formation. You are its rightful and *exclusive* owner.

Secondly. *Moral character is the only measure of man's real worth.* Conventionally, men are regarded as great or otherwise, according to the power of their genius, the extent of their attainments, the amount of their social influence, or the magnitude of their secular possessions. But, really, in the sight of the holy universe, and in the estimation of " *the judge of all the earth,*" man is great or otherwise, according to the texture and quality of his moral character. If that character embody the great principles of social rectitude and godliness, then, though a hut be your home and penury your lot, you are *great—* angels are your willing servants, Jesus calls you brethren, and the ETERNAL rejoices in you as His children.

Thirdly. *Moral character is the only earthly product man will bear with him to the other world.* Our earthly possessions, our home, our friends, and even our body, we must leave this side of eternity ; for "*naked came we into the world and naked must we return.*" But moral character we bear with us to the other side, and ever with us : whilst reason and consciousness endure will it continue.

Fourthly. *Moral character is the source whence springs our lasting weal or woe.* The germ of paradise or the fuel of hell is enwrapped in every character. Character will prove to every man, either an Eden, where the spirit of beauty will appear in endless forms of enchantment, and goodness cluster in richest fruits ; or a Hinnom, whose corruptions poison the air, "*feed the worm that dieth not, and the fire that is never quenched.*"

Such, then, is the transcendent importance of *character ;* and the chief glory of Christianity is its relation to it. Its design is to produce in man a holy character : in other words, to transform the human soul into the image, and elevate it to the fellowship and enjoyment of the great God. Hence Christ, its author, constantly spake of character—was ever warning men of the false, and urging them to the true. In the passage before us He alludes to the *underlying,* or *germinant, element* of moral character.

The words suggest four thoughts in relation to this *foundation* of moral character :—

I. THAT IT IS A VITAL PRINCIPLE OF ACTION. It is not a dormant element. It was something vital in these "*false prophets,*" that prompted them to "*come in sheep's clothing ;*" something vital, both in the "*good*" and *corrupt* "*tree,*" which *operated* to the production of fruit. These allusions authorise us to infer that what the *governing* instinct is to a brute, and what the *vital* sap is to the tree, the master *disposition* of man is to his character. We have frequently stated that every man is under the sway of some *propensity* or other, whatever it may be ; in any case it is evermore the source of character. It is his *moral* heart, out of which are *the issues of his life.*

This underlying element of character, like the principle of life in all forms, *assimilates* everything to itself—turns everything into its own essence. Life in the tree turns everything it appropriates into tree, life in the animal turns everything it appropriates into animal. The rose transmutes all into rose, and the vine all things into vine ;

the wolf all things into wolf, and the man all things into man. It is the principle of life that does this. Now, the primary element of a man's character—the *controlling disposition*, acts ever in this way. If that principle be sensual, it turns everything into sensuality; if selfish, it turns everything into avarice; if religious, it turns everything into religion. Like the sap of the tree, this principle of character, runs into every branch of life, produces, shapes, colours, every part.

This passage suggests another thing concerning this *underlying* element of character :—

II. THAT IT IS EITHER RADICALLY CORRUPT OR GOOD. It is implied here, that a tree, even apart from its fruits, is either "*good*" or "*corrupt.*" The fruits are the effects, the *essence*, of the tree. It is so in relation to character. Man is good or bad, according to the moral quality of this principle of action; and that even apart from his outward acts. His external deeds are no more his character, than the fruits of a tree are the tree. It is not so much what I have *actually* done or not done, as what I have *wished* and *willed*, that determines the quality of my character. "*As a man thinketh in his heart, so is he.*"

Now, this fundamental principle is either "*good*" or "*corrupt :*" there is no middle quality—no neutralism in morals.

Another thing suggested by this passage in relation to this underlying element of moral character is :—

III. THAT WHEN IT IS CORRUPT, IT IS GENERALLY DISGUISED. The wolf comes "*in sheep's clothing.*" Man has the power to misrepresent his heart. He can make a moral mask, and wear it so as to *deceive the very elect.* But, mark you, it is the *evil* principle which he disguises, not the good; it is the *wolf* that puts on the "*sheep's clothing,*" not the *sheep* the wolf's. Vice always puts on the robes of virtue, and error speaks the language of truth; but never the reverse. In sooth, the "*corrupt*" principle dares not fully show itself; a bad man is bound by his badness to act the hypocrite. He is seldom just to his own depraved principles; he lacks the courage, he is too great a coward, to act them out in the sunlight of social life. Where is the debauchee that dare publish to the world the whole of his filthy thoughts? Where is the dishonest tradesman or professionalist, who would avow all his schemes of chicanery and craft? Where is the infidel that would venture to act fully out all his views and feelings before the eyes of his fellow-men? The truth is, unless a wicked man concealed, in some measure, his principles, and put on some of the outward forms of virtue, he would not be able to hold up his head in society. He would be shunned as a demon, and left to pine away a wretched life in dark and chilly isolation. To the honour of the moral intuitions of humanity, let it be proclaimed that a good man alone can be faithful to his principles and afford to be *un*-hypocritical. He alone can be open and natural; goodness, like the wide-spread landscape, expansive ocean, or the open heavens, unfolds itself to all, and is most beautiful when most exposed.

But Christ, in the passage before us, refers to the corrupt principle as being under the disguise of *religion*, and under the disguise of religion in its highest form. It appeared not merely in the character of a *saint*, but in the character of a "*prophet.*" "*Beware of false prophets that come to you in sheep's clothing.*" Jesus referred to the Jewish teachers of His day, who sat in the seat of Moses. In the name of divine truth they inculated vain traditions; in the name of benevolence they sought their own selfish ends; in the sacred name of religion they wrought out their own worldly aims. Evil has often robed itself in this attire. Every age has had its hypocrites in the pew, and its false prophets in the pulpit. This, instead of being an objection to religion itself, is an argument in its favour. It is sin's homage to holiness. For does not imitation always imply, in the imitator, faith in the excellence of the original? Whenever a character of distinguished excellence has arisen in any department of life—politics, science, or art, as well as religion—has there not always followed a host of sciolists and quacks?

Another thing suggested by the passage in relation to this underlying element of character is :—

IV. THAT WHENEVER DISGUISED IT MAY, AND SHOULD, BE DETECTED. "*By their fruits ye shall know them,*" &c.

First. *It may be detected.* How? "*By their fruits.*" The fruits are the test. But what is the *fruit* of a man's soul? Fruit is the natural production of a tree; it embodies and expresses its essence. Hence *all* the acts of men cannot be regarded as the *fruits* of the inner life. Sometimes human actions have no vital connection with the inner governing principles of the heart. Men sometimes act against their will; sometimes without their will; they are sometimes creatures of necessity, and sometimes the dupes of mistake. The actions, therefore, which can only be regarded as the criteria must be those which are *fruit*—the natural production, exponents, and embodiment, of the moral principle. The *fruitial* actions of a man are the average and spontaneous doings of his life. We would not judge a tree by its occasional productions; it may fail one year, and yet be a good tree. So with man's character, you must strike the average of his deeds. You must deal with it as the philosopher deals with nature, the theologian with the Bible, the judge with the evidence—look upon the whole. The average conduct, then, and not the occasional deed, is the fruit by which you are to test the inner principle of a man's heart. This is the tongue of his soul.

This test is (1) *infallible.* "*Do men gather grapes of thorns and figs of thistles?*" In the material world, like causes always produce like effects. Men reap what they sow : every tree beareth after its kind. This law holds good in the moral sphere ;—a corrupt heart will have a corrupt life. It is true that the mere occasional acts of a ͵man may not agree with its inner principles : but his *general* conduct, which is the *fruit* of his being, will ever fairly represent them. (2.) The test is *universal* in its application. "*Every tree,*" &c. It is not some particular tree that produces fruit after its own kind, but every tree: so it is not some particular man, whose average conduct expresses his heart, but it is the case with all men. He, for example, who can afford to live without prayer, whose whole energies are engaged, and whose time is engrossed, in worldly pursuits and pleasures—whatever his professions—is destitute of piety. Aye, the heart will out in the life, however strict the guard set over it. *" By their fruits ye shall know them."*

But this test will apply to other things besides character. It will apply to *systems of religion.* You may test Deism, Paganism, Islamism, Mormonism, Christianity, &c., by their fruits. It may be applied, also, to *particular doctrines* of Christianity. You may test predestination, justification by faith, &c., by their fruits. It may be applied, also, to the *methods of promoting Christianity.* The comparative value of the voluntary and coercive principles employed in the promotion of Christianity may be determined by their fruits.

Secondly. *It should be detected.* *" Beware,"* &c. Why should it be detected? (1.) Because the *evil* principle is highly pernicious to others. The primary element of a corrupt character is a *devouring* instinct. Christ compares the false prophets to the *"ravening wolves."* The allusion seems to be to the ferocity and subtilty of these creatures in seizing the unsuspicious sheep and feasting a savage appetite upon their blood, regardless of their cries and agonies. As the wolf lurks in the day and prowls forth in the night on its mission of death, so corrupt men misrepresent their principles in order to gratify their malevolent instinct. Like Joab, they profess friendship in order to stab between the ribs : or, like Judas, they kiss in order to betray. Hence the importance of being on our guard—of seeking to detect the corrupt everywhere, especially when it assumes the character of prophets,—for then it is most dangerous. Let us try the spirits to see whether they are of God : and try them not by their words, however scriptural, or their mien, however devout; but by their *fruits.* Moreover, we should "beware," (2.) Because the *evil* principle is destructive to its possessor. *" Every tree that bringeth not forth good fruit, is hewn down and cast into the fire."* This evil principle in man *insures* ruin, it produces a character only fit for the flames, it is the hell of the soul. BEWARE!

Matthew 7:21-27

Man's Religions, and their Testing Day

This paragraph is the solemn conclusion of the incomparable sermon which Christ delivered upon the Mount. The truths it contains stand out in bold relief and in impressive aspects. They are—

I. THAT MEN ARE NOW RELYING ON VERY DIFFERENT KINDS OF RELIGION. Most men have some religion. Man has been called a "religious animal." He has at once worshipping instincts and capacities. However destitute of knowledge and civilization he may be, he is generally found in possession of a creed, a shrine, and a god.

Now, this passage before us suggests no less than four kinds of religion :—

First. *The religion of profession.* " *Not every one that saith unto me, Lord, Lord, shall enter into the kingdom of heaven.*" These words imply that many of the human family would call Him " Lord, Lord." The religion of this country, we fear, is for the most part of this description. It is a thing of words, and forms, and professions. As a nation, we call Jesus " Lord." We build temples for His worship ; we swear by His religion ; we are called by His name. But as a nation does our conduct agree with our profession ? Are His laws held everywhere supreme ? No ! No ! His laws are little more than speculative ideas to us as yet. His words, perhaps, are a vague creed to us, but, certainly, *no ruling code.* For example, He has commanded us not to labour supremely for the meat that perish-eth—not to lay up for ourselves treasures on earth—not to take any anxious thought for the things of the morrow—not to return evil for evil, but to do good to our enemies, and thus imitate Him " *who when He was reviled, reviled not again.*" These are His laws, written as with a sunbeam, in His own word ; and is not our conduct in direct opposition to these injunctions ? We call Him " Lord, Lord," and that is about the sum of our religion as a nation.

Another form of religion suggested by this passage is—

Secondly. *The religion of merit.* " *Many will say to me in that day, Lord, Lord, have we not prophesied in thy name ? And in thy name have cast out devils, and in thy name done many wonderful works ?* " The spirit of this is, Have we not merited thy favour by what we have done ? There is a fearful tendency in man to attach the idea of merit to his religious conduct. How many there are who imagine that by their social integrity, their benevolent deeds, their devotional observances, they will procure the favour of their Maker ? But he who has this idea has not learnt the alphabet of Christianity. Were I as holy as an angel, as devoted as a seraph, could I ever do aught that would merit a single favour from my Maker ? No ! for the power with which I should work would be His, and the instrumentality by which I acted would be His, and the time I employed would be His, and the influence which incited me would be His ; what merit, then, could attach to my operations ? How absurd, therefore, for a sinner to attach the idea of merit to the best of his labours !

Another form of religion suggested by this passage is—

Thirdly. *The religion of hearing.* " *Therefore, whosoever heareth these sayings of mine,*" &c. This, also, has ever been a very popular form of religion. Great numbers were now hanging on the lips of Christ, and feeling, probably, an interest in the wonderful things He uttered. Never, perhaps, was the religion of hearing so general as now. Many temples of the Lord are crowded every

Sabbath-day with the hearers of the word. But hearing the Gospel is not true religion. There are many things which give men an interest in hearing the Gospel, altogether apart from the true religious feeling. There is (1) *man's active desire for excitement.* Every man has an instinctive desire for excitement ; the mind pants for it as the "*hart for the waterbrook.*" The poetry, the narrative, the discussion, the speech, the scene that will kindle the most emotion, will ever be the most welcome to the human heart. And, within the widest sweep of creature thought, are there any subjects so suited to stir the human passions, and move the human heart to its centre, as those with which the preacher has to do ? There is (2) *a native desire for knowledge.* Deeply seated in the intellect is the craving after truth,—a craving which no amount of information can gratify. Supplies only serve to quicken it; allay it they cannot. The Gospel ministry meets this desire also. The Bible contains an exhaustless mine of truth, and it is the province and duty of the minister ever to bring out things *new* as well as old.

The fact that the Gospel ministry serves to gratify these two instincts in human nature is sufficient to show, that no man has a right to infer that he is religious because he feels an interest in *hearing* the word.

It serves to explain, moreover, the fact, that there are two widely distinct classes of unprofitable Gospel hearers :—the morbid sentimentalists and the theoretical intellectualists. The former are never gratified in the sanctuary unless their passions are stirred and their animal sympathies awakened. Dramatic exhibitions of truth, terrible details of misery, pictorial sketches of hell, tragic exhibitions of Christ's physical agonies—whatever, in fact, in the heavens above, or in the earth beneath, or in the hell under all, will move the mere feelings, are Gospel to them and nothing else. Hence the preacher, however gross and material in his notions, if fluent in speech, vehement in spirit, and dramatic in style, is ever most popular with such. And the latter, namely, the theoretical intellectualists, esteem nothing as Gospel but certain doctrinal views. They feed on the dust of a metaphysical creed.

Another form of religion suggested by this passage is—

Fourthly. *The religion of doing.* "*He that doeth the will of my Father which is in heaven.*" "*Whosoever heareth these sayings of mine, and doeth them.*" This is the only valid form of religion—the only form that will obtain the approbation of Christ and stand the test of the retributive economy. Christianity is a system intended not merely to awaken excitement or instruct the intellect, but to rule the life and form the character. "*For not the hearers of the law are just before God ; but the doers of the law shall be justified.*"

The next general truth which this passage contains is—

II. THAT A CRISIS WILL DAWN WHEN ALL THE VARIOUS KINDS OF RELIGION SHALL BE TESTED. "*That day.*" The universal forebodings of humanity, men's moral reasonings on providence and analogy, concur with the Bible in teaching that such a day will come. Christ says, " that day," as if His hearers were thoroughly convinced of its coming, and were assured of its pre-eminent importance. " *That day*,"—when all the purposes of mercy shall be realized, when the mediatorial economy shall be closed, and Christ deliver up the kingdom to God, even the Father.—" *That day*,"—when the graves shall send forth their dead ; when all the men who have ever breathed this air, or· trod this earth, shall stand forth in the full consciousness of their personal identity in the presence of their Maker, and their Judge.—" *That day*,"—when the despised Galilean, the wearied traveller at Jacob's well, the malefactor on the cross, shall appear on that " *great white throne*," before whose refulgent brightness the heavens and the earth shall melt away.— " *That day*,"—when every providential mystery shall be explained, every complaint silenced, every murmur hushed for ever.—" *That day*,"—to which all other days have pointed, to which the events of all other days have flown, whose sun shall never set, and whose transactions will never be reversed or forgotten.—" *That day*,"—when an everlasting separation shall be made between the righteous and the wicked : when the redeemed universe, shaken by the storms of centuries, shall settle into a peace that no sin shall break again.—" *That day*,"—when all the bright epochs of time, which, like stars, have been glimmering out their pale and chilly rays from the benighted firmament of the race, shall be lost in the brightness of a sun that shall rise to set no more.

The other general truth contained in this passage is—

III. THAT ON THIS DAY THE TRUE AND FALSE RELIGIONISTS WILL BE MOST SIGNALLY DISTINGUISHED.

First. *The false religionists will be filled with intense anxiety, the true will not.* " *Many will say to me in that day, Lord, Lord*," &c. How agitated the false in that day, how calm the true !

Secondly. *The false religionists will be rejected, the true will not.* " *And then will I profess unto them, I never knew you*," &c. How ineffably dreadful will it be to be disowned by Him whose smile is heaven, but whose frown is hell. " *I never knew you;*"—never approved of you ;—though you heard with interest my Gospel, though you wrought great things in my name, yet I never approved of you.

Thirdly. *The false religionists will meet with destruction, the true will not.* " *Therefore, whosoever heareth these sayings of mine, and doeth them, I will liken him unto a wise man, which built his house upon a rock : and the rain descended, and the floods came, and the winds blew, and beat upon that house, and it fell not: for it was founded upon a rock. And every one that heareth these sayings of mine, and doeth them not, shall be likened unto a foolish man, which built his house upon the sand : and the rain descended, and the floods came, and the winds blew, and beat upon that house ; and it fell : and great was the fall of it.*" In Judea there are periodical rains which often continue for successive days ; these rains often fill the glens of the mountains to their overflow, and the accumulated waters rush forth and roll in foaming torrents down the hills, bearing everything before them.

The house that was built above them would be secure, but that at the base would be exposed to the utmost danger. Picture the scene of the house thus built on the sand. It is just finished and the owner has taken possession of it as his home. There he hoped to enjoy comforts which would amply repay his labour and cost. For a season all is fair. It is girded by the hills, the valleys bloom around, the genial air breathes softly by. It seems a beautiful residence, a well-chosen home. The traveller admires it on his way. But the summer months roll away, autumn succeeds, and now the dreary winter comes. There are indications of a storm, the clouds gather, blacken, and spread ; the winds howl in threatening notes, rains commence, torrents fall on the earth day after day without abatement, the glens of the mountains are full to an overflow, they come rushing down the hills with an ever-increasing force, they dash against the sides of the house, they accumulate around it, they penetrate and loosen the foundation; meanwhile the winds are raised to a hurricane and are beating all their force upon the building. At length the foundation gives way ; not a stone, a timber, escapes—it is utter ruin. "*Great was the fall.*" Such is the image which Christ employs to describe the terrible condition of the false religionists in "*that day.*"

How miserable the circumstances of this man ! Think of the *amount* of his loss. All the money, anxiety, and labour, which its erection cost him, sacrificed for ever. Think of the *time* of his loss ; the house is destroyed just at the period when *most required,*—in the tempest ; think of the *irremediableness* of his loss. The materials are probably borne away by the flood, and a re-erection is impossible.

In sublime contrast with this, behold the stately and stable dwelling of the "*doer of the word,*" up upon the rock yonder. It stands unmoved amidst the severest tempests of *that day*, and with a full consciousness of security, the tenant looks calmly out and enjoys the wild sublimity of the scene.

Matthew 7:28-29

The World's Great Teacher

The verses which now come under our notice present Christ to us as the world's Great Teacher.

There are three incidents in the passage before us which indicate the transcendent greatness of Christ as a teacher—the impression He made upon His auditors ; "*they were astonished at His doctrine :*" the reason which the Evangelist assigns for this impression; "*for He taught them as one having authority :*" and the numbers that accompanied Him after the sermon was over ; "*when He was come down from the mountain, great multitudes followed Him.*" These circumstances unite in giving us the idea, that as a teacher He stands alone in unapproachable glory. " *Never man spake like this man.*" All on whose ears His voice fell, felt this. It is said that " *the common people heard Him gladly ;*"—the common people; not the religious rabble, who are carried away with any vulgar declaimer who can excite their sensibility, but the unsophisticated millions, possessing the average amount of common sense—*they* " heard Him gladly.*" There were a freshness and a force about His statements that touched their inmost nature and woke their slumbering souls. The sermons of Jesus wafted the minds of His hearers into a new world : new stars shone above them, the landscape was new ; and the air fresh and balmy, quickened the pulsations of their souls and gave them feelings they never had before. " *They were astonished at His doctrine.*"

But what gave this power to His teaching ? What were the distinguishing features of His ministry ? This question is of such practical moment that we cannot do better than notice, briefly, a few out of many of Christ's features as a teacher.

We shall divide them into three classes:—

I. THOSE WHICH CANNOT BE IMITATED.

First. *His originality cannot be imitated.* What He taught was not derived from books, traditions, or living men, but was the production of His own mind. The truth He taught was *in* Him, as rays are in the sun—as streams in the fountain. He was truth. Perhaps you may find most of what He said wrapped up in the Jewish Scriptures. Be it so. He was, nevertheless, original. Originality does not necessarily mean novelty. A thousand minds may think the same thing, yet each be strictly original in the thought. Moreover, was not the Old Testament itself derived from Him ? Did He not speak by the prophets ? Was not His spirit in them ? " He was in the world "—in its rising intuitions, and struggling intellects—long ages before His incarnation. He was the light " *that lighteth every man.*" He illumined not only the Hebrew seers, but those ancient sages, whose philosophies, infidels would have us believe, were the fountains of His best ideas. Does the sun borrow from the ray ? Then, did Jesus borrow from our Socrates, Plato, and Seneca ? No, He borrowed not. He drew His sermons from Himself. His ideas come forth from Him, wearing the impress of His own nature. Even the ideas that had been current in the world before, He made His own,—made new. He moulded them into new forms, breathed into them new life, and gave them new voice to startle the dormant faculties of mankind, and mould men into His own image. He cut a new channel for the world's thought, ever-widening and ever-deepening, and threw into it a tide of sentiments that shall one day flood society with a new life.

Secondly : *His miraculousness cannot be imitated.* Christ taught by wonderful works as well as words. His miracles, if they did not prove the truth of His doctrines, which we are disposed to admit, called attention to them, illustrated their meaning, and symbolised their spirit. Jesus made mute nature speak for Him. He unsealed the eye of the blind, healed the diseases of the afflicted, raised the bodies of the dead, and hushed the storm, to adumbrate that spiritual light, health, life, and peace, which all His doctrines were designed and fitted to impart. This we cannot imitate. We cannot work miracles.

Thirdly. *His authority cannot be imitated.* " *He spake as one having authority.*" There was nothing like the hesitating of doubt, or the consciousness of insufficiency, in His utterance. He knew that what He stated was true, and that He had the highest authority to proclaim it. Hence He frequently prefaces the announcement of sentiments with the expression, " *Verily, verily, I say unto you :* " as if He had said, " I know that what I say is absolutely true, and have an undoubted right to proclaim it." Hence, too, He challenged attention to, and demanded credence for, His doctrines, not on the testimony of others, nor on the ground of argument, but on His own authority. He places Himself on an equality with the FATHER. " *He that receiveth me, receiveth Him that sent me.*" He states that His words would determine the future destiny of man. " *The words that I speak unto you, they shall judge you in the last day.*" He did not utter His ideas as individual opinions, but as eternal principles ; His words came as laws rather than lessons. Such was His authority, that He had only to say at any time to any men, " Follow me; " and forthwith they would leave their all and follow Him. This is an attribute we cannot imitate.

II. THOSE WHICH MUST NOT BE IMITATED.

There appear to me three features in our Saviour's ministry, which should never be imitated by other teachers.

First. *His positiveness.* Nearly the whole of His teaching is made up of positive assertion. He does not go into proof; He seldom, if ever, condescends to argument. He is oracular ; He dictates, but seldom debates. This dogmatic mode was in Him an excellency. His doctrines were amongst those *first* principles of belief which lie beyond the reach of logic, and are so congruous with human consciousness as to require no formal proof. He knew that the principles He enunciated were absolutely true,—true in themselves : and relatively true,—true to human nature. Why, then, should He deign to argue ? It was for Him only to pronounce. Let no man attempt to imitate Christ in this respect. All, since the days of the apostles, are erring men ; sin has clouded the divine page of first principles in their nature, and they have no reason to expect that their fellow-men will receive doctrines on their *ipse dixit.* They must reason, not dogmatize. If they would have their opinions intelligently respected, they must seek by just and judicious argument to make them harmonize with the dictates of conscience, the laws of reason, and the word of God. The dogmatism of the pulpit is a repellent to genuine inquirers.

Secondly. *Self-assurance.* Christ, as a teacher, had always boundless confidence in himself. He never prefaced a discourse or a remark by an apology. There was nothing like the diffidence of self-insufficiency about Him. He always felt able to sound the depths of every thought, and to span every question. This self-assurance should not be imitated by any who are engaged in the holy work of teaching. The apostles had it not; even Paul, at times, seemed crushed under a sense of his own insufficiency for a work so sublime in its nature, and so momentous in its issues. It is a sad thing to see, which you frequently may, self-sufficiency in this sacred office. Between the self-assurance of Christ and that of other preachers there is an infinite difference. They arise from opposite causes. Jesus had it because of the *perfection of His knowledge.* The whole realm of truth came within the sweep of His glance, and every object stood out in cloudless sunshine. He saw everything—everything distinctly, and in its true proportions and relations. He was the master of every theme He touched; the deepest things of God were familiar to His mind. But other teachers who have this self-assurance, have it because of their *ignorance.* The man who has the greatest dash of this in his ministry, is the man who has seen the least of the wondrous and soul-overpowering field of truth. He has but just touched the margin, and seen an object here and there in the dim twilight of old dogmas, received from tradition or from books. The less thought, the more self-confidence; sometimes the paucity of thought and intelligence beget an impudence in the pulpit which the vulgar mistake for inspiration.

Thirdly. *His self-representation.* He was constantly speaking about Himself. He was the great subject of His own teaching. Hence all He said was full of the *I.* " I and my Father are one;" " I am the bread of life;" " I am the resurrection and the life;" " I am the good shepherd;" " I am the way, the truth, and the life;" " I say unto you." His discourses are, in fact, full of the *I.* The reason of this is obvious. He had nothing greater to reveal; in Him dwelt all the fulness of the Godhead bodily; He was the centre and circumference, the soul and substance, of all truth. Now, it is not for men to imitate this *egoism* in teaching. They have to keep self in the background. Their I in the pulpit is an offence and a sin;—they become great and powerful as they become self-oblivious. Their work is to bring Christ to the front; to catch the rays of His glory, and fling them on the souls of men. *I have determined to know nothing amongst men, save Jesus Christ and Him crucified.*"

These, then, are some of the features which must not be imitated. Let me now call your attention to the other class of features :—

III. THOSE WHICH SHOULD BE IMITATED.

First. *His naturalness as a teacher.* I say natural, not in the sense of *coarseness ;*—for all His sentiments, expressions, and habits, as a teacher, were exquisitely refined. An ethereal delicacy of feeling pervaded the whole of His life. Nor in the sense of *uncultivatedness* do I apply the word to Him. His intellectual and spiritual powers were well trained. He had evidently devoted the leisure hours of his youthful life to the important work of self-culture. Somewhere, amid the solitudes of nature, He had so studied the pages of truth, that His spiritual faculties grew with His years. The mind of Jesus reached the full stature of perfect manhood, as did His body, gradually, by attending to the divine laws of growth. But I mean that His teaching was *natural* in the sense of *genuine simplicity*. How free from everything like *art* were the reasonings and the language of Christ! There was nothing of the technical scholar in the structure of His sentences, nor of the sanctimonious priest in His intercourse with His hearers. He did not formulate His thoughts by any logical rules, nor adorn them with any rhetorical ornaments. His thoughts were the rising intuitions of His own great nature, and He made the current and every-day language of His contemporaries the mirror to reflect them on the eye of others. His outward life was the faithful expression of His inward, and His inward life was ever in perfect agreement with truth and sympathy with God. Every changing note of His voice was the ring of something new within, and every expression of His countenance was the gleam of some passing thought or feeling of His soul.

I refer His constant readiness to teach to His *naturalness*. He was always ready;—He never offers an apology for unpreparedness. Never drawing His thoughts from books or memory, but from His own nature, He was never at a loss. He could speak to any class on any question, in any place, at any time; and speaking, always make himself felt; and this because He was not the creature of art, but the child of nature:—and unsophisticated nature, if interrogated, will never fail to respond; if trusted, will never disappoint.

I refer His variety as a teacher to His *naturalness*. There was nothing monotonous in His teaching. There was always something new. The same thing twice said by Him seemed different. Variety is a characteristic of nature—monotony, of art. Take the flower blooming in the landscape, and the flower painted on the canvas; or take the cedar towering in the forest, and the cedar cut down, carved, and polished, by the hand of art, to adorn some lordly mansion. The flower and the tree, abroad in the bosom of nature, are changing their forms and tints every hour, but in the cold sphere of art they remain from year to year almost the same. There seems to me as much difference between a teacher that is natural and the one that is artificial, as between the growing cedar and the polished pillar. The former is constantly varying—new branches sprout forth and new tints appear; but the latter, from its constant sameness, becomes uninteresting. The want of naturalness has always been the sin and weakness of religious teachers. They have too generally lost their nature in their art, they have merged all the idiosyncracies of their manhood in their office. Their education, instead of strengthening and developing their nature and bringing out all its strong and characteristic points, has moulded them after some conventional model, by which all are made to think in the same way, speak in the same voice, and move in the same style. Hence, people sleep under the hollow monotony of the pulpit now-a-days.

Let nature, rightly trained to think, and permeated with the godly spirit, speak in her own voice and key from the pulpit, and a spirit of hearing the Gospel will once more inspire our population.

Secondly. *His suggestiveness as a teacher.* Every sentence He uttered started some thought, or trains of thought, in His hearers. Hence the questions which were put to Him, not only at the end, but often in the midst of His discourses. There was more religious *thinking*, perhaps, in Judea during the three years of His ministry, than had been there for centuries before. He put the wheels of religious thought, which had been all but motionless for ages, into a rapid movement, which has been perpetuated ever since, and which has borne humanity on to its present advanced stage of civilization, knowledge, morality, and religion. His thoughts, like the breath of spring, swept over the mental world, and quickened its dormant germs into life. This *suggestive* teaching is the highest kind of teaching, the only teaching of any worth. He who crams the mind of others with his own ideas, however correct, does nothing to help humanity equal to him who stimulates the mind to create ideas for itself—to *think.* Jesus knew this, and His aim was to get men to think. The suggestiveness of His teaching may be traced as well to the *manner* as to the *matter* of His discourses.

There was much in the *definiteness* of His manner to account for it. He generally appeared to have some *one* point at a time which He sought to fasten upon the attention of His hearers. His habit was to state some one principle, and then draw a parable to illustrate it ; and by this means He would bring that principle so to act upon the mainspring of the soul, as to put the wheels of thought in action. In this respect His teaching differs widely from the teaching of most of those who profess to be ministers of His Gospel. They endeavour to press into every discourse the whole of their little system of theology ; they must have what they designate the " doctrines of grace " in every sermon. " Doctrines of grace ! " narrow souls ! Are not all the truths of the Bible, which lie thick as grass on each of its sacred pages, " doctrines of grace " ? Indeed, most of what you call the " doctrines of grace " were seldom, if ever, mentioned by Christ. A sermon containing all the truths Jesus uttered in His discourse upon the mount would not be considered a " Gospel sermon " by these theological censors. He who brings his own few favourite dogmas into every discourse, preaches not as Christ preached, and must have his ministry characterized more by the somnific than the suggestive.

I refer His suggestiveness as a teacher to His remarkable freedom from all that was formal and conventional in thought, expression, and manner. Everything He said was fresh with a new life ; even truths that had become stale in human creeds, and hacknied on the lips of the world's pedagogues, bloomed with new life as they flowed from Him.

Thirdly. *His catholicity as a teacher*. It is true that the particular sphere of His ministry was Judea, that the class of men He generally addressed were Jews, and that some of the forms and illustrations of His doctrines were specially suited to the Hebrew race. But His teaching, notwithstanding, was world-wide in its intent and adaptation. He spoke not mainly to a class, but to the race. His ministry was a ministry for humanity. He spoke to the Jew that, which in its spiritual relation, was equally applicable to the Gentile; to His contemporaries, that which was of equal fitness and moment to all generations of coming times up to the last hour of the world's probation. His truths were for the general intellect and conscience of mankind, and His merciful provisions for its common aspirations and wants. He was the first teacher that ever founded a school for the world. Even the broad-minded Plato had written over the door of his school, " Let none but geometricians enter here." His was a school for a small class : but Christ has written, as it were in letters of light, over the entrance to His great school, " *Come unto me all ye that are weary*," &c.

Fourthly. *His spirituality as a teacher should be imitated*. He was ever impressed with the paramount importance of spirit. Matter, to Him, even in its most magnificent and imposing forms, was nothing in comparison with mind. Worlds seemed to pass into empty shadows as He dwelt upon the value of souls. Hence He never sought to awaken the animal sympathies, nor please the sensuous part of His audience. He was ever appealing to the inner spirit—the moral sympathies—the conscience. He taught that the object of worship was a Spirit, and that true worship was not a formal service, but a spiritual devotion. He taught that religion was not in overt acts, but in hidden principles ; not in the outward propriety of the Pharisee, but in the inner penitence of the Publican. He did not prescribe rules for the external conduct, but inculcated principles to govern thoughts and control emotions. He directed His hearers to holy principles, purposes, and spiritual habits, as the true riches ; and warned them against labouring mainly for worldly wealth. He was a spiritual teacher. The God, the wealth, the kingdom, the honour, and the happiness, He spoke of, were all *spiritual*. His words were " *spirit and life*."

Fifthly. *His tenderness as a teacher should be imitated*. His treatment of the woman taken in adultery ; His tears at the grave of Lazarus ; His pathetic lament over Jerusalem ; His last conversation with His disciples ; His gracious notice of Peter on His first meeting with him after the denial ; His prayers ; and His address to His mother on the cross ; are a few examples of His exquisite tenderness. His tenderness was not the simpering of an effeminate nature,—it was the nerve of a mighty mind, who looked into the heart of things, having the deep consciousness of its solemn and strange relations. It could roll the thunders of faithful rebuke as well as breathe the words of soothing sympathy and hope. His tenderness was as the sap of oak,—the strength of His nature.

His tear was the exudation of moral force. Let all teachers imitate the Great Teacher in this. Tenderness is the soul of eloquence; it tunes the voice into music; it breathes our thoughts into the hearts of our hearers, and makes them one with us.

Sixthly. *His faithfulness as a teacher should be imitated.* Though poor, friendless, despised, and persecuted, He stands erect before the greatest men of His age;—confronts them, and spares them not. He takes off their mask and brings out into the light their long-hidden sins. The voice which whispered in accents of love to His disciples, " *Let not your hearts be troubled," resounded in thunder elsewhere.* He had no soft and courtly forms of speech for the respectables of His country—the Pharisees, the Scribes, the Lawyers, the Priests, the Rulers. Without mincing, in broad vernacular, and with the emphasis of honest indignation, He told them what they were,—"a wicked generation;" "whited sepulchres;" "hypocrites;" " blind guides;" "fools;" "serpents;" and "vipers." He treated pretence as infamy; seeming sanctity, as a damning crime.

Seventhly. *His consistency as a teacher should be imitated.* His doctrines were drawn out in living character. He exemplified the spirit He inculcated, He embodied the truths He taught; His life illustrated, confirmed, and enforced His language. *He was truth :* —breathing, living, speaking, acting truth. This consistency is an element of power which every teacher should devoutly and habitually seek.

Eighthly. *His devoutness as a teacher should be imitated.* Christ was ever full of the great idea of God, and, therefore, ever full of the spirit of prayer and worship. Frequently do we find Him withdrawing into some secluded spot,—to a "mountain," to a "solitary place," to a "desert place," to a "garden," to pray. . He felt the Eternal Father ever with Him; encircling, nay, filling, the whole sphere of His being,—sunning and warming the entire atmosphere of His soul. He always spoke as in sight of God, and always spoke, therefore, with the unction of devotion. Herein is speaking power. Sermons are mere intellectual productions until they are bathed in the life-giving current of devout emotions. Ideas become instinct with life as the soul grows prayerful. It is the *felt* idea of God alone that gives life, energy, unity, to all the parts of a sermon.

Matthew 8:1-4

The Great Physician

It would seem, from chapter iv., verses 23, 24, that Jesus had effected numerous extraordinary cures,—"healing all manner of sickness, and all manner of disease, among the people,"—prior to the cure of the "leper," recorded in the passage now under notice.

But the case of this leper is the first miraculous cure which Matthew narrates in detail. Jesus had now finished His sermon on the mount. That sermon had evidently made a powerful impression upon the listening assembly; for "as He came down from the mountain great multitudes followed Him." His thoughts had polarized their hearts, and so long as the new impressions lasted, they were drawn after Him as by a magnetic force. The "leper" came within this new and mystic circle of influence, felt the attractions of Christ, approached Him, "*and worshipped Him, saying, Lord, if Thou wilt, Thou canst make me clean.*"

We shall look at Christ healing the leper as an illustration of *His healing souls.* There are three reasons which justify us in turning it to this use. (1) Because physical evils in · man are the effects and emblems of spiritual. We do not say that the particular evils of any given individual arise from his particular sins; but that the physical evils of all have moral evils as their roots. Human suffering springs from human sin. These physical evils, moreover, are not only effects, but emblems. Diseases of the body *represent* the diseases of the mind. Blindness, deafness, debility, pain, are the body's portraits of the soul's woe. (2) Because Christ's physical cures were generally effected on spiritual conditions and for spiritual ends. As a rule, Christ required the patient to have faith in Himself before He performed the cure. He generally gave the mind an impulse before He touched the body; and, moreover, spiritual good was the manifest design of all His physical cures. He sought to win the soul through kindness done to the body; and He often did so. (3) Because Christ's physical cures are admirably suited to represent His healing of souls. And assuming, what we are far from believing, that they were not *intended* for this purpose, their wonderful adaptedness justifies us in thus using them.

The passage, looked at in this aspect, suggests four remarks in relation to Christ's curative power :—

I. HIS CURATIVE POWER IS EQUAL TO THE WORST CASES OF HUMAN DISEASE. Amongst the physical ills which afflict humanity, perhaps that of leprosy may be regarded as the very worst. It covers the body from the crown of the head to the sole of the foot with disgusting pustules; it roots itself into the system, and is seldom eradicated; it is transmitted from sire to son, through many generations; it debilitates the whole system, and produces a most oppressive sense of prostration. Sometimes it is so virulent that it mutilates the body and separates the joints and the limbs. It makes the wretched victim repulsive to society, so that his nearest relatives and friends shun him with disgust; and it renders his mind restless, gloomy, desponding, so that his "*soul chooseth strangling rather than life.*" But malignant as is this disease, it does not surpass the curative power of Christ. This poor leper came to Him having, perhaps, the malady upon him in its most virulent form and offensive aspects; and Christ had only to say, "*I will—i.e.,* I am willing—*be thou clean; and immediately his leprosy was cleansed.*"

Let this leprosy stand as a picture of sin in its most aggravated forms; let the leper be taken as the type of the "chief of sinners," and the glorious truth illustrated is," HE IS ABLE TO SAVE TO THE UTTERMOST." What a glorious word is this "uttermost!" Who shall gauge its dimensions? *It compasses all sins.* Whatever their class, whether of omission or commission,—of ignorance or knowledge,—against the teachings of nature or the spirit and provision of the Gospel; whatever their degrees of enormity, and whatever their number; though they be more heinous than those connected with the infernal deeds of Calvary, and more numerous than the sands on ocean's wide-spread shores, this word "uttermost" stretches beyond them all, covers them all, and has ample room for more. *It compasses all periods of life.* It extends over all the years of our mortal existence, and touches the last moment of our probationary career. It takes hold upon the dying thief and rescues him, just as the pendulum of life was making its last vibration on the side of time, and as the deathless soul was about sinking into the flames. Zaccheus, the rapacious tax-gatherer; Peter, the lying blasphemer; the converts on the day of Pentecost—men who had imbrued their hands in the blood of Jesus; Saul, the infuriated persecutor; and the proverbially dissolute and depraved Corinthians ;— all, and myriads now on earth, and millions more now in heaven, attest the Almighty energy of the Son of God to heal the worst diseases of the soul. "*He is mighty to save.*"—HE IS ABLE; HE IS WILLING.

II. HIS CURATIVE EFFICACY HAS ITS SOURCE IN HIS OWN WILL. "*I will, be thou clean.*" "I WILL." This is the fiat of Omnipotence; —the fontal force, the spring of all the impulses and movements in the creation, but those of sin. This is the ultimate reason of things; the final resting-place of logic and love.

In order to see the greatness of Christ's *will*, look at it for a moment in connection with ours. We have all a will. We can all say "I will; " we do say so ; and by saying so with earnestness, we often effect something of more or less importance. But, the "I WILL " of Christ is different from ours.

First. *His will can act without any instrumentality, ours cannot.* We may *will* hundreds of things, but there is not one thing that we can do simply by willing. We must employ means—we must work by instrumentalities. The body itself is but a system of instrumentality by which we give effect to our volitions. The curative power of earthly physicians is in the fitness of the means they employ, not in their will ; their will, however resolute and earnest, has no effect whatever of itself. Not so with Christ. The curative virtue is *in His will*, and not in instrumentalities. He hushed the storm, healed the sick, and raised the dead, without any instrumentality at all :—simply by volition. In the following verses we have an account of His healing the servant of the Centurion, without ever touching or seeing him. There was Almightiness in His will. The whole universe is more thoroughly at the command of His will than our bodies are at the command of ours.

Secondly. *His will gives effectiveness to all instrumentality, ours cannot.* We not only cannot do anything without instrumentality, but we can do nothing, even with the most right and fitting instrumentality, merely by our own will. His will is the effective force of all useful instrumentality. It is so in nature. The machinery employed for maintaining order in the universe, generating and sustaining life, watering the fields with rain, and warming them into beauty and fruitfulness with sunshine, is made effective by His will. His will is the spring of every wheel, the fructifying virtue of every sunbeam and shower. It is so in the spiritual system. Institutions fitted for usefulness, the most powerful books, the most evangelical sermons, the Bible itself, will never answer their end unless they have the "I WILL" of Christ. He quickens whom He *will.* Let us learn to look to His WILL as the mainspring and nerve of the universe, the rule of our duty, and the only hope of sinners.

III. HIS CURATIVE SUCCESS REQUIRES THE MENTAL ACTION OF THE SUFFERER. The leper now approached and entreated Christ with a resolute and earnest will. Perhaps most, if not all, the cases of healing which we have recorded of Christ, followed the mental action of the sufferer, as a condition. It is true, that this does not always appear. In the case, for example, of the Centurion's servant, recorded in the following verses, it is not stated that he had any feeling or will concerning Christ; but then it must be remembered that he did not apply to Christ in person. His master was the applicant, and the probability is that his master applied not merely with his concurrence, but *by his request.* The same may be said of other cases. The woman who had been diseased for twelve years received the curative virtue, after an act of resolute and earnest will in pressing through the multitude to touch the hem of His garment. The two blind men on the roadside received their sight, after they had made a most importunate appeal to Christ.

One might ask, Why did Christ so frequently, if not always, make His cures dependent upon the state of the sufferers' mind? Was it because the producing of a certain mental state was necessary as means to an end? That such is the connection between soul and body, that the recovery of a patient is oftentimes greatly dependent upon the state of mind that can be produced, is a physiological fact. Strong faith in the ability of a physician has often done what no medicine could accomplish. But since Christ can effect His purpose independent of means, we are not disposed to regard this as a reason. Our view rather is, that it was intended to adumbrate the great truth, *that an earnest will directed to Christ is an essential condition of spiritual healing.*

The great law of spiritual healing is this: no soul can be cured of the malady of sin, either against its will or without its will, or even by its will directed to any object for the purpose, but to Christ. The afflicted soul must come to Christ, as did the leper now. Do you ask why souls are not healed? Not (1) because Christ has not willed their restoration. In the mission He undertook, the suffering

He endured, in the provision He has made, in the invitation He has given, I hear Him say to the diseased world in language most unequivocal, and in emphasis most thrilling, "*I will, be thou clean.*" His will is the instinct—the fiat of a world-wide philanthropy. Nor (2) because Christ has willed an impracticable mental act on man's part as a condition. He has not only willed that men should be morally cured, but that they should be morally cured in connection with their own free and earnest application to Him. And whilst we would not presume to say that He could not heal souls without this condition, we do say that we cannot see the possibility of His doing so. But is the condition *impracticable?* Has not man the natural power; and has he not in the Gospel all the means and motives to excite him to this earnest application to Christ?

IV. His CURATIVE RESULTS WILL BEAR THE SCRUTINY OF HIS MOST INTELLIGENT AND INVETERATE ENEMIES. "*See thou tell no man; but go thy way, shew thyself to the priest, and offer the gift that Moses commanded, for a testimony unto them.*" The reason for this injunction was, obviously, that the priests, the recognised authorities in such cases, should attest the validity of the cure. When they had done so, there would be no further room for doubt on the subject. It is true that other purposes were served by this injunction It served (1) to show the unostentatiousness of Christ in all His doings. He did not wish the leper to trumpet the healing marvel abroad among the multitude, to awaken their applause. He made no parade of His doings; He did not cause His voice to be heard in the streets. It served to show (2) That the reception of a special mercy from heaven requires solitude. It the leper had mingled at once with the multitude, the impression which such a favour made upon the mind would have been speedily eradicated. Solitude is the scene for nursing impressions into virtuous principles. It served to show (3) That He had no desire to invade the rights, or enjoy the immunities of any human office. "*Go to the priest*"—he is regarded as an authority; get his judgment; but in doing so, render to him what he considers, and what society considers, his rights; "*offer the gift that Moses commanded, for a testimony unto them.*"

But whilst such purposes as these were answered by this injunction, the design was evidently *to prevent any suspicion as to the validity of the cure, by having the attestation of those recognised authorities, who were enemies to Him.*

Christ's moral cures will bear the test of the most shrewd, enlightened, and inveterate enemies. Saul of Tarsus, Bunyan of Bedford, Newton of Olney, are types of the millions that Jesus has cured of the leprosy of sin. Who amongst the most determined foes of the Christian scheme can gainsay the validity of such cures? And are they not the most cogent and decisive proofs of the power, mercy, and divinity of Jesus?

Matthew 8:5-13

The Centurion; or, the Representative Believer

Jesus was now in Capernaum, a city, situated in a triangular and fertile plain, on the north-western side of Gennesareth's memorable lake. Here, amidst luxuriant vales and imposing hills, mountains, and streams—in the presence of the beautiful and grand in nature, He seems to have spent the greater portion of His public life, wrought most of His "mighty works," and proclaimed most of His soul-transforming truths.

The incident recorded in the historic fragment before us as having taken place on Christ's entering Capernaum, is one of great spiritual significance. Judea, being at this time in subjection to the Roman empire, had garrisons of soldiers in all its chief towns and cities. One of the officers who had the command of a hundred soldiers, a Centurion, residing at Capernaum, where, probably, Roman troops were garrisoned, hearing of Christ's arrival into the city, applied to Him on behalf of an afflicted domestic : he besought Him, saying, "*Lord, my servant lieth at home sick of the palsy, grievously tormented.*" The narrative shows that, though a heathen, he had, like many of the pagans of his age, out-grown his religion, and was possessed of something higher. Paganism with him had evidently become obsolete; it was a soul-garment worn out and folded up ; his heart had laid it by, and he had advanced, not only to Hebrew theism,—for Luke tells us that he had built a synagogue,—but was looking out still for a higher and purer faith.

The promptitude with which Christ attended to his request, and the high testimony which He bore to the greatness of his faith, when He said, "*I have not found so great faith, no, not in Israel,*" leads us to regard him as a *representative believer.*

We shall look, then, on this narrative as an illustration of the man's great faith ; and we observe :—

I. That it was characterised by an unbounded confidence in the divine capability of Christ. In order to appreciate the extent of his confidence in Christ's divine ability, let us analyse his language, and we shall find that his faith includes three things :—

First. *A belief in Christ's capability to direct all forces.* "*Speak the word only, and my servant shall be healed. For I am a man under authority, having soldiers under me; and I say to this man, Go, and he goeth ; and to another, Come, and he cometh ; and to my servant, Do this, and he doeth it.*" The idea of this Roman officer obviously is : that as my hundred men are under my absolute command—for as soldiers they have no will of their own—they are bound to fulfil my behest as their military chief ; so, all things, all laws and events, all forces and operations, all things and beings, all agents and agencies, visible and invisible, are at Thine absolute disposal. Thou art the great CHIEF of the universe : Thou canst marshal all its forces at Thy pleasure. This is faith in Christ as the King of kings and the Lord of lords. Here is—

Secondly : *A belief in Christ's capability to direct any forces to a specific end.* He believed that Christ could despatch some invisible healing messenger to his home, and to the sick-bed of his poor afflicted domestic. There are some who, while they regard Christ as the Head of the universe, seem to speak of Him as if He did nothing more than superintend the universe in working out its pre-established and immutable laws ;—merely watch, as it were, the workings of the machine. Such was not the faith of this Centurion. He regarded Christ as having power to despatch, at that moment, some invisible healing power to his poor afflicted domestic. He did not regard Christ as so bound to any set of governing laws as to allow Him no discretionary and divergent action, nor so taken up with the vast and the grand as to have no interest in the minute and the humble. Here is :—

Thirdly : *A belief in Christ's capability to direct His forces to a specific end by mere volition.* " *Speak the word only, and my servant shall be healed.*" Thou needest not employ any means, Thou needest not even come to my house. Distance is no obstruction, either to Thy knowing or working. All that is wanted is Thy WILL. " *Speak the word only.*" Thy word is almightiness. What a sublime faith in Christ is this ! How broad and firm its grasp ! What clear and comprehensive views of Him does it involve ! How keen and far-seeing the eye to discover in the poor Galilean this almighty energy and absolute dominion ! What Hebrew, what child of believing Abraham ever displayed such faith in Him during His mortal sojourn here ? Well might He say, " *Verily I say unto you, I have not found so great faith, no, not in Israel.*"

II. HIS FAITH WAS ASSOCIATED WITH A DEEP INTEREST IN HIS DOMESTICS. " *Lord, my servant lieth at home sick of the palsy, grievously tormented.*" Luke says, " That he was sick and ready to die," and that he " *was dear unto him* "—the Centurion. The exact nature of the servant's disease cannot be propounded with certainty. John supposes it to be a " Cramp, which in Oriental countries is a fearful malady, subjecting the patient to exquisite sufferings, and inducing death in a few days." The narrative teaches that it was intensely painful in its nature, and fatal in its tendency.

Now, we do not aver that the interest which this man displayed in his servant was the result of his faith. Though a soldier, he may have been a man of deep and tender social sympathies— sympathies which military studies, engagements, and habits, so destructive to all that is genial and loving, as well as to all that is morally just and honourable in our nature, had failed to obliterate. Nor do we assert that the feeling of sympathy here manifested could not exist apart from faith in Christ. Fallen and depraved as our nature is, examples are not few of individuals who have no connection with Christianity who possess, and practically develop, a tender and benevolent interest in the afflicted of their species. But what we assert is, *that wherever there is true faith in Christ, there will always be the display of the deepest interest in our race, and especially in our domestics.* You may find such kindly feeling as the Centurion's where there is no faith in Christ, but you will never find *genuine* faith in Christ where those generous and sympathetic feelings are not. Faith in Christ *involves* convictions, necessarily tending to deepen, widen, and strengthen the social sympathies to the utmost extent. Does it not involve convictions as to the brotherhood of the race—the essential equality of the race, the moral guiltiness of the race, the priceless value of each member of the race, the self-sacrificing love of Christ for the race? If these convictions are involved in an intelligent faith in Christ, how is it possible for such faith to exist without the profoundest sympathies with our fellow-men?

What shall we, then, say of Christian slave-holders, so-called, who work their fellow-men like beasts of burden, and trade in them as cattle? Nay, what shall we say of those employers nearer home who call themselves Christians, but who are heartless, arrogant, petty CZARS in their little domestic and mercantile empires; who speak to their servants and assistants with the imperialism of an autocrat, work them through the hours which nature has appointed for recreation and sleep, and are practically regardless alike of their physical and spiritual interests? Say of them? They are hypocrites! Their social conduct gives the lie to their religious professions. *If a man has faith in Christ, he must have loving sympathy with men.*

III. His FAITH WAS ASSOCIATED WITH A DEEP CONSCIOUSNESS OF PERSONAL UNWORTHINESS. His consciousness of unworthiness is seen, First: In the fact that he does not presume to approach Christ directly, and in person, at first. "He sent unto Him elders of the Jews" (Luke vii. 3). "The Centurion," says Olshausen, "impressed by the circumstance of his being a Gentile, dared not venture on approaching the Messiah in his own person; wherefore, he sought the intercession of the representatives of the old covenant, with whom he was closely connected." The doctrine of mediators is very congruous with, and indeed springs from, a profound but mistaken sense of humility. His feeling of personal unworthiness is seen, Secondly: In the language he expresses, "*Lord, I am not worthy that thou shouldest come under my roof.*"

Man in office is given to highmindedness. When "dressed in a little brief authority," he is prone to swell out with the feeling of conscious greatness, strut and swagger, and play the little lord. But this Centurion, though the commander of a hundred brave Romans, felt his insignificance in the presence of Jesus. A profound consciousness of moral unworthiness is an essential concomitant of faith in Christ. Faith in Christ is the finite mind in the felt presence of the Infinite; the corrupt and guilty mind in the felt presence of absolute holiness and eternal rectitude. Can any mind be in such a posture without experiencing the profoundest sense of unworthiness? Impossible!

IV. HIS FAITH WAS FOLLOWED BY AN INTRODUCTION INTO THE GRACIOUS EMPIRE OF GOD. "*And I say unto you, that many shall come from the east and west, and shall sit down with Abraham, and Isaac, and Jacob, in the kingdom of heaven. But the children of the kingdom shall be cast out into outer darkness : there shall be weeping and gnashing of teeth.*" Whether "the kingdom of heaven" here means the spiritual reign of God over the soul on earth, or in the celestial state, does not matter, inasmuch as the former is the germ and pledge of the latter. He that has come under the gracious reign of God here, already participates in the ethereal felicities which are perfected in the upper world.

The words present three thoughts in reference to the introduction of this Centurion into this blessed state :—

First : *It was an introduction to a scene which he would share with vast multitudes, from different and opposite parts of the world.* "*Many shall come from the east and the west;*" and Luke adds (xiii. 29.) "*from the north to the south,*" meaning, of course, from every part of the globe—from every clime and zone. "Many," not a few. Morbid pietism says a *few*. Narrow-hearted bigotry says a *few*. A soulless sainthood says a *few*, and a scribe-theology says a *few*. But Christ says, "*I say unto you;*"—I who know all things, who know every man of every generation that shall ever be, I, who *now* distinctly see the immeasurable heavens, with all their "*many mansions,*" completely populated as they shall be after the great day of judgment has passed by and become a distant fact in history ; I say unto you that "MANY *shall come.*" When we think of the vast proportion of our race that die in infancy, and remember that "of such is the kingdon of heaven;" when we think of the probability that our world is but in its childhood; and that the sun of *many* ages more must shine, and the vital air of many ages more must flow, to train it into manhood; when we think of the moral birth of "nations in a day," and the many glowing visions which the inspired prophets had of numerous generations that are to come, all of which "*shall be righteous;*" when we think of the infinitude of restorative provision in Jesus Christ, and of the pictures that Jesus drew of the final state of humanity, in which He shows that there was but one out of three stewards who abused the trust—only one found at the wedding feast who had not on the qualifying costume; and when we further think, that in the days of John, eighteen hundred years ago, the multitudes of the saved were such as " no man could number;"—when such subjects as these pass under our review, we get the deep and soul-uplifting faith that the saved will far out-number the lost, as stars out-number the passing meteors of the sky.

Another thought which these words present in reference to the introduction of this Centurion to this blessed state is,—

Secondly : *That it was an introduction which would insure to him the most glorious society.* These millions, gathered from all ages and lands, shall "*sit down with Abraham, Isaac, and Jacob ;*" and, by implication, the Centurion with them. "*Shall sit down.*" * The spiritual enjoyment of Christianity and heaven are frequently set forth in the scripture under the image of a festive banquet. Sitting down or reclining on the couch at the banquet of celestial joy implies, (1) *Social equality.* Jesus, in thus representing Gentile people from remotest parts as coming into the kingdom of heaven and sitting down with the chief of the Jewish patriarchs, most probably intended to strike an effective blow at that narrow prejudice of the Jews, which led them to regard the Gentile as too inferior and unclean for social intercourse with them. Jesus would teach that His system was for Gentile as well as Jew, that heaven would be the home of men and not sects ; and that all there would be on a *blessed equality*—they would *sit down* together. The little social and religious distinctions—all the "partition" walls of conventionality, which divide society here into little formal and cold-hearted sections are "broken down" by *practical* Christianity, and are not found in the upper world of perfected humanity. All there are in their "Father's house ;" a child-like sympathy, a brotherhood of sentiment, a community of interest in the One Father, GOD, and the One Elder Brother, CHRIST, make the mighty millions ONE in spirit and in aim. "Sitting down," (2) implies *Social repose.* There is, there, none of that want of confidence in each other ; none of that suspicion about each other's veracity, affection, and honesty, which, like a serpent coils about social circles here, and darts its rankling poison into the very veins of earthly friendship ; nor any of that painful feeling of inferiority which, in the social circles of earth, the *would-be* great are constantly seeking to produce ; nor any of that diversity of sentiment and aim, which here leads to painful collision, to envy, and rivalries. But all that cheerful and unbounded trust, thorough at-homeness, and hearty identification of motive and purpose, which give to the humblest member of the glorious circle a blessed feeling of ease and repose. Ah me ! What imagination can picture the social blessedness of that state ? What will it be after all the toils, and trials, and turmoils, of this earthly scene, to sit down with the greatest spirits of all ages—poets, sages, prophets, historians, orators, authors, apostles, reformers, martyrs, and ministers ; to listen to the narration of their experiences during the long centuries that have passed over them, to hear their great and lofty thoughts about God and His universe, to respond lovingly

---

* Literally, shall *recline with.* "The Oriental posture at table is not like ours, a sitting, but a recumbent, one. Those who eat recline on couches."— *Livermoor.*

to their divine impulses and suggestions, to blend sentiment and and intermingle soul with them !

Another thought which these words present, in reference to the introduction of this Centurion to this blessed state is,—

Thirdly : *That it was an introduction to a scene of blessedness, from which some of the professed people of God will be excluded.* "*The children of the kingdom shall be cast into outer darkness : there shall be weeping and gnashing of teeth.*" The children of the kingdom, literally, refers to the Jews, who were, as STIER expresses it, "*born in the typical kingdom* of God." Many of them were excluded—were "cast off," while the Gentiles came in. It is suggested, that exclusion from this kingdom is a *lamentable catastrophe.* The kingdom of heaven is compared to a Jewish feast, generally celebrated in large, splendid, and well-lighted apartments. In contrast with this is the condition of the excluded. Cold, dark, and terrible. *Outer darkness,* where the excluded would weep with disappointment and remorse, *and gnash their teeth ;* referring either to the chattering of teeth produced by the intense cold, or the effect produced by the agony and rage of the self-excluded soul. What a picture of hell is this, and how sad the thought that it is the doom of many of the professed people of God ! How many of the men that worshipped in the temple at Jerusalem are there ! How many members of churches are there ! How many that prophesied and taught in the name of Christ are there ! "When we come to heaven," says Matthew Henry, " we shall miss a great many there that we thought would have been going thither."

V. HIS FAITH WAS REWARDED BY THE FULFILMENT OF HIS DE-SIRES. "*And Jesus said unto the Centurion, Go thy way ; and as thou hast believed, so be it unto thee. And his servant was healed in the self-same hour.*" Here is a practical illustration of this principle.

Let us cultivate faith in Christ as strong as this representative believer—then we shall appeal to Him in all our trials—we shall be humble—we shall be introduced into the kingdom of God, and we shall have our desires fulfilled. "LORD, INCREASE OUR FAITH !"

Matthew 8:14-22

The Ability and Inability of Christ

These verses are a record of several incidents that have no very marked connection of any kind with each other.* We take them

* If we look merely to the sequence of events the chapters viii. to xiii. are very irregular. We need not be surprised at this if we remember that chapters viii., ix. are all that Matthew has recorded of our Lord's ministry for nearly a year and a-half. If, moreover, we consider this Gospel as especially the gospel of the kingdom, iv. 23, *i.e.,* the good news about Messiah's kingdom ; and that the writer's object,

together simply because they will supply sufficient thought-materials to illustrate an important subject. Each of the events before us is significant. *Christ taught by incidents*—incidents suited to start the deepest thoughts by their strangeness, and to excite the profoundest feelings of gratitude, admiration and awe, by their wonderful goodness and almighty power.

For the sake of order and distinctness, we shall divide these incidents into two classes—those which illustrate the *ability* of Christ and those which illustrate His *inability*.

I. THOSE WHICH ILLUSTRATE THE ABILITY OF CHRIST. Those contained in the first four verses belong to this class; and they teach—

First: *That Christ can, with ease, remove the various physical ills of humanity.* He was still at Capernaum, where, as we have stated in our last *section*, He cured the servant of the Centurion. While here on this same occasion He enters *"Peter's house."* And this house becomes the scene of extraordinary cures. First, there is *"Peter's wife's mother,"* who was afflicted with a fever; He healed her, and *"she arose and ministered unto them."* All the symptoms of disease are gone, and with the vigorous pulse of full-toned health, and a heart, doubtless, overflowing with gratitude, she blithely moves about the house and ministers to Jesus and the family. This wonderful cure was soon known through the neighbourhood, and, according to Mark, it occurred on the evening of the Sabbath-day. *"And when evening was come they brought unto Him many that were possessed with devils: and He cast out the spirits with His word, and healed all that were sick."* However various and virulent their diseases, He healed them. He dismissed none uncured, and the whole cure was done with *ease.* How did He heal Peter's wife's mother ? He merely touched her hand. How did He deliver the others from their maladies ? He merely spake a word. *"He cast out the spirits with His word."* All this shows the *ability* of Christ to ransom the body from all the ills to which it is subject through sin. All are prophesies and pledges that He will one day redeem it from the power of the grave. He is a corporeal as well as a spiritual Redeemer. He will swallow up death in victory; and the bodies of His people He will fashion like unto His own glorious body, through that almighty power by which He is able to subdue all things unto Himself. The passage teaches,—

Secondly : *That Christ can fulfil all the ancient predictions of Scrip-*

under the guidance of the Holy Spirit, was to set forth the real kingship and kingdom of Christ, we may trace the following connection. The Sermon on the Mount propounds the laws and ordinances of the King. Successive chapters set forth His authority, viii. His gracious character, ix. The open proclamation of His kingdom, x. Its relation to the forerunner, xi. Its conflict with Jewish rebellion and unbelief, xii. Its future development and final triumph, xiii. The miracles in chap viii. are selected as specimens to call attention to the fulfilment of prophecy and to illustrate the leading idea in v. 17. We may trace in them a moral gradation ; the personal application of the lesson; the vicarious requests of the Centurion and of Peter ; the sullen adjuration of the Demoniacs of Gadara resisting the power, the wisdom, the mercy of God.

ture concerning Himself. " *That it might be fulfilled which was spoken by Esaias the prophet, saying, Himself took our infirmities, and bare our sicknesses.*" Of course it is not meant that these cures were effected in *order* that this prophecy might be fulfilled. The motive in Christ was pure benevolence; His ultimate purpose the amelioration of human woe, and the promotion of human happiness. But it means that in the spontaneous outworking of His world-wide philanthropy, things which the inspired prophet had predicted of Him met with their realization.* Matthew applies the language of the prophet to express the removal of physical sufferings from humanity : and Peter (1 Epistle, ii. 24), applies it to express His removal of moral guilt. The discrepancy admits of various explanations. It may be referred to that latitude which inspiration evidently granted to the sacred writers in the use both of their faculties and materials of information ; or, to the common consciousness of the writers, as Jews, that physical diseases always involved sin; and that, consequently, to speak of the removal of the one would, by implication, be to speak of the removal of the other.†

The general idea suggested is, that *Jesus fulfills the prophecies concerning Himself.* He has fulfilled many ; he has given substance to mental visions, body to ideas, historical import to prophetic dreams. He has taken up much of the Old Testament in Himself, embodied the ritualism of its priesthood, and accomplished the predictions of its seers. He will fulfil the whole. He has ability for this, and He will do it. Do you see in the prophetic region of the Old Testament glowing outlines of a moral world; whose tenants are all holy, whose wildernesses blossom as the rose, whose flowery fields and fruitful forests bloom on without blight, and whose sun is never dimmed by mist nor cloud ;—a world whose whole character will be so glorious that the former " heavens" will no more come into remembrance?— He will fill up this outline. He will make this vision real. He is now at the work; the process of the new creation is going on ; and the day will come when there will be a new heaven and a new earth, wherein dwelleth righteousness. "He will not fail, nor be discouraged," until the work be accomplished.

These incidents, then, show CHRIST'S ABILITY in two things at least : His ability *to redeem*, with ease, the human body from all the various complicated and distressing ills to which it is subject through sin; and His ability to realise all that the old prophets predicted concerning Him ;—to fill up the whole prophetic outline, to exhaust and make palpable the whole prophetic sense. *He is mighty to redeem the body ; He is mighty to fulfil the Scriptures,*—to translate the most

---

* See Dr. Davidson : " Quotations of the Old and New Testaments ; " and the Remarks, especially, on the formula ὅπως πληρωθῇ, in his SACRED HERMENEUTICS, p. 484.

† All the miracles of Christ were redemptive acts by which He showed His mission to destroy moral and physical evil. We may look on them all as pledges that the work of salvation shall be fully carried out, for what are diseases but so many partial deaths? By these manifestations of mercy and power the Lord of Life exhibited His credentials as the restorer of man, and the conqueror of death.

glowing productions of past ages into the glorious history of a renovated and beatified world.

We pass on now to the other class of incidents before us, which are :—

II. THOSE WHICH ILLUSTRATE THE INABILITY OF CHRIST. What! is there any limit to the ability of Christ? Are not all things possible with Him? Is it not derogatory to predicate inability concerning Him? There is a limit to His power; and in the very limitation of His power we shall see the highest aspects of His character and glory. What *cannot* He do? I reply, *summarily*, He cannot en*courage nor tolerate wrong states of mind.* This is illustrated in each of the incidents contained in verses 19-22 : where we learn—

First: *Christ cannot encourage the selfishly ambitious.* As Jesus, in consequence of the great number that gathered around Him, was about leaving the scene where, on this Sabbath evening, He had performed so many cures, and was making His way towards the Galilean sea, in order to cross to the other side, we are told that a certain scribe came and said unto Him, " *Master, I will follow thee whithersoever thou goest.*" From the impulsive and hasty utterance of the scribe, and the language of Christ in reply, it is but too obvious that his spirit was rather that of a *selfish ambition* than a genuine love for Christ. He had witnessed Christ's displays of miraculous power in healing all manner of diseases; he beheld the crowds that thronged about Him, and the numbers that were still streaming towards Him through every rural lane and public road; and he probably thought, as a keen-sighted and legally-educated man would be likely to think, that He who had this wondrous power and rapidly growing popularity, would soon be on the throne of Israel, if not of Rome; have David's sceptre, if not that of Cæsar: and as an ambitious man, thirsting for power, exclaims, under the impulse,—" *I will follow thee whithersoever thou goest.*" The honest paraphrase of his real sentiments, would probably be,—I want power and influence in the world : the most effectual way to realise these, is to follow thee—" *I will follow thee,*" therefore, " *whithersoever thou goest.*"

How did Christ meet this state of mind? Did He utter a word of sanction, or encouragement? No! He said what must have struck a revulsion into the heart of this scribe; " *The foxes have holes, and the birds of the air have nests; but the Son of man hath not where to lay his head.*" * As if He had said: Don't follow me; I have

---

* This title is used by our Lord, of Himself, sixty-one times in the Gospels. Stephen uses it, Acts vii. 56; and John, Rev. i. 13. On the hypothesis that the Saviour was a *mere* man, the title is most unmeaning; but to those who acknowledge our Lord's Divinity, the title is most expressive; for it intimates that His original form of existence was not in human nature; and it glances at His present humiliation, as preparatory to His future exaltation. From John xii. 34, it appears that the Jews understood the term to mean the Messiah; and from Luke xxii. 69, 70,—that they considered the Son of Man to mean the same as the Son of God. This is the expressive word by which our Lord designates Himself as the Messiah, —the Son of God manifested in human flesh, the second Adam, the Lord from heaven.

nothing for thy state of mind; I *cannot* encourage thee to move one step with me; I have no *worldly* power nor pageantry; of all beings on earth I am the most destitute. "*The foxes have holes,*" &c. I wish you to observe, that Christ seems to announce *His secular poverty as a discouragement and check to this selfishly ambitious state of mind.* Indeed, herein, perhaps, you may find the *rationale* of Christ's destitution when on earth.

But how does Christ's secular poverty discourage and check this selfish ambition, which we suppose this lawyer to have possessed? Let this be the question for the earnest thought of a few moments; and in reply to it, I observe,—

First: *That Christ's secular poverty checks all selfish ambition, by showing that true greatness is something independent of all external circumstances, and can co-exist with the utmost secular abjectness.* In Christ we have the *highest* form of greatness. In the whole history of the past, there is no one in moral majesty to be compared to Him. That earth's greatest sovereigns and sages, philanthropists, heroes, and reformers look mean in His presence; that He towers in moral grandeur above all the great men of the ages that are past, like some tall cliff lifting its head above the pebbles of the shore, is what the greatest sceptics have admitted. If the display of moral virtues determines a man's greatness, whoever displayed such high virtues in such high forms as Christ? Or, if the extent of influence upon the world, is any gauge of a man's greatness, whoever wielded such influence as Christ? His ideas have reformed governments, created institutions, changed the character and destiny of the millions of every age; are admired by the greatest thinkers, and devoutly cherished and advocated by the best men of modern Christendom. He is, even apart from His divine nature, the greatest being that has ever appeared in the history of the world; shining out amid the generations that are gone like the central light amongst the planetary orbs. Now, what was the secular condition of this truly majestic being? *He was the poorest of the poor.* A stable was His birth-place; the wife of a humble mechanic His mother; His daily associates the lower classes. "*The foxes have holes, and the birds of the air have nests; but the Son of man hath not were to lay His head.*" What does this teach? Why, it speaks to humanity with the tongue of thunder; that true greatness is independent of external circumstances; and may co-exist with secular destitution: it says that greatness is not in *having*, but in *being*; not in external circumstances, but in internal states: that man, stripped of all that the world can give, having nothing under these heavens but sheer existence, may be great, happy, and divine.

In answer to the question we have mooted, we observe,—

Secondly: *That Christ's secular property checks all selfish ambition, by showing that the spirit of true greatness may even require the sacrifice of all secular possessions.* What is the spirit of true greatness? What is that which gives a moral beauty to every attribute of character, that evermore inspires the great heart of the true hero?—

the man who excites the respect, admiration, and reverence, of his race? It is *disinterestedness*. It is only as we see, or think we see, this in men that they command our esteem, and prompt our praise. If you make manifest selfish motives in the world's great heroes, whatever may be the sacrifices they have made, or the services they have rendered, they fall at once from their lofty pedestal. Hence all the would-be-heroes robe themselves in the livery, and speak the language, of disinterestedness.

Now, Christ's secular abjectness, was the result of *disinterestedness*. It was not a misfortune He could not avoid,—it was a position He selected. Might He not have been born of royalty, lived in palaces, and spent His life amidst the luxuries and splendours of the secularly great? The choice of parents, birth-place, and secular circumstances, which none of the other sons of Adam ever had, Christ had. He chose poverty; and disinterested love prompted and required that choice. *He became secularly poor, that we, through His secular poverty, might be made spiritually rich.*

We have said that Christ's disinterested love—the spirit of true greatness—*required* that He should be secularly poor. Indeed, it is difficult to see how He could, as a Redeemer, who was to save by a living *example*, as well as by a propitiatory death, accomplish His work without becoming poor. Humanity required, at least, three things to save it: (1) *A conviction that its well-being is not in externalities.* Men's crime and curse have been in looking for happiness in the possession of worldly wealth, power, grándeur, and influence. Had Christ, therefore, lived in secular opulence and magnificence, would not this soul-destroying tendency and habit have been encouraged and strengthened? (2) *A practical and soul-penetrating display of a spirit opposite to that which inspired it.* Selfishness is "the spirit of the world,"—that which prompts and directs its every movement. This spirit is eternally incompatible with virtue and happiness. It must be exorcised ere the world can be saved. And how can it be expelled? Only by the opposite. Satan cannot cast out Satan. Now, had Christ lived in affluence, where would have been the display of the opposite spirit—disinterestedness? (3) *A conviction of the universal practicability of the saving principles inculcated.* Had Christ lived amongst the higher classes, it might have been said as an excuse for neglecting His teaching, "The principles He inculcates may be practicable to His own class, who have luxury and leisure; but not to us, the children of indigence and toil." But the Divine Teacher, being the poorest of the poor, has for ever precluded the possibility of such an objection.

These remarks, whilst they serve to show, in some measure, the *rationale* of our Saviour's secular poverty, bear powerfully in support of our position, *that Christ cannot encourage the selfishly ambitious spirit.* His whole secular life was a protest against it; the genius of His religion is against it; there is nothing in His system to sanction it. Its imperial voice to every man is, Deny thyself, and take up the cross, and follow Him who had nowhere to lay

His head. Christianity *has* glory for its disciples; but not the pretentious and tawdry glory of gilded and highly decorated externalities.

We observe, in relation to the *inability of Christ,*—

Thirdly. *That He cannot tolerate the half-hearted in religion.* This appears from the incident recorded in the twenty-first and twenty-second verses. Another person on this occasion approaches Christ, and manifests a desire to follow Him. It appears from Luke that Christ commanded him to do so. The man, however, though partially inclined, is not thoroughly disposed. A *stronger* sympathy holds him to another course. There was another object nearer his heart than Christ. " *Suffer me first,*" says he, " *to go and bury my father.*" It is not necessary to suppose that his father was actually dead, and his body at home awaiting interment. There are reasons to believe that this was not the case. The meaning, probably, is, let me go and live with my father until his death, and then I shall be free, and will follow thee. May not his state of mind be thus paraphrased ?—I love my father dearly ; the infirmities of years are growing on him, symptoms of approaching dissolution are appearing, he cannot live very long, my heart will not permit me to leave him now when he most requires the succour and the guardianship of filial love ; I will wait his end, fulfil the last offices of affection, and see him borne reverently to his " eternal resting-place ; " then, when this attraction of home is gone, " I will follow thee." Will this do ? Does Christ accept it as a valid cause ? Hear Him. "*Let the dead bury the dead ; follow thou me.*"

What does this strong figurative language mean ? Not either of the three following things : Not (1) that Christ had no respect for parental claims. The feeling displayed towards His Mother on the cross, and the whole spirit of His religion, show that He could not mean this. Not (2) that He was indifferent to the condition of those who were spiritually dead ; supposing that our Saviour meant to say what some suppose—" Let the spiritually dead bury the corporeally dead." We cannot entertain the idea for a moment that He was indifferent to the condition of those who were " *dead in trespasses and in sins.*" Not (3) that the duties of His religion are incompatible with filial obligation. Real duties never come into collision—to follow Christ is to fulfil *all* righteousness. What, then, does this language mean ? *That religion must be everything or nothing.* That father, mother, houses, land, &c., must be held subordinate to Christ. Religion is not *mere* love to God. Perhaps, all men feel some kind of love to God at times. His goodness, sometimes, awakens their gratitude ; and thoughts of His grandeur call up their reverence. *Love to God only becomes religion when it becomes* SUPREME. In all other stages it is destitute of moral worth, and unacceptable to our Maker.

Christ cannot *tolerate half-heartedness,* then, in religion. He must have the whole heart or nothing. By why cannot He tolerate half-heartedness ? First, because there is no moral excellence in half-heartedness. Moral thoroughness is the only soil in which divine seeds of heavenly virtue grow. Secondly, because there is no true happiness in half-heartedness. A divided heart is the arena of conflict—the fountain of every bitter stream. Thirdly, because there is no power for true usefulness in half-heartedness. He only is powerful to promote religion, whose heart is in it.

Matthew 8:23-27

The Disciples in the Tempest; or, Soul Storms

The extraordinary cures which Christ had effected at Capernaum had, it would seem, attracted to Him throngs of people from all parts of the neighbourhood. In His personal ministry there was a fulfilment of a prediction which had been uttered some twenty centuries before. Jacob, on his death-bed, wrapt in prophetic vision, had said that unto "Shiloh shall the gathering of the people be." During the brief period of Christ's public life, "*great multitudes gathered about Him.*" Wherever He went, whether to the quiet mountain, the secluded village, or the solitary shore, He attracted crowds. His life was a magnet drawing to itself all that came within the sweep of its influence. All the attraction, however, of His personal ministry on earth is but a faint representation and pledge of that more spiritual and higher influence which He is destined one day to exert upon all the nations under heaven. He "*will draw all men unto Him.*" The day will come when the whole population of the globe will have their thoughts, sympathies, and souls, centred in His person, and guided by His will.

It is remarkable that Christ, at various times, seemed anxious to avoid popularity. The incident before us is an example. In the eighteenth verse, we are distinctly told that when " Jesus saw great multitudes about Him, He gave commandment to depart unto the other side." And forthwith He enters into a ship in order to cross to "the other side." This desire to escape notoriety, which He on several occasions manifested, is a subject which, though it may lead to interesting speculation, is, we consider, of not much practical importance. Whether it arose from that instinct to shun, rather than to seek, popularity, which has ever characterized all truly great men, or from some prudential reason, we stay not to enquire.

The scene before us needs no elaborate description. In a few sentences of exquisite simplicity the evangelist presents an event of most stirring sublimity and suggestive significance. Had a modern biographer of the popular stamp to represent some such a scene as this in the life of his hero, how much labour and time would he expend in order to work it into effect! How many fine words he would employ! How many allusions to other scenes which would

serve to show off the superior character and extent of his reading
How many pages would he fill! And how much of the precious
time of the reader would he waste with his tawdry pencillings!
But the evangelist sketches this magnificent scene with a few simple
strokes, in such a way as to prevent all wise expositors from making
any effort to heighten its effect. The men who wrote this Book
were not book-makers. They had too much to communicate to be
such. The writers and speakers who have the most thoughts have
always the fewest words. Verbosity is always the offspring either
of vagueness or vacuity.

We take this incident of Christ and His disciples in the tempest,
to illustrate *the mental distress of the good.*

I. MENTAL DISTRESS FREQUENTLY COMES UNEXPECTEDLY. The distress of the disciples, now in the tempest, came upon them by
surprise. When they embarked that night, and moved off from the
shore, there was, perhaps, every prospect of a safe and happy voyage. The stars, it may be, shone upon them from a peaceful sky,
and their bright images seemed to sleep upon the calm bosom of
the azure wave. But this serenity was temporary. A storm was
brooding. The scene soon changes. Matthew tells us, " *There arose
a great tempest in the sea,* insomuch that the ship was covered with
the waves." Mark describes it as a " *great storm of wind;* " and
Luke says, " *there came down a storm of wind on the lake.*" There is
no need of supposing that this storm was miraculous. The Galilean
sea, being surrounded by mountains and hills, was naturally subject
to sudden storms. It was evidently a most terrific scene. The
billows dashed over the vessel, threatening every moment to fill and
engulph her. Thus their distress came *unexpectedly.*

Is not this frequently so in the history of man? How often men
enter on some new enterprise, period, or relation of life with every
prospect of much enjoyment and prosperity; all things seem to
smile on them with promises of an auspicious future: when suddenly, some storm obscures the lights of their sky, lashes their sea
into commotions, and threatens them with ruin! Abraham, Job,
and David are striking examples of this, on the side of the good;
and on the other side, such names as Belshazzar and Judas may
stand. How strikingly does this fact show *that our destiny is ever
in the hands of another.* " *We know not what a day may bring forth.*"
In imagination, our to-morrow may be a period redolent with bright
joys; but let it come, and we may find it a day of thick darkness
and sorrow. The path of our history is filled with the vestiges of
frustrated plans and blighted hopes. " *The lot is cast into the lap;
but the whole disposing thereof is with the Lord.*" "The horse is prepared against the day of battle, but safety is of the Lord." As
there was an invisible power beyond the hills that bounded the
Galilean sea, working up a storm at the moment everything seemed
bright and calm to the disciples, so there is always a mighty spirit
beyond our sensuous horizon, who can at any moment lash the calmest sea, on which we glide along, into the wildest fury of the tempest.

II. MENTAL DISTRESS OFTENTIMES INDUCES EARNEST PRAYER. How earnestly now do the disciples cry to Christ for help! Jesus was asleep. The benevolent toils of the day had fatigued Him; and participating in our natural infirmities, He retires to the hinder part of the ship, lays His weary head on some wooden pillow, and sinks to repose. The storm disturbs Him not; its most furious blast bore no alarm to Him. Innocence can calmly sleep in storms. There is no room for fear in that heart whose sympathies and aims are ever in concert with the Infinite Will. But whilst Jesus sleeps, the disciples are in an agony of fear; they hasten to Him, rouse Him from His slumbers, and exclaim, "*Lord save us, or we perish.*" "*Carest thou not for us?*" "*Master, Master, we perish!*" Here is earnest prayer.

We may look at this appeal to Christ, under these circumstances, in two aspects,—

First. *As a tendency in human nature to call upon God when exposed to imminent peril.* History abounds with examples of this. The heathen crew of the ship in which Jonah embarked for Tarshish cried every man to his god in the midst of that terrible storm which threatened their destruction. The Psalmist states, as a general truth, that those that go down to the sea in ships, and do business in the great waters, "*Cry unto the Lord in their trouble.*" Now, the fact that men do this, whether they be theists or atheists, their character depraved or holy, is very significant. It shows (1.) *An instinctive belief in the Divine existence.* There is such a belief in man, and no infidel logic can argue it away. (2.) *It shows a belief in God's connexion with individual history.* If man did not feel Him near, he would not pray. It shows (3.) *A belief in His power to help;—else why invoke His aid?* And (4.) *A belief in the efficacy of prayer.* These beliefs seem to me involved in the fact that men do *involuntarily* cry to God for help in danger. And do not these beliefs lie at the foundation of Biblical truth?

Look at the case in another aspect,—

Secondly. *As an indication that these disciples had an impression of Christ's superhuman power.* Had they regarded Him to be, what He appeared, a poor man worn out with the fatigues of the day, and glad to rest His weary frame in some secluded spot of that humble ship, would they have appealed so earnestly to Him now? Would they have called Him "*Lord*" and "*Master,*" and thus humbly and importunately implored His help? We trow not. The supernatural energy of Christ was not a mere article in their creed; it was a deep and practical conviction of the heart; a something that had become more powerful than any native impulse of the soul. They had heard such divine things flow from His lips, and seen such stupendous deeds effected by His power, that they could see in that tired, sleeping frame of His, the might and majesty of a God.

III. MENTAL DISTRESS GENERALLY ORIGINATES IN UNBELIEF. Jesus arose, and saith unto them, "*Why are ye so fearful, O ye of little faith ?"* Mark expresses the idea, that the want of faith was the cause of their fear, more forcibly still. *"Why are ye so fearful ? how is it that ye have no faith ?"* As if He had said : Had you faith, you would not be in all this trepidation ; but you would be calm, brave, self-possessed. The fact, that they approached Christ with the prayer, *"Lord save us, or we perish,"* indicates, as we have already said, that they had some measure of faith in His supernatural energy ; but their faith was still defective and weak. What is the faith that is wanted ? The faith that will make one calm and truly brave in difficulties—that will save us. Not a mere belief in the doctrines of Christ's teaching, or the facts of His life. This is common. But an *all-confiding trust in the love of His heart, in the might of His arm, in the truth of His word, in the rectitude of His administration, and in the benevolence of His aims.* This is the ennobling faith—the faith that will give us heroism of soul. What examples we have in the Bible of its power ! See Abraham, with knife in hand, offering up his son Isaac. See Moses at the margin of the sea. See Job bereft of all—property, friends, children, health ; yet hear him say, *"The Lord gave,"* &c. What is the cause of this calmness ? Here it is : " Though He slay me, yet will I trust in Him." See Paul at Ephesus—how dark his prospects, but how calm is he ! *"None of these things move me,"* &c. What is the cause ? Here it is : *"I know in whom I have believed,"* &c.

How true, then, is the idea, which is here implied in the words of Christ, that distress arises from unbelief ! History tells us that Julius Cæsar was at sea in a little boat when a terrible storm came on. He sought to inspire the courage of the men who plied the oars, by telling them that their little boat bore Cæsar and his fortunes. Let us be encouraged by feeling that if we are *genuine* disciples, Jesus is on board the barque of our being, voyaging with us on the mighty sea of existence. He holds the helm in His hand, and winds and waves obey His voice.

IV. MENTAL DISTRESS CAN BE EASILY ALLAYED BY THE INTERPOSITION OF CHRIST. *"And He arose and rebuked the winds and the sea."* There are two ways of doing it,—

First. *By removing the external causes of distress.* This He did. Now He hushed the outward storm. He has all power over our external circumstances, and if we trust in Him, He will one day remove from them all that has a tendency to pain or agitate the heart.

Secondly. *By removing the internal susceptibilities.* What are these ? *Selfishness—guilt—dread* of death. Christ removes these : and where these are not, mental distress cannot exist. No storm can make an angel fear.

Friend ! thou art on the sea of life. A sea, not like the Sea of Galilee, lying within small limits ; thy sea stretches into the infinite —new billows are ever rising up from the great eternity. There are rocks, quicksands, shoals, and other dangers in thy way. Who can pilot thee safely—who is able to steer thy barque ? It must be some one that *knows* that sea—knows its soundings, its boundaries, and all its perilous points—and has, at the same time, power to guide thy fragile and complicated ship, and control the mighty elements that play around thee.

Matthew 8:28-34

The Devil and the Swine; or, the Power of Evil over Humanity, and the Power of Christ over Evil

This is one of the strangest incidents in the history of the marvellous—the life of Christ. It naturally starts at once two questions: first, whether these two men were actually possessed with devils, or the subjects of some species of mental insanity, such as hypochondria, epilepsy, or lunacy. This is a question of no practical moment, though it has originated a large amount of controversy, and is capable of originating a great deal more.* The second question is, of what spiritual service can the record of such incidents as these be to us, the men of this age? As it is inscribed in this world-book, it is natural to suppose it bears in it something of value for humanity. What use is it intended to serve? To gratify the sense of the marvellous within us, or to start abstruse discussions, either as to the influence of certain conditions of the atmosphere upon the brain, or the influence of disembodied spirits upon mankind in the world? It does these two things assuredly. But we scarcely think either or both uses are of sufficient importance to account for its being recorded in a Book intended for humanity.

* Some cling to the opinion that the Demoniacs were not literally possessed with devils, but were merely afflicted with ordinary diseases, as epilepsy or madness. With reference to this opinion we may remark, that as our Lord was manifested to destroy the works of the devil, it is quite reasonable to conceive that during His life on earth, and in the land of His ministry, the fallen spirits were permitted to display their malice and power in a peculiar way over the bodies of men. It may be contrary to our experience that such possessions still exist, and history may not record similar instances in other times and countries; but we do not know the nature and intent of diabolical agency, and it is admitted that the symptoms agree with the combined effects of epilepsy and madness. Celsus and others imputed these miracles to magic, but never denied the fact of their occurrence. The adversaries of Christ ascribed them to a like mysterious influence, by asserting that He derived His power from the prince of the devils. As by curing disease our Lord showed His power over physical evil, so by casting out evil spirits He manifested His power over moral evil. Attention to these general considerations will dispose us to admit as historical facts, that the Demoniacs are distinguished by Christ Himself from the afflicted with ordinary diseases. In the language of Christ and the answers He received, the person of the possessed is carefully distinguished from that of the evil spirit.. When the devils go out they enter into other creatures. The devils had a clearer knowledge of Christ at the beginning of His ministry than was shown by others. The silence of John gives tacit consent to the construction put on these narratives by the Church in his day.

It is, I think, charged with a lesson which urgently requires the earnest study of every man that is, or ever shall be. What is that? *The baneful power of moral evil over human nature, and the blessed power of Christ over moral evil.* Whether these men were literally possessed, or were the mere subjects of a mental disease, it matters not to this lesson; the great lesson in either case comes out with equal prominence and force. It is independent of all the controversies that have ever been raised on this subject.

I. THE BANEFUL POWER OF MORAL EVIL OVER HUMAN NATURE. Whichever hypothesis bo correct, possession or disease, *moral evil* is the cause of all the sad and terrible feelings of these two men. If they were *possessed*, the devils entered them because they were sinners;— evil spirits find no dwelling-place in holy natures: or if it were mere *disease*, diseases of all kinds spring from sin. Misery never springs from holiness. All natural evils grow out of moral, as the branches of the oak out of the acorn. Looking upon the incident as expressing the baneful power of sin upon man, we have four of its baneful tendencies developed,—

First: *Its deranging tendency.* They were "*coming out of the tombs.*" The tombs of the Jews were very frequently excavations in the rocks, and were sometimes very spacious, containing different compartments for the dead. They were sometimes the haunts of robbers, and sometimes places of refuge, whither the frightened resorted in times of war. These men were so mentally deranged, that instead of dwelling in the ordinary habitations of their class and attending to the duties of life, they tenanted those tombs, and filled, perhaps, their imagination with ghastly images of the dead. Supposing that they were diseased, rather than possessed, they fancied that there was within them a "legion," a mighty multitude of the spirits of those men whose bodies crowded those tombs. What aberration!

Now, although this is a very wonderful, and an extreme, case of deception, it may fairly be regarded as indicating the tendency of moral evil, or sin, to deceive. *Sin is deceptive.* The apostle speaks of the "*deceivableness of unrighteousness.*" What delusive ideas it gives men about life, and happiness, and glory, and God! Souls, under its influence, are everywhere living among the tombs. Instead of being out in the bright and happy universe of true life, filling their right place, and discharging the high duties of being, they are down in the tombs of dead souls. There is one class of persons which these two men, especially, represented, and that is those who, in religious matters, are constantly living in the sepulchral region of ideas, dogmas, and ceremonies, which belong to other ages. There is a large number of men whose thoughts are so antique, and whose minds are so gloomy, that you may say, almost without figure, that they are living "*amongst the tombs.*"

Secondly: *Its malicious tendency.* "*They were exceeding fierce, so that no man might pass by that way.*" All the kind instincts of their nature had become extinct. Their whole soul was in flames of wrath. The sight of suffering would delight them, the throes of agony would fall as music on their malignant ears. The tendency of sin is to make men malicious, to destroy "*natural affection*," to eradicate all the kindly sympathies of the heart, to set man against his fellow, as well as against his Creator. The apostle in sketching the character of sinners says, "*The poison of asps is under their lips; their mouth is full of cursing and bitterness; their feet are swift to shed blood; destruction and misery are in their way; and the way of peace have they not known.*" Does not the history of the world show this to be true? What is the history of man on earth, but a history of oppression, cruelty, bloodshed, and slaughter? You see the malicious, fiendish spirit, not merely in the men who are actually engaged in slaughtering each other, but in a form as bad,—and for many reasons worse, because of the mean cowardice associated with it,—in those who heartlessly advocate war, while they lounge at home on the couch of ease. Sin and benevolence are eternal opposites.

Thirdly: *Its foreboding tendency.* "*What have we to do with thee, Jesus, thou Son of God? Art thou come hither to torment us before the time?*" Whether this be the utterance of infernal spirits which had possession of these men, or that of their own insane and aberrated minds, you have in both suppositions the idea that sin is connected with terrible forebodings of the future. The Bible gives us to understand that devils are looking forward with awful terror to some future: they are "*reserved in chains of darkness unto the judgment of the great day.*" That judgment will make their chains more firm and galling, their midnight sky more black; raise their tempestuous storm of wrath to higher degrees of fury and anguish. In the case of men and devils, sin imparts a dread of the future. "*Art thou come to torment us before the time?*"—As if they had said, We know that there is a time of torment before us, we have no doubt of that; we have no hope of escaping that. "Art thou come to torment us before the time?" Sin is cowardice. It unmans the soul. It makes it afraid—afraid of death—afraid of God —afraid of the future—afraid of its own visions, and of its own self. It makes it the miserable victim of fear.

Fourthly: *Its degrading tendency.* "*And there was a good way off from them an herd of swine feeding. So the devils besought him saying, If thou cast us out, suffer us to go away into the herd of swine.*" The tendency of sin is not to ascend from the lower to the higher, but to descend from the higher to the lower; it does not aspire to rise from the man to the angel, but inclines from the man to the brute—the swine. The request of these maniacs, or demoniacs, if you will, strange though it sounds, *is only an expression of the general downward tendency of sin.* Sin brutalizes. Sin gives the soul an appetency for the *unclean*—a swine-ward direction. It is by no means uncommon to see human souls running into a low animalism. Through the *media* of worldliness, sensuality, and voluptuousness, the moral metempsychosis takes place every day, and souls transmigrate brute-ward. A has made his fortune in the city, and has retired into the aristocratic suburbs, to pamper appetite and to live in luxury. He has past the noon of life, and is gaining animalism every day. Thirty years ago he had an active intellect, fine susceptibilities—there was something like genius beaming in his looks and playing on his brow. But where in him do you see any of these mind-traits now? He is dull, coarse, plethoric. Whither is his soul gone? It has run *swine-ward.* Is not this A the type of a numerous and growing class that populate the suburbs of large cities and towns? The first chapter of Paul's letter to the Romans is an illustration of the swine-ward tendency of souls under sin.

Here you have, then, a picture of the ruinous influence of moral evil, or sin, upon humanity. It makes it morally mad—it puts out its kindly sentiments, and inspires it with the malignant—it fills it with forebodings of the future and degrades it into the brutal forms of life. *Sin is ruin.*

II. THE BLESSED POWER OF CHRIST OVER MORAL EVIL. The passage suggests two thoughts in relation to Christ's power over evil,—

First: *He has power to eradicate evil from man, and by so doing restore him.* "*And He said unto them, Go.*" And they went. The evil, whether it was *principle* or *person,* was expelled. Mark gives the history of one of these men after the expulsion of the evil; and, probably, what he says of one, was true of both—that "*he sat at the feet of Jesus, clothed, and in his right mind;*"—sat as a studious listener and devout worshipper. He tells us, also, that he began to publish what Christ had done for him through Decapolis. We rejoice that Christ has power to eradicate the evil, and to expel the devil from man. He does it now, as truly as He did in the case of these men: not, it is true, by miracle, but by His regenerating and sanctifying truth. And where this is done we find a wonderful change in the individual's history. Like the prodigal, he *comes to himself,*—to his right mind; he listens to Christ, and publishes His fame abroad.

Secondly: *He has power, not only to eradicate evil from human nature, but to destroy its very existence.* "*And behold the whole herd of swine ran violently down a steep place into the sea, and perished in the waters.*" Perhaps this was intended to symbolize the fact, that Christ will one day destroy evil itself; and that the works of the devil, error and wrong, selfishness and impiety, will one day be utterly destroyed;—will be buried for ever in the great swelling sea of intelligence, rectitude, and truth.

Two remarks are here suggested in relation to Christ's way of destroying evil: (1) *That His method of doing it sometimes involves the sacrifice of human property.* These people lost their swine. But what was the sacrifice to the good effected? The delivering of one soul from the devil is worth all the cattle upon a thousand hills. Much secular property must always be sacrificed in the process of destroying moral evil in this world. (2) *That through this destruc-*

tion of property, Christ's work will meet with opposition from interested parties. "*And they that kept them fled, and went their ways into the city, and told everything, and what was befallen to the possessed of the devils. And, behold, the whole city came out to meet Jesus: and when they saw Him, they besought Him that He would depart from their coasts.*" Why did they beseech Him to depart from their coast? One might have thought, that seeing He could rid humanity of such tremendous evils, that they would entreat Him to dwell amongst them, in order to relieve others of their afflicted neighbours. They were, most probably, afraid of losing more of their property; *they cared more for their swine than for their species.* It has ever been so. The true spiritual reformer, if His teaching in any way interfere with secular interests, though He may bless hundreds of devil-ridden souls, is earnestly desired, if not compelled, to leave the coast. Paul must leave Ephesus, because the "craft is in danger;" and Christ must leave Decapolis, because the inhabitants value their swine. When will the time come that men shall say, Let our craft and cattle, our property and position, go, so long as men are being delivered from devils?

Matthew 9:1-8

Christ—His Pardoning Prerogative

These verses present Christ to us in an aspect most interesting in itself, and fitted to our circumstances, as condemned and depraved. Let us look devoutly at it in the light of this short fragment of His illustrious history. Christ forgives the sins of a palsied invalid, and asserts that "*the Son of Man hath power on earth to forgive sins.*" The following truths are here obviously taught in relation to this glorious prerogative:—

I. THAT HIS PARDONING PREROGATIVE IS EXERCISED ON THE CONDITION OF FAITH. "*And Jesus seeing their faith said unto the sick of the palsy, Son, be of good cheer; thy sins be forgiven thee.*" The conduct of those who bore the sick man, "lying on a bed," indicated their strong faith in the miraculous curative power of Christ. It was not the mere faith of intellect, that expends itself in words and has but little influence upon practical life. It was a faith that had become a mighty impulse to action.* To what

---

* It is interesting to observe in the narratives of our Lord's miracles that the faith which received blessing from Him was an impulse to action. Take the faith of the blind men, ix. 27, and see how active the principle was, ἠκολούθησαν κράζοντες. And when Jesus entered the house they renewed their application. So was it with Bartimæus, who cried the more earnestly as the people commanded him to be silent, Mark x. 48. Their views of our Lord's person and rank might be obscure, but their faith, such as it was, brought them to Him, and He in His pity and grace cured them, not merely from physical but, as we may believe, from moral evil. Faith was the means of deliverance, as it brought them to the Saviour, who made them whole. Attention to these simple facts of the narrative shows the im-

strenuous exertions it now stimulated ! what obstacles it surmounted !
In the house, at Capernaum, where Christ now was, " *There was no
room*," says Mark, " *to receive them ; no, not so much as about the door.*"
" *Pharisees and doctors*," says Luke, " *were there who had come out of
every town of Galilee, and Judea, and Jerusalem.*" Yet, through the
force of faith these four men pressed their way into the presence of
Jesus. " *They sought means to bring him in and to lay him before
Him.*" And what were the means ? Let Mark answer the question. " *And when they could not come nigh unto Him for the press,
they uncovered the roof where He was, and when they had broken it up,
they let down the bed whereon the sick of the palsy lay.*"

" Entrance by the door " says Neander, " was impossible ; but
the Oriental mode of building afforded a means of access to which
they at once had recourse. Passing up the stairs which led from
the outside to the flat roof of the house, they made an opening by
removing part of the tiles, and let the couch down into an upper
chamber. Who knows the distance they bore him, the repulses
they met with, the sneers and insults of the Pharisees, and doctors,
as they pressed their way ; the amount of contrivance and physical
exertion brought out in their generous endeavour ? What but a
deep settled loving faith in Christ's curative power could stimulate
them and sustain them in their efforts ? Christ saw their faith."

But whilst the faith of the four men who bore the paralytic
attracted the attention and elicited the respect of Christ, we must
remember also that the sick man himself had faith to receive the
blessing. The words of Christ, addressed to the sick man, " *Son, be
of good cheer*," would imply this. " He saw," says Stier, " in *him* a
state of mind and feeling *different* to theirs; aiming at an object distinct from that of the bearers, who only sought for his bodily healing.
In the breast of this palsied man Christ saw that moral state of mind,
mingled penitence and faith, which the Infinite sovereign has made
the settled condition of human forgiveness." " *He that believeth
shall be saved.*" The faith of the four men who bore him on the
couch might have induced Christ to have effected the poor man's
physical recovery, but nothing but his own faith would prompt the
Son of God to pardon his sins and save his soul. The exercise,
then, of Christ's pardoning prerogative towards men depends upon
their faith.

II. HIS PARDONING PREROGATIVE IS NECESSARY TO FREE MEN FROM

portant difference between an *otiose* intellectual assent and that living faith which
proves its vitality by energy and exertion. In this cure the three Evangelists
attribute the deliverance to the faith of those who brought the paralytic. A blessing is conferred on the sick man as an honour to the faith of his friends, and as an
encouragement to us to promote the spiritual welfare of our children and of all who
are connected with us. They sought for a temporal blessing, but a spiritual is
granted in order to exhibit more vividly the Saviour's virtue and grace. Perhaps
the extent of their knowledge was that He was the son of David, that He could
heal, that He was merciful. Acceptance depends not so much upon a creed as upon
faith, not so much upon belief about Christ as on a personal application, and consequent relation to Him.—*Webster.*

THEIR SUFFERINGS. This man was brought to Christ to be healed of his physical infirmity. Christ does this by freeing him from his sins. Between human and divine forgiveness we know but of one point of analogy, and in this point the resemblance is seeming, rather than real. The end of both is to *separate the forgiven from merited punishment.* A human governor pardons the criminal, and with the pardon the merited punishment is averted. God pardons the sinner, and the merited punishment is averted. So far there is a seeming resemblance. But even under this resemblance there is a *radical* difference. The punishment in the case of the human governor is averted by the mere merciful act of the sovereign—there is no necessary change in the mind and purpose of the criminal. In the other case the punishment is avoided by such a thorough change in the criminal's heart and life as separates him for ever from his past sins. Divine forgiveness is literally an absolution—*an absolval*—a setting free—a releasing, not from obligation but from the enthralling dominance and penal consequences of sin. No impression seemed more prevalent and deep amongst the Jews, than that suffering is the offspring of sin ; and therefore that the removal of the latter required the forgiveness and the blotting out of the former. And is there any truth more obvious than this ? Is it not affirmed by the consciousness of humanity, taught in almost every chapter of the Bible, and implied in the mediation of Christ ? In *individual* cases there may be—there frequently is—suffering, where there is not sin ; but in every case suffering is traceable to sin. When we see suffering, we may ever ask, " *Who did sin, this man or his parents ?*" This fact shows two things: (1) *The infinite value of Christ's work.* He is the " *Lamb of God that taketh away the sins of the world.*" He came " *to destroy sin in the flesh ;*" " *to put away sin by the sacrifice of Himself ;*" to dry up the fountain whence all the streams of human misery flow ; to tear up the pestiferous upas by the roots. The fact shows, (2) *The paramount importance of connecting every scheme for the improvement of man with the work of Christ.* A pseudo-philanthropy is ever fertile with its remedies for human ills. It creates institutions, prescribes its nostrums, and ordains offices of relief. All is quakery. The cause of the disease is neither met nor recognized. It is a solemn trifling with the patient. It is a mere drugging humanity with opiates, to deaden its sensibilities, enervate its powers, intoxicate its imagination, and fill it with the airy visions of vanity and falsehood. All schemes to help the world should be based upon the principles, and be instinct with the spirit, of Christianity—should be grafted in it as the living vine. Then they will grow and give life to the world ; —not otherwise.

III. HIS PARDONING PREROGATIVE IS SOMETIMES DENIED ON THE GROUND OF UNSUSTAINED ASSUMPTIONS. " *And, behold, certain of the Scribes said within themselves, This man blasphemeth ;*" and then in Luke, they are represented as saying, " *Why doth this man speak blasphemies ? Who can forgive sins but God only ?*" Who was it that thus repudiated this prerogative, and charged the Son of God with blasphemy ? *Not the man who was pardoned.* No! he had the proof in his own soul. The words addressed to him, " *Son, be of good cheer ; thy sins are forgiven thee,*" carried into his deepest consciousness the conviction of the Godhead of the speaker. They broke on the chaos of his soul with omnific energy, brightening his gloomy heavens into sunny azure, and tuning the long jarring and discordant chords of his heart into music. The mighty influence of these words, in his experience, would induce him to address Christ henceforward for ever, " *My Lord, and my God.*" The forgiven never doubt the possession of this prerogative by Christ. They have the witness in themselves.

It was the Scribes and Pharisees who now denied this prerogative to Christ. And their denial was based on two *arrogant assumptions.* They assumed things which they could not prove. First, that no being but the absolute God could forgive sins. " *Who can forgive sins but God only ?* " This might be true, or it might be false, so far as their power of proof was concerned. How could they know but that God delegates to some of His creatures this prerogative ? Did not He delegate Nathan to proclaim pardon to David, saying, " *The Lord hath put away thy sin : thou shalt not die* " ? The second assumption was, that Christ was not God. They could not prove this : and they had in His history many circumstances and manifestations which rendered the converse highly probable. Because of these two assumptions their denial was of *no logical worth.* If they could prove that God never delegated the power of forgiving sins to any being—that it was a prerogative which He always exercised Himself exclusively ; this of itself would have given no logical force to their denial : they must have proved, in connection with this, the second thing, namely, that Christ was not God, to have given their denial any argumentative validity. It is on such assumptions as these, that men now deny this prerogative of Christ. How can you prove that God only forgives sins ? I am not disposed to doubt this in any way : on the contrary, my faith is, that it is His exclusive prerogative. But how can you prove it ? And then, if you prove it, your objection is of no value unless you prove that Christ is not God; and we defy you to prove that. To prove that, you must prove that it is impossible for the Deity to be personally identified with the nature of man. And is there anything " too hard for the Lord ? " You must prove that Christ, who spent His life amidst thousands of enemies, who were ever anxious to detect in him some falsehood in expression, or some defect in conduct, but who unanimously declared that they could find no fault, was an impostor ; and you must prove that His biographers were the most clever of deceivers, and that His apostles were either the veriest impostors or fools. When you say that Christ was not divine, you say what we dare you to prove.

IV. His PARDONING PREROGATIVE IS ATTESTED BY THE HIGHEST PROOF. There were three kinds of proof in support of this displayed in that crowd in the house at Capernaum. (1) *That of consciousness.* This we may suppose to have been possessed by the poor palsied sinner who was forgiven. This man required no further evidence of Christ's power to pardon. He was pardoned—he *felt* its heavenly influence. This is the highest proof: but the proof which the pardoned only can experience. (2) *That of Christ's testimony.* "*The Son of man hath power on earth to forgive sins.*" If the value of testimony depends upon the *intellectual* and *moral* competence of the testifier, who in the history of the race was ever so competent to bear testimony to anything, as Christ was to bear testimony of His power to forgive? A thousand disinterested witnesses, from His and every subsequent age, unequivocally affirm that He was the most intelligent and holy personage that ever came within the sphere of their observation and knowledge. If Christ's testimony is not to be taken, whom are we to believe? If you doubt His testimony, you are bound to repudiate all history. (3) *That of miracle.* This was a species of evidence which Christ condescended now to give to meet the prejudices of these men. When Christ had proclaimed the pardon of the poor sufferer, these sneering Jewish sceptics wished to be understood that this was a mere blasphemous pretension. Their thoughts, perhaps, after Christ had pronounced the forgiveness, might be thus paraphrased: It is very easy for this pretender to pronounce the man forgiven; He knows that we have no means of contradicting the infamous assumption; words are cheap; the poor sufferer wants to be healed; He cannot heal him; and to conceal His weakness, He assumes a divine prerogative, and pronounces the man forgiven. He finds it easier to pronounce forgiveness than to restore the sufferer. And Jesus knowing their thoughts, said, "*Wherefore think ye evil in your hearts?*" "*For whether is it easier to say, Thy sins be forgiven thee; or to say, Arise, and walk?*" As if he had said, It is a greater `work to forgive sins than to perform miracles; but you are too ignorant to understand this, and in condescension to your ignorance, I'll cure the man:—"*Arise, take up thy bed and walk.*"

The miracle thus came as that *kind* of evidence which they challenged and would be most likely to feel. They had the belief—a belief which seems to me *inherent in humanity*, that no being can work a miracle but God; Christ, therefore, by working a miracle, would do that which would be most suitable to impress them with His divinity; and if they believed that, there was no blasphemy in His pronouncing the forgiveness of sins.

V. HIS PARDONING PREROGATIVE DOES NOT ALWAYS LEAD TO THE IMMEDIATE REMOVAL OF SUFFERING IN THE PERSONS WHO EXPERIENCE IT. It would seem from the narrative, that this paralytic was allowed to remain for some little time in his physically diseased state, after Christ had pronounced his forgiveness. Hence the cause and meaning of the inuendo of the captious Pharisees, that it was " easier " blasphemously, to pretend to pardon, than to perform the desired miraculous cure. They were, perhaps, disposed to ask the question,

If the pardon is granted, why does the suffering continue?—If the cause is annihilated, why does the effect continue?

The fact that the removal of the man's sufferings did not follow *immediately* the pardon of his sins, suggests, whether intentionally or not, the general idea, that the *sufferings of man may continue after his forgiveness.* It does not follow, therefore, that because a man is afflicted he is not pardoned. It is true that the subjective character of his afflictions changes at once with the pardoning act; they are no longer punitive, but corrective; their penal character is merged in the disciplinary; the sufferer *feels* in his pains, not the stroke of justice, but the rod of love; not the rigidly just treatment of an offended sovereign, but the merciful chastisement of an affectionate father. Whilst pardon does not *immediately* terminate the existence of suffering, it immediately terminates the punitiveness of suffering.

VI. HIS PARDONING PREROGATIVE WILL ULTIMATELY INSURE THE ENTIRE RESTORATION OF THE SOUL AND BODY OF THE INDIVIDUAL WHO EXPERIENCES IT. *"And he arose and departed to his own house."* Mark says, *"And immediately he arose, took up the bed, and went forth before them all; insomuch that they were all amazed, and glorified God, saying, We never saw it on this fashion."* A new current of life ran through his veins; his dead limbs revived; he stood up buoyant and hale; walked to his home with the step of vigorous manhood and the bounding heart of a pardoned saint.

In this restored man, here, "before" the "amazed" multitude, strong in the might of manhood, and happy in the blessed consciousness of eternal love, I see a picture and a pledge of the myriads of the redeemed, who shall rise from their graves, with bodies formed for unending life, and *"fashioned like unto the glorious body of Jesus Christ."*

Matthew 9:9-13

The Feast in Matthew's House; or, Christianity in Relation to our Social Instincts

"Every man," says Bishop Butler, "is to be considered in two capacities—the private and the public; as designed to pursue his own interest, and likewise to contribute to the good of others." We may add, as almost a corollary to this dictum of the profound primate, that every man is made for two distinct spheres of being—solitude and society. Each of these, as a realm of mental action, is of equal importance to the discharge of human responsibilities, and to the cultivation of the human character. They are not opposed to each other. They are mutually advantageous—necessary to man. He who gives himself up to either, exclusively, will damage himself, fail to benefit his species, and miss his noble destiny. To retire from the world, to close the ear to its jargon hum, and the eye to its fantastic forms; and to revel in the sublime abstractions of thought, would meet with the approval of the profoundest minds. " A lodge in some vast wilderness—some boundless contiguity of space," has been sighed for by the Cowpers of every age. The anchoristic life meets something profound and solemn in the instincts and reflections of human nature. The hermit, there, in his unbroken solitude, is a living sign of invisible worlds. His strange, dreamy eyes seem to be looking into the spiritual—he sees through the sensuous veil—he lives in the invisible. He is a living, breathing, world of thought, not common to men.

But complete solitude, whilst it would gratify some of our pro-founder instincts, and shut out from the heart much that is worthless, would stunt, if not destroy, other great powers of our nature, and exclude much that is of primary importance to the interests of our being. Whilst solitude might exclude much that is evil, it would also exclude much that might be turned to a practical account. The man of anchoristic tendencies would do well to remember three things : First, that he has an individual force within him, not only to counteract social evils, but to trans-mute them into good. Had we no such power—were we but a lump of clay in the moulding hand of society—then society being corrupt, the more solitude the better. But he has this inner force —a force to form all the unhealthy exhalations of social life into clouds, and break them into refreshing showers upon the soul ; a power, like that of the bee, to transmute the bitterest plants of society into a honey-comb for the soul. He should remember, secondly, that his nature cannot be either fully satisfied or deve-loped without society. The soul shut up from society, is like the seed shut up from soil, and air, and dew, and light. Hence the faculties of the ascetic saint have always been like the shoots that break from those roots of flowers which the seedsman has left in the dark, confined, and airless cellar—soft, textureless, and without colour. His thoughts run into dreams, his emotions into super-stition, the strength of his manhood goes off in sentiment. He should remember, thirdly, that he has no *right* to abdicate society. The better a man is, the more public he should be. He should be out in the opening field, scattering the seed of the kingdom ; up the mountain height, catching the first rays of morning, and flinging them on the dwellers in the valleys.

These thoughts are suggested by the *feast-scene* in the house of Matthew. We shall look at the narrative as an illustration of the *relation of Christianity to our social instincts.*

I. WE INFER FROM THIS SCENE THAT CHRISTIANITY STIMULATES OUR SOCIAL INSTINCTS. We are told in the ninth verse, that " *as Jesus passed from thence*"—from the scene where He cured the paralytic— " *He saw a man, named Matthew, sitting at the receipt of custom : and He saith unto him, Follow me. And he arose, and followed Him.*" It would seem from Luke the sixth, that Matthew had been called into the number of the Twelve Apostles before the Sermon on the Mount commenced. Matthew, probably, after this first call mentioned by

Luke, returned to his office, as Peter had to his net. Now Christ repeats the call, and makes it *thoroughly* and *permanently* effective.* This "FOLLOW ME" now turned the whole current of his thoughts, emotions, activities, and being, fully and for ever, Christward. "The call of a publican to be a follower of Christ, and a herald of His religion, was a sign of the sublime superiority of the new faith, in its. impartiality and mercy, over the bigotries of the old; and evinces the discernment and independence of Jesus in selecting a worthy disciple from an order of men among whom common opinion had pronounced that there was no worth to be found."

Mark, now—for this is the point—the influence of Christ's words upon the *social nature* of Matthew. His social sympathies open under the influence of Christ, as flowers open to the sun. He makes a feast. "And Levi," that is, Matthew, "*made Him a great feast in his own house; and there was a great company of publicans and others that sat down with them.*" (Luke v. 29.) With the modesty of a truly generous nature, Matthew does not tell us that "he made the great feast." True hospitality never talks of the "*great feasts*" which it makes for its friends. The pleasure in beholding the brightened countenances of happy guests, and mingling in the warm, genial, sparkling flow of social life, overwhelms all the miserable financial ideas about the entertainment. It is the mock hospitality, like all other mock excellences, that vaunts its doings.

But *how* does Christianity stimulate the social in man? There are three things which in their very nature powerfully tend to stimulate us to seek intercourse with our fellow-men. First, the possession of an intelligent interest in them. There is an instinct which attracts man to his race, and induces him to blend his feelings and his being with others, which we must not dignify with the title —*social*. It is but that gregarious appetency which belongs to the mere corporeal nature, and which we have in common with the lower orders of being. It is a kind of animal magnetism. Much of what is called society and friendship, in the world, can be easily resolved into this. True social feeling is not a mere sympathy with the body; that is gregariousness : but a sympathy with the soul— with man in the entirety of his faculties and relations. Whatever, therefore, deepens my interest in man, stimulates my social interest. Secondly, the possession of ideas which are felt to be of importance to our species, serves also to stimulate the social in us. It is the instinct of an idea to seek for utterance—to struggle for dissemination ; thoughts cry for language. When those ideas vitally relate to the interest of our species, their communicative tendency becomes sometimes resistless ; sometimes, as in the case of the old prophets, when they are suppressed, they are like "*fire shut up in the bones.*" Thirdly, the possession of happy feelings that may be enjoyed by our species, tend also to stimulate the social in us. Happiness, like its highest emblem—light—is diffusive. Happy beings ever seek to make others participate in their joy. The happy lark pours its

* See Stier's "Words of the Lord Jesus," *in loco.*

music from the skies to wake its joyous feeling in all the listeners below. The bright spirits of heaven descend and minister to the sorrowing souls of earth in order to lift them to their felicities. The EVER BLESSED ONE "fainteth not, neither is weary," in creating existences in order to impart His bliss. The happier a being is, in the truest sense, the more social. Misery isolates, seeks solitude, and strives to shut up all its dark and horrid feelings within the door of its one victim, spirit; but happiness unites, seeks society, and endeavours to ring out in notes of music its own delectable sentiments to the world.

If these *three* things thus tend to incite the social instincts, who does not see the power of Christianity for this purpose ? What an ntelligent interest does Christianity give us in our species ! In what moving and endearing aspects does it present to us our race! What inspiring ideas does it give us, which we feel to be of primary importance to mankind ; ideas which, if we daily realise, will make us feel like Peter and John before the Sanhedrim, who said, " *We* CANNOT *but speak the things which we have seen and heard.*" And what happiness does it yield—what joy unspeakable and full of glory ;—happiness which makes the soul cry out to its vast brotherhood, " *O taste and see that the Lord is good.*" Never, we may suppose, did Matthew have such feelings as now at this "*great feast*," with the publicans and sinners, the disciples and their Master, about him. Man now appeared to him in the light of those spiritual ideas and joyous feelings which the words of Jesus had awakened in his mind. His conversation with his guests, we presume, would be, not about the viands on the table, the state of business, or the gossip of the day, but about the new light that had broke on his soul, and the new delights that had risen in his heart, and the purpose to which he was now going to consecrate his energies and his life.

II. WE INFER FROM THIS PASSAGE THAT CHRISTIANITY AFFORDS FULL SCOPE TO OUR SOCIAL INSTINCTS. The guests at this banquet were of different classes. They were welcome there, not because they were rich or poor, ignorant or learned, saints or sinners, but because they were *men*. The obnoxious tax-gatherers, the notorious sinners, as well as the disciples, were there. Even the Pharisees, probably, were welcome : the doors seemed open to all that the room could contain. The fact that Christ thus socially mingled with this indiscriminate party, does intimate to me the ample and unrestricted scope which Christianity allows to our social nature. It seems to say, Don't confine yourselves to cloisters, nor restrict yourselves to cliques ; but mix and mingle with *men*.

Two things are noticeable here,—

First : *The Pharisaic opposition to this social freedom.* "*And when the Pharisees saw it, they said unto His disciples, Why eateth your master with publicans and sinners ?*" As if they had said, You are Jéws as well as we; you know that our rabbis prohibit us from eating with publicans and Gentiles ; you know that for our nation to eat with a person is an expression of sympathy and regard; your Master, in eating with these infamous publicans, is acting against the religious feeling of the country, and plainly proving that He is as corrupt as they. What an empty blasphemous pretender He must be to set Himself up as the model of virtue and the anointed of God, and yet socially mingle with the corruptest of the corrupt! He! the Christ indeed! He! the glorious Messiah of whom our noble prophets in sublimest vision, spoke! Don't believe it; don't be so infatuated; don't be so fooled. He is an impious impostor, an associate, a friend, you see, of publicans and sinners. This is strong language, but not stronger than their feelings. The strong feeling, however, against Christ is bad; but there is a spirit manifest, in the method of expressing that bad feeling, as bad, if not worse: it is *under-handedness*. It is that disingenuous, mean, and cowardly spirit that carries the javelin under the cloak of friendship, and that, with the basest villany, stabs in the dark. " *They said unto His disciples!"* Why did they not speak to Him? They were too craven-hearted for this; they sought to damage His reputation and undermine His influence by that basest of instruments—*innuendo.*

Secondly: *The true defence of social freedom.* " *But when Jesus heard that, He said unto them, They that be whole need not a physician, but they that are sick,"* &c. The great truth which Christ puts forth in vindication is, that His conduct in His social relation with men was governed, not by a *just regard to their merit, but by merciful regard to their need:*—that He mingled with men, not because of their worthiness, but of their wants. This he illustrates (1) by a *proverb* —"*They that be whole need not a physician."* I am come as a Healer; this I have always professed. According to your own showing, therefore, I am in my place, in being with those whom you regard as being the vilest of the vile. The physician must not shun the disease, however virulent and contagious. The world is a moral hospital, and the worst of its wards draws most on my heart. (2) He illustrates His vindicating truth, by a *divine principle. Go ye, and learn what that meaneth,* " *I will have mercy, not sacrifice."** You Pharisees are rigid in ceremonies, but lax in morals; you think much of rituals, but care nothing for righteousness. Go and learn what the God of your fathers has said, " I will have mercy, and not sacrifice." You are particular in offering sacrifices; I delight in showing mercy;— and mercy to man is more acceptable to Him than the most costly offerings on the altar. (3) He illustrates His vindicating truth by a declaration of His mission.—" *I am not come to call the righteous but sinners to repentance."* There seems to me a caustic irony in this statement. The object of my mission is not for you,—you are right- eous: there is nothing in the code of heaven that you have not ful- filled,—you need no repentance: you are full of moral health, you need no physician—you are above my help. I am come to call sinners to repentance. My mission is to sinners. The greater the

* See the observations of Stier on the point and pertinency of this quotation from Hosea, *in loco.*

sinner, the more he requires my help, and the more ready I am to help him. Blessed declaration, this!—*I am come to call sinners.* We would not have this announcement erased from this Book for worlds; it is a bright star of hope in the dark firmament of fallen humanity. Let it shine on until every sinner respond to the call.

III. WE INFER FROM THIS PASSAGE, THAT CHRISTIANITY GIVES A RE-MEDIAL MISSION TO OUR SOCIAL INSTINCTS. Why should we go into the society of all classes, even into that of the most wicked and corrupt? For mere gustatory enjoyment? That is to act the animal, not the man. There are men so sunk in the brute-direction as to value society for the sake of its feasts; the esculents are their chief themes of social converse, and their chief elements of social attraction. "*Their god is their belly; they mind earthly things.*" For what purpose, then, should we go into society? For mere amusement? To indulge in humourous talk, to join the sensuous songs, and move in the giddy dance? No! this would be derogatory to our nature, and a reckless expenditure of our short, and ever-shortening, day of probation. No! the incident teaches that we should go to relieve and bless the spirits of mankind. The benign and merciful spirit of Jesus should inspire us whenever we mingle with Publicans and sinners. We should mingle with men as He did, in order to CALL SINNERS TO REPENTANCE. Their restoration, and not our gratification, should be our aim. In the social circle, when the heart expands with kindred sympathies and the tide of genial feeling runs high, then, is a favourable time to cast the seed upon the waters; and after the waters have receded, we may, like the Egyptian husbandman, find the fruit of our labours when the Nile is dry again.

Matthew 9:14-17

The New Religion; or, Lessons to the Ascetic and Ceremonious

The question here put to Christ, by the disciples of John, exhibits that same base spirit of disingenuousness, which the Pharisees had shown, as seen in the preceding narrative. As the Pharisees sought to damage the reputation of Christ by a mean and wicked insinuation to His disciples, so the disciples of John animated by the same miserable spirit, endeavouring to impugn the piety of His disciples by a question put in a suspecting and clandestine manner to Christ, "*Why do we and the Pharisees fast oft, but Thy disciples fast not?* We and the Pharisees attend punctually and frequently to religious fasts but Thy disciples fast not. On the contrary, they feast with "*Publicans and sinners.*" Surely they cannot possess the true religion. It is a law, that the less of the true a man has in him, the more suspicious he is of others; and the more he is under the influence of evil, the more disposed he is ever to wear the masque, and to injure others in the dark.

Christ, instead of scathing these carping, censorious, persons with the flash of an indignant look, or hurling at them the thunders of denunciation, mercifully condescends to give them that calm, comprehensive, beautiful, and suggestive reply, which you have in the fifteenth and two following verses :—" *And Jesus said unto them, Can the children of the bride-chamber mourn as long as the bridegroom is with them ?*" &c. How much of the sublime and precious truth which Christ announced, came forth in answer to the objections of His enemies ! This is the third instance of it in this very chapter. The glorious doctrine of His " pardoning prerogative " was proclaimed as a reply to the cavillings of the Scribes. The doctrine of Christianity, in relation to the social instinct, was propounded in answer to the imputations which the Pharisees cast upon Him as He sat at the banquet of Matthew ; and now the lessons which He gives to the ascetic and ceremonious, come forth in consequence of the unfriendly question of John's disciples, The interest of truth is thus often promoted by the questionings and reasonings of its enemies. Error brings out the latent energies of truth, as steel brings fire from the flinty rock.

The passage contains three lessons to the ascetic and ceremonious :—

I. THAT EXTERNAL SERVICES, IN CONNEXION WITH THE NEW RELIGION OF CHRIST, MUST EVER BE THE EXPRESSION OF THE INDIVIDUAL HEART. Jesus here teaches, that the reason His disciples did not fast was, that fasting was not in accordance with their state of mind. True fasting, the fasting which God approves, is the *effect* and *sign* of sorrow. His disciples were happy—jubilant ; and therefore, feasting, and not fasting, would be the honest expression of their hearts. Were they to fast, they would misrepresent the true state of their souls, and would be hypocrites. The Jews generally, and the Pharisees especially, had got into the habit of engaging in religious services as a matter of custom and routine. Their religious economy enjoined numerous rites and ceremonies ; and they had come to regard a mere external observance of these as the full discharge of their obligations both to man and their Maker. Their acts expressed no individual convictions ; their words were charged with no individual thinking; their prayers breathed no individual thirstings after the living God. They were mechanical, hollow, and soulless, in their religion ; they would offer sacrifices without any feeling of personal guilt, perform ablutions without any consciousness of moral uncleanness, bestow alms without any generous sentiment, and fast without any humiliation of soul before God. Their religion was " *bodily service.*"

Now, Christ taught the utter worthlessness, the base hypocrisy of all this. The all-prevailing theme of His teaching was, that the religion he came to inculcate was to be the imperial inspiration and power of the heart. He saw worship, not in the external services of the temple, but in the spirit and truth of the devout soul. He saw benevolence, not in the abundance which rich men cast into the treasury, but in the feeling expressed in the widow's mite. The suppressed sigh, He regarded as prayer; the generous desire, as true alms-giving; the devout aspiration, as the acceptable oblation. From the fact, that the external services of the new religion must ever be thus the expression of the individual heart, it follows that the same external service which would be praiseworthy in one, would be a sin in others. Men who are in deep sorrow for sin, would do well to fast;—their fasting would be a *natural* consequence, and a suitable expression of their state of heart; but where this sorrow is not, fasting would be unnatural and sinful. It is right for some men to be baptized, to partake of the Lord's Supper, to engage in public devotions, and in the holy work of the ministry ; but it would be heinously wrong for others, whose hearts are not in the same state, to enter for an instant into such engagements. The service of the new religion must be the expression of the individual heart. " *He is not a Jew,*" &c. Rom. ii. 28, 29.

II. THAT THE PREDOMINANT FEELINGS AWAKENED BY THE NEW RELIGION OF CHRIST ARE OF A JOYOUS CHARACTER. " *Can the children of the bride-chamber mourn so long as the bridegroom is with them ? but the days will come when the bridegroom shall be taken from them, and then shall they fast.*" The three remarks which are suggested by this language will illustrate the general sentiment we have just expressed,—

First : *That the relationship between Christ and His true disciples is a very intimate and tender one.* The children of the bride-chamber, the Paranymphs, were the most intimate friends of the bride and bridegroom ; none but the dearest objects of their hearts were admitted there. But in other places of sacred writ, the relationship of Christ to His disciples is represented as nearer even than this. There it is that of the bridegroom to the bride. " *Thy Maker is thine husband, the Lord of Hosts is His name :*" and the forming of the relationship is spoken of as a marriage : " *I will betroth thee unto me for ever : yea, I will betroth thee unto me in righteousness, and in judgment, and in loving-kindness, and mercies.*" The blessings of the Gospel now, and the felicities which spring from them in the future world, are spoken of as a marriage feast. But no human relationship is sufficiently close and tender fully to set forth the vital, and intimate spiritual, connexion subsisting between Christ and His people. Friend, brother, husband, father, are all ineffective figures. If we are His disciples, we are in Him, and He is in us. We are grafted into Him as the vine in the root; and from Him we derive our energy and life.

Secondly : *That the conscious presence of Christ, on the part of His disciples, is ever connected with the highest joy.* " *Can the children of the bridechamber mourn as long as the bridegroom is with them ?*" Marriage is the season for the most bright and bounding sentiments of joy. Amongst the Jews, the marriage festival was a scene where hearts overflowed with the tide of happy feeling— it streamed like sunlight from the eye—it flowed as sweetest music from the voice. This happiness is the figure which Christ employs here to intimate the joy which His disciples experience when in His presence. How happy must they have been with Christ—how happy as they walked the fields, ploughed the sea, or sat at the table with Him. What thrills of ecstacy must have run through them from every glance of His benignant eye, and every word that fell from His blessed lips! He did not seem to be able to give them a higher idea of heaven than the idea of being *with Him*. "*Where I am, there shall ye be also.*" Paul caught the idea. To be with Christ was his highest idea of heaven. The good in every age have felt this.

Thirdly: *That when this consciousness of Christ's presence is disturbed, the joy of His disciples is interrupted.* "*When the bridegroom shall be taken from them, then shall they fast.*" He here refers, undoubtedly, to His death; as if He had said, When I am gone, when I am taken by the wicked hands of my enemies and crucified, it will be a terrible hour in their history: they may well fast then: the sword that will awake against me will "*scatter the sheep.*" They will feel themselves for a time as sheep without a shepherd, in the midst of wolves. But I am with them now, and they are happy. This little interruption to their joy was not for long. According to His promise, He visited them, and was with them for forty days after His resurrection from the dead. And then on the day of Pentecost He came to them, spiritually, to be their constant guest.

These remarks serve to show that the *predominant* feelings awakened by the new religion of Christ are those of a *joyous* character. This new religion is fellowship with Christ, and fellowship with Christ *is* heaven; and this fellowship we may enjoy now.

III. THAT THE PRINCIPLES OF THIS NEW RELIGION OF CHRIST REQUIRE TO BE KEPT DISTINCT FROM ALL OTHER SYSTEMS. "*No man putteth a piece of new cloth unto an old garment,*" &c. The idea is, that the rites of the old religion must not be blended with the principles of the new.

We make two remarks here,—

First: *That there has ever been a tendency in man to connect some of his old forms with Christianity.* These disciples of John now wished Christ to enjoin on His followers the rite of fasting. You see the tendency on the side, both of the Jew and the Pagan, in the first ages. The Jewish convert was anxious to bring as much of Judaism as possible into his new religion, and the Pagan convert sought to bring as much of heathenism as possible. From these two sources the corruptions of Christianity have come. The Greek and the Romish church are illustrations of this huge evil. In both you see *new wine in old bottles; new cloth upon old garments.* Indeed, Christianity has been dealt with in this fashion in every age. How often do we see men endeavouring to patch their old dogmas to some of its glorious doctrines, to put its new wine into the rotten bottles of their old institutions and creeds. Men do not like to take Christianity in its naked simplicity. They are anxious to combine it with something else—some old notions, rites, or ceremonies.

Secondly : *That against this tendency we must strive, as against a tremendous evil.* The new wine is lost by putting it into old bottles. The new cloth which would clothe and adorn the spirit, becomes worthless by being cut into pieces, and attached to old worn-out garments. How its doctrines have been injured by being worked into old creeds and systems of theology ! Take up any system of theology, even the most fresh and orthodox, and you will discover but little of the new and inspiring wine which you have in the biography of Christ and the writings of the apostles. There are so many cracks in your logical divinity, that nearly all the new wine leaks out. Look at any church organization, and amongst the rules and rites of the "Conferences," "Convocations," "Synods," "Unions," you will find but little of the fresh wine which you discover in the upper room at Jerusalem, and in the first churches planted by the apostles. Men have treated Christianity as if it were but a system of logical dogmas. But it is a life—*it is the seed of life.* A seed does not require you to give it an organization. The acorn does not ask you to give it trunk, branches, and form. No ! give it soil, and sun, and air, and it will build out of the elements about it a majestic structure for itself.

Christianity must be kept *distinct.* The doctrine of depravity must be proclaimed without any modification; the doctrine of salvation by faith in Christ alone must be proclaimed without any modification; the doctrine of sovereign influence must be proclaimed without any modification; the doctrine of God's free love to the world must be proclaimed without any modification; the doctrine that there is one God, and one Mediator between God and man, the Man Christ Jesus, must be proclaimed without any modification.

Brother ! throw away thy " old " rotten " bottles " of dogmatic sentiment, conventional prejudices, and self-merit. These will never contain the new and ever-fermenting wine of " *the truth as it is in Jesus.*" However much thou takest in, every drop will leak out, and leave nothing but the dry leather. Get the new bottles of earnest inquiry, of child-like docility, of self-renunciation, and then get in the " new wine," and thou shalt have within thee that which will give the loftiest inspiration to thy faculties for ever. Don't waste thy precious time in patching thine " *old garments* " with little pieces from this new religion. The " *new cloth* " which the Son of God has woven by His doctrines and His deeds, by His life and His death, has enough within its majestic roll to clothe thy soul complete—clothe it with the lustrous and flowing robe of eternal virtue and blessedness. Aye, aye, enough, thank God ! to enwrap within its ample folds every child of man— a universe of souls !

Matthew 9:18-35

Old Specimens of Ever-recurring Facts

We take these four cases together,* because they contain so much that is common to one another, and the general meaning of each will gain power and prominence by the combination.

I. HERE ARE SPECIMENS OF THE IMMENSE AFFLICTIONS WHICH ARE EVER PRESSING ON THE RACE. There are four specimens recorded in these verses, and we shall take them, not according to their *supposed degree of aggravation*, but according to the order in which they are here recorded.

The first case is the death of the ruler's daughter. "*While He spake these things unto them, behold, there came a certain ruler, and worshipped Him, saying, My daughter is even now dead.*" The name of this ruler, according to Mark and Luke, was Jairus. He was a person of distinction, having the control of the affairs and worship of the synagogue. Here is death—death in the young. The fair girl—the delight, perhaps, of the father, and the hope of the mother, the "only daughter"—is a lifeless corpse, and the whole house is in sadness and confusion. "*All wept and bewailed her,*" says Luke.

The second case is the woman with the "issue of blood." This woman's disease seems to have been of an aggravated character. She had been the subject of it for "twelve" long years. During that period she had tried all likely and available means of restoration; all the physicians, probably, within her reach had been con-

---

* In this chapter the Evangelist pourtrays the gracious character of the King. See how this beams forth in all the incidents here recorded, according to the analysis of its contents which we adopt from Dr. Goulburn's *Thoughts on Personal Religion*, Part III. chap. 4 :—" Jesus is interrupted in the midst of a discourse by the appearance of a couch with a palsied man upon it. Far from accounting the interruption unreasonable, He first absolves, then heals the patient, and thus secures glory to God from the multitude. He passes out into the open air, perhaps for refreshment, and His eye catches Matthew sitting at the receipt of custom. He calls him, and Matthew follows. Our Lord accepts his invitation to a meal ; sits down with publicans and sinners, and speaks of the powers of His grace. In connexion probably with His appearance at a festival, the disciples of John ask Him why *His* disciples did not fast. He explains why. Jairus comes to solicit His merciful interference in behalf of a dying daughter. Jesus follows him, when to another interruption, which to the feelings of Jairus must have been extremely galling, the woman with an issue of blood steals a cure from Him on the road. Jesus stops to draw from her an acknowledgment of the benefit, and to dismiss her with a word of consolation and blessing. Then He resumes His former errand of love, arrives at Jairus's house, and raises the dead maiden., Coming out, the blind men follow Him into the house, and receive their cure. They have scarcely gone out when the man possessed with a dumb devil is brought to Him and restored. Thus our Lord is faithful to the plan of God, as hourly developed by the workings of His Providence. His object is not to carry out schemes preconceived by Himself, but to study God's guidings, and to be true to God's occasion and God's inspirations."

sulted, had tried, and failed. MARK says, she "*had suffered many things of many physicians, and had spent all that she had, and was nothing bettered, but rather grew worse.*" The many physicians, as is too often the case now, had, by their ignorant experiments on human life, and their rapacious cupidity, both aggravated her disease and exhausted her funds. They had, under the garb of the "healing art," injured her constitution and rifled her purse. Added to this, her disease was of that kind which according to the Levitical law, rendered her ceremonially unclean, so that she was not allowed to enter the courts of the Lord's house, in order to obtain the comforts connected with the public ordinances of religion. Her condition was, indeed, a pitiable one : without health and without the means of subsistence, wasted, worn, and shunned, the child of suffering and want, fast sinking into the chilly gloom of despair.

The third case is the "two blind men." "*And when Jesus departed thence, two blind men followed Him, crying and saying, Thou Son of David, have mercy on us.*" The disease of the woman was bad, but the case of these two blind men, we think, worse than either. What a calamity is the loss of sight ! What tides of pleasurable sensations flow to us from sea and sky, mountain and mead, and the million forms of life and beauty that encircle us, through the eye ! It lets into our hearts a rich fountain of delight. From every object in the horizon it brings to us something which either charms us with its loveliness, cheers us with its brightness, awes us with its grandeur, or inspires us with the evolutions of its force. To lose the eye is to lose the best part of the physical universe. The sun shines and landscapes bloom in vain to a sightless man : he is in starless midnight.

The fourth case is the "dumb man possessed with a devil." The faculty of speech is one of the choicest gifts of heaven. It enables us to relieve the mind of thoughts, anxieties, and feelings, which, if kept "pent within," would so burden the spirit as to destroy its powers, and make existence intolerable. It introduces us into a world of souls, and enables us to win their wisest counsels, their warmest sympathies, and most friendly help. A dumb man is, to a great extent, denied all this. He may, it is true, by signs and writing, get something like compensation, but all such artificial inventions are miserable substitutes for the natural power of speech. Here was a "*dumb man.*" Whether he was dumb from a defect in the organs of speech, or from deafness, or from that species of nervous disease which the Jews referred to Satanic possession, it does not matter. He was dumb, and as such was a miserable object. He was "*possessed with a devil.*" The devil being the primal originator and agent of sin, and sin being the cause of all disease, wherever there is a disease of mind or body, there are the proof and presence of a devil. Though the dumbness of this man, however, was a serious affliction to himself, it was rather a blessing to others, so long as he was under the special influence of this devil. "Of the two," says Matthew Henry, "better a dumb devil than a blaspheming one." It would be well, perhaps, for the world if all who are the special subjects of Satan had less tongue. Dumbness, in thousands of instances, would be a blessing to the race.

Thus these verses give us a few specimens of the *immense* afflictions of our race. Here we have the loss of health in the woman; what is worse, the loss of faculties in the dumb and the blind; and what is worse still, the loss of life in that young girl. The afflictions you have in these verses are such that mankind, in every age, are subject to: they are but a few samples of the woes and miseries of our kind. Under all that is bright and gay connected with our earthly existence, suffering still reigns; amidst all the displays and inspirations of life here, death still reigns. Suffering and death may at times be concealed from us under the fair forms of pleasure and life, but they are ever at work; ever are the poisonous streams rolling through the under-channels of life, and insidiously working their way into the homes and natures of all the sons of men.

II. HERE ARE SPECIMENS OF THE MANNER IN WHICH CHRIST REMOVES THE AFFLICTIONS OF THE RACE. Christ removed all the afflictions which are here recorded. He raised the daughter of the ruler to life, and thus filled the hearts of the sorrowing parents with gladness. He healed the diseased woman, and made her hale as ever. He opened the eyes of the blind men, and thus ushered them into a new world of joyous feeling. He cast out the devil, and caused the dumb man to speak. There was no case that He refused to help, or that over-reached His skill. And He "*went about all the cities and villages, teaching in their synagogues, and preaching the gospel of the kingdom, and healing every sickness and every disease among the people.*"

But how does He heal the woes of the world? From the cases of restoration before us, we learn three things in answer to this question,—

First: *He heals the afflictions of men with the utmost ease.* By the mere "touch."* of His garment, the disease of "twelve years'" standing left for ever the poor woman. The daughter of Jairus started from the cold sleep of death, as He "took her by the hand;"† the blind men received their sight, and felt as if ushered into a new universe, as He "touched their eyes;" and with equal ease did He expel the "dumb devil," and the man spake. In none of these cases do we find the slightest effort; nay, in none of the miraculous cures ever wrought by Him do we discover anything approaching to an exertion. By a word, or look, or touch at most, restoration from the most aggravated disease, and even from the icy grasp of death, is effected. Who

---

* "Somebody hath touched me: for I perceive that virtue is gone out of me" (Luke viii. 46). "The physical virtue which passes over does not go from Him without His *will*. That will is always disposed; stands, as it were, always open and prepared for approaching faith; and *this* is the reason why that which occurred could take place. Further: not without His *knowledge*, as is immediately shown. The touch which cleared the virtue from Him was assuredly unexpected; but He *marks* it immediately, knowing it within Himself, rejoicing over the *faith*, by which He is well pleased to allow Himself even to be thus *touched*."—*Stier.*

† See *Resurrections*, a work in which all the resurrections mentioned in the Bible are discussed; published by Kent and Co.

does not rejoice to know that, however varied and aggravated the woes of our afflicted race may be, there is One, who wears our nature that can remove the whole with the utmost ease ? Such instances as those before us, I take as foretokening that bright future of our planet, " *when He will destroy the face of the covering cast over all people, and the veil that is spread over all nations ; swallow up death in victory, and wipe away tears from off all faces.*"

Secondly : *He heals the afflictions of men from the purest impulses of benevolence.* How *promptly* and *tenderly* does He attend to those cases ! It is impossible for the most unfriendly and lynx-eyed critic to detect the slightest indication of selfishness in these, or any of the curative acts of Jesus. GAIN, so dear to the selfish heart, He never sought. Had He sought it, the number and magnitude of His healing works would have made Him the Crœsus of Judea in a few short days. FAME, which the self-seeker has ever prized, He shunned as an enemy. " *See that no man know it,*" said He to the man whose eyes He had opened. He made no parade of His illustrious achievements. Nothing but the most disinterested commiseration with sufferings influenced Him in all His remedial achievements. "His bosom," says Robertson, in one of his incomparable discourses, "was to mankind what the ocean is to the world. The ocean has its own mighty tides ; but it receives and responds to, in exact proportion, the tidal influences of every estuary, and river, and small creek, which pours into its bosom. So in Christ : His bosom heaved with the tides of our humanity ; but every separate sorrow, pain, and joy, gave its pulsation, and received back influences from the sea of His being."

Thirdly : *He heals the afflictions of men on the condition of their believing application to Him.* "*Thy faith,*" said He to the woman, " *hath made thee whole.*"* " *Be not afraid, only believe,*" said He to the father of the maid who lay dead ; and before He cured the blind men, He demanded faith on their part. "*Believe ye that I am able to do this ?*" They said unto Him, Yea, Lord. Then,"—mark, *then,* not before—"*touched He their eyes, saying, According to your faith be it unto you.*" " The miracles of Jesus," says the noble thinker before quoted, "were not arbitrary acts ; they were subject to the laws of the spiritual world. It was, we may humbly say, impossible to convey a spiritual blessing to one who was not spiritually susceptible. A certain inward character—a certain relation (*rapport*) —to the Redeemer, was required to make the mercy efficacious. Hence in one place we read, ' He could not do many miracles there, because of their unbelief.' The only touch which reaches God is that of faith. The multitude may throng and press ; but heart to heart, soul to soul, mind to mind, only so do we come in actual

---

* " We can only apprehend this spiritual-physical virtue through taking into account this spiritual relationship. The people generally throng and press Him without *that relation,* but the timid touch, which scarcely laid hold of His garment, brings healing to the sick woman, because she has faith to be healed." —Stier.

contact with God." Faith is the condition of Christ's healing agency.

III. HERE ARE SPECIMENS OF THE STATES OF MIND IN RELATION TO CHRIST, WHICH PREVAIL AMONGST THE RACE. We have specimens of four classes of mind, in relation to Christ, in the facts before us,—

First : *Here is a specimen of the thoughtless unbeliever.* We see this class represented in the persons who were in the house of Jairus when Jesus entered. Mark states three things of these people :—That they " *wept and wailed greatly ;*" "*laughed* " Christ " *to scorn,*" when He said, " *The damsel is not dead, but sleepeth;*" and that they " *were astonished with a great astonishment,*" when they saw that Christ had actually raised her to life. These three circumstances, here recorded, of these " minstrels and people," give us three characteristic facts of *thoughtless unbelief*—facts which always mark its history. (1) *That it has no consolation under bereavement.* Probably, some of those who " *wept and wailed greatly* " were those who, according to the custom of the East, hired themselves as mourners. But why should I say, according to the custom of the *East ?* To our disgrace, be it said, it is according to the custom of our little Western Isle, even in these times of civilization. We have our own hired mourners—persons who, for " lucre," exhibit the symbols and countenance expressive of those sorrowful emotions, befitting the hour and scene of bereavement, but which, for the time, are foreign to their natures. However, though this might have been the case with some of those who " *wept and wailed greatly,*" it was not so with all. There was, undoubtedly, much genuine grief ; and even the very affectation of it showed the sad and gloomy idea they had of death. Their very mock sorrow suggests the fact, that unbelief has no consolation under bereavement. How can it have consolation ? It has no faith *in the future reunion of friends.* Death to them is eternal separation—extinction. Nor has it any faith in the *paternal superintendence of God* in the event. All is reckless fortuitousness or iron-hearted fate. It cannot say, " *The Lord gave and the Lord hath taken away.*" The circumstances in this house of mourning suggest another fact in connexion with thoughtless unbelief. (2) *That it has generally a disposition to ridicule what it does not understand.* "*They laughed Him to scorn.*" They could not understand how that pale, frigid, motionless, breathless corpse was " *asleep;*" and because it did not seem clear to their unthinking minds, instead of asking for an explanation, they " *laughed.*" As ridicule always marks the mean in spirit and the destitute of argument, it is ever the attendant upon thoughtless unbelief. To ridicule what we do not understand is, 1, *unphilosophical;* for reason, *a priori,* infers necessary incomprehensibilities to the finite intellect. Is, 2, *inconsistent;* for to be consistent, if we ridicule one thing we cannot understand, we should ridicule all, and this would lead us to laugh at the universe, and everything in it, and at GOD, the ever-blessed Maker of all. It is, 3, *presumptuous;* for it is to set up our puny understandings as the test and standard of all truth. The other fact suggested by the circumstances, as associated with thoughtless unbelief, is (3) *That it is destined to be overwhelmed with astonishment.* When, by the fiat of Christ, the girl arose, and stood before them with all the flush and vigour of new life, "*they were astonished with great astonishment.*" Infidelity is doomed to this. "Behold, ye despisers, and wonder," &c. The things it denies and ridicules now, will one day rise before them as palpable and tremendous realities. The old world, that ridiculed the teaching of Noah, was *astonished* when the windows of heaven were opened. So with the men of Sodom and Gomorrah, who laughed at the warning of Lot; and so it must ever be. How *astonished* will the atheist be when he shall confront the EVERLASTING ONE in judgment! How *astonished* will the deist be when he shall know that every part of his most private life was under the eye and control of the supreme Lord of heaven and earth! How *astonished* will the materialists be when they shall see Hades sending forth all the myriads of departed souls, to rejoin bodies which had become dust in oceans, cemeteries, and battle-plains! Let the thoughtless unbeliever look at his true picture, and take warning in time.

Secondly: *Here is a specimen of earnest seekers.* Jairus besought Christ earnestly for his daughter. "*I pray Thee come and lay Thy hands upon her.*" (Luke.) The woman was in earnest. She pressed through the crowd, and said, "*If I may but touch the hem of His garment, I shall be made whole.*" The blind men were in earnest. "*They followed Him, crying, and saying, Thou Son of Daid, have mercy on us.*" All these earnest seekers were *humble, believing, persevering;*—and these are ever the characteristics of the class.

Thirdly: *Here are specimens of the transiently impressible.* "*And the multitudes marvelled, saying, It was never so seen in Israel.*" So long as these people heard Christ speak, and witnessed His benevolent work, they were impressed in His favour, and would shout laudations; but their impressions soon passed off, like morning clouds and early dew. They flowed with the stream. They were only impressed with the things of the hour. Are these not a type of a large class of the hearers of the Gospel? The preacher works on their hearts at the time, but their impressions die away with his voice.

Fourthly: *Here are specimens of inveterate antagonists.* The Pharisees said, "*He casteth out devils through the prince of the devils.*" Savagely *envious* at His growing popularity, they maliciously ascribed His miraculous cures, which were attestations of His divinity, to Satanic agency. The characteristic crime of those men was *ascribing the operations of Christ to wrong moral causes;* and this is what infidels in every subsequent age have been doing. They either endeavour to disprove the facts of Christianity, or resolve them into wrong causes. The old Pharisees and the modern infidels here meet in common sympathies, doings, and ends;—they are moral brethren.

Brother,—are not these old facts, which have now passed under review, like all the facts of the Book in which they are found, a wonderful mirror? Have you not seen specimens of suffering humanity? specimens of the conduct of the great Physician of mankind? and specimens, too, of states of mind which have ever prevailed amongst the race in relation to Christ? How true is it that the Word of God is a "glass!" In it we see the only true reflection of *the ages past and to come.* Here is photographed the panorama of the world's history; and here are visions of the things that "shall come to pass hereafter."

Who can say that the eternal future is uncertain in the light of this book?

> Great God! beam on this mirror Thy Spirit's light;
> And in it let us see, as we devoutly wish to see,
> Ourselves, the world, Thyself, and Thy Bless'd Son, aright!

Matthew 9:36-38

Society to the Eye of Christ

"*When He saw the multitudes, He was moved with compassion on them*," &c. We may suppose that there was nothing in the external appearance of these multitudes which, to the common eye, would indicate the sad. We may suppose that they were "well-fed and well-clad," and that their hearts, under the influence of numbers, as is generally the case, were buoyant with pleasurable excitement; that good humour sunned their countenances and enlivened their talk, and that—both to themselves, and to the ordinary spectator—they were a happy folk. But He who seeth not as man, looked through all the outward,—looked even down through the superficial stream of pleasurable excitement which now flowed and sparkled, and saw—*what?* Intellect enslaved, reason blinded, moral faculties benumbed, souls "faint" and lost,—"*scattered abroad as sheep having no shepherd.*"

We infer, from this passage, two lessons:—

I. THAT A RIGHT VIEW OF HUMAN SOCIETY IS VERY AFFECTING. "When He (Christ) *saw the multitudes, He was moved with compassion;*" His great heart heaved with those commiserating sentiments which, over Jerusalem, burst forth in tears. What was the view that thus affected Him?

First: *He regarded them as being in a deplorable spiritual condition.* There were (1) the subjects of spiritual *faintness*. "*Because they fainted.*" What do we mean by spiritual faintness—the want of intellectual vigour, imagination, or genius? No; there may be mental powers sufficient to prosecute the profoundest inquiries, genius whose creations shall eclipse the most magnificent productions of past times, and yet, allied to the whole, there may be the most utter spiritual prostration. Spiritual *faintness* is the want of power to feel and do the right. Paul declares the world, apart from Christianity, to be "*without strength ;*" that is, without strength to bear trials with magnanimity, and to prosecute duty without fear ; "*without strength*" to battle manfully with the wrong, and to side ever with the right ; "*without strength*" to rectify our moral errors, to roll off the load of guilt that presses upon the conscience, and to appear with acceptance before our Maker. This is the weakness— the faintness—that Jesus saw, and which now moved His compassion. And this is general. It belongs to all ages and lands ;—it is a calamity common to the race. In connexion with the corporeal strength of Samson, the intellectual vigour of Bacon, the poetic energy of Burns, the military force of Wellington, you see utter spiritual faintness—the want of power to restrain a passion, or to crush a lust. The souls of these men were "faint" indeed. The moral within them was the sport of the animal; conscience was submerged in the warm and turbulent wave of sensual feeling. Their moral souls rode faint and helpless on their impulses and passions, like an infant on an untrained, unbridled, and fiery steed, gasping for life, and every moment exposed to destruction.

(2) They are the subjects of spiritual perversity. Christ saw them not only "faint," but "*scattered abroad, as sheep having no shepherd.*" A sheep is one of those animals that seem to have a propensity to wander from their home, and to go astray ; nor does it seem to have any instinct to stimulate and guide it back to its lost pasture and position. Ascend some lofty height in nature, and behold the multitudes of sheep that are scattered, far away from the shepherd's care, and wide apart from each other, over the whole scene. One stands on an awful precipice, another on the frightful declivity of a bleak mountain, another is entangled in the thickets, another is assailed by a furious beast,—all are "faint" with hunger, and in peril. A short time ago you might have seen them all commingling together in one fold, under the beneficent care of a devoted shepherd, but now they have no connexion with each other. The great flock is split into sections—into individualities ; they have no interest in each other, and without proper pasture, shelter, and guardianship, they are weak, and exposed to ruin. Thus human souls appear to Christ. Sheep thus "*scattered*" were to Him types of men in their alienation from God and each other. They have left the fold of heaven ;—the golden tie of love which once bound them to each other is broken, and they are split into miserable unities, and are "*scattered*," one by one, over all the bleak scenes of selfishness, ignorance, and guilt. Though men are bound together by compacts, crowded together in populous cities, organized into companies and empires,—their souls, if sinners, are divided from each other, and scattered wide as the poles asunder.

This was the view of society which touched the heart of Christ. It was the moral state of the soul that affected Him ; and just as we assimilate to Him, will society affect us in this way. Lot's right-eous soul was grieved as he beheld the men of Sodom, and Paul's spirit was stirred within him as he looked into the heart of the philo-sophic and polished Athenian.

Secondly: *He regarded them as inadequately supplied with spiritual helpers.* " *The harvest truly is plenteous, but the labourers are few.*" The idea is not, we think, that they were *especially ripe for religious instruction,* but that the amount of true instruction they required far outstripped the capacity of existing teachers. There was no proportion between the vastness of the work and the fewness of the labourers. What errors, what prejudices, what habits, what propensities, in the case of each of the millions of the Jewish people now required to be worked off, and superseded by the principles of truth and the spirit of holiness, and how few were the men con-secrated to the work! Though labourers have greatly multiplied since the days of Christ, and though, perhaps, they are more numer-ous than ever, the disproportion here lamented by Christ, between the work and the workers, is as great to-day as ever. Who can think upon the multitude of sceptics, the millions of worldlings, the crowds of mere nominal Christians, the teeming myriads of heathens, in connexion with the few earnest Christian reformers, without exclaiming, " *The harvest is plenteous, but the labourers are few* "? Have we now one *true,* faithful, laborious Christian teacher to a hundred ?—to a thousand ?—to ten thousand ? The question, indeed, tends to oppress the energies and darken the hopes of the philanthropic soul. This disproportion between the work and the workers is, I confess, one of the most humbling and discouraging thoughts that steal over this doubting soul of mine.

II. THAT THE PHILANTHROPIST WHO DESIRES TO IMPROVE SOCIETY MUST DEVOUTLY LOOK TO HEAVEN FOR SUITABLE AGENTS. " *Pray ye therefore the Lord of the harvest, that He will send forth labourers into His harvest.*" But why should they look to Him?

First: *Because He has the deepest interest in the work.* He is "*the Lord of the harvest.*" All souls are His. The soul of the father as well as the soul of the son. Every grain in the great harvest-field of soul belongs to Him. Souls are " His husbandry." Who feels such an interest in an object as its proprietor ? Who can feel such an interest in the human soul as God ?

Secondly : *Because He alone can supply the men suitable to the work.* All men come from God—are His creatures—His property— His offspring. Each soul is a fresh emanation from Him. There is, indeed, nothing *new* beneath the sun but souls. Even the materials of the body we possess are old enough—as old as sun and stars —old as material nature itself. But our souls are new. They were never before we had them. New souls are streaming out from the eternal fountain of being every moment. But whilst all souls thus come forth from God, those that are fitted for spiritual labour are His children and messengers in an especial sense. He endows them with those particular attributes which qualify them for the work,—

He moulds their characters and inspires their faculties by His gracious influence. When Christ ascended up on high, He gave some to be apostles, &c. Great men—the men to do the spiritual labour of the world—must come from God.

Thirdly : *Because He gives the men suitable to the work in answer to prayer.* "*Pray ye,*" &c. Erect schools, found colleges, establish universities, promote the means of education to the utmost of your ability, if you will, but unless you get men of the right stamp, you have done but little to help the world. You have merely furnished tools, but you have no workmen to use them efficiently. One true man, fitted with the right faculties, and baptized with the true spirit—of the stamp of Elijah, or Paul, or Luther—would do more to help on the world than all your religious libraries, schools, and colleges. God's plan is to improve, elevate, and save man, by man. The want of the world is not so much better books, institutions, schools, churches, chapels, as better men—men of a higher and diviner type.

As God helps the world by men, I would suggest the following line of action to the Church. Let it have an agency whose mission it shall be to select from the humble classes of society—we say, the humble classes, because they are most obtainable—those children who are the *choicest specimens of the race;* children with the *largest supply of brain and heart, and physical vigour*—whose whole conformation is of the *highest type.* Let those, at the earliest possible age, be placed under the tuition and superintendence of teachers of the highest intellectual and moral mould, whose aim it shall be not to artificialize nature, or tie it down to any particular standard, but to develop its every power, afford scope to its every idiosyncrasy, and inspire it with the love of truth and freedom, humanity and God. Boys of this highest natural order, thus selected and trained, would, under God, become the kind of labourers the world wants. As God works by means, we believe that, through such an agency as this, in connexion with prayer, *He would send forth labourers equal to the work.*

Matthew 10:1-4

The True Labourers ; or, the Men for Saving Souls

One of the most solemn and practical questions that can engage our attention is this;—" *Who are the men to save souls ?* " The great want of man is *salvation.* The great end of Christ's mission to the world is *salvation.* " *This is a faithul saying, and worthy of all acceptation,*" &c. But who are the most suitable men for this work ? Who are the men who will be the most successful in presenting the Gospel, so as to save souls from the sway, guilt, and consequences of sin ? Now, in answer to this momentous question, I think it justifiable to infer, *that the men Christ personally and immediately appointed to the work were men of the most suitable description.* He did select, as a fact, certain men for this very work. If these men were not of the right description, it must be for one of three reasons; either (1) that He was ignorant of the kind of agency most suited, or (2) He was deceived in the attributes of the persons He appointed, or (3) that there were no others of a better kind that came within the reach of His choice. Now, we cannot entertain for a moment either of these hypotheses. Men are often guilty of the first. We often select improper men for certain departments of action, because we have not been able to form a correct judgment of the most suitable kind of agency. But this could not have been the case with Christ: He knew what was in man. Men are also often guilty of the second. How often are we deceived in men? How often do we suppose that they are able to do what they are entirely incompetent for? And as to the third, our range of choice is very restricted; we are obliged to select the best men we can get. But Christ had all men at His command. The men on philosophic chairs, and on imperial thrones, were as much at His command as the clerks at the receipt of custom and the fishermen on the shores of Galilee. We are, therefore, I say, justified in looking at these men He selected as the right class of men for saving souls.

Taking this view of the case, we infer :—

I. THAT IT IS NOT NECESSARY THAT THE MEN TO SAVE SOULS SHOULD BE DISTINGUISHED BY ANY PARTICULAR ADVENTITIOUS CIRCUMSTANCE OR ANY PARTICULAR MENTAL PECULIARITY. *Were they distinguished by anything adventitious?* Were they men who could boast of an illustrious ancestry? Were they possessors of princely fortunes? Were they of those who had won some of the splendid prizes of scholarship? or of those who held some high position in social or civil life? If so, it would be only natural to infer that such distinctions were necessary qualifications for the momentous work of saving souls, and that those only who were in possession of them were under the slightest obligation to attempt any effort in that direction. But such distinctions were foreign to these men. They were all of the humbler class, unknown to fame—toll gatherers, fishermen, and struggling sons of toil.

But although they were not men marked by any particular adventitious distinction, they might still, perhaps, be men distinguished by some one *particular* characteristic of mind. Was this so? All minds are not of the same order. Some are distinguished by the predominance of one faculty, and some of another;—some are marked by the imaginative and some by the metaphysical, some by the logical and some by the intuitional propensity and power. Did all these apostles belong to any one of these mental types? If so, one might conclude that the work of saving souls is limited to one particular order of mind, and that all others are perfectly free from the obligation. But these men did not belong to any *one* specific class of mind. Look at the utterances and acts of these men, so far as they are recorded. Their leading features of mind differ widely from each other. They seem to belong to every specific class. Some are, like Peter, greatly led by imagination, impressible and impulsive— ready to believe without evidence, and to act without thought; others, like Thomas, are reflective and enquiring, withholding faith until the most convincing evidence is brought. Some, like John, have those spiritual intuitions which enable them to feel that they are in God, and He in them; others, like Philip, are in intellectual search of the absolute, and refuse to be satisfied without proof. Their cry is, "Show us the Father, and it sufficeth us."

Now, if no particular adventitious distinction nor mental characteristic is necessary to save souls, we infer, *That souls, under God, are to be saved by man as man;* not by man as a scholar or sage; as a thinker, poet, or orator; as a sovereign, or a judge; but by man. The *obligation* is therefore on all.

II. IT IS NECESSARY TO BE INDOCTRINATED WITH THE PRINCIPLES, ENDOWED WITH THE POWER, AND GUIDED BY THE RULES OF CHRIST.

First: *It is necessary to be indoctrinated with the principles of Christ.* These were all "*disciples*" of Christ before He gave them their commission. "*When He had called unto Him His twelve disciples,*" &c. They had been taught by Him before He gave them their commission to teach; they were His pupils before He made them apostles; He made them disciples before He commissioned them to be His preachers. We infer, therefore, that Christian discipleship is a necessary qualification for Christian evangelship.

But what of Judas? Was he a *true* disciple? Yet was he not one of the apostles? His case was, confessedly, an exception to our principle—a wide exception too. Christ made no mistake in electing this man. The function of Judas, as one of the twelve, was perhaps, in usefulness, inferior to none. Though he served Christianity unintentionally, still the service he unwittingly rendered was of immense importance. Two facts will show the value of the service which Judas rendered to the holy cause. First: *Any suspicion of the moral purity of Christ's character would go greatly towards the obstruction of His system in the world.* If depraved men—either in the age of the apostles or afterwards— could have had the slightest ground for questioning the morality —the chastity, truthfulness, honesty, disinterestedness, and piety, of Christ, it is manifest that they would readily avail themselves of such a suspicion, to justify the most hearty and strenuous opposition to that class of doctrine and code of morals which are ever repugnant to the feelings of the corrupt heart. Secondly: *The sincere and spontaneous testimony to the perfect rectitude of His character by one who proved to be His greatest enemy, but who was allowed all the same intimacy with Him as that enjoyed by His most attached friends, would be the surest means to preclude the possibility of such a suspicion.* Had each of the twelve, who were privileged with all the intimacies of His friendship, and who were commissioned to promulgate His truth, been true to Him, the adverse world might have said, when it heard their eulogiums on His character, These men's judgments are either blinded by their feelings, or there is a deep and unyielding collusion between them ; and thus a suspicion might have been awakened which could not easily be put down. But when we find one of the number—one who had been let into the inner circle of His social life ; one who heard the very whispers of His heart—throwing off the mask of friendship, and coming forth as His fell betrayer and foe, but still bringing not the slightest charge of immorality against Him ; nay, when we find this same hypocrite, after his betraying act, stung with such a remorse of conscience as to make life intolerable, instead of being able to refer to the slightest impropriety in Christ's life in order to justify his wicked act, and appease, in some measure, his indignant conscience amidst his dying throes, involuntarily exclaiming, "*I am guilty of the blood of this just person,*"—when we find, I say, such a case as this, there seems an impossibility to entertain the shadow of a suspicion concerning the rectitude of Christ's character. Judas was a useful member of these twelve. Christianity required him, and Christ knew it.

His case, therefore, is no objection to our position. *That Christian discipleship is a necessary qualification for the work of saving souls.* The labourers wanted by the world must go forth from the school of Christ.

Secondly : *It is necessary to be endowed with the power of Christ.* "*He gave them power against unclean spirits,*" &c.

Some might say that if the apostles are the true specimens of men for saving souls, then their counterparts cannot be found; for they were endowed with miraculous power, and such endowments are not to be had now. It is true that the apostles had those supernatural endowments, which were confined to their own class and age ; but two thoughts will show that the *moral* power which Christ imparts now is far more than a compensation for the loss of the miraculous. First : *Much of what is true of the miraculous is also true of the moral.* (1) Was the miraculous something superadded to the natural energies of the soul ? So is the moral. Man has not, constitutionally, true moral force of soul, force of profound devotion, race-wide sympathy, and holy resolve—force whose root is in an identification of soul with the Great Will. (2) Was the miraculous specially derived from Christ ? So is the moral. There is no true moral force that comes to the soul of man that does not come from Him. (3) Was the miraculous given for the removal of spiritual and material evils—the casting out of "unclean spirits," and healing of "all manner" of bodily diseases ? So is the moral. Christ gives moral power for the very same purpose ; —for the purpose of removing all the evils that afflict the body, and expelling all the devils that infest the soul. Secondly: *What is not equally true of both shows the superior importance of the moral.* (1) The possession of the miraculous was no virtue. Wicked men might have been endowed—were, perhaps, endowed—with miraculous power, and did many "*mighty works.*" There was nothing more praiseworthy in a man being able to effect, by a power given to him at the moment, a supernatural deed, than in the little wire for transmitting the electric element; but true moral power is virtue. It is a praiseworthy thing for a man to be strong in his sympathies with the true, the beautiful, and the good. (2) The miraculous power cannot rectify or reach the moral springs of the soul. No miracle can change the current of feeling, destroy the moral habits, or turn the will. Miraculous power may cleave the mountains or arrest the stars, but it cannot reach the moral springs of soul. The soul is throned back in a pavilion into which no miraculous power can travel; but moral power—the power of truth and love—finds it out, reaches it by a whisper. Its still small voice can reverse its mightiest currents, and make its tempests cease. (3) The necessity of miraculous power might be superseded. Indeed miracles, to be of any service in the cause of truth, must cease at a point. Their constant occurrence would destroy their effect. But nothing can ever supersede the necessity of moral power: it is necessary to the man himself, necessary to society, necessary to the universe.

These remarks are sufficient to justify us in inferring, from the endowments of the apostles before us, that the men to save souls must be endowed with power from Christ. If the first apostles required miraculous power, much more do all successors in the holy work require moral. *Miraculous power is but the emblem and the handmaid of the moral.*

Matthew 10:5-42

The Laws, Issues, and Encouragements of an Evangelical Mission

In our last "disquisition" we noticed the twelve men whom Christ called to be His apostles. From His selection we inferred the kind of men required to save souls. We concluded, from the fact that He chose such men as these twelve, first, That it is not *necessary* that the men to save souls should be distinguished by any particular adventitious circumstance, or any particular mental peculiarity; and, secondly, That it is necessary that they should be indoctrinated with the principles, endowed with the power, and guided by the rules of Christ.

It is this last—*the rules or laws which Christ enjoined upon these twelve* when He " sent them forth"—that we shall first consider now.

Believing as we do, with Stier, that whatever Christ "spoke from time to time, He spoke for futurity, even to its final end; yea, even to eternity itself;"—that "the present and the immediate are the type of the more remote;"—and that, in sending forth these "twelve" He contemplates all later missions of these apostles and their successors; regarding, I say, Christ's commission in this light, I feel warranted in looking at these verses as giving the *laws, issues, and encouragements*, of an evangelical mission in every age.

I. THE LAWS OF AN EVANGELICAL MISSION. Every Christian is professedly an evangelist. And the question therefore is of general importance: How is the evangelical mission to be worked out? Has Christ laid down any laws to guide us in the work, or is it left to the mere caprice of every individual? Churches and individuals have acted as if no definite rules existed. As in the working out the evangelical mission in these times, it is not frequently that you can discover the intelligent, regular, and harmonious operations of law, it is natural to ask, Are there laws specifically applicable to the enterprise? If so, it may be that in the Church's neglect of these we may find much of its want of success.

Now, regarding the principles which Christ enjoined upon "the twelve," when He "*sent them forth*," as equally binding upon all Christians, in every age, we shall proceed to specify these principles as laws which should rule every Church in its endeavours to propagate the Gospel.

We infer, from this commission of Christ to His apostles, the following laws,—

First: *That the chief sphere of its labours should be the nearest its home.* "*Go not into the way of the Gentiles, and into any city of the Samaritans enter ye not: but go rather to the lost sheep of the house of Israel.*" The fact that Jesus Himself confined His labours to Judea, and that in the commission He gave to His disciples before His ascension to heaven, He distinctly commanded them to "*begin at Jerusalem*," and thence on,—acting ever on the most proximate,—fully authorises us in regarding this injunction to the twelve as an expression of a *general law* that should regulate all evangelizing efforts. This law is not an arbitrary impost; it is founded in the truest *love* and *wisdom*. Genuine LOVE says, If you have a favour to bestow, offer it first to those of your own kin and neighbourhood. *Home first*, is the dictate of a true philanthropy. That feeling which induces man to cross seas, and to traverse islands and continents, to offer blessings which he has never presented to his own neighbours, who stand in equal need, is the simpering sentiment of a morbid and diseased mind, not the manly love of a true heart. The law is the dictate of WISDOM as well as love. (1) We have greater facilities for giving the Gospel to our neighbours than to foreigners. They are within our reach, they understand our language, they can appreciate our mode of reasoning, they can test the sincerity of our motives. (2) Our neighbours, when evangelized, would become more effective allies than foreigners. The stronger the forces in the centre, the more powerfully the influence will be felt at the extremities. All this is especially true where the neighbours are the men of this metropolis. What city—to use the language we have elsewhere employed *—would be such an auxiliary to help the glorious work as London, were it converted? It is the fountain of an influence whose streams meander through all the institutions, cities, towns, villages, mansions, and hovels of the civilised world. You cannot fight the moral battles of the Gospel unless you get London as your faithful and loving ally. When the Church wins London, it wins the world!

Another law binding on the Church, in its evangelizing efforts, which we discover in this commission, is,—

Secondly: *That the material wants of mankind are to be attended to as well as the spiritual.* "*And as ye go, preach, saying, The kingdom of heaven is at hand. Heal the sick, cleanse the lepers, raise the dead, cast out devils.*" The command to preach "*the kingdom of heaven*" implies: (1) That the great *spiritual* want of mankind is the *reign of God* over all the powers of the soul—the making of the human will in everything cheerfully obedient to the divine. (2) The gospel is the system by which this reign is established: hence it is called "*the kingdom of heaven.*" It is not a system merely to excite the sensibilities, or to enlighten and discipline the intellect: it is the *reign* of God in the soul. (3) The work of the Church is to bring the Gospel to man for this purpose. This is its work, so far as the spiritual necessity of mankind is concerned.

But, then, while attending to this work, do not be regardless of the *material* exigencies of humanity. "Heal the sick," "raise the dead," &c.

Now, the fact that the apostles were endowed with power to remove the physical evils of mankind in their evangelical mission, and commanded to employ them, does certainly give the idea that the Church, in her endeavours to propagate the Gospel, must be mindful, at the same time, of the corporeal and temporal requirements of men. This principle was acted upon in the ministry of Christ, and is everywhere implied, and often explicitly enjoined, in the writings of the apostles. St. Paul tells us to "*bear each other's burdens, and so fulfil the law of Christ.*" St. James tells us, that "*pure and undefiled religion before God and the Father is this, to visit the fatherless and widows in their affliction;*" and St. John says, "*Whoso hath this world's good, and seeth his brother have need, and shutteth up his bowels of compassion from him, how dwelleth the love of God in him?*" This is a principle, obedience to which seems almost indispensable to success in the promotion of Christianity. (1) Corporeal evils are obstructions to the reception of the truth. Men suffering under disease, poverty, slavery, oppression, are certainly not in the best position to receive the Gospel. The natural tendency of corporeal evils is to strengthen depravity, close the heart against God and man, and nurse misanthropy and impiety into a chronic state. (2)

* See *Homilist*, vol. v., p. 37.

Earnest efforts to remove the corporeal evils of a people are amongst the most likely means to dispose them to listen to our doctrines. These evils are *felt;* and he who generously removes them is hailed as a benefactor, and the heart opens to his words. Job says, that when the ear heard him, it "blessed" him. Why? Because he "*delivered the poor that cried, and the fatherless, and him that had none to help him.*" Had the Church always acted upon this principle ;—had it endeavoured to give bread to the hungry as well as Bibles to the ignorant; had it sought to deliver man from the social and political despotism of his fellow as well as from the despotism of Satan ; had it struggled to redeem the body as well as the soul ; had it appeared to men more as a secular benefactor, and less as a theological belligerent, an ascetic devotee, or a sectarian partizan ; had the world seen it more in the acts of a genial messenger of a deep and genuine philanthropy, penetrating the darkest scenes of trial with a word to cheer and a hand to bless, and less in pompous ceremonies, conflicting creeds, and affected pietisms ;—I say, had this been the past history of the Church, it would have been now the sovereign of the world.*

Another law which we discover in this commission to "the twelve," binding on all Christians in their efforts to propagate the Gospel, is,—

Thirdly : *That the same disinterested benevolence which has made us the recipients of the blessing, should animate us in its communication.* "*Freely ye have received, freely give.*" This does not refer merely to the miraculous power of healing, &c., but includes the spiritual power of preaching as well. What you have received for this work, you have received freely, without merit, without recompense. From disinterested love you have received all, therefore give what you have received from the same principle. Three ideas are implied in the words : (1) That whatever good we have is the free gift of God. (2) That the good we possess we have the power of communicating; and (3) That, in the communication, we should be actuated by disinterested benevolence. "*Freely give :*" don't make a gain of your ministry. The disciples would have a temptation in this direction. Endowed with such extraordinary powers of healing, as well as with soul-expanding doctrines, many of them whom they benefited would be likely to offer them splendid presents. The prohibition, therefore, was specially tiresome. Christianity can only be effectually propagated by *disinterested* efforts. It must be given "*freely,*" not for the sake of office, sect, or gain, but for the gain of souls. "*Freely give ;*"—"a comprehensive and most

* See *Homilist,* vol. ii. The success of modern missions may be attributed in a great degree to the fact that missionaries have been recognised as secular benefactors. Though they have not been able to work miracles as their credentials of their mission, many have secured attention for their message by their skill in the treatment of bodily disease, by the introduction of domestic arts and manufactures as well as of improved systems of agriculture. They have been the physicians, the legislators, the political economists, the promoters of trade, commerce, and industry, in addition to their especial function of religious teachers.

pregnant position, which cannot be too much laid to heart by God's ambassadors, even to the present day; condemning all improper, methodical, and commercial stipulations in preaching God's grace; all payment that surpasses the limit of their need (ver. 10); and all those unbecoming perquisites which are ungracefully attached to the direct ministration of the word and sacraments."*

How little of this free and spontaneous action have we in the Christian Church! How much is done from sympathy with a sect, the spirit of worldly competition, the love of gain, power, and praise! How few work "*freely*" under the inspiration of that divine benevolence which swallows up all ideas of self and sect in sympathy with the general good and the glory of God!

Another law which we discover in this commission to "*the twelve*," binding upon all who are engaged in evangelizing efforts, is,—

Fourthly : *That there must be an entire freedom of mind from all secular anxieties in the work.* "*Provide neither gold, nor silver, nor brass in your purses, nor scrip for your journey, neither two coats, neither shoes, nor yet staves : for the workman is worthy of his meat.*" Naturally enough might the disciples have thought, when the command came, upon preparing a suitable outfit for the journey. They were to leave their homes, and go amongst strangers, and that with a message not likely at first to win their favour. Should not provision be made? Surely they thought, when the message came, that an equipment of money, food, and raiment was necessary, and they would feel anxious how best to make it. But Christ checks at once their rising solicitude. Provide nothing, He says : go as you are. Put not an additional fraction in your purse. Don't take a second garment with you, nor even provision for the next meal. Start at once, as you are. Now, probably it would be a " narrow perversion —a fanaticism of the letter,"—to regard this prohibition as *literally* binding upon all who are engaged in evangelizing labours; but the spirit and meaning of the command—namely, *entire freedom of mind from all secular anxieties*—are undoubtedly binding on all evangelists. Solicitude about gold or silver, purse or scrip, should have no place in the minds of those who endeavour to convert mankind to the religion of Christ. There are two things which should always exclude this anxiety: (1) Faith in the munificent providence of our Master. He is ever with His true servants, and always able to guard them in every peril, and to supply their every want. (2) Faith in the power of the Gospel to dispose those amongst whom we labour to render the necessary temporal provisions. Men who are rightly influenced by the ministry of a man will feel that " the workman is worthy of his meat." Indeed, it seems to me that Jesus here throws the support of His apostles upon the people they would preach to ; as if He had said, Don't be anxious about temporal provisions. By a law of the human mind, a *feeling of moral obligation* to support you will be awakened in those whom you bless by your message. The Gospel " workman is worthy of his meat." Worthy indeed !

* Stier.

What temporal return bears any proportion to the good which a man conveys to another who is instrumental in breaking the moral slumbers of the mind, unsealing the fountains of spiritual feeling, rolling off the sepulchral stone that entombs the soul, unswathing it of its death robes, and raising it into fellowship with God?

Another law we discern in this commission to the "twelve," binding upon all their evangelizing efforts, is,—

Fifthly : *That our conduct towards men should be ever regulated by their moral condition.* "*And into whatsoever city or town ye shall enter, inquire who in it is worthy; and there abide till ye go thence. And when ye come into an house, salute it. And if the house be worthy, let your peace come upon it; but if it be not worthy, let your peace return to you,*" &c. (1) Their visits to men were to be determined by their *spiritual* state. When they entered a city, they were to inquire, not for the rich, influential, and secularly distinguished, but for those who were inwardly worthy of their message. The worthy were not those who *deserved*, but those who *desired* the blessings they had to offer. Those who were hungry in soul—who were *waiting for the consolation of Israel.* (2) Their treatment of men was to be determined by their spiritual state : if the "house be worthy"—if the family are those who are thirsting after the true peace, give them the benediction; but if the family be not "worthy," let the peace return to you. "The blessing will cling to the place where it meets with welcome :" but where it meets with no resting-place, "it returns to those that pronounced it, as to its source of life. "*Whosoever shall not receive you, nor hear your words, when ye depart out of that house or city shake off the dust of your feet.*" The ἐκτινάσσειν κονιορτὸν —shaking off the dust—is a mere symbolical representation of total and utter separation and renunciation. (Acts xiii. 51 : xviii. 6.) To express an idea by means of an act is, in the Old Testament as well as in the New Testament, and, indeed, throughout the whole of the East, a very common process. This kind of language or speech is, to the sensuous man, more impressive than words. (Compare Matt. xxvii. 24.) The symbolical action expresses, perhaps, three ideas : (1) A disavowal of all connexion. (2) A horror of taking away aught that belongs to them, not even "dust." (3) A renunciation of all participation in their guilt.

The great principle of the whole is, *That our conduct towards men should be regulated by their moral character, not by their secular circumstances.* Whoever the man is, if he is "worthy," visit him, bless him, dwell with him, if convenient. If not "worthy," however rich or influential, have nothing to do with him : shake off the dust from your shoes. *Know no man after the flesh.* As evangelists, we have to do with souls, and the only distinction we have to recognise is the distinction of character.

Another law which we discover in this commission to "the twelve," binding on all engaged in evangelical labours, is,—

Sixthly : *That the highest intelligence should be blended with the purest character.* "*Be ye therefore wise as serpents, and harmless as doves.*" As serpents were proverbially sharp-sighted, and doves proverbially inoffensive, the two are selected to show the importance of uniting *purity* and *intelligence* together; guilelessness of character with sagacity of judgment; subtilty of intellect with simplicity of heart. The nature of the serpent and that of the dove are to be united in the true evangelist. These two poles of character are to be brought together. The worth of each in character, depends upon their combination. The mere dove-simplicity alone in a man would be little else than childlike inanity; and the serpent-sagacity alone would be nothing but cunning and craft. Temper them both together—let the ingenuous and the philosophic be properly blended—and there will be the qualifications of an evangelist. Alas! these are not frequently found in their true combination in those who are seeking to propagate the Gospel. Sometimes you see a disingenuous sagacity, which interests with its feats of cleverness, but more frequently repels the heart by its selfish cunning, and always fails to win the soul by its appeals. And sometimes you see a simpering non-intelligent simplicity which excites the contempt and ridicule of the thoughtful. Oh for a coalition of these attributes, now so separate! May purity of principle and wisdom of policy soon wed and work in every church.

Christ here gives a good *reason* why these two elements of character should be united:—" *I send you forth as sheep in the midst of wolves.*" You are to labour amongst a population as malignant and as cunning as wolves; therefore be as "*wise as serpents and as harmless as doves.*" As if He had said, The malign emotion can only be borne down by the inoffensive and amiable; be harmless as doves, therefore. The cunning can only be met and mastered by superior wisdom; be wise, therefore, as serpents. The general truth is, that *intellect in the world must be met by intellect in the church, and depravity in the world must be met by purity in the church.* An intellectual age will never bow to a weak-minded ministry; a depraved age will never be reformed by a corrupt church.

Another law we discover in this commission to "the twelve," binding upon all in their evangelizing efforts, is,—

Seventhly : *That confidence in the paternal providence of God should be strong enough to raise us above the fear of men.* Christ commands them not to be afraid of either of the two following things: (1) Not of the accusations of enemies. " *They will deliver you up to the councils, and they will scourge you in the synagogues; and ye shall be brought before governors and kings for my sake, for a testimony against them and the Gentiles. But when they deliver you up, take no thought how or what ye speak : for it shall be given you in that same hour what ye shall speak. For it is not ye that speak, but the Spirit of your Father which speaketh in you.*" As we become *self-oblivious*, absorbed in universal love and piety, we become the true organs of the Divine. Let our own selfish thoughts vanish, and the Spirit of our Father will speak through us, and speak the things suitable to the hour. *We grow divine in thought as we feel dependence upon the infinite in-*

tellect. Man gets divine inspiration only by losing himself in the divine will. (2) Christ commands them not to be afraid of the malignity of enemies. "*Fear not them which kill the body, and are not able to kill the soul: but rather fear him which is able to destroy both soul and body in hell.*" This verse, analyzed, would give the following ideas. First: that human nature is made up of body and soul. Some beings have body only; some perhaps, have soul only; —man unites them both. Secondly: that the corporeal part may be destroyed, whilst the spiritual remains uninjured. "The soul, secure in her existence, smiles at the drawn dagger, and defies the point." Thirdly: That the honest working out of a divine commission may expose the body to destruction, but the neglect of the duty would expose both body and soul to the destruction of Satan.* Fourthly: As an inference from the last, that the only "fear" which a good man should have is of that dereliction of duty which would place him in the power of Satan, the fell destroyer. Fear not man, but fear the devil; fear not bodily injuries in duty, but fear moral ones; fear not suffering, but fear sin. You may kill your soul by saving your body, if, in doing so, you neglect a duty or commit a wrong; and, on the other hand, you may save your soul by allowing your body to be martyred in the prosecution of the right.

Such, then, are the LAWS OF EVANGELIZATION which Jesus inculcated in this commission, and which we regard as binding upon the church in all ages. If these have been neglected or transgressed, it is certainly no wonder that the evangelizing work has made but little progress. The case stands thus: Christ committed the work of evangelizing the world to the church, and gave distinct and enlightened directions how it was to be carrried out. The church has been aiming and struggling for the end, but it has been comparatively regardless of the method. Is my allegation unfounded? Then I ask, Which of the seven laws which I have specified has the church not transgressed? Has it always *made the chief sphere of its labour the nearest its home?* On the wings of a mere sentimental charity, it has often left the masses in its neighbourhood to expend its energies in distant scenes. It has gone abroad to destroy evil when evil was most rampant at its own door. Has it always sought to attend to the *material wants of mankind as well as the spiritual?* Has it not *frequently*, and almost *systematically*, separated the two interests; cared little or nothing

---

* Stier regards Satan as referred to here. First: Because the fundamental idea of the whole discourse is not to be afraid of God, but to confide in Him. Its spirit is, Trust in Him who can protect you, but fear him who would destroy you. Secondly: Because, as the two members of the sentence run parallel, it is not allowable to use φοβεῖσθαι in two distinct senses. Thirdly: The destruction of the soul is never spoken of as being the work of God. Fourthly: The true and more profound sense of the whole saying cannot be developed on the other supposition. It would be very strange and inexplicable to unite in one the command to fear God, who casts into hell, and to trust Him as a merciful Father. But the two clauses are not exactly parallel, as ἀπό occurs in the first, but not in the second; the same word is often used in the same sentence in different senses; θόεος includes filial fear and servile dread. (See *Dean Alford.*)

about the political oppressions, the physical wants, and the domestic trials of men, while it pretended to be filled with unutterable concern for their souls? It has acted the part of the Levite in relation to man's body: left it lying in agony on the road, plundered and mangled by robbers and thieves, when it should have acted as the Samaritan. Has the same *disinterested love which God displays in imparting religion to man, actuated the church in its endeavours to propagate it?* Has it " freely " given? Has it not been actuated more by the love of gain, or praise, or sect, than by the free love for souls and God? Has it *always had a mind free from solicitude about purse, and scrip, and gold?* Has there been no worldly spirit displayed in its operations? Has its *respect towards men been always governed more by their spiritual worthiness than secular respectability?* Has it gone, in its visitations, more to the morally worthy than to the secularly rich? Has it *blended the highest intelligence with the purest character?* Has it not sometimes displayed nothing but the " craft " of the serpent, and sometimes nothing but the weak inóffensiveness of the dove? How seldom have you seen the two attributes in their true proportions? Has *faith in the paternal superintendence always raised it above the fear of men?* Let the church, instead of being regulated by the policy of little human organization, go back in spirit to Capernaum; stand, with " the twelve," before Christ; listen to His commission, and pledge itself to carry that commission out according to His directions ;—let this be done, and the dawn of the brightest era will commence—the key-note of the highest harmony will be struck.

These verses bring under our notice—

II. THE ISSUES OF AN EVANGELICAL MISSION. As it is always our endeavour to elicit the *general* truths of a passage, we frequently find it inconvenient to follow the exact order of the words : that is, to expound verse by verse *seriatim*. This, in many cases, would lead to much tautology and confusion of thought.

What are the results on human souls which the proper working out of an evangelical mission will produce? In other words, What moral effects on men will arise from the promotion of Christianity in the world? The chapter under review enables us to answer that the effects are threefold :—*Spiritual peace to the receiver, augmented guilt to the rejecter, and great trials to the promoter.*

First : *Spiritual peace to the receiver.* "*And into whatsoever city or town ye shall enter, inquire who in it is worthy ; and there abide till ye go thence. And when ye come into an house, salute it. And if the house be worthy, let your peace come upon it*" (11–13). We have already remarked upon these verses, so far as they relate to the behaviour of the evangelist. The point to be noticed now is, that they were, as the messengers of Christ, the communicators of *peace* to those who properly received their message. "*Peace be to this house*" or family. These words were not to be used as the empty phrase of etiquette and conventional greeting, but as the spirit and burden of their mission; as the expression of the profoundest desire of their souls, and the highest end of their office as the apostles of Christ.

The apostles, then, in their salutation, expressed the grand object of Christianity, which is to give "*peace.*" Its language to every family and soul it addresses is, "*Peace be unto you.*" Its author is the "Prince of Peace." The celestial song that announced His nativity proclaimed "*peace on earth;*" the last legacy He left the world was peace. His word is the "gospel of peace;" His empire is "peace in the Holy Ghost." To all who yield to His benign teachings and gracious influences, He imparts a "peace that passeth all understanding." What is this peace? Though it can only be fully appreciated by experience, it may be—it often is—misunderstood. What is it? It stands opposed to four things: (1) *To the moral quiescence of the thoughtless.* There are souls whose consciences are in a torpid state. Their passions work, and their intellectual powers play, but their moral sense—the heart of their being—is dormant. Its eyes are closed: it sees not the sad portents that everywhere cloud their moral heavens. Its ears are sealed, and deaf to those distant moanings in the atmosphere which are prophetic of awful tempests. This is not peace; it is the sleep of the lion, which invigorates impulses that shall wake into augmented fury. It is that unhealthy quiet of nature which forges thunderbolts and collects fuel for the lightning. True peace is the peace of a quickened, active conscience, that has done battle with lusts and evil habits, won the victory, and obtained the throne of the soul; ruling all by the harmonious will of God. True peace stands opposed (2) *to all anxieties of soul.* Men are harassed by four kinds of anxiety—*speculative, secular, social,* and *spiritual.* There are anxieties arising from our utter incompetency to solve many of the problems which the Bible, history, and experience, press heavily on our hearts. There are anxieties arising from the circumstances of ourselves and families in relation to corporeal wants; there are anxieties arising from the injustice of society, the faithlessness of professed friends, the bereavements of death; and there are anxieties arising from a sense of guilt, and a desire for salvation. True peace is opposed to all these anxieties. It expels all anxious thoughts. The intellect trusts to the wisdom and goodness of God for a solution of all perplexing problems; the heart confides in the paternal providence of God for all necessary temporal good; the spirit is divinely guided to form those friendships which, when dissolved on earth, will be renewed in heaven; and the soul trusts implicitly to the merits and mercy of Christ for complete salvation. He that believeth entereth into a rest from all these harassing anxieties. True peace stands opposed (3) *to all religious inactivity.* Inaction and true peace are opposite states. Peace of soul, like the peace of planets, consists in harmonious action. The "God of peace" is ever at work. "He fainteth not, neither is weary." The moral rest of God is right action. The "Prince of Peace" went about doing good. True peace of soul is not the peace of a stagnant lake, but the peace of a flowing river, too deep to be rippled, too strong to be resisted.

To give the world this peace is the grand aim of Christianity, and this is one of the results of its operations.

Another result of an evangelical mission is,—

Secondly. *Augmented guilt to the rejecter.* "*Let your peace return to you. And whosoever shall not receive you, nor hear your words, when ye depart out of that house or city, shake off the dust of your feet. Verily I say unto, It shall be more tolerable for the land of Sodom and Gomorrah in the day of judgment, than for that city.*" (13–15.) These words suggest two ideas touching the augmented guilt of the rejecter :—(1) *That his guilt is no injury to the minister who has offered him the blessing.* His peace shall "*return*" to him. The stream of pacific sentiment and desire which he sent forth from the depths of his heart, when it finds no resting-place, shall flow back, in all its plenitude, into his own soul. The idea, perhaps, is, that the attempt to do good, even if it fail in its object, is nevertheless no injury to the agent. The honest effort of usefulness, reacting upon the agent, comes back to his own soul with interest. The attempt to do good is good to him who makes the effort, even though the object be injured by it. Notwithstanding this, ministers are not to waste their time and energy upon the incorrigible. "*Whosoever shall not receive you nor hear your words, when ye depart out of that house or city, shake off the dust of your feet.*" The Hebrews were accustomed to express truths by dramatic actions. Isaiah walked three years naked and barefoot, to express the utter destitution and shame that would befall the Egyptian and Ethiopian captives. (Isa. xx. 2–4.) Elijah, for many days, ate his bread by weight, and drank his water by measure, to intimate the terrible famine that was about to visit the land. Jesus took up a little child, and placed him in the midst of the assembly, to express the importance of meekness and simplicity of character. The Bible, in fact, abounds with such specimens of dramatic teaching. In accordance with this custom, the apostles are commanded to perform a dramatic act towards those who neglected their heavenly overtures, in order to express their horror at the guilt of their conduct. Another idea which the verses under review suggest in relation to the guilt of the rejecter, is—(2) *That his guilt will be fully manifest at the judgment day.* "*Verily I say unto you, It shall be more tolerable,*" &c. This verse contains four solemn truths. First: *That there is a period of retribution to dawn on our race.* It is here called "the day of judgment." The state of the world requires such a day ;—oppressed virtue cries out for such a day ;—the Bible distinctly declares that there will come such a day. Every day of our life has some gleams of retribution that prophesy and mirror something of such a day. Secondly : *That men of remotest ages will be concerned in the transactions of that day.* The men of Sodom and Gomorrah, as well as the men of our Saviour's age, will be there. Two thousand years had passed away since Sodom and Gomorrah were destroyed; but Jesus teaches here that they are not gone out of existence; they shall appear agian on the day of judgment. All will appear then. Thirdly: *That amongst the myriads who will appear on this day, there will be an immense variety in the degree of guilt.* "*More tolerable,*" &c. Every land, and age, and individual, will have their peculiarities of guilt. Some of the sinners will appear almost innocent in comparison with others. Fourthly: *That diversity of guilt will, in a great degree, arise from the amount of religious opportunity abused.* Sodom and Gomorrah will appear guilty. They had nature in her most suggestive and poetic forms; they had Lot to preach to them. But their guilt will appear as nothing to the guilt of those who had the teachings of Christ and His apostles.

The Gospel, then, augments the guilt of the rejecter, as well as imparts true peace to its receivers. It is the "*savour of death unto death,*" as well as of life unto life. But it produces life by *design* and *adaptation*, death only by contingency. It is the moral *cause* of life; it is only the *occasion* of death.

The other result is—

Thirdly: *Great trials to the promoter.* Christ here states the great trials which His apostles would meet with in their endeavour to promote His doctrines. These trials would arise :—(1) *From the spirit of the world in relation to His system.* The spirit of the Jews, in reference to Him, was like that of a *wolf* (ver. 16)—selfish and savage. As this ravenous beast prowls about in search of its prey, the Jewish people pursued the Lamb of God. From this spirit, Christ tells His disciples, great trials would come to them. They would be delivered up to "*the council;*" they would be "*scourged in their synagogues;*" they would be "*brought before governors;*" they would be "*hated of all men*" for His "*name's sake.*" This savage spirit would thus express itself. Mankind, in their depraved state, have always more or less of this spirit in relation to the Gospel; and from it has always arisen to the disciples of Christ persecution in some form or other. The other cause which is here suggested as producing trials to the evangelist, is (2) *the influence of His system in producing social divisions.* "*The brother shall deliver up the brother to death, and the father the child: and the children shall rise up against their parents,*" &c. "*Think not that I come to send peace on the earth. I came not to send peace, but a sword.*" "*I am come to set a man at variance with his father,*" &c. Three considerations will perhaps explain this language,—which sounds somewhat strange on the lips of the Prince of Peace :—(1) That, as a matter of fact, His doctrines do create divisions amongst men, even where there is the closest physical relationship. In the same family the receiver and the rejecter separate most widely in soul—pass off into opposite moral directions of thought, sympathy, and purpose. The cause of this is not in Christianity, but in the depravity of the rejecter. Christianity is simply the occasion of its development. Nutritious food may be hurtful to a diseased stomach, light may be most injurious to a diseased eye, music most distressing to a diseased brain : and so Christianity, which is designed and fitted to produce peace, will always produce the opposite in the heart of the rejecter. (2) The feelings which these divisions create are generally, on the part of the rejecter, most malignant. Matthew Henry justly says :— " The most violent feuds have ever been those that have arisen from difference in religion. No enmity like that of the persecutors : no resolution like that of the persecuted." The struggle is always fierce and invincible. (3) As the result of all this, the promoters of Christianity are to expect opposition, and even persecution. " *I am come not to send peace, but a sword.*" As if the Divine Reformer had said, Do not expect that, because my doctrines are essentially pacific, and because my grand aim is peace, and your mission is peace, that you will meet with no opposition. Awful and bloody wars will frequently, though always *incidentally*, come out of your pacific mission. The moral atmosphere of the world is so charged with impurities, that bitter storms must come before men can have the salubrious and sunny influence of celestial peace.

Now, the fact that Christ warned His disciples of all this opposition, shows four things :—(1) *His thorough honesty.* He wished them thoroughly to understand the difficulties of their work before starting. He was no deceiver. (2) *His knowledge of human nature.* He knew exactly what influence His system would have upon the heart of the world, and what moral tempests it would evolve from the soul of depravity. (3) *The strength of the disciples.* The fact that they went forth at all with such terrible prospects shows the strength of their faith. (4) *The necessity for encouragements.*

This leads us to the third and last general division of our subject :—

III. THE ENCOURAGEMENTS OF AN EVANGELICAL MISSION. Christ here supplies them with an unsparing hand. Let us briefly elicit them.

First : *The cause for which the true evangelist suffers is most honourable.* Jesus says that they are " *for my name's sake.*" (Ver. 22.) We might well ask, What was there in the *name* of Christ, to excite malignant feelings against His friends ? There are infamous names in history suited to awaken the profoundest contempt and the most indignant ire of humanity. But Christ's name stands for all that is amiable in spirit, immaculate in character, sublime in purpose, Godlike in beneficence and majesty. To suffer for the sake of mere worldly heroes might be a disgrace; but to suffer for Christ's sake is the greatest honour for man this side of heaven. The apostles, and confessors, and martyrs, felt this amid their severest tortures. They thanked God that they were " *counted worthy.*" To suffer for Christ is to suffer for the promotion of truth, rectitude, benevolence, and happiness, amongst men.

Secondly : *The example which the true evangelist has in His suffering is most glorious. " The disciple is not above his master, nor the servant above his lord. It is enough for the disciple that he be as his master, and the servant as his lord. If they have called the master of* *the house Beelzebub,*** *how much more shall they call them of his household ?* " (Verses 24, 25.) " The various etymologies of Beelzebub, or Beelzebul," says Stier, " about which contention is raised, do not affect the subject; for this is certain, at least, that it was a name of the chief of the devils, and a particularly scornful one, used by such as would not do him the honour of his more dignified name, ' Satan,' —διάβολος." By giving this name to Christ, therefore, His enemies expressed the most malignant contempt. Here, then, is the example of the true evangelist—His sufferings. But how does the fact that Christ suffered in His public ministry give an encouragement to all evangelists under their sufferings ? (1) Because if the Master suffered in His work, these sufferings are no proofs, in themselves, that they are disqualified for their mission. (2) Because if their Master suffered in His work, these sufferings were not necessarily connected with any disgrace. There are ignominious sufferings. (3) Because if their Master suffered in His work, their sufferings were no necessary indications of Divine displeasure. (4) Because if their Master suffered in His work, there would be hope that their sufferings would issue in the same glorious results. They would hope to overcome as He overcame.

Thirdly : *The success of the cause for which the true evangelist suffers is most certain.* " *There is nothing covered, that shall not be revealed ; and hid, that shall not be known. What I tell you in darkness, that speak ye in light : and what ye hear in the ear, that preach ye upon the housetops.*" (Verses 26, 27.) The idea here is, that the doctrines which were comparatively concealed, shut up in the breasts of some twelve men, should one day become fully and universally known. He assures them (1) that they *would* spread. " What I tell you in darkness *shall* be known," &c. We are engaged in no doubtful enterprise : the little " cloud " shall cover the heavens, the little " stone " shall grow into a mountain, the " mustard seed " shall become a majestic tree. Those doctrines, which Jesus quietly whispered in the ear of twelve poor men, shall one day roll in streams of rapturous music through the world. He assures them (2) that they *ought* to spread. He not only predicts that they shall, but commands His disciples to set in earnest to the work. " *Preach ye upon the housetops.*" Jesus had not one doctrine for the initiated, and another for the commonalty. His truths were for the race, and race-wide should be the proclamation. Here, then, is encouragement. " *Therefore be ye steadfast, unmoveable,*" &c.

Fourthly : *The providential care of God over the true evangelist in*

---

* Beelzebub—German, Fliegen—*Baal* (2 Kings i. 2), was an Ekronitish deity ; so called because a power was ascribed to him of removing troublesome flies. Zeus —" Jupiter "—had the cognomen or epithet, ἀπόμυιος, " the driver away of flies ; " μυίαγρος, " fly-catcher."—*Olshausen.* How this particular name of an object of heathen worship came to be used among the Jews as a title of the Evil One, does not appear. The principle of such an adaptation is to be found in the contemptuous titles as " an abomination," " vanity," " lie," employed to denote idols, and in the fact stated by Paul from Moses, and generally received among the Jews, that the things which the Gentiles sacrifice they sacrifice unto devils (1 Cor. x. 20).

suffering is positively guaranteed. "Are not two sparrows sold for a farthing ? and one of them shall not fall on the ground without your Father. But the very hairs of your head are all numbered. Fear ye not therefore, ye are of more value than many sparrows." (Verses 29–31.) The argument in these verses may be thrown into three propositions, which they either imply or express :—(1) That in the estimation of the great God, some of His creatures are more valuable than others. Men are more valuable than birds. *" Ye are of more value than many sparrows."* (2) That over those of His creatures which are the lowest in the scale of value, He exercises a benevolent providence. Not one of the sparrows *"falls on the ground without your Father."* Over all life, even plantal life, He exercises care. *" The lilies of the field,"* &c. (3) That the fact that He exercises a benevolent providence over the *least* valuable, is an assurance that He does so over the *most* valuable. If He takes care of the lesser, He will surely take care of the greater." Hence *" the very hairs "* of His children's heads *"* are all numbered." Here, then, is encouragement to the true evangelist under suffering. He may say, with Job, *" He knoweth the way I take,"* &c.

Fifthly : *The reward of the true evangelist for all sufferings will be most glorious at last. " Whosoever therefore shall confess me before men, him will I confess also before my Father which is in heaven. But whosoever shall deny me before men, him will I also deny before my Father which is in heaven."* (Verses 32, 33.) These words contain three ideas :—(1) The function of true discipleship. To " confess " Christ ;—to confess Him as the Messiah—the redeeming God. To confess not merely with the lip, but *practically* with the life; not in solitude, but *" before men "* on the open theatre of life; not merely in the temple, but in the market, the senate, at the bar—everywhere. (2) The temptation of true discipleship. There is a temptation to be *"ashamed"* of Him, and to *" deny "* Him. This arises from two causes—the natural tendency of the individual to bow to the opinions of the multitude, and the fact that the opinions of the multitude are generally against Christ. Herein is the temptation. In heaven, where all love Christ, there is no such temptation. The influence flows in the other direction. (3) The reward of true discipleship. *" Him will I confess also before my Father which is in heaven."* I will acknowledge Him before the Eternal and His assembled universe, as my devoted disciple, my faithful servant, my beloved friend. What a reward is this !

Another encouragement is,—

Sixthly : *That if actuated by the right spirit, the true evangelist will find the greatest trials the greatest blessings. " He that taketh not his cross, and followeth after me, is not worthy of me. He that findeth his life shall lose it : and he that loseth his life for my sake shall find it."* Three ideas are contained in these remarkable words :—(1) That self-denial is a necessary condition of Christian discipleship. The *" cross "* is the most powerfully expressive symbol of self-denial ; and this cross, says Christ, must be borne, painful though it is, ignominious though it may seem. (2) That this self-denial may involve the sacrifice of our present animal well-being. "*He that loseth his life;*"—*i.e.*, not *existence*, but animal happiness or well-being. By following Christ, a man may lose—men often have lost —all their physical pleasures and comforts:—their support, liberty, energy, health, and even animal life itself. This Christ's own self-denial led to; and this self-denial has led to in the case of martyrs. (3) That the self-denial which leads even to the sacrifice of animal well-being, is the greatest blessing, if inspired by due respect for Christ. "*He that findeth his life shall lose it: and he that loseth his life* FOR MY SAKE *shall find it.*" Olshausen thus paraphrases the words :—" He that findeth his (fleshly) life shall lose it (that is, the spiritual life) : and he that loses his life (the fleshly one) shall find it (the spiritual one)." There is a *selfish* self-denial which may lead a man to sacrifice his animal well-being, and have nothing in return;—lose all. There is a self-denial for the sake of friends. Christ does not say, You shall find your highest life in this. There is a self-denial for the sake of obtaining heaven. Heathens will sacrifice their lives for this, and many selfish professors of Christianity sacrifice much for this. Christ does not promise that such persons shall find their highest life. The men who seek their happiness as an end will assuredly lose it. Self-seeking is self-ruin. This doctrine is true to the laws of mind, the experience of mankind, as well as the teachings of Christ. What, then, is the self-denial that ends in man's highest well-being? "FOR MY SAKE." Which is the same as to say, For the sake of eternal rectitude—universal benevolence; for the sake of the well-being of others, and the honour of God. He who acts from this inspiration, whatever sacrifices he makes here, shall gain the highest life and happiness by it.

Another encouragement is,—

Seventhly : *That the interests of the true evangelist are thoroughly identified with the interests of Christ.* (Verses 40-42.) He assures them of three things :—(1) That he would receive those who would receive them, as if they received Himself. "*He that receiveth you receiveth me, and he that receiveth me receiveth Him that sent me.*" I shall regard the treatment that you meet with, kind or otherwise, as if it were offered to me. I go with you;—blend my sensibilities and interests with yours. Those that persecute you persecute me. (2) He assures them that those that would receive them as *His* true servants, should meet with their reward. "*He that receiveth a prophet in the name of a prophet,*" &c. He who receives them merely as men, or in some other capacity, will not have the reward. He who receives under his roof a truly good man, gets a blessing in many ways. His ideas, his spirit, his example, his prayers, are all blessings. He assures them (3) that even those who render the humblest service to the humblest of their number shall be rewarded. A "*cup of cold water*" to one of the "*little ones*" will secure a blessing.

We have thus rapidly reviewed Christ's commission—a portion of Divine revelation which the Christian church, in its evangelical efforts has practically set at nought. Space has forced us to be most condensed in our expository thoughts. There are germs for volumes here worthy the study of every man ; there are elements for a legislation here which should regulate every church in its endeavours to evangelize the world.

Matthew 11:1-15

John the Baptist ; or, Phases of Moral Worth

The reader who desires a verbal criticism of these verses, clause by clause, must look elsewhere. Our object is to give their most salient moral lessons, which are, for the most part, independent of any such literary operation. Our work with the mere *words* will be to make them give prominence and effect to what appears to us the great lessons they are intended to teach.

We discover three facts here in relation to *moral worth* :—

I. That moral worth, even in its more advanced stages, is often associated with much that is profoundly trying. John was now in prison. "*Now when John had heard in the prison,*" &c. (Ver. 2.) The cause and issue of his imprisonment you have stated in Matthew xiv. 3–12 ; Mark vi. 17–29. He was there, not because he had transgressed any law, human or divine, but because —from fidelity to his age, his conscience, and his God—he reproved Herod for his immoral and licentious conduct. But though he was in prison, *he was a man of advanced moral worth.* Did John deserve this incarceration ? What was his character? He who trieth the reins, weigheth the actions, and knoweth what is in man, gives, in the passage under review, a striking and satisfactory answer to this question. (Verses 7–14.) He teaches that John was a man of *distinguished* excellence ; distinguished in three respects :—(1) In his *moral attributes.* "*And as they departed*"—as the "two disciples" whom John had despatched were returning to their master with the answer of Christ—"*Jesus began to say unto the multitudes concerning John, What went ye out into the wilderness to see ? A reed shaken with the wind ? But what went ye out for to see? A man clothed in soft raiment ?*" &c. As if the Heavenly Teacher had said, Don't suppose that, because John has sent this message to me about my Messiahship, he is fickle and inconstant ; that the man you saw in the wilderness is "*a reed shaken with the wind.*" No ! he is a man of *moral stability.* He is not one of your temporizing men, who bow to outward circumstances, as the frail reed on the Jordan to the gusts of heaven. Though the crowds that went forth to the wilderness to be baptized of him had no deep-rooted faith—were inconstant and shifting as the winds—he stood as firm in his faith as the everlasting mountains, whose cooling shadows screened him from the scorching sun. Neither suppose from his message, which you have heard his disciples deliver me, that he is one of those effeminate souls that cannot endure trials for truth's sake. He is not one of those men who study luxury and ease, and desire to be " *clothed in soft raiment.*" You will find such empty fawning men in kings' houses ; but such is not John. Wrapped in his camel's hair, and incarcerated in his dungeon, he is greater than Herod in his gorgeous robes and magnificent palace. The language of Christ implies that John had reached that stage in moral excellence which made him superior to external circumstances : that a vacillating age could not turn him from his purpose ; that a prison could not conquer his soul ; that the gaieties and pleasures of the world had no charms for him. Christ refers (2) to his *spiritual function.* " *But what went ye out for to see ? A prophet ? yea, I say unto you, and more than a prophet. For this is he, of whom it is written, Behold I send my messenger before Thy face, which shall prepare Thy way before Thee. Verily I say unto you, Among them that are born of women there hath not risen a greater than John the Baptist : notwithstanding he that is least in the kingdom of heaven is greater than he.*" The idea is, that John sustained an office in the kingdom of redemptive truth, although inferior to the office sustained by those under the Gospel dispensation, superior to all the ancient prophets. He was the *forerunner* of Christ :—like the heralds of the ancient kings, he prepared His way. He was the *introducer* of Christ. On the banks of the Jordan, when the Messiah first appeared, he pointed the multitudes to Him, and said, " *Behold the Lamb of God.*" He occupied a point in the history of divine revelation which no other man ever did. Those who preceded him saw the moon of Judaism, but not the sun of Christianity. Others who succeeded saw the sun of Christianity, but not the moon ;—the moon had gone down. But John lived just in that hour when the two bodies appeared in the heavens at the same time. He saw the moon of Judaism sinking beneath the horizon never to rise again ; and the sun of Christianity rolling up the East, to fill the heavens so long as men shall be on the earth. He was the *baptizer* of Christ. Such was the office of John—"the Elias, which was to come." Christ refers (3) to his *religious usefulness.* " *From the days of John the Baptist until now the kingdom of heaven suffereth violence, and the violent take it by force.*" Since the days that John began to preach—since he began to call the world to repentance—there has been a rush into the kingdom of truth. Men, roused from their spiritual slumbers—startled by a sense of their sin and ruin—have earnestly applied for pardon and salvation. The echo of the words he proclaimed on the Jordan still lingers and rings in the souls of men, and the result is a pressing every day into the empire of redemptive truth.

Such is the view which Christ gives of John. He cannot speak either ignorantly or flatteringly of his character. John, therefore, was a man of signal excellence—a "*burning and a shining light.*" But notwithstanding this, he was now *in prison.* Great excellences here do not exclude us from trial. Tribulation is the lot of the good. Prisons have often been the home of virtue. Some of the noblest characters that ever appeared amongst men have been consigned to chains and dungeons by their contemporaries: Joseph, Jeremiah, the apostles—Jesus Himself. "*In the world,*" said Christ, "*ye shall have tribulation.*"

II. THAT THE TRIALS ASSOCIATED WITH MORAL WORTH ARE FREQUENTLY SUGGESTIVE OF SPIRITUAL DIFFICULTY. John, in prison, sent two of his disciples to Christ, to put the question directly to Him as to whether He was the Messiah or not. "*Art thou He that should come, or do we look for another?*" Three different reasons are suggested for inducing John to send his disciples with this message to Jesus. First: That he did so for the sake of his disciples. It is supposed that some of their number were not satisfied that He was the true Messiah, and that he sent two of the doubters directly to Christ Himself, in order to have the difficulties removed. Secondly: That it was on account of John's own personal misgivings. His imprisonment and trials, it is supposed, had tended, in some measure, to raise the question in his own mind as to whether He was the true Messiah or not. Even on this hypothesis, the question implies that his faith in the existence of *a* Messiah, and in the obligation of man to look out for Him, remained unshaken. The only point on which he wanted satisfaction was, Was He *the* Messiah? How, in reply to this supposition, it is asked, could a man like John, who had been previously privileged with such visions and experiences of Christ's Messiahship, have a moment's question on the point? He who knows much of human nature—who has marked its tendency, in most cases, to reactions, and especially in such cases as John's, where the emotional element predominates, and is capable of tremendous excitement—will not see much difficulty here. Still less will he who understands much of Christian experience discover any great improbability in a good man, with a strong emotional tide constantly flowing through his nature, falling, under great trials, into doubts, even after the highest experiences of Christian certitude and joy. "In the life of every believer," says Olshausen, "are to be found moments of temptation, in which even the most firm conviction will be shaken to its very foundation. Nothing is more natural than to conceive such moments or periods of internal darkness and abandonment by the Spirit of God, even in the life of St. John." In his gloomy prison, at Machaerus, a dark hour, no doubt, surprised the man of God,—an hour in which he was struck with the quiet, unobtrusive ministry of Christ, and wherein he fell into internal conflict concerning the experiences he heretofore had. It was natural for his circumstances to start those doubts. In his cold and dreary prison he might have reasoned thus with himself:—"I am sent as a messenger to prepare the way of the true Messiah. I saw, I baptized, a Personage who professed to be the true Messiah; but can it be so? If it be He, why does He allow me to pine away in this miserable dungeon?" The other reason assigned for the question is, Thirdly: That John sends the disciples as a deputation to Christ, not on account of any doubts that either he or his followers entertained, but in order to stimulate Jesus to greater haste in the carrying out of His plans. Christ was acting too unostentatiously and quietly to suit the enthusiastic nature and hopes of John, and he was anxious for a grand manifestation at once.

Whichever supposition is the correct one,* you have the trials associated with moral worth starting difficulties to the mind. The trials of virtue have, in every age, perplexed the judgment of the godly. (1) Why, under the government of a wise, just, and merciful God, should the virtuous be impoverished, imprisoned, and sometimes martyred, by the wicked and corrupt, as was now the case with John? (2) Why should the true and the right be so slow in their progress, as they appeared now, probably, to John in the history of Christ?

III. THAT THESE DIFFICULTIES CAN BE EFFECTUALLY REMOVED BY AN EARNEST APPLICATION TO CHRIST. *"Go and show John again those things which ye do hear and see: the blind receive their sight, and the lame walk, the lepers are cleansed, and the deaf hear, the dead are raised up, and the poor have the Gospel preached to them. And blessed is he, whosoever shall not be offended in me."* Observe—

First: *Christ meets the difficulty not by logical reasoning, but by palpable facts.* He does not take John's disciples into the realm of theological thought, and there gather up considerations, in order to satisfy. No! He points them to what they could *see* and *hear*—to *facts.* The history of what Christianity has done is the best evidence of its truth. Point the infidel to what it has achieved!

Secondly: *The facts by which Christ meets the difficulty are most demonstrative.* (1) They are *supernatural in their character.* "*The blind receive their sight,*" &c. No one but the true Messiah could do those works. (2) They are *merciful in their genius.* Mere supernatural work would, of itself, be no evidence. If the work was *malevolent,* it would be so contrary to the consciousness of man that "God is love;" that, though supernatural, it *could not* be received as Divine. But the supernatural agency in Christianity is wielded for benevolent purposes. It is not striking men with blindness or deafness, &c. All is mercy. (3) They are *spiritual in their aim.* "*The poor have the Gospel preached to them,*" &c. If the *benevolent miracle* was merely for the good of the body, and had no reference to the good of the soul, which is the offspring of God, one might have some difficulty in cordially receiving it as divine. But Christianity has *miraculous* facts—miraculous facts

* The second supposition is confirmed by the personal nature of our Lord's reply, "Go and tell John," and by the admonition, "Blessed is he, whosoever shall not be offended in me;" for it is conceivable that his faith began to waver under the severe trial of his imprisonment, and that he shared to a great degree the common notions about the reign of the Messiah. (See Webster and Wilkinson on Matt. xi. 2, 3.)

essentially benevolent in character—and their benevolence aiming mainly at the good of the soul.

Thirdly: *Those that are satisfied with the demonstration of His Messiahship are blessed.* "*Blessed is he, whosoever shall not be offended in me.*" The question of John's disciples implied a kind of "*offence*"—a difficulty of thoroughly believing in Christ's Messiahship—somewhere, either with John or his disciples; and therefore Christ says, "Blessed is he that is not offended in me." As if He had said, I know that there is a danger in the corrupt heart to be offended with me. My poverty strikes at their pride—my doctrines at their prejudices. My life condemns their lusts, their selfishness, their worldliness. Therefore "Blessed is he that is not offended with me;"—blessed because it implies a true insight to my history, a living faith in my doctrines, and a thorough sympathy with my Spirit.

Matthew 11:16-19

Children in the Market-place; or, The Two Sides of Truth, and the Two Sides of Human Life

There are three general truths deducible from this remarkable passage:—

I. THAT GOD, IN HIS DISPENSATION OF TRUTH TO MAN, PRESENTS IT UNDER A TWOFOLD PHASE—THE SEVERE AND THE MILD. John was the representative of the one, Jesus of the other. John did not come "*eating and drinking;*"—he displayed no genial sympathies; no sweet strains of love fell from his lips. His life was one of isolation and ascetic severities. He was *law and terror*—the embodiment of the rigorous: the rigorous in habit, speech, and spirit. Sinai seemed the home of his nature. He folded himself in its clouds; he shot forth its lightning; and rolled its fulminations. On the contrary, Jesus was *love and hope.* It is true, that at times, Jesus assumed the severe; and His words were scathing and terrible in the extreme. But this was the exception. Mildness was the characteristic of His ministry. His great theme was the love of the INFINITE FATHER. The breath of His prayer, the spirit of His work, the import of His sufferings, the reason of His death, was *love for man.*

Now, divine truth has always these two sides. Like the Hebrew pillar, it has a dark and a bright side. In other words, it has law as well as love; justice as well as mercy. There are the principles of everlasting rectitude, as well as the provisions of redeeming grace.

First: *Analogy would suggest that truth has these two sides.* What is NATURE but a revelation of truth? But nature has its bright and dark side—its mild and severe aspects. It has its days of sunshine and serenity, when the earth smiles in beauty under genial skies, and all life overflows with joy. But it has, on the other side, its earthquakes, that engulf cities; its vapours and simoons, whose breath is destruction; its furious storms, that spread devastation over sea and land. What is HUMAN EXPERIENCE, too, but a revelation of truth? Every day of a man's life is a new chapter of divine revelation. But this experience has its two sides. It has days of health, prosperity, and friendship, when "*the cup runneth over;*" and it has days of sickness, adversity, and bereavement. Thus, both *nature* and *experience* suggest that there are law and justice in the universe, as well as love and mercy.

Secondly: *Variety in the temperament of God's ministers, indicates that truth has these two sides.* There is a manifest difference in the organisations of men. Some are cold, reserved, doubting, gloomy; others are warm, sociable, confiding, cheerful. Some are, like John the Baptist, too morose and reserved to eat and drink with men; others, like Jesus, have a genial nature, disposed to identify itself with all. Now, I take it that there is no organisation *necessarily* unfitted to communicate truth; and perhaps there is no character of temperament that God has not, as a fact, employed for the purpose. But it is manifestly impossible that these different organisations could give exactly the same aspects. Truth, like the river, receives its colour and taste from the channel through which it flows. Peter, with his impetuous and defiant nature, could not give exactly the same shade of truth as the reserved and contemplative John.

Thirdly: *The moral circumstances of the race seem to require these two sides of truth.* Some sinners—those especially of the lower class of mind—are only moved by the terrible. The preacher, either to awaken or interest them, must deal much with the appalling. The day of judgment, the solemnities of death, the agonies of hell,— these are their subjects; and the minister, in every age, who can deal the most fluently and dramatically in these, will be to this class the most acceptable. There are others—the reasoning and the cultured —whom these subjects will scarcely touch. The love of God, the beauties of holiness, the example and claims of Jesus, are what will excite and reform them. The world, therefore, wants these two views of truth. It must have the rigorously ethical and the tenderly benevolent.

Fourthly: *The structure of the Bible represents these two sides of truth.* In almost every chapter you will find these two aspects. You will find the *severe* in the history of all judgments, in the denunciations of sin, in the threatenings of approaching wrath; and you will find the *merciful* in the record of gracious interpositions, pathetic entreaties, and glorious promises. Mercy and judgment run through every page of this heaven-inspired book.

Another truth deducible from this remarkable passage, is—

II. THAT THERE IS A CLASS OF MEN WHO WILL FIND FAULT WITH GOD'S TRUTH, UNDER WHATEVER FORM IT MAY BE PRESENTED. "*But whereunto shall I liken this generation? It is like unto children sitting in the markets, and calling unto their fellows, and saying, We have piped unto you, and ye have not danced; we have mourned unto you, and ye have* *not lamented. For John came neither eating nor drinking; and they say, He hath a devil. The Son of Man came eating and drinking; and they say, Behold a man gluttonous,"* &c. Children, in the days of Christ, and in Judea, as children now and everywhere, derived their sports and amusements from the habits and customs of adults. Among the Jews it was customary on marriage or other joyous occasions, for some musician to strike up some jubilant air for the company to join in, or dance to; and at funerals, for the functionary to commence some solemn dirge, and for the company to respond by beating their breasts, and other signs of sorrow. The children observed these things, as they were constantly going on around them. Childlike, they turned the realities of men into play. They made funerals and marriages their amusement. They had the musician with his pipe for the wedding dance, and the official mourner to stimulate and direct the expressions of funereal grief. Jesus observed the sports of little children. Nothing connected with humanity, in its humblest stages of development, was uninteresting to Him. We may suppose Him standing for a few moments in some *"market-place,"* and marking with interest a little group of children assembled for play;—some full of the genial and the jocose, and anxious to commence the sport. They propose one game after another. The wedding and the burial, the gay and the solemn, are suggested to their companions; but they, with an ill-natured fastidiousness, refuse to join in either. In the conduct of these sulky and perverse children, whom their good-natured companions could not please, Jesus saw an image of the adult population amongst whom He lived and wrought.* Nothing would please them. *"John came neither eating nor drinking,"* &c. He lived in rigorous abstinency: seldom ever ate in the presence of men,—never with them; and because of this, your fastidious people would not receive his doctrines. You say that *"he had a devil,"*—that he was mad. I have come eating and drinking; I mingle with men; I am social and free; I join them at their festive board; I have nothing of the austerity of John in my nature or habits; and because of this, you will not receive my doctrines. You say that I am *"a man gluttonous, and a wine-bibber, a friend of publicans and sinners."* John, the preacher of repentance, lived as an ascetic, and called for mourning; I, the mes-

---

* Olshausen remarks, that "the whole figure would be misunderstood, were it to be viewed as though the children, who are speaking, represented Jesus and St. John—the representation of mildness and severity; while the other children addressed or spoken to, represented the capricious people. Both classes of the children—the speaking ones and those spoken to—on the contrary, are to be considered as representatives of the capricious contemporaries of Jesus; so that the meaning is, This generation resembles a host of ill-humoured children that cannot be pleased in any way; the one part desiring this, the other part that; so that, after all, no degree of useful activity is attained by them." For our own part, we do not see how the happy children proposing the play, and endeavouring to please their companions, can in any way represent the Jewish people, to whom Jesus refers; nor can we see that it is necessary to regard them as *representative* in any respect; *i.e.*, representative of Jesus and John, or the Jewish people. It seems to us, that the fastidious children spoken to, are *representative*, and they only.

senger of salvation, join you in your social enjoyments, and invite you to cheerfulness; but you reject us both.

As it was with sinners in the days of Christ, so it has ever been, and so it is now. *God cannot please them.* No dispensation of events will please them; no dispensation of truth will please them; no ministry will do. The sermon is either too crude or too finished, too doctrinal or too practical; the minister is either too intellectual or too commonplace, too sombre or too cheerful, too reserved or too free. No true ministry can please sinners. The ministry popular amongst them is not the ministry of God. *Why cannot a true ministry, under any form—severe or mild—please the sinner?*

First: *Because of the self-dissatisfying power in the sinner's own soul.* A good man is satisfied in himself; he rejoices in himself. Not so with an ungodly man; he *cannot* be satisfied with himself. His heart and his conscience are always in antagonism, and under moral excitement the conflict is fierce and terrible. What the conscience approves the heart condemns, and the reverse. What pleases one part of the nature, so long as each part is in conflict, cannot· please the other. Because the sinner is thus dissatisfied with himself, he is dissatisfied with everything else. The self-dissatisfied man *must* be a fault-finder; he cannot be otherwise. He is a cynic in the universe.

Secondly: *Because of the self-gratifying impulse in the sinner's heart.* The sinner is always bent on his own gratification. His· own pleasure is everything to him. This is the centre point of his soul. A true ministry, whether severe or mild, strikes directly against this. It denounces selfishness in all its forms, and demands a crucifixion of " *the old man, with all its corruptions and lusts.*" The ministry of John and the ministry of Christ agree in this. Sinai and Calvary blend their voices in the command to deny ourselves. The sinner, therefore, cannot be pleased with it.

Thirdly: *Because of the sin-exonerating tendency in the sinner's heart.* In order to reconcile conscience to the depraved likings and gratifications of the heart, the sinner's mind is ever disposed to seek excuses. The intellect is ever in search of palliations. It is always, therefore, ready to find fault with the dispensations of God, in order to justify to the conscience its wicked ways. What son in the family is most ready to find fault with the parent? It is the most undutiful; because fault in his father would help him to reconcile himself to his own disobedient life. What servant is most ready to find fault with his master? It is the most indolent and worthless. What pupil is most ready to find fault with his teacher? It is the most indocile. For this reason the most wicked spirits are the most disposed to find fault with God.

III. THAT WHILST THERE IS A CLASS WHO WILL THUS FIND FAULT WITH GOD'S TRUTH UNDER EVERY FORM IN WHICH IT IS PRESENTED, THERE ARE OTHERS WHO HEARTILY APPROVE OF IT IN ALL ITS ASPECTS. "*But wisdom is justified of her children.*" This proposition will show its truthfulness in the light of the following facts, which are implied in the expression.

First: *That this varied manifestation of truth to man is ascribable to the highest* WISDOM. It is that wisdom which, in the natural world, has appointed darkness and light, cold and heat, attraction and repulsion; that in the spiritual has arranged these varied phases and ministries of truth. The diversity is neither accident nor mistake, but the arrangement of wisdom:—indeed, the "manifold wisdom of God" in the dispensations of biblical truth.

Secondly: *That this* WISDOM *has a certain class of men on earth who are to be regarded as its offspring.* "*Her children.*" Who are the children of this heavenly wisdom? They are evidently persons whom our Saviour regarded as being in contrast with those perverse and fault-finding persons who rejected truth under all its forms, and whom He likens to fastidious children playing in the market-place. The children of "*wisdom*" are those who have been regenerated by the doctrines which wisdom thus dispenses. They see things in the light in which wisdom points them out, and they pursue a course of life agreeable to that which wisdom directs. They are *the children of wisdom*,—having a spirit of reverence and obedience for that heavenly wisdom displayed everywhere in the Bible.

Thirdly: *That these children of* WISDOM *thoroughly approve of the truth in whatever form it comes.* "*Wisdom is justified of her children.*" The dark and bright sides are both approved by the children. They have experienced the worth of both sides. When they were indifferent and ungodly even as others, it was the terrible aspects of truth that broke their guilty slumbers, and alarmed them with their danger. Afterwards, when through fear of hell they were about sinking into despair, it was the mild and loving displays of truth that came to their relief. And even subsequently the two sides are useful to keep their spirits in a proper balance between extreme doubt and extreme confidence. They say, "*Even so, Father,*" under all manifestations. Whether the Great One speaks to them in earthquakes or in the whispering breeze, from behind the cloud of adversity or in the sunshine of prosperity, from Sinai or Calvary, all is right. Wisdom is ever "*justified of her children.*" *

---

* Those who are truly wise will acknowledge the justice, propriety, and wisdom of the courses pursued by our Lord and the Baptist. It was fitting that the forerunner whose office was transitory, whose example served one specific purpose, should raise attention and excite inquiry by an abstemious mode of living, different from that which generally prevails. It was fitting, too, that our Lord, whose office was perpetual, whose example was to serve as an universal model, should adopt a course capable of imitation by all classes of men, in all ages and countries (Webster and Wilkinson on Matt. xi. 19).

Matthew 11:20-24

Mighty Works; or, Diversity in the External Spiritual Advantages of Mankind

From this terribly significant utterance of Christ the following truths are fairly deducible:—

I. THAT GOD VOUCHSAFES A GREATER MANIFESTATION OF HIMSELF TO SOME MEN THAN TO OTHERS. The men of Chorazin, Bethsaida, and Capernaum were made the spectators of mightier Divine works than ever came within the observation of the men of Tyre, Sidon, or Sodom. The "*mightier works*," of course, we suppose to mean, not the works of nature, but the works of *redemptive providence*. Indeed, the mighty works of God in nature are more or less the same in every age and land. "*The invisible things of God from the creation of the world are clearly seen, being understood by the things that are made, even His eternal power and Godhead.*" But in His redemptive providence His works have varied greatly in different times and scenes. (1) "Mighty works" were wrought to redeem man in the days of the Patriarchs:—works of judgment and of mercy. The expulsion from Eden, the dawn of mercy in the first promise, the translation of Enoch, the deluge, the call of Abraham, and all the Divine visions and discoveries made to him and his successors. (2) "Mighty works" were wrought to redeem men in the *Jewish* age:—emancipation from Egypt, the miracles in the wilderness, the victories in the promised land, the organising of a magnificent system of worship—which stood for ages as the glory of the world—the works of holy priests and inspired prophets, and devoted saints, were "mighty works" of God. (3) "Mighty works" were wrought to redeem men during the personal history of Christ. The works that Jesus performed in His own person, the works to which He now refers, were "*mighty works;*" so numerous that if they had been written in a book the world itself would not contain the volumes. (4) "Mighty works" were wrought to redeem men in the Christian age:—the wonders of Pentecost, the glorious triumphs which attended the preaching of the Gospel in the first three centuries, and all the moral revolutions accomplished by it in different parts of the earth to this hour, are the "mighty works of God." God has not ceased to perform His "mighty works" before the children of men. Every false system demolished, every error exploded, every truth enthroned, every soul converted, is the "mighty work" of God.

These *four* classes of "mighty works" vary much in their character. The first, we think, would not be so great as the second, nor the second as the third; and we, the men who witness the fourth, have the advantage of all. Through this Divine word we witness the *whole* that is past in connexion with all that is now going on.

II. That the design of all these mighty works is man's spiritual reformation. "*If the mighty works which were done in you (Chorazin, Bethsaida), had been done in Tyre and Sidon, they would have repented long ago.*" This language implies not merely that Tyre and Sidon, in common with all people, needed *repentance*, but that the grand object of God's mighty works, through all ages and in all places, is to effect a moral reformation. Ever since the fall, the designs of God in His dealings with mankind have been this. The turning of their thoughts, emotions, and activities into the channel of truth, rectitude, and blessedness has been His end. "*All these things worketh God oftentimes with man to bring him back from the pit to enlighten him with the light of the living.*"

III. That the mighty works which would prove effective to reform some, have no saving effect upon others. Jesus distinctly avers that the works which He had wrought in Chorazin and Bethsaida, and to no useful effect, would have worked out the spiritual reformation of Tyre and Sidon. This is not the language of exaggeration—not the language of one who judges from probabilities, but the language of one who knew with absolute certainty that of which He spoke. He was set up from everlasting—His delight was always with the sons of men. He knew those men of Tyre and Sidon, who lived many ages back; He felt that the works which He was performing now about the shores of Galilee would, if they had been wrought before the men of Tyre and Sidon, have effected their conversion.

This fact, which we are bound to receive on the authority of Christ, is profoundly significant. What does it show? Does it not show (1) the diversity in souls? Though all souls are similar in their general attributes, relations, and responsibilities, they are nevertheless so different, either in some particular feature of their nature or in the degree of depravity, or both,—that means which would be effectual in the reformation of some, are impotent upon others. Does it not show (2) the moral freedom even of depraved souls? So free has the Almighty left the action of the human spirit, even in its fallen state—that even His "mighty works" cannot effect their moral design without its consent. It may be popular, because gratifying to the native indolence of the corrupt nature, to preach that the sinner is powerless; but the fact that he can, that he does, resist the moral influence put forth in the "mighty works" of God for his repentance, impress me with the wonderful energy of his freedom to act. Does it not show (3) the sovereignty of God in His dealings with men? If the men of Tyre and Sidon would have been converted had they witnessed the mighty works which came under the men of Chorazin and Bethsaida, why did He not furnish them with such displays of His power? Why were not the shores of the Mediterranean made the theatre of Divine actions as mighty as were the shores of Galilee? I have no answer to the question but this—"*Even so, Father, for so it seemeth good.*" Does it not show (4) that we must not depend too much upon "mighty works" to convert? Some men in our age have pronounced the moral system of Christianity a failure, and are looking forward, as their only hope of the world, to a miraculous dispensation, a dispensation of "mighty works," to do that which the preaching of the Gospel has failed to accomplish. We say to those men, if "mighty works" can necessarily convert, why were not the men of Chorazin, Bethsaida, and Capernaum saved?

IV. THAT THE GUILT OF THE UNCONVERTED IS MEASURED BY THE DIVINE WORKS THAT HAVE BEEN WROUGHT AMONGST THEM. The guilt of Tyre and Sidon, and Sodom, was great. And if we may judge from the physical doom they met, we may well stand appalled at the enormity of their guilt. Where are Tyre and Sidon now? In the days of David and Solomon they were a prosperous people— their "merchants were princes;" they furnished materials and workmen for the Temple of the Lord. Where is Tyre now? Read the doom which justice pronounced upon it through the prophets Isaiah and Ezekiel. Read the record of travellers and see how it has been realised—not a vestige of its former glory remains: only a few fishermen live amongst its ruins now. The waves of the ocean dash on the lonely rocks, from which, long ago, towered those magnificent palaces of Sidon, in which its prosperous people moved in pomp and revelled in pleasure. Where is Sodom, which was once as the "*garden of the Lord*"? The judgment of heaven consumed it with its fires. But the physical doom of these people, terrible though it was, is only a faint type of their far more tremendous spiritual destiny.

But the language of Jesus implies that the guilt of Chorazin and Bethsaida and Capernaum was greater still. "*Woe unto thee*," &c. What words are these? They are the expressions of a mind that fully gauged the dimensions of their guilt, and fully comprehended the miseries that awaited them. "Woe." What meaning is in this "Woe"? Does it express indignation or pity? Does it mean that He would have them damned, or that He was in the anguish of unutterable commiseration at their coming doom? It is, methinks, the profound articulated sigh of compassion at the oceans of misery and the ages of torment which rolled before His all-seeing eye, and which awaited the men He addressed.

V. THAT THE RELATIVE DEGREE OF GUILT BELONGING TO SINNERS WILL FULLY APPEAR ON THE DAY OF JUDGMENT. "*It will be more tolerable for Tyre and Sidon*," &c. It is implied here—First: *That there is a day of judgment appointed.* Secondly: *That on this day men of remotest times and lands will meet.* On this day Tyre and Sidon, and Sodom, Chorazin and Bethsaida, and Capernaum shall appear before the Judge. These men are living. The judgment that destroyed Tyre and Sidon did not destroy the souls of the population. The fires that consumed Sodom left the souls of the people untouched: all the men that ever have been are still living, and will stand in their "*lot at the end of days*." "*We must all appear before the judgment-seat of Christ*," &c. Thirdly: *That the mighty concourse of men that will meet on that day will be treated according to the measure of their respective guilt.*

Let us realise our advantages, and act worthy of them in time. Were Christ to address us here in this country and age, He might say, "If the mighty works"—the works of tract distribution, Bible circulation, religious education, Gospel preaching,—were done in heathen lands that are now being performed in Britain, those heathens would have repented long ago.

Matthew 11:25-27

The Wise, the Prudent, and the Babes; or, the Hidden and Revealed

If we regard, as I think we are justified in doing, this utterance of Jesus as immediately following His pronunciation of "Woe" over Chorazin, Bethsaida, and Capernaum, we shall be at no loss to determine what is meant here by "*these things,*" which He gives us to understand are "*hid from the wise and the prudent, and revealed unto babes.*" They were what the "mighty works" expressed and embodied. The works of a being are the fullest, strongest, and most unmistakable expressions of his spirit, principles, and purposes. They are *living* words—words uttered not by one member, the tongue, but by the whole being. God does not reveal Himself to us merely by verbal utterances. His words are generally the revelation of His works, and His works are the revelation of Himself. His "mighty works" of redemptive providence are intended and suited to reveal to the soul His moral character, His love for man, and His purpose to save him. And these are "*the things*" of which our Saviour here speaks : and "*these things,*" which are the *meaning* of the "mighty works," are the soul-transforming powers.

Jesus teaches us to look upon "*these things,*" *i.e.,* the spirit and substance of the Gospel, in two aspects,—as hidden from some, and as revealed to others.

I. As HIDDEN FROM SOME. They were "*hid from the wise and the prudent.*" There were some of our Saviour's hearers, it is to be feared by far the majority, who, although they had the Gospel brought under their notice by Himself, by works and words, did not *see* it. Like those whom some of the old prophets addressed, whose spiritual senses were closed against the message ; like "*the natural man*" of whom the apostle speaks, who cannot "*discern*" spiritual things. Thousands there are of such in this age, who are in attendance upon the ministry of the Word. What does this concealment arise from ? In answer to this question, the circumstances of the people of whom Jesus now speaks as having these spiritual things hid from them, enable us to say,—

First : *That they were hidden not from the want of an external manifestation.* Spiritual truth had been presented to them in all the forms in which it could appear. Not merely in living words and wonderful works, but in the example of Him who was truth itself. And yet they did not discern the things thus represented. They were like blind men under the bright heavens, and deaf men amidst flowing tides of music. That *these things* are hidden from heathens is no wonder, for they have never had the external revelation of them;—they cannot see them, because there is no light thrown upon them from the heavens. But that they should be hidden from those who live amongst the utterances and forms of revelation, is passing strange and solemn.

We infer from the circumstances of these people—

Secondly : *That they were not hidden for the want of intellectual ability to discern them.* It was "*from the wise and the prudent,*" not from idiots or dolts, that they were concealed. Had the men to whom Jesus refers been destitute of *natural capacity,* men of no intellect, we could not have wondered. Though the sun shine in the sky, if the man has not the organ of vision, nature will be hid from him. Intellect is the eye of the soul, and though the sun of external revelation throws its radiance about him, if he has not the intellectual eye, the whole field of truth will be hid in densest obscurity. But the persons to whom Christ alludes possessed in an eminent degree this intellectual vision. They were "*the wise and the prudent;*"—men, some of whom had distinguished themselves in culture and learning, and were not, perhaps, a little proud of their supposed superiority in genius and attainments. They had the power of understanding these things intellectually,— of throwing them into a system of theology, and probably some of them did so; and yet, spiritually, they were "*hid from them.*"

We infer from the circumstances of these people,—

Thirdly : *That they were not hidden by any influence exerted by God for the purpose.* It is true that the words as they stand would give the superficial reader this impression. The words are, " *Thou hast hidden them from the wise and prudent.*" Were we to assume that this rendering is most faithful to the original,* we should still reject the interpretation which gives the idea that Jesus here teaches, that the Great Father exerted any influence to conceal these things from the wise and prudent. Three considerations are sufficient to show that such an idea is not to the slightest extent admissible. (1) *That the Bible recognizes a sense in which God may be regarded as the Author of things that are even contrary to His will and influence.*† " Is there evil in a city and the Lord hath not done it ? " In the same sense we may ask, is there evil in any part of the universe and the Lord has not done it ? He not only permits it, but He imparts the energy which commits it. Even the Prince of Evil derives his existence and energy every moment from Him. On this principle

---

* Exod. vii. 3, 4. 2 Sam. xii. 11, 12, 24. 1 Kings xxii. 22, 23. Isa. vi. 10.
† For the difference in meaning between κρύπτω and καλύπτω, see *Homilist,* vol. iii., New Series, p. 420.

He is said to have hardened Pharaoh's heart; to have put a "lying spirit" in the mouth of certain prophets; and to have commissioned Isaiah to make the hearts of those who would resist his ministry "fat," and "their ears heavy," and to shut their eyes "lest they should see with their eyes, and hear with their ears, and understand with their hearts, and be converted and healed." The idea merely is, Go and proclaim my truth, which shall have this blinding and hardening effect upon their gross and perverse *natures*. But it is, after all, only in a very accommodative sense that God can be said to be the Author of that which is against His holy nature, against His revealed will, against the whole of His creative and providential system of action. MORALLY and TRULY, a being is only the author of that which he produces by *purpose* and *agency*. (2) *That to conceal spiritual things from the sinner's soul does not require the agency of God. They are hid.* His agency is required, not to conceal, but to reveal. Infinite wisdom works not superfluously. (3) *That as a fact, the Divine agency amongst those to whom Jesus refers was to reveal.* Through the life, doctrines, and miracles of His Son, He brought those spiritual things most palpably and impressively under the notice of these men of Chorazin, Bethsaida, and Capernaum. We cannot, therefore, for a moment entertain the idea that there was either on God's part a positive influence exerted to blind the minds of these Jews, or the withholding of any influence required to enlighten them unto salvation. Such a supposition robs the history of Jesus of its benevolent meaning, and stains with hideous blot the lovely character of God.

Jesus here teaches us to look upon these things,—

II. AS REVEALED TO OTHERS. They were "*revealed unto babes.*" The passage gives certain particulars in reference to this spiritual revelation which will, as we examine it, throw much light upon the whole of this important subject.

First: *That the revelation of "these things" is something besides both the external manifestation and the intellectual ability.* We have seen that the men to whom the Saviour refers had both. They had the external manifestations: The Prophets—John the Baptist; and now Christ had brought "these things" most powerfully under their attention. They had, too, sufficient intellectual power to understand "these things"—they were the wise and the prudent; and yet, with all this outward light, and with all their intellectual power of vision, they saw not "these things." They were like men standing in the midst of a magnificent landscape, with a bright sun shining about them, and with eyes too, and yet all the beauties of the scene concealed from them. A man may be well acquainted with the Bible, he may attend the ministry which brings out in the strongest light the great doctrines of the Gospel,—and he, too, may have intellectual power to view them in their right, philosophical, and logical relations,—and yet not *see* the things. A man may be a theologian and yet have the *things* of the Gospel hid from him.

Secondly: *That the revelation of "these things" depends upon the state of the heart.* It is "*to babes*" that they are revealed. Not babes in years, not babes in mental feebleness, not babes in knowledge; but babes in heart-attributes,—guileless, humble, docile, loving, impressible, truthful.

Man may be said to have three distinct powers of vision : the *sensational,* by which impressions of the *form* of things are conveyed to the consciousness; *intellectual,* by which impressions of the *idea* of things are conveyed to the consciousness; and the *spiritual,* by which impressions of the moral and divine *spirit* of things are conveyed to the consciousness. It is only as man sees, in the *last* sense, that he truly sees "these things"—sees as a man. Every part of the universe has a *spiritual significance;* but this can only be seen by the spiritual faculty. Neither the mere sensuous man nor the mere intellectual man can discern, either in nature, or history, or the Bible, "*the things of the Spirit*"—they are *spiritually discerned.* All men with physical eyes see the wide-spread earth, and all men with minds can understand something about the science of nature, but only those with a certain spiritual sensibility can see and feel the overpowering loveliness and spiritual significance of the landscape. The musician may fill the air with strains of melting melody, but it is only those with a certain spiritual sensibility can *feel* the music; to others, even if they understood the theory of music, it is mere sound. Nature to the physical eye is but *form,* to the intellectual eye it is but *doctrine,* to the spiritual eye it is a divine *spirit.* Or, to use another illustration—To understand and feel the theory of a man's life, you must have something of the spirit of that man in you. Unless you have something of ambition, you will never understand the life of Napoleon. Unless you have some benevolence in you, Howard's life will be an enigma. If you have not some love for truth, the history of the martyrs will be shrouded in mystery from you. For this reason, true Christians in every age have had to say, "*The world knoweth us not.*" "*He that loveth not, knoweth not God, for God is love.*" Here is the philosophy of spiritual blindness. Our native sympathy with the right, the good, and the divine, must be awakened if we would know the things that are of God.

Thirdly : *The revelation of these things calls for the profoundest gratitude to God.* "*I thank thee, O Father, Lord of heaven and earth, because Thou hast hid these things from the wise and prudent, and hast revealed them unto babes.*" The profound thankfulness here expressed is not *that they were hid* from "the wise and prudent," but that, while they were hid from them, they were revealed unto babes. A similar form of expression to this you have in Romans vi. 17 : "*But God be thanked, that ye were the servants of sin, but ye have obeyed from the heart that form of doctrine which was delivered unto you.*" We are not to understand, of course, that Paul thanked God that they were the servants of sin, but that they, having been the servants of sin, were now "obeying from the heart," &c. In like manner does Christ thank the Almighty Father, not for hiding "these things from the wise and prudent;" but that, though hidden from them, they were revealed unto babes: that whilst men of culture and refinement, sages and statesmen, bards and orators understood not "these things" spiritually, the simple-hearted and child-like—like the fishermen of Galilee—did.

But why this profound gratitude for the revelation of "these things"? (1) *Because of the immense good involved in the revelation of these things to man.* When "these things" are revealed to a man, it is the imparting to him a new existence—a new universe. Vast is the difference between the brute and the man—they live in different worlds: vast is the difference, too, between man in a savage state, and a man endowed with the genius and blessed with the attainments of a Milton; but far greater is the difference between the most elevated mind from whom these spiritual things are hid, and the humblest to whom they aro revealed. There is a gulf between them: the one is in "the gall of bitterness and in the bond of iniquity," and the other is "sitting down in heavenly places in Christ Jesus." (2) *Because of the wonderful condescension on God's part in the revelation of these things to men.* "*Lord of heaven and earth!*"—The universal Proprietor and Sovereign. He who was before all—is in all, and over all—condescended to reveal these spiritual things to the hearts of poor sinful men. This is God's work. Paul felt this—"*It pleased God to reveal His Son in me.*" He must therefore have the praise.

Fourthly: *The revelation of these things is made to the soul through Jesus Christ.* "*All things are delivered unto me of my Father, and no man knoweth the Son but the Father, neither knoweth any man the Father save the Son, and he to whomsoever the Son will reveal Him.*" There are four thoughts here in relation to Christ as the revealer of these things to the soul. (1) *That He is a Divinely authorised revealer.* "All things are delivered unto me of my Father." All spiritual things: all spiritual truth and influence—for His Redemptive Mission are the things, probably, meant. As Mediator, He is thus Divinely qualified for this work. (2) *That He is a transcendently glorious revealer.* "No man knoweth the Son but the Father." He is so mysteriously great in His nature, relations, offices, and aims, that there is but One Being in the universe that *fully* understands Him, and that is God. He is the WONDERFUL to all finite intellect, in all worlds. (3) *That He is an absolutely perfect revealer.* "Neither knoweth any man the Father save the Son." He knows the Father and He only. "*No man hath seen God at any time; the only begotten Son of the Father, He only hath declared Him.*" The old fathers and prophets knew a little of God: angels know a little of God. No finite being, after the study of millenniums, will ever know Him fully. Christ knows the Father, He knows Him perfectly*—He alone comprehends the Infinite. (4) *That He is the indispensable revealer.* "No man *can* know the Father, but He to whomsoever the Son will reveal Him." Christ is the LOGOS.

* The word is ἐπιγινώσκει, know fully or thoroughly. The distinction between this and γινώσκω is marked in 1 Cor. xiii. 12.

The sinner will be for ever ignorant of God unless He reveals Him. It is He alone that "opens the Book" of the Divine character and history to the universe, and page after page expounds.

Matthew 11:28-30

Invitation to the Heavy Laden; or, the Spirit of Christianity

In the three preceding verses, which we have already noticed, Christ appears in His relation to the Great God. He stands before us there, as *the devout worshipper, exclusive comprehender, authorized and indispensable* revealer, of the everlasting Father. Here He appears in His relation to humanity. As the divine philanthropist, He looks with an eye of unutterable tenderness and love upon an afflicted and sin-burdened world, and earnestly invites every distressed soul to come to Him for rest.

The language of the text is figurative, and the imagery is borrowed from the agriculture of the time and place. The Jews were accustomed to cultivate the land with oxen, which were yoked together for the purpose. Perhaps Jesus now beheld this operation going on in a neighbouring field: He saw the oxen, with heavy yokes, drawing the heavy implements, tired and well-nigh exhausted, and still obliged to work. This, to Him, was a picture of the sinners of His age—they were under a heavy yoke of iniquity, wearied and almost exhausted, but still pursuing their wretched course. His benevolent heart overflows with sympathy, and He invites them to Him for rest. The depth and glow, the universality and tenderness, of the love expressed in this utterance are enough to induce a fear, in a thoughtful expositor, lest he should not do justice to this love—lest his coldness should conceal its ardour; his selfishness, its freeness; his narrowness, its universality; his hardness, its exquisite pathos. It requires benevolence to preach benevolence; tenderness to preach tenderness; pathos to preach pathos; the spirit of Christ to preach Christ.

The words teach us three truths in relation to Christianity.

I. CHRISTIANITY IMPLIES MORAL DISTRESS. It addresses itself to those who "*labour and are heavy laden.*" In order to understand clearly the class to whom Christ appeals, we may glance at the various classes of moral intelligences. They are divided into three:—

First: *Those who have no burden.* These are angels and sainted men. They pursue the path of destiny with blithe and ever-strengthening soul. "They mount up as on the wings of eagles; they run and are not weary, they walk and do not faint." Christianity is not addressed to these. Angels never require it: the original religion of the universe has ever been theirs, and that religion does not imply moral distress. Sainted men once required it, but it has done its redeeming work with them—they have passed into a higher world, and are placed under another and a sublimer dispensation.

Secondly : *Those who have heavy burdens, but which are not removable.* The Bible gives us to believe that there are spirits in some dark and accursed part of this universe who are sinking everlastingly beneath a load of guilt, and for whom there is no hope. How appalling the aspect, how crushing the weight, how galling the pressure of that mountain of guilt, which rests upon the spirits of the lost! Wretched spirits! they *labour and are heavy laden,* and no invitation of mercy is addressed to them—no hope of relief is held out to them!

Thirdly : *Those who have heavy burdens, but which can be removed.* These are sinners on earth. There are heavy burdens resting upon men here. None but God can tell the amount of trial that is surging through human souls every moment. Some are suffering under one burden and some under another. There are millions on this lovely earth to whom life itself is a burden—a heavy crushing burden. There are *physical* burdens—infirmities and diseases of the body ; there are *social* burdens—the care of the family, the claims of business, the inconstancy of friends, the hollowness and selfishness of the world ; there are *political* burdens—the enactments of injustice and the tyranny of despotism are heavy burdens upon the hearts of nations ; there are *religious* burdens—the unmeaning routine, the painful pilgrimages, the costly sacrifice, imposed by a wily and wicked priesthood, are burdens on the spirits of millions. Such burdens as these often make life intolerable, and induce men to exclaim with Job—"*I loathe life, I would not live always.*" But all these burdens may be felt, and often are, where there is no *deep sense of sin.* The victims are weary of these burdens, not because of the sin which is the cause of them, but because of the inconvenience and pain which they produce.

But that which gives pressure and galling force to all these burdens is *a sense of sin.* There are men under these fair heavens, on this earth, where the Saviour of the world lived and laboured, suffered and died, and where His blessed Gospel is faithfully preached, who feel that *sin is the burden of all their burdens.* They are sick of pleasure, they are tired of their life. They are found at the altar of Paganism, in the mosque of the Mahomedan, as well as in different parts of Christendom, crying out in different languages, but with the same emphasis of soul—" *Wherewithal shall we come before the Lord, and how shall we bow ourselves before the most high God ?*"

This is the class which Christianity addresses—which Christ here invites. Blessed be God for providing a remedy in Christianity for this class ! O ye distressed souls, tried by the world, tempted by Satan, smitten by conscience, ashamed of the past, afraid of the future—whose heavens are cloudy and seem charged with storms, listen to the invitation of Christ and accept it. " *Come unto me, all ye that labour and are heavy laden.*"

II. CHRISTIANITY PROVIDES MORAL RELIEF. " *Ye shall find rest unto your souls.*" Rest for the soul. It does not promise that those who come to Christ shall be at once released from all *corporeal* burdens incident to our mortal life. The laws of the material universe are regardless of moral distinctions. The good and evil, the just and the unjust, material nature treats alike.

But what is the rest for the soul ? Is it a deadening of the sensibilities, so as to prevent us from feeling so acutely the evils of life ? No. Christianity, instead of deadening our sensibilities, quickens them. Nor is it the rest of inactivity. The rest of the soul is not the rest of inaction, it means neither insensitiveness nor inactivity. What is it then ?

First : *It is rest from all self-seeking.* All men are working : labour is a Divine institution ; the world is full of action. Man's curse is not that he labours,—labour itself is a blessing,—but that he labours from the unhappy impulses of selfishness. Every man is seeking his own—each individual makes himself an end. This is the source of distress. Because of this, the individual worker is full of a thousand anxieties ; and because of this, society is ever in commotion. There are as many conflicting interests as there are men. The man who comes to Christ, whilst he does not cease from work, ceases " from his own work." He works from love to God and His universe —his meat and his drink are to do the will of his Father. Whether at his desk, behind the counter, in the field, at the hustings, in the exchange, at the festive circle, or in the temple, the same generous and unselfish motives govern him. He rejoices in the increase of wealth, and power, and influence, not on his own account, but because they will enable him to do more for the common good and the glory of God. *True benevolent labour is rest to the soul.* Every act is in harmony with the constitution of the mind, with the laws of the universe—with the will of God. Every such act is a note which swells the music of life and heightens the harmonies of creation. Whether worldly adversity or prosperity attend the labours of such a man, he says, " *The Lord gave, and the Lord hath taken away ; blessed be the name of the Lord !* "

Secondly : *Rest from all secular anxieties.* How much distress is in our world from this source ! Our own countrymen especially are *heavy laden* with worldly cares. These cares bend the strongest frame and disfigure the most lovely countenance. These worldly cares are lying as a mighty incubus upon the population of our country. Jesus will give rest from these anxieties to all who come unto Him. He does it by pledging His disciples every needful blessing : " *Seek ye first the kingdom of God,*" &c. He does it by inculcating upon them to " *Take no anxious thought for the morrow ;*" " *To be careful for nothing,*" &c. He does it by assuring them of a parental Providence that adorns the lilies of the valley and feeds the birds of Heaven. He does it by giving them the consciousness that this

The wicked borroweth, and payeth not again... Psalms 37:21

world is, in their case, preparatory to a better, and that "all things work together for their good." "Thus they glory in tribulation;" they know that Jesus is their guide—that the Eternal is their Father; that the universe is their home, and that everlasting life is their heritage.

Thirdly : *Rest from religious sacrifices.* By religious sacrifices I mean, whatever a man does in connexion with religion, not cheerfully and happily. How much of this kind of work is done in connexion with religion! Most men are anxious to realise some paradise beyond the grave. They work for this, and they feel it a burden. The Pagan will present costly offerings for this—the Mahomedan performs painful pilgrimages for this—the Romanist attends to painful penances for this—the Protestant gives his money for this. *Whatever a man does in religion for the sake of an ulterior good, and not for its own sake, is a sacrifice, and is a burden.* The world is groaning under this. Religious duties are burdens. The religion of Jesus frees us from them. A true loving disciple blots the word sacrifice from his practical creed. What he gives is a gratification to him. I protest against the argument that is sometimes used to induce men to give to the cause of Christ. We must make sacrifices, it is said. This idea is crippling our religious institutions. The church is "heavy laden" because of these sacrifices. Because of this she moves as a wearied traveller, with stiff limb and slow step. In every church there is the complaint of too many collections. Why is this? Not because the demand is really too great, but because the spirit of religion is gone. You must translate the idea of sacrifice into that of thanksgiving, and religious burdens will be removed. Then the church will move more cheerfully—she will take the wings of an angel, sweep the hemispheres of the globe, and preach the everlasting Gospel to all nations and kindreds of people.

Fourthly : *Rest from all legal obedience.* There are two kinds of obedience to law—the literal and the spiritual. The former depends upon specific directions; it is doing just as much as is in the letter, and *because* it is in the letter. This obedience is merely outward and mechanical; it is in the knee, tongue, or head, but not in the heart. It is always a burden. This was the observance of the Jews. The other is spiritual. Supreme love to the Lawgiver is the motive and inspiration. This is happiness. There are two sons, children of the same father, living under the same roof, subject to the same domestic laws; one has lost all filial love, his father has no longer any hold upon his affections. The other is full of the sentiment, the filial instinct in him is almost a passion. How different is the obedience of these two sons! The one does nothing but what is found in the command, and does that merely as a matter of form; he would not do it if he could help it. The other does it not because it is in the command, but because it is the wish of him he loves. He goes beyond the written law, he anticipates his father's will. Obedience is burden in the one case, but delight in the other. Much of the work now being done in the Christian church is like the obedience of the unloving son. It is done because it is commanded; done grudgingly and unhappily. Christ removes this : He breathes that spirit of love that makes obedience blessedness.

Fifthly: *Rest from all forebodings of conscience.* A guilty conscience is the burden of burdens. It makes the soul gloomy and tempestuous. It makes death terrible, the grave a land of darkness, eternity an intolerable idea. Christianity removes this. "Therefore being justified by faith," &c. *D ECLS/O*

III. CHRISTIANITY REQUIRES MORAL EFFORT. "Come unto me," &c. If the burden is to be removed, *something must be done.* And what ? Three things :—

First : *A spiritual approximation to Christ.* "*Come unto me.*" It would be trite to say, this is not to be regarded in a material but in a spiritual sense. As spiritual beings we have capacities to visit scenes and persons separated from us by countless leagues :—mind defies both time and space. On the wings of thought it can cross centuries in a moment, and visit scenes which no human eye hath seen. We are often doing so. Eden, Sinai, Jerusalem, Calvary—how often in our religious exercises do we visit these ? Abraham, Moses, David, Paul, Luther—we often feel ourselves standing side by side with these. We can come even now "*to an innumerable company of angels,*" &c. Thus we are come to Christ. Through His biography we come to His sentiments, to His sufferings and His death, to His principles, to His heart, to Himself.

Secondly : *A spiritual learning of Christ.* Of all things nothing is so important to man as learning. Without some learning he is little better than a brute. Of all learning there is none so important as religious learning. It alone touches the soul. Of religious learning there is none to be compared with that taught by Christ. He is the LOGOS. "Never man spake like this man."

Thirdly : *Spiritual obedience to Christ.* "*Take my yoke,*" &c. Every man has a moral master. He is under some yoke. The governing passion is your moral master. *Sensuality, worldliness, fame, and superstition.* These are yokes, heavy yokes, too. Christ's yoke is easy; it does not exhaust your strength, it gives new energy. It does not gall, it inspires with happiness. Come to Christ. *Mourner, doubter, backslider, penitent,*—come to Christ.

Matthew 12:1-13

Well-doing is Sabbath-Keeping

"*At that time Jesus went on the Sabbath-day through the corn.*" Thus opens our narrative. A walk in the corn-fields on the holy day of God, with a sea of ripened grain waving in the balmy breeze, must have been a soothing and refreshing exercise to Christ and His disciples. That walk was not the walk of the mere idler, who with a dead and thoughtless soul is frequently seen sauntering in the fields on the sacred day of rest; nor yet the walk of the mere sentimental admirer of nature, from whose mind the impressions of the grand and good evaporate in rhapsodic utterances. The mind of Jesus unquestionably was fully alive to the grandeur and goodness of the scene, and under His influences the disciples too, no doubt, participated, to some extent, in the lofty sentiments which stirred within Himself. The corn-field to them was a scene of worship; a temple radiant with the glory of God.

The disciples, being hungry, began as they walked the fields to pluck the corn and to eat. The captious Pharisees, whose eyes were ever following them and their Master, in order to discover some fault, seized with malignant avidity this act, and represented it to their Master as an act of Sabbath-breaking. "*Behold, Thy disciples do that which is not lawful to do on the Sabbath-day.*" The language of affected surprise and horror at His disciples, was evidently intended as a reproach of Himself. As if they had said— The impiety of Thy disciples, which fills us with amazement and horror, plainly shows what a blasphemer their Master must be! Christ meets these cavilling hypocrites in the spirit of magnanimous calmness; first, *by quoting authoritative examples from their own history.* The examples are taken from an incident in David's life; and from the work which the priests had to perform on the Sabbath-day. "*Have ye not read what David did, when he was an hungered and they that were with him; how he entered the house of God and did eat the shew-bread, which was not lawful for him to eat, neither for them that were with him, but only for the priests?*" The incident here referred to, you have recorded in 1 Sam. xxi. There is a powerful relevancy in this example to the case in point. As if Christ had said, You profess to be governed by the Scriptures, and to have a profound reverence for David: have you not read what he did? Do you not know that he and his men, in fleeing from the face of Saul, to satisfy their hunger, partook of the sacred food which had been placed on the table of shewbread, and which the law prohibited to all but the priests and their families? My disciples have only done what David and his men did,—violated the letter of a precept from the instinct of hunger. If you condemn my disciples, you should condemn David also. Moreover, "*have ye not read in the law, how that on the Sabbath-day the priests in the Temple profane the Sabbath and are blameless?*" Every Sabbath-day (Num. xxviii. 9) they have much labour in slaying victims and presenting offerings. If labour is a profanation of the Sabbath, then those very priests profaned the Sabbath; but they did not profane the Sabbath—they were held "*blameless.*"

He meets them also, secondly, *by propounding a true theory of the Sabbath.* He gives them to understand that the design of the Sabbath was not to prevent men doing what necessity and benevolence would dictate, but to subserve man's true interest. In every respect it was "*made for man.*" From the narrative I infer,—

I. That it is the ordination of God, in relation to man, that a certain portion of his time on earth should receive special religious attention. We find in the narrative that not only the Pharisees recognise the Sabbath, but Christ Himself, who emphatically speaks of it as having been " *made for man.*" The probability that the seventh day was observed from Adam to Moses to commemorate the glorious work of creation ; the fact that it was enjoined in the decalogue and regularly observed through the whole of Jewish history ; that Christ Himself, in such passages as the one under notice, recognised its existence ; that the apostles, whilst changing the day from the period of the resurrection of Christ, regularly devoted a seventh portion of their time to special religious devotions ; and that down through all the subsequent periods of the Christian church the disciples of Jesus have followed the example ;—such considerations as these, without mentioning others, which tell in the same direction, are sufficient to satisfy me that the great Author of our being intended one day out of seven of our existence on earth for special religious exercise. It is for man ; not like the Temple, for the Jew only. It is for *man ;* man in all ages and lands. " So long as man lives," says Stier, " he is to have a Sabbath of God : the necessity of his nature, and the ordinance of the Creator require this." We say, for man *on earth :* for in heaven, we presume, no such arrangement is needed. All days are Sabbaths there. The eternity of the good is one Sabbath. We say *special.* We do not mean, of course, that men are not bound to be religious on other days ; but that this day is to be used so that the religious feelings may get strength to rule us through *all* other days. The arrangement may be looked upon in a three-fold aspect :—

First : *Secular labour is an institution of God.* By secular labour I mean, the labour put forth to promote our material interests in this life. It is obvious to all that without such labour our existence here, for any length of time, would not be possible. It is by mental skill and muscular force that we draw from nature the sustenance of our physical being. The Sabbath implies this labour. It is a provision of rest " for man." I do not see how those who lounge away their existence in utter idleness can enter into the meaning of this day. Food is for all, but the hungry alone can enjoy it. The Sabbath is for all, but the worker alone can appreciate it.

The appointment of the Sabbath implies,—

Secondly : *That man has other interests than those to which secular labour is directed.* The direct end of secular work is for the body. The fact, therefore, that our benevolent Maker requires that on one day out of every seven of our earthly existence all the ordinary secular engagements of life shall be suspended, shows that man is a being that " *cannot live by bread alone ;* " that he has other relations than those that connect him with matter ; other wants than those which the world can supply. Man has an intellect to be cultivated, a heart to be disciplined, a soul to be saved. The Sabbath implies the existence of such claims.

The appointment of the Sabbath implies,—

Thirdly : *That there is a danger of secular engagements leading man to neglect the higher interests of his soul.* Otherwise, why should this day be devoted entirely to other than secular engagements? We have already stated that, as a rule, man can only live here by physical labour : the law is, "*he that does not work, shall not eat.*" By the sweat of our brow we are to eat our bread. As the population increases and competition heightens, the struggle for mere existence will become more urgent. Visit your factories, your fields, your exchange, your commercial thoroughfares, and ask, Why all this earnest and perpetual effort? The answer is, *To live.* Is this state of things an accident? · Is it a contingency that has sprung up uncontemplated by the plan of God? No. Our Maker saw all this. He saw the pressure of secular engagements to which we should be subject; and He, in mercy and wisdom, appointed one day which should be devoted to other and higher purposes ; lest in all this necessary whirl and bustle in order to preserve the body, the soul should be entirely neglected. God commands us to pause in our secular engagements every seventh day. Some men talk as if the world had out-grown the need of a Sabbath. Verily it becomes more and more necessary to our spiritual existence, as commerce increases its pressure on man. Let the Sabbath of England go, and the soul of England will soon sink under the turbid wave of materialism, to rise no more.

From the narrative I infer,—

II. That in the Jewish system this seventh portion of man's existence was enforced in all the precision and rigour of law. "*Behold, Thy disciples do that which is not lawful to do upon the Sabbath-day.*" In that law, which was given to Moses amidst the terrible manifestations of Sinai, called the decalogue, the precept respecting the Sabbath is introduced by the word "*Remember ;*" which, I conceive, implies that the obligation to observe it was known before. But now it came in all the definiteness and rigour of a positive enactment. The law refers not merely to the mere duty of its observance, but to the mode. On that day there was to be an entire cessation from "*all manner of work.*" There was to be no buying or selling ;* no food was to be prepared ;† no fire was to be kindled ; ‡ he who did any work, if it were only the gathering of a few sticks, was to be put to death.‖ The legal form in which it thus came to the Jew was local and temporary. It did not thus appear to Adam, nor does it come in such a garb to the Christian. It is done away in Christ.

Why was the Sabbath given to the Jew in this rigorous form of law, guarded by such terrible sanctions? I presume not to find out all the reasons of the Divine conduct, but I can discover certain uses which the arrangement subserves. It was not, of course, because a rigorous conformity to its mere letter was a virtue. Virtue

* Nehemiah x. 31.   + Exodus xv. 5, 22.   ‡ Exodus xxiv. 4.
‖ Numbers xv. 32.

was the same then as now, and will always be the same:—it is as immutable as God Himself. And virtue is chiefly a state of the heart. But this strictness, nevertheless, had its uses.

First: *This legal method of enforcement served to transmit its memory to posterity.* So corrupt in heart and forgetful of God were the Jews, that unless they had been thus bound at least to a ceremonial observance of this day, it would soon have passed into disuse and forgetfulness. But through these legal and ritualistic regulations it was preserved, as the tables of the law, the pot of manna, and Aaron's rod that budded, were guarded and transmitted by that mysterious chest that was covered by the mercy seat. So this seventh day which God "made for man," was guarded and transmitted through long centuries by the ceremonial regulations of Judaism. Or, to change the figure, these regulations were a kind of ark that preserved it amidst the floods of depravity, and bore it down through all the ages that followed.

Secondly: *This legal method of enforcement served to expose the depravity of the human heart.* One might have thought that it would only have been for man to *know* of such a day, in order to keep it with gratitude and delight: that he would have hailed its return and rejoiced in its sacred hours, and blessed his Maker for its merciful appointment. But no, he will not respect it at all unless he is forced. The cupidity of the world would have long since destroyed this day, had not the mercy of God maintained it, and maintained it by force. He wrenched it from the hands of cupidity.

Thirdly: *This legal method of enforcement served to impress upon man the importance of regarding it.* Mark the strict observance which the Hebrew race, for long centuries, rendered to this day. No work was done: the plough was still, the shops were closed, and the wheels of secular life were motionless. A deep and suggestive stillness hung over all the districts of Judea during its sacred hours. Mark the severe punishment which, without delay or mercy, was inflicted on those who dared so far to violate even the letter of the law, as to gather a stick to kindle a fire, in order to prepare their repast, or to warm them in the cold. What meaneth all this? Not that there was any virtue in this mere external observance, but that the *right observance of this day is of primary importance to humanity.* This was the lesson which the great God sought to impress upon the ages through the rigorous observance which He made the Jew, then in Palestine, for so many centuries to render to the Sabbath. What a true lesson is this! Philosophy and history combine to show the importance of the Sabbath to man. Where would be the religious sentiment of the world without the Sabbath, and what would the world be without religious sentiment?

I infer from this narrative,—

III. THAT A SUPREME REGARD TO THE SABBATH, AS A MERE LEGAL ENACTMENT, HAS NEVER, UNDER ANY DISPENSATION, BEEN TRUE SABBATH-KEEPING. This is implied in the cases before us. The Scribes and Pharisees had a supreme respect for the letter of the law. They

would not walk a single inch on the Sabbath beyond the space prescribed by the letter; the last moment of the holy day must have
expired before they would do "*any manner of work.*" They were
true to the letter in every point. Yet did they keep the Sabbath?
What was the state of their souls on this day? Was there a Sab-
batic calmness within? Were their spirits rapt in devout meditation
on the works of Him who "*rested on the seventh day and blessed it?*"
Did their hearts rise Godward in loving and prayerful sympathies for
their race on that day? No, no. They were saints without, but
fiends within. Their spirits were a troubled sea, heaved by the infernal tides of malignity. Deep hatred to Christ and His disciples
prompted them to rise early on this Sabbath morning in order to watch
their conduct, hoping to detect some fault, "*that they might accuse
Him.*" Luke gives us to understand that this malice grew to a passion which overstepped all bounds; "*they were filled with madness;*"
and Matthew says, "*they held a council against Him how they might destroy Him.*" Were there greater Sabbath-breakers on the round earth
that day, than were the Scribes and Pharisees, although they kept it
to the letter? On the other hand it is implied that whilst Christ and
His disciples did not pay much attention to the letter of the Sabbath,
they truly kept it. Christ seemed to have worked unusually hard this
day. "*Great multitudes followed Him, and He healed them all.*" Perhaps He did this in a measure to show these hypocrites that whilst
the letter of the law required that there should be "*no manner of
work,*" that hard labour was not necessarily a violation of its
spirit.

Mere formality has never been, and can never be, acceptable to
God. It is of itself a crime rather than a virtue. "*Thou desirest not
sacrifice, else would I give it thee; thou delightest not in burnt offering:
the sacrifices of God are a broken spirit; a broken and a contrite heart,
O God, thou wilt not despise.*" We here in England complain sadly
of the profanation of the Sabbath on the Continent. We draw a
comparison between Paris and London, in Sabbath sanctity, to the
spiritual advantage of the latter. May it be so! But let us not
forget that the closing of our shops, senate-houses, and theatres, is not
Sabbath-keeping. Men may be out of shops and yet in the business;
out of the senate-house, and yet in politics; out of the theatre, and
yet in amusements. Cessation from the outward pursuits of business and attendance on public worship are not Sabbath-keeping. In
pews, men's brains teem with business ideas, and their hearts heave
with the spirit of the market. Conventional Sabbath-keeping may
be, and often is, moral Sabbath profanation.

IV. That true Sabbath-keeping, under all economies has always been moral well-doing. "*Is it lawful,*" says Christ, "*to do
well on the Sabbath-day?*" The vital question here is, What is moral
well-doing? We can, I think, draw a satisfactory answer to this
question from the narrative before us.

First: *We infer that well-doing requires us to hold the positive and
formal in subjection to the moral and spiritual.* The positive and

the moral seemed now to come into collision. The positive pro-scribed "all manner of work," but the moral now required a certain kind of work. There were two moral principles which now urged work—*self-love* and *social love* : the one prompted the disciples to "*pluck the ears of corn*" to allay the cravings of hunger, the other prompted Christ to heal the "*withered hand*" of a diseased man. These two principles, as Butler has shown us, and our experience testifies, are innate. They are two imperative forces that our Maker has implanted within us ; and they must be obeyed. They are not like positive enactments, contingent, local, temporary:—they are necessary and universal. They are "*greater than the temple ;*"—greater than all ceremonies and institutions. They were before all positive enactments, and will live in the universe when all such en-actments are absolute. The Pharisees adhered to the positive, Christ, to the moral ; and the voice of unsophisticated humanity says Christ was right. He quotes a passage from the old Testament (Hos. vi. 6 ; 1 Sam. xv. 22). "*I will have mercy and not sacrifice,*" The spontaneity of love, and not the coercion of fear ; right affec-tions, not ritualistic acts ; the out-going heart not the mechanical hand, are what He requires. To exalt the positive above the moral, the form above the spirit, is a sin : to do otherwise even when there is a collision, is well-doing. Love is the royal law of the moral universe, from which all commandments take their rise, and to it all our positive institutes must give way.

Secondly : *We infer that well-doing requires that we should regard Christ as the Head of all institutions.* "*I say unto you that in this place is one greater than the temple.*" Jesus does not say, "I am greater;" but with much modesty, "there is something" (the original is in the neuter gender) "greater." Greater may mean either greater than the priests who served in the temple, of whom He had spoken in the preceding verse; or greater than the whole system which the temple represented. Either is true. In the 8th verse His superior-ity over positive institutions is still more distinctly and emphatically stated :—"*The Son of Man is Lord even of the Sabbath-day.*" The Son of Man is a significant and glorious title. It intimates His common relationship and sympathy with universal man. He is not called the Son of a Jew or a Gentile, but the Son of Man :—equally related to us all. He is the head of all positive institutions. He can modify them, or annul them, or multiply them. Positive pre-cepts, unlike moral principles, can be abrogated. Their appeal would create no vacuity in the universe, and would imply no contra-diction. Christ could do away with the Sabbath if He pleased, or make it occur once in five days, or once in five hundred years, or in any other period; but He could not do away with moral principles. He is not the Lord of them. He cannot abrogate the obligation of a moral being to speak the truth, to love God, and to act in all things righteously. Now *we do well* when we regard Him as the Head of all positive institutions. To follow Him, to imbibe His spirit, embody His principles, and regard Him as our Head in all things, is to do well. Follow Him, though in your path you tread positive institutes in the dust. " *He is Lord of all.*"

Thirdly : *We infer that well-doing requires that we should respect the claims of public worship.* " *And when He was departed thence, He went into the synagogue.*" Synagogues were places where the pious Jews assembled on Sabbath and festive days, for the purposes of prayer, reading, and expounding the Scriptures. Jesus attended these scenes of public worship, and once (probably on this occasion) officiated. Luke iv. 16. In attending public worship, He has left us an example. Public worship does not rest for its authority upon positive enactments, it *is a moral necessity.** The social heart of the devout man craves for it; and the mutual blending of souls in worship tends to the spiritual culture and elevation of each. To attend public worship is to " *do well.*" Men sometimes say, as an excuse for neglecting public worship, that they can worship God at home. My own impression is, an impression founded not only on observation but on the laws of mind, that he who neglects the public worship of God is not likely to worship Him at all.

Fourthly : *We infer that well-doing requires that we should always be ready to ameliorate the woes of men.* In the synagogue " *there was a man which had his hand withered : and they asked Him, saying, Is it lawful to heal on the Sabbath-day ? that they might accuse Him.*" It is not necessary to suppose that this incident occurred on the Sabbath-day on which Christ and His disciples walked in the corn-fields. It was probably on the following Sabbath. " This man," says Bengel, " had either come thither of his own accord that he might be healed, or else he had been brought by others with an insidious design." Here was another opportunity these captious hypocrites thought favourable to their malignant ends. He meets them in two ways. First, *by argument.* His argument is based upon two points, which they would be compelled to grant—(1) That if one of their sheep was in danger, they would seek to rescue it on the Sabbath. Self-interest, if not kindness, would impel them to make an effort to save the suffering and endangered animal. (2) That human life is more valuable than brute life. " *How much better is a man than a sheep !*" Their pride and their religion would prevent them from denying this. Man has reflection—conscience—responsibleness—immortality. Man is better than a sheep. The cattle upon a thousand hills are not to be compared with him in value. From these points the argument is—if it is not wrong to save the inferior, can it be wrong to restore the superior ? Nay, would it not be breaking the Sabbath not to do it. " *Is it lawful on the Sabbath-day to do good or to do evil, to save life or to destroy it ?*"

---

* Though public worship is a moral necessity, it may be doubted whether we are justified in satisfying this want without regard to the moral necessities of others. Many of those who travel to a distance to attend public worship would do better to show their respect to the letter of the Fourth Commandment by frequenting a house of prayer nearer their residence, or by denying themselves the exercise of this privilege, lest they put a stumbling-block in the way of the weak, the prejudiced, the ignorant, and the ungodly.— *Webster.*

The words imply, that the work of helping a suffering creature is well-doing; and that every omission of the work, where the opportunity occurs, is *evil-doing.* He meets these cavilling Scribes and Pharisees—Secondly, *by a curative act.* " *Then saith He to the man, Stretch forth thy hand : and he stretched it forth; and it was restored whole as the other.*" Here is an illustration of three things. (1) *A recognised capability of volition.* The command implies that the diseased had the power of *willing.* Man can will. (2) *The true law of volition.* The will of Christ; not circumstances. If this man had yielded to circumstances, to ideas of his own weakness and infirmities, he would not have resolved. (3) *The value of obedient volition.* He obeyed Christ and his volition sent blood, life, and energy into his *withered hand. Let us will what Christ commands,* and mighty will be our achievements.

Sabbath-keeping, then, is well-doing, and well-doing is what we have propounded. It is not adherence to the letter, but living in its spirit. Listen to the illustrious Dr. Arnold, in his letter to Justice Coleridge on this subject. He says—"Although I think that the whole law is done away with, so far as it is the law given on Mount Sinai, yet as far as it is the law of the Spirit, I hold it to be all binding; and believing that our need of a Lord's-day is as great as ever it was, and that, therefore, its observance is God's will, and is likely, so far as we see, to be so to the end of time, I should think it mischievous to weaken the respect paid to it."

Matthew 12:14-21

The Glory of True Gentleness as illustrated in Christ

It would be difficult to decide, with certainty, the exact place which this passage holds in the chronology of Christ's life. The probability, however, is, that it follows the healing of the man in the synagogue on the Sabbath-day, who "had his hand withered," and which is recorded in the paragraph that engaged our attention in the last " Section." *Then,* after He had performed this wonderful cure on the Sabbath-day, " *Then the Pharisees went out and held a council against Him how they might destroy Him.*"

It is my intention to use this little fragment of Christ's life, and the remarks of His biographer upon it, to illustrate the Glory of Gentleness. We shall leave the necessary verbal explanation to come out in the course of our observations upon the general subject. "The glory of gentleness!" Who, it may be said, ever heard of such a title, who ever heard of such a thing? The world sees glory in those who with a daring self-confident aim step into the most prominent and responsible positions of life, and play their part with great tact and more parade. But glory in connexion with that meek and retiring man who does his rightful work in the shade, shrinks from the noisy tongue of fame as from an unheavenly sound—is a strange thing at present to our proud world. Still it is a reality. It is the only glory on earth of any worth, or of any lasting duration. Let us look at this gentleness as it appeared in Christ, the Heavenly Teacher—the model man, as well as the redeeming God.

From this passage we infer in relation to this subject—

I. THAT THE GENTLENESS OF CHRIST EXISTED IN THE PRESENCE OF HIS MOST MALIGNANT ENEMIES. The Pharisees, we are told, " *held a council against Him how they might destroy Him.*" " *They were filled with madness,*" says Luke. Their rage overbore their reason. They were frantic with indignation. Yet, notwithstanding this, Jesus was gentle. His breast was not perturbed by fear, nor shaken by the surges of revenge. He was not, of course, indifferent to life. The instinct of self-preservation lived and acted in Him as in all men. Indeed, the fact that He now withdrew from the presence of His infuriated enemies shows that He had that respect for His own preservation, which is common to our kind. " *When Jesus knew it*" —knew the indignation of His enemies, He retired to the quiet shores of Galilee. *He withdrew Himself from thence.* He " *withdrew.*" He did not, impelled by fear, flee from them. We never hear of Him, like some of the old saints, " fleeing from His enemies." He peacefully retired, passed off with the calm majesty of an heroic soul. There is a species of gentleness that is serene amidst the friendly and propitious, but which rushes into turbulent excitement in the presence of the adverse. Such gentleness is but the storm sleeping in the stagnant air. True gentleness is that which can look calmly on the face of a frowning multitude, and maintain a quiet mastery over the passions amidst the most terrible events. Such was the gentleness of Christ; and in such gentleness I see the highest grade of glory.

From this passage we infer—

II. THAT THE GENTLENESS OF CHRIST WAS SUSTAINED AMIDST THE ACTIVITIES OF IMMENSE LABOUR. " *And great multitudes followed Him, and He healed them all.*" Mark says, " *A great multitude from Galilee followed Him, and from Judea, and from Jerusalem, and from Idumea, and from beyond Jordan; and they about Tyre and Sidon, a great multitude, when they had heard what great things He did, came unto Him. And He spake to His disciples, that a small ship should wait on Him because of the multitude, lest they should throng Him. For He had healed many; insomuch that they pressed upon Him for to touch Him, as many as had plagues. And unclean spirits, when they saw Him, fell down before Him, and cried, saying, Thou art the Son of God.*"

The shore of Galilee, whither He withdrew from the malignant Pharisees, teemed with men gathered from all districts of the country. The diseased among them He healed, the ignorant He taught. For His convenience He enters a little skiff, which, perhaps, was floating on the margin of the beach; and from that skiff, as from a pulpit, He spoke to the vast multitudes that thronged the shore—spoke words which served to heal alike the diseases of the body and the mind. Here is labour amidst the most *exciting* scenes; yet how *gentle* the Great Worker! He is not elated by His popularity, He is not harassed by the multiplicity of engagements. There, amidst the stirring grandeur of nature and the still more exciting appearance of restless crowds of men, whose anxious eyes, centering on Him, met His glance at every turn, He prosecutes His divine mission with all the ease of a moral master. This gentleness, which we ever see developed in Christ, in the midst of immense labour, is the gentleness with which I associate the idea of glory. There is a gentle mien and bearing—a certain ease and gracefulness of manner much approved in modern society as forming the "gentleman," which are often nothing more than a certain lackadaisical effeminacy. The ringed and delicate hands cannot labour. The slightest trials destroy its equanimity. The graceful ease is mechanical, not moral, measured by the laws of etiquette, not directed by the gentle motions of a heaven-attuned soul. It is but a miserable mockery of that thing which men are made to admire, that which Christ embodied; namely, the gentleness of a great soul lifted above the mercenary and the servile, moving in conscious harmony with the universe, itself, and God.

From this passage we infer—

III. THAT THE GENTLENESS OF CHRIST APPEARED IN THE UNOSTENTA-TIOUS AND TENDER MANNER IN WHICH HE PROSECUTED THE SUBLIMEST MISSION. "*He shall not strive, nor cry, neither shall any man hear His voice in the streets: a bruised reed shall he not break,*" &c.

First: *Observe the mission in which He was engaged.* There are two expressions used here to designate it: "*Show judgment unto the Gentiles,*" and "*Send forth judgment unto victory.*" That is, "until he make the cause of judgment and truth completely victorious." What a work is this! What revolutions does it involve;—social, political, ecclesiastical, and moral! Enthrone rectitude in human institutions and human souls, and earth will bloom as paradise once more.*

Secondly: *Observe the spirit with which He pursued it.* (1) *Unostentatiousness.* The whole life of Christ is marked by this. How unostentatiously He came at first into our world. No cannons roared, no bells pealed to announce His birth. He came in the quiet of morning, before the slumber of the world was broken, nor did His advent break its hush. One might have thought that His birth would have been announced by signals that would have startled the nations with awe. Few babes were ever born in more obscure circumstances—few babes, on entering life, awoke less sensation than He. His public ministry is marked by the same spirit. "*He made himself of no reputation.*" He appears not in the aspect of a sovereign, but in "*the form of a servant.*" He descends into the

* See *Homilist*, vol. vi., p. 35.

lower parts of the earth, mingles with the lowest grades of society, enters into the sorrows and the trials of the poorest of the poor. In His sermons, there is none of the vociferation of the popular declaimer, none of the ornament of the ambitious orator. All is free and familiar. " *His doctrines distil as the dew.*" Whether you see Him talking with the woman of Samaria, or sitting down with the promiscuous multitude on the mountain brow, or eating at the table of the publican, or entering for the last time the metropolis of His own country, you are struck with His modest and unostentatious bearing. He leaves the world in the same way. Instead of rousing its attention to His departure, He goes out early in the morning to the Mount of Olives, while mankind are yet asleep, takes with Him His disciples, and after spreading His benevolent hands over them, and pronouncing His last benediction, quietly leaves the world; leaves it until those ages pass which gracious Heaven has allowed for His redemptive work : and then He will come again, and " *every eye shall see Him.*" (2) *Tenderness.* " *A bruised reed shall He not break, and the smoking flax shall He not quench.*" A reed is in itself a frail plant : not like the ash or the oak, of firm and solid structure. But this is a *bruised* reed, whose vitality has been checked and whose head bows to the earth. So tender, however, is Christ, that He will not injure this frail and delicate life. Nor will He " *quench the smoking flax.*" The full flame of the lamp may stand before a strong gust of air, but as it flickers with exhausted oil and wick in its last stage, the softest breath will put it out. And so tender is Christ in His methods of redemptive agency, that He will not hasten the extinction of the dying flame. There are men in society, like the broken reed and the flickering lamp—ex· ceedingly frail. Some weak in circumstances, depressed by trials and privations; some weak in body—the springs of health have failed, and life is ebbing out; some weak in intellect, having neither the power nor the means to get broad and lofty views of truth; and some weak in piety—babes in Christ. But with all these the Great Physician deals with the utmost tenderness. He will raise the " *bruised reed,*" and give it strength to bear the scorching sun and stormy wind, " *He gathers the lambs with His arm and carries them in His bosom, and gently leads those that are with young.*"

What a display of true gentleness you have here! Here is a Being engaged in the most momentous works, the work of showing "*judgment unto the Gentiles,*" and bringing forth " *judgment unto victory,*" who, instead of wearing some badge of earthly glory—and no badge, however magnificent, could adequately express the real greatness either of His being or mission—appears as the poorest of the poor. Instead of lifting His voice with the air of a hero or a sovereign, His voice is scarcely heard in the street. He does " *not strive;*" there is no display of violence in grappling with His foes. He does " *not lift up His voice in the street*" to gather and touch the souls of multitudes. He eschews all the miserable tricks of the candidate for popularity. Nor does He, on His triumphal march, haughtily pass by the frail and the tried—no: the "*bruised reed He does not break, nor quench the smoking flax.*"

From this passage we infer—

IV. THAT THE GENTLENESS OF CHRIST DEMONSTRATES HIS SPECIAL CONNEXION WITH GOD. His quietly withdrawing from the malignant Pharisees, retiring unostentatiously to the sea-side, and there, with modesty as distinguished as His love, doing good to the multitude that followed Him, and His charging them that "*they should not make Him known,*" reminded Matthew of what had been predicted of old concerning the specially chosen, beloved, and qualified servant of God—the model servant: "*That it might be fulfilled that was spoken by Esaias the prophet, saying, Behold my servant, whom I have chosen, my beloved, in whom my soul is well pleased: I will put my Spirit upon Him, and He shall show judgment unto the Gentiles.*" This does not mean, of course, that Jesus worked thus in order to fulfil the prophecy, but that, in acting so, this prophecy was so illustrated that it at once reminded Matthew of it. The fact that he does not quote it with verbal accuracy either from the Hebrew, or the Septuagint version, shows that it was a passage in Matthew's memory which this gentleness of Christ most vividly recalled.

There is, perhaps, no greater proof of a man's close moral connexion with God, and of His divine mission and endowments, than true *gentleness* of soul. God is a "*God of peace.*" The universe may be in the utmost commotion but it wakes no ripple on the Divine nature. He *sits* in sublime tranquility "*above the flood.*" All His operations are gentle. In the working of human machinery, the grating noise and the rattling din are often insufferable to the ear; but, how noiselessly works the stupendous and complicated mechanism of the great universe! Scarcely à sound is heard where God's hand is most manifest. He, who, in the moral domain, works most gently, works in closest contact and nearest sympathy with the GREAT ONE. The more removed from Him we are, the more turbulent in soul—the more blustering in action we become. The most noisy Church is the least divine—the most blustering members, the most vociferous preachers—though the most attractive for the hour, are the least in harmony with the ordinary operations of God. Noise is not power. It is the little shallow stream that you hear rattling among the hills; the deep rivers roll on in majestic calmness. It is not the exciting flash of lightning that melts the snowy mountains and clothes the earth with verdure—it is the gentle sunbeam. It is the little lamp kindled by man that flickers in every wind: the stars lit up by God burn steadily and brightly amidst the fiercest hurricane.

From this passage we infer—

V. THAT THE GENTLENESS OF CHRIST WILL ONE DAY WIN THE CONFIDENCE OF THE WORLD. "*In His name shall the Gentiles trust;*" or, as paraphrased by Doddridge, this gentle and gracious administration shall cheer mankind in so sensible and irresistible a manner that *the Gentiles shall confide in His illustrious name.*

Three remarks may serve to illustrate this remarkable passage:— First : *That man is essentially a trusting being.* Like all creatures he is dependent, and this dependence he is made to feel every day. He has wants which require supplies from without ; he has affections which require repose in something without. As the ivy twines around the oak, the human affections twine around some outward object. Every man's soul has an object of chief love and reliance. Some trust in one thing and some in another—some in gold, some in " *chariots, and some in horses:* "—all trust. Secondly : *Man's condition is evermore determined by the character of the objects in which he confides.* He who places implicit reliance upon objects incapable of meeting the instincts and exigences of his being—the false, the unworthy, and the frail, must inevitably suffer. Thirdly : *The name of Christ is the only object of trust that can secure man's well-being.* His name is Himself. He is *supremely worthy* of trust. His character commends itself to man's highest admiration. He is an *adequate* object of trust ; His wisdom can guide in every perplexity ; His power supply every want. He is a *lasting* object of trust. " *The mountains shall depart and the hills be removed,*" but " *He is the same to-day, yesterday, and for ever.*" Fourthly : *The gentleness of Christ is adapted to win the world to a confidence in His name.* Gentleness is *love.* Selfishness and malevolence are never gentle, they are turbulent and clamorous ; but love is gentle and ever winning—it is the magnet of the soul. Gentleness is *holiness.* Sin is never gentle ; it heaves the soul like a troubled sea : but rectitude is ever gentle and ever attractive ; men are made to admire the righteous. Gentleness is *moral majesty.* It is the state of a soul raised above fear and sin, sitting down as it were at the right hand of God ; and this moral majesty has ever a power to fascinate and win the heart.

Brother, it is only as we represent the gentleness of Christ that we shall draw the world to Him. The Church has too often been the scene of arrogance and clamour. We have had the harsh tones of the bigot, the pompous jargon of the blustering dogmatist, and the wild raving of the ignorant declaimer ; but how little of the gentleness of Him, who, when on earth, " *did not strive or cause His voice to be heard in the street,*"—who does not break the " *bruised reed, nor quench the smoking flax.*" Once, in the ages that are gone, " a great and strong wind rent the mountains, and break in pieces the rocks before the Lord, but the Lord was not in the wind ; and after the wind, an earthquake, but the Lord was not in the earthquake ; and after the earthquake, a fire, but the Lord was not in the fire ; and after the fire, a still small voice :" and it was in this still small voice that the word of the Lord was conveyed. " *The Kingdom of God cometh not with observation.*"

Matthew 12:22-30

The Satanic and the Divine

All the different parts of this paragraph can, we think, be conveniently explained under these four general ideas ;—ideas which are fairly and clearly deducible from the entire passage :

I. THAT GOD AND SATAN ARE BOTH AT WORK IN CONNEXION WITH MANKIND IN THIS WORLD. " *Then was brought unto Him one possessed with a devil, blind and dumb : and He* (Christ) *healed him, insomuch that the blind and dumb both spake and saw.*" Here was a man on whom Satan acted, and on whom the Great God, in the person of Christ, acted also. What Satanic possession really meant in *those days* has been noticed elsewhere, and is not our question now. We take the case before us as the type of a fact common to human nature in this world ; namely, *that God and Satan are acting upon it ;*—that it is everywhere subject to the agencies of these two Beings.

First : *Humanity is morally possessed of the devil.* If I were asked to exert my ingenuity to discover the best emblem to represent the moral state of the world, I could not do better than take a man deprived of eyes, and the power of speech, his ears sealed, his reason gone, the creature of a wild fancy, and of fiery and uncontrollable impulses. Just such is the emblem which the New Testament furnishes us in these demoniacs. The world is morally "*possessed.*" I infer this, because I find it everywhere pursuing courses of action, adopting theories, controlled by motives, inspired by passions, *inconsistent with its own reason, with its own conscience, and with its own well-being.* I infer this, because it is in manifest hostility to the mind and will of its Creator :—in His judgment "*every imagination of its heart is evil continually.*" I infer this, because it is attested by universal experience. The uncivilised has it as a feeling that the Evil One is upon him, the philosopher adopts it as a doctrine, and the saint wrestles and struggles against it as "*a law in his members warring against the law of his mind.*" I infer this, because the Bible teaches it. It teaches us that "*the prince of the power of the air worketh in the children of disobedience;*" that "the field" of the world is open to him, and that whilst men sleep he is " sowing the tares " of evil and ruin. You pity, or perhaps you stand aghast with horror at, the demoniacs who figure on the page of evangelical history ; sometimes blind and dumb, as in the case before us, sometimes raging and furious as wild beasts, tearing their own bodies, haunting the deserts, and dwelling amidst the ghastly tombs. But all this, believe me, is but a faint emblem of the moral influence which Satan has over our world. The world is but a huge moral demoniac. It is spiritually blind, deaf, dumb, mad.

Secondly : *Humanity thus morally possessed of the devil is benevo-*

lently acted upon by God. "*He healed him, insomuch that the blind and dumb both spake and saw.*" God does not leave humanity in this Satanic state. Were He to do so the world would become a pandemonium. No! he strives with men : strives by the influences of nature, by the events of history, by the dictates of conscience, by the truths of the Gospel, by the Spirit of Christ. Every act a man does has either the Divine or the Satanic character. We are the organs, the agents, the representatives, of one or other of these invisible powers. Children of the prince of darkness or of the Father of Light we are all. Hell and heaven meet and battle in man.

II. THAT THE EJECTION OF EVIL FROM HUMAN NATURE IS AN INCONTROVERTIBLE PROOF THAT THE ACT IS DIVINE. When the Pharisees heard that Christ had expelled the evil spirit from the man, they said, "*This fellow does not cast out devils, but by Beelzebub the prince of the devils.*" But the absurdity, to say nothing at present about the astounding impiety, of the allegation, will appear manifest if we just notice several things in the passage.

First: *The nature of Satan's work.* His work is not to deliver men from evil, but to afflict them with it. The case before us is a specimen of his work upon men in general; it is to make them "*blind and dumb.*" He is a destroyer, not a Saviour. The blindness, deafness, dumbness, and oftentimes madness, which marked these demoniacs, were but illustrations of the effects of Satan upon the souls of men. How he blinds their understandings so that they cannot see the spiritual realities of the spiritual world! How he seals their ears against the voices of heavenly wisdom! How he takes away their power of speech for God and truth! How he warps their judgment and deranges their understanding, so that in relation to spiritual things they are like madmen! This is the work of Satan upon the soul. He help to eject evil from man,—he aid in casting out devils! No, no, his work is to make men devils. Like begets like, the universe through. "*The prince of the power of the air*" breathes an atmosphere impregnated with the elements of hell.

Secondly: *The impression of the people.* "*All the people were amazed, and said, Is not this the Son of David?*" that is, Is not this the true Messiah; He of whom it was predicted that He would "*open the eyes of the blind*"? &c. The impression of all unprejudiced men would be, that God is in the expulsion of evil. We are not disposed to admit that this of itself would be conclusive, for popular impressions are frequently, perhaps generally, wrong ; but taken with other considerations it undoubtedly increases the power of the evidence.

Thirdly: *The reasoning of Christ.* The reasoning of Christ involves an appeal to three things : (1) To the common sense of men. "*And Jesus knew their thoughts, and said unto them, Every kingdom divided against itself is brought to desolation, and every city or house divided against itself cannot stand : and if Satan cast out Satan he is* *divided against himself ; how shall then his kingdom stand ? "* It is here implied that Satan would not do it. Would a king destroy loyalty in his subjects? Would the head of a family introduce division into the family circle? Would Satan as an intelligent being war against his own interest? Would he aim at the overthrow of his own empire? The power and influence of his empire consist in propagating and strengthening evil ; to expel evil, therefore, is to weaken his authority. Is it likely that he will do so? Then as Satan could not do it, Christ asserts that it *is done by some stronger power.* *"How can one enter into a strong man's house and spoil his goods, except he first bind the strong man? and then he will spoil his goods."* The power of Satan in a depraved man is strong. The heart of a corrupt person *" is a strong man's house,"*—the devil is there. He has taken possession. He has built around it strong defences, he has bolted the doors with more than iron bars. He has got possession, and he is strong there. No mortal man can get him out. If ever he is to be expelled it must be by some one who has power to bind the strong man, to spoil his goods, and take possession of the habitation. God only can do this. The reasoning of Christ involves—(2) An appeal to their professions. There were men amongst the Jews recognised as good men by these Pharisees, who professed to cast out devils. Jesus asks, *" By whom do your children "*—your disciples—*" cast them out ?"* You believe that they do it by the power of God. Why, then, should you say that I do it by Beelzebub? The reasoning of Christ—(3) appeals to a universal truth : *" He that is not with me is against me ; and he that gathereth not with me scattereth abroad."* There is no neutrality in morals ; no neutrality in moral principles : all things are right or wrong. No neutrality in moral actions : they are either good or bad. They may have a good form, and yet be bad. No neutrality in moral positions : all are either on the side of God, or on the side of the devil. No neutrality in moral influence : it is either useful or injurious. *Moral neutrality is impossible.**

III. That notwithstanding the manifest distinction between divine works and satanic, there are men perverse enough to confound the difference. These Pharisees did so now. They said, *" this fellow,"* &c. There are two great evils which men commit on the question of moral causation :—

First : *Some ascribe bad deeds to God.* The warrior who has rifled cities and slain his thousands appears after his bloody achievements at the altar, to return thanks to that God who has commanded us not to *kill,* and declared that all wars arise from *" the lusts "* of the wicked heart. The priest who presumes to stand between God and the people, by his sacerdotal services professing to propitiate Almighty justice, ascribes his crafty deeds to God. The Islam and the Mormonite leaders, who impose upon the credulity of the ignorant, profess to have derived their authority and doctrines from heaven. How much kingly despotism, military slaughter, priestly craft,

* See an excellent sermon of Vinet's, in his " Vital Christianity," on the subject.

religious imposture, and international plunder and oppression are enacted in the sacred name of God.

Secondly: *Some ascribe good deeds to Satan.* These cavilling and malicious men did so:—irritated with jealousy at the impression which Christ's miracle made upon the people, so favourable to His own growing popularity, they said, with contemptuous indignation, " *This fellow doth not cast out devils, but by Beelzebub, the prince of the devils."* They could not deny the miracle, it was too patent to all; the only plan they had, therefore, to resist its influence amongst the people was to ascribe it to Satanic agency. This they did. They traced a good act to a bad cause, a Divine act to the arch-foe of God. This was heinous sin. Yet the principle of this has been too common in every age. What is the conduct of those who assign all the good effects which Christianity has produced upon the world, the moral miracles it has achieved amongst the various tribes and nations of the earth to the ingenuity and craft of impostors, and who designate the Bible a *" cunningly devised fable ? "* What, too, is the conduct of those who, alas! abound in all times and lands, who are ever disposed to ascribe good acts to bad motives, and brand as hypocrites the most holy and useful men ? Why, such conduct is exactly the same in principle as that which these blaspheming Scribes and Pharisees now committed. Whilst we stand appalled at the enormous wickedness of these men who ascribe the benign miracles of the Son of God to Satanic agency, let us remember that the principle of this conduct has ever been rife in the world, and may, peradventure, be even yet in our own deceitful hearts.

Whilst God and Satan are here working on our fallen nature, let us not mistake the agency; let us not confound the working of beings so infinitely dissimilar. I know not which is the greater enormity of the two, to trace earth's crimes to heaven, or earth's virtues to the " Evil One; " but both, I know, are common sins. Proud reason! boast no more of thy philosophy. In man depraved, thou art the vassal of a wicked heart, worked to justify a guilty life and hush a crying conscience.

Matthew 12:31-32

The Unpardonable State

The miracle which Jesus had just performed was so manifestly real that His greatest enemies, " *the Scribes and the Pharisees,"* were utterly unable to account for it on any natural principles. The supernaturalness of the act was incontrovertible. They felt that no mere human power could have achieved it. What then were they to do in order to *maintain* the opposition which they had assumed towards Christ ? There was evidently only one course before them, namely, the ascribing of the miracle to Satanic agency. If they ascribed it to Divine power, then it would be a proof of His Messiahship, and their position would be destroyed. If they were to retain their hostile attitude, therefore, they were "*shut up*" to this course; and this course they adopted.

In the preceding verses, which we noticed in our *last section*, Christ gives a triumphant refutation of that explanation of His miracle which referred it to Satanic agency. After this, He adds in these verses a declaration which might well strike the utmost terror into their hearts :—"*Wherefore I say unto you, all manner of sin and blasphemy shall be forgiven unto men : but the blasphemy against the Holy Ghost shall not be forgiven unto men,*" &c.

The overwhelmingly solemn question which now meets us is, What is this sin that seals for ever a man's fate, that places him for ever beyond the pale of forgiveness, that shuts him up for ever beneath the ever-blackening firmament of condemnation ? What is the downward step that can never be retraced ? The act starting from an impulse that can never be overcome, but which must gather new hellward force for ever ?

There are at least two theories deserving notice : * the one is, that the act was such that the Pharisees, in consequence of the peculiar circumstances in which they stood to Christ, could *alone* commit; and the other is, that it was such opposition to the Spirit of God as all are liable to who reject the offers of mercy through Jesus Christ. The latter seems to me the more probable. (1) Because there is no positive proof that the Pharisees did really commit the sin. Jesus did not say so, nor does His language necessarily imply it. Moreover, if they had been guilty of this unpardonable sin, why did He continue to preach to them ? And why on the Cross did He pray for their forgiveness ? (2) Because assuming that they committed this sin the latter hypothesis is sufficiently comprehensive to involve their particular act. They wilfully referred Divine phenomena to Satanic cause,—they traced the productions of God to the agency of evil. All who state, knowing better, that Christ is an impostor, and that the Bible is a fable, commit in spirit the blasphemous deed of these Pharisees. (3) Because the latter hypothesis agrees with other passages in the New Testament which must be regarded as of general and permanent application. The Bible does certainly teach that man may here arrive at a point in sin when salvation becomes impossible—that the day of grace closes with some before the day of life.†

Now, although we would not presume to define with precision this *unpardonable state*, yet we think that *some light* may be thrown upon it by the following course of thought :—

I. THAT THE ONLY OBSTRUCTION NOW EXISTING TO THE FORGIVENESS OF MAN ON EARTH IS IMPENETENCY OF HEART. There are three things necessary to the remission of sins.

* Those who wish to see a statement of all the views that have been propounded should consult Knapp's "Theology," section 84.
† See Heb. vi. 4–6, x. 29 ; 1 John v. 16 ; 2 Pet. ii. 22.

First : *That the righteous Sovereign should be disposed to pardon.*
Forgiveness is the exclusive prerogative of the Supreme Ruler
whose laws have been violated and whose authority has been con-
temned. If, therefore, He is *indisposed* to the exercise of this sovereign prerogative, forgiveness must be necessarily unattainable.

Secondly : *That there be a ground honourable to His character and
safe to His government on which the pardon can be dispensed.* It is easy
to conceive of a sovereign having a disposition to dispense forgiveness to a criminal, and yet having no way of doing so without clouding his justice, weakening the motives to obedience, and endangering
the order of his kingdom.

Thirdly : *That there should be a proper state of mind in the criminal
for the reception of the pardon.* Let the sovereign be *disposed* to pardon, let him also have an *honourable way* in which to dispense it, yet
if the disposition of the criminal remains the same as that which
prompted the crime, there would be the strongest reason to withhold
the remission.

Now as we can only conceive of these *three* obstructions to human
forgiveness, the question is which of these exist ? Is it the first ?
Is the Infinite Sovereign indisposed to the exercise of pardoning
mercy ? Listen to His own declaration : " *Let the wicked forsake his
way and the unrighteous man his thoughts, and let him return unto the
Lord, and He will have mercy on him, and to our God, for He will
ABUNDANTLY pardon.*" Is it the second ? Listen again. " *The blood
of Jesus Christ, His Son, cleanseth us from all sin.*" " *He is a propitia-
tion for our sins, and not for ours only, but for the sins of the whole
world.*" " *He is able to save to the uttermost all them that come unto
God through Him.*"

The last, then, is the only alternative, namely, the state of the
sinner's heart. Men are not forgiven because they do not repent.
"Repentance and remission of sins " go together. " *Repent and be
converted, every one of you, that your sins may be blotted out, when the
times of refreshing shall come from the presence of the Lord.*" This is
no *arbitrary* condition. Pardon without repentance would be a
licence to further crime, would be worthless to the individual himself,
and an injury to the universe. Let the world repent, and from the
throne of God there will go forth the pardoning words of love, " *Thy
sins which are many are all forgiven.*"

II. THAT FAITH IN CHRIST, AS THE INFALLIBLE REVEALER OF THE
ALMIGHTY SOVEREIGN, IS ESSENTIAL TO THE REMOVAL OF THIS IMPEN-
ITENCY OF HEART.

This will appear from two facts—

First : *That a conviction of God's love towards the impenitent is indispensable.* How can repentance towards God be produced ? From
the laws of our spiritual nature, it is required that to awaken *new
emotions* you must produce *new beliefs.* If you change a man's faith
in relation to any object, you change the whole character and current
of his feelings in relation to that object. Get faith that the man
you hate is estimable in character, generous in sympathy, and bene-

volent in purpose towards you, and forthwith your hatred gives place to love. From the constitution of our nature, a deep impression of the fact that He whose laws we have transgressed and whose authority we have opposed, loves us with infinite depth and tenderness, is necessary to break the impenitent heart into gracious affections towards Him. And this, be it observed, is repentance. Mere moral regret, awakened by a revelation of law, is not evangelical penitence;—Judas had this—hell has this;—*but a change in the controlling dispositions and affections of the heart towards God.* Now, nothing can in the nature of the case produce this but a conviction of God's love towards us.

Secondly: *That faith in Christ as the infallible revealer of God is essential to this conviction.* Where do we learn that God loves man in his *sinful* state? Does nature reveal it? No; nature reveals the general goodness of God. Nature says nothing as to God's feelings towards the *sinner.* The volume of Nature was published *before* the fall. It is Christ that teaches it. He teaches that His love and tenderness are expression and proof of God's love; that because God loved the world, He sent Him—His only begotten Son—that "*whosoever believeth in Him might not perish but have everlasting life.*" It may be said that the prophets and the apostles teach the same. The reply is, that the former learnt it from the " *Spirit of Christ that was in them,*" and the latter directly from His own teaching. *The conviction that God loves the sinner is derived from Christ exclusively.*

But is He the infallible revealer of God? if not, I cannot accept His teaching on the subject. Nay, if not, I have every reason to reject it. For He having revealed Himself as such is the greatest of impostors, and therefore not to be trusted. Hence faith in Him as the infallible revealer of God is indispensable to give us that conviction of Divine love which is necessary to produce that genuine penitence without which there can be no forgiveness.

III. THAT ALL THE EVIDENCE NECESSARY TO THIS FAITH IN CHRIST AS THE INFALLIBLE REVEALER OF GOD MUST BE REGARDED AS FURNISHED BY THE HOLY SPIRIT. The evidence in favour of the fact that Christ is the infallible revealer of God is drawn from at least three sources :—

First : *From His own character, doctrines, and works.* His character in every part commends itself to our moral intuitions, answers to our ideal of moral excellence and glory. His doctrines are so consonant with our reason, so true to our experience, and so adapted to our sense of the sublime, that we feel that He was a teacher sent from God. His miracles are so uniformly merciful, so profoundly significant, and so overwhelmingly grand, that we feel that no one could do such works unless God were with Him.

Secondly : *From the remarkable relation of all the sacred writers to Him.* They all, or nearly all, refer to Him. Those who lived ages before Him, those who were His contemporaries, and those who lived after Him, for the most part, refer to Him as the principal subject. And although many of them lived in different climes and ages, all their statements about Christ agree with what He actually was. He actualised in His own being and history the ideas of all ; took up their conceptions, embodied them, drew them out in living characters, and thus fulfilled " *the law and the prophets.*" This remarkable congruity is mighty evidence.

Thirdly : *From the effects which His system has produced upon the world.* Its influence has been wide, purifying, and religious ; has always been to turn men to God—to assimilate them to Christ. The history of Christianity in the world is an inconvertible evidence of its Divinity.

Now, is not the Spirit of God to be regarded as the *author of this threefold description of evidence ?* The character, doctrines, and worth of Christ are refered to the SPIRIT, which was given to Him "*without measure.*" The writings of prophets and apostles are to be ascribed to that Spirit, who inspired them to write, moving them thereto. The triumphs of the Gospel in the world are to be ascribed to that Spirit, without whose aid Paul may plant and Apollos water, but all would be in vain. Every event, every statement, every consideration that serves to convince that Christ is the infallible revealer of God, must be ascribed to the Divine Spirit. It is one of His special functions to CONVINCE ; and He supplies and arranges all the necessary evidence for the work.

IV. THAT A WILFUL REJECTION OF THIS EVIDENCE IS SUCH A TREATMENT OF THE SPIRIT AS MUST IN THE NATURE OF THE CASE EXCLUDE THE POSSIBILITY OF FORGIVENESS. This follows as a necessary inference from the three former propositions. If penitence is necessary to forgiveness, if a conviction of Divine love is necessary to penitence, if faith in Christ as the infallible revealer of Divine love is necessary to this conviction, if the evidence to produce this conviction is the work of the Spirit, then it follows as a necessity that a wilful rejection of this evidence is such a treatment of the Spirit as must in the nature of the case exclude the possibility of forgiveness. He that trifles with the evidence trifles with the Spirit ; he that resists the evidence resists the Spirit ; he that contemns the evidence contemns the Spirit. The man that continues to do this *can never be forgiven, in this world or the world to come.*

Blasphemy means disrespect, irreverence, calumny, indignity. The greatest sin you can commit against a man is to blaspheme him, to traduce his charcter, to injure his reputation, to treat him with contempt. The man that steals your reputation is of all felons the greatest ; and yet this felony goes generally unpunished, and is too often practised, even in the so-called religious circles and journals. And this blasphemy or calumny is the greatest sin you can commit against man, so it is the greatest sin you can commit against the Spirit.

It is the *climax* of iniquity. A lower state of depravity is not conceivable than that state in which a man scorns the most sacred things, and speaks contemptuously of the most glorious manifestations of God. Such a state of mind is in other places represented as hopeless. "*He that reproveth a scorner getteth to himself shame.*"

" *Reprove not a scorner, lest he hate thee.*" " *A scorner seeketh wisdom and findeth it not.*" " *Judgments are prepared for the scorner.*" " *He scorneth the scorner, but giveth grace to the humble.*"

We have approached, I think, near enough this *unpardonable sin.* There must, of course, be some one last act of sin which brings man into this terrible condition : the act which takes the soul over the probationary line of hope, that seals its fate for ever. I would not presume to pronounce what that *precise* act is, I would not have it distinctly and unmistakably defined.

The Bible leaves a haziness over it, and I for one would not have that haziness removed. There are rocks in the ocean, well known to the mariner, covered with everlasting mists, so that their outlines are never seen. The sailor knows their position, and steers clear of the danger. This sin is one of those rocks in the sea of our probationary life. There is a mysterious mist enfolding it. Still we know its whereabouts. Under the light of Divine revelation we can see sometimes its dark shadow sleeping on the wave. We know in what moral direction it lies. All sinners are moving about it and gradually approaching it. It is not far from that sceptic who wilfully shuts his eyes to evidence—from that scorner that sneers at the sacred—from that Gospel-hearer who is growing more and more unimpressible every Sabbath—from that backslider, who, having once " *tasted the good word of life and the powers of the world to come,*" continues to " *fall away.*" Sceptic, scorner, Gospel-hardened backslider, take care ! your barque is sailing in the direction of that fatal rock—you cannot see it, it is mantled in mists :—take care, you are within its shadow !

" *Whosoever shall speak a word against the Son of Man, it shall be foriven him ; but whosoever speaketh against the Holy Ghost, it shall not be forgiven him, neither in this world, neither in the world to come.*" The men " who denied" Christ, " the Holy One and the Just, and desired a murderer to be granted" to them in His stead, and who killed the Prince of Life, had " *repentance and remission of sins*" preached to them on the day of Pentecost, and thousands of them received the blessings. Their heinous sins against Christ were forgiven. But such forgiveness is here denied to those who so treat the Holy Ghost. There is no hope for such either here or hereafter—" *in this world, or in the world to come.*" Make this blessed Book, then, your chart to guide you over the ocean of life. There is no safety only as you move according to its light.

> " Most wondrous Book ! bright caudle of the Lord !
> Star of Eternity ! the only star
> By which the barque of man could navigate
> The sea of life, and gain the coast of bliss
> Securely ; only star which rose on Time,
> And on its dark and troubled billows still,
> As generation, drifting swiftly by,
> Succeeded generation, threw a ray
> Of heaven's own light, and to the hills of God—
> The everlasting hills—p)inted the sinner's eye."—Pᴊʟʟᴏᴋ.

Matthew 12:33-37

The Morality of Language

Human language is looked upon in different aspects by different men. Some look upon it *grammatically*, trace its etymology, and arrange its words and sentences according to the conventional rules of speech; some look at it *logically*, study it in its relation to the laws of human reasoning; some look upon it *philosophically*, view it in its relation to the nature of the things it is intended to represent; and some look upon it *morally*, contemplate it in its relation to the laws of conscience and God. *Grammatical* language is mere conformity to acknowledged rules of speech; *logical* language is conformity to recognized principles of reasoning; *philosophical* language is conformity with the order of nature; *moral* language is conformity with the moral law of God. There is a regular gradation in the importance of these aspects of language. The first is of the least importance, the second next, and the third next, and the last the most important of all. It is strange and sad to see that the amount of attention which men pay to these aspects is in the inverse ratio of their importance. The first, the least important, is the most attended to, the second next, the third next, and the last, the most important of all, almost entirely neglected. In the department of speech we have more grammarians than logicians, more logicians than philosophers, more philosophers than honest saints. It is to this moral aspect of language that Jesus now calls our attention. *We have here the heinous enormity of some language, the true function of all language, the only method for reforming corrupt language, and the responsibility associated even with the most trifling language.*

I. THE HEINOUS ENORMITY OF SOME LANGUAGE. Some "*speak against the Son of God*," and "some *against the Holy Ghost*." We have already spoken about the danger of such conduct; we have only now to speak of its moral turpitude. Such language involves—

First: *The grossest injustice.* The language of strong invective and denunciation against some men may be, to some extent, justified by their unrighteous principles and unworthy conduct. But not so here. What fault can any find in the Son of God or in the Holy Ghost? Secondly: *The foulest ingratitude.* What have the Son of God and the Holy Ghost done for us in our salvation? The suggestion of the question is enough. Thirdly: *The greatest profanity.* Against whom are they speaking? To speak against a human sovereign is sometimes a capital offence. But this is against the Eternal Prince of the Universe. Fourthly: *The maddest hostility.* When you hear a man speak against another, you may be sure that there is strong feeling of malignity at the root. We deal tenderly with the characters of those we love. We speak *for* them, when accused, to the utmost of our power. When men, therefore, are found "*speaking against the Son*" and "*against the Holy Ghost*," you may be sure that there is a profound feeling of hostility at the root. But how mad, how irrational is the feeling! There is no *reason* for such enmity; on the contrary, there is every conceivable reason against it. *Right* and *expediency* are equally against it.

How heinous, then, is language when thus used against God! And yet, alas! it is not uncommon. You have it from the pen of the infidel in treatises, poems, orations, and from the blasphemous lips of the scoffer and profane.

II. The true function of all language. " *Either make the tree good, and his fruit good; or else make the tree corrupt, and his fruit corrupt: for the tree is known by his fruit.*" The idea suggested is, that language is to be to the real heart of man what fruit is to the tree —*the exact expression of itself.* The fruit embodies and represents the very essence and heart of the tree. Even so should language. The function of words is faithfully* to represent the soul; they should be to man's inner being what the beam is to the sun, the fragrance to the flower, the stream to the fountain, the fruit to the tree—faithful exponents of itself.

If this is the true function of language, there are two sad and general perversions of it.

First: *When words are used without meaning.* "Words are but air" is a current expression, and too often is truthfully applicable to the utterances of men. In the idle chat of gossip, the formal expressions of etiquette, the vapid compliments of society, you have words that do not stand for any real sentiments in the soul. As a rule, perhaps, where you have the most talk you have the least soul, the most profession the least principle, the most loquacity the least spiritual property and power. Language is perverted—

Secondly: *When words are used to misrepresent.* They are frequently so used. They are employed not to reveal, but to conceal what is within; they are masks to misrepresent the face of the heart. Such words as dishonest tradesmen use in striking their bargains, the seducer in rifling the virtue of his victim, the ambitious candidate in winning the suffrages of the people. The world truly is full of such perversion.

The fact is, that so depraved is society that it cannot afford to be sincere; cannot afford to show its real heart in its language. It feels compelled to use the divine faculty of speech, one of the choicest gifts of Heaven, to misrepresent the true state of its mind. What a change would come over society at once were no words used but what were "*the fruit*" of the heart! Let every man in England to-morrow begin to show his *real* sentiments, and feelings in his language, let every word be the true mirror of the soul, and English society would be shaken to its foundation. What contracts founded in deception would dissolve! What friendships based upon false professions would be ruptured! Souls which had mingled together in social intercourse, when they came by faithful speech to see each other face to face, would start asunder with mutual repulsion, and rush away with instinctive horror and indignation.

How great, then, is the depravity of our world, that we are bound to throw over it the drapery of falsehood! We have reached such a state that there seems to be a felt necessity for lying; we are either afraid or ashamed to use our words as the sun uses its beams —to show its nature.

III. THE ONLY METHOD OF REFORMING CORRUPT LANGUAGE. *"O generation of vipers, how can ye, being evil, speak good things? for out of the abundance of the heart the mouth speaketh. A good man out of the good treasure of his heart bringeth forth good things; and an evil man out of the evil treasure of his heart bringeth forth evil things."* What treasures are in the heart! What unbounded productiveness of thought, feeling, and action! The inference of Jesus from this is—*"make the tree good and his fruit good."* The Scribes and Pharisees spoke blasphemously, because their hearts were bad. They were true to their hearts: if they had spoken otherwise they would have spoken hypocritically. Therefore, reformation of language must be preceded by reformation of heart.

This will appear further evident if we consider the elements of correct moral language. These elements we deem to be, *sincerity* and *purity*. By *sincerity* we mean the strict correspondence of the language with the sentiments of the heart; and by *purity* we mean the strict correspondence of those sentiments with the principles of everlasting right. Sincerity without purity, were it possible, would be of no moral worth. But sincerity of expression without purity of sentiment seems to us, as we have already intimated, all but socially impossible. A corrupt man is both ashamed and afraid to expose the real state of his heart to his fellow-men. But let the sentiments be *pure*, let the passions be *chaste*, let the thoughts be *generous*, let the intentions be *honourable*, let the principles be *righteous*, and then, instead of there being any motive to insincerity of language, there will be all the incentives to the utmost faithfulness of expression.

The condition, then, required for correct moral language is, what Jesus here teaches, purity of heart. For *"How can ye, being evil, speak good things?"* Unless the fountain is purified, the stream will ever be tainted; unless the tree be made good, the sap, that lies in the root, will give a tinge to the foliage and a taste to the fruit. Would we, then, have a correct language? Would we have the kind of language amongst men which the Bible enjoins?—speech *"seasoned with salt, ministering grace unto the hearers;" "pleasant words which are as a honey-comb, sweet to the soul and health to the bones;"* a tongue amongst the people which shall be as *"choice silver"* and *"a tree of life?"* Would we have this blessed state of speech, we must struggle to produce that moral regeneration which Jesus so constantly and earnestly enforces. The *"cup"* and *"platter"* must be cleansed *"within;"* the people must have *"a new heart and a right spirit;"* they must be *"renewed in the spirit of their minds;"* sinners must *"cleanse their hands,"* and the *"double-minded"* must *"purify their hearts;"* the heart of humanity must be "*cleansed by the washing of regeneration and the renewing of the Holy Ghost.*"

IV. THE RESPONSIBILITY ASSOCIATED EVEN WITH THE MOST TRIFLING LANGUAGE. "*I say unto you that every idle word that men shall speak, they shall give account thereof in the day of judgment.*" The Pharisees might have imagined that as they had but spoken, and had perpetrated no real act of enormity, no guilt was contracted. Christ disabuses them of such an impression by assuring them "*That every idle word,*" &c. Every idle word; not merely the profane and impious language of the scoffer and blasphemer, but every *idle* word —words that have little or no meaning; the most airy words of wit and humour spoke in jest, not to delude or pain, but simply to please. "*Every idle word,*" &c. "*For by thy words thou shalt be justified, and by thy words shalt thou be condemned.*"

There are three considerations which may serve to show us the responsibility that attaches to *idle* words—their *reactive force*, their *social influence*, their *Divine recognition.*

First: *Their reactive force.* So constituted are we, that our expressions, every one of them, must have a reflex influence. "Those things which proceed out of the mouth come forth from the heart, and *they defile the man.*" The man who indulges in idle and frivolous talk damages his own mental faculties and moral sense thereby. In such speech there is no demand for the reflective powers, and they become impotent; there is no development of the sentiments of truth—benevolence and religion, the very stamina of our moral nature—and they become more and more inoperative and dead. In idle talk the soul in every way is injured; its rich soil, capable of producing trees of knowledge and of life, is wasted in flowery, it may be, but still noxious weeds. Whatever we do that is unworthy of our nature damages our own powers and interests.

Secondly: *Their social influence.* Science affirms that every movement in the material creation propagates an influence to the remotest planet in the universe. Be this as it may, it seems morally certain that every word spoken on the ear will have an influence lasting as eternity. The words we address to men are written not on parchment, marble, or brass, which time can efface, but on the indestructible pages of the soul. Everything written on the imperishable soul is imperishable. All the words that have ever been addressed to you by men long since departed are written on the book of your memory, and will be unsealed at the day of judgment, and spread out in the full beams of eternal knowledge.

Thirdly: *Their Divine recognition.* The Great Judge knows every word we have spoken. Not only "*the hard speeches*" which ungodly men have spoken against Him will He bring into judgment, but also "*every secret thing.*" "*Out of thine own mouth will I judge thee.*"

Matthew 12:38-42

The Religious Sign-Seekers

This passage supplies us with three facts, which are both instructive, as subjects of speculative inquiry, and practical, as indications of human obligation.

I. THAT THERE IS A TENDENCY IN MAN TO LOOK FOR THE MIRACULOUS IN RELIGION. " *We would see a sign from thee.*" This tendency was strikingly manifest in the Jewish character. " *The Jews require a sign.*" They required a sign in connexion with Christ's mission, not merely because of the marvel-seeking tendency which they had in common with all men, but because all their great teachers in past ages had accompanied instructions with miracles. Moses, Samuel, Elijah, and others—all wrought wonders amongst them. They, therefore, naturally expected that the Messiah would do that which all the great teachers had done heretofore.

We might get illustrations of this tendency in man from all religions; Hindooism—Islamism—Catholicism—as well as Judaism abound with them. But I wish to point to some of its developments amongst *us*—the men of this age and of this land.

First: *It is seen in the objections of sceptics.* " *Where is the promise of His coming, for since the fathers fell asleep,*" &c. The spirit of this is, If there be a God, why does He not give a " sign" that will silence all doubt? Why does He not interrupt this everlasting order of things, break the dead silence of the universe? Why does He not write upon the open heavens, as He wrote of old, with visible hand, upon the wall of Belshazzar's palace? Their cry is, " *We would see a sign from thee.*"

Secondly: *It is seen in the conduct of those who are waiting for some extraordinary power to convert them.* Multitudes of those who hear the Gospel do not yield to the *moral* influences that are brought to bear upon them; they are expecting that in some mysterious way God will come and change their hearts. They are like the diseased folk on the banks of Bethesda, looking up for some mystic angel to descend and trouble the dead fountain of their being. Their cry is, " *We would see a sign from thee.*"

Thirdly: *It is seen in the visions and aspirations of premillenarianism.* There is a class of Christians who are looking for the personal and speedy advent of Christ, to restore the Jews to their own country, establish a temporal empire, and by a series of miracles effect that universal spiritual reformation which the Gospel had failed to accomplish. These millenarians, as they are called, are indeed seeking after a " sign." They are a generation whose spirit is thoroughly *Judaic*, so far as sympathy with the marvellous and material, in this respect, is concerned.

II. THAT THIS TENDENCY IS PROVIDED FOR IN CHRISTIANITY. The passage suggests two remarks in relation to this point :—

First : *That in Christianity this tendency is adequately provided for.* Indeed, the history of Christ is a history of *"signs."* His existence itself was a miracle; and mighty wonders fill the narrative of His glorious life. He was the WONDERFUL. These hearers of Christ could not, in conscience, plead the lack of "signs" as a reason for their unbelief. The miracles of Moses and the prophets pale their fires before the miracles of Him who was now addressing them. Still, He here condescends to promise them yet one more sign—tho *crowning* one, and that is His *resurrection* from the dead. *"The sign of the prophet Jonas."* The resurrection of Christ is of itself a sign sufficient for the most credulous.

Secondly : *That in Christianity this tendency is finally provided for.* *"There shall no sign be given to it."* Why would not Jesus give them more signs? Not from the want of power. What He did in the way of miracle was nothing compared with what He could do. His miracles were but *"parts of His ways,"* the *"hidings of His power."* By a mere volition He could make the solid earth beneath our feet reel, and bound, and plunge, like a frail barque in the tempest; or, He could lift it into another orbit, link it to another system, make it roll round another sun, and give it new heavens. What could He not do in the way of wonder? When one thinks for a moment upon the infinite variety of wonders which Christ *might* have wrought, we may justly conclude that He had some good reason for restricting this kind of agency, and for saying to His generation, *"No sign shall be given to it."* We can discover two reasons for this :—

1. *Because a frequent occurrence of miracles would destroy their intended effect.* The power of miracles is not like the power of an army—increased by numbers; their power lies in their rarity, rather than in their abundance. After a given point, they weaken as they multiply. Let a comet sweep the heavens every month, and it shall awaken no more stir in the human population than the rising of the new moon. And—

2. *Because the cultivation of this sign-seeking tendency would be inimical to man's spiritual improvement.* This tendency takes man *out* of himself, whereas his interest lies within. Our progress requires us to live and work within—to commune with our own hearts—to hold converse with those thought-visitants that are constantly passing through us, and to decipher those pages of eternal truth which are written on the tablet of our consciousness. Our God and heaven are to be found within. But this tendency takes us out of ourselves —out into ceremonies and phenomena. This tendency serves to develop the sensuous rather than the spiritual, and leads us to rely more on *events* than truths—*forms* than principles—the *transient* than the eternal.

It was merciful in Jesus to deny more signs. We do not want more *outward* attractions. We want to be thrown back upon ourselves, and to be *self-reliant* on eternal truth and God. For this reason it was expedient for the disciples that Jesus Himself should go away. While He was with them they were dependent upon His person rather than on His principles. Hence the change for the better which came over them soon after His ascension. Compare Peter's conduct in the hall of Caiaphas on the night when he denied Christ, with his conduct after the day of Pentecost before the Sanhedrim. Compare Luke xxii. 55–62 with Acts iv. 2–22.

III. That dissatisfaction with the miraculous provisions of Christianity indicates a character most corrupt in principle; and fearful in responsibility.

First : *It indicates a character most corrupt in principle.* Christ calls them *" an evil and adulterous generation."* * The fact that they asked for more signs showed their *ingratitude.* What signs He had already given them—signs abundantly sufficient to satisfy every honest inquirer that He was the true Messiah ! It showed moreover their *perversion.* All the signs they had witnessed went for nought. Their unbelief arose, not from intellectual causes, but moral ; not from the want of more evidence, but for the want of a right disposition of heart to appreciate evidence. This is ever the case.

There are many who say they would believe, if they had more evidence. Have they properly weighed what they have ? If not, more evidence would be of no service to them. He that is unjust in the least, would be unjust in the much. *" If they believe not Moses and the prophets,"* &c.

Secondly ; *It indicates a character of fearful responsibility.* *" The men of Nineveh shall rise in judgment with this generation, and condemn it,"* &c. In illustration of this, observe two things :—1. That men had been convinced with far less evidence than they had. The Ninevites had been convinced by Jonah, and probably the queen of the south had been convinced by the arguments of Solomon. But neither Jonah nor Solomon is to be compared to Christ. Both Jonah and Solomon were imperfect men, but He who preached to them was the perfect Son of God. Both Jonah and Solomon were strangers to the persons they addressed, but He who preached to them, was one of their own nation and neighbourhood. Both Jonah and Solomon had but a short connexion with the parties they addressed. Jonah preached but one sermon, and Solomon had, probably, but one interview with the queen. But Jesus was with them from day to day, preaching the kingdom, and healing all manner of diseases. Both Jonah and Solomon were incapable of corroborating their doctrines by miracle ; but Christ's miracles were so numerous that

---

* " The expression must here be explained in accordance with the prevailing Old Testament manner of speaking, according to which everything of an unbelieving and unholy character is regarded as born of unholy love, implying therefore a separation of the soul from the Lord. This spiritual turning away of the soul from the Creator to the creature is represented as adultery, according to a profound mode of viewing the relation existing between the soul and God."—*Olshausen.*

His biographer, John, tells us, that had they been all recorded, the world would not have contained the books. Men had believed with less than a tithe of the evidence and opportunity which they possessed. 2. Those who believed with less evidence, would be witnesses against them in the judgment. *" The men of Nineveh "* and *" the queen of the south shall rise up in the judgment with this generation, and shall condemn it."* Observe the truths here implied, (1) There is a retributive era to dawn upon humanity; (2) in that era, the generations of all times and lands shall meet; (3) in the meeting of these generations, the *relative* responsibility of each will be deeply felt.

Ye religious sign-seekers, ponder this passage; let these words of Jesus curb your desire for the marvellous. Why look out for more wonders, when Christianity is crowded with them? and when more would but weaken their power, and impede your progress? Since the apostolic era, the order of the universe has not been disturbed by miracle, nor shall it be disturbed again until the blast of doom.

Matthew 12:43-45

Defective Reformation

" Demoniacal possession," whether an actual occurrence, or a mere superstitious idea, was regarded as a *fact* by the Jews, and often treated as such by our great EXEMPLAR and LORD.* If a fiction, it had all the influence of a *fact* upon the Jewish mind, and never did Jesus seek to counteract its force. Popular errors, so long as they are truly believed, will serve the purpose of illustration in teaching, better than real truths that are not generally accepted. Be it fiction or fact, it does sometimes admirably bring out, in bold and impressive form, some of the great practical truths of Christianity.

See, for example, the picture before us. There stands a man whose bosom, a short time ago, was the home of a vile demon. The dark spirit is, however, now expelled, and is gone abroad into his wonted haunts, *" seeking rest;"* and the man is free, alike from his presence and his influence : the place he occupied, is "empty, swept, and garnished." But it is not for long; the Evil One has no rest in those *" dry places."* He determines to return to his old abode. Anticipating a difficulty in regaining his lost possession, he takes with him *" seven other spirits more wicked than himself."* They approach the old dwelling; and instead of finding it as they expected—guarded and fortified—they find every gate open, no sentinel on the watch, all empty, and prepared for their reception. *" They enter in and*

---

* Those who would see the two sides of this question presented fairly and succinctly, should consult an article on the subject, by the Rev. J. F. Denham, M.A., in the " Cyclopædia of Biblical Literature."

dwell there;" and now *"the last state of that man is worse than the first."*

Whose horrid portrait is this which Jesus draws? It is that of the Jewish nation. The departure of the evil spirit refers to some reformation which had taken place in their history. Perhaps the reference is to that revolution which occurred after their emancipation from Babylon, when the demon of idolatry seems to have left them; or that which occurred in the days of John the Baptist, when the demon of apathy was exorcised by the righteous fulminations of the great reformer. And the return of the evil spirit with *"seven other spirits"* expresses some great moral relapse, when the impulses of evil would work more fearfully and powerfully in them, and show themselves in some more terrible form. It may be that the allusion is to the stupendous tragedy of the crucifixion. Truly, a sevenfold force of evil appeared in that miracle of sin.

I. THAT A DEFECTIVE REFORMATION CONSISTS RATHER IN THE DISPOSSESSION OF SOMETHING WRONG, THAN IN THE IMPORTATION OF WHAT IS RIGHT. *"The unclean spirit is gone out"* of the man, and there is a *visible* improvement. The house is swept of its filth, and garnished with many ornaments; but this is all. An *evil* spirit is gone from the man; but no *good* spirit has come in its place. Where is the heavenly occupant for whom the house was originally built?—the spirit of love for eternal truth and goodness; where is it? This man represents a reformation by no means uncommon. We find evil spirits leaving men, but no good spirits taking up their place. (1) The *"unclean spirit"* of *barbarism* may go out from man. People that were once gross, loathsome, and savage—the mere creatures of brute instinct—become enlightened in intellect, prolific in invention, and refined in manners. *Civilization* sweeps the house of social impurities, garnishes it with outward moralities and artistic beauties; but it is still *"empty,"* so far as moral worth is concerned. To be able to read Homer, and to trace the logical steps of Euclid; to travel by steam, and make electricity convey our thoughts; to maintain outward order by laws, and make machinery save our muscles and our limbs; are advantages which accrue to the civilized world, by the expulsion of the old barbaric spirit. But let us not overrate these; they are not *virtues:* they co-exist with a morally empty soul. Perhaps the civilized world is *morally* as *"wretched and miserable, and poor, and blind, and naked,"* as many parts of uncultured heathen-land. (2) The *"unclean spirit* of a *false theology* may go out from man. A country may renounce Polytheism, or Islamism, or Popery; and a correct theoretic system of faith may sweep the house of all idolatries, sacerdotalties, and such-like abominations; and garnish it with the forms of Christian theism; and the house may still be *"empty"* in a moral sense. Of what advantage to the *moral soul* of man is *nominal* Protestantism, compared with Popery; or *nominal* Christianity compared with heathenism? (3) The *"unclean spirit"* of *intemperance* and *profanity* may go out from man. The drunkard may be so impressed with the evils of in-

temperance, that he may banish the demon, and sweep his house of
the disgusting habits of intoxication, and garnish himself with the
forms of sobriety; and the profane man may abandon his blasphemous language, cease to desecrate the ordinances of heaven, sweep
his house of all odious irreverences, and garnish it with the forms of
piety; and yet, in both cases, the house may be left empty, entirely
unoccupied with any virtuous and religious emotions.

Such are the *spurious and defective reformations.* They are of no
real service to man, as an offspring of God, a citizen of the universe,
a candidate for eternity. Let a man put away all mere intellectual
and outward evil from him; let every demon of error and habit
depart; let his conversation and conduct be swept of all that could
offend the eye of the most refined spectator; nay, let him be garnished with such external attributes as would command the esteem,
and even admiration, of society; still, if the "house" be "empty"
—if the "*Spirit of Christ*" is not in it—his reformation is radically
defective, and morally worthless. All his outward excellences are
but as flowers about a corpse, serving to hide a little the hideous,
and to relieve the noisome from the spectator, but leaving to death
his undisputed sway. In true reformation, the evil spirit goes out
because the *spirit of goodness* has entered. The new life infused
expels the old spirit; and the man throws off the old, as trees throw
off their foliage, by the rising force of a new life. True reformation is like the moulting of the "fowls of heaven:" the old feathers
give way to a lovelier plumage, by the inward working of a fresh
supply of vital force.

The picture suggests—

II. THAT SUCH A DEFECTIVE REFORMATION IS NO GUARANTEE AGAINST
FUTURE DEGENERACY. "*I will return to my house from whence I came
out,*" etc. There are four circumstances suggested which will
render the subject of this defective reformation liable to a fearful
relapse :—

First: *The moral emptiness of the soul.* The soul was left *unoccupied;* there was nothing there to guard its rights, interest its sympathies, or engage its powers. The true spirit was not there to
"*lift up a standard*" against the enemy. An empty mind—a mind
without a great affection, thought and purpose—will always be as-
sailable by the enemy, at every point. There is but one thing in
the universe that can fill up a soul, and that is, *supreme love to God.*
This will so occupy it as to allow no place for aught besides. This
affection, like fire, consumes everything opposed to its own nature,
and transmutes all into its own essence. It acts as the great Redeemer
acted in the Temple of old—expels all those buyers and sellers who
desecrate the holy place. Another thing suggested, which renders
the subject of this defective reformation liable to relapse, is, secondly,
the constant restlessness of evil. This unclean spirit is represented
as "*walking through dry places, seeking rest, and findeth none.*"
There is no repose in evil. It is like the troubled sea: the mind
under its influence is never at rest, nor ever can be. An ejected

spirit, like the wild beast disappointed of its prey, prowls about the creation with heightened appetite and quickened speed. Satan is represented as a roaring lion; as going up and down the earth; as the enemy, who steals clandestinely into the fields, scatters tares, and thus frustrates the plans and blights the prospects of the moral husbandman. Another thing suggested, which renders the subject of this defective reformation liable to a relapse, is, thirdly, *the disposedness of the spirit to it.* The unclean spirit, on its return, instead of finding the house bolted and barred, found it "*swept and garnished*" as if awaiting his return. Partial reformations always have their *reactions.* The man who abandons any vice to which he has been addicted, from pride, fear, expediency, or any other motive not virtuous in itself, is only preparing his heart for the *return* of the evil spirit. Any change accomplished from any motive save love to God, is but the giving up of one sin for another; is but one evil spirit casting out another. Fourthly: There is yet another thing suggested which renders the subject of this defective reformation liable to a relapse, and that is, *the vast resources of evil.* "*Then goeth he, and taketh with himself seven other spirits more wicked than himself.*" The agents of evil in this world are far more numerous than those of virtue. The restless spirit of evil can always muster not merely "seven" but seven thousand, emissaries to help it in its work. Whilst virtue, on this planet, has but its units, vice has its millions.

III. THAT THE DEGENERACY WHICH FOLLOWS SUCH A REFORMATION LEAVES THE SUBJECT IN A WORSE CONDITION THAN EVER. "*And the last state of that man is worse than the first.*" First: *his guilt is augmented;* secondly: *his susceptibility to holy motives is deadened;* thirdly: *the obstructions to a thorough change are increased.*

This subject brings out several valuable thoughts to view. Does it not present *a true test of character?* It shows that moral worth is not in negatives, but positives; not in the abdication of vices, but in the cultivation of virtues; not in the mere ejection of a bad spirit, but in the reception of the good. True worth is the good expelling the bad, and filling up the soul. Does it not also present *a true explanation of apostacy?* What is technically called "*falling from grace,*" seems to me nothing more than a soul that had once swept itself of some vices, and appeared clean for a time, receiving back others in its place; it is the *reaction* of a temporary dormant evil, not the *extinction* of positive good. Does it not, moreover, present *the true method of reformation?* What instrument can effect a true reformation in man? Manifestly that only which can infuse into the soul a new disposition—fill it with love to God, the very spirit of all goodness. There is but one *power* in society, one instrument in the world, that historically *has* done this, or that philosophically ever *can* do this, and that is CHRISTIANITY.

Matthew 12:46-50

Spiritual and Material Kinships

It appears from the parallel passages that Jesus was now surrounded by a dense multitude (Mark iii. 20), and that in the breasts of many there existed the most malignant feelings.* His mother and brethren, apprehending danger from the perilous position in which He stood, made their way towards Him, in order, if possible, to rescue Him. We are not to understand by the language in the text that Jesus depreciated natural relationships, or that he had no regard for the claims of kindred. He was dutiful to His parents, He was affectionate to His brethren. His filial sympathies were strong. In His dying hour His last looks were directed to His mother. He committed her to His most beloved disciple. *"Behold thy mother,"* said He, intimating His desire that John should take the broken-hearted woman, and treat her henceforth with all the affection of a son. But whilst the words do not teach that natural relationship should be depreciated, they do teach the following lessons in reference to natural and spiritual relationship.

I. THE EXISTENCE OF SPIRITUAL KINSHIP. Jesus here uses the words, *"mother, sister, brother,"* in two very different senses. The one a *natural* sense, the other a *spiritual* sense. There are some beings whose connexion with each other is simply and entirely that of physical relationship;—such are the irrational creatures around us : and there are some beings whose relation is exclusively spiritual;—such are the angels in heaven. No tie of consanguinity unites them—*"they neither marry nor are given in marriage."* Man is capable of these two relationships; he is united to his fellows by natural ties, and he may be united by spiritual affinities and interests. His natural relations, father, mother, brother, sister, unspeakably

* There seems to be no necessity for resorting to the supposition that malignant feelings worked in the breast of the multitude. It is mentioned in Mark iii. 20, 21, that Jesus and His disciples had no leisure to partake of food, or to refresh themselves ; that His friends, or rather His *relatives,* came forth to check Him ; they said "He is beside Himself; " *i.e.,* His zeal and ardour carried him onward to the injury of His health, and the neglect of ordinary rules of prudence. As our blessed Lord still went on teaching, Mark records, in ver. 31, the arrival of His brethren and His mother. What more natural than that the Virgin came under the lawful impulse of maternal anxiety, with the same object as His friends in ver. 21? On two former occasions, Luke ii. 49, John ii. 4, the Virgin made similar attempts; from which the Church is taught, that the mother of our Lord had no right to interfere with Him in the exercise of His earthly ministry. By a comparison of these three passages it will appear that in regard to His work as a Saviour, and all actions connected therewith, the Virgin had no closer relation to our Lord, no more right to prefer a request, or exercise authority, than any other person. On every occasion her advances were repelled. As this was the case when our blessed Lord was upon earth, *à fortiori* we conclude that the Virgin has no right of interference or intercession, no authority of any kind, now that "All power is given unto Him in heaven and in earth."—*Webster.*

important and precious as they are, are only symbols of spiritual relations which he might have, and which he should cultivate. There are spiritual fathers and spiritual brothers. Paul calls Timothy his "son"—John directs his letters to his "little children." There is a spiritual family on earth, ever multiplying, of which Christ is the head, and all Christians are brethren. Spiritually, they are begotten by the same Spirit, they have the same filial and fraternal instincts, the same family sympathies and interests.

II. THE GROUND OF SPIRITUAL KINSHIP. Observe,—*Ecclesiastical unity is not the ground of spiritual relationship.* Men may belong to the same Church, adopt the same polity, use the same ritual, and yet not be spiritually related. Secondly: *Theological unity is not the ground of spiritual relationship.* We may hold the same creed, be zealous in obtaining the same faith, yet not be doing the will of our Father. *Doing the will of God is the bond.*

III. THE SUPERIORITY OF SPIRITUAL KINSHIP. Natural relationship, our Saviour held as secondary to the spiritual. His disciples, for the moment, were more important to Him than His natural mother or His brethren. Wherein is the superiority of the spiritual over the natural?

First: *It is more close than the material.* Strong is the tie of natural relationship. What sacrifices, for example, will not the parent make for the child at the dictate of this instinct. Notwithstanding this, it is not the closest; it does not bring moral oneness. The closest union of man with man is the union of soul, the union of moral sympathy with goodness, and truth, and God. Where this union is not, the connexion of man with man is only as the connexion of beast with beast—a connexion by gregarious sympathies. It often happens that those who are united by mere natural relationship, are alien in heart, alien in soul; there are husbands, wives, parents, sisters, living beneath the same roof, feeding at the same table, engaging, perhaps, in the same occupation, whose souls are as far off from one another as the poles. They have different mental homes and associates. But where there is a spiritual relationship, heart is bound to heart, and soul to soul, united spirits are alive to the same virtues, consecrated to the same service, have sworn fealty to the same king. Their affections gather round the same objects. The attachment of the Ephesians to Paul is an illustration.

Secondly: *It is more delightful.* The Great Author of our existence has, in the exercise of His goodness, connected happiness with every relationship. With all natural relationships there are sources of happiness. But the happiness springing from mere natural affection is often little more than animal pleasure, and it often changes into sorrow and distress. David's love for Absalom, which at one time was ecstacy, passed into anguish. How many children every day are breaking the hearts of their parents, and "bringing down their grey hairs with sorrow to the grave!" But spiritual relationship *is* happiness. It unites us to the good, to those who love us without feigned love—love us without dissimulation; to those in whom we can repose our utmost confidence, who mingle their tears of sympathy, and blend their songs of praise with ours.

Thirdly : *It is more dignified.* By natural relationships, men are sometimes introduced into stations which are conventionally high and honourable in rank. Sometimes the circles are low, slaves, paupers, culprits. But in all cases spiritual relationship introduces us into the great family of God—makes us " heirs of God and joint-heirs with Christ;" makes us "kings and priests unto God ;" enables us to call Christ our Brother, the Creator our Father, the Universe our Inheritance.

Fourthly : *It is more extensive.* Natural relationship only gives us a small circle. The largest family circle is but very small compared with the generation, and the generation small compared with the whole race. But spiritual relationship introduces us to the good of all ages of the world, of all classes and grades. It unites us to patriarchs, apostles, prophets, martyrs. It unites us to "thrones, to principalities and powers." It unites us to the great congress of the good.

Fifthly : *It is more durable.* Natural relationship, unassociated with the spiritual, is very evanescent. Many things destroy the affections even on earth. A mutual hate between those who are domestically related is, alas ! of too frequent occurrence. Death, however, will inevitably dissolve all natural relationship. But spiritual relationship lives for ever. Souls united in doing the will of God are more firmly united than planets to the sun. From the whole we learn—(1) There is no foundation for the doctrine of virgin worship. " *My mother,*" as if Christ had said, " *is nothing* to me if she does not the will of God." This is the principle that should always govern our affections. " Do not I hate them," says David, " that hate Thee ?" (2) There is but one principle that unites men together in the true Church—obedience to the Divine will.

Matthew 13:1-9, 18-23

God's Word, and Man's Soul

This parable with its explanation, and several others in this chapter, were delivered to " great *multitudes* who stood *on the sea shore.*" A ship, either resting on the beach or gently floating on the waves that broke at the feet of the crowd, was the Great Preacher's pulpit on this occasion. The scene is grand beyond description.

There are four great general truths which this parable brings up to our minds, and which introduce us to a good view of the classes of Gospel hearers here brought under our notice.

First : *That there is a constitutional affinity subsisting between Man's Soul and God's Word.* The soil is made to receive, germinate, and unfold the seed : and the seed, in its turn, to clothe its surface with loveliness, and enrich it with fruit. The parable implies a similar connexion between the Word of God and the human Soul. The most glorious fact in our nature is, that we have a capacity to receive and develop a *word* from the INFINITE.

Secondly : *That, notwithstanding this affinity, they are often found existing in a state of separation from each other.* In the scene before us, you have the field ploughed and harrowed, but no seed in it : the seed is in the sower's basket, until he throws it out. It is so in relation to the Word of God and the Soul. There are millions of cases where they exist apart; and these minds, like the untilled acres of unpeopled lands, are "a wilderness and a waste."

Thirdly : *That there is an agency in operation to bring the two into a right connexion.* The sower has gone forth to put the seed into the soil. This represents an agency employed to bring God's Word into contact with Souls. What is that agency ? who is the spiritual sower ? Our answer is, The Christian teacher. The old prophets, Christ, the apostles, ministers, and all who, in every age, of whatever sect, who from Christian motives—by writing, preaching, or conversation—disseminate Gospel truths, are represented by this "sower." Thank God, there is an agency at work in this world to bring truth and Soul together—to lodge the germs of Christianity in human hearts. Whilst we deplore its present feebleness and manifest inadequacy, we anticipate the day when it shall tread every field of every island and continent of the globe, and scatter the "incorruptible seed" over all the zones of human life.

Fourthly : *That the connexion which the agency forms between God's Word and human Souls is of various kinds.* There are four kinds of connexion brought before us in this parable :—

I. THE CONNEXION OF THE WORD WITH THE UNTHINKING SOUL. "*Some fell by the way side, and the fowls came and devoured them up.*" In many of the cultivated fields of Judea there were pathways left for travellers : through them the ploughshare was not driven, and the glebe remained too hard to receive the seed. The seed from the hand of the sower fell on it, rested there for a little while, and that was all. It was soon crushed by the foot of the traveller, or borne away by the fowls of heaven. What class of Soul, brought into contact with the Gospel, does this "way side" represent ? The UNTHINKING. Jesus explains this in the 19th verse :—"*When any one heareth the Word of the kingdom, and understandeth it not, then cometh the wicked one, and catcheth away that which was sown in his heart.*" *He understandeth it not.* This is the cause of its being left on the hard surface until "*the wicked one*" "*catcheth*" it away. Men hear, but do not *think*: the word vibrates for a moment on the ear, and then dies away. It falls on the senses, but, for the want of reflection, it does not sink into the Soul. In the nature of the case, the Gospel can take no effect upon the Soul without *thought.*

Thought is necessary both to break up the hard glebe of our nature, and to take the precious seed as it falls upon the outer senses into the Soul, where, amidst the prolific soil of moral feeling, it may lie beyond the reach of the "fowls," and there germinate and grow. There is—

II. THE CONNEXION OF THE WORD WITH THE SENTIMENTALLY IN-TERESTED SOUL. This connexion is marked by four things :— *Superficiality :* The Word hath not "*root in himself,*" but merely in his emotions. It has not been digested by the intellect, and then deposited in the Soul and conscience. It merely floats on the surface— does not sink into the rich mould beneath. *Precocity :* The seeds that fell into this ground * soon made their appearance : "*forthwith they spring up.*" The mere sentimental effects of the Gospel are very rapid in their development. *Joyousness : "Anon with joy receiveth it."* Full of rapture for a time : all hymns and music. *Transitoriness : "And when the sun was up,"* &c. How accurately these things characterise all mere *sentimental* hearers !

III. THE CONNEXION OF THE WORD WITH THE WORLD-DIVIDED SOUL. *"Some fell among thorns ; and the thorns sprung up, and choked them."* Not amongst thorns full grown, but where they were in germs; for in Luke it is said, *"they sprang up with it."* They grew up together, but the thorns overtopped the seeds, shut them out from the air and light, extracted the moisture and nutriment from the earth which they required for their nourishment, and thus they pined away in the shade. The *soil* here seems to have been good ; it is neither represented as hardened or superficial. No fault is found with it. This represents, therefore, those into whose *moral* nature the Word goes ; those whose consciences are awakened, and partially developed by it ; those who understand something of its *rationale,* and feel something of its moral grandeur and power, but Christianity has not an *entire* possession of their souls : there are other things interesting it—other germs growing in the soil, which injure the seed of the kingdom, and prevent it from producing fruit. *"The care of this world, and the deceitfulness of riches, choke the word, and he becometh unfruitful."*

IV. THE CONNEXION OF THE WORD WITH THE TRUE-HEARTED SOUL. *"Other fell into good ground,"* &c. In Luke, we are told that the good ground are those who, *"in an honest and good heart, having heard the word, keep it, and bring forth fruit with patience."* These are men who allow it to possess their entire souls : it fills

---

* "A soil mingled with stones is not meant; for these, however numerous or large, would not certainly hinder the roots from striking deeply downward, as those roots, with the instinct which they possess, would feel and find their way, penetrating between the interstices of the stones, and would so reach the moisture below; but what is meant is ground where a thin superficial coating of mould covered the surface of a rock which stretched below it, and presented an impassable barrier, rendering it wholly impossible that the roots should penetrate beyond a certain depth, or draw up any supplies of nourishment from beneath."— *Trench.*

them, and they produce fruit according to their opportunities and capacities. " *Some an hundredfold,*" &c.

Which of these connexions sustainest thou to the great soul-saving WORD ? Is it the *unthinking* one ? Then thy nature is a " *way side,*" exposed to the hardening tread of every moral footpad ; and the winged ones of the air will bear away every germ of truth and goodness that Heaven's sowers are scattering over the field of the world. Or is it the *sentimentally* interested ? Does the *word* find but a lodgment in thy feelings ? Has it no grand form of rational thought—no breath of soul-inspiration—no controlling principle of moral life ? Is it nought but a thing of sigh, and song, and unctuous talk ? Then it has no root. The blade and bud will soon be scorched by the sun. Or is it *that of the divided soul ?* Has it taken root in thy understanding and heart in connexion with germs of worldliness ? Does it but share thy nature ? Are there other antagonistic principles growing with it in the soil ? Then it will one day be choked, and thy nature will be like the field of the slothful, *covered over with nettles and thorns.* Or is it the connexion of the truehearted ? Then it shall flourish and grow, and produce abundant fruit. It shall cover thy inner and spiritual world with the loveliness of Eden once more, and adorn again the tree of life with rich and eternal fruit.

Matthew 13:10-17

The Revealment of the Gospel

The subject which the present paragraph presents is *The Revealment of the Gospel;* and it gives us three things in relation to this revealment which we shall notice with the utmost brevity :—The evident necessity of its revealment; the parabolic method of its revealment; and the different spiritual results of its revealment.

I. THE EVIDENT NECESSITY OF ITS REVEALMENT. " *And the disciples came, and said unto Him, Why speakest thou in parables ? He answered and said unto them, Because it is given unto you to know the mysteries of the kingdom of heaven, but to them it is not given.*" The mysteries of the kingdom may be regarded as meaning the *elements of the Gospel,*—its cardinal truths and provisions ; these, until they are revealed, are *secrets,* or mysteries. It is important to remark, that there is a *distinction between the Gospel and its revelation.* The Gospel is something existing independent of revelation. As astronomy is something independent of all astronomical books, as geometrical truths are independent of Euclid, so the Gospel existed before a revelation. There are the germs of many sciences existing in the world that have as yet found no revealment. But apart from the revelation the Gospel would be a *secret*—a mystery.

The principle, the manifestation, and the personal application, of the Gospel are all mysterious until revealed. The principle is God's love for apostate man; the manifestation is the incarnation of Christ; the application is the work of the Spirit.

Now, the necessity of its revelation will appear obvious from these three facts :—

First : *That the Gospel can only benefit us as it is believed.* Faith in its "*mysteries*" or secrets is the necessary condition of spiritual salvation. It is no arbitrary arrangement which leaves our destiny dependent on faith, "*He that believeth shall be saved, he that believeth not shall be damned.*"

Secondly : *That there can be no belief without knowledge.* We have no faith, we can have no faith, in anything that has not come within the range of our consciousness. "*How can they believe in Him of whom they have not heard ?*"

Thirdly : *That without a revealment the realities of the Gospel could never have been known.* The truths of the Gospel are not like the truths of science, written on the pages of nature for men to decipher and to interpret. They transcend human discovery. "*Eye hath not seen, ear hath not heard,*" &c. From these three facts the necessity for a revealment is obvious.

II. THE PARABOLIC METHOD OF ITS REVEALMENT. Christ, in order to reveal the "mysteries," the cardinal elements of the Gospel, dealt largely in parables. There is a rich cluster of them in this one chapter. Instead of enunciating them in mere logical propositions, He brings them out from the realms of abstraction, clothes them in a body, and makes men see, feel, and hear them. We have thus the *reason* of this parabolic method. In answer to the question, "*Why speakest thou to them in parables ?*" Christ replies, "*Because it is given unto you to know the mysteries of the kingdom of heaven, but to them it is not given.*" "I speak to them in parables : because they seeing, see not; and hearing, hear not," &c. The reason is, *the spiritual obtuseness of sinners.* I am aware that many expositors, Olshausen and Doddridge amongst them, interpret the words of our Saviour as meaning that He taught in parables *in order* to conceal His meaning from His ungodly hearers. I cannot entertain this thought, for the following reasons :—

First : *The language does not necessarily imply this idea.* Jesus does not say, I speak to them in parables because I want to hide from them my meaning—want to render more dense the atmosphere, more impenetrable the veil of their hearts. No ; He says that it is because they are already so blind that He thus teaches. He gives parables not to produce moral obliquity, but because moral obliquity existed ; "*they seeing see not,*" &c.✱

✱ Ver 13. "'Therefore speak I to them *in parables.*' This direct answer to the question of the disciples has hitherto, it is to be regretted, received very generally a one-sided explanation from the following ὅτι, although it must first of all be understood as an evident consequence from the *foregoing* ὅτι, together with all that follows. How has this truth, as earnest as it is friendly, been obscured by the one-

Secondly : *This idea is essentially inconsistent with the nature of parabolical teaching.* The very nature and design of a parable are to make an obscure truth clear,—to *illustrate.* Had He spoken in intricate allegories and enigmas, or in scholastic technicalities, there might be some show of reason in supposing that Christ spoke in order to conceal.

Thirdly : *This idea is incompatible with the character and mission of Christ.* Does it comport with His kindness to suppose that He sought to intensify the darkness of the human spirit ? An attempt on Christ's part to do this would have been superfluous, and inconsistent with all our notions of His character and purpose. We hold therefore to the principle that He taught in parables because of the existing spiritual *obtuseness* of His hearers. Had their spiritual intuitions been clear they would have caught His meaning by a simple sentence, and they would not have required such time spent in illustrations.

Besides making Divine truth clear to the ignorant, parables serve other subordinate and auxiliary purposes. (1) They serve to reflect the manners and customs of the ancients. Christ's parables are pictures taken from olden times. (2) They serve to show the mercy of Jesus in thus condescending to meet the benighted condition of our minds. (3) They serve to invest the Bible with all the charms of variety and life. Christ's teachings, being parabolical, are full of nature and human life. (4) They serve to show the importance of adapting our methods of teaching to the conditions and capacities of our hearers.

III. The different spiritual results of its revealment. The passage teaches that there is a difference both in the *kind* and *degree* of the result.

First : *There is a difference in the kind of result.* Some perceive it, and some do not; " *seeing they see not, hearing they hear not.*" Some feel it and some do not. Their heart is " *gross,*" their ears are " *dull,*" their eyes are " *closed.*" Man has a threefold vision;—the sensuous, the intellectual, and the spiritual. The last is that which makes the object real, brings it home to the heart, and makes it part

---

sided explanation which has been given to it, as if Christ here speaks to them in parables, *in order that* they may not understand ! Only read what the very unjustly slighted Mark (iv. 33) says truly by the Holy Ghost : ' He spake the word to them *as they were able to hear it.*' (Compare John viii. 43.) Does that mean ' not understand ?' Christ does not merely say in what follows, as will soon appear, ' Therefore speak I to them in parables, *because* they do not understand;' nor has He in ver. 12 said, ' Therefore, *that they may not* understand.' Either of these as separated from the other is ' in no sense a justifiable idea,' the latter still less so than the former. The truth takes both together, as Christ's word here stands between what precedes and what follows. Does Christ then speak purposely to the wind ? Are not parables given to be heard ? and if they may yet possibly be rightly heard to be understood. Christ does not light His lamp in vain, as He assures us in Mark, ver. 21, 23. To what purpose is it, then, that He lets it shine until the night comes when none can see to work, and that He so patiently and diligently instructs this people also even to the last ?"—*See Stier on " The Words of the Lord Jesus.*"

of our nature. Unless a man sees the Gospel in the best sense, he is injured by it; he seeing sees not. The Gospel ministry is a damning as well as a saving process. It has made millions of Pharaohs. Observe three things in relation to this moral obduracy :—

First : *Its figurative representation.* "This people's heart is waxed gross." In Isaiah, the word "fat" is applied to the heart instead of "gross." Fat,—the most unfeeling and encumbering part of the animal creature ; a man distinguished by grossness and fatness, is dull, heavy, unimpressible. *Insensibility* is the idea. The Bible represents the sinner as having a hardened heart, a stony heart, &c.; and represents him morally as being asleep, dead, sometimes "*twice dead.*" The moral heart of the sinner is so fat with pride, selfishness, carnality, and worldliness, that it is almost "past feeling." The moral nerves are buried in the "fat." This moral insensibility is : (1) *Criminal.* It is not the normal condition of the soul; it is the result of a sinful course. It is (2) *Dangerous.* It is a moral disease of the most alarming character. It is (3) *Temporary.* It will not continue for ever. The heart must one day be quickened, either by the convictions of the Gospel, or by the flash of retribution.

Second : *Its universal symptoms.* "By hearing ye shall hear, and shall not understand," &c. (1) *Want of spiritual understanding.* They hear the Law and the Gospel; hear the echoes of Sinai and of Calvary, but they do not understand the spiritual import. All that the most powerful sermons do, is to ring on the hearing nerve, and then die away in sound. There is no understanding. The condition of the soul is too dull and heavy, too "*fat,*" to put forth any effort to penetrate the Divine meaning of what is heard. It recoils from thinking on religious subjects in a religious way. (2) *Want of spiritual perception.* "Seeing ye shall see, and not perceive." Pictures of Divine things, both in nature and in the Bible, are brought close to the eye of sense, and yet the soul sees them not. Rational statements of Divine things are brought close to the eye of understanding, and yet the soul perceives them not. The spiritual eye is full of evil, and all is dark within. The soul can only see in the object what it brings to it, and as it has not the Divine spirit of things in it, it sees not the Divine in outward objects. A thick haze of sensuousness and sin hides the spiritual from the soul's eye.

Third : *Its grand discoverer.* "*In them is fulfilled.*" Or, *is being* fulfilled, is now in the course of illustration, what the old prophets said. It is here taught that the great discoverer of the moral insensibility of the sinner is the teaching of Christ. *The life and teaching of Christ have brought out to the view of the universe, in aspects of hugest hideousness, the moral insensibility of the sinner's soul.*" Take the conduct of the Jewish nation, or rather the Sanhedrim, as the representative of that nation in relation to Christ, as exhibiting the hardness of the human soul. The members of that Jewish council had, by the teaching and life of Christ, the divinest things brought in the most powerful way to their ears, and in the most commanding form to their eyes, and yet they understood not, neither did they perceive. They witnessed His miracles, they heard His sermons ; they knew the unearthly tenor of His life, and yet they were so blind and hard, that they went on, in the face of all, to crucify Him. More, they witnessed the wonders of His cruci- fixion ; they were convinced of His resurrection. The wonders of the Pentecost must have assured them that He was gone to heaven; and yet, blind and hardened, they continued to persecute, even unto death, the disciples who advocated His cause. Truly this child was set for the rise and fall of many in Israel, *and the thoughts of many hearts were revealed by Him.* Christ revealed the moral heart of His age, and His Gospel ever since discovers the awfully hardened con- dition of man. Man's awful moral insensibility is seen in two ways. (1) *In his opposition to the Gospel.* His infidel calumnies and his bloody persecutions, &c., show this. (2) *In his indifference to the Gospel.* The fact that millions upon millions hear the Gospel and see it, and yet have no vital sympathy with it, is an awful illustra- tion of the fact that " *the people's heart is waxed gross.*" Oh, haste the day when the Gospel trump shall not only be heard throughout the land, but when its blasts shall grow so loud and startling. as to reach the dullest ear, and rouse into living action the dullest soul !

In these two opposite results it is important to remember three things. (1) The Gospel benefits by design ;—it does not injure by design. (2) The Gospel benefits by adaptation ;—it does not injure by adaptation. It has no aptitude for this. (3) The Gospel bene- fits by divine influence ; it does not injure by divine influence.

Secondly: *There is a difference in the degree.* " Many prophets and righteous men desired to see those things which ye see," &c. The disciples had a fuller manifestation and a richer enjoyment of the Gospel than the prophets and righteous men of whom Christ speaks.

Matthew 13:24-43*

Wheat and Tares ; or, Good and Evil

Good and evil are in this world. This is one of the distinguish- ing facts of its moral history. We know of no other world in the universe where they both exist together. In heaven, good exists, and good alone—unmixed, ever-advancing good. In hell, evil, and evil exclusively. But on earth you have both : the tares and the wheat grow in the same soil. This parable presents us with three facts in connexion with good and evil in this world : *their implant- ation, their growth, and their maturity.*

* The parables of the mustard seed (31, 32) and the leaven (33), which come between the parable of the wheat and tares, and its explanation, are noticed sepa- rately in the following sections.

I. THE IMPLANTATION OF GOOD AND EVIL. " *The kingdom of heaven is like unto a man which sowed good seed in his field; but while men slept his enemy came and sowed tares among the wheat, and went his way.*" Christ's interpretation of this is,—" *He that soweth the good seed is the Son of Man; the field is the world; the good seed are the children of the kingdom; but the tares are the children of the wicked one; the enemy that sowed them is the Devil.*" Both evil and good in men are to be traced to an *implantation*. Neither is inbred. The seeds of evil are not constitutionally in man; and the seeds of good, though once constitutional, have been all but entirely eradicated by sin. Wherever you find, therefore, either growing, you may be sure that the seed has been implanted by some outward agent, *i.e.*, " the Devil," or " the Son of Man." Between these two great sowers, or implanters, there are certain striking points of contrast :—

First : *The one has a right to implant, the other has not.* " *The Son of Man* " is the owner of the field. It is here called " *His field,*" and the servants recognise it as His field. " *Didst thou not sow good seed in thy field?*" All souls, with all their capacities to receive, incorporate, and to develop the good, both in theory and practice, doctrine and duty, are His :—His by creative power and redemptive love. To unfold their resources, to bring out their faculties into the bloom and fruitfulness of virtue, is His unquestionable right, as it is His pleasure. But Satan has no right to any part of the field. He has no right to touch a susceptibility, or to influence a power. He is a moral marauder.

Secondly : *The one works clandestinely, the other openly.* " While men *slept.*" When the sable curtain of night veiled the world's vision, and men, wearied with the toils of the day, lay in the refreshing arms of sleep, the Devil stole in and began his work. *It is only as men sleep that the agents of evil can succeed.* In proportion to the dormancy of the human faculties, and the general drowsiness of the soul, evil spreads. Like some of the predatory animals, evil works in the dark, and skulks away at the opening eye of day. The reverse of this is true in relation to the right and the true. Christianity requires all the wakefulness and activity of thinking souls.

Thirdly : *The one is inspired by enmity, the other is not.* The sower of the tares is called an " *enemy.*" Oriental travellers inform us, that even to this day, in Judea, enmity gratifies itself in the way which is here indicated. The agriculturist who happens to have an enemy, is watched by him with a vindictive eye as he ploughs his field, in order to avail himself of the first favourable opportunity to cast into the soil some noxious seed. Christ would give us to understand that it is thus with the Devil. Christ has come into the field; He has ploughed its hardened soil, and in it sown the seed of everlasting truth and right. But the *enemy* has watched Him, entered the field, and scattered the seeds of error and wrong. Enmity inspires the promoter of evil, but love, pure and unbounded, the promoter of good. "An *enemy*," says Christ, "hath done this;" as if He had said, I have not sown these tares, the wheat only I have sown. Christ is neither the author nor agent of evil.

So much for the *implantation* of these antagonistic principles; one under an agency which is *unjust, clandestine,* and *malignant;* and the other, under that which is *righteous, open, benevolent.* Youth is especially the season of this implantation. It is when the conscience is susceptible, when the emotions are warm, when the imagination is vivid, when the judgment is unfettered and free, that these principles are generally implanted. After-life is but the growth and development of what we received in our youthful days.

We have here—

II. THE GROWTH OF GOOD AND EVIL.

First: *Both are susceptible of growth.* Both the tares and the wheat, having been sown, germinated and grew. The soil of the heart quickened both. Though man's nature is made for truth and right, it will grow error and wrong. It can develop a wrong abstract idea into a upas tree, which shall spread its baneful branches over empires. All the social, political, and religious institutions that curse the world, are but principles received from the devil, and grown by the human heart. Man, thou hast soil in thy heart to grow the upas, as well as the tree of life !

Secondly: *That in their growth their difference is seen.* "*Then appeared the tares also.*" In the seed they appeared indistinguishable : in size, shade, and shape they were much alike. But as they came out in the stalk and green blade, the difference became obvious. Frequently, wrong principles, as they stand in propositions, appear in books, or flow from the lips of eloquence, are scarcely to be distinguished from the right. But let them grow into the forms of acts, habits, and institutions, and the dissimilarity becomes obvious. You will have great difficulty in convincing the foolishly indulgent parent, who ministers more to the bodily appetites and fantastic wishes of his child than to the conscience, who instils the principles of pleasure rather than duty, that he is wrong; but let the boy or girl reach maturity, and he shall have heart-breaking proofs of his error. You may have a difficulty in convincing an Atheist that his principles are bad, but let them grow and become embodied in the life of a nation, and, as in France, the enormity shall be written in blood and proclaimed in thunder. The difference between good and evil principles appears more and more as they are left to grow.

Thirdly: *That although the difference appears in the growth, a complete separation cannot be effected during growth.* "*Let both grow together until the harvest.*" What is meant by this ? Not (1) That we are not to endeavour to root out the tares of evil from our own hearts. This is the most urgent duty of every man. Christ solemnly enjoins it. (Matt. v. 29, 30.) Not (2) The non-excommunication of the detected hypocrite from the fellowship of the godly. This is also a duty. Not (3) The ceasing from moral efforts connected with the preaching of the Gospel and the dissemination of truth to destroy evil in the world. This also is a duty. But *it means that no effort of force and violence is to be made, in order to remove bad men from the world.*

The desire of these servants seems to have been to clear the field entirely of the tares, to tear them up root and branch, and to leave nothing in the whole field but wheat; which means, perhaps, the destruction by martyrdom of all wicked men, and leaving the world entirely in the possession of the good. To this wish Christ utters an emphatic No;—" lest *while ye gather up the tares, ye root up also the wheat with them.*" As the roots of the tares and the wheat are so intertwined in the soil that the pulling of the one would involve injury to the other: so men in this world are so interblended by their relationship of country, family, and friendship, that the martyrdom of the bad would injure the good. The mixture of the good and bad in this world is of service. (1) It is of service to the bad—it keeps them in a position of improvement; and (2), It is of service to the good. Holy character is strengthened and perfected by contact with palpable evil.

We have here—

III. THE MATURITY OF GOOD AND EVIL. Here notice the period in which they shall reach maturity; the forms they shall assume in maturity; the treatment they shall meet with in maturity.

First: *The period in which they shall reach maturity.* " The harvest is the *end of the world.*" When will the moral principles which have been scattered over the world for ages, idolatry, superstition, infidelity, and worldliness, as well as principles of an opposite and holy character, reach their *full maturity ?* Jesus tells us— in " *The end of the world.*" Then all principles will wave in ripeness and invite the scythe of Heaven. What ends are involved in this " *end of the world !*" The end of all human enterprises :—commerce, politics, arts, and professions will be no more. The means of moral discipline will find an end in this end; no more churches built, or sermons preached, or books written, or pardons granted, or sinners reformed, or souls sanctified and saved :—" *the harvest is the end of the world.*"

Secondly: *The forms they shall assume in maturity.* What forms shall these principles assume in the last day? Will they appear in books, speeches, or institutions ? No! All will appear in two classes of mankind ; " *The children of the kingdom, and the children of the wicked one:"* the former, those who are born of incorruptible seed, and the latter, of the principles of evil. In that day, all principles both good and evil will have passed from books, from talk, from memory, from theories, INTO MAN. On the great day of judgment you will look on the left hand and see in the horrid faces, expressions, and characters of the lost, all the evil principles that have ever been at work in this world during all the ages that are past, incarnated, and embodied in "*The children of the wicked one.*" And on the right hand of the Judge you will see a living embodiment of all the good principles that have ever operated in this earth in *"The children of the kingdom."*

Thirdly : *The treatment they shall meet with in maturity.* *" The Son of Man shall send forth His angels,"* etc. Observe (1) The treatment of the evil. *" He will bind them in bundles to burn them."* This may convey the idea that the wicked will not be conveyed to misery in one great indiscriminate mass, but there will be a classification : they will be grouped together on some principle ; perhaps, according to their ages, their countries, their associations, and their relative amount of guilt. *" To burn them !"*—Hell is a tremendous reality. Observe (2) The treatment of the good. *" They shall shine as the sun in the kingdom of their Father."* It is a mercy to live in a good kingdom, but a greater mercy to live in a father's empire ; to have a father on the throne, to obey a father's laws, exult in a father's victories, adore a father's majesty.

The good *"shall shine as the sun"* in this kingdom. How pure the sun ! his beams are undefiled by all the pollutions of this polluted earth ; the good shall be *"without spot or wrinkle or any such thing."* How useful the sun ! he lights distant worlds with his beams, he is the life of the system. The good shall serve God and His universe day and night. How glorious is the sun ! he stands alone in the heavens, the object of universal admiration. The good shall be *"made kings and priests unto God."* *" They shall shine for ever,"* saith Christ ; yes, and ever brighten as they shine. The sun has not increased in splendour for thousands of years, nor does it light any more worlds than it did at first ; but the good shall *increase* in splendour, they shall advance from glory into glory, they shall brighten their lustre, widen their orbits, and extend their influence through the boundless future.

Friend, our subject is pre-eminently practical. The principles that are now implanted in thy bosom will grow, and one day reach maturity, and in that maturity thou wilt find thy heaven or thy hell. Nothing so momentous as principles. As sure as August shows the work of the farmer, so sure thy futurity will show the principles thou art cultivating now. "Buy" then "the truth ;" buy it at any cost ; for any amount of labour, sacrifice, or talent, buy it, and when thou hast it, sell it not ! No, sell it not for pleasure, for prosperity, for fame, or for life. Get holy principles and thou shalt get the pinions of an angel, which shall bear thee above all the clouds and storms of earth, into the sunshine and the calm of eternity.

Matthew 13:31-32

The Mustard Seed; or, Christianity a Life

These verses give us three things in relation to Christianity.
I. THE APPARENT INSIGNIFICANCE OF ITS ORIGIN. " *The least of all seeds.*" This does not mean that the mustard seed is the least of all seeds, or that when grown it becomes the greatest of all trees. This is contrary to fact. But inasmuch as the ancients specially marked, in this case, the wonderful difference between the small grain and the full developed tree, "*small as a grain of mustard seed*," became a proverbial expression amongst the Jews. Its smallness was felt not by comparing it with other seed, but with the big tree which grew out of it. It is therefore a suitable figure to represent the general idea that out *of small beginnings great things arise.* Did ever a system come before men in such a humble aspect as Christianity? Who was the founder? The despised Galilean. —" *He was as a root out of the dry ground.*" Of the people there was none with Him. "*He was despised and rejected of men.*" He was born as a pauper, and He died as a malefactor. The first promoters of His system, who were they? None of the conventionally great or even respectable, but for the most part men of the humbler class in life. But though apparently insignificant, though the seed was small in size and mean in form, it was full of vitality,—inextinguishable vitality. An eternal series of celestial harvests slumbered in its shell. Men have always been anxious to give grand forms to things. They found their schools and inaugurate their administrations amidst the pomp of imposing ceremonies. They garb their thoughts in rhetoric and propound their laws in formulas of hazy solemnity. The reason of this is, the want of faith in the vital truth of their ideas. Truth, like life, will make its own form; —error only lives as it is wrapped in fine clothes. Christianity was a principle of living truth, " *a seed;* " and though small, only give it soil and it will build up structures for itself. The little acorn will build in oaken forests for itself a home, before which the most magnificent palaces of kings shall appear mean, and that shall flourish in strength and beauty when those palaces are dust. Truth never studies appearance, error does; truth is content with the form of a mustard seed, error seeks all the pageantry that art can invent and wealth procure.
II. THE WONDERFUL EXTENT OF ITS EXPANSION. "*When it is grown it is the greatest among herbs.*" The proportion between the little mustard seed and the full-grown tree is one of the marvels of nature. There are in nature smaller seeds and bigger trees in abundance, but we are not sure whether you will find in nature a larger tree starting from a smaller seed. " *When it is grown it is the greatest among herbs.*"—Greatest in proportion to its seed—

"and becomes a tree so great that the birds of the air come and lodge in the branches thereof."* "The idea," says Olshausen, "which this parable is obviously designed to set forth is simply this—That in the manifestation of what is Divine, the beginning and the end of its development stand related to each other in an inverse ratio. Springing from invisible beginnings it spreads itself abroad over an all-embracing field of operations." The little seed which Jesus and His disciples sowed shall one day grow to proportions more vast than that tree which the prophet beheld in vision whose "*height reached unto heaven and the sight thereof to the end of all the earth.*" All the other productions of the world shall be small in comparison with it. Or, to change the figure, "*the little stone cut out of the mountain without hands*" will roll on and grow in every revolution until it becomes a great mountain to fill the whole earth.

From this destined expansion of Christianity let us learn :—

First : *Not to despise things of humble appearances and beginnings.* Our question should be, in relation to all systems and measures, not, Are their forms imposing or respectable ? not, What great names stand in association with them ? but Have they the vitality of truth in them ? If they have, treat them with becoming homage, for they are Divine ; oppose them not, for they are destined to grow : they will spread out their majestic branches over your grave. "*Despise not the day of small things.*" †

From this destined expansion of Christianity let us learn :—

Secondly : *The duty of patient perseverance in our efforts to promote truth.* Christianity is confessedly slow in its progress ; but it does progress. It does not grow fast, but it does grow. As a general principle in life, science, and institutions, the greater the thing the slower its growth. Every kind of life, philosophic, social, and political, as well as vegetable and animal, has its mushroom and oak ; the one reaching its perfection in a few hours, the other requiring the growth of long centuries. Since Christianity appeared how many systems of religion have sprung up, reached their maturity, and passed away ! But Christianity is growing still, its roots are deeper, its branches stretch over more territory, and are

---

* "In hot countries, as in Judea, the mustard tree attains a size which it is never known to reach in our colder latitudes, sometimes so great as to allow a man to climb up into its branches (though this, indeed, is mentioned as a remarkable thing) or to ride on horseback under them, as a traveller in Chili mentions that he has done. Maldonatus assures us that in Spain he has himself seen great ovens heated with its branches ; he mentions further that birds are exceedingly partial to the seed, so that when it is advancing to ripeness he has often seen them lighting in very great numbers on its boughs, which, however, were strong enough to sustain the weight without being broken. This fact of the fondness of the birds for the seeds, and the manner in which, therefore, they congregated in the branches, was probably familiar to our Lord's hearers as well. They, too, had beheld them congregating in the branches of the trees, whose seed thus served them for meat, so that there must have been a singular fitness in the image which the parable presented to their minds."—*Trench.*

† See a characteristic sermon of John Foster on this text.

clad in richer foliage to-day, than ever. Let us then toil on : we cannot labour in vain.

III. The necessary condition of its expansion. *" Which a man put into the soil." " Except a corn of wheat fall into the ground and die, it abideth alone : but if it die, it bringeth forth much fruit."*

First : *There is an affinity subsisting between the human soul and the Gospel, analogous to that subsisting between the earth and the seed.* The earth is invested with powers to quicken, nourish, and develop the seed. The human soul can take in the Gospel and turn it into a living and regnant power. There is beautiful fitness in the Gospel to the constitution and condition of the human soul. There are some systems that suit some souls in some respects but do not suit others. Christianity suits all—it is fitted to universal mind as the earth is fitted for the seed. It can grow in souls of every zone, from the equator to the poles.

Secondly : *The extension of the Gospel requires that it should be committed to the soil.* *"Unless,"* says Christ, *"it die, it will abide alone."* Christ was a sower of the seed. He sought to put the truth into human hearts. He did not commit His thoughts to books but to souls. Christianity as it works in the heart is mightier than it is when explained and enforced in a thousand volumes. Christianity in books is like seed in the granary, dry and all but dead. It is not written, but living, characters that are to convert the infidel. The life of good men and not the library of theologues is the converting power.

> " O, let me speak the thoughts of Christ !
> And then my words like seed shall grow
> In hearts, when I am gone:
> In nobler forms and widening spheres
> To beautify and bless, shall they appear:
> Harvests out of them shall come
> To help the millions yet to be."

Matthew 13:33-34

Leaven ; or, Christianity an Influence

From this we learn :—

I. That Christianity is an imported power. The leaven is " taken " from somewhere, and put into " the meal." It is not an *inherent* element. Christianity is not a force *native* to the world. It is something *brought* to it and *put into it.* *" My kingdom,"* said Christ, *" is not of this world ;"* it does not rise out of the world as other kingdoms have done. It is a foreign importation. The world could not produce it, for it could not produce that which was *dissimilar* in spirit and *opposed* in aim to itself. Christianity is of Divine origin.

II. THAT CHRISTIANITY IS A HIDDEN POWER. The leaven is "*hid in the meal.*" This is illustrated by the silent manner in which Christ entered the world, and the unostentatious way in which He passed through it: "*He was in the world, and the world knew Him not:*" by the manner in which His system works—"*His kingdom cometh not with observation.*" Subjectively it begins working as a quiet power in the heart. Its reformative energy begins not with outward institutions and forms, but with inner principles, and then works on gently until it reaches the extremities of the external, and fashions all to its own ideal. ·

III. THAT CHRISTIANITY IS AN ASSIMILATING POWER. *The leaven makes the lump like itself.* Christianity makes all it influences like itself. It gives men the spirit of Christ. What a glorious state will the world be in, when it shall have realised its mission! Each of the millions of men on this earth Christ-like in all that is moral. If the Gospel has not leavened us with its spirit it has not realised its end in our case.

IV. THAT CHRISTIANITY IS A DIFFUSIVE POWER. "*Leaven leaveneth the whole lump.*" (1) *Gradually diffusive.* From particle to particle it moves. It works from the centre gradually to the circumference. Christians in their efforts too often overlook this order. They have transported Christianity over masses, instead of working from man to man. (2) *Universally diffusive.* "*The whole lump.*"

Matthew 13:44-46

The Treasure and the Pearl ; or, Christianity the Highest Good

I. As A TRANSCENDENT GOOD IN ITSELF AND APART FROM MAN. It is here represented as a *treasure* and a *pearl.* "*A pearl of great price.*" Looking at it *apart* from man it is "*a treasure,*" a good in itself :— it has *intrinsic* worth. But it is "*a hid*" treasure—hid in the field of revelation. It is "*a pearl*" in the sea of Divine events. There are material treasures in those hills around us, and pearls beneath the waters that roll at our feet, sufficient, could we but obtain them, to invest us with the wealth of a Crœsus. It is so with spiritual things. There are elements of good in the Scriptures and in religious literature, and in the Church of God, which, if men could only discover and possess, would enrich and ennoble them for ever. "*The unsearchable riches of Christ,*" like treasures concealed by the earth, or pearls buried in the waters, are in our world ; but they are unseen and unowned by the millions.

There are four criteria by which we determine the value of an object—*rarity, verdict of competent authorities, durability, usefulness.* First : *Rarity.* This makes gold more valuable than brass or iron, pearls and diamonds more valuable than ordinary stones. In this sense Christianity is valuable. It is perfectly unique. There is nothing like it. Amongst all the systems of the world there is but one Gospel—amongst all the books but one Bible. "*There is no other name given,*" &c.

Secondly : *The verdict of competent authorities.* Whatever article in the markets of the world is pronounced valuable by men, whose judgment is considered most correct on such subjects, derives at once a value from the fact. The opinions of such authorities will invest almost any article, however intrinsically worthless, with a commercial value. Intrinsically worthless books, if praised by those who are considered judges of literature, will pass as the most precious productions of genius. Apply this to Christianity. The greatest sages, the sublimest poets, the purest saints, have all pronounced Christianity to be of incomparable value. They have felt with Paul, who said, "*I count all things but loss,*" &c.

Thirdly : *Durability.* The duration of an object often gives it value. The thing of ephemeral existence is not esteemed of much worth. The Gospel is durable. It is the *incorruptible* seed. "It is the Word of God that *endureth for ever.*"

Fourthly : *Usefulness.* We value an object according to the service it is capable of rendering. Metals and plants, animals and men, are estimated by this rule. What has rendered such service to humanity as Christianity ? We need not speak of its intellectual benefits, and show how it has broken the monotony of thought and set the mind of the world in action. We need not speak of its political benefits, and show how it has flashed and frowned upon injustice and tyranny, and moulded governments according to the principles of rectitude. We need not speak of its social benefits, and show how it has evoked and refined the best sympathies of our nature, given man a kindly interest in his fellow, and laid the foundation of social order and progress. We speak of its *spiritual* blessings. How it purifies the fountains of life, how it pacifies the guilty conscience, how it fills the soul with the sunshine of Divine love, how it raises our nature above the fear of death, and enchants it with glowing visions of an ever-expanding and brightening futurity.

Blessed Gospel ! It is indeed "*a pearl of great price.*" Take it from us, and you will freeze up the fountains of our spiritual energy and blight the springing germs of our hopes; you will turn our landscapes into deserts, and our hemispheres into midnight. Take it from us and what are we ? Frail barques struggling with the heaving billows of life, without a chart to direct us, or a star to break the darkness that enshrouds us on the surging wave.

II. As a transcendent good in the process of appropriation by man. It is interesting to look upon Christianity as an infinite good *in itself;* but it is more interesting to look upon it as a good *appropriated by ourselves.* Such is the view we now pass to. The appropriation includes two things. *Discovery and joyous surrender of all for it.* First : *Discovery.* The pearl and *treasure* were "*found.*" In two very different ways : one by an *apparent accident,* and the other by an *intelligent purpose*. (1) There is apparent accident in the discovery of the treasure. It is not said that the man was in search of it. Perhaps the man as he was digging, or driving his plough-share through his land, in the process of its cultivation, turned up the treasure unexpectedly.* This man represents those who meet with the saving power of the Gospel at a time when they had *no intention* of so doing. These are the men who are found of Christ though they ask not for Him. Such was the woman of Samaria, at Jacob's Well; such were Peter and Andrew "*casting a net into the sea ;*" such was Nathaniel "*under the fig-tree.*" How many have been converted in a seemingly casual way! Christ has come to them in a tract, or a conversation, or a sermon, or in some other event, in an unexpected manner. The inestimable treasure has been found in a most casual way—casual to the finder, but pre-arranged by heaven. (2) There is *intelligent purpose*. The merchant was engaged in "*seeking goodly pearls.*" This man believed in the ex-istence of "*goodly pearls,*" he strongly desired them, and visited all the markets within his reach in quest of the same. † This re-presents the men who believe in a higher good than they have

---

* "The circumstance which supplies the groundwork of this first parable, namely, the finding of a concealed treasure, must have been of much more frequent occur-rence in an insecure state of society, such as in almost all ages has been that of the East, than, happily, it can be with us. A writer on Oriental literature and customs mentions that in the East, on account of the frequent changes of dynasties and the revolutions which accompany them, many rich men divide their goods into three parts : one they employ in commerce, or for their necessary support ; one they turn into jewels, which, should it prove needful to fly, could be easily carried with them ; a third part they bury. But while they trust no one with the place where the treasure is buried, so is the same, should they not return to the spot before their death, as good as lost to the living, until by chance a lucky peasant, while he is digging his field, lights upon it. And thus when we read in Eastern tales how a man has found a buried treasure and in a moment risen from poverty to great riches, this is, in fact, an occurrence that not unfrequently happens, and is a natural consequence of the customs of these people. Modern books of travels continually bear witness to the universal belief in the existence of such hid treasures, so that the traveller often finds great difficulty in obtaining information about antiquities, and is sometimes seriously inconvenienced, or even endangered, in his researches among ancient ruins, by the jealousy of the neighbouring inhabitants, who fear lest he is coming to carry away concealed hoards of wealth from among them, of which, by some means or other, he has got notice. And so also the skill of an Eastern magician in great part consists in being able to detect the places where these secreted treasures will successfully be looked for. Often, too, a man, abandoning the regular pursuits of industry, will devote himself to treasure-seeking in the hope of growing, through some happy chance, rich of a sudden."—*Trench.*

† "This appears to indicate the antiquity of a still Oriental profession, that of a travelling jeweller, a person who deals in precious stones and pearls, and goes about seeking for opportunities of making advantageous purchases or exchanges, and taking journeys to remote countries for this purpose, and again in another direction to find the best market for the valuables he has secured. In the course of their operations it frequently happens that they meet with some rich and costly gem, for the sake of obtaining which they sell off all their existing stock, and every article of valuable property they may possess, in order to raise the purchase-money. Something similar may sometimes occur in the transactions of stationary jewellers, but not so often as among those who travel : indeed, the jewellers of the East, as a body, are perhaps the greatest travellers in the world."—*Pictorial Bible.*

reached,—anxiously search for it in science, in literature, in worship, —and at last find it a rich prize. " We have, perhaps," says Trench, " no such a picture of a noble nature seeking for the pearl of price, and not resting till he had found it, as that which Augustine gives of himself in his ' *Confessions* ; ' though we, also, have many more, such as Justin Martyr's account of his own conversion, given in his dialogue with Trypho, in which he tells how he had travelled through the whole circle of Greek philosophy, seeking everywhere for that which would satisfy the deepest needs of his soul, and ever seeking in vain, till ho found it at length in the Gospel of Christ."

Though, however, the chief good is often found *casually*, no one has a right to expect it without acting as the merchant did. Nay, every man incurs guilt who acts not thus. A man must go into the field, and not merely upturn its soil with the ploughshare of cursory thought, but he must *dig* and *delve* as a miner. He must not merely look into the face of the waters for a pearl, he must dive to the sandy bed on which it rests. He must prosecute an earnest quest for it. " *Yea, if thou criest after knowledge, and liftest up thy voice for understanding : if thou seekest her as silver, and searchest for her as for hid treasures ; then shalt thou understand the fear of the Lord, and find the knowledge of God. For the Lord giveth wisdom : out of His mouth cometh knowledge and understanding. He layeth up sound wisdom for the righteous : He is a buckler to them that walk uprightly.*"

Secondly : *A joyous surrender of all for it.* " *He selleth all that he hath and buyeth that field.*" The merchant did the same, and bought the pearl. The only condition on which you can obtain this transcendent good is by *selling all you have ;*—your preconceived notions, old habits and selfishness, pride, time, talents ;—your all. It must be regarded of more worth than all other things put together. We say a *joyous* surrender of all for it. " *With joy,*" &c. The purchase must be made—not mechanically, reluctantly, but joyously, with an exultant heart. " *What things were gain to me,*" said Paul, " *I counted loss,*" &c.

Matthew 13:47-50

The Net ; or, Christianity a Collecting Force

" *Again, the kingdom of heaven is like unto a net, that was cast into the sea,*" &c. The great idea here is, *that Christianity is a power to collect men together.* The existence of Congregations and Churches throughout Christendom, from the apostolic days to these, attests its congregating force. There are two facts suggested here in relation to its collecting capability.

I. THAT IT COLLECTS TOGETHER ALL CLASSES OF MEN, GOOD AND BAD. The net is not thrown into a channel or bay, but into the wide sea.

Christianity is for universal man—it is to be thrown into the vast ocean of souls, " *amidst the noise of the seas, and the tumult of the people.*" Thus acting upon the world, it gathers " *of every kind.*" Because Christianity appeals to so many impulses in the human mind men are drawn to it from improper as well as righteous considerations.

First: *There is the love of excitement.* Men have a strong instinct for excitement. This is the philosophy of most of the entertainments of the age. Race-courses, dances, theatres. Christianity appeals powerfully to this. Used with a little dramatic skill and eloquence, nothing is so exciting as Christianity.

Secondly: *There is the love of happiness.* " *Who will show us any good ?*" The heart of the world has no deeper cry than this. All are in search of enjoyment in some way or other. Christianity appeals to this deep instinct. It reveals the hell to be avoided—the heaven to be obtained.

Thirdly: *There is the love of study.* The desire for knowledge and intellectual action is a strong instinct. Men are made to desire and to admire truth. Hence the tremendous propensity to believe, —the credulousness of men. Christianity appeals to this instinct. It gives a system of truth adapted to engross and charm the intellectual nature.

Fourthly: *There is the love of power.* Men naturally desire influence among their fellow-men. Now, in this age, in Christendom, Christianity appeals to this instinct; for men cannot obtain much power who are in avowed hostility to it. " *The offence of the Cross*" has ceased long ago in this respect. It is an ornament in dress, a condition of greatness, a pledge of worth. Men must use it now to get influence.

Fifthly: *There is the love of right.* Men are made " *to delight in the law of God after the inward man.*" Christianity appeals to this sense.

Now these are the forces by which Christianity *collects* men of all classes.

The fact teaches (1) That the moral character and primary end of Christianity are not to be judged of by the character of the men it collects into assemblies. There are good fish in the net, and there are bad ones also. There are good men in the visible Church, but there are also many bad ones. On the whole, perhaps, more bad than good. " *They are not all Israel who are of Israel.*" In the great house of the Church " *there are not only vessels of gold and silver, but also of wood and of earth ; and some to honour, and some to dishonour.*" Like the bad fish, some are so small as to be worthless, and others so unclean and putrid as to be offensive and injurious. You would not judge of the design and usefulness of " *the net*" by the bad fish, but by the good; why then judge of Christianity by the bad men that from unworthy motives attach themselves to it ? And yet men do so. There is no visible Church that gives a correct representation of Christianity. Individuals may be selected who do so, but not communities. The fact that Christianity thus congregates men, teaches (2) The great importance of all its adherents giving themselves to self-scrutiny. It is no proof that we are good, that we have been drawn into Christianity and are held by it. The question is, *What* in Christianity has drawn us, and *what* in Christianity holds us?

II. THAT THERE IS A PERIOD TO ARRIVE WHEN THE COLLECTED MULTITUDE SHALL BE SEPARATED. " *When it was full, they drew to shore, and sat down, and gathered the good into vessels, but cast the bad away : so shall it be at the end of the world,*" &c.

First: *The separation will be deliberate.* This is indicated by the statement that *" they sat down."* There will be no precipitancy, none of the confusion of haste in this work. Each individual fish in the net was minutely examined to ascertain its value or worthlessness. So it will be with men at last; each will be strictly examined : every man shall " *give an account for himself.*" Secondly : *The separation will be solemn.* (1) Think of the period in which it will take place. " *The end of the world.*" What overwhelming descriptions does the Bible give of this period ! (See 2 Peter iii. &c.) (2) Think of the agents employed for this purpose. " *The angels shall come forth.*" We cannot agree with those who, like Olshausen, regard the "angels" here as denoting the ministers of the Gospel. The parable does not require such a construction, and other parts of the Scripture distinctly teach that to be the work of angels in the proper sense. (Matt. xiii. 41 ; xxiv. 31; xxv. 31; Rev. xiv. 18, 19.) " *They shall come forth ;*" they have seldom been visible to men ; their visits have been proverbially " few and far between." But they shall COME FORTH now in broad sunlight before the open eye of an assembled universe. (3) Think of the final results of the separation. " *The good gathered into vessels,*" but " *the bad cast away.*" The good are taken care of, they are received " *into everlasting habitations,*" into " a city that hath foundations," " the heavenly Jerusalem." The bad are " *cast away.*" Thrown into " *a furnace of fire.*" This is a figure, but a figure of a terrible something. What?—Who shall answer?

Matthew 13:51-52

Christianity a System for Thought

" *Jesus saith unto them, Have ye understood all these things ? They say unto Him, Yea, Lord. Then said He unto them, Therefore every scribe which is instructed unto the kingdom of heaven is like unto a man that is an householder, which bringeth forth out of his treasure things new and old.*"

I. CHRISTIANITY IS A SUBJECT TO BE INTELLECTUALLY UNDERSTOOD. " *Have ye understood these things ?*" There are some who act as if

Christianity could save them without their understanding it. Such are,—

First, the *sacramentalists*, who fancy that saving grace is mystically communicated through the sacraments. Such are,—

Secondly, the *sentimentalists*, men who come to the house of God not to understand but to *feel;* who never think of being taught— never wish it. The titillation of the sensibilities is all they look for. Such are,—

Thirdly, the *fatalists*, who expect to be converted in some miraculous way in God's own time. That Christianity is to be understood is evident from four things. (1) It has a written revelation. (2) It has an interpreting ministry. (3) It can rightly influence men only as it is understood. (4) It inculcates the duty of study.

II. That the better men understand Christianity the more qualified they are to minister it. "*Every scribe which is instructed unto the kingdom of heaven is like unto a man that is an householder, which bringeth forth out of his treasure things new and old.* Three remarks will bring out the spirit of this passage.

First: *That the function of a true minister is to provide for the spiritual wants of his people.* He is a "*householder.*" We do not agree with those, who, like Neander, regard the work of the householder here as consisting in showing "his visitors his jewels, exhibiting in pleasing alternation the modern and the antique, and leading them from the common to the rare." We are disposed to think that his work is of a more useful description, namely, spreading on his table various articles of food for his family, agreeable to their diversified tastes and wants. The work of the minister is to spread out before his people the provisions of the Gospel.

Secondly: *That the provisions which he presents should be characterized by variety.* "Things new and old." "Things," says Henry, "of this year's growth and last year's gathering." Man wants variety for his body, and God in nature hath provided for it; man wants variety for his soul, and God in Christianity has provided for it. There are truths here for every grade of intellectual power, every phase of spiritual experience, every stage of religious growth —for the child, the young man, and the father. The rustic and the sage may study together here.

Thirdly: *That an increasing acquaintance with the things of Christ will qualify the minister to furnish this variety.* Christ's words are *seeds* of thought. When a man begins to treat Christianity in a devoutly philosophic way, he will discover on every page truths of such suggestive force as will be perpetually opening his mind to new and nobler views. One true thought, in the very nature of mind, is the fountain of myriads. If preachers were truly thoughtful, the pulpit would never be *monotonous;* it would be a perennial source of life and beauty. From what source can truths so fresh and vigorous be obtained as from the Scriptures !

Matthew 13:54-58

Nazarene Prejudice ; or, A Social Sophistry

This fragment of history has no necessary connexion with any preceding portion of this chapter ; it is not, therefore, necessary that I should remind you of any remarks in connexion with our past exposition of this Gospel.

Jesus was now at Nazareth, here called " His own country." Capernaum was designated " His own city," because there He spent the largest portion of His public life, and performed most of His mighty works. Nazareth, however, was the home of His friends, and the scene of His early days.* Here He passed through all the

---

* The Rev. Arthur Penrhyn Stanley, M.A., who himself visited scenes of sacred history, thus describes Nazareth in his admirable work :—

" Fifteen gently rounded hills ' seem as if they had met to form an enclosure ' for this peaceful basin ; they rise round it like the edge of a shell to guard it from intrusion. It is ' a rich and beautiful field ' in the midst of these green hills— abounding in gay flowers, in fig-trees, small gardens, hedges of the prickly pear ; and the dense rich grass affords an abundant pasture. The expression of the old topographer, Quaresmius, was as happy as it was poetical : ' Nazareth is a rose, and, like a rose, has the same rounded form, enclosed by mountains, as the flower by its leaves.' The village stands on the steep slope of the south-western side of the valley ; its chief object the Great Franciscan Convent of the Annunciation, with its white campanile and brown enclosure.

" From the crest of the hills which thus screen it, especially from that called Nebi-Said, or Ismail, on the western side, is one of the most striking views in Palestine : Tabor, with its rounded dome, on the south-east ; Hermon's white top in the distant north ; Carmel and the Mediterranean Sea to the west ; a conjunction of those three famous mountains probably unique in the views of Palestine : and in the nearer prospect, the uplands in which Nazareth itself stands, its own circular basin behind it ; on the west, enclosed by similar hills, overhanging the plain of Acre, lies the town of Sepphorieh, just noticed as the Roman capital, and brought into close and, as far as its situation is concerned, not improbable connexion with Nazareth, as the traditional residence of the Virgin's parents. On the south and south-east lies the broad plain of Esdraelon, overhung by the high pyramidal hill, which, as the highest point of the Nazareth range, and thus the most conspicuous to travellers approaching from the plain, has received, though without any historical ground, the name of the ' Mount of Precipitation.' These are the natural features which for nearly thirty years met the almost daily view of Him who ' increased in wisdom and stature ' within this beautiful seclusion. It is the seclusion which constitutes its peculiarity and its fitness for these scenes of the Gospel history. Unknown and unnamed in the Old Testament, Nazareth first appears as the retired abode of the humble carpenter. Its separation from the busy world may be the ground, as it certainly is an illustration, of the Evangelist's play on the word, ' He shall be called a Nazarene.' Its wild character high up in the Galilean hills may account both for the roughness of its population, unable to appreciate their own Prophet, and for the evil reputation which it had acquired even in the neighbouring villages, one of whose inhabitants, Nathanael of Cana, said, ' Can any good thing come out of Nazareth ? ' There, secured within the natural barrier of the hills, was passed that youth, of which the most remarkable characteristic is its absolute obscurity ; and thence came the name of NAZARENE, used of old by the Jews, and used still by Mussulmans, as the appellation of that despised sect which has now embraced the civilized world.

stages of life up to the ripest manhood. Thirty years He seems to have spent amongst its magnificent scenery and rough society in study, toil, and worship. Hence He is called " Jesus of Nazareth," and " the Nazarene." It was an obscure place, and one of low reputation. It was one of the most disesteemed villages in that Galilee which was itself the most disreputable part of Palestine. The reasons for its standing so low in the estimation of the Jews were various. The rough, uncouth, and strange dialect of its inhabitants, and the moral corruptions which reigned amongst them, both of which arose from the mixture of provincial Jews with Egyptians and other foreigners who resided there, rendered it a place of odious notoriety. Hence the name of Nazarene stood for a low, ignorant, and uncultured person. The question of Nathanael, " *Can any good thing come out of Nazareth ?* " was by no means an unnatural one.

We find, by reference to Luke iv. 16–30, that Jesus had visited this place before as a teacher. It was on a Sabbath-day, and He entered the synagogue as He was wont to do. The book of the prophet Isaiah was put into His hand, and He opened it, and His eye fell upon that beautiful passage, " *The Spirit of the Lord,*" &c. On that occasion He met with a most unhospitable and cruel treat-

" It was not to be expected that any local reminiscences should be preserved of a period so studiously, as it would appear, withdrawn from our knowledge. Two natural features, however, may still be identified, connected, the one by tradition, the other by the Gospel narrative, with the events which have made Nazareth immortal. The first is the spring or well in the green open space, at the north-west extremity of the town, a spot well-known as the general encampment of such travellers as do not take up their quarters in the Franciscan convent. It is probably this well—which must always have been frequented, as it is now, by the women of Nazareth—that in the earliest local traditions of Palestine figured as the scene of the angelic salutation to Mary, as she, after the manner of her country-women, went thither to draw water. The tradition may be groundless, but there can be little question that the locality to which it is attached exists, and that it must have existed at the time of the alleged scene. The second is indicated in the Gospel history by one of those slight touches which serve as a testimony to the truth of the description, by nearly approaching, but yet not crossing the verge of inaccuracy. ' They rose,' it is said of the infuriated inhabitants, ' and cast Him out of the city, and brought Him to a brow of the mountain ' (ἕως ὀφρύος τοῦ ὄρους) on which the city was built, so as to ' cast Him down the cliff' (ὥστε κατακρημνίσαι αὐτόν). Most readers probably from these words imagine a town built on the summit of a mountain, from which summit the intended precipitation was to take place. This, as I have said, is not the situation of Nazareth. Yet, its position is still in accordance with the narrative. It is built ' upon,' that is, on the side of a ' mountain,' but the ' brow ' is not beneath but over the town, and such a cliff (κρημνὸς) as is here implied, is to be found, as all modern travellers describe, in the abrupt face of the limestone rock, about thirty or forty feet high, overhanging the Maronite convent at the south-west corner of the town.

" It is needless to dwell in detail on the other lesser scenes of our Lord's ministrations in the neighbourhood of His early home. Nain, at two or three hours' distance, in the Plain of Esdraelon, has been already mentioned. The ' parts,' or ' borders ' of Tyre and Sidon are too indefinite to be dwelt upon. The claims of Cana are divided between the two modern villages of that name, the one situated at some distance in the corner of the basin of Sepphorieh, the other nearer in an upland village to the east of Nazareth." (Page 365.)

ment. " *They were filled with wrath, and rose up, and thrust Him out of the city, and led Him unto the brow of the hill whereon their city was built, that they might cast Him down headlong.*"

Now He visits them again: their enmity towards Him has not quenched His love for their souls. Their proverbial unkindness will not prevent Him from entering into their midst. The Good Shepherd came to seek the lost; the Great Physician to heal the diseased. What was the result of this second visit? One might have thought that a calm reflection upon what He said to them when He stood in their midst, the Almighty power and the benign temper which He then displayed, and the ingratitude and indignity with which they treated Him:—I say, one might have thought that such a reflection would have softened them into penitence, pre-pared them to hail Him to their midst on a second visitation, and to listen with earnestness to every word which He would then pronounce. But was such the fact? No. They heard Him in their synagogue again, and nothing that He uttered could they gainsay. Every word commended itself to all that was intuitive within them. They were impressed with the force, charmed by, and astonished at, the sublimity of His doctrine. But that was all. They believed Him not, and He departed from their midst without the performance of any mighty works, because of their unbelief.

Now it is to the *cause* of this, that I wish to call your attention. What was it that rendered this second visit of Jesus a failure? What was it that thwarted the gracious purpose of this second mis-sion? What was it that repelled mercy again from their midst, and resisted the Almighty arm of love, outstretched to save? Was it a something local and temporary—an evil which was confined to that age and place; or was it something common to all the depraved generations of our race? It was, I conceive, the latter. It was *pre-judice*. The prejudice may be expressed in one sentence. *The incompetency of a man of humble rank to teach his neighbour.* The spirit of these Nazarenes may be thus expressed :—Is not this the poor carpenter, the humble mechanic, who has been toiling amongst us for His daily bread. We knew His mother and His brethren; " *Whence hath He this wisdom ;* " He has never had any scholastic advantage ; He has never been to our schools ; never sat at the feet of any of our rabbis ! What, then, can this poor neighbour of ours know about souls and truth, immortality and God? We must be as well acquainted with these things as He is : and who is He, therefore, that He should presume to teach us? Now there is, as I shall have an opportunity of showing, a great deal of what is common in all this ; it is very much the language of men generally. It is one of those popular *social sophistries* that exercise a most pernicious influ-ence amongst men, and that require to be exposed and denounced. Men somehow or other disparage the teaching of their neighbour, especially if he happen to be poor. Poor labouring mechanics,—what can they know ?

The passage suggests four things in relation to this *Nazarene prejudice, or social sophistry.*

I. IT IS REMARKABLY FORCEFUL. The impression which Jesus made upon them was evidently powerful. " *They were astonished, and said, Whence hath this man this wisdom ?*" His doctrines carried their reason and their consciences with Him. They could raise no argument against His position ; their moral constitution bound them to approve of the principles which He inculcated. Notwithstanding this, there was a something in them which induced them practically to resist the whole. A something in their minds which, like water, quenched the fire of His doctrines, as it fell upon their hearts ; a something in the soil of their natures that destroyed the life of the seed as soon as it dropped into their bosom. What was this something ? The stupid prejudice, that *a poor neighbour could not be a great teacher.* This notion, which seems to have been wrought into their souls, prevented them receiving even what their judgment and consciences approved. Though they felt that there was a wonderful teacher before them, the old prejudice soon overcame the impression. Prejudice has always this neutralising power. In whatever mind it dwells it acts in relation to truth as alkali in relation to acids, neutralising its very power. Arguments the most cogent, discourses the most powerful, can be neutralised at once by some prejudice in the mind.

II. IT IS MANIFESTLY FOOLISH.

First : *Because the merits of a doctrine are absolutely independent of the circumstances of the teacher.* The grand want of man's nature is truth. It is truth that he requires to solve his difficulties, answer his questions, quicken his nature, develop his power, and guide his being. The business of his life ought to be, to " *buy the truth*"—to " *get wisdom.*" The truth he especially requires is moral—that which refers to duty and to God. Moral truth is the same everywhere, in whatever age it appears, or by whomsoever proclaimed. The truth or falsehood of a moral doctrine is independent of the person who proclaims it. That there is a God, that men should love and serve Him, that there is a hereafter of retribution—these and cognate principles are true. They are as true when proclaimed by the meanest peasant as when uttered by the greatest prince. As true when proclaimed by the most untutored rustic as when taught by the most learned doctor of theology The rational question, therefore, of every man in listening to the doctrines of a teacher should be, not, Is he a neighbour or a foreigner ? not, Is he scholastically educated or self-trained ? not, Has he sprung from the loins of rank, or risen from obscurity ? These are mere contingencies ; but, Is the doctrine *true ?* If true, however humble the man, his doctrine has a majesty before which I must bow ; if false, however great the teacher, his doctrine I must treat with contempt. It is foolish :—

Secondly : *Because such circumstances, particularly in relation to Christ, were peculiarly favourable to the proving of the divinity of His doctrine.* Suppose two individuals to appear amongst us as teachers of the same doctrine, and that doctrine such as commends itself to our reason ; one we shall know as a foreigner, high in rank, well trained in the first institutions of his country, the other shall be one of our neighbours, with whose humble origin and relatives we are well acquainted, and who has never been blessed with any educational advantages. Let both proclaim the same doctrines with the same clearness, propriety, and force—which of these men would it be more rational to regard as connected with supernatural endowments? Would it not be our poor neighbour ? In the other case we might refer the man's power to the extraordinary advantages which he had received in his own country. But in this case we could refer it to nothing of the kind. The very idea that such a poor man at our very door should rise up and proclaim doctrines which no sage had ever announced, would, we think, naturally impress us with the fact that the teacher was connected in some special way with God. The very reason therefore which induced these Nazarenes to reject the doctrine, was one which in itself was the most adapted, if they had used their reason, to impress them with its divinity. It is foolish :—

Thirdly : *Because some of the greatest teachers in the world have sprung up from the lowest ranks of life.* It is a *physiological* fact, that the muscular exercise which an individual who has to labour for his livelihood puts forth, is conducive to the health and vigour of the brain ; and as is the brain so will be the mind. It is a *social* fact, that those who are dependent for their livelihood on their own exertions must employ many of their intellectual and moral powers. In such a case there must be forethought, plan, invention, patience, perseverance, and all these are helps to intellectual development, which the man of opulence and ease has not. Hence we find that it is an *historical* fact, that many of the great teachers of all countries have been for the most part poor. Necessity has urged them onward. Jesus might have reminded these men of their great teachers. He might have pointed them to Elisha, who was taken from the plough ; to Amos, who rose to prophetic distinction from the sheepfold ; and to David, who ascended from the lower walks of life, and became the greatest bard, hero, and monarch of any time.

III. It is proverbially common. Jesus intimates this : " *A prophet is not without honour, save in his own country.*" Why is this ?—Why is it that the home teacher, especially if he be poor, is so generally depreciated ?

First : *Because the defects of a home teacher are more observed than his excellences.* Our eyes are keen to mark the improprieties of our neighbours; their vices are generally more noticeable to us than their virtues. From this tendency it is not a little that tells in favour of the purity of Christ. None of His neighbours could charge Him with any moral defect. They could not say, Is not this the intemperate, the false, the dishonest ? The best of men have their defects, and the nearer we come to them, the more disposed we are to say, " *We have seen an end of all perfection.*" Men whom we have loved and almost worshipped in the distance, have, as we approached them, appeared but men.

Secondly : *Because the home teacher has not the advantage of our imagination.* Imagination will give the stranger a number of fictitious attributes. *His position, attainments, studies, virtues,* are all magnified by the imagination. If he says great things we think him great ; wonderful things, we think him wonderful.

Thirdly : *Because the home teacher is more likely to awaken feelings of opposition.* It was so now. *Pride and envy* are evolved. It is humbling and mortifying to vanity to find our own poor neighbour outstripping us in power, merit, and influence. We wish to be the greatest in our own little neighbourhood, if possible. Such are some of the reasons which give popularity to this prejudice, and induce men to reject, and even martyr, those of their neighbours whom the foreigner will praise and posterity will bless.

IV. It is lamentably pernicious.

First : *It prevented them from believing on Christ.* Prejudice is always opposed to faith. The first thing that Bacon had to do was to eject the various prejudices which he called idols. These are fetters that enslave the intellect, clouds that obscure the vision, bolts that shut out the truth.

Secondly : *Their not believing on Him prevented Divine operations.* It is so in everything. Would the agriculturist have God to perform mighty works on his fields, covering it in autumn with abundant crops ? then he *must have faith* in the laws of nature, and in the capacity of his soil. Would the poor man have God to perform mighty works for him, raise him from penury and obscurity to wealth and influence ? he must have faith in the principle that " *the hand of the diligent maketh rich.*" Would the statesman have God to perform mighty works for his country ? he must, in all the measures he proposes and the laws he enacts, have faith in the truth that "*Righteousness exalteth a nation.*" It is so in everything. "*He that hath faith as a grain of mustard seed, shall say unto this mountain,*" &c. Would you like to know what God has done through faith ? Read the eleventh chapter of the Hebrews.

Matthew 14:1-11

Herod and John the Baptist ; or, The Power and Weakness of the Sinner

This is a sad fragment of human history. The gross sensuality, daring impiety, and cold-blooded homicide, here recorded, are sufficient to redden us with blushes, on account of the depravity into which our nature has fallen. We would have omitted this scene in our exposition, we would have drawn a veil over it, were it not for the conviction that the lamentable facts would not have found a record on the inspired page, were they not of importance for us to observe and study. Assuming that this book, as a whole, is the word of God, I cannot believe that any portion of it is useless. Each item has a function of its own in the great sphere of human culture. Such facts as these in the inspired volume are beacons which Heaven has erected on the high rocks of history, to warn every subsequent voyager on the ocean of life, of the perils that beset his course. The particulars of the scene here are so minutely expressed as happily to require no explanation. Any remarks, therefore, on the details would be more likely to offend the delicacy than brace the nerves of virtue. I take the narrative as illustrating the *power* and *weakness* of sinful man.

I. THE POWER OF SINFUL MAN. What freedom of action did the Divine Ruler of the universe now allow to Herod ? He was allowed a free opportunity to carry out his base purposes.

First : *He was allowed to reach regal authority.* Herod was the ruler of Perea and Galilee. He had reached the highest worldly position in the country in which he lived. He was, in fact, the civil ruler of the greatest and holiest personages that ever trod our earth, or breathed our air. Jesus was a Galilean, and politically subject to this man's authority. Antecedently, one might have expected that He who is the " prince of the kings of the earth " would have put an interdict upon the ambition of such a man as this ;—that if He condescended to prolong the life of such a wretch, He would, nevertheless, keep him in the lowest ranks of obscurity, where he could have no power for injuring his species ; and that he would never have been allowed to grasp a sceptre or to wear a crown. One might have thought that in proportion to the reckless workings of a man's depravity, would be the restraint which Heaven would put on his liberty. Such, however, is not the case. The history of the world furnishes us with innumerable examples similar to that before us ; and they serve to impress us with that liberty of action which the great God allows on earth. A man as corrupt as Herod shall rise from the humblest walks of life to opulence, municipal authority, aye, even imperial sway, if he will only play well and earnestly his part. Let moral principles and the claims of conscience be treated as idle puerilities, let the schemes be comprehensive, let the plot be well laid, let every tide be watched and caught at the flow, and the chances are that if life is spared he will reach his point.

Secondly : *He was allowed to exercise his civil authority in the imprisonment and death of one of the greatest of God's servants.* Of those born of woman there had not appeared " one greater than John the Baptist;"—the sturdy reformer, the faithful preacher, and the herald of the Captain of Human Salvation. His principles were as firm as the mountains that threw their shadows on the Jordan that rolled at his feet. He pointed his age away from the ritualism of the past, to the righteousness that was to be for all, and for ever, by saying, "*Behold the Lamb of God that taketh away the sins of the world.*" Antecedently again one might have thought that tyranny would never be permitted to put its ruthless hand upon such a man as this—that the man who dared to injure such an one in the slightest degree would be crushed with some thunderbolt from heaven;—that as the men of Bethshemesh fell dead as soon as they touched the Ark, tyrants would be paralysed as soon as they put forth a hand to injure God's saints. But such is not the fact. The Herods, the Neroes, the Bonners, the Lauds, the Jeffreys, how they have revelled in the blood of martyrs!

Thirdly: *He was allowed to murder one of the greatest of God's servants for actually doing what was right.* John had reproved him. For "*John said unto him,*" &c., not, It is not honourable or safe, but not "*lawful.*" As if John had said, Though thou art a ruler of men, thou art subject to God; thou art bound by moral obligations, and in thy domestic connexion thou art trampling on the laws of thy Maker. Such a reproof as this indicated John's high sense of virtue and his heroic faithfulness. It is not uncommon for men to reprove the poor and the humble in society for their offences, but it is a rare virtue to charge crime, with unflinching fidelity, upon the higher classes. To get up services and lectures for the poorer classes is popular now-a-days. The poor are lectured on all hands, and the most contemptible clap-traps are adopted to catch their ear. But where are the Johns to lecture the rich and the royal—the Herods? Perhaps there was no other man living who had such an attachment to right, and noble boldness of mind, as to do what John did now—confront his sovereign, and charge crime home on his conscience: yet for this he was imprisoned, and for this was he put to a cruel death.

These facts show what scope for free agency God grants to wicked men on this earth. He allows them an opportunity for working out what is in their hearts, whether it be to behead a prophet or to crucify a Saviour. Sinful men are everywhere on this globe carrying out their wishes and giving full play to all their intentions. The liberty thus afforded to the sinner—(1) Serves to show the depth of human depravity. To the extent in which men use this liberty is the revelation of moral corruption. What streams of pollution emanate every day from the free working of the corrupt heart! As we watch the actions of the sinner, we feel the truth of inspiration, "The heart is deceitful above all things, and desperately wicked." (2) It serves to show the efficacy of the Gospel as the only remedy. What can purify a heart so vile as that which Herod here displays? Law, science, education, poetry, philosophy, all these have tried in vain. The Gospel can do it. In thousands of instances it has done so. It has turned the lion into the lamb, it has made the sensual spiritual, the high-minded humble, the profligate religious, the cruel kind—transformed the demon into a saint. It is, indeed, then, "The power of God unto salvation." We value it as the only antidote to our evils, the only balm for our wounds, the only purifier of our souls. (3) It serves to show that there must come in the government of God a rectifying period. It can never be that evil will always have such a scope. It can never be that under the government of a righteous being the wicked shall for ever tyrannise over the good. There must come a day when "the rod of the oppressor shall be broken;" when the martyred Johns shall be raised to honour and to immortality, and the persecuting Herods visited with everlasting destruction *"from the presence of the Lord, and the glory of His power."* (4) It serves to show what sin will lead to when all restrictions are removed. Great as is the scope allowed for human action in this world, there are, nevertheless, checks and restraints existing in all civilised countries. There is the check of holy example—evil ever grows faint in the presence of virtue; there is the check of public sentiment—in such a country as ours, whatever may be the amount of practical depravity, the general sentiment amongst us is in favour of morality, and the public sentiment is like a spell on the heart of vice. There is the check of wholesome legislation. We say not that legislation can create virtue, nor that it can destroy vice, but that it can prevent it from coming out in such diabolical forms as that which the conduct of Herod exhibits. When we remember all the restraints here set on sin, we heartily adopt the words of Herbert, not the least of Britain's sacred bards:—

> ' Lord, with what care hast thou begirt us round !
> Parents first season us: then schoolmasters
> Deliver us to laws ; they send us bound
> To rules of reason, holy messengers,

> " Pulpits and Sundays, sorrow dogging sin,
> Afflictions sorted, anguish of all sizes,
> Fine nets and stratagems to catch us in,
> Bibles laid open, millions of surprises,

> " Blessings beforehand, ties of gratefulness,
> The sound of glory ringing in our ears ;
> Without, our shame ; within, our consciences ;
> Angels and grace, eternal hopes and fears."

Let these checks be removed, and the imagination stands appalled at the array of evils that must be developed. These checks are to the corrupt heart what the embankments are to the ever-accumulating waters—they shut them up for a time; but let those embankments be broken down, and the long pent-up waters shall rush forth as a flood, spreading devastation and ruin through the whole district. There is a world where these checks exist not; a world where there is no holy example, no public opinion for morality, no wholesome legislation; but where the spirits are let loose, in all the fury of their passions, to prey with vulture appetite on the peace of each other, and to rebel with a demon's rage against the righteous authority of the universe.

II. THE WEAKNESS OF SINFUL MAN. This Herod, though he had the power to rise to civil authority, to use that authority in destroying the greatest servant of God, and doing so simply on account of his virtuous conduct;—I say, though he had all this scope of action, he was, nevertheless, in the most emphatic sense, a *slave*.

First: *He was a slave to his own lusts.* The man who could make such a promise as Herod made to the wretched and worthless woman that danced before him, must be regarded as the mere creature of corrupt affections. His reason, his conscience, all the great elements that made him a man, were led captive by the very lowest of animal instincts. His soul was submerged in the hot, rolling tide of sensual feeling. Here was a man who arrogantly and unrighteously presumed to rule a country, who was too powerless to rule his own low lusts. He was " *carnal, sold under sin.*" Is not this a too true representation of men ? We look around us, and we see men everywhere governed by some lust;—some by the lust of sensuality, some by that of power, some of fame. " *He that is born of the flesh is flesh.*" Far be it from me to libel my species or to judge my contemporaries uncharitably, but I cannot shut my eyes to the fact that everywhere the body reigns;—" the old man," with his corruptions and lusts, is everywhere on the throne. Animalism is enthroned in politics, and the universal law is not the absolute right, which alone can give true freedom to man for ever, but the temporally expedient, which may serve his material interests for a day. It is enthroned on the exchange, and " *What shall we eat, and what shall we drink, and wherewithal shall we be clothed ?*" are the questions which determine the movements of manufacturers and merchants. It is enthroned, too, in our literature ; far more than half of the literature of the present day is for the animal, not for the moral, in man. The poetry and the fictitious prose read by those who are regarded as persons of taste and refinement, if analysed, would be found to have but little in them that did not minister to the low passions of humanity. Thus man's fleshly lusts are ever warring against the soul.

Regeneration is a dethroning of the animal and the raising of the spiritual into power. " *He that is born of the Spirit is spirit,*" his soul is resuscitated, &c.

Secondly : *He is a slave to public sentiment.* We learn from this narrative, that public opinion at first prevented him from putting John to death. " *He feared the people.*" But after that he gave his word, his " oath," to do so, and public opinion then seemed to act upon his mind to propel him to the deed. " *His word's sake.*" What matters thy word, Herod ? If thou hast made an improper vow or " oath," the sooner thou breakest it the better ! Ah ! but it was not because he feared the wrongness of breaking his oath, but the unpopularity of it. It might be laid down as a general truth that all men without religion are very much the creatures of popular thoughts and opinions. They are swayed and moulded by the general sentiment that prevails around them. They follow the mass, they think as others think, they are more ruled by the applause of men than the claims of conscience and of God. They give alms, they keep fasts, and pray to be seen of men. " *How can ye believe*," says Christ, " *which receive honour from man ?*" This is slavery; a slavery from which true religion emancipates us. The great question of a religious man is, " *What wilt thou have me to do ?*" not, What will people think? what will meet with the public patronage ? The Hebrew youths, and Peter and John, are examples of superiority to this.

Thirdly: *He was a slave to his own conscience.* " *At that time Herod the tetrarch heard of the fame of Jesus, and said unto his servants, This is John the Baptist; he is risen from the dead ; and therefore mighty works do show forth themselves in him.*" What was it that led Herod to this conclusion? Was it his *creed ?* It is generally supposed that he was a Sadducee, and that therefore he, theoretically, denied the doctrine of the body's resurrection. But were this not the case, supposing that he believed in the doctrine of the general resurrection, that belief by no means involved the belief that any *one* man would rise before another. His creed, therefore, could not have led him to this conclusion. Was it his *wish ?* Had he a strong desire that John should rise again? That he, whom at one time he was delighted to hear, but whom he murdered, should visit his courts again as the Prophet of the Lord ? It is proverbial that a man is very anxious to believe what he enthusiastically desires. But Herod could not have had this desire. His desire must have been never to see his face again—to bury the very memory of him if possible. Let all the buried generations start to life, but let John sleep on for ever in his grave. This would be his feeling. The only way to account for this is, the *guilty conscience.* The tidings of a mighty worker that was again treading the region of Galilee startled the conscience of the monarch with the memory of John— " *This is John the Baptist, whom I beheaded.*" The guilty conscience evoked from the regions of death his murdered victim, brought him to his eye, and made his prophetic voice to fall again upon his ear; the mountains around him seemed to ring with the prophet's voice. (1) An awakened conscience will preach to a man doctrines which he never believed before. There is something in man mightier than poetry, philosophy, or logic; it is CONSCIENCE. (2) An awakened conscience will bring scenes the most repulsive to your view. It will haunt you with the ghosts of forgotten crimes. It will open the grave of the past, bring old sins to life, and make them look us in the face.

Matthew 14:12

John's Burial ; or, The Trials of Humanity

Our remarks on Herod and John in the preceding section preclude the necessity of any preliminary remarks in this place. We shall at once, therefore, proceed to notice the general subject which the verse before us suggests and illustrates. Our subject is, *The Trials of Humanity*. "*And his disciples came*," the disciples of John, "*and took up the body*," the body of the martyred Baptist and Reformer, "*and buried it, and went and told Jesus*." There are two things which strike us about the trial which the disciples of John were now called upon to endure :—

I. THAT IT MUST HAVE BEEN A VERY PAINFUL ONE. It must have been painful—

First : *To their affections as social beings.* Tender, numerous, and strong, are the ties by which a thoroughly honest and enlightened religious teacher binds the hearts of his loving and docile disciples to himself. Such a teacher, in fact, from his access to the arcana of the soul, and the constant influence of his spirit and ideas upon its most vital parts, roots, to a great extent, the mind of his pupils in himself. They live in him, they draw their spiritual nutriment from his great thoughts. Such, pre-eminently, we presume, was the connexion between the Baptist and his disciples. The fact that they followed him shows that they loved him ; and if they loved *such a man* at all, their love must have been decided and strong. For John, like all great men, had those salient, bold, marked attributes of character, which would evoke in the minds of those he affected at all no half-and-half emotions. For such men there are no apathetic or sentimental friends or foes ; they are sure to have from society either intense hate or intense love ; out-and-out censure and opposition, or out-and-out approval and co-operation. A moral reformer of John's type, intrepid in purpose, inflexible in principle, defiant but unostentatious in bearing, fiery in zeal, must ever reveal the hearts of men, and make society positive and intense in their feelings towards him. John, therefore, must, we conclude, have been ardently loved by his followers. Though one greater than their master came, even Jesus, of whom their master was but the harbinger, they still adhered to John. They fasted when he was in prison, and no doubt often prayed with many tears for his deliverance. What, therefore, must have been their grief now, as they looked upon, handled, bore to the grave, the mutilated remains of their most beloved teacher and friend ? They "*took up the body and buried it.*" But this trial—

Secondly : Was not only painful to their affections as social beings, but *to their faith as religious beings.* What questions concerning God and His government would this murder of John be likely to start in the mind of his bereaved disciples! Questions tending to shake the very foundations of their religious faith. Even John's imprisonment seems to have shaken his own faith. Though on the banks of the Jordan he had borne such a noble testimony to Christ when he said, "*Behold the Lamb of God,*" &c., yet his incarceration led him to doubt as to whether He was the true Messiah or not. "*When John heard in the prison the works of Christ, he sent two of his disciples and said unto Him, Art thou He that should come, or do we look for another?*" If John by his mere imprisonment was thus tried, it is natural to suppose that much more must have been the trial of the faith of his disciples at his cruel martyrdom. I can imagine them looking at the mutilated body of their beloved teacher, and asking themselves, in utmost agony of heart, Can it be that there is a God who judgeth in the earth? If so, why does He allow the perpetration of such enormities? Is He ignorant of what is going on amongst mortals? Has he withdrawn all providence from this planet? If not, why does He permit such terribly iniquitous and bloody scenes to be enacted? Has He no controlling power over the purposes and doings of men? If so, why does He not thwart the designs of the wicked and frustrate their infernal plans? Has He any interest in the progress of right and truth on this earth? Is it His desire that the true and the righteous shall triumph over the false and the wrong? If so, why does He allow the vilest to sit on thrones, and thus oppress and murder the good? Such questions would be natural, and such questions would tend to shake the foundations of that old religion which was the loved home and the glorious temple of their hearts.

The other point which strikes us about their trial is—

II. THAT ALTHOUGH IT WAS VERY PAINFUL IT WAS MORALLY USEFUL. After they had buried the body of John, laid him in some quiet grave, they "*went and told Jesus.*" With hearts full of sorrow and anxiety they wisely and rightly went to "*The Consolation of Israel.*" "*They told Jesus.*" What? Not merely, we think, the painful incidents connected with John's martyrdom, but unbosomed to Him their own sad feelings. They told Him, we presume, what they thought and what they felt. This is a sight I should like to have witnessed; I should like to have seen those poor disconsolate men standing around this blessed Comforter and unfolding their tale of woe. I should like also to have seen His sympathising looks as He listened, and to have heard the soothing and balmy words that fell from His lips. Perhaps He wept with them. We may be certain that He pointed them to comforting truths, and to the ever-pitying Father of souls. We may suppose that He assured them of three things: (1) That that mutilated body was not John—that their master was living in higher realms: (2) That even that mutilated body should not be lost—that He would raise it up at "*the last day:*" and (3) If they truly followed the teaching they had received they would meet their master again.

Inasmuch as this trial led them to Christ, it was morally useful.

Whatever trials lead poor humanity to Him are blessings in disguise. He is the centre and the Eden of the soul. If the destruction of property, the loss of health, the death of friends, lead us to Him, all will be well. Would that little child, whose heart is full of gloomy sorrow on account of having done something contrary to its mother's wish, obtain relief, let it go and tell its mother, unbosom its little heart, and confess its offence; and in the responsive love of the mother's genial look a calm sunshine will overspread its being. This is the Divine principle of relief under trial. Weeping soul, go and tell Jesus.

Matthew 14:13-21

The Feeding of the Five Thousand; or, the Compassion of Christ

"*When Jesus heard of it, He departed thence by ship into a desert place apart.*" The expression, "heard of it," does not refer to what John's disciples told Him; nor, we think, to the statement of Herod, in the second and third verses of this chapter, where the narrative dropped, in order parenthetically to relate the murder and burial of John; but to what His own disciples had told Him, on their return from the mission on which He had sent them. From Mark's account, and also from Luke's, it appears almost certain that this was the case. Mark says, "*And the apostles gathered themselves together unto Jesus, and told Him all things, both what they had done and what they had taught.*" The words of Luke are, "*And the apostles, when they were returned, told Him all that they had done; and He took them and went aside privately, into a desert place belonging to the city of Bethsaida.*"

Indeed, perhaps the two communications, the one from the disciples of John concerning the tragical end of their master, and the other from His own disciples about their ministries, were all but coincident. As the bereaved and sorrowing deputation withdrew, probably the other appeared, flushed with the memory of their moral victories, though physically fatigued with their arduous campaign. "*When Jesus heard it, He departed thence by ship into a desert place apart.*" * Various reasons may be assigned for the withdrawal of Jesus into this desert place. Bloomfield, who supposes that ἀκούσας refers to John's death, and Herod's opinion of Himself, says that "it was on both accounts, as well as to avoid the imputation of blame for any disturbance which might be expected to follow."

---

* Luke says that the desert place belonged to the city called Bethsaida. "This town," says Olshausen, "must not be confounded with the city of the apostles (John i. 44), which lay on the western shore of the sea. This second Bethsaida was situated on the eastern bank, close to where the Jordan flows into the lake. At first it was a village, but Philip the Tetrarch raised it to the rank of a city and named it Julias."

Let us now attend to some particulars of that compassion of Christ which are displayed in this narrative.

We infer from this narrative—

I. THAT HIS COMPASSION EXTENDS TO ALL THE DIVERSIFIED INFIRMITIES OF OUR NATURE.

First : *Here are the sufferings of the afflicted which engage His compassion.* "And Jesus went forth and saw a great multitude, and was moved with compassion towards them, and healed the sick." The "*multitude*," we are informed in the preceding verse, were the people that followed Him on foot out of the cities. Mark says, "*ran afoot.*" The word is not used in contrast with riding, as would at first appear, but in contrast with going by sea on ship. Jesus sailed across the lake, whilst the people went round by land to the place where He went ashore. Here in crowds they stood around Him. Many of them were afflicted with diseases more or less distressing. He saw in the deep-sunk eye, in the withered cheek, in the tottering frame, of many in that multitude great suffering, and His heart was touched with sympathy, and "*He healed the sick.*" Christ feels for human suffering.

Secondly : *Here is the fatigue of His disciples which engages His compassion.* He looks at His disciples, worn and jaded with their labours, and He says to them, "*Come ye yourselves apart into a desert place, and rest awhile : for there were many coming and going, and they had no leisure so much as to eat.*" "He," says Stier, "speaks not of His own, but of the disciples' rest;" and because they were somewhat too full of all the things that they had done and had taught, He kindly leads them into the solitude where is the true rest. They are not to create such a sensation or make such a noise among the people on their return to them. "Come ye also now into retirement, as I am wont to do, and even now have need of it for myself; rest yourselves from your journey, because ye, too, have laboured." But when Christ permits or commands rest, He yet significantly adds—a little. More is at present not yet granted them : labour soon again sought out Him and them. "*He knoweth our frame, He remembereth that we are dust.*" He knows that we require rest even from our honest labours. He is no hard master. His "*yoke is easy, and His burden is light.*"

Thirdly : *Here is the spiritual destitution of the people which engages His compassion.* Mark says,—*And Jesus when He came out saw much people, and was moved with compassion toward them, because they were as sheep not having a shepherd : and He began to teach them many things.*" It was the state of their souls that stirred His heart the most. Spiritually they were without *food* and without *protection*,— as "*sheep without a shepherd.*"

Fourthly : *Here is the physical hunger of the multitude which engages His compassion.* "*And when it was evening, His disciples came to Him saying, This is a desert place, and the time is now spent; send the multitude away, that they may go into the villages and buy themselves victuals.*" These words would give us the impression that the benevolent desire to prepare food for the hungry thousands arose first in the minds of the disciples. But such impression would be manifestly false. John, in his account of the case, gives an incident which the other evangelists omitted, and which shows that the desire arose in the merciful mind of Christ. "*When Jesus then,*" says John, "*lifted up His eyes and saw a great company come unto Him, He saith unto Philip, Whence shall we buy bread that these may eat?*" Christ puts the question, not of course because He did not know what to do, but that He might "prove" to the apostle himself, and prepare the minds of all to appreciate, the magnitude of the miracle He was to perform. And He addressed the interrogation perhaps to Philip rather than to the rest, either because, as some suppose, that Philip was the disciple who took charge of the food; or, which is more probable, his somewhat materialistic temperament (John xiv. 8) rendered it specially desirable.* True to his sensuous tendencies, Philip began to calculate how much money would be required to procure such a quantity of food. "*Two hundred pennyworth of bread is not sufficient for them,*" said he. Now, after the appeal had been thus made to Philip, and he had spent perhaps some time in his calculation, "*and when the day was now far spent,*" or, as Luke has it, "*began to wear away,*" the other disciples began to feel anxious. "*And they came to Him, saying, This is a desert place, and the time is now past; send the multitude away, that they may go into the villages and buy themselves victuals.*" What a soul-bracing thought it is, that there is ONE who feels for earth's woes, and is "*mighty to save!*"

We infer from this narrative:—

II. THAT HIS COMPASSION IS ASSOCIATED WITH AMPLE CAPABILITY TO RELIEVE. The incident shows:—

First: *That His capability to relieve transcends their conception.* Perhaps He allowed His disciples to tax their invention to the utmost to find out how the vast hungry multitude could be fed; and after they had failed, He says, "*They need not depart. Bring them* (the five barley loaves and two fishes) *hither to me. And He commanded the multitude to sit down upon the grass.*" Mark says, "*He commanded them to sit down by companies upon the green grass. So they sat in ranks, by hundreds and by fifties.*" Behold the wondrous scene! Five thousand men, besides women and children, seated on the *green grass*. There is none of the confusion generally attendant on crowds in this scene. There is no jostling, no intermingling, no noise. All is exquisitely arranged by the Master:— they sit down *in ranks, by hundreds, and fifties.* All eyes are centered on Jesus—a silent wonder reigns through the crowd. He takes the five barley loaves and the two fishes, He looks up to heaven, blesses these simple articles of food, and then divides them among all, and "*they all eat and are filled.*" "Few miracles," says

---

* It may be that our Lord put this question to Philip from conceiving him to be better acquainted with the neighbourhood than the other apostles. Some would translate πόθεν, in John vi. 5, from what "fund?"

Livermore, "could be less exposed to cavil than this, which not only addressed the eye, but which satisfied the appetite of thousands." What could have been more morally sublime, or a higher proof of Divine authority, than the creation, so suddenly, of an immense quantity of food to relieve the famishing crowd? The incident shows :—

Secondly : *That His capability to relieve transcends their necessities.* They only required food for the occasion, but they had much more. "*They took up of the fragments that remained, twelve baskets full.*" His gifts are never exhausted ; there always remains something over. He gives nothing with a niggardly hand. To show the immeasurable depths of His love and the amplitude of His power, He always gives more than is required. In nature it is ever so. Less light would illumine the world, less water fertilize the earth, less air would feed the world's great lamp of life. Nature, which has fed the generations that are gone, has as much, if not more, for the generations that are to come. The fragments that remain are always greater than the stock that has been used. In the Gospel it is so. In the Gospel He has supplied the need of millions, but He has "*unsearchable riches*" in it still. Nay, His blessings seem to increase by consumption. The more they are used, the more they multiply and grow. Thus God's great universe grows richer every day.

We infer from this narrative :—

III. That Christ's compassion is never exercised to encourage wastefulness. "*Gather up the fragments, that nothing be lost.*" Although He miraculously creates a wondrous profusion of food, He inculcates the lesson of frugal use. "*Let nothing be lost.*" Use all —abuse none. In one sense, nothing can be lost, not an atom of matter, not a thought of mind; nature, both in the material and spiritual realm, allows nothing that once comes within its grasp to escape. In a moral sense, however, a thing is lost when it is not rightly used. Food is lost when it is allowed to rot; Truth is lost when it lies dead in the soul; the soul is lost when it does not serve its God. The lesson is—do not let Heaven's blessings run to waste, appropriate them to the right purpose : those that rightly use them shall have more; those that abuse them shall lose what they have.

We infer from the narrative :—

IV. That Christ, in the exercise of His compassion, would direct men to the infinite source of all good. "*And looking up to heaven, He blessed, and brake, and gave the bread to His disciples.*" He blessed God for the food. This was a custom among the Jews. "Blessed be thou, O Lord our God, the King of the world, who hast produced this food from the earth." That was the form. But it was not from custom that Christ did it. It was heart with Him. His spirit rose in gratitude to the Infinite Father. And He assumed this heaven-turned attitude, and used words, in order to impress the minds of the multitude that they must turn their hearts to Heaven as the source of all good.

Every part of this wonderful narrative demands a thoughtful pause. It is instinct with Divinity; it heaves with suggestions about suffering man and the redeeming God. It is a little mirror, reflecting the world and its heavenly Helper. Let us ever look at them both together. I know the world is burdened with woes. Deep throes of anguish rise from the heart of humanity every day:—

> "Each new morn
> New widows howl, new orphans cry—new sorrows
> Strike Heaven in the face, that it resounds."

But, thank God! I know, too, that there is one come from heaven to "heal the broken-hearted."

Matthew 14:22-23

Christ's Acts of Devout Isolation

Christ, as we have seen, had, in the exercise of His compassion, just fed the multitude, by a miracle the most striking and incontrovertible. No less than "*five thousand men, beside women and children,*" both witnessed with the eye and felt in the satisfaction of their hunger the supernatural act. There was no gainsaying the fact. All believed, and felt, that in the multiplying of the loaves and fishes, His omnipotence was as conspicuous as His compassion. The multitude being fed, "*straightway Jesus constrained His disciples to get into a ship, and to go before Him unto the other side, while He sent the multitudes away. And when He had sent the multitudes away, He went up into a mountain apart to pray; and when the evening was come, He was there alone.*" Here we have what we may call an *isolating act of Christ.* He separates Himself from the multitude, He extricates Himself from society, and withdraws into the depths of solitude. In this act, as here recorded, four things are observable—First: *Unostentatious kindness.* He had performed a noble work: and His praise was on the tongue of all:—the applauding shouts of the multitude filled the air. But He does not, like the vain lover of praise, pause to feast His ears with the plaudits of the populace. He had done a noble deed; and He was satisfied with its performance. Goodness is its own reward. "Our consideration," says Bengel, "ought not to dwell on things which we have well done." No; having done them, whether men censure or praise, it matters not, let us pass on: we have wrought a work for the universe and the ages. Another thing observable in this isolating act of Christ, is— Secondly: *Resolute determination.* He "*constrained*"—ἠνάγκασεν, compelled—"*His disciples to get into a ship.*" No doubt the reluctance to go into the ship without Him, and to sail alone, was great. The multitude, too, most probably, were strongly inclined to remain longer with Him. Indeed, John tells us that they wanted "*to take Him by force and make Him a king.*" (vi. 15.) They were so entranced with Him for the time, that they were anxious forthwith to enthrone Him as their monarch. So that to get the disciples into the ship, and to send the teeming multitude away, required no little determination. If our resolves be right, let them be firm, let them be too adamantine for the fiercest fires of persecution to destroy. In this isolating act of Christ, we observe—Thirdly: *Moral might.* How did He turn thesc multitudes to His resolve? Each one of the thousands had a will of his own, and that will was to tarry longer with Christ. How did Jesus reverse the wills of these thousands and turn them to His purpose? Not by material force. He could have commanded the winds, the lightning, or some other material agent, to come and bear them off. But these forces, though they might have transported hence their bodies, could not change or touch their wills. It was His moral influence; the moral majesty that sat upon His brow; the moral energy that went forth in His word, the moral electricity that darted from His looks—it was this subtile but sublime power that did it. When I see this Jewish peasant bowing the wills of thousands to His own, I feel that He must be "*God manifested in the flesh.*" Once more, in this isolating act of Christ we observe—Fourthly: *Religious devotion.* "*When He had sent the multitudes away, He went up into a mountain apart to pray; and when the evening was come, He was there alone.*" He retired from impure humanity to the Holy Father—from the finite to the Infinite—from acts of social benevolence, to acts of religious devotion. On a mountain at night, alone! The eye of day is closed; nature, wrapped in the sheets of darkness, is silent in the arms of sleep; inviolate stillness reigns over the whole scene: there, in the noiseless depths of retirement, with the awing spirit of solitude upon His heart, there He is alone with the Infinite in prayer.

> " He was there alone—when even
>   Had round earth its mantle thrown
> Holding intercourse with Heaven—
>   He was there alone :
> There His inmost heart's emotion
>   Made He to His Father known,
> In the spirit of devotion
>   Musing there alone."

Matthew 14:24-33

The Disciples in the Storm; Soul-disturbing Forces, and their Victorious Master

Whilst Jesus was alone, on the mountain, in communion with the Infinite Father, and the wondering multitude whom He had fed by a miracle had retired to their respective homes, the disciples, whom

He had "*constrained to get into a ship,*" were in the midst of the sea tossed with waves.

The stirring incident before us, viewed in connection with the facts immediately preceding what we have already noticed, forces at once on our attention two important considerations :—

First : *The great changes to which human life is every hour exposed.* How sudden the change to the disciples ! A few hours before, they were on the "*green grass.*" There was everything to delight them. The day was bright. Nature, perhaps, was in one of her most genial moods ; her breath was warm with love ; her face was bright with bliss. The scenery about them, too, including hill and dale, beach and billow, was picturesque and stirring ; and the social influences were exhilarating in a high degree. They were in company with their holy and loving Master, and with those thousands of men and women who, for a time, were enraptured with Him to whom they had given their hearts. They must have been happy. But now, after the lapse of an hour or two, where are they ? In the midst of the sea, "*tossed with waves,*" overwhelmed with terror, struggling for life. Such is a picture of life. Perpetual vicissitudes, successive trials make up our brief history.

The other truth suggested by this incident, viewed in connexion with the preceding fact, is—Secondly : *The difficulties that meet us even in the path of duty.* Had they gone to sea that night, contrary to the will of their Master, such tempests and terrors they might have justly expected. For he who moves against the will of Heaven must encounter storms of the direst kind, sometime or other. Mercy, it is true, for a time, may hold back the tempests, and restrain their fury, hoping that the rebel may retrace his steps ; but if he persist, come they must in ever-increasing violence, and dash upon his naked soul for ever. Every step the sinner takes, he challenges Omnipotence, and provokes the forces of the universe to wake in thunder against him. This seems reasonable and right. But for those to encounter difficulties and dangers who are following out the Divine will, does not, at first sight, appear agreeable to our notions of the wise in policy, or the righteous in principle. The whole Church was in that vessel ; and thus it was treated. It is ever so. "*In the world ye shall have tribulation.*" Seldom, perhaps, has there passed from earth to heaven a human soul, who has not had reason so say, with Israel's imperial bard, as it pursued its course—

> " Save me, O God,
> I sink in deep mire,
> Where there is no standing—
> I am come into deep waters,
> Where the floods overflow me."

We shall now turn to this narrative in order to illustrate two subjects :—*Soul-disturbing forces and their victorious Master.*

I. SOUL-DISTURBING FORCES. The disciples appear before us in the greatest agitation and horror ; "*they were troubled, they cried out for fear."* What raised this inner tempest ? A few hours before, they were calm and happy with their Master. What produced the change ? We discover here two classes of disturbing forces—the *outward* and the *inward.*

First : *The outward.* The wild fury of the elements, the boisterous winds and the raging waves, on this dark night, disturbed them. *"The ship was now in the midst of the sea, tossed with the waves, for the wind was contrary."* The sea of Tiberias, it seems, is constantly exposed to sudden and violent storms, from the mountains that lie around it. The vessel had well-nigh gone *half* the distance. At no point is the lake more than ten miles in length ; " and they had proceeded," says John, " *about twenty-five or thirty furlongs*," *i.e.,* about four miles, according to our method of measurement. Here, then, literally in " *the midst* " of the sea, they were at their wits' end, battling with the tempest.

This may be fairly taken as a *representative* case. External nature is constantly disturbing the human soul ; baffling its efforts, thwarting its purposes, and arousing its fears. By blights and droughts, by floods and hurricanes, by thunders, lightnings, earthquakes, and other such unpropitious manifestations, it is perpetually agitating the heart of humanity with distressing emotions. The elements of nature and the " *stars in their courses* " often seem to fight against man. Nor does nature in all this pay any deference to piety. It treats the sinner and the saint alike. Her storms shall wreck the vessel bearing missionaries and Bibles to the heathen, as well as the fleets of blood-thirsty warriors or mercenary merchants ; her pestilential blasts shall sweep from the earth the virtuous and the useful, as well as the vile and the worthless.*

The fact that nature thus disturbs the heart of humanity, whilst too obvious and patent to require proof or illustration, is profoundly significant. It suggests to me, that man is not in his original state. For whose notions of infinite goodness will allow him to suppose that nature was made thus to disturb the peace of souls ? Does the world in which angels live break the tranquillity of their spirit ? I trow not. Man has fallen, and God in mercy makes nature thus the perpetual monitor of the awful fact.

The other class of soul-disturbing forces which you have displayed in this narrative is :—

Secondly : *The inward.* We discover three things in connexion with the mind of these disciples at this time which tended greatly to their agitation and distress : (1) *Error of judgment.* "*And in the fourth watch of the night, Jesus went unto them, walking on the sea ; and when the disciples saw Him walking on the sea, they were troubled, saying, It is a spirit!*" This implied that they believed in spirits—and who does not ? It is an instinctive and therefore a universal belief. Spirits crowd the air we breathe—the great universe was built for souls. It implies also their belief that spirits had the power to do them an injury. This also may be true, but

* See *Homilist,* vol. vii.

these disciples, notwithstanding, made two mistakes. They were mistaken in supposing that the figure they saw walking on the foaming water was a spectre, and also in supposing that it came to do them an injury. They mistook in regarding the incarnate God as a ghost, and their best friend as an object of dread. Thus, through *their errors*, the very event intended to calm and cheer them, became a source of distress. They regarded Heaven's highest messenger of mercy to them as some fell spirit of destruction. Errors are soul-disturbers. Errors about life, and God, and duty, fill the world ; and, like tides in the ocean, keep the soul in a ceaseless surge.

The other thing we discover here in connexion with mind which tends greatly to agitate and distress is :—(2) *Guilty foreboding.* "*It is a spirit! and they cried out for fear.*" But supposing it to be a spirit, why be afraid of it ? Had they not spirits, and did they not belong to the great spiritual kingdom themselves ? Is not the Great God "*the Father of Spirits,*"—and are they not ever under His benign control ? Men have always thus been afraid of spirits. It is true that the poet, painter, and sculptor represent angelic spirits as very beautiful creations. But their pictures are not true to the human conscience. Man dreads a spirit. Why is this ? Why fear a spirit more than a body ? The reason is a guilty conscience. Men feel that they have violated the laws of the spiritual kingdom, and incurred the righteous displeasure of God, and therefore they forebode evil from the spiritual realm. They expect that a messenger of Justice must one day come ; and everything like spiritual manifestations makes them tremble, lest it should be Heaven's just avenger. Ah! it is the *guilty* " conscience that makes cowards of us all."

The other thing which we discover here in connexion with the mind of the disciples which disturbs the soul is :—(3) *Lawless impulse.* This is seen *especially* in the case of Peter. His distress was greater than the others, he was actually sinking beneath the yawning wave, and crying out, "*Lord, help me.*" What brought him into this special distress ? His characteristic impulsiveness. "*Lord,*" said he, "*if it be Thou, bid me come unto Thee on the water.*" There is no reason in such a request. What right had he to expect a miracle to confirm his own faith ? How Peter-like, impulse overbearing judgment! Jesus, probably to reprove him for his folly and to correct his impetuosity, encouraged him to do so ; and he soon finds out his mistake. He is soon overwhelmed in horror. This distress came from *impulsiveness.* And this is ever a soul-disturbing power. How much of the mental distress of the world arises from hasty and unreflecting action! How often are men plunged into the billows of anxiety and trouble for life, by some one impulsive act!

Such, then, are the soul-disturbing forces which this narrative discloses. It is true that there are others, in the world, which are not developed in this incident. But all can be brought under one of these heads—The *Outward* and the *Inward*. In truth, the power of the outward to distress us depends upon the inward. If the mind was free from errors of judgment, guilty forebodings, lawless impulses, and other spiritual evils, the external would have little if any power to disturb us. But so long as the mind of the world is subject to these evils, the soul of humanity will be in constant commotion, " *like the troubled sea.*"

Let us pass on to notice—

II. THEIR VICTORIOUS MASTER. Is there any one who can deliver man from these soul-disturbing forces, or must they beat on the heart and agitate the spirit for ever ? Thank God for the answer we can give to these questions ! He who appeared now walking on the boisterous billows, and saying, " *It is I, be not afraid,*" has undertaken the task and is equal to it.

There are four remarks which the narrative suggests in relation to Christ in connexion with this work :—

First : *However corporeally distant He may be from us, He is perfectly cognizant of all our disturbing forces.* Though He seems to have been away at some distance amongst the mountains, in prayer, He knew all about the pains and perils of His disciples. There was not a wave that rolled, not a gust that blew, not an anxious thought or painful feeling that arose in either of their minds, of which He was not cognizant. So it ever is. Corporeally, Christ may be at an immeasurable distance from us,—far up the highest heights of this stupendous universe, still He knows everything pertaining to our individual history. " *He understands our thoughts afar off.*" By His Spirit He is with us always, and will be even to the end. He is the Head of the Church, and is vitally conscious of the existence and feelings of every member.

Secondly : *He graciously approaches us in good time for our deliverance.* Though they were in the midst of the sea, at the height of the tempest ; though, perhaps, the shattering barque was about going down the yawning deep ; and though, perhaps, they had given up all hopes, and resigned themselves to the fate of a watery grave, they were not gone. Though on the boundary line of eternity, they had not passed it; and at this critical moment Christ appeared. Though the case was terrible to the last degree, He was not too late. The soul may feel itself sinking beneath the waves of its own dark thoughts, moral corruptions, and terrible forebodings, as Peter felt himself now sinking beneath the billows ; still, if Christ approach by His word and spirit, it is not too late.

Thirdly : *When He appears His power of deliverance is equal to every emergency.* "*But when he saw the wind boisterous, he was afraid; and beginning to sink, he cried, Lord, save me. And immediately Jesus stretched forth His hand, and caught him, and said unto him, O thou of little faith, wherefore didst thou doubt ?*" He has power to deal with the *external* and the *internal*. His dominion extends over matter and mind. He expels the inward or mental forces of agitation and distress *by revealing Himself as the all-sufficient deliverer.*

"It is I, be not afraid." There is no reason to be afraid where I am ; my mission is to disarm the soul of all its fears. It is I, *be not afraid of spirits;* they are under my absolute control. I have the key of their empire at my girdle; they go and come at my bidding. It is I, be not afraid *of Divine vengeance ;* no officer of justice can do you harm, for I have satisfied all the claims of immutable rectitude.

> " These raging winds, this surging sea,
> Bear not a breath of wrath to thee,
> That storm has all been hushed by me—
> 'Tis I, be not afraid."

It is I, be not afraid of *these tumultuous elements of nature.* "I hold the winds in my fist, and the waters in the hollow of my hand."

Fourthly : *His success in ridding humanity of its soul-disturbing forces demonstrates the divinity of His nature.* " *Then they that were in the ship came and worshipped Him, saying, Of a truth Thou art the Son of God.*" Every soul that Christ has delivered, and He has delivered millions, and will deliver millions more from its disturbing forces, is a witness to His divinity, a witness whose evidence is incontrovertible and invincible. The asseveration of every converted soul is :—" *Of a truth Thou art the Son of God.*"

Brother, the sea of human life is a sea of depravity, and, like the sea of Tiberias, is ever subject to storms. It is the sea of tempests. Many a struggling bark it has engulfed. Blessed be God, a DE-LIVERER has appeared walking on the turbid and multitudinous wave. He has trodden the billows at the height of their fury, and left abundant proofs of His power to subdue the wildest tempest, and save the most imperilled voyagers. Even those who, like Peter, feel themselves sinking beneath the swelling surge, shall be saved, if, like Peter, they turn their eyes to Him and cry : " *Lord, save me.*"

> " Thou Framer of the light and dark,
> Steer through the tempest thine own ark ;
> Amid the howling, wintry sea,
> We are in port if we have thee."—KEBLE.

Matthew 14:34-36

The Saviour at Gennesaret

The storm is over, the agitated minds of the disciples are hushed in peace, and the little ship, with its precious cargo, has safely reached Gennesaret. The designation " land of Gennesaret " was given to the western shore of the lake. According to Josephus, the district extended thirty furlongs in length, and twenty in breadth ; the climate seems to have been exceedingly mild, and the soil fertile ; to this delightful spot Christ now retired. The practical lessons of this incident are few but important; we shall do little more than state them.

First. THE ADVANTAGE OF SEIZING OUR OPPORTUNITIES. "*When the men of that place had knowledge of Him, they sent out unto all that country,*" &c. His appearance there, perhaps never again to occur; they seized it at *once*, they caught the tide of mercy at the flood. It was their hour, and they used it rightly. There are auspicious crises in every man's history, which, if promptly seized and rightly used, would bless our being for ever. These neglected, destiny darkens. (1. The period of early sensibility is an auspicious crisis. 2. The period of moral impression is an auspicious crisis.)

Second: THE INFLUENCE WE ARE CAPABLE OF EXERTING FOR GOOD. These men of Gennesaret, not only personally availed themselves of the blessing, but "they sent out into all the country round about, and brought unto Him all that were diseased." Through them multitudes who otherwise would have remained ignorant of His appearance, and suffering in their afflictions, got the intelligence of His coming, and were relieved. What these men did is the duty of all: (1) To inform their neighbourhood of Christ's mission in their midst. (2) To persuade their neighbours to avail themselves of His help.

Third: THE POWER THAT MEASURES OUR SUCCESS. "*They besought Him that they might only touch the hem of His garment: and as many as touched were made perfectly whole.*" Wonderful *faith* was this! They did not expect any manifestations or effort on Christ's part. They did not expect the striking of the hand on any place, as Naaman did. (2 Kings v. 11.) Their touch of His garment they felt to be enough. How came they to this *faith?* Perhaps they had heard of the woman with the bloody issue, who probably lived in their district, who was cured by touching the hem of His garment. But, great as was their faith, the success they met with was exactly equal to it; they believed that the touch of the hem of His garment would do it. "*As many as touched were made perfectly whole.*" The result was measured by their faith; so it ever is: great faith will achieve great things; it ever has done so, and so it will again. Virtue streams through every avenue of the universe from Christ: the touch of faith will bring it to ourselves.

Matthew 15:1-9

Traditional Religionists

There are two things very remarkable in this fragment of evangelic history. We have here—First: *Moral rectitude in connexion with conventional sin.* "*Then came to Jesus Scribes and Pharisees, which were of Jerusalem, saying, Why do Thy disciples transgress the tradition of the elders? for they wash not their hands when they eat meat.*" We cannot give a more clear and succinct account of the "elders" and "traditions" here mentioned, than by quoting an exposition from one, with some of whose theological opinions we have a strong antagonism, but who has few to equal him in the lucid, terse, and telling way in which he frequently gives you not only the literal explanation but the genius of the passage. " The elders are those distinguished for their wisdom and virtue, who had flourished in the past ages of the Jewish commonwealth. Their wise sayings and maxims relative to the Mosaic law and institutions had acquired, in the course of time, great authority among the Jews. They were attributed to Moses, who, it was said, received from God an oral, as well as a written law, at Mount Sinai. The oral communications were explanatory of the written laws. They were said to have been given by Moses to Aaron and his posterity, passing from one to another, through priests, prophets, and rabbis, to Rabbi Judah, in the second century of the Christian era, who committed to writing the traditions, as the oral law was called, which existed in the time of Christ, and are referred to in the text, and thus formed what is now called the Mishna, which means miscellanies. The volume contains explanations of all the precepts of the Mosaic law. About a century after, another Jewish rabbi, Jochanan, composed another volume, supplementary to the Mishna, called Gemara, *i.e.*, completion, or perfection, which contains illustrations and comments on the Mishna. These two, the Mishna and the Jewish Gemara, compose the Jerusalem Talmud. Long after, Rabbi Asa composed the Talmud of Babylon, in a celebrated Jewish school near that city. This consists of the aforesaid Mishna in the text, and a new Gemara, as commentary or supplement. These works are all written in the Hebrew language, and are even in higher estimation among the Jews than the Scripture itself. In these Talmuds is found the Cabala, or mystical method of explaining the law, by which abstruse and mysterious significations are formed by ingenious combinations of letters composing a word or words in the law. The criminality, in the judgment of the Scribes and Pharisees, of transgressing any precept of the elders, may be estimated from these sentences in their writings :—' The words of the Scribes are lovely above the words of the law, for the words of the law are weighty and light, but the words of the Scribes are all weighty.' 'The words of the elders are weightier than the words of the prophets.' 'The written law is narrow, but the traditional is longer than the earth and broader than the sea.' The Jews compared the Bible to water, the Mishna to wine, and the Gemara to hippocras.—Wash not their hands when they eat bread, or eat food. The Scribes and Pharisees, according to Mark, had already observed that the disciples ate bread with unwashen hands. In the Talmudical writings, there are many minute and ridiculous directions given respecting washing the hands, upon the ground that some uncleanness may be contracted. He was thought worthy of excommunication and even death, who broke the custom. An evil spirit, called Shibta, was said to sit on the food of him who ate without washing, and to make the food hurtful. A story is related in the Talmud of a man perishing in prison, because, part of the water brought him being spilt, he preferred using the rest rather to wash than to drink. Mark, writing for the benefit of the Gentiles, goes into a fuller account of the ceremonies of washing than Matthew, who was writing for the Jews, where these customs were known."

Now, it was an important ceremonial principle, with these elders, that they should not eat before they washed their hands. Mark says, " *that the Pharisees, and all the Jews, except they wash their hands oft, eat not.*" Not to do this, was to transgress their rules, was to commit a *conventional sin.* As a practice it was good. Physical cleanliness is seemly and useful, in every way useful to body and heart. But to enforce it as a religious rite, and attach to it a superstitious importance, was wrong : this they did. The disciples, perhaps on this ground, ignored the principle, and practically repudiated it. They seem to have acted rightly in this, for Christ virtually vindicates their conduct. Conventionally these disciples were wrong, but *morally* they were right. The lesson is,—Do not condemn others because they conform not to your religious formalities ; it may be that they are not only not wrong in not doing so, but are right in setting your little polities at defiance. Many a conventional schismatic is a true saint, many a conventional heretic is a veritable hierarch in the universe.

The other remarkable thing which we have here is—Secondly : *Conventional rectitude in connexion with moral sin.* The spirit which these punctilious men here display, the charge and the denunciations which Christ directs against them, unmistakably indicate that, however formally righteous, they had not the root of moral rectitude within them. They were but *Traditional Religionists;* an order of men who are found in all ages, and in all churches, modern as well as ancient.

These Scribes and Pharisees, as they appear here, are the types of a large class of men who are found in the churches of every age. The passage leads us to notice three things concerning them :—

I. Their miserable spirit, as displayed by themselves. Their spirit, as displayed here, was marked by hollow punctiliousness, captious officiousness, and impious assumption.

First : *They display a spirit of hollow punctiliousness.* The only thing they noticed in the conduct of the disciples of Christ, and the only thing about them in which they felt any interest, was their disregard of one little point of ceremony—namely, the " *washing of hands.*" The divine spirit His disciples breathed, their high-toned conversation, the holy principles on which their character was organised, the honesty and honour, the rectitude and religion, that rung in their utterances and shone in their lives, went for nothing in the estimation of these hollow-hearted traditionalists. The clean heart was nothing to them, the clean hand was all they thought of. Thus it has ever been with their class—the letter is exalted above the spirit, punctilios above principles. It matters not how good a man is, he may be as earnest as Paul, as meek as John, if he belong not to their sect, subscribe not to their tenets, respect not their canons and rituals, they are nothing, they are worse than nothing, they are heretics, deserving nothing but denunciation and abuse.

Secondly : *They display a spirit of captious officiousness.* What business had they to interfere with the disciples ? Why could they not leave these good men to pursue their own course and regulate their own conduct ? It was the cavilling spirit which inspired them. Your traditional saints, the men who live in dogmas and ceremonies, have always displayed this spirit of cavilling interference. Show me the member of a church who is more taken up with the forms and proprieties of religion than with its spiritual importance and claims, and you will show me a man whose captious spirit is ever disturbing the harmony of the fellowship to which he belongs. It is an historical fact, that those sections of the Christian church which pay most attention to form and ceremony, are the most censorious in their spirit, the most bitter in their sectarianism, and the most successful of agents in creating schisms in the ranks of the good.

Thirdly : *They display a spirit of impious assumption.* Their every interference implied a feeling, on their part, of authority on such questions. They act as if they were the judges of character, the arbiters of destiny. Why this arrogance ? Simply because they were traditionalists. They lived in the mere externalities of truth and godliness. They had not penetrated the spirituality of things. Surely we have good reason to ask, who are the men who have ever been the most ready to arrogate to themselves this power ?—the most ready to arraign and punish their brethren for heterodoxy ? Have they been distinguished either by great spirituality of soul, liberality of thought, or a philosophic insight into the laws of the mind, the doctrines of the Gospel, and the principles of God's administration ? No; they have been men whose conceptions have been narrow, superficial, material ; men whose Gospel has been a little bundle of crude notions, attractive to the thoughtless, but, verily, repulsive to all other minds.

Such, then, is the spirit which these traditional religionists displayed in the days of Christ, and such is the spirit their class has ever displayed. In denouncing these Scribes and Pharisees, let us remember we are not denouncing obsolete characters; they are living now.

The passage leads us to notice :—

II. THEIR ARROGANT ASSUMPTION, AS IGNORED BY THE DISCIPLES.

The disciples were true men, and they practically set at nought the punctiliousness of these religionists. To wash hands, when at meat, was not only a harmless custom, but proper and useful on material and social grounds ; had it rested merely on these grounds, the disciples would undoubtedly have respected it. But these Scribes and Pharisees had exalted it to a religious ritual, had invested it with a superstitious importance. On this ground the apostles repudiated it. We will make two remarks on the conduct of the disciples here :—

First : *It was justifiable.* The fact that Christ, instead of intimating in the slightest degree that the disciples were wrong in neglecting this rite, criminates and denounces their accusers, clearly shows that they had done no wrong. We are always justified in disregarding a custom or ordinance, in itself innocent, and in its place useful, when raised to an unnatural position and clothed with an unnatural importance. The brazen serpent was good as an emblem, and should be studied ; but when regarded as a god, it became a curse whose destruction was a duty. We remark,—

Secondly : *That it was natural.* The more men's souls advance in a knowledge of spiritual principles, and a sympathy with God and the universe, the more indifferent they naturally become to the mere letter and etiquette of religion. Ecclesiastical rubrics, like the shell of the acorn, will remain intact until the germ of spiritual life within begins to grow, and as it grows it will burst the shell, and leave its remains to rot in the dust, while it rises into the open air, and struggles towards the sun. Thus the Hebrew Christians left Judaism ; thus the Reformers left Popery ; thus the Puritans, and in later times, Wesley and Whitefield, with their followers, left the Anglican Church ; and thus now there are rising spirits in every church that are practically indifferent to its little points of ceremony and minor shades of creed.

The passage leads us to notice :—

III. Their hideous character, as unmasked by their Judge. *" Christ answered and said unto them, Why do ye also transgress the commandment of God by your traditions ? For God commanded saying, Honour thy father and mother. He that curseth father or mother, let him die the death,"* &c. The appeal of Christ shows four things concerning these Scribes and Pharisees :—

First : *That however orthodox they appeared before men, they were heretics in the sight of God.* These men prided themselves on the accuracy of their religious opinions ; they were regarded as authorities in such matters : like the technical theologians of every age, they would have it believed that they had fathomed the depths of all truths essential to human belief and practice. But notwithstanding this, they were heretics that understood not the A, B, C, of true theology. They had no *experimental* acquaintance with the principles of rectitude and godliness. Nay, so far from having any practical knowledge of these, their traditional views led to their utter disregard—they *" transgressed the commandment of God by their tradition."* A mere traditional faith is not merely a substitute for, but an obstruction to, all spiritual belief. Traditional faith is, indeed, *"the letter that killeth."* How many in the church, in these times, are to be found who hold traditionally the doctrine of the trinity, election, justification by faith, &c., who, in the name of religion, will coerce conscience, sanction war, defend slavery, and develop a spirit, mercenary and mean, selfish and sordid? Moral heresy is often associated with intellectual orthodoxy.

The appeal of Christ shows :—

Secondly : *That however socially upright they appeared befo·e men, they were dishonest in the sight of God.* Christ gives a case here to show their moral unsoundness, and to prove that by their traditions they did transgress the laws of God. "*But ye say, Whosoever shall say to his father or his mother, It is a gift, by whatsoever thou mightest be profited by me, and honour not his father or his mother, he shall be free. Thus have ye made the commandment of God of none effect by your tradition.*" Observe here two things—(1) *The divine principle of duty.* This principle is, that it is the duty of children to honour their father and mother. The word "*honour*" does not mean merely a sentimental sympathy, or a respectful behaviour, or an external obedience, but includes a care and maintenance of the parents, should it be required. A reference to 1 Timothy v. 3–17, will show that this is included in the word "*honour.*" This duty is enjoined by a fearful penalty—"*He that curseth father or mother, let him die the death,*" &c.: that is, let him surely die. The word "*curse*" must be regarded as standing in contrast with the word "*honour.*" This divine principle of filial obedience is congruous with the dictates of reason and nature. That having derived our being, support, protection, and all the blessings of early life, from our parents, we should return such obligations by ministering to their comfort, should they require it, is a duty unmistakably clear and absolutely binding. Observe, (2) *The violation of this divine principle by these traditionalists.* "Ye say, Whosoever shall say to his father or his mother, It is a gift," &c. The gift here refers to what Mark calls "*corban,*" which means something devoted to the service of God. Property thus devoted went to the coffers of those who had the conduct of the religious institutions of the country. These Scribes and Pharisees were interested in such donations, and the selfishness of their class forged the tradition, that if a child devoted his property to religious uses, he was "*free*" from the obligation to support his parents. The property once devoted could not be recovered,—it was "*corban*" for ever. Thus, by their tradition, they violated this principle of filial obligation. In the name of religion, they extorted from children the property that should have gone to the succour and support of indigent parents. Such pious frauds have, alas! been too common in every age. Property that should have gone to feed the hungry and clothe the naked has, by traditional religionists, been employed to build costly cathedrals, to support ritualistic pageantry, and feed plethoric priests. The appeal of Christ shows :—

Thirdly : *That however religious they appeared before men, they were infidels in the sight of God.* "*Ye hypocrites, well did Esaias prophesy of you, saying, This people draweth nigh unto me with their* *mouth, and honoureth me with their lips; but their heart is far from me."* They were confirmed hypocrites. And the case here referred to by Christ, of turning property, which morally belonged to needy parents, to their own use, and that in the name of piety, was but one of the many proofs of the fact. The language here quoted from Isaiah most aptly describes their character.* They had no heart. They were verily religious in the estimation of society. They were not *" as other men are, extortioners, unjust, adulterers."* They fasted twice in the week, and gave tithes of all they possessed. They were punctual in all their religious devotions. Most pious men were they before the eye of the world. But to God's eye they were *infidels,* moral atheists :—*" their heart is far from me."* Their religion was nothing but sound and form. These traditional religionists are practical atheists. They are " without God" in the heart. There is no atheism so bad as the atheism of the mere lip-worshippers in the church. The mere theoretical infidel you may vanquish by argument, but all your reasoning goes for nothing with the lip-worshipping infidels. I believe that if there was no moral atheism in the church, there would be no theoretical atheism in the world. Every worshipper would be such a living witness for God, that bold infidelity would everywhere turn pale, and die. The appeal of Christ shows :—

Fourthly: *That however valuable their religion appeared before men, it was utterly worthless in the sight of God. " In vain they do worship me, teaching for doctrines the commandments of men."* "They paid," says Bengel, "little regard to the commandments of God, and that little they defiled by observing the commandments of men." No doubt, those men were regarded as model saints, and the conservators of public religion. But to Him that searcheth the heart their religious services were utterly worthless. *" In vain do they worship me :"* there is no heart in their devotions, and therefore no virtue. *" God is a Spirit, and they that worship Him must worship Him in spirit and in truth."*

Brother, " in vain " is thy theological creed, however scriptural its basis and philosophical its structure ; " in vain " is thy ecclesiastical polity, however it may accord with the principles of the New Testament, and be adapted to church edification and order; " in vain " are thy forms of devotion—thy hymns may breathe seraphic piety, thy liturgies may be inspired, thy prayers may be fashioned after the great model prayer; " in vain " is the punctuality with which thou attendest to religious services, and the propriety with which thou dost join in the exercises of the great congregation,—in vain all, and for ever in vain, if " thy heart is far from God." In all thy religious engagements thou art only sowing the wind, and thou wilt reap the whirlwind.

---

* Between the passage, as given here, and as found in Isaiah xxix. 13, there is a little difference: " Since this was taken from the Greek Septuagint, and not from the original Hebrew, the declaration of Isaiah is introduced, not as implying the fulfilment of a prophecy, but as a description given by the prophet of his time, which was applicable to the Jews of that period."

Matthew 15:10-20

Things that go into a Man ; or, Man's Moral Character determined, not by his Receptive, but Transformative Power

In this passage Jesus turns from the TRADITIONAL RELIGIONISTS, and makes the ceremonial spirit, which they had displayed in their complaint of the disciples eating with "*unwashen hands,*" the subject of a profoundly significant address to the "*multitude.*" "*He called the multitude, and said unto them, Hear and understand ; not that which goeth into the mouth defileth a man ; but that which cometh out of the mouth, this defileth a man.*" And again He says, in the further illustration of the point, to Peter, "*Those things which proceed out of the mouth come forth from the heart ; and they defile the man. For out of the heart proceed evil thoughts, murders, adulteries, fornications, thefts, false witnesses, blasphemies : these are the things which defile a man : but to eat with unwashen hands defileth not a man.*"

Now we deem it necessary, at the outset, to guard this passage from, at least, three opinions, which a mere cursory reader would be in danger of attaching to it.

First : *The opinion that it is a matter of perfect indifference what we eat and drink.* If the words, "*not that which goeth into the mouth defileth,*" are to be taken in the strict literal sense, the drunkard and the glutton may get something like a divine sanction for their intemperate indulgences and habits. The influence, however, of intemperance, not only upon the body, but upon the intellect and heart, the numerous prohibitions of the Bible on the subject, and the teaching of Christ Himself, in which He warns us not to be "*overcharged with surfeiting and drunkenness,*" unmistakably show, that such an idea must not be for a moment attached to His words. We would guard this passage against the opinion :—

Secondly : *That the things that go into the mouth are to be regarded as exclusive of all other external things.* It is true Christ only mentions that which "*goeth into the mouth,*" because the dispute with the Pharisees arose about *eating ;* but He evidently mentions this, not to the exclusion of other externalities, but rather as a specimen or representative of all outward circumstances. The language must be interpreted as proposing what "*goeth into the mouth*" as an example of all that comes *from without* to the man—all that goes in through his eye, and ear, and touch, as well as through "*his mouth.*"

We would guard this passage against the opinion :—

Thirdly : *That external circumstances are matters of no importance to man.* It is certainly of consequence to man as to whether he should be surrounded by the pure and the true, or by the impure and the false. What else is the meaning of the prayer, "*lead us not into temptation*" ?

The idea is, that the source of moral character is not in the *external circumstances* of the man, but in his inward mental life. Or to put it into a more subjective form, *a man's moral character is determined, not by the receptive, but by the transformative, powers of his nature.* "Unto the pure all things are pure : but unto them that are defiled and unbelieving is nothing pure, but even their minds and consciences are defiled."

Man is necessarily *receptive.* Every moment impressions are made upon him ; there is not a point of time in which the outward does not impart something. His senses are channels ever filled to over-flow with things which they are conveying from the great ocean of outward circumstances to the deepest depths of his nature. But the outward things which he thus receives do not necessarily form his character. He has within him what we shall call, for the want of a better term, a *transformative* power ; a power which takes action upon the impressions which the external makes upon the soul, and which action, in the form of words or deeds that "*come out,*" makes the moral character ; a power which transmutes all that comes to him from without into moral good or evil. A power by which "*a good man out of the good treasures of the heart bringeth forth good things, and an evil man out of the evil treasures bringeth forth evil things.*"

Taking the principle, *that man's moral character is not determined by the receptive but by the transformative power of his nature,* as the great truth of the passage, we shall proceed to notice a few consider-ations which the words of Christ suggest in relation to it :—

I. THAT THIS PRINCIPLE DEMANDS THE ATTENTION OF ALL MEN. "*He called the multitude, and said unto them, Hear and understand.*" The heavenly Teacher enforces it on the notice of all. Why is universal attention to this principle so important ? We may assign two or three reasons :—

First : *Because the principle displays the goodness of God in the nature He has given us.* Were our moral characters determined by the things that *come into* us from without, or, in other words, by our receptivity, it is obvious that in a world like this, where there is so much *moral corruption* surrounding us on all sides, we should become inevitably and hopelessly corrupt : the depraved language, manners, and spirit of the social world into which we are born, and in which we are bound to live from day to day, would be our ruin. But as we have this power within to deal with all the impressions that are made upon us as we think fit, we are delivered from this terrible necessity. This power is one of the distinguishing attributes of our being. It enables us, not only to bend circumstances to our will, but to get good out of evil ; to turn outward dissonance into music, deformity into beauty, poison into nourishment. Let us adore our Maker for this wonderful endowment ;—an endowment which guards us from the coercion of outward forces, secures to us an inward freedom of action, and enables us to put all outward things in subjection to our own spiritual selves.

The principle demands universal attention :—

Secondly : *Because it serves to counteract man's propensity to plead circumstances as a reason for his conduct.* The power and universality of this tendency are seen in the readiness with which man will refer to external events, sometimes to palliate his offences, at other times to justify his conduct, and at other times to account for the moral inferiority of his life as compared with that of others. It is this tendency that has made what in philosophy is called *fatalism*, and what in modern theology wears the name of hyper-Calvinism, so popular amongst the weak and untutored in all ages and lands. So long as men regard themselves as powerless instruments in the hands of circumstances, there is no possibility of their spiritual elevation. The moral feebleness of professing Christians arises from their *undue* dependency upon the outward ordinances of religion. They too often act as if sermons and sacraments would do everything for them, independent of the earnest activity of their own spiritual natures. This crippling tendency of the soul can only be destroyed, as you work into the heart of the people the mighty principle to which Christ now calls the attention of the " multitude."

The principle demands universal attention :—

Thirdly : *Because it shows the indispensable necessity of the right use of our spiritual powers.* As food, however nutritious, cannot administer strength to a man's body without the digestive and appropriative power, so no external influences, however good and useful in themselves, can raise a man's soul, without the right action of its faculties. Man cannot be made good. His body may be borne to the summit of a lofty mountain without the use of his limbs, but if his soul is to ascend " *the holy hill of the Lord,*" he must climb it every inch himself. Fortune or patronage may raise him to some eminent social position, but he cannot reach a single stage of moral dignity—the true dignity of man—apart from his own earnest endeavours. The transformative power of the soul is, to external circumstances, what the builder is to the materials out of which he rears his edifice. The choicest materials may be brought together, —gold, marble, and cedar : but unless the builder use them with artistic skill, they will never take the form of a beautiful structure. So, the providence of God may gather around man all the facilities and elements for the raising of a noble character ; but unless he use them with his own spiritual hand, he will never produce such a structure.

Such are some of the reasons why this principle should be proclaimed to the *multitude* and enforced on their attention.

The passage suggests :—

II. That this principle is repugnant to the ceremonialists. " *Then came His disciples, and said unto Him, Knowest thou that the Pharisees were offended after they heard this saying ?* " The Pharisees, like all religious formalists, practically, not of course theoretically, held the doctrine that man was the creature of circumstance : —upon the reception of such dogmas, attention to such rituals, obedience to such regulations, they made the destiny of men to depend. Men were good or bad, dignified or degraded, according to their teaching, in proportion to their conformity or nonconformity to their traditional creed and ecclesiastical rule. The principle which Christ lays down, strikes a blow at the root of such notions; —hence it is no wonder they were " offended." But, perhaps, they were more " offended " at *the fact of Christ pressing this principle on the multitude,* than at the principle itself—which must have accorded with their reason and their conscience. Well they knew, that if the multitude would practically accept this principle, their power would depart. Priests, who obtain their livelihood and influence by exalting the ceremonies of their own church ; rabbis, who regard their views as the standard of orthodoxy ; sects, which regard themselves as special favourites of heaven,—will always feel offended at the propagation of such a principle. Preach the doctrine, in all the breadth of its meaning, that it is not the sermons you hear, not the sacraments you celebrate, not the sect you join, that necessarily determine character and destiny,—but the use of your own spiritual powers,—and you will be sure to incur the displeasure of Pharisaic religionists.

The passage suggests :—

III. THAT THIS PRINCIPLE IS VITAL TO MAN AS A SPIRITUAL BEING. *" He answered and said, Every plant which my heavenly Father hath not planted shall be rooted up. Let them alone : they be blind leaders of the blind ; and if the blind lead the blind, both shall fall into the ditch."*

From these words we infer three things, showing the vital importance of this principle :—

First : *That whatever in the history of man implies the practical disregard of this principle is not of God.* The men, or class of men, who act upon the principle that their characters are necessarily moulded by externalities, either of a secular or spiritual character, must be vitiated in all their ideas of duty, unsound in all their habits of life. The principle is so *cardinal* that everything pertaining to man's life must be influenced by it. And it is so radically wrong that nothing that grows out of it can be Divine. The religious dogmas and ritual observances based upon a notion that what goeth into a man defiles him, wherever they exist—in Judaism or Christianity, in Popery or Protestantism, in the Church or in Dissent—are not of *our Father's planting :* they are worthless, noxious weeds of moral depravity.

Secondly : *Whoever practically disregards this principle is blind in relation to spiritual things.* Our Saviour says of those Pharisees, *" they be blind leaders of the blind."* They were blind to the omnipresence of God ; to the spirituality of His law ; to the free and responsible action of the human soul ; to the eternal condition of moral progress ; and to the essence of virtue and vice. And thus blind must all men be who act upon the idea that what goeth into a man will necessarily defile him. The recluse, who retires from the world, hoping to avoid its defilement, and the religious formalist, who is perpetually moving through a routine of ordinances in order to make his heart clean, are blind in relation to the great facts of spiritual being and relations.

Thirdly : *The practical disregard of this principle exposes us to a terrible calamity.* Whatever creed, system, character, institution, and enterprise have grown out of its neglect, are " plants that the Father has not planted," and they must be *uprooted.* "Every plant," says Christ, "which my Father has not planted shall be rooted up." Oh, how much there is in human society, even in its Christian department, that our heavenly Father "has not planted"! There are not only worthless weeds, thorns, and briars in every path, but broad acres of moral hemlock and mighty forests of upas-trees. Thank God, they shall be uprooted. *"The Son of Man shall send forth His angels, and they shall gather out of His kingdom all things that offend and that do iniquity."* The blind, too, shall *"fall into the ditch."* Inevitable ruin awaits those who are framing a character according to outward rules, rather than cultivating one by the right exercise of the soul's affections and powers.

The passage suggests :—

IV. THAT THIS PRINCIPLE IS BUT IMPERFECTLY APPRECIATED EVEN BY THE TRUE. *"Then answered Peter, and said unto Him, Declare unto us this parable; and Jesus said, Are ye also yet without understanding ?"* Peter was a representative member of the most true and spiritual society on earth—*the disciples.* Notwithstanding this, he did not fully compass the meaning of this principle. So strong is the tendency of man to over-estimate the outward, and to over-look the transcendent importance of the Divine world of his own soul—the world within, the world of thought, emotion, and will, where character is formed and destiny is settled—that even the most *spiritual* have difficulty in fully appreciating the principle, that it is not that that goeth into a man that defileth him, but that which cometh out. Hence the exaggerated interest which almost all sections of the Church display in the external. The zeal, the wealth, the energy, of churches are expended in creating and sustaining that which must be regarded as the mere machinery of religion, rather than in spiritual efforts to generate and foster those principles of the soul which are the essence of godliness, the spirit of all true power, and the glory of man.

In conclusion :—

First : *Our subject suggests the best means for religious parents to guard their children against the corrupting influence of society.*

It is always a deeply anxious period in the history of a pious parent, when the time comes to send his children out into the wide world, to engage in such pursuits as may be the most conducive to their advancement and usefulness in life. This profession is thought of and given up, because of the temptation with which it is associated. That business, though lucrative, is renounced because of the fallacious and dishonest principles on which it is conducted, and the depraved circles with which it stands connected. There is not a single department of secular life that can be thought of as suitable for his child, that is not beset with perils to his innocence and virtue. And when, after much anxious thought and prayer, he decides on that which is least objectionable on moral ground, still he is anxious. Which is the way to meet this parental difficulty? Teach the child that his Maker has endowed him with powers of mind and thought that will enable him to stand against all outward temptation; that if he is true to the spiritual nature which kind Heaven has given him, he can pass through the most fiery assaults of the devil unscathed, move through the most polluted scenes without a moral taint. Teach him that his safety is in reliance upon the right use of his own faculties and in the blessing of his God. Teach him that it is not the unchaste conversation, the filthy song, the profane expression, that may go into his ear, that will defile him, but the use he makes of these. Teach him that he has a power to turn this very wickedness to his own spiritual advantage.

Secondly: *The subject suggests the only method by which man can reach a blessed destiny.* How is he to secure his present and everlasting well-being? By endeavouring, like the anchorite, to avoid outward evil? Whilst no man should put himself in the way of temptation, no man should be afraid to confront evil, to go into its most malarial regions, if duty call. In truth, if man's well-being depended upon escaping outward evil, it could never be realised; because to live in the world he is bound to live in its midst, and evil must stream into him every day. How, then, is he to reach a blessed destiny? By endeavouring to frame his life according to the outward rules of morality and religion? No; but by a right use of his own spiritual powers. There is a power in the body, when in a healthy state, to appropriate whatever goes into it from external nature that is wholesome and necessary, and to expel that which is noxious and superfluous. The soul has a power analogous to this: a power to appropriate the wholesome and to expel the injurious. This power we call the transformative. Let us use it rightly—use it as Noah used it, who, amidst the blasphemy and ridicule of a corrupt generation, walked with God, and fulfilled a noble destiny; as Paul used it at sceptical Athens and dissolute Corinth, and in pagan Rome, who, from experience, left the world this testimony—"*all things work together for good to them that love God.*"

Brother, practically realise this wonderful power of thy soul; a power that may

> " Gather honey from the weed,
> And make a moral of the devil himself."

Matthew 15:21-28

The Syro-Phœnician Woman; or, the Difficulties and Triumphs of an Earnest Soul in Search of Divine Help

After Jesus had addressed " the multitude " on the subject of what really determines moral character—a subject raised by the captious spirit of the Scribes and Pharisees, the traditional religionists of the day,—He leaves the neighbourhood, and departs into " *the coasts of Tyre and Sidon,*" cities that lie on the shore of the Mediterranean. "Each," says Stanley, "stands on a promontory; that of Sidon running out from a mass of rich gardens and palms; and that of Tyre from a somewhat wider extent of plain, with Lebanon and Hermon both in view far in the distance." The object of Christ in retiring to this region was, perhaps, to avoid, for a time, the snares of Herod, and the growing malignity of the Scribes and Pharisees. Mark says, " *that He would have no man know the place where He was.*" On His entrance into this new and Gentile sphere, He was accosted by an importunate suppliant. " *Behold, a woman of Canaan came out of the same coasts, and cried unto Him, saying, Have mercy upon me, O Lord, thou son of David; my daughter is grievously vexed with a devil.*" Mark designates this woman, " *a Greek, a Syro-Phœnician by nation.*" Though the Phœnicians descended from the Canaanites, the country, having been conquered by Alexander, whom history, in its ignorance of true dignity, calls " the Great," was now governed by the Greeks. The region in which Tyre and Sidon were situated was called Phœnicia; and was included in the more general name of Syria. Hence the inhabitants were called Syro-Phœnicians, as distinguished from the " Phœnicians of Libya,—Carthaginians."

I shall take this deeply interesting narrative to illustrate *the difficulties and triumphs of an earnest soul in search of Divine help.*

I. THE DIFFICULTIES OF AN EARNEST SOUL IN SEARCH OF DIVINE HELP. The help which this noble-hearted woman, this brave heatheness sought, was the restoration of her child. Maternal compassion for a suffering child fired her nature, and nerved her heart with the courage of a heroine. " *Have mercy on me, O Lord, thou son of David; my daughter is grievously vexed with a devil,*"—a demon. Whether the disease mentioned here, and so frequently referred to elsewhere in the New Testament, was some supernatural possession, which evil spirits obtained, peculiar to the scene and period of our Saviour's ministries, or some malignant nervous distemper of a natural kind to which all men are liable, is a question on which the most competent and devout critics are divided; and one which seems to us as destitute of any practical importance, as it is of sufficient means to furnish a solution in which all Biblical students must agree. Anyhow, the affliction of this woman's child was felt by her to be of the most painful and dangerous description. For this she sought the merciful interposition of Christ. Now in the effort, she meets with *four difficulties*, which, it seems to me, are very much like the difficulties which all earnest souls have to encounter in their efforts to obtain that special help from Heaven which they require.

First: *The apparent disregard of the* GREAT ONE *to her efforts.* While she was crying in an agony of entreaty for help, it is said, that "HE *answered her not a word.*" As she looked with eyes of flame and spoke in beseeching words of fire to Him, He appeared, perhaps, impassive and unmoved. Whilst we repudiate as a revolting impiety the suggestion that He intended by His silence to misrepresent the real state of His heart towards her, we are far from supposing that His silence was that of indifference to her passionate entreaty. Indifference to the cries of suffering humanity on His part, would be to the last degree un-Jesus like. Idle, if not presumptuous, would it be to speculate on the *reason* of His silence; it is obvious, that it served to bring out before the disciples and before the ages an example of the persevering and victorious power of genuine faith. It is also clear, that she must have felt it as a *difficulty* at the outset of her endeavours.

This *apparent disregard of God* to the efforts of earnest seekers at the outset of their career, has always been a difficulty deeply felt by them. They strive for knowledge, they aspire after virtue, they struggle for the right, they supplicate Heaven; but there is no apparent response. The Great One seems indifferent. Though they search in His Revelations for knowledge as for hid treasures, though they agonize to enter in at the strait gate of truth and virtue, though they resist unto blood, striving against sin, though they are importunate in prayer for help, they receive, perhaps, no indication that they have made any impression on God. Nature goes on as ever; the heavens seem brass, God is silent, and He answers not a word. What religious inquirer, what earnest seeker, has not felt this at the outset of his career? He expected responses at once: but he had them not.

Another difficulty which this woman met, and which all true seekers have to encounter at the outset, was:—

Secondly: *The conduct of Christ's disciples.* See the way in which the disciples treated her. "*And His disciples came and besought Him, saying, Send her away, for she crieth after us.*" These men interposed, not out of compassion for her, but from a desire for their own comfort and convenience. Her clamour annoys us; and we entreat thee to dismiss her anyhow, with or without her request; or as Stier expresses it, "Pray, make haste, and rid us of her and her crying." The unchivalrousness, unmanliness, cold harsh selfishness, of all this must have rendered their conduct anything but grateful to her feelings or encouraging to her efforts.

Scarcely a greater difficulty does the religious seeker encounter at the outset of his career, than the conduct of what are called religious professors. The narrow prejudices, the bitter sectarianism, the cold, mean-hearted selfishness, the hollow sanctity, and the gloomy grimace, which they often discover in connexion with those who *profess* to be devoted adherents to a system which encourages the utmost freedom of thought, breathes universal benevolence, denounces insincerity, inculcates a virtuous manly naturalness, and inspires its true disciples with genuine happiness of the highest kind, is one of the greatest stumbling-blocks which young inquirers find in the commencement of their path.

Thirdly: *The apparent restrictedness of Divine grace.* In reply to the request of the disciples, Christ said, " *I am not sent but unto the lost sheep of the house of Israel.*" These words, referring to the limitation of His mission to Israel, are, as Bengel has it,—"to be understood, not with reference to the whole mediatorial office, but only our Lord's preaching and miracles." Whilst it seems to have been the ordination of the Eternal that Christ's personal ministry, during His sojourn on earth, should be circumscribed within the pale of Israel, it was at the same time His purpose that the doctrines He taught, and the spiritual blessings He procured by His mediation, should be commensurate with the world. Still, though the words were not intended to convey a limitation of mediatorial mercy, falling as they undoubtedly did, on the ear of the woman, and, probably, with the intention of Christ, they must have sunk as lead upon her heart. The inference that she would be likely to draw from these words would be " *Then I am excluded,*" and " *Can there be any hope for me ?*" This is another difficulty which she had to encounter.

This, too, is a difficulty which the young inquirer meets with. He sometimes receives a deep and distressing impression that Divine grace does not extend to him, that Christ was not sent to save him. He thinks of the few in every age that have been converted, the multitudes that have remained reprobate; he remembers the enormity and multitude of his own sins; and he seems to hear a voice something like that which now fell on the woman's heart—" *I am not sent to thee.*"

Another difficulty which she encountered, was :—

Fourthly : *A current religious opinion.* After she had again pressed her request, He answered and said, " *It is not meet to take the children's bread, and to cast it to the dogs.*" In this, Christ manifestly utters, not His own idea, but a popular prejudice among the Jews. They were wont to regard themselves as the children of God, — the special favourites of Heaven; they looked on all other peoples with cold contempt. The most opprobrious epithets were used to designate them. All other nations were " dogs," they only were children. This moral superiority to every other tribe was with them a reigning religious belief. Jesus simply quotes it, not to express His opinion—far from it—but only to try her faith, and obliquely strike at the foolish prejudice which still existed in the minds of his disciples, as Jews. But though, in quoting it, Christ takes away the edge of the insult, softens the rude harshness of the language, by using in the original, the diminutive, *little dogs,* yet the opinion even in the mildest form, when addressed to her, in answer to her request, must have been felt as a repulse.

What young inquirer has not met with difficulties arising from some religious ideas especially current in his own circle of life? Perhaps reprobation is the reigning idea, or sacramental efficacy, or some such unreasonable and heart-repelling absurdities. We speak from experience when we say, that some of the theological dogmas, which meet the young seeker after God, are amongst his greatest hindrances. Like thick mists upon the landscape, they hide the bright lights above and the living beauties below; they darken the path, they distract and confound the traveller. Would that some breeze from the holy heavens would sweep through Christendom, and clear the atmosphere of all the vapours and fogs of traditional theology!

Having noticed the difficulties, let us now direct attention to,—

II. THE TRIUMPHS OF AN EARNEST SOUL IN SEARCH OF DIVINE HELP. This woman surmounted all these difficulties; she had that faith before which mountains flee away. She attained her end: *"And her daughter was made whole from that very hour."* Her success serves as an illustration of several important subjects:—

First: *Her triumph serves as an illustration of the character of genuine faith.* The faith of this woman was obviously of the right type, for it both succeeded in its object and gained the approval of Christ. *"Great is thy faith."* What is true faith? One example will give a better idea than a thousand definitions. Here is a veritable example; here it is drawn out in the living actions of human life. Her faith was marked by three things. (1) *An unbounded confidence in Christ.* She addresses Him as the true Messiah—*"Have mercy on me, O Lord, O Master, Thou Son of David."* There was no question in her mind as to who He was; she had no debate with herself about His Divinity or His Messiahship. All these points were settled. She "knew in whom she believed." She wanted mercy, and she knew that He was Heaven's chosen messenger of mercy to the earth. This is ever a feature, or rather the *essence*, of true evangelical faith. It is not a belief in something *about* Christ—in certain views which men have propounded about Him in treatises, creeds, and catechisms—but an unbounded trust in HIM as the Son of David, the Sent of God, the Saviour of the world. "Ye believe in God; believe also in Me." (2) *Her faith was marked by invincible perseverance in her course.* Difficulties, instead of crushing her spirit, only stimulated its energies. The apparent regardlessness of Christ at first to her request, then the cold selfish spirit displayed by His disciples, then the intimation that Christ's mission was confined to the lost sheep of Israel, and then, lastly, the popular idea that she belonged to the mere dogs of society, instead of cooling her ardour, re-fired it; instead of depressing her spirit, raised it to an indomitable force. This is ever a mark of true faith. Doubting souls are morally little; they tremble before the shadow of opposition, they are "*afraid of that which is high,*" they spend their time in lisping about difficulties as a reason for their indolence and inaction. Souls of great faith are morally great. They are all-conquering and unconquerable. At their fiat the hills are removed, at their fire the mountains melt. Difficulties only nurse them into the majesty of a martyr's power. They rise with a swelling buoyancy under the pressure of opposition, as the waves of ocean bound beneath a nation's fleets. (3) *Her faith was marked by an entire renunciation of all self-conceit.* When Christ by implication classed her amongst the dogs, did she repel the insinuation as an insult? or, did she show any symptoms of mortified pride? No. But with an unfeigned humility and with child-like simplicity she said, "*Truth, Lord; yet the dogs eat of the crumbs which fall from their master's table.*"* As if she had said, I readily acknowledge my utter meanness; I am not worthy to be ranked amongst thy children. Nor do I ask for the bread of children, but the crumbs that fall from thy rich table of mercy. Humility is ever associated with true faith. All vain and proud notions of self will vanish in the light of that faith which brings the soul into contact with the Infinite, as the drops of dew evaporate in the beams of the summer's sun.

Secondly: *Her triumph illustrates the severe aspects which mercy sometimes assumes towards man.* There is an evident air of severity about Christ in His treatment of this woman, at first. He appears somewhat cold and repulsive. But the severity is only in appearance; it is mercy in disguise. All the while His loving heart

---

* She cleaves to the friendly word, "little dogs," in which Christ has betrayed His heart to her—"she catches Him in His own words" (Luther); "takes the sword out of His hand and slays Him with it" (Heinr. Müller); "drives back the arrow into His heart" (Rieger). *Yes,* Lord! thus speaks humility; pride would say—No, I am not a dog; I will not be cast out among them! No; pride says, in many even to this day; but "No, Lord," too, when the Lord accuses, rejects all claim, shuts thee out as unclean from the family rights of the heavenly Father's dear children. Oh, that then, at least, all might surrender themselves with all-conceding acknowledgment: *Yes, Lord!* Oh, that we might learn from the woman at all times to *connect* with this as closely the powerful importunate "*yet*"! In the connecting together of these two words is involved the whole order of salvation and prayer. Such faith finds the promise in the very refusal, makes the unworthiness, precisely as the neediness, the plea for favour. "The dogs," hast thou said? Well, then, the dogs are and remain beneath the table when they are hungry; and do not let this little place in the house be taken from them. When the children break their bread, Mark has now παιδία for τέκνα, when from their master's table ψιχία fall (double diminutive, little crumbs) there is then no need, properly speaking, for λαβεῖν καὶ βαλεῖν, which I am not asking, for the dogs are contented even with the smallest share, if only they do not starve with hunger! I am even now, O Lord, not far from the table: even now there falls for us Gentiles a crumb of bread from Israel's table; I see that Thou art on our boundary; the dogs eat—well, I too may eat: it is done, and there is no preventing it. Thus, does the word of the woman outbid all refusal on the part of Christ; and to understand and feel this aright, belongs to the right understanding of His reply in which He acknowledges Himself all at once overcome.— *Stier.*

heaved with the warmest and tenderest sympathies. Her cries rang on all the nerves of His benevolent nature. He assumed the severe for her good, to bring out her soul more earnestly towards Him. It was His mercy that made Him appear severe. The GREAT ONE often deals thus with true souls. He seems deaf to their prayers,—He appears to them rather as the cold Judge than the warm-hearted Father. "*Clouds and darkness are round about Him.*" He is in the whirlwind and storm of affliction. Still all is mercy. Thus it was with Abraham, thus it was with David, and thus it has been with the good in every age and clime. The heart of every afflicted saint has sung a thousand times :—

> " The thorn it was poignant, but precious to me :
> 'Twas the message of mercy,—it led me to Thee."

Thirdly: *Her triumph illustrates Christ's regard for true suppliants.* (1) *He commends her faith.* "*O woman, great is thy faith.*" (2) *He grants her request.* "*Her daughter was made whole from that very hour.*" It seems from Mark, that the mother found her daughter restored when she returned home. Christ did it by a *volition :* the volition took effect instantaneously, without the employment of means, and without any personal contact. It was an undoubted miracle, as expressive of His Almighty power as of His tender compassion. This answer to her prayer is another of the striking and ever-accumulating testimonies to the established principles in the government of God,—that "*they that seek shall find.*"

Such, then, are some of the difficulties which the earnest seeker for Divine help has always to encounter. But these very difficulties are masterable. A genuine faith in Christ, and an invincible perseverance in the true course of action, have surmounted them a thousand times, and so they will again. When mastered they become our greatest blessings. They develope energies which otherwise would have remained dormant; they originate feelings of moral satisfaction and triumph which otherwise could never have been experienced. The mightier the foe, the more glorious the victory; the higher the mountains we scale, the grander the prospect, and the fresher the breeze.

Young seeker after Divine help, be not discouraged then by the difficulties that beset thy path. I see not how thy soul could be saved from lethargy, weakness, morbid fear, and base cowardice, without having difficulties to stimulate thy zeal, challenge thy faculties, and bring out the spiritual energies of thy being. "Tribulation " to man has ever been, since the Fall, and must ever be, the path to the empire of spiritual majesty and bliss. Imitate, then, the example of this Syro-Phœnician woman. Centre thy faith, thy soul, not on mere theories that men propound about Christ ; but on the SON OF DAVID. Though He may not for a time answer thee " a word," and the heavens above thee seem brass as thou prayest, persevere : His silence is mercy,—still cry on to the

Son of David. Though the conduct of some of His professed disciples may, at times, repel thee with their glaring inconsistencies and cold-hearted selfishness, still cry on to the Son of David. Though ideas about the restrictedness of Divine grace may ring in thy ears, and thou mayest fancy that thou art not included amongst "the lost sheep" for whom mercy has been provided, still cry on to the Son of David. Though a spurious theology may trouble thee with suggestions that thou art too worthless a creature for mercy, and that thou art excluded from the covenant of promise, still cry on to the Son of David. Let nought divert thy attention from Him. Hold on to Him with an unrelaxable tenacity amidst all the trials of life's wilderness, in the Jordan of death, and thou shalt feel on the other side that He has made thee "more than conqueror."

Matthew 15:29-39

The Healing and the Feeding of Multitudes; the Restorative and Conservative Work of Christ

Our Lord had now approached the culminating point of His public labours, and reached the zenith of His popularity. His fame now rang loudly on the ear of His age, and the minds of all classes were astir with thoughts of Him. There are two wrong opinions touching the passage now under notice. One is, that it is *un*historic, and the other is that it is *repetitious.* The former opinion, which regards it as mythical or parabolic, is, of course, entertained only by those who are falsely called *rationalistic* interpreters of the Holy Word. The other opinion, which regards it as the repetition of a fact which Matthew had before recorded (xiv. 13-21), is held by many orthodox expounders, and has some plausible considerations in its favour. A comparison of them both, noticing the points of dissimilarity, will assist the reader to reach a true judgment on a question which, after all, is of no vital moment.

As to the dissimilarity between this narrative, and that of Matthew xiv. 13-21, the following points are very noteworthy : (1) *The number of persons fed.* In the former miracle, the numbers fed by miracle were five thousand; the numbers here were four thousand. (2) *The quantity of food.* In the former case there were five loaves and two fishes ; here we have seven loaves and a few little fishes. (3) *The quantity of fragments gathered up.* In the former case there were twelve baskets full; in this case only seven baskets full. (4) *The time it occurred.* The first miracle was wrought on the evening of the first day, after the people were assembled; the second miracle, after they had been with Him three days. (5) *The locality in which it took place.* The former miracle was wrought in Capernaum ; it was in a desert place, on the eastern coast of the Galilean shore.

This miracle occurs in Decapolis. Mark says that Jesus departed from the borders of Tyre and Sidon. He came through the midst of the coast of Decapolis, that is, in the midst of those ten cities round the sea of Galilee; these cities were south of the Sea of Galilee.* (6) *The preceding and succeeding events are different.* The former occurred immediately after the disciples had brought the mangled body of John the Baptist to Him. This took place after He had granted the request of the Syro-Phœnician woman, and retired from her coast. The former miracle was succeeded by His going forth from the mountain, which He had ascended to pray, to walk on the sea and rescue His disciples from the perils of the storm. This is *succeeded* by a severe contest which He had with the Pharisees and Sadducees of Galilee. (7) *The subjects of the miracle were different.* Those composing the first multitude were those from the cities along the western shore of the lake. Those of the second assembled from the mountains on the eastern side. The expression in this passage, "They glorified the God of Israel," indicated, that part of the multitude gathered were heathen, and glorified the Jehovah in contrast with their own deities.

These striking points of dissimilarity preclude almost the possibility of regarding the two narratives as records of the same event. Looking at the passage with a practical intent, it may be regarded as furnishing a striking illustration of the RESTORATIVE and the CONSERVATIVE work of Christ. The *restorative* is revealed in the cure which He now effected in "the lame, the blind, the dumb, the maimed, and many others." He seems on this occasion to have healed all, whatever their affliction. His physical healing is the *symbol* of His spiritual. Christ came to bear away the evils that afflict humanity. He is a complete Redeemer of body and soul. The passage illustrates, moreover, the *conservative.* He not only removes all the evils that afflict men, but He grants them food to nourish and sustain them. Having *cured*, He *feeds*; He *keeps* what He *redeems*.

Matthew 16:1-4

The Sadducees and Pharisees ;—Infidelity

From this passage we may draw the following conclusions in relation to practical infidelity.

* What part of Decapolis the Lord visited, is not mentioned by any of the evangelists. Under this title were included ten cities, eight or nine of which were on the east side of Jordan, and the east or south-east of the Sea of Galilee. It is spoken of by Josephus as a well-known territorial designation, embracing towns and villages. After Syria had been conquered by the Romans, ten cities seem, on some grounds not well known, to have been placed under certain peculiar municipal arrangements, and brought directly under the Roman rule. It is probable that their population was chiefly heathen. The names of the ten cities are differently given. To the original ten cities others were probably added, though at no time do they seem to have constituted a distinct province.—*Andrews.*

I. That practical infidelity is a thing rather of corrupt hearts than of theoretic creeds, or social classes. "*The Pharisees also with the Sadducees came, and tempting desired Him that He would show them a sign from heaven.*" The following remarks of Bengel on these words are worthy of quotation:—

"The common people were mostly addicted to the Pharisees, men of rank to the Sadducees (see Acts v. 17, xxiii. 6); as at present the crowd is more inclined to superstition, the educated to atheism—the two opposite extremes. The Evangelists describe only two attempts of the Sadducees against our Lord (the first of which occurs in the present passage), for they cared less than the Pharisees about religion.—ἐκ τοῦ οὐρανοῦ (*from heaven*). Miracles had been performed from heaven in the times of Moses, Joshua, and Elijah. The reason why the Pharisees were unwilling to accept as Divine the miracles hitherto performed by our Lord, seems to have been this : that since He had not yet produced any sign from heaven, they thought that the others might proceed even from Satan (cf. ch. xii. 24, 38); and that they considered that a sign from heaven affecting the whole creation, would be greater than any signs performed on the microcosm of man."

Though these Sadducees * differed widely in social position and

* "'*The Sadducees.*' The origin of this sect is far more distinctly ascertained than that of the Pharisees. The high-priest, Simon the Just, was succeeded in the chair of the Sanhedrim by Antigonus of Sochos, who, among his instructions, was heard to say, ' Be not as servants who wait upon their master, for the sake of the reward ; but be ye like servants who wait upon their master, not for the sake of the reward ; but let the fear of the Lord rule you.' This excellent precept was grievously misunderstood and misapplied by one of his pupils, named Sadoc, the founder of the sect in question, as also by another scholar, called Baithus. When they had left their master, they said to each other, ' Our master teaches us that there is no reward or punishment, or any expectation at all for the future.' On this view Sadoc set about to deny that there was any future life or resurrection of the dead. Lightfoot, however, seems to show that this last opinion was entertained a good while before the time of Sadoc, even so early as the time of Ezra ; although it did not become the defined tenet of a sect till it was formally taught by this person. The tenet was never popular, and the sect of the Sadducees was insignificant in numbers as compared with the Pharisees ; but this deficiency was compensated by the dignity and eminence of those who embraced this persuasion, who were generally persons of the highest distinction, and several of the sect were advanced to the high-priesthood. They did not dispute the sway of the Pharisees over the multitude, and, according to Josephus, seldom took any part in the affairs of the state. Such of them as acted as magistrates and councillors seldom opposed the measures of the Pharisees, knowing that opposition would be badly received by the people, who never regarded them with much favour.

" The tenets we have stated were by no means the only distinguishing ones held by the Sadducees, and it is singular that there was scarcely a single point in which their opinions were not diametrically opposite to those of the Pharisees. They not only held that the soul of man was mortal, and perished with his body, but also denied the existence of any angel or spirit (chap. xxii. 3 ; Acts xxiii. 8). In opposition to the Pharisees, they also insisted that there was no fate, or even an over-ruling providence ; but that man enjoyed the most ample freedom of action, with full power to do either good or evil as he thought proper ; that God exercised no influence upon him ; and that his prosperity or adversity were respectively the result of his own wisdom or folly. Hence it is said that they made severe judges. Another great matter in which they were distinguished, and that favourably, from speculative religious opinions from the Pharisees, they agreed in that spirit of captious infidelity which they displayed in relation to Christ. Anomalous as it may appear, real infidelity is often found co-existing with orthodox *credenda* and godly professions. The infidelity of the pulpit, the pew, the sanctuary—that which preaches faith and repeats creeds—is the worst kind of infidelity; it exists not amongst the floating ideas of the brain, but amongst the vital roots and fibres of the heart.

We infer from this passage:—

II. THAT PRACTICAL INFIDELITY IS OFTEN IMPIOUSLY EXTRAVAGANT IN ITS DEMANDS FOR EVIDENCE. "*They desired Him that He would show them a sign from heaven.*" The impious extravagance of this demand will appear from two considerations. First: *That they disregard an immense amount of evidence already existing.* He had given them "*signs*" in abundance. The miracles of Moses and the prophets pale their fires before the miracles of Him who was now addressing them. If they would only compare His history with the predictions of their prophets they would soon be convinced that He was the true Messiah. Infidelity, in crying for more evidence, has always overlooked the abundant evidence already furnished. The impious extravagance of this demand for evidence will further appear from the consideration :—

Secondly : *That the evidence which they disregarded in favour of His Messiahship was far superior to that on which they built faith in material changes.* "He answered and said unto them, when it is evening, ye say, It will be fair weather: for the sky is red. And in the morning, It will be foul weather to-day; for the sky is red and lowring." The ancients were skilful in prognosticating the weather. This was done, as at the present day, by observing the signs of the sky, the appearance of the clouds, and the heavenly bodies. These signs of the weather which they observed were not infallible. An eminent French philosopher has said that there is no scientific principle by which any philosopher can predict what weather we shall have on the morrow. Notwithstanding this, these men trusted to these signs. Christ does not find fault with them for doing so, because, generally perhaps, they were correct, and a little attention to these would be useful in their arrangements for the morrow, but He condemns them for disregarding the moral department; the signs of the times were *trustworthy* and *transcendently important.*

We infer from this passage :—

III. THAT PRACTICAL INFIDELITY IS TO THE LAST DEGREE ABHORRENT

the Pharisees was, that they rejected every iota of that traditional rubbish on which the Pharisees set far more value than they did upon the written law. They insisted that their assent was not authoritatively required to any opinion or practice which the written law, in its literal acceptation, did not inculcate or enjoin. It has been charged upon the Sadducees that they only received the five books of Moses, and rejected all the other sacred books. But this imputation rests on no very clear foundation, and Josephus, who is sufficiently bitter upon the Sadducees, whom he often mentions, does not anywhere hint at this, although he would scarcely have failed to do so had it been true."—*Pictorial Bible.*

TO THE MIND OF CHRIST. "*O ye hypocrites, ye can discern the face of the sky ; but can ye not discern the signs of the times ?*" He shows His abhorrence here in three ways : First : *By denouncing their hypocrisy.* "*O ye hypocrites.*" If they had been sincere in their desire for evidence, they would have paid proper regard to that with which they were already furnished before they sought for more. Secondly : *By refusing their request.* "*There shall no sign be given.*"* Had they properly employed the evidence which they had, He would, perhaps, have given them more. He could easily perform wonders in the heavens. Thirdly : *By abandoning their society.* "*And he left them, and departed.*"

Matthew 16:5-12

"*Beware of the Leaven,*" &c.—*Spiritual Caution, &c.*

In reading this passage and its connexion, three things strike our attention with remarkable force. A brief mention of these things may serve as a suitable introduction to the main subjects which the passage contains, and which it will be our special purpose to develop on this occasion.

First : *We are struck with the display of a terrible kind of displeasure.* Christ was now on board a little skiff, sailing away from the shore where lived those Pharisees and Sadducees who had just tempted Him, by requesting that "*He would show them a sign from heaven.*" Having denounced their conduct, it is said, "*He left them and departed.*" He stepped on board the vessel, and left them, as an incorrigible set of hypocrites and blasphemers. Who can tell His feeling ? It is said, in Mark, that "*He sighed deeply in spirit.*" It was the sigh of love, as it passes into righteous indignation. "*He left them and departed !*" What a catastrophe for the men He thus left ! The principle that Paul inculcated, Christ now acted upon : —"*A man that is an heretic,*" said the Apostle, "*after the first and second admonition reject, knowing that he that is such, is subverted and sins, being condemned of himself.*" We call the displeasure which Christ now manifests, *terrible,* because it is the displeasure of Infinite love, and because it shuts out all hope for the recovery of the objects. The indignation of irascible natures is nothing, nor is the indignation of malign natures anything, compared with the indignation of benevolent spirits. Love in wrath is oil in flames.

Secondly : *We are struck with the power of great subjects to drown minor ones in the human mind.* The disciples who had gone on board the vessel with Christ were, it would seem, so taken up with the thoughts that Christ had addressed to the Pharisees and Sadducees, as well, perhaps, as with the absorbing ideas suggested by His

* See a Homily on "The Religious Sign-Seekers," in *Homilist,* vol. iii., p. 316.

leaving them, that they had forgotten to make the necessary temporal provision for their voyage. "*And when His disciples were come to the other side, they had forgotten to take bread.*" Mark says, "*They had not taken more than one loaf.*" It is well to see great souls absorbed in great subjects; but it is not well to see them neglect even the minor matters of life: and yet to this we are disposed from the very infirmity of our nature. Man is prone to two extremes: either to exaggerate the spiritual to the neglect of the material—as in the case of the mystics—or to exaggerate the material to the neglect of the spiritual, which is, alas! the case with the great bulk of mankind.

Thirdly: *We are struck with the readiness of Christ to seize the passing thoughts in the minds of His hearers for the purpose of spiritual impression.* The disciples as soon as they discovered their neglect began to feel anxious. Their minds were now taken up with "bread." Christ, knowing their thoughts, virtually says to them, "Do not be anxious about material bread, take care of the leavened spirit of the men I have just denounced and from whom I have just parted." "*Take heed and beware of the leaven of the Pharisees and the Sadducees;*" that is, beware of the corrupting influence of their doctrines, and their spirit, which, like leaven, though it works secretly and silently, still works with effective force. Thus Christ here as everywhere seizes the passing idea of His hearers in order to make a spiritual impression on their hearts.

In this paragraph we discover three great spiritual evils—a corrupt social influence, an infirm religious faith, and an obtuse spiritual vision. Christ, in giving His disciples a distinct and emphatic caution against the first, charges them at the same time with being the subjects of the other two.

As these evils were not confined to the disciples in Christ's day, but are common to all ages, and are in close association with us all, we shall devote this article to an endeavour to develop with the greatest brevity their baneful character.

I. Here we have a corrupt social influence. "*Then Jesus said unto them, Take heed and beware of the leaven of the Pharisees and the Sadducees.*" In the New Testament both good and bad doctrine are spoken of as *leaven*, which silently diffuses itself throughout the mass in which it is placed. "*Know ye not that a little leaven leaveneth the whole lump?*" Paul urges the Corinthian Church "*to purge out the old leaven*" of corrupt sentiment and thought. Superstition and pious pretence constituted the leaven of the Pharisees; infidelity and pride that of the Sadducees, who denied the doctrine of Providence and of a future state, both of body and soul. The warning of our Saviour suggests:—

First: *That spiritual evil in society has a leavenous tendency.* It works in society as leaven works in the mass of meal in which it is deposited,—progressively, permeating the whole; and transformingly, transmuting the whole to its own character.

The warning of Christ suggests:—

Secondly : *That spiritual evil in society may influence us unconsciously.* It is a fact as solemn as it is obvious, that our tastes, ideas, habits, manners, are always modified, and sometimes completely fashioned, by the society in which we live. The man in whose company we have been living, often leaves his spirit upon us, and it often requires a resolute effort of our own manhood to shake that spirit off. How often do we find ourselves in possession of other men's thoughts, and using other men's words and even tones. Hence the necessity of the caution given by Christ. "*Take heed and beware,*" &c.

II. HERE WE HAVE AN INFIRM RELIGIOUS FAITH. "*And they reasoned among themselves, saying, It is because we have taken no bread : which when Jesus perceived, He said unto them, O ye of little faith, why reason ye among yourselves because ye have brought no bread ?*" It would seem from this that the disciples misconstrued the meaning of Christ. They seemed to think that His caution meant that they were not to take *bread* of the Pharisees, and hence they "reasoned amongst themselves, saying, It is because we have taken no bread."

First : *Secular anxiety is a symptom of the infirmity of faith.* Had the disciples possessed an unshaken trustfulness in the power and kindness of Christ who was with them, they would have experienced no solicitude on account of the want of provision. On the contrary they would have felt that having Him they had everything they required. Anxiety about secular circumstances, about the success of our worldly plans, about our temporal morrow, about provision for ourselves in old age, for our children when we are gone, evermore betrays a lack of confidence in the Fatherly providence of that God who clothes the lilies of the field, and feeds the fowls of the air. "Wherefore, if God so clothe the grass of the field, which to-day is and to-morrow is cast into the oven, shall He not much more clothe you, O ye of little faith ?"

Secondly : *Memories of past mercies are means by which to strengthen faith.* "*Do ye not yet understand, neither remember the five loaves of the five thousand, and how many baskets ye took up ? Neither the seven loaves of the four thousand, and how many baskets ye took up ?*" Had they kept this in memory they would not have had a particle of solicitude about their being unprovided with bread. They would have felt that, having with them Him who had wrought such marvels of mercy on their behalf before, and who could do so again at any moment He pleased, they were well-provided for. Reminiscences of past mercies are amongst the best means to re-invigorate a failing faith. David felt this ; his confidence in God at one time was sinking fast ; but he bethought himself,—he recollected past mercies, and he was strong in faith again. Hear his experience : "*And I said, this is my infirmity : but I will remember the years of the right hand of the Most High. I will remember the works of the Lord ; surely, I will remember Thy wonders of old. I will meditate also on Thy works and talk of Thy doings.*"

III. HERE WE HAVE AN OBTUSE SPIRITUAL PERCEPTION. The disciples misunderstood His reference to the "leaven;" they thought that He alluded to the material bread with which they had forgotten to provide themselves. They reasoned amongst themselves, saying, "*It is because we have taken no bread.*" But Jesus, after first reproving them for their want of faith, next reproves them for their *obtuseness:*—"*How is it that ye do not understand that I spake it not to you concerning bread, that ye should beware of the leaven of the Pharisees and of the Sadducees?*" A thought is here suggested worthy of notice, namely:—*That this spiritual obtuseness arose from the secularity of their thoughts.* Why did they misunderstand Christ? The answer is clear. Because their minds were taken up with thoughts concerning their natural bread. This is ever the case. Men look at subjects through the medium of their own ideas and feelings at the time. The particular mental state in which a man is when a subject is presented to him, acts as a kind of mirror to reflect that subject to his vision. Hence it is that secular minds must ever misinterpret spiritual doctrines. The carnal mind discerneth not the things of the spirit. This principle is capable of indefinite illustration, accounts for all errors in religion, and should act as a motive for us to endeavour to clear our minds from all material thoughts when we essay to study God's Holy Word.

Matthew 16:13-20

The Rock and Key of Christianity

The Divine paragraph which we have selected for exposition has been the subject of much controversy. It is an old battle-ground of polemic theology. Hard and long Papist and Protestant have struggled here in sectarian disputation. They have done much to lay waste this "green pasture" which the great Shepherd has provided. They have trodden down its blooming verdure, and well-nigh trampled out of sight its living germs. Party feeling is a great hindrance to truthful interpretation. Every object in its horizon it tinges with the jaundice of its own eye. It builds up systems but buries Scriptures. It cares more for grammar than grace, and lives more in the roots of words than in the "reason of things." Verbal criticism is its great implement—an instrument this, though useful in its place, ever dangerous in such hands. The measure of man's words determine not always the dimensions of God's ideas. A truth-loving heart is a better interpreter than all your lexicons. The unlettered saint often seizes truths which elude the grasp of the verbal scholar. The Bible is addressed to the man, not to the critic as such. Thank God! the necessary canons of interpretation are the genuine dictates of our common souls. "If thine eye be single, thy whole body shall be full of light."

There are two or three remarks which will open up the way to our main subject.

First : *That of all the forces to which men are subject, none so important as ideas.* Man is the subject of ten thousand influences every day. His every sense is assailed on all hands and at all times ! In the fields of nature, and in the circles of society; in the bustle of business, and the quiet of home—everywhere he receives impressions that exert some moulding force upon his character, some impulse to quicken his moral pace, to lift him up or to press him down. "Thou hast beset me behind and before, and laid thine hand upon me :" the utterance, this, of true philosophy, as well as of conscious theism.

But of all the forces the force of an *idea* is the most important. Impressions move the senses, ideas the soul. Public sentiment has never yet attached sufficient importance to ideas. The man who has faith in them as such, it has ever stigmatised as a visionary enthusiast; or an utopian dreamer. Whilst on the other hand, the machine-man—who has no theory of his own, who arrogantly contemns the theories of others, and moves on in the same routine of practical operations as his forefathers pursued—it readily compliments as the real practicalist, and the true utilitarian. It is time for this vulgar prejudice to be crushed. It is the chief of the false prophets among the people. In it despotism has its stronghold, and human progress finds its chief barrier. As thinking men, we can scarcely overrate the importance of ideas. They are the seed of character, and the soul of history. They lift the savage to a sage, and turn the sinner into a saint. They create the difference between the wild man of the woods and the Newton of the stars. They are the pathway from the kingdom of darkness into the empire of Gospel light—the steps by which a sanguinary persecutor rises to a paragon of meekness, and an apostle of love. They are our masters —absolute autocrats. As they move, the world moves. The individual ideas sway the individual man. The national idea is the national sovereign. An ancient sceptic once referred this fair and million-formed universe to a fortuitous concourse of atoms, that through indefinite ages had been coursing about the immeasurable fields of immensity. We smile at this imbecility. But we are truly philosophic in tracing up all that is fair and useful in the civilized world of man to the ideas that have been floating about the fertile brain of humanity from the beginning. Our fleets and our cities, our mechanical inventions, our mercantile arrangements, our political systems, our social institutions—all the arts, in fine, that bless and beautify our lives, are but ideas that have taken form; plants that have sprung from the germ of thought. The world of modern civilization, like the coral islands, has been reared by the constant working of invisible powers. Your mere practicalists, who glibly talk against abstract principles and visionary schemes, are men that eat the fruit, but trample the life-seed in the dust—a generation of such men would soon waste up the world.

Secondly : Another remark which we would offer as introductive, is, *that of all ideas to which men are subject, none so important as the religious.* The religious element in man appears to me the chief part of his nature. It is *the* fact of his being—not an attribute, but the stamina—the foundation of all his powers. It penetrates, underlies, and pervades his entire self. The reason of his reasoning —the soul of his soul. Hence we find, that under no impulse will he move with such potency as under this. Religious excitement will do what no other excitement can—enlist all the faculties on its side, and concentrate all the inner powers to its point. Let a man believe that he is doing God service, and under the influence of that belief what will he not do ? He will fight with the desperate energy of a crusader, suffer with the indomitable heroism of a martyr, and labour with the self-immolating spirit of an apostle. Whatever idea, therefore, moves this element, is the greatest, and this idea is the religious. Other ideas will rouse certain faculties ; some the intellect, some the imagination, some the emotions; but this the entire *man.* Other ideas act upon human nature as the rays of winter upon the soil; under their influence only a few germs will be evolved, and a few plants will grow; but this, like the glowing beams of the vernal sun, will penetrate the deepest depth with its quickening energy, cause every seed-bud in nature to burst into life, and rise into fruitfulness. " *These be thy gods.*" Their influence is co-ordinate with the race. Have not all generations bowed to them as the ripened fields of autumn to the winds of heaven ? False or true, they are our potentates. When false, they ruin. The majorities of all ages sink into the miserable abysses of superstition beneath their weight. When true, they redeem. Gradually do they raise the world to spiritual intelligence, freedom, and power. They " create all things new." Every chapter and every verse of the history of their influence upon the world, whether for good or evil, is a protest against the impious assertion of atheism. The theistic ideas have ever been the greatest reality to human souls ; their amazing energy makes it a solemn thing to propound them, and truly great is the responsibility associated with the religious teacher. Yes, the mystic rod of Moses was not so mighty as the instrument he wields. He lives nearest the heart of the world. He is up at the head-springs, out of which proceed the issues of life. He turns and tinges the out-gushing streams. His hand is on the helm of the barque—on the mainspring of the machine. God give him light—and help him to be faithful !— clothe thy priests with righteousness !

Thirdly : *That of all religious ideas, none so important as the right idea of Christ.* This brings me to the subject of our Scripture, and must occupy the remainder of our attention. " Whom do men say that I the Son of man am ? " Twice does Jesus put the question, not for the sake of information, for " He knew their thoughts," but in order to impress upon them the importance of entertaining a *right* opinion concerning Him. Various notions were afloat on the subject. People were busily thinking about Him. He woke up the mind of His contemporaries, and opinions grew rife. Nature, the morning on which the babe of Bethlehem was born, was scarcely more still in torpor than was the Jewish intellect when Christ began His mission. But the wonderful works He wrought, and the sublime doctrines He proclaimed—His unearthly demeanour and Divine Spirit broke its slumbers. He found the mind of Judea like a lake without a ripple; He left it heaving under impulses that have been moving the world ever since; is moving it now; and will one day work out its reformation.

The opinions which now obtain concerning Christ, are not less various and conflicting than those which obtained amongst the Jews in His own day. Canvass the ideas of our Christendom on the subject; what a contrariety would you have developed? To the question, "Whom do men say that Jesus is?" replies of every hue of sentiment—uttered in every tone of voice, would come. Some with impious arrogance would say, that He was a clever impostor, and the prince of deceivers. Others, with a pseudo-philosophic air would aver, that He had no existence but in the imagination of a superstitious people—that his history is not fact but fable—a *myth*. Some, in mock reverence, would admit the veritableness of His existence, but declare Him to be nothing more than a great man—one to be placed side by side with the heroes of the world—Confucius, Socrates, Mahomet, Luther, and Cromwell. These are the men of His type. Others, rising as they suppose to a sublime conception, would admit that He was more than man—super-human—but not Divine—"the chief of the creation of God." Some would state that He was the sinless representative of the moral Divinity. Others, that He was the immaculate incarnation of the personal and the absolute God—God-man in HIMSELF. Yes, and amongst those who believed in the Divinity of His person and the priesthood of His office, there would still come out a large variety of sentiment.

Since, then, there is such a diversity of ideas concerning Christ, what is the right one? This is the question—the vital question. The reply of Peter, "Thou art Christ, the Son of the living God," contains the *true* idea. This is beyond debate, if we assume the Divine authority of our Scripture. Christ in His address to Peter after this confession, most unequivocally declares by implication, that he had risen to the true conception. What the *real* idea of Peter was, can only be ascertained by a legitimate interpretation of his language. The two terms employed are not tautological, but express two distinct ideas—the word *Christ* designates His *office* as the Messiah or Redeemer; and the expression " Son of God" designates His *nature* as *Divine*. In this view all our best Biblical scholars agree. Those who would satisfy themselves with the reasons for this interpretation, should consult Smith's "Testimony of the Messiah,"—a work as profound in its erudition, and philosophical in its structure, as it is magnanimous in its polemics and Christian in its spirit. The idea then of Peter, expressed in popular

language, would be—thou art the REDEEMING GOD. This I take to
be the right idea of Christ. It is the fundamental element of tho
Bible, the summary of Christianity; the deep want of man, the
CORE OF CREEDS. Volumes of thought are wrapped up in it. It
implies what we are; and what we want—the extraordinary position
in which we have fallen; and the extraordinary character which
God has assumed to meet us. It is that which gives to revelation
its life, unity, power, aptitude, and worth.

The words of Jesus suggest four thoughts in relation to this
idea.

I. THAT THE IDEA OF A REDEEMING GOD IS AN ELEMENT OF
PERSONAL BLESSEDNESS. " *Blessed art thou, Simon Bar-jona.*" Great
is the power of an idea upon the mind, for weal or woe. From the
sunshine of hope, and the pinnacle of enjoyment, the mind has often
been hurled, with a giant's force, by the entrance of some idea. A
single thought has often lashed the calmest spirit into a storm, and
caused the bravest heart to quail with fear. Nor is its capability to
raise, invigorate, and bless less manifest and great. Mark the
perplexity of that tradesman yonder. How embarrassed! He has
reached a point in his business where all is dark. What steps to
take he knows not. An idea darts into his mind, and like a flash
from Heaven dispels his gloom and lights up his path. Look off in
the field of science on that student. He is in difficulty, he has
arrived at a stage in his investigation where problems start up which
he cannot solve, phenomena appear which he cannot reconcile with
adopted theories. An idea comes to him, and with its advent all is
sunshine. But true ideas bless us in more ways than one. They
strengthen, as well as enlighten. They arm us with power over
matter, and with control over self. They hush the tempest of tho
soul. They kindle hopes which cheer us in the gloom, and open
fountains which refresh us in the desert.

Now, of all the ideas that can enter the *fallen* mind of humanity,
none so *beautifying* as that of a *Redeeming God.* It is to it what the
corrective property in medicine is to the man for whose disease it
is an infallible antidote—*the thing.* That the thought was which
broke in upon the perplexed intellect of the old Grecian Sage, when
he sprang into ecstasy and exclaimed, *Eureka, Eureka*—the solvent
of difficulties. What the mystic stream from Horeb's Rock was to
languishing Israel—the identical element for the emergency.

Now to help us in estimating the felicitating influence of this idea
upon the fallen mind, let us take a few specimen cases of distress,
to which it is ever subject, and then mark its operations in meeting
the precise exigency and administering the necessary relief. The
first shall be that of *intellectual solicitude* on religious subjects. The
man is in the region of speculative theology. He is there, not as an
idle theorist, but as an earnest labourer: not for amusement, but
for relief. Conscious necessity, not curiosity, has urged him thither.
" Who is the Lord ? " " Where shall I find Him ? " " Wherewith
shall I come before the Lord ? " " If a man die, shall he live

again?" These and cognate questions are pressing on him. To his interrogative cries there is no response. He is unhappy; for sincere scepticism is always painful, and earnest doubting is real suffering. The distress, however, is always heightened in proportion to the felt importance of the subject. This man's subjects are the most momentous, and the deepest throes of intellect are expressed in his questions. Now, what can relieve that man's mind? As a matter of philosophy I know of nothing so fitted for the purpose as the idea of a *Redeeming God*. Whether the idea is true or false, is not the question now. All I say is, that you have nothing so adapted to meet that man's case. Who does not see, that if he comprehend this in all its bearings, grasp it with all the tenacity of an earnest faith, his doubts will vanish, his anxieties will cease. It will light up the whole region of thought. It will explain the facts of his history, the mystery of providence, and the condition of the world. It will throw a radiance on the character of God, and point out his way to life everlasting. Henceforth it will be to him a veritable criterion, by which to test every religious theory; an anchorage, holding him steadfast amidst all the surges of sceptical suggestions; a nucleus, around which all his after-thoughts will gather, and in which they will find their centre and their home. It will crystallize all his other ideas into a transparent whole, which as a mirror will reflect the glory of God, in the face of Jesus Christ.

There is another case; a specimen-case of the mental sufferings of our fallen nature. The man's *conscience* is awakened to a sense of guilt. Self-reproaches and terrible forebodings fill him with the most poignant anguish. Distressing as were the anxieties of the intellectual inquirer in the former case, they are not to be compared with the anxieties of the morally awakened man in this case. No questions so painful as those which start from an excited conscience. They come not as propositions, from the calm realm of philosophic study; but as fiends, from the tumultuous regions of a self-condemned spirit—regions where all above .lower and blacken into fiercer storms, and all below yawn and roar with more than volcanic rage. The man is alarmed, for he feels himself on the confines of Hell, and exclaims, "O wretched man that I am, who shall deliver me from that gathering tempest, which looms before me in the distance, threatening to scathe me with its lightnings and to shiver me with its thunders?" Is this an overdrawn picture? Is it taken from the imagination, rather than from the common history of the race? I trow not. The existence of this sense of sin, all writers admit in theory, all nations have felt in fact. Pagan altars, Islam pilgrimages, Jewish ritualisms, and the multiform creeds of Christendom —all unite in proclaiming that a sin-convicting conscience is common to humanity. How is this to be removed? How is this tempest to be hushed? Where is the voice that can speak it into calmness and brighten it into sunshine? How is this virus to be extracted from the writhing heart of our nature? Like the man of old, "who went down from Jerusalem to Jericho, and fell among thieves, which stripped him of his raiment, and wounded him, and departed leaving him half-dead;" this self-convicted man before us, lies prostrate in agony on his way to eternity. Neither Priest nor Levite can help him if they would—away with them—let them pass by " on the other side." Is there a Samaritan near at hand?—one who will heal his wounds, raise him to his feet, set him on the high road, and free his passage to a happy home? Quitting the figurative, what in simple language can relieve the guilty conscience of this man? This is the question. And without pausing at present to canvass the various methods that have been propounded by superstition, or priestcraft, or philosophy, I unhesitatingly affirm, that the idea of a Redeeming God is an infallible antidote to such a guilt-stricken spirit. A JUST GOD AND A SAVIOUR. It is the idea of a *just God* that terrifies the conscience, and it is the idea that He has become a *Saviour* that pacifies it. Satisfy the man that He whose laws he has violated, and whose displeasure he has incurred, has assumed a character exactly corresponding to his sinful relation— that the great Arbiter of the universe has mercifully condescended to become the Redeemer of Man, and forthwith he has relief. His tumults are calmed, and his sorrows are soothed. The darkness is past, and the true light shineth. This is no pious vaunting—no rhetoric swell—no sentimental outburst. The true mental philosopher will see the aptitude of the means to the end, and he will grant it as a theory. The enlightened scripturalist will discover it in the Bible, and he will hold it as an article in his creed; and the genuine Christian will realise it in his experience, and avow it as the greatest fact in the history of his consciousness.

Take yet another case of distress common to our fallen nature : the case of *conflicting affections.* Here is a man, in whose emotional nature there is a mighty schism. His inward impulses have no common end. They heave in opposite directions. His inward currents flow at right angles, not in parallel lines. Each susceptibility has its own objects, and these, instead of lying along the straight line of virtue, are in all moral directions. Hence within him, what crossings of currents! What streams dashing against streams! What wild and foaming tumults down in the deeps of his being! Now this purpose is formed, and anon another. To-day he sins, and to-morrow repents to sin again. In the morning one impulse is on the throne, and in the evening another grasps the sceptre. His soul is "a kingdom divided against itself;" reduced to a little province for contending powers. He has "gods many, and lords many." This is a case of distress far more general than either of the other two. These conflicting affections are co-extensive with wickedness. " The wicked are like the troubled sea, when it cannot rest, whose waters cast up mire and dirt." What can relieve a man it this state? What can produce a coalition between these hostile elements within? What can create a channel in his nature deep and broad enough for all susceptibilities to flow on serenely ? What can unite his divided heart ? On the ground of mental science I aver, nothing but the idea of a Redeeming God.

There are four facts capable of vast amplification, but which I can only mention now, in order to make my position clear. First, that the *governing* affection of the soul is the only uniting power. As in matter so in mind, the greater force is the only centralizing one. The master affection is to the heart what attraction is to the material world; that which binds into a firm cohesion all its parts. Secondly, no *governing* affection will unite the whole soul that does not secure the full *concurrence of the conscience.* The mere existence of a supreme affection will not ensure harmony within. All have a supreme love, but few an affectional concord. The reason is, that the master affection is not such as to ensure the sanction and sympathy of the higher nature. Conscience goes not with the predominant affection of the unconverted man. Thirdly, that the concurrence of the conscience can never be obtained in any supreme affection which is not *directed to God.* Depraved as human nature is, the moral element will never give its consent to the loving of any object supremely, but the Supremely Good. Unless man loves God paramountly, he will always have his moral instincts against him. My fourth fact is, that a sense of guilt will necessarily prevent the supreme affection being set upon God, unless He appears in a *redeeming* aspect. When Christ said, " No man can come unto the Father but by me," He stated not an arbitrary arrangement, but a necessary truth. As the great Creator and just Governor of the universe, the guilty conscience arrays Him in all that is dark and terrific. The natural workings of fear ever repel and hurry off the soul. " Whither shall I flee ? " This is its deep cry. Fear crushes the genial sympathies of the soul, and bars up the heart against God. But let the JUST ONE appear in a redeeming attitude—let Him bow the heavens and come down in the form of love—let Him say convincingly to the conscience, "fury is not in me;" "I am come that ye might have life;"—I say, let Him appear thus, and who does not see that there is opened up a " new and living way," by which the guilty conscience might return in loving sympathy to Him. This is what He has done in the history of Jesus. This is the *redemptive idea*—an idea which, when lifted up in the soul, will act as a magnet to draw back its *entire* nature to that God in whom alone it can find its centre and its rest.

For all these cases, then, of that mental distress to which our fallen nature is subject, this idea is an infallible antidote. It is the *panacea* for all mental woes, the elemental germ of human blessedness. Pronounce it fiction, if you will; it is a fiction that out-rivals all other reliefs for wounded souls. Fiction, though it be, can we dispense with it ? No ; with the tenacity of a death-grasp we must hold it, until you give us a fact that will answer the same purpose. Blessed fiction ! Thine introduction to the soul is ever a bright era in its history. It is the dawn of a spiritual jubilee. The imprisoned faculties are set at liberty, and the spirit enfranchised for ever. It is the rising of the morning star on the stormy darkness of our depravity—reflecting and heralding that greater light in whose sunshine is the consummation of our bliss. " This IS life eternal, that they might know, thee, the only true God," and Jesus Christ whom thou hast sent.

II. THAT THE IDEA OF A REDEEMING GOD IS A SUBJECT OF DIVINE COMMUNICATION. "*For flesh and blood hath not revealed this unto thee; but my Father which is in heaven.*"

In a sense all true ideas are communications from God. He supplies the means, motives, and capacities for their formation. Rays from the great " Father of lights," and the medium of mental vision, are they all. Whatever we see of self, the universe, and God, is through their light. As they widen and clear, the circle of our being expands and brightens, "In thy light shall we see light."

But there is, I think, a *special* sense in which He must be regarded as imparting *the idea* under consideration. This, perhaps, will be rendered manifest, if we determine what is meant by the communication of this idea? What is it to have it revealed *unto* a man, as Peter now had it revealed to him? It seems to me that there are three distinct stages in its revelation—the *sensible, logical,* and *spiritual.*

First : I observe that its revelation unto a man is something more than the *sensible.* The redeeming God appeared in person to men. He revealed Himself to their senses. " That which was from the beginning"—says John—" which we have heard, which we have seen with our eyes, which we have looked upon, and our hands have handled, of the word of life." A more wild and baseless notion never entered the brain of humanity, than that which represents Jesus as a *poetic impersonation* of the spirit of His age; a phantom. His biography appears written, as if to prevent the possibility of any infidel imagination soaring to such a height of extravagance; or rather would I say, from diving into such depths of blasphemy. The artless narrative wears the impress of fact, and breathes the breath of life. There is nothing of fable in its structure, nothing of poetry in its hue. Never did a subject of any biography appear so prominent and real, as Jesus appears on the pages of the Evangelists. It is the hero, not the writer, that you see. It is the incident, not the composition, that enchains you. It is not the polish of art, but the bloom of nature, that gives the Gospels their beauty and their charm.

Add to the *artlessness* of the narrative the *impression* which the subject has left upon the world. Jesus produced a mighty effect upon His own age. He did not insulate Himself from His contemporaries, nor seclude Himself in a solitude where only a few would have occasional access to Him, whose opinions would be the only means by which the mass would form their notions of Him—notions which they would swell and colour according to the tendencies of their imagination. No man, perhaps, was ever better known by the people of His time, than Jesus. On the open theatre of Judea He acted out the drama of Redemption. He proclaimed His doctrines, performed His miracles, endured His sufferings, and breathed His last before the open eye of His country. Nor did the people merely see Him. Their interest in Him was intense. By a mysterious instinct, they were drawn after Him. The roads through which He passed were thronged with travellers. The quiet shores of Galilee teemed with life when He was there. On the lonely mountains, busy crowds stirred with anxiety when He climbed their heights to perform a miracle or proclaim a truth. He broke the monotony of villages when he appeared, and cities startled into enthusiasm when His tread was heard in the streets.

But the effects of His history after His departure far transcend anything that occurred during His lifetime.' The day of Pentecost was a type and pledge of His influence upon every subsequent age. During the apostolic era, His influence permeated the living world, and formed men into associations by impulses they never felt before. Thirty years roll on; and in Judea, Galilee, and Samaria, in Asia, in the islands of the Mediterranean, in Greece, Italy, and Africa, we find flourishing churches celebrating His name and triumphing in His history. Tacitus, who was prætor of Rome about eighty years afterwards, in giving an account of the burning of the imperial city by Nero, says, "The Christians had their denomination from Christus, who, in the reign of Tiberius, was put to death as a criminal, by the procurator Pontius Pilate. This pernicious superstition, though checked for a while, broke out again and spread not only over Judea, the source of the evil, but reached the city (Rome) also." Justin Martyr, who lived about one hundred and six years after Christ's ascension, writes, "There is not a nation of Greeks or barbarians, or by whatever name they are called, even those who wander in tribes and live in tents, among whom prayer and thanksgiving are not offered up to the Father and Creator of the universe, in the name of the crucified Jesus." Tertullian, about fifty years afterwards, says, "We are but of yesterday, and we have filled your cities, islands, towns, and boroughs, the camp, the senate, and the forum." The celebrated Origen, who writes about thirty years after Tertullian, says, "In every part of the world, throughout all Greece, and in all other nations, there are innumerable and immense multitudes who, having left the laws of the country and those whom they esteemed gods, have given themselves up to the law of Moses and the religion of Christ." Eighty years after this, Constantine, recognising its mighty influence upon the world, adopted it as a religion of the State. Though checked in its progress by this fact, still, from that day to this, the history of Jesus has not ceased its operations. It is still in conflict with heathenism, its old antagonist. Though it has levelled many temples in the dust, and ground many gods into powder, its energy is not exhausted. It has sapped the foundations of Pagan systems, and they are tottering to the fall. In its brightness, the crescent has become dim. It has stripped priestcraft of its mask, and thrown light into the spectral realms of superstition.

Systems that once held the world in awe it has exploded. It has stabbed autocracy to the heart, and the death-throes of despotism are everywhere heard. The seed of liberty it has scattered over the two hemispheres. It has given laws to the ruling empires of the world. The first geniuses of the race have been kindled into splendour with its themes. It has coloured the literature of the world, and tempered the spirit of the age. Its symbol is the chief ornament in Christendom. It is hung in the halls of science, and the palaces of sovereigns. It is interwoven into the thoughts and hearts, into the hopes and fears, into the designs and doings, and general experience of that race of men who are inevitably destined to become the civil, intellectual, and moral masters of the world.* The day must dawn, therefore, when the history of Christ will be the history of humanity; the biography of Christ the life of the world.

Why have I thus referred to the influence of Christ's history upon the world? In order to impress you with the *reality* of His earthly existence as the Redeeming God, and expose the monstrous absurdity of that notion which reduces His biography to a fable. He who can believe that a fictitious personage could do all this—could colour and direct the streams of human history for eighteen centuries, and put forth an influence, which, in the tenor of things, is destined to permeate the world, must be beyond the pale of reason and the reach of argument. Nor is the idea, that the history of a *mere* man could effect this, much more reasonable. I could as soon believe that a human hand gave the ocean its boundaries, or piled up the Andes, as believe that the history of a frail mortal could effect what the history of Jesus has achieved.

But to recur to our point. Though Jesus had thus an actual earthly existence which placed Him within the range of the senses, His being revealed *unto* Peter was something more than this. To have the senses impressed and the physical sympathy awakened by Christ will profit but little. Christ in the senses is not Christ in the soul. He is in the outer court of our nature, not in the inner sanctuary there. If He advance no farther, we have but a *sensuous Christianity*, which I esteem a sore evil—a disease which emasculates the mind—turns its emotions into superstition, its worship into forms, steals all manliness from its thoughts, all vigour and health from its influence.

Secondly: I observe, its revelation *unto* a man, is something more than the *logical*. In this stage, the sensuous impressions are wrought into the forms of intelligible notions. These notions the reflective faculty defines, classifies, and reduces into systems. Christ is conducted from the region of feeling into the calmer region of thought. His history is translated into propositions. All the incidents of His life are arranged under some general terms. The man has now a creed—a theological Christ. Would I complain of this? Would I intimate that the *idea* of a Redeeming God ought not to

---

* See a beautiful article "On the Present State of Humanity," in the Philosophical Essays of the celebrated Jouffroy.

assume this form, or pass through this stage? By no means. It is according to the tendency of our nature. One of our greatest faculties is for this very purpose. The power which turns the wild sounds that thrill the savage breast into scientific music, and converts into astronomic truth the countless stars, which stir with awe and wonder the soul of the rustic shepherd on the plain, will in the same way reduce to theory the impression which the history of Christ makes upon the heart. Peter, I have no doubt, had his theory. What he had seen and heard of Christ, had taken some speculative form in the understanding, and so far as his logical notion was true, it was a Divine revelation. The unaided efforts of " flesh and blood " could never give to the human mind the conception, either of the Redemptive relationship, or the moral character of Jesus. From what source in nature could we derive the idea that the Creator of the universe had assumed a character correspondent with the lost state of humanity? Nature reveals God as the Creator, and universal history as the Governor.

But does either utter a syllable about the Redeemer? Here they are mute. The same is true as to His *moral character.* To say that the ideal of moral goodness embodied in Him was an aggregation of the moral elements of His times, is a reckless assertion. Do not all the facts of His age rise in evidence against it? Between His spirit, and the spirit of the period in which He lived, was there the slightest affinity? Was there not an impassable gulf? His character was not moulded by education. The rich forms of virtue developed in His life sprung not from seeds imparted. They were the out-growth of germs within Him. He was not the moral child of His age. If like begets like, then on this round earth He had no moral parent. He was an incarnation from some other scene. His character was a living miracle in their midst. He moved amongst His contemporaries as the mystic pillar moved amidst the Israelites in the desert when the sun went down—a strange light broke the darkness, and threw its radiance on the face of all. Did the fiery pillar grow out of the Arabian desert? Prove it, and I will believe that the character of Jesus sprang from the character of His age. If the idea, then, transcends the discovery of " flesh and blood," it must come to the man who has it as a Divine communication. The Bible is its revelation. To unfold the Redeeming God, as nature unfolds the Creating God, is its sublime function.

But is this *logical* notion, however correct, the revelation of Christ *unto* a man? Was this the whole of what Peter had? No? Of what service would this have been to him? When the idea stops at this stage, when Christ remains only in the understanding, when Christianity is simply a thing of intellect, it is, to say the least, of questionable value. Faith, when it leads to right works, is an incalculable blessing; but when it fails of this, it is a great bane. " The letter killeth." Some of the greatest crimes ever perpetrated under these heavens have had their impulse and licence from *logical Christianity.* It has frequently been in association with most arrogant despotism, intolerable bigotry, and fiendish persecution. The *mere* creed-man the world is beginning to shun, as a social pest. Thinking men look at him in the light of ecclesiastical history, and feel that he has more respect for his own opinions, than for human rights—would sooner brand a brother with ignominy, than allow him to question the orthodoxy of his views. But if the revelation of this idea *unto* Peter was something more than a sensible impression, or a logical judgment, what was it? It was a *spiritual sympathy*. There seems to be three distinct classes of sympathy in our complex nature : the sensuous, or sympathy with material forms ; the intellectual, or sympathy with theoretic doctrine ; and the moral, or sympathy with the principles of everlasting right. Christianity appeals to all. It has a form, and it can wake the passions. It has a system, and it interests the intellect. It has moral principles, and it can engross the soul and win the man. We have seen that neither the first nor the second is religion. As means, they are useful and necessary; as ends, they are gigantic evils. Christianity appeals to them in order to get admission into the interior of our being, and set up its empire there. Both the senses and the understanding are but stages through which it passes on to its destination. Woe to the man that detains it at either point! Let the High Priest pass into the inner sanctuary, and not tarry in these courts. "I thank Thee, O Father, Lord of heaven and earth, because Thou hast hid these things from the wise and prudent, and revealed them unto babes !" The things of which Jesus speaks were not hid either from the senses or the judgment; but from the spirit—their moral meaning was not apprehended.

The revelation of this idea to Peter thus, was a revelation unto his moral consciousness—*himself*. He knew the moral meaning of what he said. The Redeeming God had become the great reality to his spirit. His universal principles harmonised with, and developed into action, his moral intuitions. His doctrines had solved his difficulties. His provisions had met his wants. His promises rose to the full height of his highest aspirations. His moral loveliness had won his heart. He was the centre of his affections. His spirit had become the inspiration and the soul of his soul. He was one with Christ. Identical with this was the revelation which Paul had. "But when it pleased God, who separated me from my mother's womb, and called me by His grace, *to reveal His Son in me*, that I might preach among the heathen; immediately I conferred not with flesh and blood." Here it is most distinctly taught, that the revelation was *in* the soul ; that the revelation was made in the soul by God, and that the revelation thus made produced a thorough change in his history. Henceforth he knew no man after the flesh—not even Christ. His Christ was not the material Christ of the ceremonialist, nor the theological Christ of the technical professor, but the spiritual Christ—the embodiment of *law* and *love*. The *spirit* of Christ was his religion. This lifted him from a Jew, to a man : raised him above all conventionalities ; made him a citizen of the world, and a servant of God. When I think, that this is the *only* true religion, and look at that amongst us which is popularly considered such—a thing which is more ritual than righteous —more technical than truthful—having more regard to sects than souls—makes more sceptics than saints—my spirit sinks within me. I am confounded. I feel that Christianity is libelled, and men are the victims of a most jeopardizing delusion.

Now, the idea of the Redeeming God revealed in this ultimate and perfect form—brought into the soul and there enthroned, is not the result of " flesh and blood." The Infinite Father, who brought Him personally before the *senses* of Peter, and who in His word brings Him before the *judgment* of all, brings Him now by His Spirit into the *heart.* The Bible is full of this doctrine ; and so is the ever-growing book of Christian experience. Good men vary in their notions as to the mode ; but one are they all as to the fact. And what a fact ! To reveal Christ to the moral consciousness— has the Highest a higher aim with man than this ? Such a revelation is at once the brightest reflection of Himself, and the sublimest boon to souls. In its light man sees his Maker and himself. Like the sun, it uncovers the boundless heights that encircle us with their starry splendours, and sheds at the same time its radiance upon our persons and our paths.

III. THAT THE IDEA OF A REDEEMING GOD IS FUNDAMENTAL TO ALL TRUE ASSOCIATION. *"And upon this rock will I build my church, and the gates of hell shall not prevail against it."* It is scarcely necessary to remark, that whilst the generic meaning of the term church is an *assembly,* the New Testament meaning is generally more restricted. It designates the assembly of the good, sometimes in its local sections, and sometimes in its entire aggregation. Here it signifies the " general assembly " of the pious—the vast and ever increasing assemblage of holy men, in whatever age, locality, or world they may exist.

There are three general thoughts suggested by the Scripture at the head of this section.

First : That the grand purpose of Christ is to bring men into this holy association. " *I will build my church.*" The well-being of social man requires the cordial love, entire confidence, and pure fellowship of his species. The happiness of the world demands that each unit should feel in sympathy, will in harmony, and act in concert, with the general whole. The growth of the human family in the elements of knowledge and the principles of goodness—in science and virtue, depends upon *fellowship.* Man in solitude is like seed without soil,—a dry germ deprived of all influences that can either quicken or develop. Man in uncongenial and antagonistic society grows in selfishness, and lives in suspicion. The cordial comminglings of sympathies, and free interchange of thoughts—the identifying of heart with heart, and the blending of soul with soul, constitute the necessary condition of human advancement. But our world has lost this. The social temple is riven to its foundations. There is scarcely "one stone left upon another." "The middle wall of partition" everywhere rears its head, and throws its gloomy shadows abroad. Mutual suspicion, civil caste, worldly rivalry, religious sectarianism, and false nationality, stand up between man and man in all circles. The earth, which the Great Father furnished as a lovely home for His children, has become an arena of bitter strife and sanguinary conflict. "No man careth for my soul." Language this, whose application, alas! is world-wide still.

Now the great work of Christ is to heal the breach, and to restore vital unity. Every "middle wall of partition" He is breaking down. The scattered sheep from the wildest scenes and bleakest mountains He is collecting into one fold. The various members of the race disjointed, like the dry bones in Ezekiel's dream, He is bringing together into one body. *One* spirit shall animate that body, and by one head shall it be governed— HIMSELF. The shivered temple He is building up. Stone by stone, slowly but surely, the superstructure rises. The day will come when "He shall bring forth the headstone thereof with shouting, crying, Grace, grace unto it." Then shall earth's antipathies be annihilated—earth's groans be hushed. Its discords lost in music, its contentions exchanged for the greetings of brotherhood—Christ's prayer answered, and redemption finished.

Secondly: That Christ brings man into this true association through the instrumentality of the idea contained in Peter's confession. Upon "this rock," &c. What is the antecedent to the "this"? Such a child's question I am almost ashamed to write. One might have thought it almost an impossible thing to have got two answers to this question. Still more impossible, three. But party criticism is fertile in invention. *This*—not Peter—not Christ, but the subject about which Jesus was speaking—the idea which Peter had expressed in the 15th verse, and which Jesus in the immediately preceding sentence assured him had not been revealed by "flesh and blood." Indeed, if the language could bear any other interpretation, the truth would nevertheless be, that the *idea* is the foundation. Christ is the foundation of the Church no farther than He is the *subject* of the correct idea. Where He is not known, He has no moral influence to this end; and where He is not known correctly, His influence would not bind men into that association of which we are speaking. If you say, Peter was the rock, I again reply, that in the nature of things, he was no further the rock or the foundation of the church, than he was the correct representative of this idea. Abstract this idea from his soul and speech, and you strip him of all power to lay one single stone on the temple of the world's unity.

Now, if we can prove that the idea of a Redeeming God is indispensable to the building up of this church—that it is not an arbitrary arrangement which requires this, but that in the nature of the case, no true human association can be realized in its absence, our interpretation will be confirmed, and the passage will have to us, at any rate, a truly momentous and tangible meaning. In pursuance of this object I would state three undeniable facts.

First, that *moral* love is a necessary element in all true association. Men are only really united, so far as they have mutual confidence in each other's principles, mutual esteem in each other's character, mutual sympathy with the moral desires, aims, and enterprises of each other. There are, I am aware, other elements at work in society, which tend to a kind of union. There is *animal* sympathy—a kind of magnetic influence existing between persons of certain organisations. The physical forms, tones, styles, habits, fascinate and attract, and produce a species of union. The conjugal association is too frequently based exclusively upon this element. But such union as this is the union of animals, not men. The moral soul of parties thus conjoined may be—often is—as far asunder as the poles. There is *secular* sympathy. Persons associate on the ground of interests. A selfish policy is the uniting bond. Commercial companies and political organisations are based upon this principle. But this is the union of money-makers, not of men. There again is *intellectual* sympathy. There is an identity of mental tastes and habits. The same class of subjects is admired, and the same mode of viewing things pursued. The same principles embraced, the same creeds adopted. Literary clubs, theological sects, and philosophic schools are thus founded. But even this is not real union. It is the association of thinkers, not of men. MORAL SYMPATHY—sympathy with the principles, dispositions, aims, and souls of men, as children of the same Father, subjects of the same administration, candidates for the same eternity—this is the only really uniting bond. This is an associative power, which has to do, not with the colour of a man's skin, the style of his dress, the dogmas of his belief. It heeds not his lineage, takes no inventory of his goods and chattels, cares neither for the size of his dwelling nor the character of his nation; but fastens its interests upon *himself*. A bond this, which, like the arch of heaven, stretches beyond all conventional distinctions and material barriers. It unites *souls* in bonds mightier than adamant, but finer than the finest web—too weak to fetter, but too strong to break.

Secondly, that moral love can only exist in connexion with moral excellence. How is this love, which alone can unite men, to be obtained ? How is this divine element to be evoked ? Let us narrow the question. How is that love to be awakened in the Christian church, which will heal all its schisms, and make its sections one ? This is a popular query now, and one deeply interesting to a large class of excellent men. Will exhortation to love one another do ? No. You may, with all the eloquence of an Apollos, exhort me to love another, and doomsday would dawn before you would succeed in awaking a spark of affection. Sentimentalism, the bane of the church, you may evoke, but not love.

Your oratory might charm or perchance tantalise me, but certainly not enlist my love for your client. It is more likely to be repelled than drawn forth in this way. To beg for love, must ever be as useless as it is unphilosophic and mean. The love worth having never comes thus.

How, then, is this union to be produced? by forming organisations for the purpose, and agreeing to love those who will subscribe to your theological test? Consult your own consciousness. Have you ever loved another with that soul-identifying affection of which we are speaking, and which is essential to union, on the ground of his subscribing to the tenets of your faith? On the contrary, does not your nature recoil with disgust from some who hold all that is most precious in your theology? There is much uniformity of faith where there is mutual antipathy of spirit. Love is an involuntary state of mind. It does not come by volition. It springs up spontaneously at the view of the object suitable to awaken it. If you would have me to admire music, you will never succeed by your exhortation or your beliefs. Bring upon my ear the sweet harmony of your notes, and the emotion will start up forthwith. And if you would have me to love any class of Christians you may select, you need not waste a breath of your eloquence. Let them show me the lovable, and no power on earth can prevent the upspringing of the affection. "If we walk in the light as He is in the light, we have fellowship one with another." In these few words you have the philosophy of true union. There is no cordial fellowship—no spiritual oneness existing between any two minds—where there is not the mutual recognition of the light of holiness. It is either sentimental weakness, or black hypocrisy, to profess moral affection for a man in whom we do not discover moral excellence. Integrity of principle, purity of motive, generosity of spirit, nobleness of character, a heart bowing in enlightened and filial veneration before God, and expanding in warm and genial love for the world—these elements, which I express in the one word GOODNESS, are the only powers that can awaken this love. In all souls the great Author of our being has implanted susceptibilities to love these elements of moral excellence. The race through all its ramifications herein agree. These are the attractive forces. That individual or community who embodies them in the highest form has the most of the world's affection. If the Baptist, Wesleyan, Independent, Episcopalian, and others, would get more united, let them attend a little more to the culture of their hearts. Let some of them commence the practice of the first principles of justice, to say nothing of charity. Let them all strive more to become love-worthy and then the love will arise. I do not complain of the want of love between churches. To me it seemeth good that there is not more love where there is not more excellence. Were love to go in advance of goodness, would it not be an immense calamity? Would it not argue a depravity too blind to mark moral distinctions, and therefore beyond hope? If, then, excellence is the condition of love, the men, whether they belong to your unions and alliances or not, who are most successful in improving the spiritual morality of a population, are the best agents in uniting men. In philosophic investigation, it is down in the region of detail that the mental battlings go on. The higher men ascend the line of generalisation, the more united in thought. There is a harmonious confederation of intellect, far up in the realm of first principles. So it is down amidst the quibblings, technicalities, ceremonies, offices, and sects, that you have the contentions and strifes. The men who rise the highest in the scale of morality are the most harmonious. The truly good of all sects are already one. The Fénelons and Penns, though ecclesiastical antipodes, must ever clasp souls.

Thirdly, that moral excellence is found only in connexion with the *idea* embodied in Peter's confession. I lay it down as an axiom that there is nothing love-worthy, or really love-awakening in any character, only just so far as it seems to spring from disinterested motives. Array an individual in all the outward attributes of the most perfect moral character. Let him converse like a Pascal, or act like a Howard, yet if you discover that the whole has sprung from personal consideration—that into pride, interest, ambition, or some such selfish purpose, you could resolve the whole; would not his externally beautiful character awaken disgust rather than affection? The remark of Volney, that there is no "merit or crime in intention," is opposed to the universal consciousness of mankind. Do not men everywhere estimate acts according to the intentions which they are supposed to represent? Now I state a fact when I say that Christianity—of which Peter's idea is the summary—is the only system on earth that either requires or generates this disinterestedness. I look to the moral systems of the world's philosophy, and Shaftesbury's opinion is the spirit and type of them all: *that all the obligations to be virtuous arise from the advantages and disadvantages of vice.* I look to the various systems of religion, and I find that hope and fear—elements which can never generate the truly beautiful, are nevertheless the only elements which they appeal to and develop. Their temples are markets, their altars are stalls, and their worship is bartering of the most avaricious kind. On the contrary, to destroy selfishness in all its forms,—to turn the emotions into a free, clear, and even active fountain of love,—to bring the entire man under the master influence of charity, is the sublime aim of Christianity. Would space permit, it would be interesting to show that, philosophically, the idea of a Redeeming God is the only idea that can turn the selfish heart into that benevolence which is the spirit of all that is morally lovable. That it is the only system that actually does, facts in abundance show. Where can you find character on which the heart can repose in full confidence and love, where Christ is not known as the great Redeemer? Point me to the tree of virtue on spots where Christianity has not shone. I would not depreciate other influences of spiritual culture—nature, science, law, art, literature—we thank God for these quickening and raising forces ; but neither of them separately, nor all conjointly, can beget in the soul this vital germ of moral goodness. Helps they may be, but not causes—auxiliaries, but not substitutes. The soft earth, the glowing atmosphere, the falling showers, and the various gales, of themselves could do nothing towards the life of the world. Add to their influence the sun, and at once they will clothe continents with life, and upstart majestic forests on the barren hills. So the varied elements of civilized life ; alone they are useless to this end, but let them be combined with the creative light of this divine idea, and the moral wilderness will blossom as the rose.

If, then, there is no true church—that is—no thorough association amongst men—where there is not moral love ; and if there can be no such love where there is not moral excellence, and if the *idea* we are discussing is essential to moral excellence, the inference is undeniable —that the idea of Peter is fundamental to all real union amongst men. It is the rock, and the only rock, on which in the nature of things the church *can* be built. "Other foundations can no man lay" that will sustain the temple of true union. All human organisations, for whatever purpose, are based upon some recognised idea or ideas. But the idea which combines the holy men of all places and periods into unity of spirit is the idea of a *Redeeming God*. If the friends of union, the emissaries of peace, and the lovers of man, would have their aspirations realised, let them in all their self-denying efforts seek mainly to bring this centralising truth into living contact with the heart of churches, nations, and the world. The other idea suggested by that part of the passage now under notice, is—

Thirdly : That the association which Christ effects amongst men by this idea, is proof against the most formidable opposition : "The gates of hell shall not prevail against it." The expression, disrobed of its figurative dress, means, that not even death itself shall prevail against it. Ah, what disruption does death produce ! That merciless power, which dissolves the intimate connexion between the soul and body, rends at the same time every tie that unites us to our race—save the tie of moral love. Political associations, religious sects, intellectual clubs, benevolent societies, mercantile companies, physical relationships—these unions the " gates of hell " challenge —over these they win a triumph every hour. Day by day, each man not united to the great church of the good, death dissevers from all his connexions. Poor man ! he is left a social wreck to float on the waves of desolation, without a heart to love or an attribute to be loved : without a friend—without a God, he must endure his desolate doom ! But the bond of mutual moral love is *indestructible*. Before men thus united can be separated, one of three things must take place—either the annihilation of their existence, or the destruction of their goodness, or the loss of the capacity to appreciate the goodness. If none of these things transpire, which we must now assume, their union is eternal. Rivers, oceans, islands, continents, worlds, divide not the good. They are one, as the planets are one—they mingle their bright beams together—they revolve round one centre, obey one law—the radiance of one glory they receive and reflect.

IV. THAT THE IDEA OF A REDEEMING GOD QUALIFIES FOR THE HIGHEST OFFICE. *"And I will give unto thee the keys of the kingdom of heaven; and whatsoever thou shalt bind on earth, shall be bound in heaven; and whatsoever thou shalt loose on earth, shall be loosed in heaven."*

What is the *exact* idea contained in this highly figurative statement? It is important, for the sake of explanation, to observe what is not expressed here. It is not said, first, that I will give thee "the keys" which I will give to no other apostle. It may be true or false that, Peter was invested with an authority which the other apostles had not. These words are entirely mute on that subject. *They say nothing concerning the other apostles.* Nor, secondly, is it here said, I will give thee keys, which will place thee in authority over the other apostles. Christ may have made Peter the "primate of the apostolic college"—as Horsley has it—or not, for anything that is here stated on the subject. *The words say nothing about authority over men.* Nor, thirdly, is it here said, I will give thee keys, which thou shalt transmit to thy successors, who in all future times shall have power to open and shut paradise as they please. This may be a sublime truth or a huge falsehood. *This passage says nothing about succession.* Nor, fourthly, is it here said, I will give thee keys which belong to the apostolic character and age—a power that is special, local, and temporary. This, again, may be true or false. *The words predicate nothing about classes or places.* I deny that any of these notions are contained in, or sanctioned by, these words of Christ. It comes not within my purpose to discuss the merits of these opinions. I say nothing about their truth or falsehood. All I aver is,—that this passage does not teach any of them—that if you hold either, you must look for support to some other quarter. Neither the scope nor grammar of Christ's language can justify you in identifying it with such notions.

What, then, is the exact idea? Let us understand the figures. The word "keys" is expressive of *authority*. When the Jews authorised any man to become a teacher of the law, they put into his hand the key of the closet in the temple, where the sacred books were kept. Thus intimating that they had entrusted him with power to explain the Scriptures. The phrase "kingdom of heaven" was an expression which Jesus commonly used to designate His system—the Gospel. The expressions to "loose" and to "bind" mean to permit and to prohibit. The sense is—says Bloomfield— "whatsoever thou shalt forbid, or whatsoever declare lawful and constitute in the church, shall be ratified and held good." To open up what is right for men, and to forbid what is wrong, comprehend the great work of the Christian teacher—a work which must ever accord with the will of heaven, for moral truth is the same in all worlds. Stripping, then, from the passage, its figurative garb, the idea I take to be simply this—I will authorise thee to expound my system.

Now my position is, that the idea contained in Peter's confession qualified him for this high office. Two remarks will illustrate this: First, *that Peter's qualification was the ground of the authority now committed to him.* Christ raises no one to an influential post in His kingdom who has not been previously qualified. In human states men are frequently lifted to an office whose functions they are incapable of discharging. Unjust judges, ignorant teachers, servile kings—with such anomalies human society has ever been too familiar. Outward patronage, not inward power, is too frequently the stepping-stone to high offices. This is a sore evil. It injures the functionaries themselves. Little men, in great offices, are more the objects of commiseration than envy. They often lose their nature in pretence, and their soul in vanity. They become dizzy on the altitude to which some false hand has borne them. Nor is it less injurious to the commonwealth. In such cases, merit is at a discount; the motives to self-culture are weakened, and the general conscience is insulted. But in Christ's empire, the man always determines the office. You have no commission, unless you have the power. *The divine " call " to any ministry, is the capacity to discharge its functions.* Peter was now authorised to expound Christ's system, because he had now reached the qualification.

My second remark is, *that Peter's qualification was grounded on this idea.* This idea qualified him first *intellectually.* Without this idea, I maintain that no man could ever expound the Scripture. It is the key by which alone we can enter into this kingdom of truth. Take away the idea of a Redeeming God, and all the other biblical ideas will mingle coldly and confusedly together, like the rude elements of the world before the first sun arose upon the long and frigid night of chaos. The Bible, in the absence of this idea, has no meaning. It is unintelligible jargon. Its gorgeous ritualism, sublime predictions, and extraordinary facts are all inexplicable. The Shasters of the Hindoo, or the Koran of the Mussulman, would be scarcely more incoherent. This is the principle by which alone you can make sense of this blessed book. In getting this idea, Peter got the key by which he could unlock the whole empire of truth—throw open its gates, and expose it to the eye of reason, and the heart of the world. With it, in fact, he did unlock those mystic gates. He stepped within the precincts of the great kingdom—looked around —saw the "unsearchable riches"—felt that the provisions were commensurate with the wants of the world: and forthwith "he opened his mouth, and said, of a truth, I perceive that God is no respecter of persons: but in every nation, he that feareth Him, and worketh righteousness, is accepted with Him."

This idea, secondly, qualified him *spiritually.* We have seen that intellectually it is the one key-truth: that, without which, the whole kingdom of revelation would be shut up in impenetrable mystery;

but we should err if we imagined that a mere intellectual under-standing of the Bible would qualify any one for the high office of a correct expounder. Given, that a man has a theoretical knowledge of the biblical economy; that he can propound it in the most lucid verbal propositions, and present it, as a logical whole, to the under-standings of men; unless, in connexion with this, he has a spirit wrought into sympathy with its genius and designs, he would miser-ably misrepresent that which he sought to explain. He would have no right to the *keys*—the office. There is a spirit, necessary both to discern and expound the "things of the spirit." The spirit of a speaker often speaks without words—always gives its own meaning to words. The gesticulations, tones, and looks of a cold, selfish ex-pounder of the Gospel, contradict his every statement, blunt the point of his every argument, and caricature the system which he seeks to make plain. If I would become a correct expounder of God's Word, I feel that I must lose my own will in its vast designs; its genius must become the inspiration of my soul; and its aims the intensest aspirations of my heart. Thus it was, I presume, with Peter. He understood the system spiritually, as well as intellec-tually. It had impregnated and quickened his moral consciousness. In the clear light of the idea of a Redeeming God, his Jewish pre-judices gave way—his heart burst through all sectarian bonds—all conventional distinctions faded off his horizon; and his spirit rose into unconquerable sympathy for the world. He concluded, with Paul, " that because one died for all, then were all dead : and that He died for all, that they who live, should not henceforth live unto themselves, but unto Him who died for them and rose again." Oh that all teachers looked at the world thus—viewed it in the broad light of Christ's universal love, as the Redeeming God ! But how few look at humanity through this medium ! One teacher looks at it through an ecclesiastical system ; another through a petty sec-tarianism, and another through a dogmatic theology. Thus it is, that man is not seen as MAN—not seen in the depths of his soul, in the breadths of his relations, in the vastness of his responsibilities, and the deathlessness of his being. Would that some mystic hand, like that of old, which rent asunder the veil of the Temple, and ex-posed its hidden things, would rend these false media from the eye of the church, and lay bare the great world of men in the clear, strong light of the Redeemer's love !

Christ then authorised Peter to expound His truth because he was qualified, and he was qualified because he had risen to and realised the idea that He was the Redeeming God. Do you ask then, how you shall get these keys—how you shall receive Divine authority to open the great empire of truth to a perishing world ? I tell you, not by striving to put yourself in the line of apostolical succession—the vile invention of a crafty priesthood ; this will but make you the dupe of a wicked, and, thank God ! a waning system, and turn your vigorous manhood into a sickly sacerdotalism. Not by any official inauguration to the office of teacher—no ordination of any church, however scriptural; the laying on of no hands, however holy, can invest you with these keys. Not, in fine, by formally identifying yourself with any system or church, but by becoming *morally qualified as a man to teach your brother man.* Christ makes qualifications the necessary condition of office. He authorised Peter to teach, because he was qualified. He gave him the keys, because he knew how to use them. The humblest man that walks our streets, may have the real keys, when prelates and popes have nothing but the name.

Do you ask how you shall obtain this qualification ? By getting, as Peter got, the right idea of Christ—getting it not merely in its logical form, but also in its spiritual impression and reality. You can only open the kingdom as you rise to the true idea of Christ. A profound truth Jesus taught when He said, " By ME if any man enter in, he shall be saved, and he shall go in and out and find pasture."

Let me urge you, in conclusion, to promote the influence and speed on the march of this IDEA. Would you defend spiritual Christianity against the assaults of its foes ? This is the sure palladium. To battle with men's creeds, to scowl at heretics, to pile uncharitable allegations on the head of the erring, to evoke the arm of coercive power, to raise a fume of popular passion—passion too largely compounded of the emotions of sickly pietists, crafty factions, and thoughtless men and children. * What ! is this the way to defend Christianity ? Can you adopt such means ? Will your *philosophy* allow you to believe that one error *can* be annihilated in this way, or that a system of love can be accelerated by the wild fury of strife ? I could as soon believe that you could break adamant by argument, as believe that the foundations of error and wrong can be broken up by such instrumentality. Will your *Christianity* allow you to believe that such means *ought* to be employed? Where in the life of Jesus, in the history of the apostles, in the genius of the system, do you find a sanction for such methods ? There is a passage which seems to me to express the spirit of the whole system on the question—a passage which I would fulminate —no, not fulminate—softly whisper in England's dinned ear at this moment—whisper in the benign accents of Him *whose voice was not heard in the street,*—it is this, BRETHREN, IF A MAN BE OVERTAKEN IN A FAULT, YE WHICH ARE SPIRITUAL RESTORE SUCH AN ONE IN THE SPIRIT OF MEEKNESS, CONSIDERING THYSELF LEST THOU ALSO BE TEMPTED.

Be it yours to draw the attention of the thoughtless masses, and point the hopes of your suffering race to the redeeming God. Lift up the idea of Peter as the great panacea for the woes of the world —"lift it up, be not afraid." Stand as the Baptist stood of old amongst the masses of your countrymen, and say, "Behold the Lamb of God which taketh away the sins of the world." Your great mission is, not to censure your brother's creed, but to save his soul.

* This was written during the No-Popery agitation.

I believe, that the man who saves one soul, does a greater good to the universe than he who would merely disorganise one of the vilest systems on earth. As the conscious self of man lives and acts more vigorously after the disorganisation of his body in death, so the vile spirit of a system may be resuscitated into new energy after its old forms have been shivered into atoms. But *save a soul,* and you crush an evil spirit—you tear up by the roots a baneful upas from the universe, and plant a germ in the garden of God, whose fruit will tend to the healing of the nations—you dry up a malarial stream, and open in this desert world a new fountain of quickening influence—you mitigate the darkness of the world, and create a new light in the moral firmament of the race—you crush a tormenting demon, and give birth to a spirit that shall ever rejoice over the repentance of sinners, and minister unto the heirs of salvation.

Matthew 16:21-23

The Sufferings, Death, and Resurrection of Christ foretold and vindicated by Himself

" *From that time forth began Jesus to show unto His disciples, how that He must go unto Jerusalem, and suffer many things of the Elders and Chief Priests and Scribes, and be killed, and be raised again the third day.*" The events which Christ here predicts as about to occur in His personal history, are events not only of vital moment to man, but of profound interest to the universe. They are things into which " *the angels desire to look ;*" they are the foundation-facts of that Gospel which makes known " *the manifold wisdom of God*" unto " *the principalities and powers in heavenly places :*"—that Gospel which to man is " *the power of God unto salvation unto every one that believeth.*"

I. THESE EVENTS ARE HERE FORETOLD BY HIMSELF TO HIS DISCIPLES. The fact that Jesus should thus lay so distinctly before the minds of His disciples the stupendous events about transpiring in His history is suggestive of at least three things :—

First : *It is suggestive of His super-humanity.* Christ gives here a specimen of His thorough knowledge of His own futurity. The scene of His sufferings, " *Jerusalem :*" the multiplicity of His sufferings, " *many things ;*" the instigators of His sufferings, " *the Elders, the Chief Priests, and the Scribes ;*" and the mortal termination of His sufferings,—His being " *killed,*" were all distinct objects in His horizon, and were all now fully laid under the notice of His disciples.

> " O suffering Friend of humankind !
> How, as the fatal hour drew near,
> Came thronging on Thy holy mind
> The images of holy fear,—

Gethsemane's sad midnight scene—
The faithless friends, the exulting foes,
The thorny crown, the insult keen—
The scourge, the cross! before Thee rose."

Yes, and what is more wonderful still, even the *fact* and *period* of His resurrection were clear to His vision. Surely such knowledge of the future of our individual life does not belong to our simple humanity. As men, an impervious veil conceals our future. We know not what shall be even on the morrow. All beyond the present, so far as our *individual* life is concerned, is black as midnight. We can see nothing. No ray falls to light the next approaching hour. But it is not the mere knowledge of His future that suggests to us the idea of His super-humanity, but the calm magnanimity with which He looked upon the stupendous events which were appoaching Him. With the nameless indignities which awaited Him at Jerusalem, the mysterious horrors that would roll their blackest clouds over His heart in Gethsemane, and the infernal assaults and tortures that would come upon Him as He hung upon the Cross, spread out in all their immensity of anguish before His eye, He was sublimely equanimous in spirit. The gathering tempest, with its sky-blackening clouds, and its wild boding winds howling about His soul, ruffled Him not. What mere man could stand calmly in the presence of such a future ? I would not have my coming year, nay, my coming week revealed ; I fear its revelation would paralyze my reason, disorganise my frame, and entirely unfit me for the duties of life.

Secondly : *It is suggestive of His voluntariness in suffering.* With such a knowledge of what awaited Him some months on in the future, could not He whose word had just hushed the storm upon the Galilean lake have escaped them ? Undoubtedly. His sufferings were not accidental, He was not the victim of iron necessity—of resistless fate. He was free. "*I have power to lay down my life and to take it again : no man taketh it from me.*"

Thirdly : *It is suggestive of His considerate kindness towards His disciples.* Why did Christ thus foretell His sufferings to His disciples ? Not, as some do, for the sake of parading His sorrows and His trials. Far from it. Great sorrows, like great loves, court silence rather than speech. Why then ? Evidently for their good. They required to have their minds disabused of certain wrong impressions which they had entertained concerning His mission. They clung to the hope that He would assume the pomp and power of worldly dominion—that as a triumphant conqueror Ho would take His sword, slay the Romans, and make Jerusalem the mistress of the world. He here disabuses their minds of these material notions. He brushes away these illusions from their brain. Still more, they required to be prepared for those wonderful events in His history, so that when they came, instead of having their faith in Him shaken by them, they would have it established, by regarding them as the fulfilment of His prediction. It was for their good that He thus foretold His future.

II. These events are here indicated by Himself to Peter. " *Then Peter took Him, and began to rebuke Him, saying, Be it far from Thee, Lord : this shall not be unto Thee. But He turned and said unto Peter, Get thee behind me, Satan, thou art an offence unto me; for thou savourest not the things that be of God, but those that be of men.*"

In this conduct of Peter and our Saviour's address to him, four things strike our attention :—

First : *The rapidity with which good men can pass from a proper to an improper mental mood.* In the preceding verses, 16–19, Peter appears in a glorious attitude of soul. He confesses Christ to be " *the Son of the living God;*" for which Christ pronounces him blessed, inasmuch as he had been instructed by the Father, had grasped the foundation-truth on which the true Church was to be built, and was now invested with the key to unlock the great kingdom of grace and truth. But here this same Peter passes almost at once into a spiritual mood in which Christ denounces him as an adversary. Now it is true that Peter had a peculiarly impulsive nature, his transitions were rapid and extreme ; in a momen he could pass from the equator to the pole, in feeling. Albeit, to such changes we are all more or less exposed in this life; we are now on the mount of hope, and now in the vale of despondency ; now glowing with affection, now cold in indifference ; now valiant and now timid. Yet inasmuch as these improper mental states are not cherished, they are rather as bubbles raised on the stream by the outward breeze, than plants growing naturally out of the soil.

Another thing which strikes our attention in Christ's conduct with Peter is :—

Secondly : *The equal readiness of Christ to mark both the proper and improper in the conduct of His people.* The voice which blessed Peter when in the proper mood, denounced him now. It is mercy in both. To chastise the wrong in us is as useful as to commend the right. But what was there in Peter's conduct to call forth this apparently severe reprehension ? (1) *There was an arrogant irreverence.* Peter took Him, probably, by the hand,* and began to " *rebuke Him.*" It would seem as if Peter had been so elated with the benediction which Christ had pronounced upon him, and the commission He had entrusted to him, in the preceding verses, that he had forgotten himself, forgotten the position he really occupied. He rebuked Christ! What arrogancy! The torch censuring the sun. (2) *There was a culpable ignorance.* " *That be far from Thee.*" Far from Him, Peter! Why, for this He came into the world. If these things are not to occur to Him, hell forthwith must open her fiery jaws and swallow thee up, yea, thy race as well! " *O fools, and slow of heart to believe,*" &c. (3) *There was false sympathy.* We must do Peter the justice of supposing that something like com-

---

* Προσλαβόμενος αὐτόν. This controverted passage is best interpreted, " Taking Him by the hand," an action naturally accompanying advice, remonstrance, or censure.—*Bloomfield.*

passion for Christ prompted this. But Christ is no object of compassion. He does_not suffer against His will. Whether the Cross is on His shoulders or He is on the Cross, He is not an object for pity. Sentimental tears of compassion He repudiates as out of place, not required, and even offensive. " *Weep not for me,*" &c. In His deepest agony, He is an object for praise, not pity—commendation, not commiseration. He suffered not as a helpless victim, but as a free and an almighty champion.

Another thing which strikes our attention in Christ's conduct to Peter is :—

Thirdly : *The character we should regard as acting a Satan to the soul.* " *But He turned and said unto Peter, Get thee behind me, Satan, for thou art an offence unto me : for thou savourest not the things that be of God, but those that be of men.*" Mark says, that He "*turned about and looked at His disciples.*" What a look ! What mingled feelings were in that flashing glance ! What unutterable meaning and mystic force that *look* threw into those words of withering rebuke—" *Get thee behind me, Satan.*"

Σατανᾶς signifies an evil adviser, an adversary ; and as such Peter now acted, and Christ, with characteristic honesty, denounces his conduct as offensive and Satanic. Mark well the moral of this. He who gives us advice to tempt us from the path of duty, however attached to us and however friendly his motives, is a *Satan to us in that act*. Nay, his Satanic power over us is in proportion to his love. The ill-advice of an enemy is the devil without power.

> " 'Tis love that makes the tempter strong,
> And wings his thoughts into the heart."

The devil is never so strong as when he works through the affections of a tender mother, a noble father, a brave brother, a beautiful sister, a generous lover. Let us learn to say, even to the most loving and the most loved, when they seek from a false affection to turn us from a noble path of usefulness and duty, because it taxes so much our energies and demands from us such sacrifices, " *Get thee behind me, Satan.*" Brother, keep Satan in the rear, and leave him farther and farther behind, until the impassable gulf of eternity shall lie between !

Another thing which strikes our attention in Christ's conduct with Peter is :—

Fourthly : *The supreme work of human life.* What is it ? Devotedness to " *the things of God.*" " *Thou savourest not the things that be of God, but those that be of men.*" The views of Peter savoured of selfish ease and power. Such were not the things of God, which are self-sacrificing love, unswerving truthfulness, and supreme sympathy with the infinitely good. What are the things of God ? " *Whatsoever things are true, whatsoever things are honest, whatsoever things are just, whatsoever things are pure, whatsoever things are lovely, whatsoever things are of good report :*"—such are the things that be of God, and he is our Satan who seeks to turn us from them.

Matthew 16:24-28

*The Three Great Valuables—the World, the Soul, and Christ-like
Love*

Amongst the many great things which Christ refers to in this
passage there are three to which I would specially invite your
attention :—The *World*—the *Soul*—and *Christ-like Love.* The first
is great, the second is greater, and the last, for many reasons which
will hereafter appear, is greater than either.

The World is great. All men, though for very different reasons,
are impressed with its greatness. It is great to the poet, whose
imagination glows in the presence of its scenes of enchanting
beauty and aspects of stirring grandeur. It is great to the
philosopher, who in every step of his research is amazed with the
subtlety of its elements, the regularity of its operations, the fitness
of its means to its ends, and the boundless variety of its combinations and its life. It is great to the Christian, who feels its moral
significance, regards it as vocal with the thoughts, overflowing with
the goodness, filled with the presence, and radiant with the majesty,
of the Great Father of all. It is *great* even to the miserable worldling. He navigates its oceans, traverses its shores, cultivates its
soils, and works its mines, in order to appropriate to himself as
much of its treasures as is possible. In the language of Christ, he
seeks to "gain the world." The world is great.

The Soul is greater. Christ distinctly teaches this in the passage
before us. "What shall a man give in exchange for his soul?"
The word which is translated "soul," in one of the verses under
notice, is translated "life" in others. It would seem that our
translators regarded the terms as convertible; and so they are. The
soul is man's life. Take that essence from us which we call soul,
that which thinks, feels, recalls the past, and anticipates the future,
which reproves of sin, makes us tremble sometimes at death, and
turn pale when we think of the crimes we have committed and the
retributive judgment that is coming on : take, I say, this soul from
us, and we cease to be men ;—we are brutes, nothing else. In Luke,
the idea that the soul is the man is fully expressed, and instead of
the phrase "lose his soul" we have "lose *himself."* To lose the
soul, then, is to all intents and purposes to lose one's self. Now, this
soul is greater than the world. The world cannot think of its
Creator, the soul can ; the world cannot act contrary to the will of
its Creator, the soul can ; the world will not exist for ever, the soul
will. Ancient philosophy and modern science encourage the belief
in Peter's declaration concerning the destruction of the world :
"The heavens shall pass away with a great noise," &c. As a leaf
this planet shall fall from the great forest of existence ; as a passing
cloud in the sky it shall melt into thin air. But the soul has an
imperishable existence.

> " This spirit shall return to Him
> That gave its heavenly spark ;
> Yet think not, Sun, it shall be dim
> When thou thyself art dark !
> For it shall live again and shine
> In bliss unknown to beams of thine ;
> By Him recalled to breath,
> Who captive led captivity,
> Who robbed the grave of victory,
> And took the sting from death ! "—CAMPBELL.

O brother, however feeble thy talent or humble thy world's position, thou art greater than the globe beneath thy feet or the great stars that roll above thee.

Christ-like Love is greater than either. " If any man will come after me, let him deny himself, and take up his cross and follow me." Here is a material representation of a spiritual principle. It does not mean, of course, that we are literally to "take up the cross ; " but that we are to be swayed by the same principle of action as that which led Christ to take up the cross. *There must be an identity of moral disposition.* The question is, What was the principle that induced Christ to endure such ignominy and suffering? He could have avoided all this ; He could have appeared in more than royal affluence and splendour. What influenced Him otherwise ? Here is the philosophy :—" Ye know the grace of the Lord Jesus Christ," &c. The principle of self-denial is often enforced from pulpits, but seldom rationally and scripturally explained. It is popularly supposed that it is the principle that prompts us to give up one good in order to obtain another, and a higher ; to give up the world in order to get *heaven.* This is selfishness in its most iniquitous form. What is it then ? It is that sympathy with the claims of God and His universe which makes us delightfully oblivious of all mere personal considerations. Christian self-denial is not painful but pleasant ; it is not slavery but freedom. Christ's "yoke is easy." The greatest happiness of moral beings is in *loving.* And the greatest happiness of loving is giving. The sweetest thrill of pleasure springs from the greatest sacrifice of love. How happy is the affectionate mother, when ministering to her sweet suffering infant the produce of her hard earnings. Her nights of refreshing sleep, all her personal comforts, she sacrifices with a hearty pleasure, in order to soothe the anguish of her afflicted babe. The martyr throws his life upon the flame in song.

Now this Christ-like love, which sacrifices the material to the spiritual, the personal to the universal, from an overflowing love to God and His creation, *is true religion, and nothing else is.* It was " the love of Christ," the Christ-like affection that *constrained* Paul, that was in truth His inspiration ; and this Christ teaches, by inference, *is greater than either the world or the soul.*

The passage leads us to make four remarks in relation to the *greatness* of this principle :—

I. THAT OUR SAFE RELATION TO CHRIST DEPENDS UPON THE POS-

SESSION OF THIS CHRIST-LIKE LOVE. "If any man will come after me, let him deny himself, and take up his cross;"—*Let him have the principle, that will qualify him to do that which I am doing.* Two remarks will illustrate this proposition:—

First: *That our everlasting well-being depends upon following Christ.* Unless we follow Him, act as He acted in relation to God and man, we must inevitably fail of a happy destiny. He is the only perfect example, the only safe guide;—there is no other way to blessedness but that which He trod. "No man can come unto the Father but by me."

Secondly: *That without the love that influenced Him we cannot follow Him.* Indeed we cannot *understand* Him without it. Love alone understands love. Where there is no love in the heart, there is no eye to see the forms and manifestations of love without. For the want of this, the world understood not Christ and His apostles. Moreover, without this, we cannot be *attracted* by Him; for those who have not this love, He has no charms. "He is to them a root out of a dry ground." The magnetic force of His character can only act upon kindred souls. Indeed, without this love, you have not a foundation on which a Christian character can be built; not a soil on which a Christian character can grow. Human virtues, since the Fall, have never grown elsewhere.

II. THAT THE WORTH OF OUR EXISTENCE ITSELF DEPENDS UPON THE POSSESSION OF THIS CHRIST-LIKE LOVE. "Whosoever will save his life shall lose it; and whosoever will lose his life for my sake, shall find it." To lose this life or soul, does not mean, of course, to lose its *existence—consciousness or moral obligations.* All this would seem impossible—but to lose its *well-being*—to lose all that makes its existence worth having. The idea does not seem to me to be, that he who sacrifices his bodily life shall secure his spiritual life, and *vice versâ;* but that he who seeks his own happiness from *selfish* considerations in life, will lose it: whilst he who from love to God and man—*Christ-like* love, forgets himself in the great cause of piety and benevolence, will secure the blessedness of his being. This is an undeniable truth. The laws of our nature render it impossible for a selfish man to be happy. Happiness can never come by seeking it as an end. (1) Moral approbation is necessary to happiness. Where conscience does not approve, can there be any blessedness? Impossible. But conscience never has said, never can say, "Well done" to a selfish purpose, a selfish act, still less to a selfish life. (2) The approbation of others is essential to happiness. The consciousness of *being loved* is an element of gladness. But whilst society may flatter a selfish man, it can never love him. (3) The approbation of God is essential to a happy life. His "well done" is indispensable. "In Thy presence," &c. But He never has approved, and never will approve, of a selfish life. (4) The harmonious development of our spiritual powers is essential to a happy life. But this can never take place under the government of selfishness.

It is an eternal law, therefore, that Christ here propounds. The soul that seeketh happiness as its end, is like a man seeking to grasp his shadow; the swifter he runs the swifter runs the shadow. Thus, if we would be happy, we must *repeat in our own life the sacrifice of Christ;* we must give up ourselves to the common cause of benevolence. Indeed, unless *we* thus sacrifice, His sacrifice is worthless; unless we give *ourselves,* His giving Himself is of no avail to us. He *alone* understands and appropriates the sacrifice of Christ who has thus sacrificed Himself.

III. THAT THE VALUE OF THE WORLD TO US IS MEASURED BY THIS CHRIST-LIKE LOVE. "What is a man profited, if he shall gain the whole world, and lose his own soul?" &c. There are three remarks suggested here:—

First : *The possession of the whole world would be useless without this.* Avaricious men are constantly striving to gain as much of the world as possible; but though a few sometimes gain much in comparison with what others have, the greatest possessor holds but a fraction of its vast treasures. But take the supposition; invest a selfish man, or a man destitute of this Christ-like love, with the whole world: Is he happy? No; it has only increased his anxieties, augmented his responsibilities, pampered his appetites, carnalized his nature.

Secondly : *Nothing in the universe would be of any real service without this.* "What shall a man give in exchange for his soul?"—his happiness? The whole universe of God is of no avail without it.

Thirdly : *With it, you really gain the world, and secure the soul.* With this love everything is valuable to man; and in a true and glorious sense, everything belongs to him. "The world is yours, all things are yours."

IV. THAT THE DAY OF JUDGMENT WILL MANIFEST THE IMPORTANCE OF POSSESSING THIS CHRIST-LIKE LOVE. "For the Son of Man shall come in His glory," &c. He will come in overwhelming glory, come to wind up the affairs of the globe, come to raise the dead, to judge the world, "to render unto every man according to his works." Now, if you will refer to a representation of the Day of Judgment, contained in the 25th chapter of Matthew, you will find that the everlasting destiny of all on that day will be determined by the possession or non-possession of this principle. "Inasmuch as ye did it (*or* as ye did it not) to one of the least of these my brethren, ye did it (*or* ye did it not) to me."

> " No work shall find acceptance on that day,
> When all disguises shall be swept away,
> That square not truly with the Scripture plan,
> Nor spring from love to God, or love to man."—COWPER.

Christ tells them that they would have a display of His glory, even before the Day of Judgment; nay, that such a manifestation was just at hand: "*Verily I say unto you, there be some standing* *here which shall not taste of death till they see the Son of Man coming in His kingdom.*" Most probably the transfiguration which was about to take place, and which Peter, James, and John would witness, is referred to here.* Peter speaks of that illustrious event as "*the power and coming of our Lord Jesus Christ.*"

Mark then, brother, well the fact, that this Christ-like love is thy chief good. Without it, thou canst not "follow" Him one step, who is the only true guide of thy being; without it, thy soul, thyself is *lost*—lost to virtue, to usefulness, to true felicity, and to God; without it, even the world itself, couldst thou possess it, would conduce nothing to thy real enjoyment; it would only be as music to the deaf, beauty to the blind, luxury and liberty to the paralytic; without it, the approaching day of judgment will be a terrible day for thee. Get, then, into thy soul this principle; it is the life of Christ; it is the soul of goodness; it is the philosophy of the universe; it is the inspiration of God. There abideth then these three:—the world, the soul, and Christ-like love; but the greatest of these three is *love*. The world is nothing without the soul, and the soul is nothing without love. Fill thy soul with love, and thou wilt fill thy universe with all that is good and glorious.

> " The soul, whose sight all-quickening love renews,
> Taketh the semblance of the good she views ;
> As diamonds, stripped of their opaque disguise,
> Reflect the noon-day glory of the skies."

Matthew 17:1-8

Transfiguration; the Visions and Voices of Christianity

Redeemed men from heaven and redeemed men on earth here meet, on one of Palestine's mountains, the glorious Redeemer of both. Whether Tabor, so eloquently described by Stanley,† or

---

* Reference may be made to the fall of Jerusalem, and to John as a survivor. The destruction of the temple removed the great impediment in the way of the Christian dispensation, as the ritual of Moses could no longer be observed.—*See Webster and Wilkinson.*

† " This strange and beautiful mountain is distinguished alike in form and in character from all around it. As seen, where it is usually first seen by the traveller, from the north-west of the plain, it towers like a dome ; as seen from the east, like a long-arched mound, over the monotonous undulations of the surrounding hills, from which it stands completely isolated, except by a narrow neck of rising ground, uniting it to the mountain range of Galilee. It was not what Europeans would call a wooded hill, because its trees stand all apart from each other. But it is so thickly studded with them as to rise from the plain like a mass of verdure. Its sides much resemble the scattered glades in the outskirts of the New Forest. Its summit, a broken oblong, is an alternation of shade and greensward, that seems made for national festivity ; broad and varied, and commanding wide views of the plain from end to end."

the southern slope of Hermon, hard by Cæsarea Philippi, was the scene of this wonderful meeting, I am neither competent nor anxious to decide. We would not have the haze of mystery, which conceals the exact locality of this mountain, blown away by the breeze of certitude; this would only add a new impulse to the superstitious tendencies of humanity.

The apparent discrepancy between the account as to time which Luke gives of this wonderful meeting, and that presented by Matthew and Mark, is easily disposed of. Luke includes in his "eight days" both the day from which the event is dated—namely, the prediction in the last verse of the preceding chapter—and the day of the ascent into the mountain. The other evangelists do not include these two days in their calculation, and hence the difference.

Very diversified are the views which have been propounded in relation to the scene. Some regard it as a record of *sensuous illusions*—the visions were optical deceptions, and the voices, too, were only fancies of the ear. The imagination, highly excited by the strange circumstances of the hour, exerted an unnatural influence upon the hearing ear and the seeing eye. Some regard it as a record of *mental visions*—the whole had no objective or outward existence, the scenes and sounds were perceptions of the mind. The whole was a dream. This supposition, if the vision is regarded as a Divine production, does not destroy the reality of the scene. No vision is so real to man as a mental one. But the fact that all the disciples had the same vision is fatal to the hypothesis. Some regard it as a *mythical fabrication*—it is to be classed, not with the verities of history, but with the fables of a fabulous age. It is fiction, not fact. The historical air of the whole record repudiates such an unfounded notion. Others regard it as the record of a *historical fact*. In this view all the most competent and acknowledged critics agree. But though a fact, it is in a sense an allegory. God's allegories are not like the allegories of men; they are founded upon actual occurrences, not upon mental inventions.

We shall take the narrative to illustrate some of the chief VISIONS and VOICES with which Christianity favours its genuine disciples.

I. THE VISIONS. There are three visions here : Christ ; the departed good ; and the manifestation of God.

First: *Here is a vision of Christ.* He was transfigured before them. "The verb μετεμορφώθη," here rendered, "*was transfigured*," says Bengel, "implies that our Lord always possessed the glory within Himself." "*His raiment became shining, exceeding white as snow, so as no fuller on earth can white them.*" "*His face did shine as the sun, and His raiment was white as the light.*" Up to this point in His history the glory of His divinity seemed to be enshrouded by His suffering humanity. For the most part He had been hitherto seen as the "*man of sorrows and acquainted with grief,*" but now divinity burst into effulgence.

This glorious manifestation would serve to impress the disciples with the unmistakable divinity of His nature ; with the illustrious majesty with which He will appear for ever in the celestial world in the midst of the universal church ; and with the idea of the change which would be wrought in themselves on the resurrection morning, when their "*vile bodies would be fashioned and made like unto His own glorious body.*"

Secondly : *Here is a vision of departed saints.* Moses, Israel's great lawgiver, and Elijah, its most illustrious seer ;—representatives of the "*law and the prophets.*" Many centuries had run their course since the unknown grave in "*the valley of Moab*" closed upon the body of the illustrious lawgiver ; and also since the prophet of sublime intrepidity, without seeing death, ascended to heaven in "*the chariot of fire and the horses of fire.*" But these centuries had not impaired their energies, nor weakened their interest in earth. They are here on this mountain now ; here, perhaps, as the representatives of those myriads of the Old Church who had reached their celestial homes. The beauty and the excellency of Christianity are, that it reveals to us the existence of the *departed good.* We are left in no suspense on the subject. It opens the doors of heaven, and shows us "*the great multitude which no man can number,*" &c.

Thirdly : *Here we have a vision of Divine glory.* "*The cloud overshadowed them.*" This was the well-known, the usual, and expressive symbol of the Divine presence and glory. It gleamed in the sword of the cherubim at the gate of Eden ; it flashed on Sinai ; it lighted the Israelites through the Wilderness, across the Red Sea into the Promised Land ; it often filled the tabernacle with its mystic radiance ; shone for ages over the mercy-seat ; and like a strange star it glided through the heavens, and guided the wise men to Bethlehem, where the King of the Jews was born. Now it lighted up the mountain in a blaze. It was the manifestation of the Divine glory. Christianity, however, gives us a more real and full display of the Divine glory. *It gives the incarnation of Himself.* "*The brightness of His glory.*"

II. The Voices of Christianity. "*And there appeared unto them Elias with Moses, and they were talking with Jesus,*" &c.

First : *Here is a voice of social converse.* "*They were talking with Jesus.*" What was the great theme ? Luke tells us ;—"*The decease which He should accomplish at Jerusalem.*" They call death a "*decease,*" which means, not a destruction, but a departure—not an extinction, but an exit. Christ's "decease" at Jerusalem, or the Cross, is the great central truth of revelation—that which gives unity, life, worth, to the whole. Take this fact from the Bible, and you take the foundation-stone from the superstructure, leaving ruins ; the soul from the body, leaving a putrid carcase ; the sun from the system, leaving blackness and chaos. The Cross is the great theme of discourse between the good in all worlds ; it is the chorus in heaven's anthems ; it is the key to interpret all the mysteries in the moral empire of God.

Secondly: *Here is a voice of Divine affection.* "*A voice came out of the cloud, saying, This is my beloved Son,*" &c. This utterance reveals the glorious fact that the Creator *loves;* He is neither insensitive nor malevolent, He *feels;*—and His feeling is *love.* And the utterance reveals, moreover, the *object* that has undoubted claims to universal love. Whatever the Creator loves most, demands the paramount affection of the creature. This object is Christ. "*The Father loveth the Son.*" God loves Christ, let man love Him too; and then the Divine heart will meet and mingle with the human, and man and God be one in Christ. Since this utterance from heaven has been made, no one need be in doubt as to what object should be supremely loved, nor need any wonder at the terrible words of the Apostle, who says, "*If any man love not the Lord Jesus Christ let him be Anathema Maran-atha.*"

Thirdly: *Here is a voice of imperative duty.* "*Hear Him.*" He who at sundry times and in divers manners spake in times past unto the fathers by the prophets, is now in "*these last days*" to speak unto us by His Son. Moses and the prophets, who had hitherto been the only authoritative organs, must now retire into a secondary place. This voice would undoubtedly remind Moses of the voice that descended on his soul in the solitariness of the desert many centuries before: "*The Lord thy God will raise up unto thee a prophet from the midst of thee, of thy brethren, like unto me; unto Him ye shall hearken.*" "*Hear Him.*" He is the oracle, the prophet, the lawgiver. Test everything by His utterances. The deductions of reason, the traditions of the past, the pronouncements even of evangelical ministers, ay, and even the statements of Moses and the prophets, must be tested by His word. Whatever agrees not with His *dicta* must be repudiated without compromise, denounced without mercy. Ye men of inquiring thought, "*Beware lest any man spoil you through philosophy and vain deceit, after the traditions of men, after the rudiments of the world, and not after Christ.*" And ye thoughtless millions take heed that ye "*Refuse not Him that speaketh. For if they escaped not who refused Him who spake on earth, much more shall not we escape if we turn away from Him that speaketh from heaven; whose voice then shook the earth, but now He hath promised, saying, Yet once more I shake not the earth only but also heaven.*"

There are three remarks which we shall now offer upon these VISIONS AND VOICES.

First: *That their appreciation requires a true Christian discipleship.* Of all the millions of men on earth, of all the disciples, there were but three that Christ honoured with this wonderful scene:—Peter, James, and John—the sons of thunder and the man of rock. Mark says, emphatically, "*that He suffered no man to follow Him,*" but these three. The reason why Christ selected only three of His disciples and no more, and these three rather than any of the others, does not appear; but the reason why He selected *disciples* rather than others is obvious enough. They alone were morally qualified to appreciate and enjoy the scene. "*The carnal mind discerneth not the things of the Spirit.*" There is an ear for moral voices, there is an eye for moral visions.

The world is full of these Divine voices and visions; the mount of transfiguration is only a specimen of what holy souls may find on every spot of the globe. Let the moral ear be opened, let the moral eye be unsealed, and the world will blaze with the radiance, and echo with the voices, of the Transfiguration. The presence of these disciples on this occasion, and no others, significantly proclaims the fact that none but His disciples will be admitted to the enjoyment of His fellowship and glory in the heavenly world. "*He is to be admired in His saints.*"

Another remark which we will offer on these VISIONS AND VOICES is :—

Secondly : *That their impression upon the disciples was very deep.* Peter was entranced. "*He wist not what to say;*" and in the mysterious ecstasy of his emotions, he exclaims, "*Lord, it is good to be here: if Thou wilt, let us make three tabernacles, one for Thee, and one for Moses, and one for Elias.*" He felt himself very near heaven. The disciples never forgot this impression. John wrote afterwards and said, "*we beheld His glory;*" and Peter too, after the lapse of many years, writes of what he heard and saw upon "*the holy mount.*" It must have been truly delightful for them to have felt themselves in the presence of that Moses whose wondrous history in the wilderness they had read in childhood; with that Elijah who had thundered in the ear of a corrupt age, opened the windows of heaven, and wrought many illustrious deeds of marvel and of love; and with that Christ now more glorious than they had ever beheld Him before. If there is such rapture as this on this cold earth with Christ, with only two of His perfected saints, and death still awaiting Him, what must be the joy of being with Him for ever amidst the countless myriads of His redeemed ones?

Another remark which we shall offer on these VISIONS AND VOICES is :—

Thirdly : *That their suggestiveness to every Christian student is very great.* Many glorious truths are suggested by this incident—we can only specify a few. (1) *It suggests the conscious existence of departed men.* The fact that Moses and Elijah now appeared shows that those who have left this world, not only exist, but exist in the conscious exercise of all their powers. (2) *It suggests the glory of the resurrection body of the good.* That body of Christ, which now coruscated in every part with the bright rays of heavenly splendour, is the model after which our "*vile bodies*" shall be formed. (3) *It suggests the fact that centralizes all redeemed souls together.* The death of Christ is that fact. (4) *It suggests the necessity of special revelation from God to qualify for special trial.* These three disciples had to go down to Gethsemane, &c. (5) *It suggests the sublime joys of the celestial world.* "*To be with Christ,*" &c.

Matthew 17:9-13

Divine Prudence in Teaching, and Human Mistakes in Learning

As Luke ix. 37 tells us that Christ and His three disciples did not descend the mount until the next day, it is highly probable that the transfiguration itself occurred during the night;—a circumstance which would heighten the solemn sublimity of the event. The conversation which now took place between Christ and His disciples, as recorded in the passage above, leads us to consider two important subjects:—*Divine Prudence in Teaching, and Human Mistakes in Learning.*

I. DIVINE PRUDENCE IN TEACHING. Jesus charged them, saying, " *Tell the vision to no man, until the Son of Man be risen again from the dead.*" This is not the only time in which we find the Heavenly Teacher indicating the expediency of silence on certain questions and events for a certain time. In the 20th verse of the preceding chapter, He charges His disciples that they should " *tell no man that He was Jesus the Christ;* " and also in His last discourse with His disciples He distinctly says (John xvi. 12), " *I have yet many things to say unto you, but ye cannot bear them now.*" Moreover, in His commission to His disciples to teach, He declared in the most impressive manner that His truths were not to be presented to men of certain mental and moral habitudes ; to present His doctrines to some men would only be to lay " *pearls before swine.*" The principle taught in these and such-like representations of Christ is that in teaching humanity, *God deals out truth only as men are able to receive it.*

Two thoughts may throw some light upon the reason of the prohibition to publish the transfiguration. (1) *The transfiguration, unless received as a proof of Christ's Messiahship, would answer no practical purpose amongst men.* The past conduct of the Scribes and Pharisees, and the people over whom they had such power, made it evident that if the disciples were to proclaim what they had seen and heard on the mountain the previous night, instead of accepting the statement in good faith, and taking it as proof of Christ's Messiahship, they would only turn it into factious quibbles, scorn, and ridicule. Evil, therefore, rather than good, would come out of its publication. (2) *After His resurrection from the dead, the transfiguration, viewed in connexion with the whole of His marvellous life, would come with well-nigh irresistible proof in favour of His Messiahship.* In the light of the crowning fact of His resurrection, all the facts of His previous life, even the most apparently trivial, would start up as incontrovertible evidence, and declare Him to be " *the Son of God with power.*" Isolated facts of His life, viewed separately, might be quibbled about and sophistically argued away ; but link them all together and join them to His resurrection, and as evidence they become omnipotent. His resurrection was a sun-fact that lighted up the whole of His previous life with the rays of supernaturalness. Hence, when Peter proclaimed it on the day of Pentecost, thousands, who before regarded Him as an impostor and blasphemer, bowed with penitential reverence to Him as the mighty Son of God. We see, therefore, good reason for the injunction, "*Tell the vision to no man, until the Son of Man be risen again from the dead.*"

But this prudential method of teaching observed by Christ, seems to me only a specimen of the plan of instruction pursued by the great "*Father of lights*" in training humanity.

In *scientific relations*, you can observe this order. One fact will not be revealed until others occur. Very gradually are the great facts of nature made known. The great Book of Science, "*written within and on the backside, sealed with seven seals*," is not laid open at once to nature's inquiring pupil. One seal is broken ; and when the contents of the unfolded document has word by word been deciphered and understood—which work may take millenniums— another seal will be broken, and thus on for ever. To the men of science the Heavenly Teacher says, "*I have yet many things to say unto you, but ye cannot bear them now.*" Yes, "*many things !*" We feel this when we remark the progress which science has made during the last few years. "Although," says one of our ablest scientific writers, "there are thousands of years on the records of the world, our Bacon, who first taught the true way to investigate nature, lived but the other day. Newton followed him, and illustrated his precepts by the most sublime discoveries which one man has ever made. Harvey detected the circulation of the blood only two hundred years ago. Adam Smith, Dr. Black, and James Watt, were friends; and the last, whose steam-engines are now changing the relations of empires, may be said to be scarcely cold in his grave. John Hunter died not long ago ; and Herschell's accounts of newly-discovered planets, and of the sublime structure of the heavens, are in the late numbers of our scientific journals. Illustrious Britons these! who have left worthy successors treading in their steps. On the continent of Europe, during the same period, a corresponding constellation of genius has shone, and Laplace is now the bright star connecting the future with the past."

In *religious revelations*, you can observe the order still more clearly. Four thousand long years were occupied in bringing the religious intellect of the world on to the full revelation of the Christian system. Through long generations Christianity remained a hidden mystery.

This method of Divine teaching (1) *arises from the necessity of finite mind.* It is only gradually and slowly that man can get knowledge. We must in all departments learn the alphabet before we can read; the first principles must be learnt before we can advance to the science. This method of Divine teaching (2) *suggests the ever-heightening blessedness of true disciples.* New revelations will appear in succession for ever;—as one volume mastered becomes obsolete to the soul, another will come challenging its attention. So on through ceaseless ages.

The other subject in this passage is :—

II. HUMAN MISTAKES IN LEARNING. "*And His disciples asked Him, saying, Why then say the Scribes that Elias must first come?*" Let us notice the *nature*, the *cause*, and the *evil*, of the mistake here recorded.

First : *The nature of their mistake.* The error was not in supposing that the advent of Elias would precede the mission of the Messiah. This supposition was true, and founded in Scripture. "The Scribes" were right in maintaining this ; and Jesus Himself admits the accuracy of the opinion when He says, "*Elias truly shall first come, and restore all things.*" Though the transfiguration seems to have convinced the three disciples of Christ's Messiahship, they still felt a difficulty, inasmuch as, according to the doctrine of the Scribes, Elias, who was to herald the Messiah, had not appeared. "If Thou art the Messiah, as we believe Thou art, where is the Elijah of whom the Scribes speak as Thy forerunner?" This seems to have been the thought. The mistake of the Scribes was in supposing that the identical Elijah of the Old Testament, who went to heaven in "*the chariot of fire,*" would reappear in order to introduce the Messiah ; whereas all that the prophecy in Malachi (iv. 5, 6) meant was, that a man of the *same spirit* as Elijah would appear. John the Baptist was, in spirit, that prophet. The mistake was twofold;—the misinterpretation of a Scripture, and the forgetfulness of a fact. The Scripture was that which referred to the coming of Elias, and the fact was the life of John the Baptist. That wonderful life which spoke in thunder, and wrought heroically amongst them, and which had just closed, they had forgotten.

Secondly : *The cause of their mistake.* The cause of the mistake may be said to consist (1) *In applying a wrong principle of interpretation to Scripture.* They "*judged after the flesh;*" they gave a material and literal interpretation to a spiritual fact figuratively expressed. (2) *In neglecting to read Scripture in the light of current events.* If they had brought the Scriptures down to every-day life, they would have seen that the extraordinary man, who, upon the banks of the Jordan, called the nation to repentance, pointed to the appearance of a higher teacher, and thus prepared the way for Christ, was indeed the predicted Elijah. Men commit this error now with the Bible ; they interpret by the light of their preconceived notions and theological standard, and not by the light of human life. It is only as we look at the Bible in the light of our own intuitions, deep spiritual wants, aspirations, experiences, current events, that we get at its living import.

Thirdly : *The evil of their mistake.* What was the evil the mistake led to? The abuse of existing mercies. They were looking for some one to come bearing the name of Elijah, and at the same time abused him who had the spirit of Elijah. "*I say unto you, that Elias is come already, and they knew him not, but have done unto him whatsoever they listed.*" Technical religionists are ever acting this foolish and wicked part; they are ever sighing after future good, and abusing the present. But the part these Scribes had acted towards John they were now acting towards Christ. They were looking for some one answering to their notions of the Messiah they found in the Scriptures, while the true Messiah was amongst them, and they were ill-using Him; "*Likewise shall also the Son of Man suffer of them.*"

Matthew 17:14-21

The Wants of the World, and the Weakness of the Church

There is a touching interest in this narrative. It is a scene where opposite sympathies play their part with all the simplicity of nature, and the fascination of charm. Christ has just descended from the Mount of Transfiguration. The mystic lustre perhaps still lingers around His person. Peter, James, and John, who on the quiet hill had witnessed the ecstatic vision, are at His side: they meet a turbulent multitude on the way, and the other disciples are in their midst. One of their number, a father, is the object of general notice and common sympathy. He has a son, the subject of a malady under whose paroxysms he foams and tears himself, seeking self-destruction by attempting to plunge into the fire, and sometimes into the water. The unhappy father bends his knee to Christ, and earnestly prays for help. The disciples had tried their power, and failed, and the Scribes and Pharisees are exultant at their non-success. With their wonted uncharitableness and hate, they seize, perhaps, the failure as another opportunity to denounce them and their Master as impostors, and to turn upon them the contempt of the multitude. Christ reproves them in language breathing the mingled feelings of indignation and tenderness. He orders the father to bring his lunatic son into His presence, and demands of him personal faith as the necessary condition of cure. The son appears; the condition is met; and the disease is forthwith removed. Humbled by their failure, the disciples approach Jesus apart from the multitude, and inquire why they could not cast him out. The significant reply is, "*Because of your unbelief.*"

Such is the short but wonderful piece of history before us. It comes not within our plan here to investigate the nature of the malady to which the young man was subject,* nor to reconcile formal discrepancies, which the critical eye of a sceptical mind may

---

* Let those who desire to go philosophically into the question study the thoughts of the great Neander on demoniacal possession, given in his " Life of Christ."

discover between the histories of the different evangelists. All this would necessarily occupy considerable space, and draw the mind too far into the region of logic and letters for spiritual and practical ends. We shall use the narrative to illustrate a subject which presses heavily on our hearts, and urgently claims the attention of all earnest men. The subject is, *The wants of the world, and the weakness of the church.*

In making this application of the scene before us, we would, at the outset, disclaim all sympathy with the practice of "spiritualizing" God's word—a practice which we regard as violating all acknowledged laws of interpretation—ministering to the most morbid sentiments of the human soul—spreading a mystic haze over the book of sublimest reason, and thus clouding the light of the world. All we do is, use the narrative as Jesus used the flowing wells, the fruitful vineyards, and the fields of waving corn —make it the organ through which to speak great truths to human hearts.

The first truth is,—

I. THAT THE WORLD REQUIRES A GREAT WORK FROM THE CHURCH. It was no trivial request that the father of this raving demoniac made upon the disciples. To remove the enraging malady—or, if you will, to exorcise the furious fiend that had gained an absolute mastery over all the faculties and organs of his son, to restore him to physical health and mental sanity, and make his existence once more a blessing to himself and a comfort to his family—was a work warranting all the earnest solicitude which the father had displayed. But greater, far greater, than this is the work which the world requires of the church. To say that the world is possessed of *devils*—that men are moral demoniacs—is not showy rhetoric, but solemn Scripture. Judged by the everlasting laws of moral reason, the conduct of the world is as reckless and irrational as that of the miserable lunatic who foams and raves, and, in frantic madness, plunges into perils. The *moral* fiends that possess its soul, inspire its energies, and direct its movements, are conspicuously manifest. They are not like the "horses and chariots of fire round about Elisha" on the mountains of Dothan, seen by none but the prophet—they are visible to all.

Let me mention two or three of the most potent and prominent of the *evil spirits* that possess society.

There is *selfishness.* This is a corruption of self-love—a principle prompting men to act ever from personal consideration—to make self the centre and circumference of all plans and operations. A selfish man is one who holds all interests cheap in comparison with his own; who receives readily but gives reluctantly, unless it be with the hope of the donation flowing back with interest to his own coffers. He views all questions in their aspect upon himself. "Loss and gain" are the fundamentals of his moral system. He weighs everlasting principles in the balance of lucre, and all is visionary and Utopian—chaff that tells not in the scales. The labourer may toil and sweat—the shopman wear away his health—the mariner hazard his existence—the warrior dye continents in blood, and tread empires in the dust;—compunction he has none, if results are favourable to his interests. Such is selfishness; and is it not the presiding genius of the world—the very mainspring of society—producing and perpetuating the motion of almost every wheel?

There, again, is *sensualism.* The apostle divides mankind into two classes—the "carnal" and the "spiritual." The great distinction between them in their relation to the body is this: the spiritual attends to fleshly appetites *as the necessities of his nature,* the carnal *as the sources of his pleasure.* If seeking pleasure from the senses is carnality, how fearfully prevalent is it! "Fleshly lusts," not spiritual impulses, move, mould, and master the bulk of the race. Esau's appetites governed his conscience, impelled him to barter away his birthright for a mess of pottage, and reduced him to beggary and tears. In his foolish conduct you have a picture of the world; in his wretched destiny you may read its doom. Amongst savage hordes, and in rural districts where education has not gone to wake the intellect to thought, and to touch the conscience into life, the reign of this power might have been expected; and there it is in its grossest forms and most disgusting aspects. But, lo! amidst civilized communities of men has it not a wide dominion? The luxurious in living, the gay in dress, the material in wealth, the animal in pleasure—where are these not coveted? where are they not sought? Sensualism is, verily, a mighty spirit amongst us. It plays a prominent part in the merchandise of the world. Art, in its higher forms, ministers to it: sculptor, painter, singer—the loftiest geniuses—stand waiting at its side, and move at its behest. It is the inspiration of theatres and the fascination of amusements. It is sung in taverns and has its music in drawing-rooms. It is the chief element in the literature of the masses. It breathes in the ballad of the beggar, and is bound in the volume of the peer. It is the talk of the vulgar in the streets; it is the reading of *refined* ones in their quiet chamber, and, in the bright days of summer, on the beach. Will any keen observer of society pronounce this exaggeration, or hesitate to admit that it falls far beneath a full statement of the case?

There is also *scepticism.* I do not mean mere intellectual scepticism. God knows, this is fearfully spreading amongst us. We have all classes of infidels: there is the anti-theist, who declares there is no God; there is the anti-biblist, who admits a God, but denies the divinity of the Bible; there is the anti-supernaturalist, who admits the divinity of the Bible in the same sense as he admits the divinity of any other true book, but who denies to it any supernatural feature: and there is the anti-propitiationalist, who professes to believe in the supernaturalness of the Bible, but denies the great doctrine of atonement. Intellectual infidelity in these various forms is working busily in our midst. It has its clubs, its platforms, and its press. Philosophy and poetry, logic and eloquence, are pressed into its service. It has the tongue of the orator and ear of the populace. But it is not of this scepticism that I speak. I refer to something deeper, broader, and mightier far—the *spirit* of which all intellectual infidelities are the effects and forms—the soil from which they spring. The scepticism of the heart and life, which no *argument* can meet, is the evil demon which oppresses me. Does not this spirit possess men? Where is the faith of the heart? I see this spiritual scepticism everywhere; not merely in the manners of the millions who sail down your rivers, travel your railroads, saunter through your streets, crowd your taverns, and perambulate your parks on the holy day of God, but in your cathedrals, your churches, and your chapels, with heartless apathy repeating its *beliefs*, muttering its prayers, and singing its psalms. It haunts our temples, it kneels in pews, and speaks from altars. "*Verily when the Son of man cometh, shall He find faith on the earth?*"

There is, finally, *superstition.* The strongest native element in the soul is the religious. In the right development of this element is man's well-being—in its perversion is his ruin. When it is clouded with ignorance, and inspired with fear; when it bows at the shrine of a false deity, and worships through the intervention of priests; when it moves by blind impulse rather than by enlightened conviction, it becomes superstition: and superstition has ever been, and still is, a mighty spirit of evil in our world; it reigns with an undisputed sway over the vast domain of heathenism, and is the empress of more than one-half of professing Christendom.

These are some of the chief spirits that possess society. How many of the phenomena of the general history of the world are traceable to them! The unrighteous tricks of business—the graspings of cupidity—the oppressions and woes of indigence—the blasphemous speculations of philosophy—the tyrannies of governments, the horrors of war—the absurdities of religion,—all spring from these spirits as streams from the fountain, as plants from the soil.

Now, *the work which the world requires of the church is to cast out these spirits*—nothing less than this. The breaking up of its heterodoxical system, or the removal of its oppressive institutions, will not meet the case. Unless you eject these spirits, they will create systems as erroneous as ever, and build up institutions as oppressive as before. What are "doctrinal errors" but head-fumes arising out of their hidden fire? And, as to outward institutions, rear churches and chapels on the ruins of operas, gin-palaces, and other public scenes of sin, and what have you done? These spirits can work as much vileness and moral devastation through a temple as a theatre, in the pulpit as on the stage. "*Neither circumcision nor uncircumcision availeth anything.*"

The second truth the narrative serves to illustrate is—

II. THAT THE CHURCH HAS SIGNALLY FAILED TO DO THE WORK REQUIRED. The disciples did not more signally fail in healing the lunatic than the church has in meeting the exigencies of the world. That the world is better in some respects through the agency of the church, admits of no question. Knowledge has been increased, and inventive genius has been developed; the social heart has been genialized, and public manners have been improved. Evils that once pressed as an incubus on the upheaving energies of mankind are buried in the grave of the past. The rights of man are recognised, and greatly multiplied are both the comforts of life and the facilities for future advancement. But looking at humanity in the full breadth of its nature, and the infinitude of its relations, we are bound to regard this as falling unspeakably short of the demands of its condition. Whilst we adopt not the sentiment of the French writer, who degrades civilized life by representing it as no better than barbarism, we cannot lose sight of the fact, developed not only in ancient history, but everywhere palpable in the life of modern Europe, that the lowest degree of moral corruption may co-exist with the highest point of material civilization. The arts may advance, and the intellect may rise where the *soul*—the man— is sinking all the while. The question we have to decide, in order to determine the failure of the church, is, *Are the evil spirits expelled?* This is its work: if it has not done this it has done nothing to the purpose.

Is the world less selfish, less sensual, less sceptical, now than it was eighteen hundred years ago? We need not ask, is it less superstitious, for the settlement of that question would prove nothing. Mere secular knowledge will decrease superstition, and often its expulsion makes way for scepticism; one demon departs to make room for another. Some maintain that there is not at this hour a larger number of Christians, in proportion to the population of the world, than existed at the close of the first century of our Lord— that Christians are not relatively more numerous now than they were then. The supposition is astounding. But we need not go thus far for evidence. Is it true that two-thirds of the earth's inhabitants are in pagan darkness, and that the vast majority of the other third is made up of Mohammedans, Jews, infidels, worldlings, and nominal Christians? Is it true that, even in Christian England, the Church is making no aggression on the world? that conversions are not as numerous as births? Is it true that, even in the vicinities of churches and chapels, the bulk of the neighbourhood are entirely indifferent to religious ordinances? Is it true that the working-men of England, comprehending a large proportion of the mind and muscle of the age, are scarcely touched by its influence? The affirmative of either of these questions is sufficient to show that the church has signally failed in her great work.

There are two thoughts which are sufficient to overwhelm a serious mind with the solemnity of this failure.

First: *That the work neglected is of the most incomparable import-*

ance. The sublimest discoveries of science—the grandest achievements that patriotism or philanthropy ever realised, are puerilities to it. So long as the world is under either of these spirits, real prosperity and true happiness are *necessarily* impossible. Can that soul whose relations are infinite, and whose sympathies were in. tended to flow forth like the light, encompassing the wide world with its beams, ever reach its well-being under the master-sway of *selfishness?* Impossible! This, like a demon, imprisons the faculties, deadens the moral susceptibilities, seals up the fountain of spiritual life, and separates the spirit from the infinite source of love and order. As the plant never reaches its perfection, but as it yields itself up to the free influence of nature, throws out its odour on every breeze, and spreads forth its beauty to every eye, so the human soul can only realise the full development of its powers as it yields itself up to universal love, and gives out its properties to the good of the great system to which it belongs. Or can man ever advance to true greatness and peace under the dominion of *sensualism?* Does not all history show what is taught alike by philosophy and the Bible, "*that fleshly lusts war against the soul?*"—that they are *necessarily* incompatible with its purity, peace, freedom, and force? Did not the great apostle feel that the keeping under of his body was indispensable to the salvation of his soul? Is *scepticism* consonant with the true interests of humanity? Does it not strike at the root of all virtue, and destroy every motive to spiritual culture? In the nature of things, can there be any spiritual life, growth, or peace, where the *idea* of God is not felt as the greatest reality of consciousness? A moral soul without this idea is a planet without a sun—in darkness, disorder, and death. Nor is *superstition* less unfavourable to the real progress of mankind—it is a cloud upon the sun, a miasma in the social air. It is a fiend that dethrones reason, perverts conscience, and stimulates to arrogant assumptions and heartless cruelties. Every page of its history is an exposition of the text, "*Their sorrows shall be multiplied that hasten after another god.*" Thus, then, the world is necessarily lost so long as these spirits are in the ascendant. It requires no Divine interposition to conduct it to misery; it is on its road, and these "*devils and their angels*" are getting strength to torment it day and night. Oh! until these demons be expelled—until selfishness give way to benevolence, sensualism to spirituality, scepticism to faith, superstition to religion—humanity, from the everlasting laws of its nature, is doomed to ruin. It can no more enjoy life, and rise to ultimate greatness, than the poor lunatic in the text. It will be foaming eternally under some new passion, and plunging itself "*into the fire, and oft into the water*" of destruction.

Secondly: The other thought which gives deep solemnity to this failure is, *That there is no other body on earth that can do the work.* Christ constituted the church the moral exorcist; gave it the Gospel as the infallible implement, and said, "*Cast out devils.*" In the first days she nobly fulfilled her mission; she spoke, and the demons fled.

The sensualism of voluptuous Corinth, the scepticism of philosophic Greece, the selfishness of the narrow-minded Jew, and the super-stition of the dreamy Pagan, were scared off at the majesty of her voice. But now these spirits sport at her side—haunt her very altars—play about her heart. I am told that the Church is fast sinking into contempt amongst the common-sense, thinking men of the world. My heart is pained at the probability, but my judgment is not surprised. High pretensions, coupled with practi-cal impotency, must necessarily produce such a result. If the dis-ciples declared their possession of miraculous power, and narrated the wonderful feats they had done, and the still greater works they could achieve, I can imagine the multitude naturally turning to them the sneering lip and the flashing eye of ridicule when they saw them fail in the attempt to cure this young man. But if *they* were ex-posed to contempt on this ground, how much more so are Christians ! How lofty our pretensions ! We talk about our commission to EVAN-GELISE THE WORLD ; we deign not to aim at anything less. We speak of our immense resources—the might of truth and the power of prayer—and our achievements are as miserable as our pretensions are sublime. The world laughs at our great swelling words and little doings, and well it may. We are taunted, not trusted : rever-ence has given way to ridicule. What is to be done ? The world is full of moral demons, and we fail to cast them out.

The other truth is—

III. THAT THE FAILURE OF THE CHURCH HAS ARISEN FROM THE WANT OF FAITH. "Why could we not cast him out ?" "*And Jesus said unto them, Because of your unbelief: for verily I say unto you, If ye have faith as a grain of mustard seed, ye shall say unto this mountain, Remove hence to yonder place, and it shall remove: and nothing shall be impossible unto you.*" The general idea expressed in this bold, figurative language, is, *that the smallest genuine faith is sufficient for the achievement of the greatest works.* The New Testament is filled with the two doctrines, that success in all human operations is from God, and that the success is ever dependent upon personal faith. It is with the latter that we have to do at present. One of the evangelists assures us that Christ could not do "many mighty works " in Nazareth, because of the unbelief of the people. Now, it seems to us that the making of personal faith a necessary condition of success is no arbitary arrangement. *It is founded in the nature of things.* It is essential to preserve intact the principle of moral merit in human operations, and also to stimulate to that species of exercise which, in the nature of the case, is fitted to gain the result. In no department of action, secular or spiritual, could Christ do many mighty works for men if they have not FAITH. Unless the husbandman has sufficient enlightened and vigorous faith in the laws and advantages of agriculture to stimulate and guide him to the proper cultivation of his land, many mighty works of God will not be done in his fields. The statesman or sovereign who has not a noble faith in the everlasting principles of *right,* has no ground to expect that, through his legislation, God will do many mighty works for his country.

There are three things indispensable to human success in any department of labour—*means, method,* and *motive :* a suitable instrument, a proper way of using it, and a sufficient motive to prompt the necessary action. Now, our position is that, *without faith,* there can be neither of these in the great work of converting the world; and that, therefore, unbelief is the cause of failure.

Faith is necessary to the means. What is the necessary instrument? The ready and general answer will be, The Gospel. We accept the reply; but, for the sake of accuracy, ask in what *form is* the Gospel the instrument? Is it in the *book-form ?* Would a correct verbal repetition of it answer the purpose? If so, why a ministry? The Gospel written on the heavens, articulated in the winds, or circulated in tracts, would do. Is it in the *form of other men's thoughts?* Will a faithful recital of the opinions and interpretations of the "old divines." realise the end? The great principles of orthodoxy I hold with a tenacious grasp; the memories of the great theologians of other times I venerate, and thank the Almighty Spirit for many of their quickening and guiding thoughts. But the *formal* repetition of them by their successors will never convert the world : God never intended any generation to act the part of a parrot. He has given mind to each. The intellectual labours of no one were intended to relieve its successor from the most earnest and indefatigable investigation of the great text-book of truth. On the contrary, they were to light them into farther deeps, and to accelerate their speed. In addition to this, so constitutionally dissimilar are the minds of men, that a proposition embodying a living conviction of one generation, would be little more than a dead dogma if *formally* uttered by another, What, then, is the instrument? THE INDIVIDUALLY DIGESTED GOSPEL : the Gospel whose evidence has been analysed and approved' by the individual reason—whose principles have been comprehended by the individual judgment—whose blessings have been appropriated to the individual experience—whose genius burns as the inspiration of the individual soul. This is the all-conquering form of the Gospel. The man who speaks this, however untutored his mind or unclassic his tongue, will speak that which will be sound in philosophy, true in experience, and all-captivating in poetry. He speaks because he believes; and speaks, therefore, not as an echo, but a living voice—speaks in the full might of his manhood. He who preaches the Gospel in any other form is like David in Saul's armour; very splendid it may be, but ridiculous to the thoughtful eye, and powerless to strike one conquering blow.

Faith is also *necessary to the method.* In art, business, and philosophy, method is of primary moment. Without method there may be colour, canvas, and brush, but no painter—shop and capital, but no tradesman—a universe of facts and a vigorous soul, but no philosopher. In like manner, the Gospel will achieve little without method. By method, of course, we mean no prescribed or patent plan : the one word LIVINGLY will express our idea. Present it in the living logic of a mind inspired with its philosophy, to meet the world's *reason*—the living rectitude of a mind inspired with its goodness, to meet the world's *conscience*—the living religion of a mind inspired with its God, to meet the world's *soul*. See you not that the Gospel presented in the *reasonable*, *righteous*, and *religious* talk of men thus inspired, would, as the summer's sun acts upon the morning mists, banish them from the scene, and leave the landscape clear ? Let the church teach thus, and her doctrines will drop on the world as the rain, and her speech distil as the dew. But can there be such a method as this without individual faith ?

Faith is, moreover, *necessary to the motive*. We may possess an instrument suited to a certain work, and be well acquainted with the proper way of using it, and yet do nothing, for the want of motive to stimulate to action. That nothing but faith can supply the requisite motive is too obvious to require illustration. Without faith in the soul—in its worth and lost condition—in the sufficiency of the atonement—in the aptitude of the Gospel—in the earnestness of the Spirit, and in the love of God, what can induce that consecration of earnest effort which the work demands ?

From the considerations which we have, with the utmost brevity, stated, does it not appear evident, that where there is not faith there must necessarily be a failure in the great work intrusted to the church ? Our faithlessness is our impotency.

"*Lord, increase our faith.*" Oh! for the faith that Elijah had, who, on Carmel's brow, single-handed, confronted and confounded the heathens of his country ;—or the faith that John the Baptist had, whose *voice* broke the moral slumbers of Judea, and roused the spirit of earnest inquiry amongst his countrymen; who, in a vacillating age, amidst men who bowed to circumstances as the "reeds" to the wind, stood as firm in principle as those hills around him that threw their shadows on the bosom of the rolling Jordan ;— or of Luther, before whose moral majesty all Europe stood in awe ;— or of our own Whitfield, who, in alternate tones of love and thunder, and in tears of unutterable emotion, drew the folded veil of matter, and brought the spiritual world in contact with the souls of men.

"Awake! awake! Put on thy strength" of heroic faith, "O Zion!" Put on "thy beautiful garments"—garments wrought of celestial virtues—"O Jerusalem," thou Holy City ! " Shake thyself from the dust " of sensuous ritualism and technical faiths. "Arise," and sit down in calm majesty on the sublime throne of moral principle, O Jerusalem ! Loose thyself from the shackling bands of worldly policy, hereditary beliefs, priestly domination, and conventional piety, " O captive daughter of Zion !" *Then shall the Gentiles see thy righteousness, and all kings thy glory ; and thou shalt be called by a new name, which the mouth of the Lord shall name : thou shalt be a crown of glory in the hand of the Lord, and a royal diadem in the hand of thy God !*

Matthew 17:22-23

The Remarkable in Christ and the Improper in His Hearers

We have already noticed a passage so parallel to this (Matt. xvi. 21–23), that it is somewhat difficult to strike from this a new line of thought. If we look at the words in order to illustrate two things, i.e., *something remarkable concerning Christ, and something improper concerning His hearers*, the difficulty may be obviated, and some practical ideas may be developed.

I. SOMETHING REMARKABLE CONCERNING CHRIST. Two things here are very remarkable.

First: His *designation* of Himself—" Son of Man." Why should He call Himself the Son of Man? Is not every man the son of man? Are not all the common offspring of the first one man? (1) Men, generally, are the children of certain *races*. All modern men, for instance, identify themselves with some or other of the chief races, such as the Asiatic, the European, the Ethiopic, &c. ; and they have the physical peculiarities of these great families. In contra-distinction to this, we may suppose that Christ was an *ideal* man *physically*. He was, in His corporeal organisation, what the original man was, and what God intended a man to be. (2) Men, generally, are the children of certain *countries*. They have *national* character-istics and predilections. They live in, and for, their Fatherland. Nationality, in them, is often stronger than humanity. They would sacrifice themselves, and other nations, for the interest of their own. In contra-distinction to this, Christ was a cosmopolitan. The round earth was His country, and all men were His fellow-citizens. He lived for MAN, not for nations. His sympathies grasped the world. In this sense He was an ideal citizen of the earth. (3) Men, generally, are the children of *sects*. They are born, and brought up, in connexion with some religious sects. They are, to a great extent, the creatures and organs of a religious system. Their religious intellect is tied to a creed. Their religious enthusiasms is bounded by sectarian limits. In contra-distinction to this, Christ's ideas came directly from the Divine and Everlasting Fountain of Truth. The Church He lived in and for, was the Kingdom of Heaven. He was an ideal religionist. " God is a Spirit," said He, " and they," &c.

Secondly : *His future knowledge of Himself.* This is a very *re-markable* thing. He here foresees His Betrayal, Crucifixion, and Resurrection. Two things here are suggested in favour of His superhumanity. (1) *His power to attain such a knowledge suggests this.* It is not given to men to know the future of their life. Even the morrow is shrouded in mystery. But Christ saw the whole of His future. The mystery of all future ages was open to His eye. (2) *His power to bear this knowledge suggests this.* Had we a revelation of even the future of one week, I question whether it would not paralyse our energies. But Christ sees His Betrayal, Crucifixion, and Resurrection, hears the facts, and talks about them.

II. SOMETHING VERY IMPROPER CONCERNING HIS HEARERS. It is said they were " exceeding sorry." Why were they sorry? Unless they were sorry on account of the enormous human wickedness which was involved in the coming sufferings of the Son of God, which is by no means likely, their sorrow was manifestly improper. What then was their sorrow?

First: *Was it the sorrow of sympathy for themselves?* Did they tremble at the loss which they themselves would sustain at His departure? It is likely they did. But even this sorrow was wrong, inasmuch as the very facts concerning His future life, which He had just stated to them, were essentially necessary to their own happiness. Poor short-sighted men, we often regret the very loss which serves our highest interest!

Secondly: *Was it the sorrow of sympathy for their fellow-men?* Did they think of what their contemporaries would lose by the departure of Christ from the world? and did this make them sad? if so, their sorrow was improper, for His crucifixion, &c., was the only power which could truly help the world.

Thirdly: *Was it the sorrow of sympathy for Him?* Did they feel commiseration for Him on account of the dreadful agonies which awaited Him? If so, then pity was ill-bestowed. In His greatest agonies He was not an object of pity, but of admiration. He was not a sufferer from necessity, but from choice. To the women who saw Him bear His cross by the way, He said, " Weep not for me, but weep for yourselves, and your children."

Matthew 17:24-27

The Political Policy of the Christian Citizen

This is an extraordinary incident in the history of an extraordinary life; and therefore, though passingly strange itself, is in beautiful keeping with the evangelical biography of which it is a part. There are four things here which at once strike our attention:—An old law meeting modern men; a characteristic act in the conduct of Peter; a remarkable lesson on the social policy of the Christian citizen; and a striking display of Christ's superhuman power. A brief word of explanation on each may be desirable as an introduction to the point on which we are anxious to fasten our attention.

Here we have—

First: *An old law meeting modern men.* Christ and His disciples had just entered Capernaum;—a city that once stood on the north-western side of the Lake of Gennesareth, and in which the Redeemer seems to have spent the greater portion of His public life—thus exalting the population to Heaven in respect of privileges, and consequently entailing on them many fearful responsibilities, the neglect of which brought on them a doom more terrible than that which befell Sodom and Gomorrah. (Matt. ix. 23.) Soon after they entered the city on this occasion, they that received tribute money came to Peter and said, " *Doth not your Master pay tribute ?* " These officers are not supposed to be the men who collected the taxes paid to the Romans for political purposes, but persons who were employed to collect subscriptions towards expenses incurred in the various sacrifices and other services of the Temple. The subscription was an annual payment of half a shekel, about fifteen-pence halfpenny of British money, levied on all Jews twenty years old. (Exod. iii. 13 ; Neh. x. 32.)*

This *old* law, which now met the apostles on their entering Capernaum, was made many centuries before; and made, moreover, to support an institution in which these disciples had lost faith, an institution which they had outgrown, and which to them was almost obsolete. Somewhat strange this, one thinks ; and yet not singular, but common. We, the men of this age, are ever met by laws made by men that have perished in their own decay many centuries ago. Some of these laws, too, such as those referring to the support of certain forms of religious institutions, the achievements of bloody war, many moderns no longer receive, but rather reject with moral indignation. Yet the *old* law, the offspring of poor fallible brains long since dust, comes to us with imperial authority, cares nothing about our new convictions, makes its demand, to which we must yield or suffer. Though I cannot see the rightness of this arrangement, nay, though a little reflection makes me stagger at its anomalies, it still seems to be the great law of Providence which we must respect.

Here we have—

Secondly : *A characteristic act in the conduct of Peter.* What was Peter's reply to these tax-collectors ? Did he, before he gave the answer, consult his spiritual Master ? or, did he pause a moment for a little reflection ? No. " He saith, YES." How Peter-like this ! How beautifully it harmonizes with the whole of his impulsive history. The unartistic record of little expressions and actions like these in the evangelical history, which so thoroughly agree with the temperament and tenor of the individual's life, is to me no feeble argument in favour of the truthfulness of the writer.

Here we have—

Thirdly : *A remarkable lesson on the social policy of the Christian citizen.* And when he, Peter, was come into the house, Jesus prevented him (anticipated—for such is the meaning of the word), saying. " *What thinkest thou, Simon ? of whom do the kings of the earth take custom or tribute ? of their own children, or of strangers ?* Peter

* See " Pictorial Bible."

saith unto Him, Of strangers. Jesus saith unto him, Then are the children free." Christ in this address to Peter would delicately suggest to the impulsive disciple that he had been rather too hasty in his reply, and that as a matter of right He might hold Himself free from the payment of such imposts. Peter knew of the general custom amongst kings not to tax their own sons, and therefore was prepared to appreciate the force of our Saviour's argument on that ground. Jesus was the Son of the universal King ; the Temple for which the tax was collected was the house of His Imperial Father ; and therefore, like the sons of earthly monarchs, He was free from the obligation to pay the tax. Yet, and this is the lesson, though on the ground of *right* He could claim an exoneration, He consents to pay. " NOTWITHSTANDING, LEST WE SHOULD OFFEND THEM." Here is His policy, waiving a personal right, in order to conciliate popular sentiment !

Here we have—

Fourthly : *A striking display of Christ's superhuman power.* " *Go thou to the sea, and cast a hook, and take up the fish that first cometh up ; and when thou hast opened his mouth, thou shalt find a piece of money : that take, and give unto them for me and thee.*" Jesus here performs a miracle to prevent giving offence. Bengel states six things to show the greatness of this miracle :—" that the fish should be caught—that it should be caught quickly—that there should be money in it—that the money should be in the first fish—that the sum should be just so much as was needed—and that it should be in its mouth."

Now, let us take up for a moment the *reigning* truth of this passage, which is *the social policy of the good.* There are three thoughts suggested by the narrative which will throw no small amount of light upon the subject.

I. THAT IT IS HIGHLY POLITIC FOR THE CHRISTIAN MAN TO FALL IN, AS MUCH AS POSSIBLE, WITH THE INSTITUTIONS OF HIS COUNTRY. The simple reason Christ here assigns for performing a miracle to pay tribute was,—" *Lest we should offend.*" And why would He have offended had He not done so ? Because the Jewish Temple was a national institution, and popular sentiment was as yet in its favour ;—as must indeed be the case with all national institutions. Popular sentiment is the life of all national organizations ; as soon as that departs, the vital sap has left the tree, root and branch, to rot. Christ acted through life upon this principle. He did not put Himself in antagonism with the recognised institutions and authorities of His country. Though he denounced, in no measured terms, dishonesties, carnalities, ambitions, iniquities, and all other moral evils, that worked like demons in the heart of society, you never find Him oppose the ordinances of the Temple, the constitution of the Sanhedrim, or even the political power which a foreign despot exercised over His country. He formed no *anti*-associations to battle with institutions. He worked in a far more philosophic and a far more effective way the ruin of all corrupt organizations : He indoctrinated the public mind with a class of truths that would so change the soil of society as to root out the old thistles and thorns, and produce trees whose fruit should be for the healing of the nations. Thus, too, the apostles acted. Whilst they were honest in their utterances, "*declared the whole counsel of God,*" and feared not the frown of kings nor the thunder of opposing dynasties, they sought as much as possible to conciliate the spirit of the age in which they lived. Hear Paul. "*All things are lawful for me, but all things are not expedient.*" Again, "*Give none offence, neither to the Jews nor to the Gentiles, nor to the church of God; even as I please all men in all things, not seeking mine own profit but the profit of many, that they may be saved.*" Again, "*It is good neither to eat flesh nor to drink wine, nor anything whereby thy brother stumbleth, or is offended, or is made weak.*"

II. THAT IT MAY BE SOMETIMES NECESSARY TO WAIVE A PERSONAL PRIVILEGE IN ORDER TO AVOID COLLISION WITH EXISTING INSTITUTIONS. "*What thinkest thou, Simon? of whom do the kings of the earth take custom or tribute? of their own children, or of strangers? Peter saith unto Him, Of strangers. Jesus saith unto him, Then are the children free.*" "Jesus," says Olshausen, "here runs a parallel between earthly kings and earthly tribute, and the heavenly King and spiritual contributions; as with kings their own sons are free from taxes, so also are the sons of heaven. For what God's children possess belongs to God—they have no property exclusively their own—they contribute out of and into their own purses; they are therefore free." Christ and His disciples were free from any obligation to pay such taxes. He might have stood upon this freedom, resisted the demand, and thus placed Himself in direct antagonism with the spirit of His age. But He did not do so; He waived the privilege in order to avoid such a position.

To guard you, however, against the idea that Christ encouraged in any way an *unprincipled temporising* policy in thus endeavouring to avoid giving social offence, two things should be distinctly observed:—

First: *That the tribute to the Temple which He now paid was of Divine appointment.* (Exodus xxx. 11–16.) It was not the tax of a heathen despot, to support a pagan temple, or to carry on the horrid trade of war. I cannot suppose that Christ would have yielded to such impious and unrighteous imposts. No; with a moral chivalry transcending that which heroic Daniel displayed, He would have resisted such iniquitous demands.

The other thing which should be observed in order to guard against mistake here, is :—

Secondly : *That Christ, in yielding to the demand, only surrendered a personal privilege.* Would Christ, think you, have sacrificed any principle of truth,—any fundamental right of humanity, any moral claim of Heaven, in order to guard against giving offence? Never. Banish the blasphemous thought! Sooner than sanction by word or deed the slightest departure from *moral* propriety, He would brave the stormiest rage of a thousand worlds. Had He been *governed* by the idea of not giving social *offence*, He could have lived and died in the warm bosom of the world's adoring love. It was because He loved principles more than applause, that He lived a pauper's rather than a prince's life, and died a malefactor on the cross rather than a world-lauded monarch in a palace.

III. THAT CHRIST'S DISCIPLES CAN AFFORD TO BE GENEROUS IN THEIR CONCESSIONS TO PUBLIC SENTIMENT. They can afford to be free and untrammeled in their intercourse with society, and liberal in their concessions to public customs and usages, for two reasons, which are here suggested :—

First : *The distinguishing spirit which inspires them.* The spirit that moved and swayed Christ and His disciples is essentially opposed to that which permeates and controls the society of the world. They are opposed, as benevolence and selfishness, sincerity and falsehood, animalism and spirituality, godlikeness and devilism. The contrast, therefore, is so great that the true disciple has no fear of being personally injured or misunderstood in any concession he may make to public usage. Christ knew that the paying of the tax would not identify Him, or His disciples, the least, either in personal feeling or in public estimation, with Temple services or Mosaic institutes. It is ever so. The more of the true Divine Spirit the man has in him, the better he can afford to eat and drink "*with publicans and sinners,*" and to regard all times and places as equally sacred. He knows that it "*is not that which goeth into a man that defileth him ;*"—"*that to the pure all things are pure.*" It is not the men, I have learnt, that make the greatest grimaces at the world, most parade their "principles," and battle with society for what they call their "*rights*" who have within them most of the divine and magnanimous spirit of Christianity. As a rule, it seems to me that the smaller a man is, in a moral sense, the more strait-laced he is in connexion with the world, the greater agitator against public institutions, and the greater censor of public conduct. As in literature the smallest intellects are the readiest critics, so in morals the smallest souls are the severest censors.

The other reason for enabling Christ's disciples to be generous towards the world, which is here suggested, is :—

Secondly : *The vast resources at their command.* Though it seems that neither Christ nor His disciples had in their personal possession the money to meet this assessment, all nature was at their service. Christ had only to speak, and kind nature would yield whatever was required. To Peter, He said, "*Go thou to the sea and cast a hook, and take up the fish that first cometh up. And when thou hast opened his mouth thou shalt find a piece of money ; that take, and give unto them for me and thee.*" He might have sent to the field as well as to the sea, to the plant as well as to the fish ; in fact, to anything in any part of nature, and He would have had whatever He needed. The miracle symbolizes this glorious truth : *That nature is at the service of the good, and is ready at any time to yield to devout generous souls just as much as is required, and no more.* Christ enunciated one of the most settled laws of His providential government, when He said, " *Give, and it shall be given unto you.*"

Brother, all nature will help thee to be just, generous, and magnanimous in thy conduct towards society and the world. As she pours her bright beams and genial influences upon all, fans the breathing lungs both of the evil and the good with her waves of vital air, she helps thee to be generous by her example; and as she is the ever-loyal liege of thy Great Master, she will help thee at His bidding, by yielding up of her treasures whatever thy love-expanding heart and liberal hand may require.

> " Great Nature, to great souls declares,
> That all she has is theirs."

Matthew 18:1-6

Moral Childhood ; or, Christ's Answer to the Ambitious

Whichever of the apostles put the question, " *Who is the greatest ?*" it is of little importance. The question is, more or less, the question of all men. Ambition is an instinct of the soul. Christ's reponse to this question—a question which, in some form and at some time, rises in every heart—must have struck the disciples as exceedingly strange. Had He said, He that is the most brave and victorious in battle, he that is most successful in merchandise, he that is most eminent in intellectual research, or he that is most popular in religious teaching, they might not have been surprised; but when He said, You must become as a " *little child,*" His reply must have clashed with all their preconceived notions of greatness.

In another place we have noticed the child-like attributes which all men must *unavoidably* possess—those it is *criminal* to possess, and those which they are morally bound to possess.* It is this last class of attributes that Christ requires as the foundation of human greatness. Christ teaches, in this passage, that this is indispensable to all greatness.

He teaches—

I. That this child-likeness is necessary to an introduction to the sphere of true greatness. " *Except ye be converted* "†—

* See *Homilist*, vol. v., p. 198.

† Some have maintained that the apostles were not converted till the day of Pentecost, but according to the usual acceptation of the word, this change was manifest when they forsook their all to follow Christ. There is but one passage (Acts xv. 3) in which the term conversion occurs in its modern sense, and there it is applied, not to individuals, but to nations. In Luke xxii. 32, James v. 19, the word expresses the recovery of a Christian brother who had been drawn aside from the right path. Continual conversion, perpetual turning from darkness to light, from the power of Satan to God, is necessary as long as we have need to grow in lowli-

that is, unless you renounce your material notions of my kingdom, and love for worldly greatness, and become as a "little child," in self-obliviousness, simplicity, and truth, "*ye shall not enter into the kingdom of heaven.*" This child-spirit is the condition of *entrance* into the kingdom of God. "*Blessed are the poor in spirit : for theirs is the kingdom of heaven.*" There must be the renunciation of three things at the very threshold of this kingdom before *entrance is possible.*

First : *A practical renunciation of all obedience to secular distinctions.* "Whosoever would be a friend of the world is the enemy of God." In the empire of Christ, "the rich and the poor meet together." The only distinctions recognised are distinctions in moral excellence. All are regarded as brethren. Lazarus, according to his goodness, is as great there as any one. The Baptist, in his cell, is in this empire ; Herod, on his throne, is excluded. Paul, in his chains, is in this empire; Felix, on the judgment-seat, is excluded. As the innocent child treats the beggar and the prince alike, so all the members of this spiritual empire act towards each other.

Secondly : *A practical renunciation of all ideas of self-importance.* Peter, when he entered the kingdom, fell down at Jesus' knees, saying, "*Depart from me; for I am a sinful man, O Lord.*" The Publican, as he entered, exclaimed, "*God be merciful to me a sinner.*" The Centurion felt that he was not worthy that Christ should enter his house. All ideas of self-merit and self-importance are left *outside* this kingdom.

Thirdly : *A practical renunciation of all ideas of self-seeking.* All ideas of self-interest and self-aggrandisement are abandoned. No man seeketh his own. The new spirit of love to God, and benevolence, must enter the soul before it can cross the threshold of this kingdom. "*He that loveth not, knoweth not God; for God is love.*" "*The love of Christ constraineth*" all in this empire. It nerves every arm, fires every heart, and governs every spirit. They that live there do "*not henceforth live unto themselves, but unto Him who died and rose again.*" From the text, we learn—

II. THAT CHILD-LIKENESS DETERMINES THE DEGREE OF ELEVATION IN THE REALM OF TRUE GREATNESS. "*Whosoever therefore shall humble himself as this little child, the same is greatest in the kingdom of heaven.*" David, who was great in this empire, felt himself to be "*a worm, and no man.*" Isaiah, who sustained in this empire an eminent position, felt himself to be "*a man of unclean lips.*" Paul, ness, docility, affiance, and innocency. The formal and stereotyped division of all men into the converted and the unconverted springs from poverty of language and of thought. These classes always exist; Scripture presents them under various aspects, and by different terms, as the children of light and the children of darkness, as the wise and the foolish virgins, the tares and the wheat, as timeists and eternalists. To present them invariably in the same aspect, and by the same term, frequently tends to "make sad the heart of those whom God would not have made sad," while they stand in doubt of their conversion; and "strengthens the hearts of the wicked by promising them life," because they think themselves, or are thought by others, to be, in a conventional sense, converted characters.— *Webster.*

perhaps, who was higher than either in this blessed realm, considered himself less than "*the least of all saints.*"

First: *He that is most child-like in this empire is "greatest" in real worth.* Real worth will always be determined by the loftiness of thoughts in relation to God. It is on the wings of lofty thoughts that we rise Godward; but the more lofty our thoughts, the more profound our humility. "*When I consider thy heavens, the work of thy fingers, the moon and stars which thou hast ordained,*" &c. The greatest creatures in the universe bow, in the profoundest prostration, before the Infinite.

Secondly: *He that is most child-like is greatest in social power.* Who, in the nature of the case, is the man who will obtain the greatest sway over the mind of his fellow-man? Not the haughty and the proud, who speaks and acts under a consciousness of his own superiority; but the man who "*minds not high things, but condescends to men of low estate.*" "*Whosoever shall be great among you, let him be your minister; and whosoever shall be chief among you, let him be your servant.*" This command involves an eternal social law. No man can ever become, really, a chief among men who does not serve. Christ Himself descended to the lowest human condition, identified Himself with the poorest, that He might gain a moral sovereignty over souls. The proud man may gain a material throne, and govern the bodies of men, but he will have no sovereignty over souls. Over the graves of the proud monarchs of the ancient world you may stand, and utter the language of the prophet:—"*How art thou fallen from heaven, O Lucifer, son of the morning!*" &c.

Thirdly: *He that is most child-like in this empire is greatest in the estimation of God.* The high and lofty One, whose name is holy, says, "*I dwell in the high and holy place, with him also that is of a contrite and humble spirit, to revive the spirit of the humble,*" &c. "*He hath respect unto the lowly.*" "*He giveth grace unto the lowly.*" "*He forgetteth not the cry of the humble,*" though "*He poureth contempt upon princes,*" &c.

III. THAT CHILD-LIKENESS IDENTIFIES OUR EXISTENCE WITH THE PRINCE OF TRUE GREATNESS. "*Whoso shall receive one such little child in my name receiveth me.*" Christ is the Head of the great empire of mind. "*He is exalted far above all principalities and powers, and might and dominion,*" &c. He is in the midst of the throne—the Centre of universal attraction, the Object of universal worship, the Source of all light and love. And yet He says, in relation to His humble disciples—

First: *That the treatment which men render to them He will regard as being rendered to Him.* "*He that receiveth them receiveth me.*" "Inasmuch as ye have done it unto one of the least of these my brethren, ye have done it unto me." The connexion between them and Christ is vital—vital as that between the members and the head. What they feel He feels.

Secondly: *That any injury inflicted on them, He will requite with the greatest punishment.* "*Whoso shall offend one of these little ones which believe in me, it were better for him that a millstone were hanged about his neck, and that he were drowned in the depth of the sea."* Christ here refers to one of the earliest forms of capital punishment as practised amongst the heathen—viz., casting into the sea. But He refers to this form of punishment here, in the strongest possible manner. Not merely is the criminal to be cast into the sea, but into the *depth* of the sea; and not only is his body to be cast into the depths of the sea, but a *stone* is to be bound around his body lest he should rise. Nor is it a mere *stone* that is to be cast around his neck, but a heavy stone—"*a millstone.*" The idea is, that this terrible and ignominious punishment will be better for a man, than that he should do any injury to the humblest of Christ's disciples.

Let us, then, brothers, cultivate this child state of heart. If we live to old age, there will come, necessarily, a second childhood—a childhood of the bodily members; a childhood of the intellectual faculties. But let us, to beautify and to bless young life and old life, life here and life hereafter, cultivate this moral childhood—the childhood of the heart. "*Let this mind be in you, which was also in Christ Jesus, who, being in the form of God, thought it not robbery to be equal with God.*"

Matthew 18:7-9

Obstructions to Vital Christianity

"That is an offence," says Matthew Henry, "which occasions guilt, which by enticement or affrightment tends to draw men from that which is good to that which is evil, and which occasions grief and makes the heart of the righteous sad." Although some modern translators rendered the term offence, "*snares,*" we do not think the word adequate;—it does not express the full meaning of our Saviour. *Obstruction,* or *stumbling-block,* would perhaps better represent the idea of the Great Teacher on this occasion. Christ is speaking of that which would hinder the progress of the new religious life which He had awakened in the heart of His disciples. *Obstruction to the Christian life* is the chief subject of the passage; and concerning it three thoughts are suggested :—

I. THAT OBSTRUCTION TO THE CHRISTIAN LIFE IS FRAUGHT WITH EVIL. "*Woe unto the world,*" &c. Some take the word "woe" rather as an exclamation of pity than a denunciation of judgment—and would render the words thus :—"*Alas! for the world because of offences.*"

First: *Obstruction to the Christian life is an evil to the world in general.* Whether the "*offences*" to Christianity come in the forms of love or hatred; in all the plausibilities of sophistical reasoning; the seductive charms of feigned affection; or in edicts of law and cruelty of persecution; it is an evil to the world. By such "*offences*" the world is led to misinterpret Christianity and to shun the only power that can really improve its condition.

Secondly: *Obstruction to the Christian life is an evil especially to those who are its chief promoters.* "*Woe to that man by whom the offence cometh.*" Whether he be a betrayer, like Judas; a persecutor, like Nero; or a slanderer, like Celsus; alas for him! he has incurred the righteous displeasure of Heaven. "*It were better for him,*" says Luke, "*that a millstone were hanged about his neck, and he cast into the sea, than he should offend.*" "Woe to the man, even were he an apostle," says Stier, "he is an *offence* and a *devil* among the twelve. Perhaps, as was the case at other times, as the anointing of Christ by the woman in Bethany, this Judas may have been the originator, or at least the promoter, of the evil thoughts connected with this unhappy dispute among the disciples. This, however, is only conjectural and uncertain; with more certainty we now apply the word of Christ with a most perfect justice to another. Woe to the φιλοπρωτεύων in the church, pseudo-Peter, and haughty *servus servorum Dei*, who with false key shuts the kingdom of heaven, offends and corrupts the faithful, nay, builds up a world full of offences (which yet is held to be the true church) as the Babylon which is afterwards to be thrown down as a mill-stone is cast into the sea!" (Rev. xviii. 21.)

Anti-Christ, whether Protestant or Papal, avowed Infidel or professedly Christian, will fall under this "*woe.*" (Rev. xvii. 1, 2.) He that, by snares or cruelties promotes these offences, tampers with the deathless interests of souls.

II. THAT OBSTRUCTION TO THE CHRISTIAN'S LIFE IS TO BE EXPECTED. "*For it must needs be that offences come.*" In Luke, Christ is reported to have said to His disciples, "*It is impossible but that offences will come.*" And Paul says, "*There must be also heresies among you, that they which are approved may be made manifest among you.*"

There are two facts here which all philosophy is bound to accept as verities; but which no philosophy can logically reconcile. One is *Divine prescience,* and the other is *human responsibility.*

Here is *Divine prescience.* "It must needs be that offences come." Christ foresaw all the opposition that in all future ages should arise to retard the onward march of His religion in the world. He knew that the eternal antagonism between the "*two seeds*" would produce these "offences." He knew that the more His truth spread the more offences would come; as the warmer and brighter the sun the more insects crowd the air. But fore-knowing does not involve *fore-ordaining.* He foresees all future evil; but He does not predetermine it. All His predestination in the matter is, that souls shall be *free;* free to obey and disobey; free to do evil and good.

Here is *human responsibility.* Though "offences" *must* come, "*woe unto that man by whom they come.*" The same idea comes out in Christ's statement concerning Judas:—"The Son of Man goeth as it is written of Him, but woe unto that man by whom the Son of

Man is betrayed." Sin may appear a *necessity* in our poor logic, but it is not so in our *consciousness*. We feel that the sinful act is ours, —that we are its originating cause,—that our moral instincts will not allow us to charge it upon any object out of us, upon any decree concerning us, or upon any arrangements antecedent to us. The simple act is ours. We *feel it;*—hence our self-crimination and remorse. No argument can destroy the feeling. Though Heaven foresaw all the demons in our nature that have figured in human history, and all the wicked deeds, even to the utmost *minutiæ*, they were not the less demons on that account. Do not ask me to reconcile Divine prescience, or Divine preordination, with human freedom and human responsibility. I cannot—no one has ever done so, no one can; he does not know his mental position in the universe who dares attempt it.

III. THAT OBSTRUCTION TO THE CHRISTIAN LIFE IS TO BE EARNESTLY RESISTED. " *Wherefore, if thy hand or thy foot offend thee, cut them off, and cast them from thee : it is better for thee to enter into life halt or maimed, rather than having two hands or two feet to be cast into everlasting fire.*" The practical meaning of this highly figurative language may be brought out in the two following remarks :—

First : *That whatever tends to injure our Christianity, however near to us, must be uncompromisingly and earnestly resisted.* Though it were as valuable to us as the hand or foot, or as tender and precious as the eye, it must be resisted. (1) *However tender in friendship the offender may be.* Dear relations, sweet companions, enthusiastic lovers, if their aim and influence be to turn us from Christian virtue and truth, away with them ! To the most endeared of them we must say, avaunt ! (2) *However near in interest the offender may be.* Though our standing in the world, our prosperity in business, the very comforts and necessities of life, may depend upon them; still, if they tend to turn us from the right way, they must go. Shops, houses, lands —even *bread* itself must go, if they thus offend. (3) *However exquisite in gratification the offender may be.* Whatever be your strongest lust, your favourite pleasure;—music, novel-reading, drinks, money-making, concupiscence—if they, in their influence, are opposed to your spiritual life, they must go. You must " *mortify the flesh.*"

Secondly : *That upon such uncompromising and earnest resistance of these offences, our future destiny depends.* " *It is better to enter into life halt or maimed,*" &c. Paul uses the same argument;—" *if ye live after the flesh, ye shall die;*" " *but if ye, through the Spirit, do mortify the deeds of the body, ye shall live.*" This, indeed, is a necessity of our nature.

Here, then, is our spiritual interest. We must leave materialism and sinful pleasures. As Abraham quitted Uz of the Chaldeans; as Moses left Pharaoh's royal court; as Paul left Judaism with all its gorgeous ceremonies, enchanting associations, great emoluments, and Pharisaic honours and delight ; declaring that what things were gain to him he " *counted loss for Christ.*"

Matthew 18:10-14

Guardian Angels

There are two things which at once strike us in this passage.
First: *That there is a tendency in the world to despise the humble Christian.* The caution which Christ here enforces against it implies its prevalence. The first Christians being poor, in a worldly sense, destitute, for the most part, of the graces of intellectual culture and social refinement, and known as the pledged followers of One who was despised and rejected by the age, were regarded with no small measure of contempt by their thoughtless contemporaries. They were everywhere spoken against. Nor is the tendency on the part of worldly men to despise the humble Christian, peculiar to the Jew in the first ages of Christianity; it has always been prevalent, and still is. Even in nominally Christian England, a poor Christian is despised. It is true, that you may see the world bowing down and rendering homage to Christian men who may be possessors of large fortunes, or occupiers of eminent civil positions, or great patrons of public institutions; but it is not the *Christian* man in them that is thus honoured,—it is the wealthy, the influential, the grand man. The Christian element seldom awakens real respect in worldly souls, even when associated with worldly grandeur;—it is often despised, and sometimes ridiculed, when associated with poverty.

The other thing that strikes us in this passage, is :—
Secondly : *That there is, notwithstanding the tendency to despise, a strong reason for honouring the humblest Christians.* Christ here assigns cogent reasons why "*the little ones*"—the most obscure and the most feeble—should not be despised. "*For I say unto you, That in heaven, their angels do always behold the face of my Father which is in heaven,*" &c.

There are two reasons in this passage why the humblest disciples should be honoured :—*They engage the services of the heavenly angels, and they are precious to the Everlasting Father.*

I. THEY ENGAGE THE SERVICES OF THE HEAVENLY ANGELS. "*In heaven their angels do always behold the face of my Father.*" There are some who suppose that, by the word "*angels,*" used here, we are to understand human souls in the heavenly state. It is true, that the term "angel" is used at least once to designate a human spirit. Some of those who dwelt in the house of Mary, the mother of John, when Rhoda told them that Peter was at the door, exclaimed, with astonishment, "*It is his angel!*" (Acts xii. 15.) But I do not see sufficient reason to regard Christ, in this passage, as speaking of the *spirits* of these little ones as their angels ;—though in a sense their spirits, as redeemed, do now behold the face of God. I accept here the generally received idea, namely, that Christ refers to the *guardianship of angels.*

Adopting this view, there are two thoughts to be observed, in order duly to appreciate the force of this reason for honouring poor disciples.

First: *They have their own guardian angels.* "*Their angels,*" (ἄγγελοι αὐτῶν). That angels minister to the good, is abundantly taught in other parts of Scripture. Thus, for example, we read, "*The angel of the Lord encampeth round about them that fear Him, and delivereth them.*" We read, "*He shall give His angels charge over thee to keep thee in all thy ways.*" We read, that they are "*all ministering spirits, sent forth to minister for them who shall be heirs of salvation.*" We read also of various services which angels have rendered to certain good men both in the Old Testament and the New. But I am not aware of any other place, besides the passage before us, where the idea is given—that the good have their *own* angels; that each true disciple has some angel or angels specially devoted to his service.

The idea (1) *Is reasonable.* If angels minister to men at all, must they not have some method of action?—something like a division of labour amongst them? Great as they may be, they are still finite; and can finite beings attend to all alike? Impossible. They must have their own spheres. Moreover, judging from analogy, may we not suppose that, as amongst men, there is a mental sympathy which gives different men a special interest in certain individuals,—and thus qualifies them to render special service, so there may be mental sympathy between some angelic spirits and certain men, which does not exist between others, and which induces and enables them to render service to them which they render not to others? In the church here below, the man that can teach and edify one class of mind, is often utterly incompetent to render any service to another class. Hence a great preacher in one church would scarcely be tolerated in the pulpit of another. There is nothing, therefore, unreasonable in the idea suggested by the passage; on the contrary, the idea beautifully harmonizes with the natural conclusions of our own judgment. The idea is not only reasonable, but (2) *Delightful.* How energizing and uplifting the thought, that, if we are the true disciples of Christ, however weak in mind, frail in body, poor in circumstances, we have still an angel guard! Whilst the great ones of the world have honourable men for their retinue and guards, the "*little ones*" of the church are attended by glorious angels.

> " How oft do they their silvery bowers leave,
> And come to succour us who succour want;
> How oft do they with golden pinions cleave
> The flitting skies like flying pursuivant!
> Against foul fiends to aid us militant,
> They fight, they watch, and duly guard,
> And their bright squadrons all around us plant,
> And all for love—and nothing for reward."

Secondly: *Their own guardian angels are in high favour with the Sovereign of the universe.* They "*do always behold the face of my*"

Father which is in heaven." In Eastern countries, kings were wont to live in pavilions, concealed from public notice. The few who occasionally were admitted to their presence, were regarded as most signally honoured. Christ, perhaps, here hints at this circumstance, in order to express the dignity of those spiritual intelligences who are the guardians of the good. They are admitted into the immediate presence of the Supreme Sovereign, they behold His face—nay, they do *always* behold His face. It is not on set occasions, nor at distant intervals, but *"always."* One of their number said, " *I am Gabriel, that stand in the presence of God."* They stand shining in the beams of His countenance, glowing with adoring love, and awaiting His behests.

Here, then, is a forceful reason why you should not despise these *"little ones."* Each has his guardian angel, and each guardian angel is ever in the conscious presence of the Everlasting Father. Ye empty worldlings, who speak in language of scorn and contempt of these "little ones!" take heed, *"for in heaven their guardian angels do always behold the face of the Everlasting Father!"*

II. THEY ARE PRECIOUS TO THE EVERLASTING FATHER.

First: *Their salvation was the object of His Son's mission to the world. "For the Son of Man is come to save that which was lost."* That humanity is "lost,"—gone from its original sphere of being and action, admits of no debate. The fact is patent to universal reason, and palpable to universal consciousness. *Materially, intellectually, morally, socially,* the world is gone astray. Christ comes to restore it. *"God sent not His Son into the world to condemn the world, but that the world through Him might be saved."* Humanity is diseased in every organ and in every limb. He is the Great Physician, who will restore it to more than its former beauty of form, robustness of vigour, and buoyancy of being. Humanity is a shattered and wandering orb in the creation; He is the moral Creator, who restores it, brings it back to its orbit, and makes it keep the time, and heighten the blessedness, of the universe. How precious, then, must those whom Christ came to save, and for whom He sacrificed Himself, be to the Everlasting Father!

Another suggestion here, which shows their preciousness to the Great Father, is—

Secondly : *The restoration of even one of them is a source of inexpressible delight. "How think ye ? If a man have a hundred sheep, and one of them be gone astray, doth he not leave the ninety and nine and goeth into the mountains and seeketh that which is gone astray ?"* &c. Christ here recognises a fact in the history of human consciousness, which is this, the power of one restored object to awaken, for the time, more delight than any number of unlost ones. The parents, who out of a large family have one little one laid on a bed of sickness, and brought nigh unto death, will rejoice more over that child the day it leaves with restored health its chamber, and begins to take its place with its brothers and sisters again, than over all the other healthy members of the family. This is human nature, and Christ knew it, and appeals to it. (See Luke xv.) For this reason, perhaps, our world, which may be the only one lost out of millions, will awaken more delight in the universe than any ninety and nine, or any number of unlost ones. It will be the restored prodigal at the table of the Great Father of the universe.

Another suggestion here, which shows their preciousness to the Great Father, is—

Thirdly : *The ruin of the least of them is repugnant to the Infinite mind.* *"Even so it is not the will of your Father which is in heaven, that one of these little ones should perish."* If the "little ones," as some suppose, refer to infants, it is a beautiful thought, and one as *true* as it is beautiful, that it is not God's will that *one* of the little infants should perish. The Infinite is benevolently interested in individual souls, and in the least of individual souls. He sees in one infant soul, germs which eternity will unfold in scenes of ever-heightening wonder. If true of infants literally, it is equally so of children figuratively ;—His humble disciples. It is not His will that they should perish. Blessed be Heaven for the declaration that it is not the will of our Father that one of the "little ones" should perish. I like it ; it chimes in with that unbounded benevolence which seems to flood the great universe of material nature ; I like it, for it accords with the most generous sympathies of my poor heart for the unhappy race to which I belong ; I like it, for it gives the lie to those theological blasphemies that come from some modern pulpits, representing the Almighty Father as predestinating the ruin of certain souls ; I like it, for it inspires within me glowing hopes concerning that future of humanity when mortality —*moral* as well as material—*"shall be swallowed up of life."*

From what I have said on these words of Christ, how forceful does His prohibition appear, *"Take heed that ye despise not one of these little ones."* Despise them not ! They have their angel guards, they live at Bethel, and from their feet a ladder reaches to the opened heavens by which these guardian angels come and go. Despise them not, they are precious to the heart of the Great Father of souls—*"He that toucheth them, touches the apple of His eye."* He regards what is done to one of the least of the "little ones" as being done to Him. Despise them not. They may be feeble in intellect, poor in circumstances, and amongst the lowest of the low in worldly rank, yet He who "feeds His flock like a shepherd, gathers them with His arms, and carries them in His bosom,"—carries them onward through life's perilous and labyrinthean path, to the blessed heights of immortality.

Matthew 18:15-20

The Policy of the True Church on Earth, and its Power in Heaven

It seems necessary, at the outset of our endeavour to reach and develop the spirit of this passage, to get a clear and a definite idea of the thing which Jesus here designates ἐκκλησία—the church. It is scarcely necessary to remark that the simple meaning of the word is an *assembly;* but in the New Testament sense it means generally, though not always, a *religious* assembly. Thus the Jews, as congregated in the synagogue, are called a "church;" and thus, far more frequently, the assemblage of Christians for religious purposes anywhere is called a "church." The term is never used to designate a *building,* * a class of *religious functionaries,* or a system either of *doctrine* or of *worship.* In the *Christian* sense it means nothing more than an assembly of Christians. The assembly may be large or small, held in a city or a village, in a public building or in a private dwelling, within the precincts of a house or in the open air.

We need not travel far from the passage under consideration in order to get a tolerably correct idea of a true church—a church in the sense in which the heavenly Teacher here uses the word. I gather from this passage—

First: *That it is a society that may be constituted of the smallest possible number.* "*Two or three.*" You cannot have a smaller assemblage; it is the smallest plurality. It is not the *number* of the assembly that constitutes the *true* church, but the *quality.* There may be no true church found in a crowded conventicle or cathedral, whilst it may be found in the humble cottage, or in the open air, where but two genuine souls have met in earnest for Christian ends. I gather from this passage—

Secondly: *That it is a society morally agreed.* Christ here indicates that the whole power of the church depends upon *unity.* "*That if two of you shall agree on earth as touching anything that they shall ask,*" &c. The agreement is not in mere *opinion*—this would be impossible and undesirable—nor in the measure or mode of operation, but in the inspiring spirit and the master aim. It is, in one word, not intellectual or mechanical, but *moral.* All having one spirit, the spirit of Christ, and all moving by the dictates of that spirit, as all the members of the body move by the volitions of the one soul. I gather from this passage—

* It is one of the blemishes of our authorised version that ἱεροσύλους, in Acts xix. 37, is rendered 'robbers of churches' instead of 'robbers of temples,' or, as in some earlier versions, 'sacrilegious.' This was objected to by the Puritans at the time, as an attempt to obtain scriptural sanction for the custom of applying the term church to the material fabric. The only similar instance of ecclesiastical bias is in Acts xii. 4, where μετὰ τὸ πάσχα is rendered 'after Easter,' whereas it clearly means 'after the Passover,' which was then in celebration. The erroneous rendering is very objectionable, as it indicates a nascent desire to judaize Christianity. — *Webster.*

Thirdly : *That it is a society always acting in the "name" of Christ.* " Where two or three are gathered together *in my name*," &c. Not in the name of king or pope, Calvin, Luther, or Wesley; not even in the name of Moses and the prophets, but in "*my* name." Everything must be done in the name of Christ. His Spirit must prompt and His ideas guide in all. The life which each lives in the flesh must be a life of faith on the Son of God.

Now, it is of this society, which may consist of the *fewest possible number*, which is ever *morally* agreed, and which does everything in the *name of Christ*, of which the heavenly Teacher is now speaking. This is the *ideal* church of which we are about to speak.

I shall take the passage to illustrate—

I. THE POLICY OF THE TRUE CHURCH ON EARTH. "*Moreover, if thy brother shall trespass against thee, go and tell him his fault between thee and him alone*," &c. We have, of course, to confine our remarks concerning its policy on earth to the case which is supposed in the passage. It is the case of an offence of one member against another. It is implied that a member of this *true* church may be overtaken with a fault, may fall into evil, and do an improper and even a wicked thing. The best men, so long as they are on earth, are liable to be tempted to the erroneous in doctrine, the unvirtuous in feeling, and the wrong in conduct. "*Let him that thinketh he standeth take heed lest he fall.*"

Now, the conduct which the offended member is to pursue towards the offender is here indicated with remarkable precision, "*Go and tell him his fault*," &c. The policy as here developed leads us to consider two things—the magnanimous benevolence of the aim, and the admirable wisdom of the means.

First : *The magnanimous benevolence of the aim.* What does Christ require you to do to the brother that has offended you ? To disgrace him, to crush him, to wreak vengeance on him ? No, but restore him. " If he shall hear thee, *thou hast gained thy brother.*" Thou hast, by morally convincing him of the turpitude of his conduct, and generously offering forgiveness on the ground of his repentance, won him back to a right feeling towards thyself and to his old relation to the church. This is admirable, this is divine. But alas ! in the history of what is called the church, this has been all but invariably contravened. What has the church—I mean the *conventional* church—been doing with offenders ? Let the ACTS AND MONUMENTS OF JOHN FOXE, with their ten thousand tongues, declare; nay, let the history of all the sections of the church, even of those who boast most of their liberality, speak, and you will find that the offending brother has generally been shunned with pietistic horror, denounced with pietistic arrogance, excommunicated with pietistic ceremony, and often martyred with pietistic solemnity. Why, even in those denominations who are ever ringing the notes of liberty, catholicity, and progress, let a brother offend even in the *mere letter* of doctrine, and a thousand hoarse, bigoted voices shall be lifted up to brand him as a heretic, and to warn mankind against him as a fearful enemy of his species. How different this from the policy which Christ here enjoins, and from that which Paul commands, when he says, "*Brother, if a man be overtaken in a fault, ye which are spiritual restore such an one, in the spirit of meekness.*"

Secondly: *The admirable wisdom of the means.* Mark the varied steps pursued for this object. (1) The offended party is to go to the offender *alone.* He is to go to him. This is not according to the ordinary conduct of mankind in such matters. We generally expect our offender to come to us, to present assurances of sorrow for the offence, and to make suitable apologies. We scarcely dream of the restoration of amity in any other way. With a proud heart we say inwardly, If he desires the renewal of our friendship, let him come to us and seek it; it is contrary to all order for us to go to him, nor shall we demean ourselves by going to him. Yet this is the policy enjoined here. And it is manifestly an admirably wise policy, inasmuch as it is adapted to the end. If you wait for the offender to come to you, the chances are, you will be disappointed; and even should he do so, he would not gain that impression of your magnanimous nature and forgiving spirit which would serve to bind him to you in the indissoluble bonds of the highest admiration and love. The policy here inculcated could scarcely be adopted without success. There is something so unique, so sublimely strange, and withal so morally divine and commanding, that it could scarcely fail to tell effectually upon the heart of the offender. It is, in truth, the conduct which the Infinite Father has pursued towards us, His offending offspring. He does not wait for us to go to Him. *He comes to us* and He presses for reconciliation. But when you have entered his house, how are you to speak to him about his fault? In the language of crimination and anathema? No, but in the calm, firm, dignified language of self-control, conscious rectitude, and Christian love. Let him feel that you are above the petty feeling of resentment, that you are more concerned about the bearing of his "fault" upon *himself* than upon you, and that your mission to him is to "*overcome evil by good.*" All this conversation, however, must, in the first instance, be strictly *private* —BETWEEN THEE AND HIM ALONE." Do not blazon the matter abroad. A *personal* and *private* interview is the best to remove misunderstandings, to allay angry passions, and to rekindle old affections.

Should this fail, what is the next step in this policy?—(2) To visit him again, in company with "*one or two*" other mutual friends. Do not let the failure of the first visit disgust or dishearten you. Follow it up by a second, and in the second take with you such a person or persons as shall sympathise with your generous object, and shall strengthen your influence for its achievement.

But should this fail, what next? (3) Bring the matter under the notice of the community of which you are mutually members. "*Tell it unto the church,*" &c. What for? That the indignation of the church may be awakened, and its thunderbolts hurled at his guilty head? No; but that it may, by its admonitions, expostulations, and prayers, help to "*gain him*" to a right state of heart, and to his old standing in the affections of the brotherhood.

But should this fail, What next? Nothing more can you do to restore him. You have brought your individual influence upon him to restore him; you have taken with you mutual friends to co-operate with you for the purpose; and, lastly, you have called in the concurrent influence of the whole Christian assembly of which he and you are members: you can do nothing more in the way of restoration. Your resources are exhausted. If the loving arguments, entreaties, and prayers of a *whole* church combined failed to raise this fallen one, what else have you? .Nothing. What then are you to do with this incorrigible brother? Coerce him by threats, persecution, or penal inflictions? No. *Leave him alone.* Separate from him. Have no more connexion with him than the old Jew would have with "*a heathen man or a publican,*"—than you would have as a religious man with a notorious sinner.

Who can conceive of a policy more admirably adapted to the end than this? Nay, it is the *only* policy that in the nature of the case can answer the end. If the end be to "*gain*"—restore the offender, rather than to destroy him, it is the exclusive policy to be pursued! All else must prove ineffectual. Severity, resentment, coercion, are in no wise adapted to *gain* the offending brother. These may kill the criminal but not the crime; destroy the enemy but not the enmity; drive your offending brother farther away from you, but never draw him nearer—never "*gain him.*" Though the mere *conventional* church has almost invariably in her practice set at nought this policy, the ideal, the *true*, church has ever pursued it;—and, inasmuch as all are bound to belong to the true church, it is binding alike upon every man.

Seeing that the principles of Christianity are of universal application, and all men are equally bound to become Christians, I regard this policy as binding upon the civil magistrate. Believing, as I do, that the grand end of civil government, in relation to offenders, should be to "*gain*" them, to bring them back to a loyal and virtuous life; to reform them, not to destroy them,—I cannot but regard the spirit of the policy which is here inculcated, as that which the very philosophy of our nature demands. It would, I trow, be well, even on political grounds, if something of this policy was adopted, in order to settle international disputes, and to regain the friendship of national offenders. The policy which is pursued for this purpose now with European powers is almost to the last degree absurd. The offended party, with a thousand tongues, dilates on its "honour," trumpets its own greatness on every breeze, blazons to the world in the most exaggerated forms the faults of the offender, employs a frozen diplomacy to negotiate terms of reconciliation, and to urge them by pointing to the cannon's mouth. Is this the way to restore friendship? O wisdom, whither hast thou fled? In the cabinets of statesmen thou art seldom found ! When the philanthropic Sturge, on whom the grave has just closed, with two kindred souls and worthy friends, visited St. Petersburg to have an interview with the great Çzar, to avert if possible that dire hurricane of war, whose thunders soon afterwards shook the world to its centre, and whose fiery bolts hurled unnumbered thousands of our fellow-men into eternity, the frothy press made the empty age laugh at him as a fanatic. Albeit he played, I am bold to aver, the most sage-like part in the terrible drama of that war-generating hour. He did what no diplomatist could do ; he passed from the kinghood to the manhood of the mighty autocrat. His quiet words of reason stirred the sympathies of the husband, the father, the man ; and the defiant Emperor, that dared the opposition of three kingdoms, wept as a child as the few true words of Sturge distilled like dew upon his manly heart. Had a few statesmen, a few of the most influential men in the offended States, " doffed " their cold officialism, obtained an interview with him, talked to him as *men*, and used the whole of their *moral* influence, that war, whose enormous wickedness eternity alone can reveal, might have been averted.* " WISDOM IS BETTER THAN WEAPONS OF WAR." War and wisdom are antipodes.

We turn now to the other side of the subject :—

II. THE POWER OF THE TRUE CHURCH IN HEAVEN. "*Verily I say unto you, whatsoever ye shall bind on earth shall be bound in heaven : and whatsoever ye shall loose on earth shall be loosed in heaven.*" Again, "*I say unto you, that if two of you shall agree on earth as touching anything that they shall ask, it shall be done for them of my Father which is in heaven. For where two or three are gathered together in my name, there am I in the midst of them.*" These words show the *true* church has power in heaven to secure three things :—*a divine ratification of its conduct ; a full answer to its petitions ; and a personal fellowship with its Lord.*

We observe that the *true* church has a power in heaven to secure—

First : *A divine ratification of its conduct.* " Whatsoever ye shall bind on earth shall be bound in heaven; and whatsoever ye shall loose on earth shall be loosed in heaven." Blomfield thus paraphrases the passage :—" Whatsoever ye shall determine and appoint respecting such an offender, whether as to his removal from the Christian society, if obstinate and incorrigible, or his re-admission into it on repentance, I will ratify." The ideal church is the organ of the Divine. Whatever it does therefore *as such*, whether it forgives or condemns, receives or rejects, its conduct is approved and ratified in heaven. " *Whosesoever sins ye remit, they are remitted unto them, and whosesoever sins ye retain, they are retained.*" The *real* church, not the mere conventional church, has power to forgive sin; —for its will is the will of Heaven. Whatever *right* thing we do here is ratified in heaven. Every true thought, every pure senti-

---

* This was written about the close of the Crimean war.

ment, every holy resolve, and every righteous act, are approved and settled irrevocably in heaven. Whatever in human conduct is *morally good* is *divine*, and whatever is divine is ratified in heaven.

But not only has the true church a power by which it secures a divine ratification of its conduct; but also a power by which it obtains—

Secondly : *A full answer to its petitions.* "*If two of you shall agree on earth as touching anything that they shall ask, it shall be done for them of my Father which is in heaven.*"

The heavenly Teacher, I presume, assumes here two things :— the rectitude of the *principle* of their agreement, and the *propriety* of the thing they asked for. Their agreement was not a mere intellectual one, an accordance in doctrinal opinion, nor a mere selfish one, a unity of desire for a certain object for personal ends. I cannot conceive that in either case Heaven would attend to the request. There is much of this union of doctrinal sentiment and union of selfish desire in the prayers of conventional churches ;—but there are no answers to them. Righteous Heaven is mercifully deaf to such prayers. The principle of agreement must be a *righteous* principle,—a principle in which all personal considerations are merged in the reigning desire to help humanity and serve the universe by following out the *will of Infinite benevolence ;*—a desire that finds its utterance in the words, "*Let the kingdom come.*" "*Let the people praise Thee, O God,*" &c. Two souls united thus will always have a mighty influence in heaven. Moreover, the *propriety* of the thing asked for seems also to be assumed in these words. The word "*anything*" here must therefore be taken in a restricted sense. The context itself indicates the boundary lines, by giving us to understand that it means anything relating to the "*loosing*" and the "*binding ;*" *i.e.*, anything relating to the interests of Christ's cause in the world.

Regarding then, as I think we are bound to, these two things as being assumed by Christ, the promise commends itself to our judgment and corresponds with the experience of the good in all ages. I venture to believe that no social prayer, where there has been the *true agreement* of soul for the *true thing*, has ever ascended to heaven unheard or unanswered. Men ask, Why is prayer unanswered ? My reply is, Prayer in Christ's sense is always answered. "*I say unto you, that if two of you shall agree on earth as touching anything that they shall ask, it shall be done of my Father which is in heaven.*" The church in the upper room in Jerusalem were agreed in asking for the Holy Ghost on the day of Pentecost, and it came with its marvellous gifts. Peter was in prison, and "*prayer was made without ceasing of the church unto God for him ;*—and the Lord brought him out of the prison.*" Peter and John arrived in Samaria from Jerusalem; they were agreed; and "*they prayed that the men of Samaria who had received the word, should receive the Holy Ghost ;*" and they did receive the Holy Ghost. Let us not say that prayer is not answered. What we sometimes call prayer is not prayer. *True prayer is always answered.* "THIS IS THE CONFIDENCE THAT WE HAVE IN HIM, THAT IF WE ASK ANYTHING ACCORDING TO HIS WILL HE HEARETH US."

We go on to observe that the *true* church has a power in heaven to secure—

Thirdly : *A personal visitation from its Lord.* "*For where two or three are gathered together in my name, there am I in the midst of them.*" The rabbinical writers say, "That if two men sit down with the law between them, the Shekinah or Divine presence is with them." This is not up to the grand reality of the Old Testament promises :—" *In all places where I record my name I will come unto thee and I will bless thee.*" Or again, "*The Lord is nigh unto all them that call upon Him, to all that call upon Him in truth.*"

Christ's presence is secured not merely by meeting together, but by meeting together in *His name.* His name—His life—Himself— must be the *reason* of our meeting, the vital bond of our communion, the theme of our converse, the object of our love, the fontal spring of our life. When this is the case, He is present. *He,* not His mere representative or influence, but He Himself. " There *am I* in the midst of them," &c. In the midst, as the Shekinah was in the midst of the mercy-seat, shedding its mystic radiance on every part; as the sun in the midst of the planets, binding all in harmony, filling all with life, adorning all with beauty, and bathing all with the beams of its own glory. " *Lo, I am with you always,*" etc. His pre- sence amongst them explains the power of their prayer. Without Christ our religious meetings, however crowded in numbers, scrip- tural in behaviour, enthusiastic in spirit, are worthless ; with Him, whatever else is absent, they are infinitely valuable.

Brothers, in our meetings, let our grand aim be to have *Him* pre- sent. It is not difficult to get crowds present. The " name " of some preacher, whose fluent audacities and pulpiteering tricks have gained him the popularity of the fleeting hour, will crowd your largest buildings to an overflow ; but what boot such gatherings if Christ be not there ? *And He will not be there unless you meet to- gether in His name.*

Matthew 18:21-35

Unbounded Forgiveness towards the Repentant Offender

Five ideas you may extract from this passage, and that without any violence to the language, which, whether true or false, it was obviously never designed to teach.

You may force from the passage the idea—

First : *That it is the duty of men to forgive injuries without any con- dition or restriction.* The reply of the heavenly Teacher to Peter

touching *forgiveness* is remarkably strong, and without any qualification. " How oft," says Peter, " shall my brother sin against me,
and I forgive him? " The answer is, "*I say not unto thee, until
seven times: but until seventy times seven.*" A definite number for
an indefinite multitude. Take the language just as it is, and deal
with it in a mere *verbal* style, and you have the idea that whatever
the aggravation or number of injuries a man may inflict upon you,
there is to be no resistance, even in the form of just retribution ;—
but an unconditional forgiveness. Now, that such an idea as this
was intended to be taught, cannot for a moment be entertained. It
not only clashes with our common sense, reason, and conscience ;
with the necessary conditions of social order, and with the general
tenor of Biblical teaching on the subject; but with the very instructions of Christ Himself, and that even in the context. In the
verses immediately preceding, Christ, in legislating for the offended
brother, teaches plainly the duty of binding or condemning, as well
as the duty of *loosing* or absolving; the duty of judicially excom-
municating an incorrigible offender, as well as the duty of mercifully
receiving a repentant one.

You may force from the passage the idea—

Secondly : *That the Almighty sanctions the principle of man holding
property in his fellow-man, and of punishing the innocent for the sins
of the guilty.* The conduct of the master here in relation to his servant, who had contracted such an enormous debt, and who could
not pay, is certainly based upon the notion that he has not only a
right to sell the debtor, but to sell his wife and children, as his property. It is true, that inasmuch as the " certain king " here is no
other than the great God, He has an absolute right to act thus.
All souls are His :—the soul of the husband and the wife, the parent
and the child, are His; but as His conduct is here illustrated by
human action, are we not bound to believe that such actions are
right ? For could that be *wicked in man* which is taken to represent
His righteous procedure ? By such plausible reasoning you may
get out of the passage the idea, that God sanctions the principle of
man holding property in his fellow, and even of his punishing the
innocent for the guilty. Such an idea, however, as this, which the
ruthless slaveholder and the tyrannic autocrat are anxious to maintain, is repugnant alike to the universal and instinctive sentiment
of social justice, and to the whole genius of Christianity. Were it
otherwise, however, were the idea true, we should still say, that is
not an idea which the heavenly Teacher *intended* to convey in this
passage.

You may force from the passage the idea—

Thirdly : *That a man who has once been pardoned may relapse into
wickedness and be finally lost.* This debtor, who, after his earnest
entreaties, was forgiven his enormous debts, instead of consecrating
the whole residue of his life to the merciful, the just, and the godly,
very soon, it would seem, commences a course of relentless tyranny.
" *He went out and found one of his fellow-servants which owed him an*

hundred pence,"—a mere fraction compared with the debt which he had been forgiven—"*and he laid hands on him and took him by the throat, saying, Pay me that thou owest. And his fellow-servant fell down at his feet, and besought him, saying, Have patience with me and I will pay thee all. And he would not, but went and cast him into prison till he should pay the debt.*" For this piece of unkindness, his lord, who had forgiven him, was "*wroth,*" revoked, it would seem, the pardon which he had granted him, and then "*delivered him to the tormenters*"—jailors, who in the East were very cruel—"*till he should pay all that was due unto him.*" Now the possibility of a good man apostatizing admits of no question. Some of the best men have fallen into grievous sins. But whether such men may be finally lost is a question which no theological controversy has yet settled; and which, I believe, is mercifully enshrouded in a haze of uncertainty. But were it certain that a man once pardoned may fall into wickedness and be finally lost, this passage was not *designed,* I think, to convey such an idea.

You may force from the passage the idea—

Fourthly: *That we are justified in regulating our conduct towards men according to their conduct to others.* Why did the lord of this servant revoke the pardon which he had granted, and inflict such condign punishment upon him? Was it not because of the inexorable spirit of cruelty which this servant had displayed towards his fellow-servant? Are we not then authorized to regulate our conduct towards men by their conduct towards others? Are we not justified in that case in being severe to them? This seems very fair reasoning from the passage; but the principle of action which is thus brought out, is certainly not correct; and if it were, it is not what the passage is designed to teach.

You may force from the passage the idea—

Fifthly: *That after a period of purgatorial endurance the wicked may be delivered from their torments.* "*And his lord was wroth, and delivered him to the tormentors, till he should pay all that was due unto him.*" Does not this shed a ray of hope upon the future of the damned? Does not the language imply the possibility of discharging the debt amongst those tormentors? The Papists have used these words in support of Purgatory. The principle of purgatory, in its application to this life, I believe in. There is something like purgatory in our passage to every state of true elevation. No true kingdom is entered but through much tribulation. It is through something like the purgatorial fires of moral thought, conviction, resolve, aspiration, that we pass into our heavens here. But I do not see sufficient reason as yet to believe that this principle is applicable to the other world. The fires there, I fear, are not purgatorial. Anyhow, the passage before us was not designed to teach that idea.

The truth is, the passage is parabolical; and a parable, like all pictures, has generally much thrown into it which has no necessary connection with the subject, but whose strokes and shades are intended to bring out the subject into a bolder relief and a more commanding attitude. The expressions and allusions from which you could draw some of the ideas we have mentioned, are mere incidental strokes of the artist, which are not to be examined separately, but viewed in connexion with the leading subject.

What, then, is the master-idea of this passage? *Unbounded forgiveness toward the repentant offender.* This is here enforced by, The strong language of Christ; The example of the great God; and, The terrible doom of the unforgiving.

I. THIS GREAT SUBJECT OF UNBOUNDED FORGIVENESS IS ENFORCED BY THE STRONG LANGUAGE OF CHRIST. "*Until seventy times seven,*" said Christ. Peter's question, which was probably started in his mind by what the Son of God had just said (15–17), concerning the manner of dealing with an offended brother, implies a twofold impression: that it was his duty to exercise forgiveness towards an offender, and that that forgiveness from the Christian should be of a marvellously generous character. "*Till seven times?*" says he, feeling no doubt that this was wondrously liberal, and would meet with the commendation of his great Master. And it was liberal for unrenewed human nature, which seldom forgives even once; liberal even for the Hebrew saint; for three times and no more did the old Hebrew religion require the exercise of forgiveness.

Peter might have been led to specify the particular number "*seven,*" because that number was a matter in discussion among the Jews, who, according to Lightfoot, pardoned the third, but not the fourth, offence. The apostle here more than doubles that number, as if to go to the greatest lengths of mercy. No doubt he considered himself prodigiously merciful in stating "*seven times;*" and confidently expected a high commendation from his Master for such an extraordinary stretch of mercy. But he was disappointed, and would soon feel humbled on account of the meagreness of his heart. "*I say not unto thee,*" says Christ, "*until seven times, but until seventy times seven.*" As if He had said, There is no limit to the exercise of a merciful disposition. In Luke xvii. 3, we hear Him inculcating the same sentiment. "*If thy brother trespass against thee, rebuke him; and if he repent, forgive him. And if he trespass against thee seven times in a day, and seven times in a day turn again to thee, saying, I repent; thou shalt forgive him.*" In other places He intimates that unless we forgive our enemies, we have no reason to hope for forgiveness from God. "*If ye forgive men their trespasses your heavenly Father will forgive you.*" How earnestly, moreover, does Paul inculcate the same unbounded mercifulness of disposition. "*Put off anger, malice; forbearing one another, forgiving one another, if any man have a quarrel against any; even as Christ forgave you, so also do ye.*"

The unbounded mercifulness of disposition which Christ here, in this *seventy times seven,* inculcates on Peter, serves two important purposes—

First: *To expose the unchristianity of the church in this respect.*

Turn over the pages of ecclesiastical history and show me where has been the display of this spirit. I read of acrimonious controversies, of uncharitable accusations, of wretched bigotries, of malicious persecutions, of sanguinary wars, in connexion with what has been called the church; but I confess that since the apostolic age I can discover scarcely a vestige of this wonderful spirit. "The eye for an eye" and "the tooth for a tooth" spirit, I see everywhere; but scarcely any sign of this *seventy times seven* spirit of forgiveness. Great Emmanuel, how the conventional church has misrepresented Thy spirit to the world!

Again, the unbounded mercifulness here expressed, serves,—

Secondly: *To indicate the vastness of His forgiving love towards the world.* He inculcated only the principle on which He Himself acted. He "*abundantly*" pardons. "*Though your sins be as scarlet,*" &c.

II. THIS GREAT SUBJECT OF UNBOUNDED FORGIVENESS IS ENFORCED BY THE EXAMPLE OF THE GREAT GOD. The "*certain king*" here represents the Almighty; and see how He acts towards the man who owed Him 10,000 talents. Sin is an enormous debt. The sum here stated, if the silver talent was meant, would be about £3,431,875 sterling; but if the gold talent, about sixteen times as much. The idea is an immense sum. "Who can understand his errors?" This enormous debt the *sinner cannot discharge.* The debtor was unable to pay a fraction towards this overwhelming amount. "Sinners," says Matthew Henry, "are insolvent debtors; the Scripture, *which concludeth all under sin,* is a statute of bankruptcy against us. Silver and gold will not pay our debt. Sacrifice and offering would not do it; our good works are but God's works in us, and cannot make satisfaction." This enormous debt unless removed will *entail the utmost ruin.* "His lord commanded him to be sold and his children and all that he had, and payment to be made." What misery is involved in all this! Only a faint picture, however, of hell. True penitence will *obtain full and instant relief.* This is the reigning truth here, and the most glorious truth to man,—the Gospel itself. The debtor offered the penitential prayer, "Have patience with me, and I will pay thee all;" and what followed? "Then"—at once, without a moment's delay—"*Then the lord of that servant was moved with compassion, and loosed him, and forgave him the debt.*" He forgave *all;* cancelled every fraction of the mighty sum. Here, then, in the example of God, you have illustrated the doctrine of unbounded forgiveness.

But this example is brought out here in bold and magnificent relief, by being placed side by side with the conduct of a mere human creditor towards his debtor; and that creditor, too, the very man whose enormous debt the king had just cancelled. "*But the same servant went out and found one of his fellow-servants which owed him an hundred pence; and he laid hands on him, and took him by the throat, saying, Pay me that thou owest,*" &c. Think of three things :—

First : *That the man who thus severely treated his debtor, had been a debtor himself; but the heavenly King has never been under obligation to any one.* One might have expected that he, a debtor so mercifully dealt with, would have been tenderly considerate of others similarly circumstanced.

Secondly : *That the man who thus severely treated his debtor had but a very insignificant claim-compared with that of the heavenly King.* The one owed only a hundred pence, the other ten thousand talents.

Thirdly : *That the man who thus severely treated his debtor was of the same class in life as the debtor,—a fellow-servant; the other infinitely superior to either, the glorious Sovereign of heaven and earth.* How does God's forgiving mercy shine forth by the comparison !

III. THE GREAT SUBJECT OF UNBOUNDED FORGIVENESS IS HERE ENFORCED BY THE TERRIBLE DOOM OF THE UNFORGIVING. Mark the conduct of the sovereign towards the servant who treated his debtor, a fellow-servant too, not only with an unforgiving spirit, but with cruel severity. *"His lord"*—the very sovereign who, with munificent generosity, had cancelled his debt of ten thousand talents—*"said unto him, O thou wicked servant, I forgave thee all that debt, because thou desiredst me : shouldest not thou also have had compassion on thy fellow-servant, even as I had pity on thee ? And his lord was wroth, and delivered him to the tormentors, till he should pay all that was due unto him. So, likewise, shall my heavenly Father do also unto you, if ye from your hearts forgive not every one his brother their trespasses."*

Four general truths are discoverable here.

First : *That the great God marks the actions of our social life.* The king had his eye upon the conduct of his servant, not merely in its relation to himself, but in its relation to his fellow-servant. Heaven sees how we act towards each other.

Secondly : *That His mercifulness towards us heightens the enormity of our severity towards others.* "I forgave thee all that debt "— *"That* debt," &c. Therefore, the peculiar aggravation of thy severity.

Thirdly : *That the punishment which will overtake the unmerciful will be very terrible.* "And his lord was very wroth, and delivered him to the tormentors, till he should pay all that was due to him." Two things here suggest the terribleness of the punishment :—(1) *Its exquisite fitness to the sufferer's sense of justice.* He only received that which he himself had inflicted upon his own fellow-servant. He had laid hands upon his fellow-servant, taken him by the throat, and, notwithstanding all the heart-rending entreaties of his victim, cast him into prison. He only gets back what he had given. He has no ground for complaint. His conscience must say, "Amen" to his doom. *"With what measure ye mete, it shall be measured to you again."* This congruity of doom with conscience is a primary ingredient in the punishment of the damned. (2) *Its utter destitution of any prospect of relief.* How long is he to remain in the

prison? " *Till he should pay all that was due to him.*" How long
will that be?—Ah, how long!

Fourthly: *That any merciful conduct to be virtuous, must be virtuous in spirit.* "So, likewise, shall my heavenly Father do also
unto you, if ye from your *hearts* forgive not every one his brother
their trespasses."*

Matthew 19:1-12

Marriage

Marriage is an institution of God; it accords with the dictates of
nature and the laws of inspiration. It is coeval with human society,
it was an essential ingredient in the happiness of happy Eden. It
heightened, it perfected, the pure, fresh, and serene joys of that
garden, the scene of every beauty and the temple of God. In mercy
it has been perpetuated to the present hour as a social blessing to
soothe and sustain our nature amidst the depressing circumstances
of our fallen state.

Jesus threw around this relationship a peculiar grandeur; He
clothed it with sublimity; to His holy eye it was a holy thing. He
ratified its contract, He guarded its obligations, He expounded its
laws. He graced its celebration with His presence: the first
miracle that His sacred hands performed was at a bridal feast.
The apostles caught the idea of their Master, and invested it with a
mystic solemnity by representing it as a type of the substantial, invisible, and everlasting union existing between Christ and His
church. It involves the most tender, close, and lasting ties that
can unite human beings together in this life. "Therefore shall a
man leave father and mother, and cleave unto his wife, and they
twain shall be one flesh." It combines the earthly interests, fortunes, and happiness of two; it may influence the eternal destinies
of many. The interests of the parties united, the triumphs of truth,
and the upward progress of humanity, are all dependent on the
nuptial bond.

Marriage is the subject of the paragraph now under our notice:
the subject is started by a question of the captious Pharisees, an
artful question put for the express purpose of ensnaring the heavenly Teacher. "*The Pharisees also came unto Him, tempting Him,
and saying, Is it lawful for a man to put away his wife for every
cause?*"

"It is probable," says a modern expositor "that the question
which the carping Pharisees now put to Christ on the subject of
marriage, was asked, not for the sake of information, but to involve
Jesus in difficulty." Two celebrated schools existed at this time
among the Jews, called by the names of two great teachers, Hillel

* Further remarks on this passage will be found in *Homilist*, vol. iii., p. 259.

and Shammai, which held different views upon the dissolution of the marriage relation. That of Shammai contended that divorce was unlawful except in the single case of infidelity in the connexion; whilst that of Hillel, more lax, permitted the union to be severed on any trivial ground, as that of dislike or discontent (Deut. xxiv. 1). The answer of Jesus, they supposed, could not be framed without exposing Him to the odium of one or the other of these parties. But the usual wisdom of Jesus did not desert Him. He refers them beyond the quibbling and jargon of the schools to the authority of the great law-giver, and the purpose of God who made the sexes, and instituted marriage as a connexion not to be dissolved for any slight cause. The heavenly Teacher did what it would be well for all Christian teachers to do in such controverted points, ignore the disputations of men on the subject, and appeal to the authority of God. The words of Christ lead us to notice, *the prescribed limitation, the tender intimacy, the conditional dissolubility, and the optional formation of the marriage tie.*

I. THE PRESCRIBED LIMITATION OF THE MARRIAGE TIE. "*Have ye not read,*" said Christ, "*that He which made them at the beginning made them male and female?*" a reference which shows that marriage is the union of *one* to *one* of each sex. The marriage tie is to be restricted to *one* and no more on either side. That this is the case appears clear from the following considerations:—

First: *The numerical proportion of the two sexes which has existed through all ages, from the creation of the first pair to the present moment.*

Secondly: *From the immense evils that have ever arisen, and that, in the nature of the case, must ever arise, from polygamy.*

Thirdly: *From the unequivocal teaching of the Bible on the subject.* Paul states in the fewest words, and in the clearest manner, the doctrine of the Bible on the subject, when he says: "*Let every man have his own wife, and every wife her own husband.*" Though polygamy was practised in patriarchal and Jewish times, it was never sanctioned by God, as Dr. Wardlaw has clearly shown.*

II. THE TENDER INTIMACY OF THE MARRIAGE TIE. "*For this shall a man leave father and mother, and shall cleave to his wife, and they twain shall be one flesh.*" The apostles take up the same idea of tender identification: "*Let every one of you in particular so love his wife even as himself, and the wife see that she reverence her husband.*" "*Husbands, love your wives, and be not bitter against them.*" "*Wives, submit yourselves unto your own husbands, as unto the Lord; for the husband is the head of the wife, even as Christ is the Head of the Church; and He is the Saviour of the body. Therefore as the church is subject unto Christ, so let the wives be unto their own husbands in everything. Husbands, love your wives, even as Christ also loved the church and gave Himself for it, that He might sanctify and cleanse it by the washing of water by the word; that He might present it to Him-*

* See Wardlaw's "Systematic Theology," vol. iii., where the whole question of marriage is discussed with great delicacy, intelligence, and thoroughness.

self a glorious church, not having spot or wrinkle or any such thing; but that it should be holy and without blemish. So ought men to love their wives as their own bodies. He that loveth his wife loveth himself, for no man ever hated his own flesh, but nourisheth and cherisheth it even as the Lord the church. For we are members of His body, of His flesh, and of His bones. For this cause shall a man leave his father and his mother and shall be joined unto his wife, and they both shall be one flesh." Hear the statements of the Apostle Peter:—" Ye husbands, dwell with your wives according to knowledge, giving honour unto the wife as unto the weaker vessel. Ye wives, be in subjection to your own husbands; that if any obey not the word, they also may without the word be won by the conversation of the wives; while they behold your chaste conversation coupled with fear." They are to be one, in interest, sympathy, and purpose. Such a union, of course, implies the existence of moral excellence on either side. For there can be no real union of soul without this.

III. THE CONDITIONAL DISSOLUBILITY OF THE MARRIAGE-TIE. " They say unto him, Why did Moses then command to give a writing of divorcement, and to put her away? He saith unto them, Moses, because of the hardness of your hearts, suffered you to put away your wives, but from the beginning it was not so." " And I say unto you, whosoever shall put away his wife, except it be for fornication, and shall marry another, committeth adultery; and whoso marrieth her that is put away, doth commit adultery." Christ's remarks here on the dissolution of the marriage tie express two things:—

First: The toleration of Moses on the subject; the license he granted in consequence of the hardness of the heart; see Exodus xxxiii. 3, 34; Deut. ix. 6, xxxi. 27; Isa. xlviii. 4; Ezek. ii, 4; Acts vii. 51; and,—

Secondly: The justifiable ground of divorce. Milton, who regarded " fornication " here as expressive of any conduct as would be equally as offensive to either man or wife, will not appear to be very far out of the way, when you consider what the marriage tie really is. What is it? Is it mere natural sympathy, that which has respect to the outward and external character? Or, is it moral esteem, that which has respect to the inner being and spiritual attributes? It is neither separately; it is both combined. Conjugal love is a compound of both. It is sinful, it is hazardous, alas! it is common to enter into this relationship by the mere impulse of natural sympathy. When this element exists alone, the affection is fickle, turbulent, and confused; but when associated in due proportion with moral esteem, love is firm, calm, and harmonious; storms may be without, but they will never reach the inner shore, they produce no ripple upon the deep and ever-rolling stream of domestic bliss. When alone, the connubial tie becomes a felt fetter, the home a prison, the only bond of union civil law; but, when combined with the other, the tie is no chain; it is mightier than adamant, but finer than the finest web; too weak to fetter, but too strong to break. When alone, it is mortal, death dissolves the union and removes the parties far and for ever apart; but when combined with moral esteem, it constitutes a principle of unity more durable than that which binds planets to their centre,—it will survive the grave and flourish in the eternal hereafter. If moral esteem be thus such an indispensable element in domestic blessedness on both sides, to promote it requires the promotion of excellence, virtue is its vital air ; and let me remind you that the way to cultivate moral excellence is to believe the doctrine, cherish the spirit, and obey the precepts of Christ. The conclusion therefore is, that personal Christianity is essential to the welfare and design of conjugal life. It sanctifies, prospers, and immortalises human friendship. This fact gives a moral splendour to the bridal day of Christians ; they enter upon this the most intimate and endearing of relationships in the possession of an intelligent and vigorous Christianity. The power that unites their hearts together is composed of an indestructible element that issues from the Cross; an element that is to bind all holy souls in harmony for ever.

While I cannot better explain the question of divorce amongst the ancient Jews, than by quoting a very clear statement on the subject from Dr. Jahn's "Biblical Antiquities" as below, I can only see the possibility of an essential dissolution, when the mutual moral esteem is departed.* As soon as ever *mutual* love has quitted the

---

* "As the ancient Hebrews paid a stipulated price for the privilege of marrying, they seemed to consider it the natural consequence of making a payment of that kind that they should be at liberty to exercise a very arbitrary power over their wives, and to renounce or divorce them whenever they chose. This state of things, as Moses himself very clearly saw, was not equitable as respected the woman, and was very often injurious to both parties. Finding himself, however, unable to overrule feelings and practices of very ancient standing, he merely annexed to the original institution of marriage a very serious admonition to this effect—viz., that it would be less criminal for a man to desert his father and mother than, without adequate cause, to desert his wife. Gen. ii. 14, compared with Mic. ii. 9 and Malachi ii. 11–14. He also laid a restriction upon the power of the husband as far as this, that he would not permit him to repudiate the wife without giving her a bill of divorce. He further enacted in reference to this subject, that the husband might receive the repudiated wife back, in case she had not in the meanwhile been married to another person; but if she had been thus married, she could never afterwards become the wife of her first husband—a law which the faith due to the second husband clearly required. Deuteronomy xxiv. 1–4; compare Jer. iii. 1 and Matt. i. 19, xix. 8.

"The inquiry, 'What should be considered an adequate cause of divorce?' was left by Moses to be determined by the husband himself. He had liberty to divorce her if he saw in her *the nakedness of a thing*—i.e., anything displeasing or improper, as may be learnt by comparing the same expression in Deut. xxiii. 14, 15 ; anything so much at war with propriety, and a source of so much dissatisfaction, as to be, in the estimation of the husband, sufficient ground for separation. These expressions, however, were sharply contested as to their meaning in the later times of the Jewish nation. The school of Hillel contended that the husband might lawfully put away the wife for any cause, even the smallest. The mistake committed by the school of Hillel in taking this ground was, that they confounded moral and civil law. It is true, as far as the Mosaic statute or the civil law was concerned, the husband had a right thus to do; but it is equally clear that the ground of legal separation must have been, not a *trivial*, but a prominent and important one, when it is considered that he was bound to consult the rights of the

breast of the wedded pair, there is a *real* divorce, whether the civil magistrate will ratify it or not. Marriage is a union, not of bodies, nor of purses, but of souls. Whenever souls separate by mutual antipathies, there is a real divorce.

IV. THE OPTIONAL FORMATION OF THE MARRIAGE TIE. The disciples, hearing these words of Christ, which bore so strongly against divorce, said unto Him : " *If the case of the man be so with his wife, it is not good to marry.*" As if they said, if the bond be so indissoluble as this, it is such a hazardous thing, that we had better not venture on marriage at all ; we may be caught in an inextricable snare, which may make us miserable all the days of our lives. To this our Saviour replies, " *All men cannot receive this saying* " (v. 11, 12). I cannot better express the meaning of these two verses than by the paraphrase of Doddridge, who says : " But He said to them, all men cannot receive this saying of yours, that it is not expedient to marry ; but only they to whom it is given as a peculiar gift to conquer those inclinations towards that state which God, for wise reasons, has wrought into the common constitution of human nature. For there are some eunuchs who are born so from their mother's womb, and whose natural temper and inclination is in this respect peculiar ; and there are some eunuchs who were made eunuchs by men's wickedness, who drive on that scandalous traffic which the luxury and effeminacy of the eastern world has rendered common. And there are some eunuchs who have, as it were, made themselves eunuchs on account of the kingdom of heaven ; that is, who, by a resolute guard on their appetites and passions, have conquered the propensities of nature, that, being free from the encumbrances of marriage, and devoting themselves to a life of more sublime devotion, they might promote the interest of my Gospel. Compare

woman, and was amenable to his conscience and his God. The school of Shammai explained the phrase, NAKEDNESS OF A THING, to mean *actual adultery.* This interpretation of the phrase gives to the law a moral aspect, and assigns a reason, as the ground of divorce, of the truest moral nature. But the truth is, that the phrase, in itself considered, will not bear this interpretation ; and the law beyond question was designed to be merely a *civil*, and not a moral one. Jesus, who did not so much explain as fill up the deficiencies of the Mosaic institutes, agreed with the school of Shammai as far as this, that the ground of divorce should be one of a moral nature, but He does not appear to have agreed with them in their opinion in respect to the Mosaic statute. On the contrary, he denied the equity, the moral correctness of that statute ; and, in justification of Moses, maintained that he suffered it to be sanctioned by his authority only in consequence of the hardness of the people's hearts. Matt. v. 31, 32 ; xix. 1–9 ; Mark x. 2–12 ; Luke xvi. 18. *Wives*, who were considered the property of their husbands, did not enjoy by the Mosaic statutes a reciprocal right, and were not at liberty to dissolve the matrimonial alliance by giving a bill of divorce to that effect. In the later periods, however, of the Jewish state, the Jewish matrons—the more powerful of them at least—appear to have imbibed the spirit of the ladies of Rome, and to have exercised in their own behalf the same power that was granted by the Mosaic law to their husbands. Josephus Antiq. xv. 7–10 ; Mark vi. 17–29 ; x. 12. In case the wife felt herself injured and aggrieved, we may infer, from the fact of the concubine's possessing that right who had previously been a maid-servant, that the wife also possessed the right of obtaining a bill of divorce from a judge. Exod. xxi. 10."

1 Cor. vii. 7, 37. He therefore, on the whole, that finds he is able to receive this saying, let him receive it ; or let him that is in his own conscience persuaded that he can glorify God most by a single life, choose it. Others may, and ought, to marry, but let none lightly rush into that state, on the supposition that the bond of it may be broken through at pleasure." From this it would seem that man is not bound to marry. Heaven has left it an optional matter.

Matthew 19:13-15

Christ and Little Children

This seems to me one of the most glorious passages in the glorious biography of the glorious Redeemer of our race. Even the most brilliant of His miracles do not impress me so much with the sublime as this. As I look at Him in this, the most stirring period of His history, with the dark events of His last agonies thickening on His horizon, condescending to take little children in His arms and bless them, I feel deeper chords in my nature touched than when I see Him hush the furious tempest, or raise the buried dead.

In this passage there are *four* pictures, which, if we look at, and earnestly and devoutly study, will not fail to exert a most salutary influence upon the soul.

I. THE PICTURE OF GODLY PARENTS. " *Then were brought unto Him little children*"—Luke says " *infants,*"—" *that He might put His hands upon them, and pray.*" It was customary among the Jews of old to lay the hands on a person's head on whose behalf a prayer was offered. When Joseph brought his two sons, Ephraim and Manasseh, to his father Jacob for his farewell blessing, the dying patriarch put his hand on the head of each in pronouncing his benediction; Gen. xlviii. 14–20. " *The imposition of the hand,*" says Bengel, " and more particularly of the hands, was employed for conferring on, and propagating to, human beings, especially children and ministers of the Gospel, bodily blessings and spiritual gifts. See Acts xx. 12 ; Heb. vi. 2 ; 1 Tim. v. 22 ; 2 Tim. i. 6." The origin of this custom I cannot divine. Did it arise from the recognition of a power which certain modern biologists maintain belongs to human nature, of one man being able to transmit to another, through the agency of the hand, a portion of his own vital energy ? It may be so. Life is too mysterious, and modern revelations are too wonderful, to authorise any one dogmatically to deny the existence of such a power. Undoubtedly there are ways by which one man can affect another, of which at present we know absolutely nothing. Thoughtful men, therefore, will be modest how

they pronounce on such subjects. The question, however, is, Who
brought these little children to Christ for this purpose? Undoubtedly the parents. It is true we are not told so in so many
words, but we are left to infer the fact as a matter of course. Who
else would do so? Now look at those parents bringing their
children to Christ, and see in that act the highest privilege and the
most binding obligation of every human parent. What they did is
the duty of all who have children. We may look at the act of these
parents in two aspects :—

First : *As the wisest service of parental love.* It is the instinct of
parental love to desire and seek the welfare of their offspring.
This is what all parents, worthy the name, are doing every day.
This instinct is one of the great springs in the complicated and ever-
acting machine of social life. It is true that very different methods
are employed for the purpose. The love of some parents employs
means that must inevitably prove ruinous to their children. Foolish
parental love has entailed ruin upon millions. It really damns the
dear objects it longs and strives to bless. My position is, that what
these parents did, is the *wisest* course for parental love to pursue, in
promoting the happiness of its object. You cannot do anything so
well for your children as bringing them to Christ ; nay, you cannot
do anything that can become a substitute for this, anything in sooth
that can be of any true service without this. This is the *essential*
thing.

In the first place, *your children have minds which will soon be
starting anxious questions which Christ alone can satisfactorily solve.*
Questions must of necessity start within them about their own
natures, relations, duties, and destiny ; about God, the great universe, and the wonderful future. The questions which have come
to all men, What am I? Whence came I? Whither am I tending?
How shall I be just with God? If a man die shall he live again?
will come to them, and stir the soul with agony. Who shall give
the answer? Sages? Priests? Oracles? No ; the world has tried
these for ages without success.

> " Sages after sages strove
> In vain to filter off a crystal draught
> Pure from the lees, which often more enhanced
> The thirst than slaked it, and not seldom bred
> Intoxication and delirium wild.
> In vain they pushed inquiry to the birth
> And spring-time of the world ; asked, Whence is man?
> Why formed at all? and wherefore as he is?
> Where must he find his Maker? With what rites
> Adore Him? Will He hear, accept, and bless?
> Or does he sit regardless of His works?
> Has man within him an immortal seed?
> Or does the tomb take all? If He survive
> His ashes, where, and in what weal or woe
> Knots worthy of solution, which alone
> A Deity could solve. Their answers, vague
> And all at random, fabulous and dark,
> Left them as dark themselves."—COWPER.

Christ alone can respond satisfactorily to them.

Take them, then, to Him; to learn of Him who is meek and lowly in heart, and find rest unto their souls.

In the second place, *your children have imitative faculties, by the agency of which the character will be formed, and consequently their destiny determined.* Man's character is formed on the principle of imitation. We become like our parents and dear associates. The loved ones with whom we mingle transfigure us into their moral image. We get their character. What is wanted, therefore, is a perfect model. And where is it to be found? Tell me where but in the evangelic biography. Christ is the only one.

In the third place, *your children will need some friend to succour them under the trials of life.* If man is born to trouble as the sparks fly upwards, dark and tempestuous days await your little ones. Disappointments, bereavements, disease, infirmities, death, are before them. They will require a friend to sustain them. Where is there an adequate friend? I know of none but Christ, a tender, faithful, all-powerful, ever-living friend—" *one that sticketh closer than a brother.*"

In the fourth place, *your children will require some one to deliver them from the difficulties in which they are involved.* They are the off-spring of a corrupt race, they inherit a nature prone to go astray, they are surrounded on all hands by seductive agents and polluting influences. As they rise into life they will feel themselves the sub-jects of guilt which they have contracted, and which will fill them with terrible forebodings of future punishment. The moral atmo-sphere they breathe is impregnated with evil. The prince of the power of the air taints it with his poisonous breath. Who shall de-liver them out of these difficulties? Who shall deliver them from the body of this death? This is the question? All experience says there is but One, and that is Christ. He is the only Saviour; One that is mighty to save. Can there then be a better way to show your love to your children than by bringing them to Christ? Nay, your love is blind and foolish, and will prove a curse to your offspring, unless you do so.

The other aspect in which you may look at the act of these parents, is,—

Secondly : *As that which is essential to the fulfilment of parental obligation.* Unless you do this, whatever else you do, you have neglected your duty. You may educate them in all the branches of human knowledge,—make them scholars and artists of the highest type ; you may by your industry endow them with splendid fortunes, and by your influence lift them to the highest position in society ; but unless you have brought them to Christ, you have neglected your duty, and will one day have to render an account for the tre-mendous omission.

But we have not only in this passage the picture of well-doing parents, but—

II. THE PICTURE OF NARROW RELIGIONISTS. " *The disciples re-*

buked" these parents for bringing their children. Why did the disciples thus repulse them? Was it from false ideas of Christ's dignity? Did they think that little children were beneath His dignity, and that therefore to present them to Him was to offer Him an insult? If they did they were greatly mistaken. An infant to the eye of Christ was an object of stupendous importance; a subject of immeasurable potentialities; a life for endless development and wondrous destinies. He saw the oak in the acorn, the waving harvest in the little seed. An infant to Him was an archangel, or arch-fiend, in embryo. It could not, therefore, be beneath His dignity to notice such. Or was it from the notion that such a presentation of children to Him was a *useless* act? Did they feel something like what some good people express in these days, when they say, Of what service is it to bring unconscious babes into connexion with religious ordinances? Did they say within themselves, Our Master is a great Teacher, and these little ones as yet have no power to grasp His great ideas, to understand His character, or to appreciate His [work; why therefore interrupt His procedure by such a useless demand? Or was it from exaggerated views of their own importance? Did they feel within themselves, He is our special friend; it is not to be supposed that He loves others as He loves us; we are His favourites, His chosen, His "dear people;" and the insolence of these rude parents in bringing their children to Him cannot be tolerated; we feel our dignity insulted in the attempt? I am very much afraid that the reason of their conduct is to be found somewhere in this direction. However, be the reason this or that, it was something that was displeasing to Christ. Luke says that "*When Jesus saw it He was much displeased.*" He felt a holy indignation. Anger is not sinful in itself. It is sometimes a holy passion. To flame with indignation at corrupt motives and base conduct is not wrong. I can scarcely conceive of virtue, living in a world like this, where there is so much that is morally oppressive, without flashing its lightnings, and hurling its thunderbolts. Christ often did so. "*Be ye angry and sin not.*"

Now, is there nothing in these days, amongst certain religionists, corresponding to the conduct of these disciples in rebuking these parents who brought the children to Christ? A bigoted churchman will rebuke you for bringing your children to Christ through a dissenting chapel; and a bigoted dissenter will do the same if you bring them hrough the church. Every narrow sect will rebuke you if you do not bring them through its little portals. The narrow sympathies, the miserable prejudices, the sectarian controversies, the cold-heartedness, the inconsistent lives—of the religionists of this age, act, I fear, as a repulse to many who attempt to bring their children to Christ.

III. THE PICTURE OF A LOVING CHRIST. But Jesus said,* "*Suffer*

---

* "The argument for infant baptism intended by the compilers of our liturgy in making this passage (Mark x. 13–16) the Gospel for the service, is very simple and sound. As little children were brought to Christ personally, were placed in

little children to come unto me and forbid them not, for of such is the kingdom of heaven. And He laid His hands on them," &c. Mark says : *"He took them up in His arms, put His hands on them, and blessed them."* Can you realize this wonderful scene? Christ is surrounded by a multitude, many of whom He had healed of their diseases. He had just delivered some thoughts of profound wisdom on the subject of marriage, in reply to questions which the captious Pharisees had put to Him, for the purpose of entrapping Him in some theological inconsistency. All around Him is excitement, and the terrible events of His last days are gathering thick about Him. His attention is at once arrested by mothers, and perhaps fathers, with the children in their arms, pressing their way through the crowd to Him for His blessing. The disciples, not supposing, perhaps, for a moment, that He will attend to them in such circumstances, rebuke them. But what does He do ? He addresses those who obstruct—*"Suffer them to come to me and forbid them not."* Anger and love both seem to ring in these words : anger towards the men, who, instead of encouraging, hinder them, and love towards the little children. Suffer them; *stand* back, clear the way, offer no obstruction, my heart yearns towards them. *"Forbid them not;"* they have as much claim to my affections as you have; I am as accessible to them as to any ;—*forbid them not.* "It was not the will of my Father that one of these little ones should perish." After He had thus addressed the obstructors, Luke tells us that *"He called them unto Him."* We are not told what He said either to the parents or the little ones. I should like to have had those sweet words recorded. With arms extended, and eyes beaming with more than earthly love, did He say, " Come hither, parents, with your dear little ones; heed not the rudeness of the crowd; be not disheartened by the cold repulse of my disciples, who ought to know better; press on; I will take them in my arms and bless them "? No; these words are not tender enough. Who can form a sentence to express His heart ? Then He takes them in His arms, looks at them with tenderest compassion, and blesses them; commends them to the loving guardianship of the great God. There

His arms, and received the imposition of His hands, which was the highest symbolical means and pledge of blessing, even so He favourably alloweth us to bring them to Him now, in the only corresponding way in which they can be brought, to receive the symbol which is administered in His name, as the means and the pledge of His blessing."—*Webster and Wilkinson.* On Acts xxi. 6, the same annotators remark: " The children then were surely considered Christians, as belonging to the household of faith. We see that they were taught to honour the word of the Gospel, and to respect the ministers of the Word; permitted to unite in an action of the church as recognised members of it, and to participate in services of an active character ; caused to make public profession of their religion with their seniors. Hence it is reasonable to conclude that they had also been admitted to baptism." In an interesting work, called " The Gospel in Burmah," an American missionary, in recording that the inhabitants of a village " received him as an angel of Christ Jesus," especially mentions how the mothers presented to him their babes to bless, and justifies his compliance with their request by referring to the conduct of Christ on this occasion.

is a sublime humanity in all this. Men of great natures have always shown an interest in children. Aye, there is more than humanity in it; there is a Godhood herein. What other teacher ever paid such an attention to children! The great teachers of past ages directed their attention more to the wealthy than the poor, more to adults than to children, and more to those distinguished by splendid talents than to those of ordinary powers. Christ preaches to the poor, and takes helpless infants in His arms.

IV. THE PICTURE OF A BEAUTIFUL HEAVEN. "*For of such*"—of children—"*is the kingdom of heaven.*" A picture is here suggested; it is the home of the *child* and the *childlike.*

First: *It is the home of the child in age.* Christ does not mean to convey the idea that heaven is only for children; no, but that heaven is *certain* for children. Adults by millions are excluded, but *never* an innocent child; and inasmuch as a great proportion of the race die in infancy, a larger portion of that age may be there than others. Not, of course, as infants; for maturity of faculty and character mark every tenant of that blessed home above. "*Of such is the kingdom of heaven.*" Blessed statement! This tends in some measure to solve the mystery of infantile suffering and death. Why do such millions of the human race just appear on earth, breathe a few hours, suffer, and then die? If the answer is, "To people heaven," I am satisfied. Let them die. "*The Lord gave and the Lord hath taken away.*" This, too, is a consolation for parents bereaved of their children. Do not mourn their loss. Rather rejoice that they are taken away from the evil that is to come, and that they have been so speedily translated to the better and brighter world.

Secondly: *It is the home of the child in character.* Whatever may be the earthly age of those who are taken to heaven, they have all the *childlike spirit;*—the spirit of docility, humility, and confidence. There are no proud haughty spirits in heaven. "Unless you repent," said Christ, "*and become as this little child, ye shall in no case enter into the kingdom of heaven.*"

Matthew 19:16-22

The Moral Characteristic; or, the one Determining Element of Character

There is a gradation in depravity as well as in excellence. Sin has its blade, its ear, and its full corn in the ear. Great injustice has been done to the cause of truth and humanity, by an indiscriminate denunciation of man. Those who are not far from the kingdom of God, almost Christians, receive the same treatment as those who are "earthly, sensual, and devilish," "twice dead," "without God and without hope in the world." If there be such a difference in depravity, it is natural and important to ask, How small may a man's depravity be, and how much his goodness, and yet he not be virtuous in the sight of God? In other words :— What is the determining element of character—that which divides into distinct classes and assigns to distinct dooms, the least depraved and the least good? What is the boundary line which throws into an impassable distance the kingdom of Satan from the kingdom of Christ? As between the life of an animal and the life of a plant, there is much correspondence, though there may be some point or points which divide them; and as between the life of a brute and the life of a rational being, there is much agreement, though at the same time there is a something which marks them off from each other; so whatever agreement there may be between the most virtuous sinner and the most imperfect saint, there is still a something which divides :—a moral *differentia*. What is it? What is that which turns the balance, that which makes a bad man good, and gives to natural virtues moral and divine worth? This momentous question we shall answer in the light of this narrative.

And we observe, negatively :—

First: *Not respect for moral goodness.* This young man, of accomplishments and fortune, paid a profound respect to the moral character of Christ. He "kneeled to Him." What did he reverence in Christ? There was no mark of worldly grandeur about Him. He was poor and despised. He saw moral goodness beaming in His looks and radiating from all the acts of His life. Respect for excellence is an amiable feature of character, especially when that goodness is found in connexion with nothing that the world considers great. It is common to see, magnify, and laud a very little virtue in a man of great worldly eminence. This little virtue will make him a great saint and hero. Sycophants will talk of it, and the press will trumpet it half the world over. It is, however, a rare natural virtue to observe and respect goodness in poverty, as this young man did now. But this is not the "one thing." What then?

Secondly : *Not correct theological knowledge.* In this young man's address to Christ he indicates a clear knowledge of three facts, which involve much correct theological information. (1) *The existence of future blessedness.* He knew more than Socrates. He not only knew of a future state, but of a future state of blessedness— "eternal life." (2) *The necessity of good works to obtain it.* "What good thing shall I do?" He knew that he could never get it by adopting a certain creed or cherishing certain sentimental feelings; but that something must *be done, and done by himself.* Unless our faith and feelings are wrought into acts and habits they are worth nothing. (3) *The capability of Christ to direct him in the right course.* "Good Master," etc. Now all this is a good portion of a good creed. But there was "one thing" wanted yet. What?

Thirdly : *Not a strong desire for future blessedness.* Neither his station in life nor his wealth satisfied him; he felt the world unsatisfying. *He desired heaven.* This is common. Heavenly desires are but the breathings of earthly selfishness. This young man desired "eternal life." But "one thing" was wanted yet. What?

Fourthly: *Not a spirit of genuine docility.* He knew much, but he sought for more information, and sought it from Christ. This is good. Many men who call themselves Christians lose their docility. They know all, and become dogmatists, not learners. It is mentally healthy; it is virtuous to keep the inquiring faculty always alive, thirsting, and actively crying for more, and yet again for more.

Fifthly: *Not a faultless external morality.* "All these have I observed from my youth." No one in society could charge him with the violation of any social right; or, the infringement of any social law. This was good; but "one thing" yet is wanted. What?

Sixthly: *Not susceptibility of conscience.* "He was sad at that saying, and went away grieved." It was the grief of conscience, for the want of heart to act in harmony with right. There may be moral susceptibility and yet the "one thing" lacking. What?

Seventhly: *Not Christ's appreciation of the good in him.* "Then Jesus beholding him loved him." All that was good in him Jesus saw and valued. He, the just one and the kind, will give the worst man credit for the least virtue that may be in him. What, then, is the "one thing"—one word expresses it. LOVE. He could not sell all that he had, and give to the poor :—he had not the heart for it. This was the lacking thing. By LOVE I do not mean *natural kindness*, mere amiability of temperament, nor *emotional charity*— a thing that rises occasionally in the heart of the most selfish in the prospect of suffering, or under the wand of some eloquent appeal— *nor conventional philanthropy* which subscribes to benevolent institutions by custom or by rule. *But that affection which has such a supreme regard for the character of God and the interests of others,* that all private interests are kept in the background and absorbed; —an affection which swallows up the material in the spiritual, the individual in the universal, the human in the Divine.

That this LOVE is the "one thing," the *substratum* of moral goodness, is obvious,—

First: *From the constitution of the human soul.* (1) The deepest craving of the heart is to love—it rests not until it finds some object on which to centre its affections. The tendency of love is to bury self in the object— to sacrifice self at its shrine. (2) The impossibility of conscience smiling on any actions but those of disinterested affection. A sycophant world may praise selfish actions, but the conscience cannot; no bribery or sophistries can induce it to do so. And if conscience approve not, what are we? (3) There is no principle but LOVE that can secure a full and harmonious development of our nature. You may as well endeavour to make the seeds in your garden grow and ripen to perfection by excluding the sun, as to endeavour to cultivate to perfection the germs of your spiritual being without disinterested love. It is obvious,—

Secondly: *From the teachings of the Bible.* The Scriptures teach that love implies "the whole duty of man," that it is, especially, the "new commandment;" and that whatever else we have, if we have not this love, we are nothing. (1 Cor. xiii.) The absence of this love from the soul, is—*chaos—disharmony—hell.*

Brother, have you this "one thing"? Remember, that without it, whatever else you may have, you are morally worthless and wretched; you are a cloud without water; you are a star wandering from your orbit, without law, without light, without life,—rushing into boundless gloom and ruin. Remember, that to love others truly and disinterestedly, you must love God supremely; that true philanthropy ever springs from piety. Remember, that to love God, you must study His moral loveliness,—for it is only as the heart muses, that the fire will burn; and remember, that to study the character of God, you must look at Him as He appears to you as a *sinner*, in the life of Him who is "the brightness of His glory, and the express image of His person."

Matthew 19:23-26

The sad Condition of Wealth-loving Men

The narrative which gave rise to this exciting and solemn conversation between Christ and His disciples we glanced at in our last section. Our space will scarcely allow us to do more than bring out with prominence the three solemn facts which are contained in these words. They teach,—

I. That the difficulties in the way of a wealth-loving man's salvation are very great. We say a *wealth-loving* man, for to such the heavenly Teacher refers,—and not to the man who merely possesses riches. In Mark's Gospel, indeed, it is so stated. It is the man "*who trusts in riches,*"—the man who sets his heart upon them, and holds them as the chief good. He who has wealth, and holds it in subordination, will find it rather facilitate than hinder his salvation. His wealth will purchase for him books, leisure, and all the necessary provisions of spiritual culture and development. It is not wealth *per se* that is the obstruction; it is the *love* of it. The difficulty which the man who *trusts* in his riches will find in the way of salvation, Christ represents in this passage in a strong and startling way: "*It is easier for a camel to go through the eye of a needle*" than for such a wealth-loving man to enter into the kingdom of God. Some expositors have very gratuitously substituted in their translation of this passage, the word *cable* for "camel," in order to avoid what they considered the unwarrantable extravagance of the language as it stands in our version. But the expression is manifestly proverbial, as Dr. Kitto has shown.* Now the difficulties in the way of salvation, to the man who trusts in his wealth, may be illustrated by the following considerations :—

First : *The disposition of heart, and habits of life which such a state of mind engenders.* The man who is wealthy, and trusts in his wealth, is almost sure to become proud, self-sufficient, unsympathetic, worldly, and indifferent alike to the claims of society and the institutions of religion. The man who trusts in his wealth, and who has more than heart can wish, is likely to "*set his mouth against the heavens.*"

Secondly : *The teachings of the Divine revelation on the subject.* Moses warned the children of Israel against the tendency of wealth to injure the soul (Deut. viii. 11, 14). Solomon says, "*He that trusteth in his riches shall fall*" (Prov. xi. 28). Christ says, "*The deceitfulness of riches choke the word*" (Matt. xiii. 22). Paul says,* "*They that will be rich fall into temptation*" (1 Tim. vi. 9). James

* "*'It is easier for a camel to go through the eye of a needle,'* &c. Lightfoot and others have shown, that to speak of a camel or other large animal—as an elephant—as going through the eye of a needle, was a proverbial expression, much used in the schools, to denote a thing very unusual or very difficult. Thus, in a discourse about dreams, to intimate that they do not exhibit things of which the mind had no previous conception, it is said, 'They do not show a golden palm-tree, or an elephant passing through the eye of a needle.' Again, to one who had delivered something which was thought very absurd, or scarcely credible, it was, said, 'Perhaps thou art one of the Pombeditha (a Jewish school of Babylon) who can make an elephant go through the eye of a needle.' Thus, also, the authors of an edition of the book of Zohar express the arduous nature of their undertaking by saying, 'In the name of our God, we have seen fit to bring an elephant through the eye of a needle.'

"A similar form of expression, or indeed the same, may be traced very extensively in the East. In the Koran, 'Until the camel shall enter the needle's eye ' (*ear* in Arabic), occurs in the same sense. 'Narrower than the eye (ear) of a needle,' is still applied to business of a difficult nature ; and even in India, 'an elephant going through a little door,' or 'through the eye of a needle,' are proverbial expressions of the same import. Some of these illustrations are important to fix the true force and meaning of the expression ; and all show the error of several Greek transcribers (followed by some translators), who, not understanding the expression as it stood, took the liberty of supposing it a mistake, and therefore altered κάμηλος, 'a camel,' to κάμιλος ' a cable,' producing the reading, 'It is easier for a *cable* to go through the eye of a needle, &c. See Lightfoot and Gill *in loc.* ; Michaelis's ' Introduction,' vol. i p. 131 ; Burckhardt's ' Arabic Proverbs, No. 396, &c.

"The real *origin* of such a proverb is a question respecting which many conjectures have been offered, a few of which we may here repeat. The Rev. F. J. J. Arundell, in his ' Discoveries in Asia Minor ' (ii. 119–123), says : ' As we ascended the hill, I saw something shining on the road, which proved to be one of the needles used by the camel-drivers for mending their camel-furniture. It was about six inches long, and had a large, very long eye. It had evidently been dropped by one of the conductors of a caravan which was some way ahead of us. . . . This association of the needle with the camels at once reminded me of the passage which has been considered so difficult to be illustrated: "It is easier for a camel to pass through the eye of a needle, than for a rich man to enter the kingdom of God." Why should it not be taken literally ? As the usages of the East are as unvarying as the laws of the Medes and Persians, I can easily imagine that even the camel-driver of Rachael carried his needles about with him to mend "the furniture," and the equipment of a camel-driver in those days could not well have says, "*The friendship of the world is enmity with God*" (Jas. iv. 4). And John says, "*If any man love the world, the love of the Father is not in him*" (1 John ii. 15). Such is the testimony of the Bible.

Thirdly : *The general history of mankind.* Does not the history of Christian evangelisation to the present hour, show that not "*many of the rich and mighty are called*"? There were two apostates in the first era of the Church,—Judas, and Demas,—and it was the love of money that ruined them. There were but two rich men that evinced any love for Christ; and they were both timid,—Nicodemus, and Joseph of Arimathea.

II. THAT THIS IMMENSE DIFFICULTY IS SUFFICIENT TO AWAKEN, IN THE MIND OF THE THOUGHTFUL, THE MOST PROFOUND SOLICITUDE. "*Who then can be saved ?*" This question arose not from idle curiosity, not as a mere proposition for speculative debate, but as a profoundly anxious problem of the heart. There were three things, perhaps, which served to make the disciples supremely solicitous on this point at this moment :—

been more simple than at [present. . . . The needle, from its constant and daily use, must have held a prominent place in his structure of ideas and imagery ; and as we all know how fertile the imaginations of these camel-drivers were in furnishing us with proverbs and legendary tales, why may not the impracticability of a camel's passing through the eye of his needle have been a common expression to denote an impossibility?'

"Another explanation, as ingenious, but much less natural and probable, is indicated by the same writer : ' Everybody has heard of the obelisks of Alexandria, called the *Needles* of Cleopatra—a name, I apprehend, anciently given to them and similar obelisks. These are usually erected at the entrance of temples. If two such obelisks were existing at Jerusalem, and so close to each other as not to admit the passing of a laden camel, and passable only by the traveller on foot, the proverb might have had its origin from hence.'

"Of the same kind, but much more probable, is the explanation suggested by Lord Nugent, in his ' Lands Classical and Sacred,' vol. i. p. 326. Entering Hebron, he says : ' We were proceeding through a double gateway, such as is seen in so many of the old eastern cities, even in some of the modern ; one wide-arched road, and another narrow one by the side, through the latter of which persons on foot generally pass, to avoid the chance of being jostled or crushed by the beasts of burthen coming through the main gateway. We met a caravan of loaded camels thronging the passage. The drivers cried out to my two companions and myself, desiring us to betake ourselves for safety to the gate with the smaller arch, calling it ' Es Summ el Kayût '—the hole or eye of the needle. If—as, on inquiry since, I am inclined to believe—this name is applied, not to this gate in Hebron only, but generally in cities where there is a footway entrance by the side of the larger one, it may perhaps give an easy and simple solution of what in the text (Mark x. 25) has appeared to some to be a strained metaphor ; whereas that of the entrance-gate, low and narrow, through which the sumpter-camel cannot be made to pass unless with great difficulty, and stripped of all the encumbrance of his load, his trappings, and his merchandise, may seem to illustrate more clearly the foregoing verse, ' How hardly shall they that have riches enter into the kingdom of God !' It also applies itself to several other passages by which our Saviour illustrates a similar subject, "Enter ye in at the strait gate," &c. (Matt. vii. 13, 14), and others.' "

* In 1 Tim. vi. 9, οἱ δὲ βουλόμενοι πλουτεῖν, they who are minded to be rich. Jas. iv. 4, ὃς ἂν οὖν βουληθῇ φίλος εἶναι τοῦ κόσμου, whoever is minded to be a friend of the world. This translation of βούλομαι, which the A. V. has in Matt. i. 19, might with advantage be preserved in many other passages.

First: *The transcendent importance of salvation to every man.* Having been with Christ for some time, they had heard His impressive teaching on the great question of the soul's salvation; and having had themselves a spiritual foretaste of "*eternal life,*" they unquestionably felt that if a man missed salvation, he missed everything in the universe worth having; nay, that the very missing of salvation would make self, Christ, and the universe, an intolerable curse to the soul. If this was their impression, it was right. "*What shall it profit a man?*" &c. And if this, moreover, was their impression, it was natural for them to feel the deepest solicitude in the question, "*Who then can be saved?*"

Secondly: *The commonness of that universal difficulty which Christ specified.* They knew that whilst wealthy men were a very insignificant minority in every country and community, yet wealth-desiring and wealth-loving men abounded everywhere. Whilst few possessed wealth, nearly all men desired it, struggled for it, and worshipped it; and it was in a state of mind common almost to the whole race that the difficulty lay. They would probably thus reason,—Since wealth-loving is such an immense obstruction to salvation, and since all men seem to have more or less of this feeling in them, "*Who then can be saved?*" Where are the men to be found free from this money-loving impulse?

Thirdly: *The rare excellences of the young man who had just striven after salvation, but had failed.* Here was a young man of considerable religious intelligence, of unblemished moral reputation, who had great respect for Christ, and a great desire for future blessedness; one, too, whom Christ loved, who had made an earnest application for salvation; but who failed, and was gone away from Christ "*sorrowful!*" Would they not reason thus,—If a young man of such rare excellences, so distinguished in certain points of goodness from the great bulk of our kind, fail, who can succeed?

We can thus account for their anxiety; would that we could adequately feel it! "*Who then can be saved?*"

III. THAT THE DIFFICULTY, THOUGH IMMENSELY GREAT, CAN BE OVERCOME BY GOD. "*With man this is impossible,*" &c. Two remarks will serve to illustrate this:—

First: *That the salvation of any man, with this state of mind, is impossible to God as well as to man.* So long as a man loves the pelf, powers, and pleasures, of the world, he cannot be saved. The tree of life and the fruits of paradise cannot grow in such a heart, the springs of "*eternal life*" cannot well-up from such a nature. In other words, God Himself cannot save a man *in* his sins.

Secondly: *That the salvation of any man, in any way, is impossible to all but God.* He alone can overcome this wealth-loving power, as well as every other element in the soul that is antagonistic to salvation. He has done so in millions of instances, and will continue to do so, *but never independently of the sinner's own agency.*

Matthew 19:27-30; 20:1-19

The Reward of Piety

WHAT SHALL WE HAVE THEREFORE? This question, thus started by Peter, and eternally echoed by selfish religionists, is the key to the interpretation of the entire passage.* Although piety, in its highest moods, disdains such a mercenary inquiry as this—is too full of gratitude to think of gain—too absorbed in the delights of present engagements, to feel aught of solicitude about future joys; still Jesus deems it proper to reply; and, in responding to the inquiry, He propounds certain great truths in relation to its rewards; and to these truths, as here developed, we shall give our present attention.

I. THAT THE REWARD OF PIETY, IN RELATION TO THE APOSTLES, WAS ASSOCIATED WITH MUCH THAT WAS PECULIAR. "Verily I say unto you, That ye which have followed me, in the regeneration, when the Son of Man shall sit in the throne of His glory, ye also shall sit upon twelve thrones, judging the twelve tribes of Israel." † There are two general thoughts contained in this passage, which will develop what was *peculiar* to the apostles in the reward of piety—

First: *That they had a special connexion with this great work of spiritual reformation.* They *followed* Christ "in the regeneration;" they were His *immediate* successors; they caught the world-regenerative words from His lips, and imbreathed the reformation-spirit from His life; they witnessed those wonderful facts of His history on which the doctrines of His renovating system are based, and by which they are illustrated and enforced. In the "upper room" at Jerusalem, they waited for that Spirit which He promised, and which descended on them, giving them "tongues of fire" to proclaim His truths, and powers of miracle to enforce the same. They first con-

---

* The word "for," with which the 20th chapter begins, plainly shows its connexion with what goes before; nor can the parable given in the first nineteen verses of the 20th chapter be fully understood, unless it be looked at as a reply to Peter's interrogation.

† The word "regeneration" we regard as designed to designate that great spiritual reformation which Christ came into the world to promote amongst men, and which, through His system, has been slowly proceeding ever since, and will continue to progress from age to age until the *moral* "restoration of all things." The period alluded to in the expression, "when the Son of Man shall sit in the throne of His glory," seems to us to refer unquestionably to His ascension to heaven, when He became invested with authority; and when, in consequence of His dispensation of the Spirit on the day of Pentecost, the "regeneration" received an impulse that should gain new force and influence from that moment to the last hour. The promise here made to the disciples to "sit upon twelve thrones, judging the twelve tribes of Israel," contains a spiritual and Christian idea enrobed in material and Jewish costume. As "the twelve tribes" comprehended the whole of the Jewish people, the expression is here used to designate the whole Christian church. James, in the first verse of his epistle, uses it in this sense; and the "twelve thrones" evidently mean, that each of the apostles should be invested with a ruling authority in that church.

veyed His glorious message of mercy " in Jerusalem, and in all Judea, and in Samaria, and unto the uttermost parts of the earth." Thus, in a special sense, they " followed " Him " in the regeneration."

Secondly : *That, in consequence of the special connexion which they had with this great work of spiritual reformation, they were invested with peculiar authority.* " Ye also shall sit upon twelve thrones." Each shall have authority amongst " the twelve tribes "—the general church.

Has not this promise been fulfilled ? Have not the apostles ever since sat on moral thrones in the church ? Have not their speeches and writings ever been regarded as of unquestionable authority ? Have not all the succeeding disciples of Jesus bowed reverentially to their words ? Are they not judges in all the tribes of our Israel? They are, indeed, the greatest moral sovereigns, Christ excepted, ever born of men. No systems of thought, however venerable with age or radiant with genius; no scheme of government, however advocated by eloquence or defended by arms; can stand long if they oppose these monarchs of Israel. They fade and melt away before the brightness of apostolic *dicta*. These apostles are enthroned in the hearts of the good : side by side they sit down with Jesus on the throne of redeemed souls. Their empire survives the ruins of time, and will one day encompass the wide world.

This *authority*, then, is an element in the reward of the apostles' piety *peculiar* to themselves. From the nature of the position they occupied in the system of Jesus, no others will ever participate of this honour. We infer, from this passage—

II. THAT THE REWARD OF PIETY, IN THE CASE OF ALL, IS INEXPRESSIBLY GREAT. "And every one that hath forsaken houses, or brethren, or sisters, or father, or mother, or wife, or children, or lands, for my name's sake, shall receive an hundredfold, and shall inherit everlasting life." Three ideas are here suggested, which will bring out our general proposition—

First : That respect for Christ is essential to the *rewardableness* of human conduct. "For my name's sake," says Christ. The expression, which is of frequent occurrence, indicates, I think, supreme respect for the spirit which He exemplified, the doctrines He taught, and the enterprise He adopted. To respect Christ in this sense is to respect the greatest truths, the most perfect goodness, the highest interests of humanity, and the sublimest manifestations of God; and this is *virtue*, and nothing else. " Whatsoever ye do, therefore," saith the apostle, "in word or deed, do all in the name of the Lord Jesus."

Secondly : That respect for Christ may frequently involve great sacrifices. At the outset of Christianity, those who identified themselves with it had to forsake "houses," "brethren," "sisters," &c.; and, up to the present moment, it has held true that the full and faithful carrying out of religion involves sacrifices in some form or other. The next truth which this verse contains is,—

Thirdly : That these sacrifices, however great, are infinitely more than compensated. An hundredfold shall be received in this life, and in the future state everlasting life. The advantages of a religious life here are infinitely more than a counterbalance to all the inconveniences that may arise out of it. What inward tranquillity! what uplifting thoughts! what buoyant energy of soul! what high aspirations! what lofty hopes! what kindling inspirations! How delightsome to feel that death is gain, that God is our Father, that the universe is our home, and that eternity is the sphere where we shall develop our powers, realise our desires, and fulfil our aims! But what is all this to the hereafter—EVERLASTING LIFE? Here are ages of enjoyment that no arithmetic can compute; oceans of pleasure, whose majestic billows rise from the depths of infinitude, and break on no shore!

This is the reward of piety for all—not for the apostles only, but for "every one." We infer, from this passage—

III. THAT THE REWARD OF PIETY IS INVARIABLY OBTAINED IN CONNEXION WITH LABOUR. In the parable, the householder rewarded none "in the evening" who had not been employed some part of the day in the vineyard. Those who continued "all the day idle" received nothing from the householder's hand at the reckoning hour. *Work* is Heaven's condition of prosperity and enjoyment in everything. Indolence brings ruin to the individual and the state, to the body, intellect, and soul. It fills our workhouses with paupers, our prisons with culprits; it keeps the intellect in the darkness of ignorance and error, and the will in the chain of prejudice and passion; it makes the moral heart of the world like the "field of the slothful," all grown over with thorns and nettles, "and the stone-wall thereof broken down." Who, then, will be rewarded "in the evening"? Not the man whose religion consisted merely in hearing sermons, seeking comfort, talking his beliefs, uttering sentimental sympathies, and offering prayers; but the man who laboured earnestly, faithfully, and devoutly, in the cause of humanity, for Christ's sake.

I infer, from this passage—

IV. THAT THE REWARD OF PIETY IS NOT REGULATED BY THE TIME ON WHICH THE LABOUR WAS ENTERED. Here are persons who commenced their labours at different hours in the day—some who entered even on the last hour—and yet all received the same sum. The common opinion concerning these "hours" is, that they refer to the different periods of *individual life*—childhood, youth, middle life, old age. Against this opinion I have two objections :—first, that such an idea does not harmonise with the design of Christ, which was to answer the question of Peter; and, secondly, that such an idea tends to weaken the motive for the present consecration, by holding out an advantage for procrastination; for if the man who adopts religion in the "eleventh hour"—in old age—will be treated the same as he who has pursued a religious course from the first of his conscious being, what motive is there for youthful consecration? It seems to me to refer not to the different periods of individual life, but to the different periods of *Gospel history.* Our Saviour is answering the question of men who entered the Christian vineyard on the first period of the history of His system—the "third hour"—the dim dawn of the Gospel day; and who seemed to feel that they had a claim to special honours on that account. Jesus reminds them, by His parable, that there was no ground for such a hope: that the people who would enter on the work in any subsequent age, up to the very last hour in the world's history, would be treated alike. This view not only gives point to Christ's reply, but a sublime grandeur to His system. His system is not for one generation, nor one age, but for all generations and all ages, up to the last. Century after century, up till the clock of time strikes the last hour, men will be entering His vineyard; and the man of the last age shall be rewarded as well as the man of the first. Thus the old proverb shall receive another illustration :—" The last shall be first, and the first last."

V. THAT THE REWARD OF PIETY IS EVER ADMINISTERED ON PRINCIPLES OF UNDENIABLE FAIRNESS. Some of those labourers in the parable who had entered the vineyard first, on receiving the same pay as those who had entered last, "murmured against the good-man of the house, saying, These last have wrought but one hour," &c.*

The murmuring affords an opportunity of showing how fair the principles are on which He bestows rewards.

First: It always agrees with the understanding of the labourer when he commenced his work. "Didst thou not agree with me for a penny?" What is the promise that Christ makes to a man on his entering His system? SALVATION. This is, indeed, all that Christ *directly* bestows. All the *peculiarities* of glory spring out of diversity of talent, position, &c. The labourer thinks of nothing more than SALVATION at the time. To have this is his highest aim; and this "penny," this reward, every true labourer shall have. "Believe on the Lord Jesus Christ, and thou shalt be saved."

Secondly: It always agrees with the manifest principles of justice. "Is it not lawful for me to do what I will with mine own?" Indeed, in Christ's labour there is no right to a reward; the very word is an accommodation. Who gave the *strength* to labour, the *time* to labour, the *disposition* to labour? Christ. Whatever blessing, therefore, comes as the result, is a sovereign gift, rather than a righteous allotment. Where, then, is the ground for murmuring? "Is thine eye evil, because I am good?"—Art thou envious, because I am so generous to all?

VI. THAT THE REWARD OF PIETY WILL BE EXTENSIVELY ENJOYED. "For many be called, but few chosen." Three different ideas have been attached to this expression. The first is, that whilst God calls many by the Gospel, He has only chosen a few to be saved; the second, that the chosen refers to the Jews, and the called to the

---

* This murmuring of the labourers is a mere stroke on the background of the picture, to show off to greater effect the main subject. All parables have such strokes.

Gentles; and the third, that the chosen refers to the few apostles selected as His first heralds, and the many to those who, by His Gospel, shall be brought into His kingdom. The first is a God-dishonouring idea, entertained by a class which, under the increasing light of intelligence, is dwindling fast. The second is an idea which is, unquestionably, true, but not, we think, the truth intended to be taught. Christ is answering a question put by His disciples, who were, in an especial sense, His *chosen* ones; and what He means, I presume, is, You, my disciples, are but very few compared with the many that are to be called to the high privileges of my kingdom.

Matthew 20:20-28

The True and False in Greatness

Jesus, in His teaching, legislated for the varied instincts of our spiritual constitution; a fact which at once proves the divinity of His mission, and gives to His system an incomparable value.

In the interesting narrative before us, we have the most unmistakeable directions concerning this native love of greatness—this ambition. We have here FALSE and TRUE greatness illustrated. The conduct of the disciples reveals the former, and the address of Jesus the latter. The conduct of the disciples suggests several things which must ever mark false greatness.

First : *That it is selfish.* The mother is here represented as seeking exaltation for her sons. In Mark she is not mentioned. They are the direct applicants; but whether they applied through the medium of their parent or not, the request was theirs, and self-aggrandisement was the idea. The mother thought only of her sons, and they thought only of themselves; even the claims of their ten brethren were overlooked. To be raised to power, to sit on the right and left hand of Christ, and receive the reverence of men, was at present their master-thought. Self has ever been the primal idea of the world's great man.

> " Fain would he make the world his pedestal,
> Mankind the gazers, the sole figure he. "

But, vain man, how false thy motive ! I lay it down as an incontrovertible principle, that *greatness can never be obtained from selfish motives.* Little motives can never make great men. He who is under the sway of self-interest is in the declining, not in the advancing scale. The self-seeking disposition enervates the moral powers, and eats as a canker into the very stamina of our manhood. You may as well expect luxuriant crops to start from untilled deserts, as to expect the highest powers of your nature to grow and flourish in the soil and atmosphere of a selfish heart. Disinterestedness is the soul of greatness.

Secondly : *It is external.* "Grant that these my two sons may sit, the one on Thy right hand, and the other on the left, in Thy kingdom." Their notions of Christ's kingdom were purely material: they thought of it in connexion with all the pomp and pageantry of an earthly sovereignty, that should shiver the sceptre of the Cæsars —make Jerusalem the empress of the world—rear for her a throne on the ruins of mighty empires ; that should govern all peoples, and flourish through all periods. From what He had just said to them about His resurrection, they thought that the hour of this illustrious power was on the dawn, and they now ambitiously sought to participate in its splendour. So grovelling and gross was their idea of greatness, that they looked for it without, not within. Ever, indeed, has this notion prevailed, and over the wide world does it reign to this hour ; and yet there shall not be found a thinking man who will stand up and seriously defend it. No ! The unsophisticated common-sense of humanity declares, what all history proves, that the true greatness of man is not in externalisms, however magnificent and dazzling. Purple robes, elevated offices, territorial possessions, armorial bearings, high-sounding titles, mitres, coronets, crowns—can any or all of these attach greatness to a human soul ? Ask me, can the paint of the artist add to the natural beauties of the landscape ? Can a spark increase the lustre of the great sun ?

Thirdly : *It is unreflective.* "But Jesus answered and said, Ye know not what ye ask." It was an unreasoning impulse of ambition that dictated their request. Had they duly considered the nature of that kingdom of which He had often spoken to them, the sufferings which He told them awaited both Him and His followers, and the sublime ideas of greatness which He often presented to their attention, never would they have made such an application as this.

Have not false notions of greatness ever been traceable to the want of reflection ? In whatever path we meet men in search of worldly distinction, we may address them in Christ's language, and say, " Ye know not what ye ask." Are you seeking greatness from *worldly riches*—endeavouring to amass wealth, and to become a man of princely fortune ? You know not what you ask, my brother. Reflect, and you will find that whilst wealth cannot make you great, it may expose you to—

" The loudest laugh of hell—the pride of dying rich."

Are you seeking greatness from *worldly honours*—striving to get that before which men will kneel in servile homage, and for which they will ring your name on the loud trumpet of applause ? Still " Ye know not what ye ask." Reflect, and you will find that the world's highest eulogiums cannot add a " jot or tittle " of greatness to your *being*. Man is not great because the world votes him so.

The wild dreams of the old astrologers did not less affect the peaceful stars, than do the laudations or denunciations of the world the real greatness of *the man*. Before serious reflection the world's lustre grows dim, and the world's famed heroes fall from their lofty pedestal.

Fourthly: *It is dissocialising.* " And when the ten heard it, they were filled with indignation against the two brethren." The concord and amity of society must ever require the recognition of general rights, and the display of general sympathy. It is not in man to be harmonious with those who infringe his rights, and disregard his interests. False greatness respects no rights, and regards no interests but its own. Its temper is proud, overbearing, monopolising. Self is its divinity—a divinity so great that earth has no oblation too precious for its shrine. Ere now mighty cities have flamed as holocausts to this implacable god. Such a spirit as this must ever tend to loosen the foundation of social order. It is like that *wind* of which añ old Hebrew spoke, which produces whirlwind. Ah, me! what desolating and confounding *whirlwinds* have sprung up in society from this *wind* of false greatness! As the spirit of the two disciples now angered the ten, so the ambition of the few has, from the beginning, socially disturbed, and oftentimes enraged the many.

Such are some of the ideas which this incident suggests about false greatness. Let us proceed now to the address of Jesus, in order to ascertain something of the nature of TRUE greatness. I remark—

First: *That Christ-like suffering is the condition of true greatness.* "Are ye able to drink of the cup that I shall drink of, and to be baptized with the baptism that I am baptized with?" You are seeking greatness when you should be expecting suffering. " Are you prepared to participate in the sufferings that await me?" This appeal of Christ struck at once at the *root* of their vain ambition, and intimated the connexion subsisting between suffering and glory. Jesus does not say, there is no throne before you; He leaves them in its anticipation; but He does assure them that suffering like His must first come. In the writings of the apostles, the principle here suggested, that Christ-like suffering is the condition of human glory, is stated with precision, enforced with power, and repeated with frequency. We read of being " crucified with Christ," of being " buried with Christ," and of being " made conformable unto His death." The meaning of all this is obvious: it is not that we are to endure the agonies or the specific forms of suffering that He endured, but that we are to have ever that SELF-SACRIFICING spirit, of which His sufferings were the effects and expressions. This is the " fellowship with His sufferings;" this is the drinking of His cup, and the being baptized with His baptism; and this is the necessary condition of true greatness. Would you get high up to the moral throne of Christ, and share in the sublime honours of His spiritual empire? You must have that indomitable sympathy with the cause of truth, right, and God, which would impel you, if need be, to sacrifice property, ease, comfort, and life itself, for its sake—a sympathy under whose influence *self*-seeking is crucified and buried, and the soul " filled with all the fulness of God." This is the basis of all true nobility. Without this spirit man can never display those attributes which the conscience of society honours, the universe applauds, and the great God approves.

Secondly : *God is the source of true greatness.* " To sit on my right hand, and on my left, is not mine to give, but for whom it is prepared of my Father." This language fully expresses the idea that God hath prepared greatness for men. Indeed, all good emanates from the Father. He is the primal Fountain of our being and blessings. The things He hath " prepared " may be divided into two classes—the *given* and the *gained;* those that are bestowed unconditionally, and those that are reached as the results of conditions. Light, air, water, existence with its varied powers and natural relationships, Jesus, and the Bible, are of the former class. They are all conferred, not procured. Luxuriant crops, mental discipline, intellectual knowledge, moral character, are of the latter class. In the nature of things, they are reached only as the results of certain human operations. *Greatness* is one of the blessings that the Father had prepared in this conditional way. Men can only obtain it from the Father as the agriculturist gets his crops, or the scholar his knowledge,—*by fitting agency.* This explanation serves two purposes : it shows that they " for whom it is prepared," are they who properly attend to the settled conditions for acquiring it ; and it shows that there is a deep truth underlying the expression of Jesus, it " is not mine to give." It cannot be *directly* given. It is like knowledge—it must come as the result of individual effort. Did the true dignity of man consist in being robed in splendour, or fed on luxuries; in being lifted to high civic offices; having titles appended to the name, or an imperial crown encircling the brow, it might be given ; the outward hand of patronage could confer the boon. It has often done so—often made civic peers of intellectual and moral plebeians, political sovereigns of mental and spiritual serfs—greatness consists in a sublime inward energy to think without prejudice, to love without lust, to will without selfishness, and to follow duty with a brave heart, ever " making melody " to God, and it can only be attained by the strivings of a personal agency. No one can carry thee up the " holy hill " of true greatness. Thou must climb its height thyself— thou must weave thine own crown— rear thine own throne. The " Father hath prepared " them for thee, but they must be wrought out of, and by the powers He has given thee.

Thirdly : *Social usefulness is the manifestation of true greatness.* " But Jesus called them unto Him, and said, Ye know that the princes of the Gentiles exercise dominion over them, and they that are great exercise authority upon them. But it shall not be so among you : but whosoever will be great among you, let him be your minister: and whosoever will be chief among you, let him be your servant." In the kingdoms of the world, men are considered great in proportion to their wishes and their wants. Hence, to break down the individual independency of men, and reduce them to mere instruments to be wielded at pleasure, has ever been the aim and effort of the ambitious and the proud. The antithesis of this is true greatness. Its measure is not determined by the numbers that servilely attend on us, *but rather by the numbers that we benevolently attend upon.* Its mission is to minister, not to master; to give, not to govern. Its sceptre is love, not force; its throne is in the heart, and its empire over souls.

Fourthly: *Jesus Christ is the model of true greatness.* "Even as the Son of Man came not to be ministered unto; but to minister, and to give His life a ransom for many." Though the reputed son of an obscure mechanic of Nazareth—though He lived on the bounty of others, had no home in His suffering life, and scarcely a friend in His ignominious death—though despised and rejected of men, a Man of sorrows, and acquainted with grief," still He was sublimely great—great in all the attributes of goodness and power. He was great in the spotless purity of His character, in the unconquerable energy of His love, in the invincibility of His will, and in His spiritual identification with the heart and plans of the Infinite Father. Under the miserable and tattered garb of worldly indigence and social degradation, His greatness was seen. He wept over the poverty of the opulent, and over the degradation of kings. His contemporaries saw His moral majesty gleaming through His mean externalism. The populace saw it on His way to Jerusalem, "lowly and riding upon an ass," and they fell in reverence, and shouted, "Hosanna to the Son of David." Pilate saw it as He stood a prisoner at his bar, and, after pronouncing the wicked sentence, washed his hands in the open court, and declared, "I am innocent of the blood of this just person." The Roman ruffians saw it under the pale moon in Gethsemane, and fell as dead to the ground. The centurion saw it sitting in majesty on His bleeding brow, as He hung upon the cross, and "feared greatly, saying, Truly this was the Son of God."

Here, amidst the deepest poverty, and greatest suffering, is the greatness I call on you to imitate—the true greatness of man. Would you become a great painter? Take the pencil, and study some Titian. Or a sculptor? Take the chisel, and study another Phidias. Or a poet? Take the pen, and study a Milton or a Wordsworth. If you would become a *great man*, take the *heart* and study CHRIST. Look at Him until, with emphasis, you can call riches dust, worldly splendour toys, worldly titles, idle dreams, and until you feel that the true glory of man is "the glory which shall be revealed IN US."

Worldly glories are but as bubbles on the troubled streams of time —we touch them and they burst; are but as clouds without water in the sky of life—though fringed with the golden beams of the

setting sun, they vanish into thinnest air ere the morning dawn.
Ah! that morning—that morning!

> " Some sink outright :
> O'er them and o'er their names the billows close :
> To-morrow knows not they were ever born.
> Others a short memorial leave behind,
> Like a flag floating when the bark's engulfed,
> It floats a moment, and is seen no more :
> One Cæsar lives—a thousand are forgot.''

Matthew 20:29-34

The Two Blind Men; Symbols of the Moral in Human History

It is noteworthy that the three Evangelists who record this event
differ in some striking particulars. Matthew speaks of *two* blind
men, Mark and Luke speak of *one*. Matthew and Mark represent
the event as taking place as Christ departed from Jericho ; Luke
says it occurred when he was " come nigh." These discrepancies
have led some expositors to the conclusion that the different Evangelists record different miracles; that one of these occurred when
Christ entered Jericho, and the other when He departed. One
method of reconciling these accounts we insert below.* Whatever
the number of the blind men, and however the accounts may be
harmonised, the lessons of the narrative remain very much the same.

* In order to reconcile these varying accounts, it is needful to remember, that
some of the Evangelists give a brief and condensed account of the very same event,
which others narrate more fully. " On this occasion two blind men received their
sight." This is expressly affirmed by Matthew. Only one is noticed by Mark and
Luke. Matthew also relates, that they were healed by Jesus on His departure
from Jericho. The óne mentioned by Mark was cured by Christ as He left Jericho.
His name {was Bartimeus. Taking the account of Matthew in connexion with
Mark's, we believe that there were in reality two blind men both restored to sight by
Christ as He passed from Jericho to Jerusalem. Let us now attend to what Luke
says : " As Jesus drew nigh to Jericho, a certain blind man sat by the wayside
begging." There is no ground for supposing that this blind man was the same as
Bartimeus, mentioned by Mark. He is not so called. It is not said that he was
Bartimeus. We believe that he was a different person. The reason of this
opinion is, that Bartimeus is said to have been healed by Christ as he left Jericho ;
whereas the blind beggar noticed in Luke's Gospel received his sight from our
Saviour when drawing nigh to the city. Thus there is no contradiction between
the narratives of the three Evangelists. Matthew relates that Christ performed
the remarkable miracle of giving sight to two blind men who sat begging by the
wayside, as He departed from Jericho, and we believe him. Mark notices but one
of these, whose name he gives ; but he does not say that Christ on that occasion
healed no more than one. His account, therefore, is not contradictory of Matthew's, though it is not so full. Luke again informs us that the Saviour, before
entering Jericho, healed a poor blind man who cried unto Him. This last individual was wholly different from either of those mentioned by Matthew. Taking,
therefore, the narratives of the three Evangelists together, we perceive from them
that three blind men received their sight from Christ during His visit to Jericho ;
one before He entered it, and two others as He left it.

We shall look upon the incident as illustrating much in connexion with the moral history of man.

I. THEIR CONDITION SYMBOLIZES THE MORAL CONDITION OF THE UNREGENERATE.

First: *They were poor.* They " *sat by the wayside begging.*" It is a sad thing to see a man living in a world where the God of nature has made such munificent provisions for the wants of all His creatures, reduced to such abject destitution as to be compelled to beg of his fellow-man. We say that poverty is not a crime; but this is only true in individual cases. Whilst the poverty of some good men is not attributable to any fault of their own, poverty always implies crime somewhere. Nature's granary is full enough for all. Be this, however, as it may, the greatest physical destitution only serves as a faint illustration of the moral destitution of the unregenerate man. "*He is without hope and without God in the world.*" He is a moral bankrupt. He has contracted immense debts, without the means of discharging one fraction of the mighty sum. The worst feature of his poverty is, he does *not know* it. He considers himself "rich and increased in goods, and having need of nothing; whereas he is poor, and wretched, and miserable, and blind, and naked." In this respect he is like the maniac pauper, who dreams that he is a king.

Secondly : *They were blind.* Physical blindness is an immense evil; for it shuts out all that is grand, beautiful, and bright, in this glorious universe. But a far greater evil is *moral* blindness, for the following reasons. (1) It shuts out greater glories. The material glories of the universe are but the ever-fading costume of Him who is "the King of Glory." Him moral blindness excludes. The man who is physically blind, like England's sightless bard, may see God and revel in the beauties of the spiritual creation. The sinner is "without God." (2) It is evermore criminal. It does not arise from the want of the organ of moral vision—for conscience is that organ; nor from the want of the medium of moral vision, *light.* Nature floods all souls with light, and the Bible, where it goes, brightens the radiance a thousand-fold. But it arises from the *voluntary* closing of the eye from the light,—hence the crime. If I shut my eyes, I am for the time as blind as if I had no eyes, or as if heaven were as black as pitch. Physical blindness is a misfortune to be pitied, but moral blindness is a crime to be condemned. (3) It is essentially unproductive of any good. Physical blindness is often turned to good account; the other senses are often so improved by it, that there is more than a compensation. Intellectual reflection and development are often stimulated by it, and not unfrequently has it been blessed to the highest spiritual ends. Our own glorious Milton, in his touching wail over his sightless condition, did not fail to recognise some of the advantages of his sad deprivation.

> " When I consider how my life is spent
> Ere half my days, in this dark world and wide,
> And that one talent which is death to hide,

Lodged with me useless, though my soul more bent
To serve therewith my Maker, and present
My true account, lest He, returning, chide ;—
Doth God exact day-labour light denied ?
I fondly ask ; but Patience, to prevent
That murmur, soon replies, God doth not need
Either man's work, or His own gifts ; who best
Bear His mild yoke, they serve Him best. His state
Is kingly ; thousands at His bidding speed,
And post o'er land and ocean without rest ;
They also serve who only stand and wait."—MILTON.

But moral blindness can be turned to no good account ; it is bad in itself, bad in all its issues, essentially and for ever bad.

II. THEIR EFFORT SYMBOLISES THE DUTY OF THE INQUIRER. These poor blind men did that which all who desire salvation should do ; they made a proper appeal to the Being who alone could help them. The appeal was proper in four respects.

First : *It was an appeal to the right Being.* They appealed to Christ as the *"Lord, the Son of David."* They recognised Him as the Messiah, through whom Jehovah, in the Old Testament, had promised to bless mankind. "I will make an everlasting covenant with you, even the sure mercies of David." (Isaiah lv. 3.) Had these poor blind men appealed to any other in the vast crowd which was passing by, it would not have been surprising ; help they wanted, and the first man they might have seized by the hand and entreated his assistance. But there was but *One* in the dense crowd they thought of, and that was the "Son of David," and to Him *alone* they appealed. In this way every inquiring soul should act, Do not dally with intermediate objects. Heed not the crowd ; there is not one amongst the millions can save you, but Christ. Through the teeming multitudes that crowd God's universe, cry out to Him, *so as to be heard*, "O Lord, Thou Son of David, have mercy on me." Their appeal was :—

Secondly : *An appeal for the right blessing.* It was for *mercy*,— mercy for a *specific* and deeply felt want. "*Lord, that our eyes may be opened.*" They felt the need of sight, and they appealed for *that* in the fewest and simplest words. This is prayer. There is no preamble, no vague utterance, no redundancy of expression, in *real* prayer. Much of what is called prayer in these modern times is nothing but a weak and windy string of sentences. Where do I find prayer ? In the cry of the publican in the Temple : "God be merciful to me a sinner ; " in the cry of Peter in the storm : "Lord, save or I perish ; " in the cry of the Canaanitish woman : "Lord, help me ; " in the cry of Saul of Tarsus : "Lord, what wilt Thou have me to do ? " Their appeal was :—

Thirdly : *An appeal at the right time.* When did they appeal ? "*When they heard that Jesus passed by.*" It was just the moment. They caught the tide at its flood. They seized the opportunity as it occurred. The *moment* they heard He was passing, "they cried out." Jesus is passing by us in the ministry of Providence, in the dispensation of His truth, in the strivings of His Spirit. "Cry out" to Him, &c. Their appeal was :—

Fourthly : *An appeal in the right spirit.* It was earnest, resolute, and persevering. "*The multitude rebuked them, because they should hold their peace.*" The populace, then, as now, was cold, haughty, and selfish. Crowds are tyrants. "These multitudes rebuked them." Why? Perhaps they wanted to monopolise the attention of the popular Teacher, or perhaps they thought these poor men beneath His notice; and that it was the height of arrogance for them to make the appeal. However, the spirit of these supplicants was not cowed by the rebuke of the heartless multitude. It rose superior to all the opposition—"they cried the more." True souls gain strength by opposition. The moral electricity within them bore them up against opposing currents; and they sail on

"Like thunder clouds against the wind."

In all these respects let us follow the example of these poor blind men, in our efforts for happiness. Let us appeal to the right Being, for the right blessing, at the right time, and in the right spirit.

III. THEIR RECOVERY SYMBOLIZES THE CONDITION OF THE REDEEMED. "Their eyes were opened."

First : *They were introduced to a new state of being.* Mark for a moment the procedure of Christ in effecting the cure. The first thing to be observed is : He is arrested in His journey.—"*He stood still.*" He who moves the universe is held by the prayer of these men. The next thing is : He "*commands them to approach Him.*" He called them to Him. This was a tremendous reproof to the crowd. He invites those whom they "rebuked." The next thing is : He asks them what they required Him to do. "*What will ye that I shall do unto you ?*" He does not ask for information, but to stimulate their earnestness, and to impress them with the fact that He was both able and willing to do whatever they needed. And the next thing is : *He touched their eyes.* "*And immediately they received their sight.*" What a change for them! The material creation is to us according to our five senses. Lessen their number and you reduce our universe; multiply them and you augment it. Of all the senses that of vision is for many reasons the most important. The sensations of colour, size, proportion, beauty, grandeur, splendour, are all dependent on the eye. When the blind man, therefore, receives sight, he receives a new universe. All about, around, and within him, is new. The great sun, the lovely moon, and the million stars of night, with all the countless objects of the glorious landscape, come to the blind man as he opens his eyes. But great as is the change in such cases, it only faintly symbolises the changes in the condition of the soul that is translated from the kingdom of darkness into the *marvellous* light of the Gospel.

Secondly : *They were started on a new course of action.* "*And they followed Him.*"

Matthew 21:1-11

The Relation of Christ to the Religious Feeling of Humanity

Christ was now about entering Jerusalem, the metropolis of Judea, the home of the prophets and priests, and the richest scene of Hebrew associations. It was on the Monday of that week on which the Jews would "fill up the measure of their iniquities" by crucifying the Son of God. It was the dawn of a wonderful week for Judea—for humanity—for the universe.

In the narrative of our Saviour's journey towards Jerusalem we discover several remarkable and profoundly significant things.

First: *The superhuman under the garb of the human.* The knowledge which He displayed about the existence, position, and owner of the ass in a neighbouring village, the right which He claimed to its use, the authority with which He despatched His two disciples, and the strange readiness of the owner to accede to His request, are indications of powers and rights more than human.

Secondly: *The majestic under the garb of the mean.* Christ as a *mere* man was great—great in intellect, heart, purpose, action;—as a Mediator, supremely great. But how does this great Being, Prince of the powers of the earth, enter Jerusalem? In a triumphal chariot?—on a stately, prancing steed, accompanied by a magnificent cavalcade? No! On an ass. The more truly kingly a man is, the less he cares for conventional pageantry. Your great men have never cared for jewellery. The more ornaments are coveted, and dress is studied, the more mean and impoverished the soul. Heart of oak requires neither veneer nor varnish. A great age has never been an age of millinery and gold rings. The kingly soul does not care for the robe or the crown.

Thirdly: *The eternal under the garb of the incidental.* It seemed perfectly incidental that Christ should have required a creature to ride upon, and that there should be such a creature at hand: but all this was but the carrying out of an eternal plan that an old prophet saw some six hundred years before. "*Rejoice greatly, O daughter of Zion!*" &c. Caprice and impulse had no part in the control of Christ's life. The life of virtue is never that of impulse or accident; it is always the unfoldment of an eternal idea.

Fourthly: *Truth enunciated by an erring crowd.* As Jesus rode on the ass, the people "*took off their garments,*" &c. They spoke about Christ with one voice, and spoke the truth. They declared Him to be "*a King.*" They represented Him as coming in the "*name of the Lord,*" and spoke of "*peace in heaven,*" and "*glory in the highest,*" in connexion with His mission. Here you have the crowd, then, for *once* uttering truth. I know of no phrase ever coined by mortals more untrue than *Vox populi, vox Dei.* The voice

of the people has almost always been the voice of selfishness—
carnality—worldliness. It has been mostly the voice of the devil,
seldom the voice of God. The people have generally rejected the
best measures, the best men, the best books, the best preachers.
So long as the populace continue what they have been, God deliver
us from popularity! The vote of majorities is no proof either of
truth or right. For this reason, even the law of a constitutional
government, being but the public voice, is not necessarily right.
Here, however, the people for once spoke the truth.

But our point at present is to look upon Christ in relation to the
religious feeling of mankind. That man has the religious element is
too obvious for proof, too trite for remark. It is the root-sentiment
of his soul—the substratum of his nature. Man has senses, man has
mental faculties, but man *is* religious. What relation does Christ
sustain to this, the soul of man's soul?

I. CHRIST ROUSES IT INTO ACTIVITY. "*Blessed be the King*," &c.
This is an outburst of the *religious feeling*. Sometimes you hear
the crowd thunder the feeling of revenge or of loyalty, or of ambition; but here it is the *religious* feeling that fills the air, and
echoes through the roads. What roused this? The appearance of
Christ. But how does Christ wake the religious feeling of men?
By *revealing God*. As the sensation of sight could never be awakened
without light, even though the eye existed in a perfect state, so the
feeling of religion could not be excited without the idea of God. It
is this alone that can touch the religious soul. Christ reveals God.

First: *He reveals His law to the conscience.* He brings the Divine
" commandment."

Secondly: *He reveals His love to the heart.* He is the expression,
evidence, and medium of the Divine love.

Thirdly: *He reveals His beauty to the soul.* His perfections are
His beauty. Christ unfolds them. "*He is the brightness*," &c.
"*The image*," &c. In " Him dwells all the fulness," &c.

II. CHRIST INSPIRES IT WITH GLADNESS. All the religious feeling
which now expressed itself was *joyous*. It was not expressed in
tears and groans, but in songs and shouts. The religious feeling is
awakened in heathen lands; but it is not inspired with gladness, it is
all gloom and sadness. The religious feeling is either the source of
man's greatest happiness or misery. But Christ sets the religious
sentiment of the soul to music.

But how does Christ inspire it with joy?

First: *He directs it to the right object of supreme affection.* Love
is happiness. From an instinct in human nature, every man has
some object of supreme affection; and this greatly determines his
happiness or misery. The supreme object to make one happy,
should be, *absolutely perfect—thoroughly happy—reciprocally loving—
equal to all the emergencies of our existence—for ever inseparable from
our being.* Such an object Christ gives—the INFINITE FATHER.

Secondly: He *directs it to the sublimest subjects of contemplation.*
Contemplation is a condition of happiness. The attributes, claims,

arrangements, works, and government of God, are happy themes for thought.

Thirdly: *He directs it to the happiest sphere of hope.* Hope is happiness. Every man has a sphere of hope, but all spheres but *one* doom him more or less to disappointment. Christ presents the highest blessings, with a certainty of their attainment.

Fourthly: *He directs it into a delightful course of action.* Activity is a condition of happiness. Doing everything for the glory of God. The course of action to insure happiness must be felt to be *worthy of our nature—agreeable to our conscience—abundantly remunerative.* This is religious action. Thus Jesus inspires the religious feeling of men with gladness. His religion is not a gloomy thing. "*I am come,*" said He, "*that ye may have life.*"

III. CHRIST ENCOURAGES ITS EXPRESSION. "And some of the Pharisees from among the multitude said unto Him, Master, rebuke Thy disciples. And He answered and said unto them, I tell you that, if these should hold their peace, the stones would immediately cry out."

First: *Christ encourages it despite the opposition of wicked men.* Wicked men have always been opposed to the expression of the religious feelings of mankind. It has condemned their conduct, it has roused their consciences, it has broken their peace. The songs of Zion fall with a revolting discord upon the ears of the wicked. Hence persecution.

Secondly: *Christ encourages it as a matter of utmost importance.* "If these should hold their peace, the very stones would cry out." The language implies two things: 1. That when properly excited the religious feeling *cannot* be repressed. The man who has it must speak it. Examples: Jeremiah, who felt it as fire shut up in his bones. Peter and John before the Sanhedrin—"We cannot," &c., said they. Paul and Silas in the prison. The spirits above cry it out vehemently—shout it in thundering strains of music. 2. That when properly excited the religious feeling *ought* not to be repressed. The feeling is right, and it *should* manifest itself. Were it wrong, Christ would repress it. A few days after this there was a burst of feeling that fell on the ear of Christ from the weeping women on His way to Calvary. It was improper, and He repressed it: "Weep not for me." Pity for Him was not the right feeling—He was above that. The expression of the religious feeling, however, is always necessary and right. The world wants this Divine power in the soul so manifested as to put down the wrong. "*Make a joyful noise unto the Lord, all ye lands.*"

Matthew 21:12-16

The Ideal and Actual Temple

The question as to whether the event recorded in this paragraph is the same as that narrated by the Evangelist (John ii. 13–17), though it has occasioned a considerable amount of discussion amongst the more verbal portion of commentators, is obviously of no vital moment ; and therefore we feel justified in dismissing it at present with a mere reference to the opinion of Tholuck.*

I shall use this strange and striking incident to illustrate three things :—*The ideal temple, or the temple as it should .be on earth— The actual temple, or the temple as it is found on earth—The cleansed temple, or the ideal temple to be realized by Christ on. earth.*

I. THE IDEAL TEMPLE, OR THE TEMPLE AS IT SHOULD BE ON EARTH. The words and actions of Christ here present us with two facts which serve to give a tolerably full and faithful description of the temple as it should be.

First : *That it is a special meeting-place between man and the great God.* The Divine Redeemer here calls it His house :—" *My house.*" The Bible in various places calls the temple the "*house of the Lord.*" In a sense, the great universe is His house ;—He lives in all, and

---

* " The identity of these two occurrences was first maintained by some English theologians, Pierce and Priestley, and subsequently by a majority of the recent writers (by Krabbe himself, c. l., p. 248). After most writers (even Strauss, 1st ed.) had contended at first for the correctness, chronologically, of the position it held in the Synoptical Gospels, the opinion now is that the position in John is the correct one, as also Strauss held in the third edition, though decidedly on the other side in the fourth edition. The Synoptists, it is supposed, had probably got an account of our Saviour's driving the dealers out of the temple, but without a complete historical detail, and as they knew of no other Passover, at least furnish an *account* of no other than the last, they ' have disposed of it ' in this place. We ask, first, Has the repetition of the action during Christ's last entry into the temple any improbability ? We can find none. We should not be surprised if the dealers had by the very next Passover renewed their evil course ; in fact, the opposite could only be anticipated in the degree to which this extraordinary appearance in the department of religion made an impression on their consciences. Perhaps, however, the disorder was abated for the second year ; if, however, in the third year, the impression from the earlier period did not remain in sufficient strength to prevent its repetition, there is nothing in this to occasion surprise. Christ, in the Synoptists, does not allude to His having acted in a similar manner before, but the tradition transmits in all cases only the more striking characteristics of the discourse. To these would especially belong what Christ says (v. 19), as we see by the repeated allusions to it, of which mention has already been made. If, now, what the Evangelists recount is the same fact mentioned by John, should we not expect to find in them this important expression of Christ ? We would lay no weight upon the other points of dissimilarity in the narratives, but that this expression is wanting in the Synoptists we must regard as an evidence that they narrate a different occurrence. It has, indeed, been thought that in Matt. xxi. 23, Luke xx. 2, we have the same thing that John (ii. 18) mentions ; but the question of the superiors there refers to the *teaching*, and occurs, according to Matthew, on the following day ; according to Luke, on one of the following days."

occupies every part of the immeasurable palace. But He has a *special* connexion with places reared by His people, according to His directions, for Divine instruction and worship. He is there in a capacity in which He is discovered nowhere else;—as the *Redeeming God*. Abroad in the universe He is everywhere seen as the Almighty Creator, Sustainer, and Sovereign, but in the temple He is revealed as the Saviour of guilty man. The temple is "His house;" in it He dwells for a certain moral purpose. He is there to meet sinners, and "to commune with them from off the mercy-seat" of Christ's mediation. Abroad in the creation He gives you the natural revelations of Himself; but in the true temple He gives you the *Gospel* revelations of Himself; and these are the revelations essential to your well-being as sinners. Man's great want is the "power of God as it is seen in the sanctuary."

The passage suggests concerning the ideal temple,—

Secondly : That it is a special meeting-place between man and God, *in man's social capacity*. The temple was a *public* building for a *social* purpose. It was not a closet for one, or even a private dwelling for a family—it was a place for the accommodation of all. It was a place where men were to meet God *together ;* not so much in their individual as in their social capacity. Here all intellectual and social grades are to intermingle, regardless of all conventional distinctions. "*The rich and the poor meet,*" under the sacred impression that "*the Lord is the Maker of them all.*" The sympathies and souls of all classes are to blend in their devotions—words of prayer and songs of praise, all mingling together. Social worship is a want of human nature, and a *wise, ancient,* and *divine* institution. It is enjoined by the authority of Heaven, and sanctioned by the example of the inspired and the good of every age.

There are many who profess to believe in Christianity, who estimate lightly public worship. They think, and sometimes say, that they read the Scriptures and worship God at home in their own dwelling ; and that they need not go abroad to unite with others in acts of *public* devotion. It is to be feared that the majority of such persons never worship at all. The man who neglects private devotion may often attend public ; but it is very seldom, I think, that the man who customarily neglects public, attends private worship. I confess to have but little faith in the private devotions of those who systematically neglect the social devotions of God's people. Public worship is not an arbitrary institution—a thing that may or may not be. It arises out of the very nature of things—it is founded upon the properties and wants of our social nature. If man were an isolated being, if he stood alone, dissevered from all beings in the universe but God, then his private worship would be all that was required. Or if he were united only to the members of his family, then his domestic prayers would be sufficiently public for him. But as he is linked to the race, as he is a social being that pants for intercourse with others, has a heart made to expand in generous sympathies for mankind, his devotions demand association with others. Public worship is a divine and necessary school to educate, purify, and perfect our social natures. Here the affections of the soul are drawn out by the sublimest influences of God upon the mind. Man loses all proud ideas of external distinction here, and feels that he stands upon the same common basis as the meanest man that walks the globe. Here the spirit is made to yearn with compassion for the woes of the sinner, and to glow with love for those who are brethren in Christ. Man requires the strong influences of "the great congregation" to take him out of the narrow circle of his own individual interests, to break down those barriers of selfhood that shut the soul up in itself, and to bring him out into the great sphere of universal interests. This is what public worship does. It draws the soul out of itself, and lifts it, by a Divine social excitement, into union with all that is true, loving, and godlike.

There is yet another thought which the passage suggests concerning the *ideal* temple, and that is,—

Thirdly : That it is a special meeting-place between the great God and man in his social capacity, *for the exercises of piety and philanthropy.* The paragraph authorises us to infer that the temple should be specially used for at least two purposes—*Prayer and beneficence.* As to the first, it is here called the "*house of prayer.*" The spirit of prayer is the realization of the creature's dependence upon his Creator; and inasmuch as this should ever be our controlling state of mind, we should pray "*without ceasing,*" pray everywhere, and at all times. Prayer should be the breath of our souls. The temple, however, is for the *special* exercise of the prayer. Here, by religious thought and concentration of soul, we are to feed the flame of devotion, that it may burn more intensely and brightly through every part of our lives. The temple is "the house of prayer," the house in which the spirit of prayer is to be generated and nurtured to an all-commanding power in our every-day consciousness. But it is not only a place for prayer, but for *beneficence.* The paragraph informs us, that "*the blind and the lame came to Him in the temple, and He healed them.*" What Christ did in the temple we may rest assured is *right* to be done within its sacred precincts. It is a scene not merely for the cultivation of the spirit of prayer, but for the cultivation of *true benevolence.* It is a scene for the unsealing of our social sympathies, and drawing them out into practical efforts to bless the needy. It is as religious to feed the hungry, clothe the naked, and heal the wounded, in the temple, as it is to pray. The true temple is the house of *beneficence* as well as the house of prayer.

Such, then, is a brief sketch of the *ideal* temple as suggested by the words and works of Christ, recorded in the passage before us. It is a scene of a special meeting between man and his fellow-men, and between him and his Maker as a social being, for the exercises of piety and philanthropy.

Having noticed the *ideal* temple, or the temple as it should be, we now proceed to notice,—

II. THE ACTUAL TEMPLE, OR THE TEMPLE AS IT IS ON EARTH. Christ found the temple now sadly polluted. There were those there who "*sold and bought*," "*the money-changers*," and those who "*sold doves*,"—all of whom Christ expels and denounces, as having turned "*the house of prayer into a den of thieves*." The department of the temple in which this business was transacted was that called the court of the Gentiles—the least sacred part of the whole building. Though it is probable that the traffic carried on in this place in the days of Christ extended to all kinds of merchandise, at first the only things commercially disposed of were such as pertained to the sacrifices. "The tables of the money-changers," which were now in this court, were no doubt at first intended for the convenience of the worshippers. The Jewish law required that every man should pay an annual contribution to the services of the temple of half a shekel. (Exodus xxx. 11-16.) This was a Jewish coin, and was to be paid in that form. But the current coin of Judæa at this time was Roman, and therefore a place seemed to be necessary where the worshipping people could change the current coin for the Jewish half-skekel. This was the business of these "money-changers." They obtained a profit on every exchange, and the multitudes who came up to the temple to the great feasts would make their employment a very lucrative affair. They conducted their business in a truly *mercenary* spirit. The same is true of those who "*sold doves*." The law required that these birds should be offered in sacrifice (Lev. xiv. 22); and hence the sale of them in the temple became a business. The priests who let out these places for such secular purposes would derive a considerable income from the traffic that was carried on. Thus the spirit of money-getting invaded the sacred inclosure. The breath of mammon became the atmosphere of the place, and there was a thorough secularization of spiritual things.

Now, suppose ye that these sordid barterers in the temple were sinners more than all the rest? Suppose ye that the principle that inspired them was confined to their sphere and to their age? If ye do, ye mistake—mistake egregiously. The principle has invaded and desecrated the temple of God on earth, in all places, through all dispensations, and through all ages. What is it? What is this element that profanes the holy and perverts the good? It is this,— *Seeking personal gain from godliness.* Subordinating religion to self-interests. That is it.

First : *The temple is desecrated when it is used as the means of temporal gain.* Those sordid barterers that Christ now denounced and expelled did this. They made a trade of religion. What millions do the same even in Christendom—ay, and in England too? Every ruler that makes religion an engine for political and secular ends; every minister who officiates in the temple for the sake of its temporal emoluments ; every person who attends the services of the temple in order to obtain a patient, a client, or a customer ;—in fine, every individual, who in any way connects himself with religion from selfish and secular considerations, commits a profanation identical in principle with that perpetrated by the mercenary men who now incurred the righteous indignation of Christ.

Secondly : *The temple is desecrated when it is used as the means of eternal gain.* Whilst this proposition will startle some and offend others, it must commend itself to every unprejudiced and earnest believer in the true theory of virtue and the teachings of the New Testament. The man who uses the temple in order to avoid for himself everlasting misery, and insure for himself the felicities of an eternal heaven, as truly desecrates it as the man who merely uses it for mere worldly gain. The principle, *selfishness*, is the same! only in the latter case it is more voracious, and more grasping. The man who wants to get heaven out of the temple, is more extravagant in his selfish greed than the man who aims to get a good secular "living " out of it. Religion is not a question of gain or loss—it is a question of obligation and right. It is supreme love to the INFIN-IFELY GOOD ONE ; and were there no heaven, no hell, no after-life, so long as He, the ALL-GOOD, and the human soul existed, religion would be imperative. Religion is not a means to an end—it is the sublimest end itself. There is nothing higher in the universe for the creature to aim at. " *He that loveth, dwelleth in God, and God in him.*"

If, then, the man who seeks gain from the temple, either temporal or eternal, pollutes and profanes it, how great is its desecration in this age and land ? It has verily become " *a den of thieves.*" Men use it for their own greedy ends. It is a market where heaven is to be purchased by sacrifice or service, rather than a scene where the Holy One is to be loved and adored for His own sake. Men are invited to it to be *saved*, rather than to be *sanctified*.

The passage further suggests to us,—

III. THE CLEANSED TEMPLE, OR THE IDEAL TEMPLE TO BE REALIZED BY CHRIST ON EARTH. The religious sentiment is the soul of humanity. That corrupted, everything in human history goes viciously and ruinously ; set that right, and all will proceed virtuously and well. To set and keep right this master-spring of human action, is Christ's mission. Hence He enters the temple now ; and thus symbolizes the fact that His grand work is to penetrate the religious life of humanity, and thoroughly purify its fountains. He is a religious reformer, and therefore a radical reformer, working from the centre to the circumference.

As a temple or a religious reformer, He appears in the passage before us,—

First: *As conscious of a Divine right in His mission.* He goes into the temple, not as a trembling worshipper, not as a religious functionary, but as the proprietor and Lord of all. He calls it, " *My* house." Christ, who is conducting the religious reformation of our world, has an absolute right to penetrate all the religious spheres of man ; to drive out all things that profane the sanctuary of God, and to regulate the religious movements of the world.

As a temple or a religious reformer, He appears in the passage before us,—

Secondly : *As profoundly impressed with the difference between the ideal and the actual.* He points these profane barterers to the ideal of worship :—" *It is written.*" They knew where, or ought to have known ;—He knew. The idea of true worship stood out in cloudless sunlight before His great intellect as the greatest idea touching the claims of heaven and the destinies of man. In the presence of that idea, how revolting to His holy nature must the corrupt state of the temple have appeared. He felt it—felt it deeply ; and His heart flamed with a righteous indignation. Christ knows what we *ought to be,* and what we *actually are ;* and the difference impresses Him ; and, under the profound impression, He consecrates Himself to the glorious work of moral reformation.

As a temple or a religious reformer, He appears in the passage before us :—

Thirdly : *As blending in His conduct severity and kindness.* His severity is seen towards these buyers and sellers. In John's account we are told " *that He made a scourge of small cords, and drove them all out of the temple, and the sheep and the oxen.*" There is no reason to believe that He either made the scourge for the men or applied it to them ; though they fully deserved a severe corporeal chastisement. The scourge was obviously for the " *sheep and oxen,*" which could not understand the force of His words, or feel the moral flash of His eyes. Whips for brutes, suasion for souls. Christ has no honied words for incorrigible hypocrites, or hardened worldlings. Terrible were His fulminations against such. But whilst there is severity there is kindness too. Whilst he drove out the corrupt amidst the thunders of His indignation, He heals at the same time " *the blind and the lame,*" who approached Him and sought His aid. Severity towards wrong is not incompatible with kindness, but necessitated by it. As kind nature requires its winters, and even the genial days of summer its tempests, the highest love must ever speak in thunder when the selfish and the wrong appears.

It is not the man who keeps an unclouded smile upon his face, and speaks only honied words in softest tones, that is the kindest at heart. The reverse is always the case. That man has the most real love in his heart that can throw the blackest frown, dart the most scathing flash, or peal out the most terrible invective against meanness, hypocrisy, and wrong.

As a temple or a religious reformer, He appears in the passage before us :—

Fourthly : *As having an all-conquering command over their guilty consciences.* What made these mercenary barterers rush away from His presence ? They were undoubtedly a numerous body, they had their priests with them and popular sentiment too. Why did this strong body of well-backed men flee at the rebuke of this poor peasant ? There is something strange here ; and yet I think I know the reason. The burning rays of rectitude flashed from His looks upon their guilty consciences. Heavens ! how men will flee as panic-struck cowards before the ghosts of their own crimes.

As a temple or a religious reformer, He appears in the passage before us,—

Fifthly : *As evoking the enthusiasm of genuine souls.* The religious natures of *"the children,"* that were now in the temple, were so wrought into excitement that they were *"crying and saying, Hosanna to the Son of David."* The Chief Priests and Scribes complained of this to Christ as something unbecoming the place. But what said the heavenly Teacher ? *"Out of the mouths of babes and sucklings thou hast perfected praise."* The ideal temple should promote religious excitement; I say *religious* excitement, not sensuous passions, nor superstitious fear; but the excitement of the moral soul in holy gratitude and devout adoration.

Matthew 21:17-22

The Withered Fig-tree : a Symbol

We cannot better introduce the lessons which we wish to get out of this wonderful incident, than by quoting from the great Neander the following explanatory remarks on the passage :—

"A remarkable occurrence in this part of the history must now be examined somewhat closely. Christ, returning with His disciples in the morning from Bethany to Jerusalem, became hungry, and saw at a distance a fig-tree in full leaf. At that season of the year such a tree might be expected, in full foliage, to bear fruit; and he walked towards it, to pluck off the figs. Finding none, he said, ' *No man eat fruit of thee hereafter for ever.*' On the second morning, the disciples, coming the same way, were astonished to find the fig-tree withered.

"In what light is this fact to be regarded ? Shall we see in it the immediate result of Christ's words; in fact, a miracle, as Matthew's statement appears to imply ? All His other miracles were acts of love, acts of giving and creation; this would be a punitive and destroying miracle, falling, too, upon a natural object to which no guilt could cling. It would certainly be at variance with all other peculiar operations of Christ, who came in every respect, ' not to destroy, but to fulfil.' Shall we conceive that the coincidence with Christ's words was merely accidental—a view which suits Mark's statement better than Matthew's ? If so, we shall find it impossible to extract from Christ's words, twist them as we may, a sense worthy of Him.

"The proper medium is to be found in the *symbolical* meaning of the act. If the miracles generally have a symbolical import (and we have shown that in some it is particularly prominent), we have in this case one that is *entirely* symbolical.

" The fig-tree, rich in foliage, but destitute of fruit, represents the Jewish people, so abundant in outward shows of piety, but destitute of its reality. Their vital sap was squandered upon leaves. And as the fruitless tree, failing to realize the aim of its being, was destroyed; so the Theocratic nation, for the same reason, was to be overtaken, after long forbearance, by the judgments of God, and shut out from His kingdom.

" The prophets were accustomed to convey both instructions and warnings by symbolical acts; and the purport of this act, as both warning and prediction, was precisely suited to the time. But to understand Christ's act aright, we must not conceive that He at once caused a *sound* tree to wither. This would not, as we have said, be in harmony with the general aim of His miracles; nor would it correspond to the idea which He designed to set vividly before the disciples. A sound tree, suddenly destroyed, would certainly be no fitting type of the Jewish people. We must rather believe that the same cause which made the tree barren had already prepared the way for its destruction, and that Christ only hastened a crisis which had to come in the course of nature. In this view it would correspond precisely to the great event in the world's history which it was designed to prefigure : for the moral character of the Jewish nation had long been fitting it for destruction; and the Divine government of the world only brought on the crisis.

" It is true, no explanation on the part of Christ is added in the account of the event above related, although we may readily believe that the disciples were not so capable of apprehending His meaning, or so inclined to do it, as to stand in need of no explanation. But we find such an explanation in the parable of the *barren fig-tree* (Luke xiii. 6–9), which evidently corresponds to the fact that we have just unfolded. As the *fact* is wanting in Luke, and the *parable* in Matthew and Mark, we have additional reason to infer such a correspondence. We cannot conclude, with some, that the narrative of the fact was merely framed from an embodiment of the parable ; nor that the fact itself, so definitely related, was purely ideal; but we find in the correspondence of the two an intimation that idea and history go here together ; and that, according to the prevailing tendencies of the persons who transmitted the accounts, the one or the other was thrown into the back-ground."

Adopting, then, the view of Neander, and regarding the fig-tree, here smitten by Christ, as symbolic, we proceed to notice the two subjects which are evidently contained in the whole passage :—

I. THE DOOM OF A FRUITLESS LIFE. The tree was now smitten to destruction by a miracle of Almighty power.

First: *The doom was manifestly just.* (1) Think of the position in which it was planted. It was in the way from Bethany to Jerusalem; probably in the district of Bethphage, whose very name signifies "house of figs," on account of the fitness of its soil and climate to grow that kind of tree. How favourable was the position of the Jewish nation for the production of moral fruit ! It was a vine planted by Heaven in a most congenial soil. It was enclosed and guarded by a special Providence, it was watered by the rays of holy ordinances, and shone on by the genial beams of Divine truth. But still more favourable is our position to the production of spiritual excellence. Truly "the lines have fallen to us in pleasant places, and we have a goodly heritage." "Blessed are our eyes," &c. "Many righteous men have desired to see," &c. (2) Think of the appearance which it displayed. It was covered with "leaves." "In fig-trees," says Stier, "it is well known that the fruit ripens ere the leaf appears." It promised fruit. The difficulty arising from the statement of Mark,—"For the time of figs was not yet," is satisfactorily met by Dr. Kitto.* Ought not such a tree to be destroyed? Where is the propriety of allowing it to occupy a position, and to appropriate nourishment, which, if granted to another tree, would result in abundant fruitfulness? Let it die. Why should its roots steal the nutriment of the soil, its leafy branches obstruct the genial rays of heaven, and prevent their falling on better plants? Justice requires that the unfruitful life should be smitten down. Usefulness is the grand end of all created existence, and the function of justice is to remove out of the way whatever answers not its original design. Justice clears the universe of the worthless. The fruitless tree it burns, the salt that has lost its savour it casts forth as rubbish, the spirit that perverts its powers it divests of its freedom and its influence, its privileges and enjoyments. Justice weeds the garden of the universe.†

But the doom is not only manifestly just, it is,—

Secondly: *Utterly ruinous.* "*Let no fruit grow on thee henceforward for evermore; and presently the fig-tree withered away.*" Christ's Will operates at once. It is Omnipotent. He requires no assistance, agencies, or instrumentalities, to give His Will effect. His words are not only "*spirit and life,*" but they are death too. When He pronounces the doom of fruitless souls, they are ruined for ever. Who shall alter His decree, or disannul His purpose? "*As the tree falleth so it must lie.*" This is almost the only act of destruction which we have recorded in the life of Christ. Its solitariness enhances its significance. Like one black cloud upon the azure vault of a night radiant with burning orbs innumerable, it shows that, however bright and peaceful the universe may be, deep darkness and fierce tempests can come if necessary. The voice of redeeming mercy can hurl the fiery bolts of justice.

II. THE CONDITION OF A USEFUL LIFE. "*And when the disciples saw it they marvelled, saying, How soon is the fig-tree withered away! Jesus answered and said unto them, Verily, I say unto you, If ye have faith and doubt not, ye shall not only do this which is done to the fig-tree, but also if ye shall say to this mountain, Be thou removed, and be thou cast into the sea, it shall be done,*" &c. Christ here avails Himself of the sentiment of wonder which His miracle had awakened in the

---

* See "Pictorial Bible," *in loco.*
† See "Homilist," vol. ix., page 146.

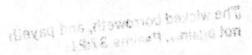

minds of His disciples, to impress them with the fact that, if they would only have true faith in God, they might have a power that would enable them to do even a greater work than the miracle with which He had just astonished them. As if He had said, "*You need not stand amazed*" at my doings ; you may do something even more wonderful by the same power—the power of God, if you only obtain the requisite faith. He teaches here at least two things,—

First : *That faith can achieve wonderful works on earth.* It can "*remove mountains.*" A strong figure this to express its wonder-working power. What has not faith done in *material civilization ?* The discoveries of Columbus and Livingstone, the engineering of Stephenson and Brunel, the conquests of Washington and Garibaldi, as well as the gigantic achievements of other great workers in the material interests of humanity, must all be ascribed to their strong faith. It was faith that gave them that clear insight of the adapta-tion of means to ends, and that indomitable will, by which they "removed mountains." The man of strong faith, in every depart-ment of secular enterprise, has only to speak and it is done ; the mountains will depart and the hills be removed. What has it not done in the department of *spiritual labour ?* The apostle celebrates many of its marvellous triumphs in the eleventh chapter to the Hebrews. But since he penned that epistle, the world has wit-nessed much greater things. Who can appreciate the achievements of the apostles who turned "*the world upside down ?*" The triumphs of reformers, confessors, martyrs, missionaries, too ? Verily, man's history abundantly exemplifies the truth, that he that has faith shall "remove mountains." Three things seem essential to great achievements in spiritual work. (1) *Faith in the universal suffi-ciency of the atonement.* (2) *Faith in the adaptation of the Gospel to man's spiritual nature and condition.* (3) *Faith in the availableness of God's Spirit to help us in this work.*

Christ teaches here,—

Secondly : *That faith can achieve wonderful works in Heaven.* "And all things, whatsoever ye shall ask in prayer, believing, ye shall receive."

Everywhere does the Bible teach the efficacy of believing prayer. "*If ye abide in me, and my words abide in you, ye shall ask what you will, and it shall be done unto you, that whatever ye shall ask the Father in my name, He may give it you.*" Again, "*This is the con-fidence that we have in Him, that if we ask anything according to His will He heareth us.*" Again, "*Ask and it shall be given you, seek and ye shall find, knock and it shall be opened unto you.*" Again, "*The effectual fervent prayer of a righteous man availeth much.*" By such prayer, to use the language of Scripture, *we take hold upon the strength* of Omnipotence ;—we move the arm that moves the uni-verse. Do you know what it is to "take hold" upon the strength of a being ? Enlist the heart of a moral intelligence, and you "*take hold*" upon all the powers of his nature, and all the resources at his command. There stands before you a man of giant frame, high spirit, and dauntless courage. He is a very Samson in might, a Leonidas in valour. Yet a very child shall take hold of the strength of this Hercules, and bend him to his wish. He is a father. He has one little rebellious son whom he determines to chastise. The rod is in his hand, and he is about inflicting the threatened punishment, when the little fellow looks lovingly into his eyes and says, " Dear father, though you beat me to death, I will love you; spare me this once, and I will never offend you again." The father's strength for inflicting the threatened punishment is gone, the rod falls from his hand, and he takes the dear boy in his arms, kisses him, and presses him to his bosom. Coriolanus, who dares the Imperial city to arms, is seized by his aged mother Veturia, and his poor wife Volumnia. Their loving entreaties " *take hold* " of his strength, and as the mighty warrior stands with the nerves of his heart in their grasp, he exclaims :—

> " Ladies, you deserve
> To have a temple built you ! all the swords
> In Italy, and her confederate arms,
> Could not have made this peace."

Thus we can " take hold " upon the strength of Omnipotence in prayer. Elijah did this, and the Heavens obeyed his will. Abraham did this, and the storm of fire stood for a time hovering over the devoted cities of the plain. Moses did this, and he seems to have held back the outstretched arm of justice;—for the Almighty said, " Let me alone that I may destroy this people." The good in all ages have done the same. True prayer *takes hold upon the strength* of the Infinite. It moves that heart whose pulsations are the forces of the universe.

Matthew 21:23-27

Intellect under the Reign of Wickedness

Rapidly now grew the hostility of both the politicians and ecclesiastics—" *the elders and priests* "—towards Christ. Not only did every fresh miracle and discourse, but every incidental expression, and smallest token of interest displayed towards Him by the people, serve to fan into an all-consuming flame those fires of malignity which had been smouldering in the breasts of these officers, from the very commencement of His public ministry. Indeed it was in full flame now. It was burning with an irrepressible violence in the Sanhedrim at this moment. His triumphant entry into Jerusalem, and the hosannas of the people; His cleansing of the temple, driving out the mercenary buyers and sellers, and money-changers; the miracles of healing which He had wrought within the sacred precincts; the enthusiastic praises He had evoked from the multitude of children who gathered around Him; and the miracle which He performed, in smiting, with an everlasting barrenness, the fig-tree—all these things which had occurred within a few hours in rapid succession, had raised the hatred of His enemies to a well-nigh uncontrollable fury. Accordingly, in order to get up such a charge of blasphemy against Him as would enable them *legally* to put Him to death, the chief Council of the nation send to Him, while in the temple, a deputation, composed of "the chief priests and elders"; representatives both of their ecclesiastical and political interests, who address to Him, in the most direct way, the question as to His *authority:*—"*And when He was come into the temple, the chief priests and elders of the people came unto Him as He was teaching, and said, By what authority doest thou these things? and who gave thee this authority?*" "The double question," says Stier, "is probably to be understood thus:—What sort of power, right, or authority, dost thou lay claim to (divine or human)?— whom dost thou give thyself out to be? And then, Who has given thee authority, who has commissioned and qualified thee to do these things, or who authenticates thee therein?"

I shall take the incident to illustrate the *hardihood,* the *cunning,* and *confusion, of intellect when under the reign of wickedness.* The intellect of these "chief priests and elders" was under the absolute reign of wickedness. Its inventive power was employed to construct wicked schemes, its reasoning power to shake belief in the true, and to defend the wicked and the false. Intellect is ever the servant of the heart:—there will be blessing or cursing according to its behests. We have intellect before us under the mastership of wickedness; and let us look at some of its phases in this condition:—

I. THE HARDIHOOD OF INTELLECT IN THIS CONDITION. This hardihood the "chief priests and elders" here displayed in two things:—

First: *In an unblushing ignorement of all Christ's past teaching.* "*By what authority doest thou these things?*" This question they had put in a little different form three years before; and He had answered it a thousand times, in such a way as would admit of no just debate. Their eye was ever on Him; and Judea for three years rang with the fame of His marvellous works and heavenly teaching. His every miracle was an answer to the question. Every deed He wrought, every discourse He delivered, the whole tenor of His life, declared that He was a "*Teacher sent from God.*" What think you of the *hardihood* that could thus put a question ignoring all the wonderful deeds and doctrines of three years? They knew the history of those three years—none knew it better. They were painfully alive to every part of it; and yet now with a marble-faced audacity they put this question. So intellect often acts when under the reign of wickedness. The infidels of this age, with a similar hardihood, put questions now concerning Christianity which have been answered over and over again, during the last eighteen hundred years, not only in convincing books, but in moral changes wrought in the life of mankind.

The hardihood of these "chief priests and elders" is seen,—

Secondly: *In a defiance of His power to read their hearts.* They knew that they put the question not for information, but in order, if possible, to entrap Him. They must have felt, too, that He whom they addressed could look into their hearts, and discern their hypocrisy, malignant feelings, and vile intent. Yet, presumptuous mortals! they dare that all-searching eye, they stand with an impious hardihood before its glance.

Such, then, is a specimen of the *hardihood* of intellect when under the rule of wickedness. It will suggest the most audacious questions, it will ignore the most palpable fact, it will challenge even the searching scrutiny of Omniscience itself. It will call Heaven to the witness of a lie. It will rush in where angels fear to tread. It will dare—

"Defy Omnipotence to arms."

The passage leads us to consider,—

II. THE CUNNING OF INTELLECT IN THIS CONDITION. Just look at the question :—

First: *It has the aspect of great fairness.* It is perfectly proper to ascertain the *authority* of a teacher before we commit ourselves to his doctrines and influence. And the more so in proportion to the greatness of the claims he makes upon our faith, faculties, and service. The claims which Christ enforces upon man being so absolute, it is only fair that we should be satisfied as to His authority. The question, therefore, in itself could scarcely be objected to. This question which appears so fair and plausible,—

Secondly: *Was conceived in order to entrap Him.* They did not want information on the question of His authority, but they wanted to ensnare Him: and it is difficult to conceive of a question more suited to this end. It is a question that He is likely to answer;—it is so fair. And they would feel that, however He may answer it, their purpose would be gained. If He say, "From earth;" inasmuch as He could not say that He derived His authority from *them*, any other answer would have been formulated into a charge. It was in truth a wily question, worthy the great Serpent himself. Thus, it is ever with intellect under the imperial sway of wickedness. An honest heart alone can afford to keep a bland intellect. Sad for thee, O intellect! ray of the Infinite intelligence and choicest gift of Heaven, when under the mastership of sin. Instead of looking through a pure atmosphere and with a clear eye at all things within thine horizon, and with an inviolable candour predicating, according to fact, thou art bound to lay out thine energies in the service of cunning schemes, logical sophistries, and hypocritical pretensions. On the battle-field where wickedness reigns supreme, thy degraded office is to construct schemes of deception. In those, alas! ever-extending regions of trade where filthy lucre sits supreme, thou art devoted to cunning tricks of fraud. And in that domain of literature, where the heart does not "*desire a knowledge of God,*" thy work is, by plausible questions and insidious hints, to undermine the truth of heaven. "If there be a God, why has He not a more visible connexion with His universe, and appear in such aspects as to preclude the possibility of any doubt of His existence?" "If there be any moral distinctions, any real difference between what is called virtue and vice, why does not the Governor of the universe make it manifest by His conduct towards men?" "If there be a Christ who has come to save the world, why are successive generations allowed to appear on this earth in sin and sorrow, spend their brief life in sin and woe, and in sin and sorrow depart to their 'eternal resting-place'?" Such are the plausible questions which the cunning intellect under the reign of wickedness is constantly starting in such literature. So it must ever be. Wickedness dares not show itself in its true colours; and it works the poor intellect in weaving veils of concealment, and drawing pictures to counterfeit realities.

The passage teaches:—

III. THE CONFUSION OF INTELLECT IN THIS CONDITION. "*And Jesus answered and said unto them, I also will ask you one thing, which if ye tell me, I in likewise will tell you by what authority I do these things. The baptism of John, whence was it? from heaven, or of men? And they reasoned with themselves, saying, If we shall say, From heaven; He will say unto us, Why did ye not then believe him? But if we shall say, Of men; we fear the people; for all hold John as a prophet. And they answered Jesus, and said, We cannot tell. And He said unto them, Neither tell I you by what authority I do these things.*" "Our Lord," says a modern expositor, "did not wish to elude the question, or merely to confound His adversaries and disappoint them, by not implicitly declaring Himself to be the Messiah as they expected. His motives were higher. According to the customs of the Jewish doctors, and even Grecian disputants, if any one proposed a captious question to another, the one had a right to ask one in return, and not to answer the question addressed to him until his own had received a reply." The question of Jesus showed with what consummate wisdom He could involve them in their own snare. "He took the wise in their own craftiness."

First: *Their confusion was occasioned by a Divine question.* "*The baptism of John, whence was it?*" The word "baptism" here must be taken as standing for the whole *ministry*. This was the question to confound them. They thought themselves wonderfully clever, perhaps, in suggesting it; but here is an interrogation starting from a higher intellect, which baffles them with sore embarrassment. On intellectual grounds they had no chance with Him. One word of His rent the curtain which their cunning had drawn, made bare their hearts, and swept their sophistries to the wind. Thus the intellect of the wicked will be kept for ever in confusion by questions which the Divinity will eternally flash through its being.

Secondly : *Their confusion was secured by the feelings of their own hearts.* Two feelings were called up by this question, from which, with all their adroitness, there was no escape—*shame* and *fear.* Shame would prevent them from saying that the ministry of John was from heaven, for they had not believed in John. They had treated his ministry with unbelief and opposition. The Baptist had come, had fulfilled his mission, was "a burning and a shining light," and had been martyred for his noble honesty and faithfulness ; and yet they had not believed. If they said, therefore, that the ministry of John was from heaven they would condemn themselves. They were *ashamed* to be truthful. *Fear* was the other feeling. "*If we shall say, Of men ; we fear the people ; for all hold John as a prophet.*" Luke informs us that they said, "*All the people will stone us.*" They were as cowardly as they were disingenuous. What, then, were they to do, thus shut up between shame and fear ? After they had "reasoned with themselves" they took the only other course, and told a deliberate falsehood. "*We cannot tell.*" What a wretched spectacle you have here ! Corrupt souls taken in their own craftiness. So we think it must ever be with the wicked. They will be confounded. Their mouth will be stopped. A wicked policy, however fair and specious for a time, will inevitably conduct to wretched confusion and contempt.

Thirdly : *Their confusion was left without the hope of remedy.* "*Neither tell I you.*" They had become incorrigible. All truthful words would only be wasted upon them.*

"*Neither tell I you.*" It is useless, it is madness, to argue with some people. Their opinions are fossilized, their minds are incorrigible. That spirit of the soul which alone can receive the truth has left them. The soil of their nature for growing truth is worn out, has been thoroughly exhausted, by the thorns, and thistles, and noxious weeds of corrupt opinions and undivine emotions. You may as well seek to grow the sweet flowers of tropic climes upon the frosty heights of Labrador, as to plant by argument a Divine truth in untruthful natures. Christ knew this, and would not argue with those men. He would not "cast pearls before swine." Terrible state this for the soul to get into ! "*Neither tell I you.*" Your question will be left unanswered. This will assuredly be the condition of the intellect under the reign of wickedness for ever. Beaten by the tempests of a guilty conscience, it will flutter for ever in the dark wilderness of confounding clouds. "*Neither tell I you.*"

* Their ignorance was pretended, that they might not be pressed by John's testimony to Jesus. That nothing might be omitted to arouse conviction, our Lord utters a series of parables, depicting their conduct and the punishment which awaited them.

Matthew 21:28-32

The two Sons: True Labour Man's True Destiny.

This parable requires but little explanation. The meaning is tolerably manifest. Jehovah is the Father, and the immoral multitudes and sanctimonious Pharisees are the Sons. The son who refused to enter the vineyard at first, but who afterwards repented and went, represents "the publicans and harlots"—persons who made no profession of religion. These persons promised nothing at first—nay, tacitly refused to have anything to do with the new religion: but afterwards, by the awakening appeals of John the Baptist, entered as labourers into the Gospel vineyard (Luke vii. 29, 30). The son, who promptly and respectfully promised, represents the Scribes and Pharisees, who, from their professions of sanctity, promised fair, but who nevertheless never engaged in the holy work. After He had drawn the picture, Jesus puts the question to them, "Whether of them twain did the will of his Father?" The son who, although he refused at first, afterwards went: or, he who promised fairly at first, but never redeemed his pledge? Little thinking that this faithless and worthless second son was the portrait of themselves, they answered, according to the unsophisticated dictates of common sense—"*The first.*" In this they condemned themselves. Like David of old, they knew not their own moral likeness. Ah! were a correct moral portrait of ourselves this day to be held before us, and did we not know whom it was intended to represent, how much in it should we all see to despise and denounce!

The subject which the words give us is, *True Labour Man's True Destiny.* God's command to all classes is, "Go and labour." "*Go, work to-day in My vineyard.*" I am aware that this subject will clash with the practical sentiments of many. Few, indeed, hold the divinity of labour. Labour is looked upon with contempt; it is considered the painful doom of the poor, the unfortunate, and oppressed. To lounge on the gilded seats of opulence, to sport in the circle of the fashionable and the gay, to luxuriate in the pleasures of sense, and to be free from the *necessity* of labour, are regarded by the world as the most desirable and most dignified state of existence. The doctrine of the text, and I believe the doctrine of the Bible, is *that true labour is the true idea of life.*

The question which now meets us is, What labour? I answer, true *moral* labour—labour in its most comprehensive sense; the labour of the muscles and the mind for *moral* ends. Man is not a class of functions; he is *one* being: everything he does is *moral;* all his bodily and intellectual acts are but the varied expressions of his moral self. Cultivating land, building houses, constructing ships—these acts are as truly *moral* as the reading of a chapter, the offering of prayer, or the singing of a psalm.

I proceed now to notice some of the general ideas which are suggested concerning this labour:—

I. THAT THE TRUE LABOUR OF LIFE HAS A DETERMINATE CHARACTER. "*My vineyard.*" This expression indicates that man's agency is to take some definite direction or course, which is not pursued by the masses of men; that God wishes him to aim at some specific object. And what is that? I answer in one word—the *moral cultivation of the soul.* The soul is God's vineyard, and it needs cultivation. It is like "*the field of the slothful and the vineyard of the man void of understanding; it is all grown over with thorns, and nettles cover the face thereof, and the stone walls are broken.*" It is open to the foot of every intruder. Man's great work is to till it into beauty and fruitfulness : to break up its fallow ground, to uproot its noxious weeds, to develop its native resources, and to build up the wall of its moral defence. Do not, however, let it be supposed that the work is limited to *our own souls.* "The field is the world." Why are we made social? Why have we access to the homes and hearts of our fellow men? Is it merely to relieve the monotony of individual solitude? or to co-operate in mere worldly pursuits? I cannot believe this. No. It is that by action and reaction of souls the general moral sentiment of humanity may be cultivated and improved. Indeed, the world has ever risen thus. The action of the patriarch's mind, and the prophet's mind, and the apostle's mind, and, above all, of Christ's mind upon the world, have raised it to its present point of morality. The influence of a holy soul upon a depraved one is like the influence of the Heavens on the earth; it tends to dispel its mists, warm its depths, and bring out its manifold germs to life, beauty, and power. It seems to me that in the providence of God there are certain minds left especially to the moral care of others. Every man seems to have an access to a certain class of mind which no other individual has. There are manifold circles in the social system. The intellectual man is above the reach of the feeble soul. The poor man's mind has seldom access to the man of fortune and rank. The *practical principle* is this—that each man has a part allotted to him in this great moral "vineyard," into which no other can enter, and for whose work no other is equally qualified. Englishmen ! who have such access to the moral heart of Britain as you? Masters ! who have such access to the hearts of your servants as you? Parents? who can enter so readily into the bosoms of your children as you? God has given to each man a key to unlock certain hearts, and enter them almost at pleasure. And the reason is, that he might cultivate them. May God enable us to fulfil our trust !

I wish here to call your attention to what I conceive a most important but a sadly neglected fact—namely, *that all the other labours of man are means to this moral cultivation.* The popular idea seems to be, that if a man would cultivate his soul, he must live as much as possible a life of quiet and abstraction ; or that if he would be morally useful to others, he must be free from labour, and give himself entirely to the work. I do not deny the necessity of what may be termed special efforts in this work; such as self-communion, religious abstraction, devout supplication. These exercises I hold indispensable; but I hold the *general* labours of life equally necessary.

Manual labour is an important means of soul improvement. Why does the Creator require us to ply our physical energies and toil hard in order to sustain our existence in this world? Why has He left us to build our homes, to weave our garments, and to dig from the reluctant earth the necessaries of life? Could not He, who adorned the lily and feeds the raven, have prepared all things to our hands? I believe the reason to be our *moral* cultivation. To work the rough elements of the world into the necessaries and comforts of life, requires a power of contrivance, an energy of will, a capacity of endurance, a self-reliance, which are indispensable to soul culture. Hence it is that amidst the working population there is a robustness about their moral virtues that you seldom find about persons not so employed. It is ignorance that considers physical labour a degraded thing. It is an institution of God. It is a condition of physical health; and, above all, it is a means of spiritual improvement. I connect it with eternity. The poor man who toils day after day to turn the barren common into fruitfulness, may at the very same time, and by the very same act, be cultivating those moral germs of his soul that may bloom around him and bless his being in the great eternity.

Intellectual labour is an important means of soul cultivation. Why has not the Eternal Father made everything plain? Why does the shadow of mystery hang over everything with which our minds are brought in contact? Why are there so many problems on all sides and at all times challenging our investigation? God could have made the general truths of the universe as clear to the intellect as He has made the landscape to the eye in the light of day. The reason, I think, is the same as the other—on account of the moral discipline it is suited to effect. What *patience, perseverance, humility, force of determination*, does all intellectual labour develop!

Mercantile labour is also an important means of soul culture. Why has the great Creator made the principles of material exchange necessary to the physical well-being of man? I believe that this also is for *moral* ends. I do not believe in the common doctrine, that business and religion are necessary opposites. God intended business to be a *means of grace*. Here principles are tested, moral battles are fought, and moral victories are to be won. A man who conducts his business as he ought, must return every day from the market a morally stronger soul. What an opportunity for social good does business afford. The man in disposing of his goods has, at the same time, an opportunity of disposing with his good thoughts, and of exporting them to the ends of the earth.

I have dwelt longer upon this point than I intended, because of its practical importance. It appears to me that until men cease to regard one part of human labour as opposed to another, until we abolish the foolish distinction between the *secular* and the *sacred*, until we feel that man is *one in all engagements*, and that all his operations are to have the one end of moral cultivation, godliness will never make much way. Oh! come the day when men everywhere shall make gain subservient to godliness, property to principle, the senses to the soul, business to religion; when religion shall be regarded as sustaining the same relation to every department of human operations that the soul does to the body,—the *all-present, all-pervading, all-presiding power.*

The passage suggests :—

II. That the true labour of life is especially binding on all. The same command was given to each of the sons; the publicans and sinners, the Scribes and Pharisees, Jews and Gentiles;— it is addressed to all *by the same authority and with the same urgency.*

First: *It is addressed to all by the same authority.* The authority is that of a "Father." There is no authority on earth so absolute as that of a "Father." The authority of a master, a magistrate, or a monarch is but a shadow in comparison with this. Neither is there any authority so kind. What other ruler feels such an interest in his subject as the parent in his child? But the *absoluteness* and *kindness* of the authority of the human father are but very faint emblems of that power and love which characterize the authority of God. We and all we have are His—absolutely and for ever. His authority extends over our bodies, our souls, our circumstances, our time, and our eternity. The human child outgrows parental authority. He rises into manhood, and in his turn becomes the head of a family; and even the man who ruled him when a child, now infirm with age, readily yields to his control. But never will humanity outgrow the authority of the Infinite Parent. There is something to me deeply solemn in the thought that we can never change our Master; never place our being under a new Sovereign; that we must be linked for ever to the same throne; watched for ever by the same eye; amenable for ever to the same tribunal; that our obligation can never be abrogated, never relaxed. Could we not associate the idea of *kindness* with this authority, the fact would be intolerable. But when we think that the Being who is thus to rule us for ever loves us more than any other being ever has, or ever can, we feel that we would not change our Ruler if we could; that whether we walk this earth, or traverse the regions of immensity, we would ever have Him as our Sovereign.

Such is the authority that enjoins it. This work is binding though it had no advantages—though there were no hell, no heaven.

Secondly: *It is addressed to all with equal urgency.* "To-day." Think upon the magnitude of the work; how much effort it requires to make our spirits "meet for the inheritance of the saints in light;" and how all that is valuable in time and happy in eternity depends upon it.

Think that all our time was given for *this very purpose*. We are sent here not that we may indulge our appetites, make fortunes, and rise to social influence; but that we should cultivate a character that will prepare us for, and secure to us, endless felicity beyond the grave. Think that the difficulties connected with the work increase the longer it is neglected. The husbandman may wait for a more convenient time for the tilling of his land; the mariner may wait for a more propitious breeze; the merchant may defer his contracts to a more auspicious day; but there is no more convenient season for this labour than now. Difficulties increase every hour. Never before were they so numerous as they are now, and never again will they be so few. Think that the present life is the only period when the work can be done. "As the tree falleth so it must lie." "There is no work, nor knowledge, nor device, nor wisdom in the grave whither thou goest." Think how much of our time has already run to waste, and how short a portion remains. Think, I say, of these things, and then will not the voice of the Eternal Father come with tremendous force,—" Son, go work *to-day* in my vineyard."

This passage suggests :—

III. That the true labour of life is greatly at the discretion of man. There is no force employed to *coerce* either of the sons to enter the vineyard. The first, a hasty, haughty, thoughtless son, said at once he would not. He did not wait to think who it was that gave the command, what the nature of the work was, what benefits would accrue to him for engaging in it, and what evils from neglecting it. Not he. All this at first seemed unworthy his notice. The other, with equal thoughtlessness, but with more respectful feeling, promised; gave the father to understand that his will should be at once obeyed. Having given the command, the father left them alone; there was no further interference—the thing was left to their discretion. The *first*, who refused, need not yet be excluded because he abruptly and unworthily said, No. The *second* was not compelled because he had promised—they had minds of their own, and they were dealt with as such. Days, perhaps years, passed away, and no work was done by either. He who had actually promised gave no indications that he intended to redeem his pledge. At length, however, the *first* began to *think*—to think, perhaps, how rash, and rude, and unfilial he had been to such a father; and the thought worked upon his heart; then his bosom glowed with a manly penitence, and he determined to go; and he went: but the other "went not."

I cannot forbear remarking here that there seems to be *a greater chance for the man who brings his mind to a position to reject, than the man who is ever promising*. There is something self-startling in the idea of saying to God, I will never try to be religious, &c. The great work is left much to our choice. There are commands, and motives, and encouragements, and helps, and every influence employed to move us morally; but there is no compulsion. " Because *I called*, and *ye refused*," &c.

This passage suggests :—

IV. THAT THE TRUE LABOUR OF LIFE DECIDES THE DESTINY OF MAN. This is the point of the parable. It is not the first refusal that decides the destiny, else the ruin of thousands on earth would be already sealed; nor is it the first promise, or else the happiness of thousands more would be secured; but it is the *work* or *no work*. Godliness is not a thing of profession, not a thing of sentiment, not a thing of comfort—it is the *work* of life. It is the " doer of the work," not the hearer of the word, that is the blessed man.

The principle which makes our destiny depend upon our labour is not arbitrary. *Physical indolence* will bring physical ruin; *Mercantile indolence*, mercantile ruin; *Mental indolence*, mental ruin.*

Matthew 21:33-46

The Wicked Husbandmen; or, the efforts of Mercy to redeem, and the appearance of Justice to punish

Inexhaustible was the mental wealth of Christ. His mind was an overflowing fountain of knowledge. "*Hear another parable*," says He. Already they had heard from His lips much more than they desired, yet not half what they needed, and nothing compared with what He had to impart. Students in the school of Christ, for centuries or millenniums indefinitely, must expect to hear *another* parable from their Great Master. Luke represents this parable as having been spoken to the *people*; Matthew and Mark as having been addressed to the Pharisees; but the fact that the former evangelist mentions (Luke xx. 19) the " chief priests and scribes " as listeners on the occasion, obviates the apparent discrepancy.

The two great subjects which the Heavenly Artist throws on this parabolic canvas are—*the efforts of Mercy to redeem*, and *the appearance of Justice to punish*. The materials of this parable are taken from the beautiful passage of Isaiah v. 1–7.

I. THE EFFORTS OF MERCY TO REDEEM. The "householder" is the Great God, who is here represented as mercifully employing means for the cultivation of His vineyard. The parable suggests several thoughts concerning those merciful efforts.

First: *They were abundant.* The abundance appears (1) From the favourable condition in which the vine was planted. "*The householder hedged it round about, and digged a winepress in it, and*

* See " Pulpit and its Handmaids."

built a tower, and let it out to husbandmen." We are not sure that these separate figures are intended to express separate ideas, probably they are used only to give a full expression to the wonderful care which the householder employed in order to secure all the conditions of fruitfulness. The abundance appears (2) From the agents employed to secure its cultivation. "He let it out to husbandmen." The "husbandmen" are supposed to represent the regularly established priesthood. They were appointed for the very purpose of taking care of God's vineyard. (Malachi ii. 7; Ezekiel xxxiv. 2.) From Aaron down they covenanted with God to do this : it was their solemn obligation. Beside the husbandmen there was another class of agents employed in this work of cultivation, called "his servants." "When the time of the fruit drew near, he sent his servants to the husbandmen, that they might receive the fruits of it." " How, it may be asked," says Trench, "are these 'servants' to be distinguished from the husbandmen? Exactly in this; that the servants, that is the prophets and other more eminent ministers of God in His theocracy, *were sent*—being raised up at particular times, having particular missions, and their power lying in their mission; while the others were the more regular and permanently established ecclesiastical authorities, whose power lay in the very constitution of the theocracy itself." From time to time, prophets and special ministers of heaven had been sent forth by God to warn, instruct, and comfort His chosen people. Mercy then was abundant in its means to secure fruitfulness in the Jewish people, and well might the great householder say, "What could have been done more to my vineyard, that I have not done in it ? " (Isa. v. 4.) If the efforts of mercy to redeem were so abundant in Jewish times, how much more so in these later times ? In what a vineyard are we placed, and how numerous the agents which heaven employs for our spiritual cultivation? These efforts of mercy to redeem were—

Secondly : *Outraged.* " *The husbandmen took his servants, and beat one, and killed another, and stoned another.*" When these were killed, other servants were sent; and they shared the same fate. Last of all, He sent His Son, and they slew Him. "They beat one." (Jer. xxxvii. 15). "They killed another." (Jer. xxvi. 23). "They stoned another." (2 Chron. xxiv. 21.) Christ refers (Matt. xxiii. 37) to their conduct towards His servants in His wail over Jerusalem :—" O Jerusalem, Jerusalem, thou that killest the prophets, and stonest them which are sent unto thee," &c. " Others had trial of cruel mockings," &c. (Heb. xi. 36.) A sight of astounding depravity this—men outraging the efforts of mercy to save them; yet, alas, a common sight. These efforts of mercy to redeem were—

Thirdly : *Persevering.* After the first servants whom the householder sent—his loyal, loving servants—were beaten, killed, and stoned, he sent others; nor did it cease here. He persevered, and made of all sacrifices the most stupendous. " *Last of all he sent unto them his son.*" Both Mark and Luke express it in terms more touching and striking.* In the former it is said, "Having yet therefore one son, his well-beloved son, he sent him also last unto them, saying, They will reverence my son." And in the latter it is said, "Then said the lord of the vineyard, What shall I do? I will send my beloved son, it may be that they will reverence him when they see him." Here is mercy persevering, to the eternal wonder of the universe. The other leading subject on this parabolic canvas is:—

II. THE APPEARANCE OF JUSTICE TO PUNISH. "*When the lord therefore of the vineyard cometh, what will he do unto those husbandmen?*" The following remarks are suggested.

First: *The crime for punishment was immense.* What ingratitude, cruelty, rebellion, are involved in the conduct of these husbandmen in martyring the servants of the householder, and at last putting his only beloved son to death. Truly the Jewish people had filled up the measure of their iniquity.

Secondly: *The time for punishment is acknowledged.* "*When the lord therefore of the vineyard cometh, what will he do unto those husbandmen?*" It is assumed that he will come. The householder, having left the care of his vineyard with the husbandmen, *went into a far country.* He had left the system of things he had established to go on. He did not appear in person amongst them. But his return from the "far country" was certain. He would come to look after his property, and settle with his servants. A time of settlement was fixed, and all understood it. Such a settling time comes at death in every man's history. Such a settling time comes to humanity at the end of this world's history.

Thirdly: *The justice of the punishment is felt.* "*What will he do unto those husbandmen? They say unto him, He will miserably destroy those wicked men, and will let out his vineyard unto other husbandmen, which shall render him the fruits in their seasons.*" Κακοὺς κακῶς, an emphatic alliteration, not easily conveyed in English. "He will badly destroy those bad men;" or, "Miserably destroy those miserable men." Thus, unwittingly, they pronounced a terrible punishment on themselves, dictated by their own consciences. It is often thus with sinners. The Great Judge will make the sinner pronounce his own doom.

Fourthly: *The nature of the punishment is terrible.* It is suggested that it will consist (1) In the utter frustration of the sinner's purposes. "*The stone which the builders rejected, the same has become the head of the corner.*" The Son the husbandmen slew, becomes the Sovereign Judge of the universe. What an element of anguish will this be to see that very cause which it has been the purpose of our life to destroy, becoming the grandest power in the universe. (2) In

---

* The language employed to describe the son marks as strongly as possible the difference between him and the servants in rank and dignity of person. (Heb. iii. 5, 6). The expression, "They will reverence my son," is one of those points which serve as an ornament or drapery to the narrative, exciting a livelier impression of its reality.

the utter loss of all our possessions. " *Therefore I say unto you, the kingdom of God shall be taken from you.*" The vineyard shall be lost for ever. (3) In present injury and ultimate ruin. " *Whosoever shall fall on this stone shall be broken; but on whomsoever it shall fall, it will grind him to powder.*" Those builders were falling on the stone now, and bruising themselves, but ultimately the stone would fall on them and grind them into powder. Their ruin would be complete. It is said in Luke, that the people exclaimed, " *God forbid,*" when they heard this doom pronounced upon those here called the husbandmen and the builders, and well might they exclaim, " *God forbid,*" for it is overwhelmingly terrible.

Brother, redemptive mercy is busy with thee now. It has placed thee in a beautiful vineyard, and favoured thee with every facility for the production of fruit. How art thou acting? Art thou rejecting the overtures of mercy, and sinning against the arrangements of grace? If so, be it known unto thee that when the Lord of the vineyard shall come, when Justice shall appear, better thou hadst never been born.

Matthew 22:1-14

The Marriage of the King's Son: A Mirror of Christendom

The parabolic method of instruction was frequently employed by Christ. In the land in which He taught it had ever been a common method of teaching. It was admirably adapted to arrest popular attention, and to convey certain infallible truths to His bigoted hearers, with a brevity and potency which no other mode could effect; and as it partook more or less of the character of life and history, it was always deeply interesting both to the learned and the rude.

The proper interpretation of a parable depends upon a knowledge of the circumstance or custom which is employed to symbolize or bring out the truth intended to be taught.

The example employed in this parable is of a peculiarly interesting kind—it is the marriage feast of a king's son. We learn from eastern antiquities, that the case which is here given, corresponds with a well-known custom of the times and country in which Jesus was teaching. In high life the making of a feast on such an occasion —the sending out servants to inform the invited guests when all things were ready—and then, after they had enjoyed the sumptuous repast, the sending out again of messengers to invite others indiscriminately, however poor, to partake of the superabundant provisions—and the preparing for those whose means would not allow them to prepare for themselves a suitable garment to appear in on such an august occasion, are all points in this parable which agree with the actual history of such events as celebrated of old in the Oriental world.

Now, with a knowledge of this custom, there is not much difficulty in ascertaining the ideas which Christ intended to convey. Who is the King?—The Supreme Ruler of the world. What is the feast? Christianity—the provision of salvation through Jesus Christ. It is frequently represented as a "feast" in the Scriptures—Isa. xxv. 6, lxv. 13, lxvi. 10; Hos. ii. 19; Matt. ix. 15; Joel iii. 29; Eph. v. 32; 2 Cor. xi. 2. Who are the persons first invited? The Jews—to them the Gospel was first preached. Who were the messengers that invited them to enter, and whom they insulted and destroyed? —Jesus and His apostles. Who were the armies that the King employed to wreak vengeance upon them, and to burn up the city? —The Roman soldiers under Vespasian. Who were those to whom the King afterwards sent out the invitation?—The Gentiles. Who were those that accepted the invitation, and that partook of the banquet?—Those who in every age constitute the true Church. Who was he in that number who had not on the "*wedding garment?*" He who enters the church without a full compliance with the vital conditions of membership—*repentance towards God, and faith in our Lord Jesus Christ.*

I cannot think that there is anything fanciful in this interpretation. All these points accord with the object which our Saviour had in view, and are also naturally suggested by the scene which He sketches. I shall look at this parable as a *Mirror of Christendom.* As there are here four orders of men in relation to this *feast*, so there are *four classes* of men in relation to Christianity. These classes make up the population of Christendom. These are:— The *inviters*, the *rejectors*, the *acceptors*, and the *intruders at the feast.*

I. THE INVITERS TO THE FEAST. These are here represented as the "*servants of the King*." Their work was of the most interesting kind: it was to *invite*. This is the work of every true servant of Christ in relation to the provisions of His Gospel. The men for this work must be men of sympathies *wide* and *warm* as the summer sky, encircling humanity—men who can speak the word "*Come*" to the world with its proper emphasis.

In the light of truth, in the estimation of God, this, though the smallest, is the highest and most useful class in society. In a sense, every Christian writer, tract distributor, Sabbath-school teacher— every man, in fact, who has imbibed the spirit of Jesus Christ, are inviters. All Christians in different forms, and modes, and spheres, are servants of the great King, inviting men to the banquet of Infinite Love. But we shall limit it to ministers.

There are two or three things suggested by the parable as to the mission of this class.

First: *It is most benevolent.* What have ministers to do? To irritate men by polemical discussions? to frighten them by horrid denunciations? to bind their intellects to their little creed, or to coax them within their pale? No, our work is that of *invitation*—a work of love. We are to invite men to a *feast—a feast of soul;*— a feast of inspiring thoughts, of upraising hopes and holy fellowships;—a feast to gratify every spiritual taste, to supply every spiritual want, and to strengthen every spiritual power. And as it is a feast provided by the Eternal King, we cannot be too liberal in our invitations. "*There is room enough and to spare*" at the royal board for all the sons of men. We want *expansive* souls to utter this invitation. "*Come*" is the watchword of our mission. *The Spirit and the bride say, Come. And let him that heareth say, Come. And let him that is athirst, come: and whosoever will, let him take the water of life freely.*"

Secondly: *It is manifestly divine.* These servants went forth by the command of their Sovereign. He directed them to the particular classes they were to invite. Some of the servants were destroyed, but He sent forth others to take their place.

All this is a beautiful image of God's operations in the case of those who are engaged in inviting men to salvation. It is by His command that they go forth. He directs them to the particular sphere in which He would have them to act. Did some of their number depart by death, He sends forth others to take their place. To invite men to salvation is in the highest sense a divine work— "it is the work of the Lord." This was the work of the prophets; but it was the "hand of the Lord" that qualified them for it, and directed and sustained them in it. This was the work of the apostles; but they received a Divine commission and a Divine qualification. This is the work of all real Christian ministers, and it is divine. "*Go ye therefore into all the world,*" &c. "We then, as ambassadors for God, beseech you in Christ's stead, be ye reconciled to God."

Thirdly: *It is purely suasive.* What means were these servants to employ? Were they authorized to employ force and violence? No. They were to state the fact that provision was made, and in the name of the King to invite them to enter. In a very similar parable, which we have in Luke xiv. 7–16, the servants are commanded to "*compel*" them to come in; that is, to use the strongest arguments in the strongest way to induce them to come in. No *coercion* but that of argument was to be employed.

It is so now. The weapons of our warfare are not to be carnal. *We are not to war after the flesh.* We have to speak the truth in love—commend ourselves to every man's conscience. Whatever in the form of force is employed in the promotion of Christ, is an invasion of the rights of man—a gross injury to the cause of truth, and a libel on that Saviour who rebuked the disciples that would have called down fire upon the Samaritans.

II. THE REJECTERS OF THE FEAST. Those who were "*bidden*" would not come; "*they made light*" of the invitation; all were taken up with their merchandise, and other secular avocations. Some of them even grew indignant towards those who invited them.

There are four things in relation to these rejecters deserving our attention :—

First: *The distinguished privileges of all*. "The king sent forth his servants to them that were bidden to the wedding." They had been *bidden* before the servants were sent forth. This second invitation, or rather admonishment, says Trench, "is quite according to Eastern manners." Thus Esther invites Haman to a banquet on the morrow (Esther v. 8). And when the time has actually arrived, the chamberlain comes to bring him to the banquet (vi. 14). These Jews had been bidden to the divine feasts, by the prophets, centuries before Christ came. Thus Isaiah, "Ho every one that thirsteth," &c. This augments the guilt of their rejection. All Christendom have long since been *bidden*. The work of God's servants here is to "*call*" those who have long since been *bidden*.

Secondly : *The shameful indifference of many*. "They made light of it, and went their ways, one to his farm," &c. The one went as usual to his field, the other to the market. The invitation to them was of no importance compared with their worldly engagements. It is so with the rejecters of the Gospel now. They "make light" of the overtures of mercy. The world, with its occupations, interests and pleasures, entirely engrosses their sympathies, their powers, and their time.

Thirdly : *The inhuman cruelty of others*. Some of them not only "made light" of the invitation, but grew malignant, *took his servants, entreated them spitefully, and slew them*. Such maltreatment of the men who invited them in the King's name to a feast, I call inhuman cruelty. The ingratitude, the illoyalty, are so outrageous, that they rather belong to the infernal than the human. And yet there have ever been men who have so treated God's servants. The Jews did so treat the first ministers.[*]

Fourthly : *The terrible doom of some*. "But when the king heard thereof, he was wrath; and sent forth his armies, and destroyed those murderers, and burned up their city." Forty years after this, the Roman army did actually "*destroy those murderers, and burn up their city*." One of the most terrible events on the page of human history is that destruction of Jerusalem. The most terrific retribution awaits those who reject the overtures of redemptive mercy. If "*he that despised Moses' law died without mercy under two or three witnesses, of how much sorer punishment, suppose ye, shall he be thought worthy, who hath trodden under foot the blood of the covenant, and hath done despite unto the Spirit of grace ?*"

These rejecters form by far the largest class in Christendom; the rejecters are worse than heathens; and their doom will be more tremendous.

Here we have :—

III. The ATTENDANTS AT THE FEAST. "*Then saith He to His servants, The wedding is ready, but they which were bidden were not worthy. Go ye therefore into the highways, and as many as ye shall*

[*] See Acts iv. 3, 18, 40 ; xiv. 5–19 ; xxi. 30 ; xxiii. 2.

find, bid to the marriage." The result of this was, that the wedding was *furnished with guests.* Two remarks are suggested concerning the happy guests :—

First : *They were chiefly composed of those who had not been previously "bidden."* They were not invited until those who had been previously ":bidden" had refused. They were gathered, not from the favoured city, but from the *"highways and hedges."* The primary allusion here is obviously to the Gentiles. The Jews have rejected, the Gentiles have the offer. Philip goes to the city of Samaria, and preaches Christ there (Acts vii. 9). Peter baptizes Cornelius and his company. Paul preaches the Gospel at Athens, and declares that *" God commands all men everywhere to repent."* As a rule, there seems to me a greater probability that those who have never been " bidden " before will accept the offers of the Gospel, than those who have been often " bidden " and rejected. The vast majority of those who will be found in heaven at last will be those who accepted the invitation *at once.* Delay is dangerous in this matter. The first rejection prepares for the second, and so on.

Secondly : *They were composed of all classes of moral character.* The servants, we are told, *" gathered together, all as many as they found, both bad and good."* So great is the difference in the moral characters of even *unconverted* men, that some may be spoken of even as good when compared with others. All are depraved, but all are not *equally* depraved. The apostle, in his letter to the Corinthians, enumerates sinners of the worst class who had been sanctified and saved amongst them. " Be not deceived ; neither fornicators, nor idolaters, nor adulterers, nor effeminate, nor abusers of themselves with mankind. Nor thieves, nor covetous, nor drunkards, nor revilers, nor extortioners shall inherit the kingdom of God. And such were some of you : but ye are washed, but ye are sanctified, but ye are justified in the name of the Lord Jesus, and by the spirit of our God." It is a blessed thought, that many from amongst the very worst characters in this corrupt world will be found in heaven. Let none despair.

Here we have :—

IV. THE INTRUDER AT THE FEAST. *" And when the king came in to see the guests, he saw there a man which had not on a wedding garment,"* &c.

Observe four things in relation to this man—his *error ;* his *detection ;* his *speechlessness ;* and his *punishment.*

First : *His error.* What was his error ? " He complied with the invitation, was present at the feast, and probably behaved with all duo decorum. In what, then, did he offend ? He had not put on the festal robe, which the king required of all his guests. But wherein is the wrong of this ? Might he not have been too poor to have provided himself with the required costume, or might not the notice of the feast have been too short to have enabled him to do so ? No! according to the ancient customs of the East, the king had no doubt prepared the festal robe for the occasion ; he was guilty, therefore,

of the affront of refusing the royal gift, as well as of the indignity
of appearing at the banquet in unseemly attire."* The spiritual
idea of which this is the emblem, is that man requires preparation
for communion with God, and fellowship with His people. To use
the language of the apostle, man is required to *put on Christ*.

Secondly : *His detection*. " When the king came in to see the
guests, he saw there a man which had not on the wedding garment."
No one seems to have discovered it except the king—neither the
servants nor the other guests ; but it struck the king's eye in a
moment. There is a scrutinizing period to dawn on humanity—a
period when the universal King shall return to examine His guests.
He will then detect all hypocrites, " discern between the righteous
and the wicked;" all hypocrites will be unmasked on the Day of
Judgment.

Thirdly : *His speechlessness*. The king, as he entered the room,
singled him out from the numbers, fastened his eye upon him,
and addressed him, saying, " *Friend, how camest thou in hither, not
having a wedding garment ?* " And the man was *speechless;* he
was struck with confusion ; his emotion for a time paralyzed his
tongue. He could not speak. If he could, what had he to say ?
What excuse had he to offer ? So it will be with sinners in the
Day of Judgment—" Every mouth will be stopped," &c.

Fourthly : *His punishment*. " Then said the king to the servants,
Bind him hand and foot, and take him away, and cast him into
outer darkness : there shall be weeping and gnashing of teeth."
Here is complete *bondage*—hands and feet bound ; here is *unmiti-
gated darkness*—" Outer darkness." The feast was generally celebrated at night. Not a ray of light ; *overwhelming anguish;*
" weeping and gnashing of teeth." Here is a mirror of Christendom. All belong to one of these four classes. To which class dost
thou belong, my brother?

Matthew 22:15-22

*The Question of the Pharisees and Herodians concerning the
Tribute Money*

We have recently had our attention directed to an attempt of
" the chief priests and elders " to entrap Christ by a question,
touching the authority of John as a teacher. We have in this
chapter three other attempts to entrap Him by questions made by
the leading classes of Jewish society—Pharisees, Herodians, Sadducees, and Lawyers. The one question, that in the passage under
review, is of a *political* character, referring to the claims of Cæsar;
the other, that of the Sadducees, is of a *social* character, referring

* See J. Kitto, D.D., *in loco.*

to the marriage relationships in the resurrection; and another, the question of the "lawyer," of a more directly *religious* character, referring to the chief obligation of humanity, "the great commandment." We shall have to examine each of these questions in turn, and shall begin with the first. The ecclesiastical authorities of Judea, having failed to entrap Jesus, by demanding the authority by which He did His wonderful works, especially as seen in His expurgation of the temple, and being incensed in consequence of the parable spoken against them, held a council against Him, and, associating with themselves the Herodians, sent an embassy to our Lord with the express but covert design of ensnaring Him in His speech, that thus they might compass His destruction.

I. HERE WE HAVE WICKED MEN, THOUGH MUTUAL ENEMIES, UNITED IN A WICKED PURPOSE. "*Then went the Pharisees and took counsel how they might entangle Him in His talk. And they sent out unto Him their disciples with the Herodians.*

First : *Mark the mutually hostile parties.* "Pharisees and Herodians." It is probable that the Herodians were a political party, friends to the Roman authority, desirous to uphold the dominion of the Cæsars over Judea, and favourable to the adoption of Gentile manners and customs. They would, therefore, be directly opposed to the sympathy and aim of the Pharisees, who were Jews to the very letter and form of the Hebrew commonwealth; who looked with contempt on all foreigners, and struggled against the Roman yoke as a stigma upon their national character.

Secondly : *Mark the common purpose which united these hostile parties.* "They took counsel how they might entangle (παγιδεύσωσιν) Him in His talk." The only time in which this word is used in the New Testament is here, and it signifies " ensnare "—having a reference to the ensnaring of birds in a net. The word "His" which is supplied by our translators, would be better omitted. Instead of " entangle Him in *His* talk," read, " ensnare Him in talk "— their talk as well as His. Their object undoubtedly was by their conversation to wrest from Him some expression that would form the strong basis of a legal charge against His life. They were "*spies sent forth to feign themselves just men, that they might take hold of His words, so that they might deliver Him unto the power and authority of the governor.*

Now the point on which we wish to fasten special attention here is, that men *mutually hostile* are brought into concert by a malignant purpose. So thoroughly did they agree in their desire to bring Christ's life and influence to an end, that all private and public animosities were buried in their endeavour to reach the common result. The Herodians might have hated the Pharisees, the Pharisees might have loathed the Herodians; but both hated and loathed Jesus of Nazareth so much more than each other, that they are now brought into earnest co-operation. Evil has a power to some extent to bring hostile souls together. Pilate and Herod were " *made friends together* " in the perpetration of the darkest crime that stains the wicked history of this wicked world. The devil yokes souls together and makes them drag his chariot, in whose breasts flame the fires of a mutual hate. Although, from the immutable laws of moral mind, there must be a mutual recoil of soul where there is a mutual depravity, still there is much mechanical union amongst evil men in this corrupt world. Greed for a common gain, lust for a common pleasure, love for a common idol, vengeance towards a common foe, are the bands by which the prince of darkness holds the various sections of this world together in something like mechanical order. Ah! not in this world only, but in every province of his dark domain,

"Devil with devil damned firm concord holds."

II. HERE WE HAVE WICKED MEN COMPLIMENTING CHRIST IN THEIR PURSUIT OF A WICKED PURPOSE. "*Master, we know that Thou art true, and teachest the way of God in truth, neither carest Thou for any man, for Thou regardest not the person of men.*"

First: *Here is a just eulogium.* This may be regarded as an exquisite epitome of our Saviour's character. Every word is expressive of truth. "We know that Thou art true." He was true—"THE TRUTH." "Thou teachest the way of ·God in truth." He did teach the way of God in truth. "No man hath seen God at any time, the only begotten Son of the Father, He hath declared Him." "He is the brightness of the Father's glory," &c. "Neither carest Thou for any man." Though He cared for the souls of all, He cared nothing for the flatteries or the frowns, the commendations or the condemnations, of any. He confronted the hostilities of His age; like the sun, He moved calmly and majestically in His orbit, while the clouds of conflicting sentiment battled around, and the black ocean of depravity roared and raged beneath. "*Thou regardest not the person of men.*" True, He was "no respecter of persons." He had no caste feeling—no social favouritism. He was the sympathizer with all sufferers, the denouncer of all wrong-doers, the friend of all who worshipped the common Father in spirit and in truth. We can scarcely conceive of a tribute more truthful in substance, and more terse and compendious in expression, than this. We can almost imagine that in the "counsel" which they took together, they were some time formulating this eulogy. One would suggest one expression, one another; and after considerable discussion on successive amendments, out came this formula of their joint wisdom. We honour their intellects in this; would that their hearts had been as true as their judgments!

Secondly: *Here we a have just eulogium wickedly rendered.* Whilst their testimony is undoubtedly just to Christ, we must suppose it was true also to their own convictions, if they had any. For we can scarcely imagine that men of common observation and conscience, living for three years in the neighbourhood where this Jesus taught His doctrines of sublime wisdom and purity, wrought His miracles of stupendous power and love, and lived His life of unclouded rectitude and goodness, could have had any conviction concerning Him inconsistent with this testimony. Still, though the tribute was true in itself, and true, perhaps, to their own convictions, it was *wickedly rendered*. They had no heart appreciation of the character they delineated. The language was not the outburst of adoring souls. There is no heart in it; it means nothing but cunning. They intended it to appeal to a something in Christ which He had not— *vanity*. Though what they said was true—for the matter of it— there was nothing but flattery and treachery in the intention of it. They called Him Master when they were contriving to treat Him as the worst of malefactors. They pretended respect for Him when they intended mischief against Him.

We recoil with horror from the conduct of these men; and we could denounce their villanous treachery in no measured terms; yet is not their sin a common one? Have not wicked men, in all ages, sought to work out wicked purposes by calling Christ Master, and rendering to Him the mere tribute of words? Is not this the veil by which tyrants conceal their unrighteous plans, and the robe in which priestcraft and hypocrisy wrap themselves, in order to impose upon the credulity of men, and gain their selfish ends? Is not this the string of that demon bow from which sectarian bigots shoot forth their arrows of calumny and anathema upon all beyond their narrow pale? When the vilest men of Christendom seek to perpetrate the vilest deeds, they are most tempted to eulogize Christ, and to call Him Master.

III. HERE YOU HAVE WICKED MEN PROPOUNDING A CRAFTY QUESTION, IN ORDER TO GAIN THEIR WICKED PURPOSE. " *Tell us, therefore, What thinkest thou? Is it lawful to give tribute unto Cæsar, or not?*" Because Julius Cæsar was the first to achieve the position of Emperor of Rome, all his successors to the imperial dominion were called by his name. All in the line of Roman Emperorships were Cæsars. Tiberius was at this time on the throne; and he was a Cæsar. The tribute which the Romans exacted from Judea, in common with the rest of their conquered provinces, being excessively galling to Jewish pride, it became a much agitated question, whether it was consistent with the Mosaic laws to pay this tribute or not. Josephus relates that Judas, a Galilean, raised a revolt, partly on this account—saying that the taxation was no better than an introduction to slavery. It was this question, with collateral and aggravated circumstances, which aroused the Jews into the last fatal conflict with Rome.

Now mark the craftiness of their question. Nothing, as far as they were concerned, could be better invented to entrap Christ in a dilemma from which He could not extricate Himself. He could not answer the question negatively or affirmatively, without, to all appearance, involving Himself in fatal and overwhelming difficulties. If He answered negatively, and said, It is *not* lawful to give tribute to Cæsar, He would incur the charge of sedition against the Roman power, and thus wake the crushing thunders of Rome against Him; he would be tried, condemned, and executed as a political traitor.

Thus His fate would soon be sealed. But if He answered in the affirmative, and said it *was* lawful for the Jew to pay tribute to Cæsar, He would rouse the vengeance of the Jewish nation against Him; the Jewish Sanhedrin would soon convict Him as the transgressor of the law of Moses. (Deut. vii. 15.) Talk about intellectual cleverness! here it is. A question more sagely suggested, and more adroitly put for the purpose, you cannot conceive. Herodians and Pharisees alike wanted to crush Christ—to bring His life and influence to a speedy end, an end, too, which legal authorities would sanction; and what plan could they have hit on better than this? Wickedness and craft are often associated. Wickedness requires a clever, scheming, acute intellect to work out its purposes and to get on. It was by craft wickedness gained a footing first in our world; and by craft it has been working from that day to this.

IV. HERE YOU HAVE WICKED MEN OVERCOME IN THE PURSUIT OF A WICKED PURPOSE. "*But Jesus perceived their wickedness, and said, Why tempt ye me, ye hypocrites?*" &c. Christ did four things now, which not only baffled their intellects and confounded their projects, but must have touched their consciences also to the very quick.

First: *He detected their malignant motives.* "*Jesus perceived their wickedness.*" They could not impose upon Him. Solomon says, "*In vain is the net spread in the sight of any bird.*" Truly in vain do men spread their crafty nets before Omniscience. Christ's eye penetrated through all the covering with which they attempted to conceal their malignant designs. His all-piercing eye looked down into the deepest depths of their nature, and saw, as in the light of day, every corrupt principle there at work. The craftiness of a devil's intellect cannot impose upon Him. He not only "knows what is in man," but "hell and destruction are before Him."

> "He disappointeth the devices of the crafty,
> So that their hands cannot perform their enterprise.
> He taketh the wise in their own craftiness:
> And the counsel of the froward is carried headlong.
> They meet with darkness in the day-time,
> And grope in the noon-day as in the night."—JOB v. 12–14.

Secondly: *He denounced their hypocrisy.* "Jesus perceived their wickedness, and said, *Why tempt ye me, ye hypocrites?*" There is a spirit of *invincible boldness* in this appeal. The Pharisees and the Herodians were influential parties in the State. In their antagonism to Christ, and their efforts to destroy Him, they were backed by the authorities of the country and the spirit of their age. Christ knew this right well; yet no amount of hostile power could intimidate Him, or prevent Him from discharging His conscience. Though poor, lonely, despised, and with the world against Him, He was unconquerable in the energy within. He confronts these hypocrites, looks them in the eye, and sends His reproving glance through every fibre of their souls. There is a spirit of *righteous indignation* also in this appeal. Justice seemed to burn in these words. No evil seemed so abhorrent to the pure nature of Christ as hypocrisy. The sight of it fired His spirit with holy antagonism. Against no evil did He fulminate more terrible denunciations. *"Woes"* against hypocrisy rolled from His lips in successive thunderbolts. (Matt. xxiii. 13–29.) Hypocrisy is sin in its worst form; it is sin becoming too hideous to show itself; sin stealing the garb of virtue, and thus daring to impose upon the credulousness of men, and to insult the Omniscience of heaven.

Thirdly: *He thwarted their intent.* " Show me," said Christ, "the tribute money." And they brought unto Him a penny. And He saith unto them, " Whose is this image and superscription?" They say unto Him, Cæsar's. Then saith He unto them, " Render, therefore, unto Cæsar the things which are Cæsar's ; and unto God the things that are God's." The "tribute money" was the coin in which the tax was paid; the penny being a Roman silver piece, of the value of sevenpence three-farthings of our money. This coin always bore an image of the Emperor's head. It is said that Julius Cæsar first stamped his image on the coin; and that the custom originated in Persia. Christ drew His answer from the coin itself ; the coin had the image and inscription of the Emperor, and was the current coin of the country, and therefore proved that they were subjects of Rome. As Christ had the coin in His hand, He seemed to say to them, This proves that you are under the government of Rome—therefore be loyal. He thus silences the seditious Pharisees, who were opposed to acknowledging their subjection to Rome, and adds a sentence that condemns also the irreligious Herodians, who were in favour of sacrificing their religion to their master. Thus He extricated Himself and confounded them.

Fourthly: *He commanded their conscience.* He plainly taught what must ever be clear to all unsophisticated consciences, that there is a line that divides the political from the religious, and that both have their respective claims,—between which there is no real opposition ; and that the duty of man is to render a right attention to each. These are truths clearly taught in the Scriptures. Render to all their dues. "Tribute to whom tribute is due. Custom to whom custom," &c.* The three Hebrew youths clearly recognised and acted upon the distinction between the claims of Cæsar and the claims of God. And they said to the king, "O Nebuchadnezzar, we are not careful to answer thee in this matter." So also did Daniel, when his sovereign makes a command, that "Whoso shall ask a petition of any God or man, shall be cast into the den of lions." No sooner does Daniel hear that such a command is signed, than he enters his house, falls upon his knees, and prays three times a day, as usual. The apostles acted on the same principle. Standing before the authorities of their nation, they said, " Whether it be right in the sight of God to hearken unto you more than unto God, judge ye." And again, "We ought to obey God rather than men."

* See Homily on Civil Government, Divine Institution, &c.

> '" Let Cæsar's due be ever paid
> To Cæsar and his throne;
> But conscience and souls were made
> To be the Lord's alone."

The principle which our Saviour thus enforced upon them, was so self-evidently reasonable and just, that it bore down with a crushing weight upon their consciences. "*And they marvelled and left Him, and went their way.*" Luke says, " And they marvelled at His answer, and held their peace." Such is the result of this malignant and crafty attack of the Pharisees and Herodians upon Christ. Their iniquitous motives were detected, their hypocrisy exposed and denounced ; their calculations were baffled, and their purposes thwarted. Their reason and their conscience were so struck with the force of its truth that they had no further word to say. " They held their peace." Thus for ever it must be. "*There is no wisdom nor understanding nor counsel against the Lord.*" (Prov. xxi. 30.)

Matthew 22:23-33

The Question of the Sadducees.—Matrimony in the Resurrection

The Sadducees were the *rationalists* of their age in the Jewish Church. They recoiled from the stiff orthodoxy of the day. The dogmatism of the Pharisees so disgusted them, that they resolved upon investigating sacred questions for themselves, and forming their own judgments. They became freethinkers, sceptics, haughty intellectualists. They looked with contempt upon the men that lived in verbalities, and uttered oracularly, as divine doctrines, subjects which they had never investigated for themselves. Dogmatism in the church will ever lead to Rationalism. Rationalism is the recoil of the reflective intellect from a mere technical orthodoxy, and a theological dogmatism in the church. As a rule, *the greatest denouncers of rationalism are the most fruitful producers of it.* As tyranny on the throne begets rebellion amongst the people, so dogmatism in the church begets rationalism amongst the thinkers. Although the Sadducees, on this account, had but little sympathy with the Pharisees—and, perhaps, not more with the Herodians— yet they agreed in their opposition to Christ. Feeling, perhaps, a little gratified with the baffled and confounded state in which their old foes (the Pharisees) had been driven from Christ's presence, they, with their self-sufficient pride, now ventured to approach Him, and assail Him with a question. " They bring," says Stier, " before Him as actual history a curious case, which was at least possible, in order to put their question in the sharpest form :—a case which was probably not then for the first time imagined, but which was already a common and hackneyed jest against the resurrection :— as, indeed, the like are current enough among the Sadducees of this day. *Moses has said :*—Thus they begin, and are proving beyond contradiction (although cunningly, scarce suppressing a smile, they afterwards only put a *question*), that this Moses, in this, as in all his laws, cannot possibly pre-suppose a ' resurrection.' Seven brothers had all married one wife successively, without issue : all those who followed married in order to raise up seed to the first; *i. e.*, according to Moses' meaning, so to speak, to raise up his after-growth out of his grave ;—beneath which, however, according to the design of the wilful inquirers, there is a half-restrained sensual sneer at the whole Mosaic ordinance. They all died, however, without effecting their object, for the woman was barren ; last of all the woman died also, as indeed all men die. And now, if with his dying all is not over, as we say, then in the *so-called* ' resurrection ' (Mark ὅταν ἀναστῶσι, ironically for εἰ), on the so-called last day, in which we would so willingly believe, if thou wouldest solve our doubts in regard to it, what a strange claim there will be on the part of seven men ; and whose will she be ? The same question might be asked in the case of every second marriage of a widow or a widower ; but they take their stand here on the *commandment of Moses*, and *therein* lies the emphasis of the question. Did *Moses*, when he made such ordinances of this life, take for granted another life after this, and prepare such confusion for that life ? We may well admire the patience, mildness, and wisdom of the Lord Jesus towards this folly, when we hear His answer."

In Christ's answer He does three things : *He charges them with error. He corrects their mistake.* And, *He convicts them out of their own Scriptures.*

I. HE CHARGES THEM WITH ERROR. " *Jesus answered and said unto them, Ye do err, not knowing the Scriptures, nor the power of God.*" Their error sprang from *ignorance*, as most errors do. " Those that are in the dark miss their way," says Matthew Henry. The blind must be expected to stumble.

First : *They erred concerning the fact of the resurrection.* They said there was no resurrection from the dead. This was one of the leading defects in their creed. " The Sadducees say that there is no resurrection ; neither angel nor spirit." Now, had they known the Scriptures as Christ explained them in this passage, and to which soon we shall have to turn our attention, or " the power of God " as seen everywhere in nature, they would not have denied the fact of the resurrection. Why did they deny the resurrection ? Was it because of the difficulties ? Did they talk as some of the modern sceptics do ? Did they pronounce the thing an impossibility ? It is true that the work of a general resurrection appears to a finite mind overwhelmingly great. How can it be, it is asked, that each man of the countless generations of the race that have ever trod this earth or breathed this air ; whose dust has been flowing in the waters, floating in the winds, and entering into combination with an indefinite variety of existences, vegetable and animal, shall stand forth in the judgment in a body, conscious that it was the same in which he spent the days of his probationary career? Is not the idea absurd? Does not the work involve an impossibility? We answer, However stupendously difficult it is, there is no impossibility at all, since Omnipotence has engaged to accomplish it. Difficulty is a thing *relative* to creatures. What is a difficulty to one being is no difficulty to another. A work that would out-measure the energies of a child, can be achieved by a man with facility and ease. The idea of impossibility to Omnipotence is a contradiction. Had we been told that there should come a resurrection from the dead, and that the work was to be effected by the combined energy of all created existences, we might have pronounced the doctrine incredible;—we might have discovered difficulties that would have baffled and outstripped the united forces of the creation. But the moment we are told that God is to do it, the idea of difficulty becomes absurd. The God who robes this earth in verdure, rolls through it new oceans of life every hour, the God who has piled up the mountains, poured out the seas, and spread out the heavens, who crowds immensity with globes and systems that no arithmetic can compute, is certainly equal to the work of calling up and reorganizing the mighty generations of the dead. Just, then, is the reproof of Christ when He said, "Ye do err, not knowing the *power of God.*" Know the power of God, as you see it everywhere in the forms and forces of nature, and you need have no doubt about the fact of a general resurrection.

Secondly: *They erred concerning the nature of the future state.* "In the resurrection whose wife shall she be of the seven?" Strange question this for men to ask who denied the *fact* of the resurrection. Perhaps their infidelity on the subject was nothing but speculative, and they had an under feeling that there was some truth in it. Or, perhaps, they put the question as a matter of idle curiosity, in order to hear what the Great Teacher would say on the subject. Or, perhaps, they put it in order to suggest the difficulty of holding such a doctrine. They would hint that the seven could not claim her, and that, on the assumption of there being a resurrection, insuperable social difficulties would be involved therein. Had they been genuine inquirers, we see nothing unnatural or unbecoming in the question. It is such a question as affection, under certain circumstances, would suggest; such a question as bereaved domestic love has a thousand times awakened in the soul. Still, whatever was their reason for asking the question, it indicated mistaken ideas on the subject. They took it for granted, that society in the future life must be organized upon the sexuous relationship of the present. Perhaps they assumed it because they wished it might be so. Should there be a resurrection, they would have a sensual Elysium. If so, it only demonstrated the dominancy of their animalism. In answering their question:—

II. He corrects their mistake. "*In the resurrection they neither*

marry nor are given in marriage, but are as the angels of God."
There are two things implied in this language of our Saviour.
First: *The existence of a high order of intelligences.* " The angels
of God." Christ makes no effort to demonstrate the existence of
these beings. He assumes the fact. He frequently referred to
them. He spoke of them as "legions," which would come at His
command; as agents ministering to the good; as beings rejoicing in
the return of a repentant sinner; and as escorts attending Him at
the last Judgment. Clearly does the Bible reveal the existence of
these lofty intelligences, and fully does it characterize their exalted
attributes, dignified engagements, and ethereal joys.*
Secondly : *The social elevation of humanity in the future state.*
Men are to be " *as the angels of God.*" Redeemed men will be as
angels in many respects. In their intelligence, purity, devotion,
powers of unwearied action, and amazing speed. But Christ refers
here to one particular,—superiority to *animal relationships.* They
" neither marry, nor are given in marriage." This implies a thorough
change in human history. From the beginning, mankind have been
"marrying and given in marriage." This tendency has been part
of the mainspring that has kept the wheels of society in perpetual
action. This impulse, however, does not survive the grave ;—it
dies with the body ;—is not known in heaven. The language suggests the completion of the human family. One end of matrimony
was the multiplication of the race. This over, increase ceases—the
human family is complete ; not one more is to be added to its number. There was a first man, and there will be a last. This circle
once completed will remain so always. No death will ever enter its
ranks, and it will require therefore no replenishment. " The children of this world marry, and are given in marriage : but they which
shall be accounted worthy to obtain that world, and the resurrection
from the dead, neither marry, nor are given in marriage : neither
can they die any more : for they are equal unto the angels, and are
the children of God, being the children of the resurrection." (Luke
xx. 34-36.)
III. HE CONVICTS THEM OUT OF THEIR OWN SCRIPTURES. "*But as
touching the resurrection of the dead, have ye not read that which was
spoken unto you by God, saying, I am the God of Abraham, and the
God of Isaac, and the God of Jacob ? God is not the God of the dead,
but of the living.*" The Sadducees professed to adopt the Penta-
teuch as of Divine authority. Accordingly Christ directs their
attention to a passage (Exodus iii. 6) which bore upon the future
state of the departed. There are three thoughts suggested by the
passage which our Saviour quotes, and by His inference therefrom,
that may serve to show to us the force of His reasoning here in
favour of a future existence.
First: *The highest property an intelligent being can possess is God,
and this property is possessed by the good.* He is the *absolute* good.
All other things are relatively valuable, and their existence contin-

* See "Homilist," Vol. iv., page 145.

gent. All things else are like the passing shadow, He the ever-abiding substance; all else are transient streams, He the unbounded and eternal ocean. To have Him is to have all. The man who can say, " *The Lord is my portion,*" can say, Infinite wisdom, love, power, wealth, are mine. This is the portion of the good. God Himself declares that He is theirs. " I am the God of Abraham." To every true soul He says, " *I am thine,*" &c.

Second : *The possession of this property implies conscious existence.* " *God is not the God of the dead, but of the living.*" Christ states this as a self-evident proposition—a thing that had only to be stated to be believed. How can a dead creature possess property ?—still less, how can a dead man possess God, the highest property ? The moment death seizes the millionaire, his property passes from his grasp,—it vanishes as a cloud. " *We brought nothing into this world, and it is certain we can carry nothing out.*" Can your rulers hold their kingdoms, or your rich men their estates, in their graves ? But if dead men cannot hold a little earthly property, still less can they hold the infinite property—God. The thing is so obvious that no wonder our Saviour did not reason on it.

Third : *The Scripture teaches that this highest property is possessed by departed men.* The passage Christ quotes was addressed by God Himself to Moses concerning the Patriarchs, long years after they had passed away. Abraham, Isaac, and Jacob had gone to dust in the cave of Machpelah long before those words, in which God declared Himself to be theirs, were uttered. What, then, is the inference ? *That though dead they were living still—for the dead cannot hold property.*

Matthew 22:34-40

The Lawyer's Question and the great Commandments

No sooner had Christ disposed of the question of the Sadducees, then the captious Pharisee again approaches Him. If David could say that his enemies " compassed him about like bees," with how much more meaning could Christ say so ? His enemies were like wasps buzzing ever about Him, and endeavouring to sting Him with their venom. The Pharisees now put forward a *lawyer.* Mark calls him one of the scribes, *i.e.*, a teacher or expounder of the law.

In this reply of our Saviour we have, *The sum total of man's moral obligation, and, The moral substance of Divine revelation.*

I. THE SUM TOTAL OF MAN'S MORAL OBLIGATION. The lawyer asks which is the great commandment in the law. It was one of the subtle refinements of the Jewish theologians to divide the law of Moses into greater and less commandments, and to determine what precepts belonged to each class, and what was the most important one. Some maintained that the ceremonial was the greatest, others that the moral was. Our Saviour's answer exposes the absurdity of such distinctions, and gives the one principle into which every righteous law must be resolved—LOVE. Whatever be the number and variety of precepts in any code of duty, they are worse than trash if they cannot be resolved into this one word, *love*. This alone gives obligation to a command. In this answer Christ clearly defines the right measure of this love, both in its God-ward and man-ward direction.

First: *In its God-ward direction.* Love is to have a God-ward direction. Men have religious affections deeply planted in their nature. They are made to love some one supremely. Who shall it be? Christ answers the question, " Thou shalt love the Lord thy God with all thy heart," &c. This is the *first* and *great* commandment. To use the language of another, "It is so in its *antiquity*, being as old as the world, and engraven originally on our very nature; in its *dignity*, as directly and immediately proceeding from and referring to God; in *excellence*, being the commandment of the new covenant and the very spirit of the Divine adoption; in *justice*, because it alone renders to God His due, prefers Him before all things, and secures to Him His proper rank in relationship to them; in *sufficiency*, being in itself capable of making men holy in this life, and happy in the other; in *fruitfulness*, because it is the root of all commandments, and the fulfilling of the law; in *virtue* and *efficacy*, because by this alone God reigns in the heart of man, and man is united to God; in *extent*, leaving to the creature what it does not refer to the Creator; in *necessity*, being absolutely indispensable; in *duration*, being ever to be continued on earth, and never to be discontinued in heaven." Or, to characterize this first and great commandment in language of our own, we may say, (1) It agrees with the conclusion of sound reason. What answer could reason return to the question, Whom should we love the most? but this—"the being that has the most excellence"? (2) It alone meets the demands of conscience. There is no being in the universe that conscience will agree for you to give your supreme affection to, but God. Against every other she enters her indignant protests, and her protests are misery. (3) It secures the necessary conditions of happiness. The happiness of a moral being is in his paramount affection. In this he lives; from it he derives his impulses to action, and his sources of joy or misery, according to the character of the object. If the object be unworthy, misery is inevitable. In order for the supreme love to ensure happiness, there must be three things. The object must be *absolutely perfect*. In proportion to the affection we have for an object, is the amount of pain the moral heart feels on the discovery of any imperfection. The object, moreover, *must reciprocate the affection*. The loving heart is in anguish until the affections are returned. The miser is miserable because he loves that which cannot reciprocate his affection. The object must *continue inseparable from the heart*. Bereaved affection is anguish.*

* See " Philosophy of Happiness:" Crisis of Being, page 76.

Secondly: *The right man-ward direction.* "And the second is like unto it, Thou shalt love thy neighbour as thyself." Who is our neighbour? He is our brother man, wherever he may be, whatever the colour of his skin or the circumstances of his earthly lot. This neighbour, Christ says, thou shalt love as thyself. How dost thou love thyself? With no mere *sentimental* affection. It is a veritable *practical* power, this love for thyself, urging thee every hour to work thy planning brain and dexterous hand. How dost thou love thyself? With no *mean* affection. It is with a passion strong as death. Love thy neighbour;—love him so that thou canst put thyself into his position, feel his woes, and appreciate his claims, and honour his worth. Love him so as thou wouldest have him love thee in return.

In this answer of Christ we have:—

II. THE MORAL SUBSTANCE OF DIVINE REVELATION. "On these two commandments hang all the law and the prophets." This is the vital stamina of the whole many-branched tree of revelation. "This is the old commandment, this also is the new." "A new commandment also I give unto you, that ye love one another, as I have loved you." (John xiii. 34, 35.) "This commandment have we from Him, That he who loveth God love his brother also." (1 John iv. 21.) "He that loveth another hath fulfilled the law." (Rom. xiii. 9.) "The end of the commandment is charity." (1 Titus i. 5.) "The fruit of the spirit is love." (Gal. v. 22.) "He that loveth not, knoweth not God, for God is love." (1 John iv. 8; John xv. 12, 13, 17; 2 Thess. i. 3; 1 Thess. iii. 12, 13; Rom. xii. 10; Gal. v. 14; 1 John ii. 9, 10; 1 Cor. xiv. 1; Col. i. 3, 4; Eph. i. 15; 1 Titus vi. 11; Eph. v. 2; Titus ii. 22; 1 Pet. ii. 17; 1 Pet. iv. 8; Phil. i. 9.) "Without love we are nothing." (1 Cor. xiii.)

Such passages as these, which are thickly scattered through every part of the Bible, abundantly show the truth of our position, that this commandment is the *moral substance of the Bible;* that "on it hang all the law and the prophets." If this be so, three things follow.

First: *That we have an infallible rule by which to interpret all Scripture.* There is much in the law and the prophets, ay, and the apostles too, difficult to understand; much that appears even contradictory. Whatever meaning we put upon any passage, if it clash with the principle that man is to love his Maker supremely, and his neighbour as himself, it is not true, not divine. It follows :—

Secondly: *We have a text by which to determine the worth of all theologies.* The theologies that give such views of God as are not calculated to evoke and strengthen this supreme affection towards Him, and such selfish views of human nature as are unsuited to awaken in man love towards his brother, whoever their authors and whatever their prestige, are the worthless and pernicious dreams of the human brain, not the inspirations of God. Theology is only of service as it acts as the handmaid to morality, as it illustrates, brings forth, and enthrones the eternal principles of virtue in the human soul. The ideas of the brain, however brilliant, serve us not, unless they act as the genial beams of heaven upon the moral heart, quickening the affections into supreme sympathy with the supremely good. The curse of Christendom has been, that men have put theology in the wrong place;—made it the sovereign when it should have been the servant. Hence in its name virtue has been trampled in the dust, and every principle of morality has been outraged. It follows :—

Thirdly : *We have a criterion by which to test the character of our religion.* By it we can test the worth of our religion as a nation as well as individuals. We call ourselves a Christian nation, yet does our national character correspond with these commandments upon which all the law and the prophets do hang? Do our commercial dishonesties, our social oppressions, our political animosities, our sectarian bickering, our passion for soldiering, our readiness to raise the successful butchers of our kind into heroes and set them on pedestals, harmonize with these commandments on which all the law and the prophets do hang? No! verily no! " *By this shall all men know that ye are my disciples, if ye have love one to another.*" " *In this the children of God are manifest, and the children of the devil : whosoever doeth not righteousness is not of God, neither he that loveth not his brother.*" " *Whosoever hateth his brother is a murderer : and ye know that no murderer hath eternal life abiding in him.*"

One thought in conclusion, and that is the *unexampled wisdom of Christ as a legislator.* No one can rule humanity that cannot rightly legislate for its love,—rule its love; for love is its fontal force. The whole history of our race is traceable to love;—good or bad, according to the objects and measure of its love. Political legislators fail because their laws can never reach this; ancient moralists, because their precepts reached no deeper than the brain. Christ touches the heart, cleanses the fountains of feeling, and sets the springs of life to right. " *Keep thy heart with all diligence ; for out of it are the issues of life.*"

Matthew 22:41-46

What think ye of Christ ?   Theological Ignorance of the Messiah

These words give us the Messiah in three aspects :—

First : They give us the Messiah as *He appears in the Old Scriptures.* He is at once David's Son and David's Lord. He was " a rod out of the stem of Jesse." He descended from " the loins of David after the flesh." He was, at the same time, the Lord of David. Though He was the " root,"—the Divine cause, as well as the " offspring," of David. Everywhere the Old Testament presents Him in this twofold aspect. The " child," and the " ancient of days," the " man of sorrows," and " the mighty God," &c.

Secondly: They give us the Messiah as *He appears in personal intercourse with the men of His age.* Three distinct questions we have seen, had been addressed to Christ, not from the desire of information, but from a malignant wish to ensnare Him. The first was a *political* question, addressed by the Herodians in concert with the Pharisees, which referred to the claims of Cæsar. The second was a *social* question put by the Sadducees, which referred to the matrimonial relationship in the resurrection. The third is an *ethical* question addressed by the Lawyer, and referred to the comparative importance of the commandments. Christ having replied to these questions, turns upon the Pharisees, who were His great enemies, and were at the root of all these factious quibblings, and appeals to them thus, " *What think ye of Christ ?* " As if He had said, There is one question that religion has to do with, besides those connected with the political, the social, and the ethical questions referring to the Messiahship. What think ye of the Messiah, the centre-point of all prophecy, and the very substance of your Moses and the prophets? What is your opinion of Him? He now turns upon them, addresses to them a question which so thoroughly perplexes them, that they could " *not answer Him a word, neither durst any man from that day forth ask Him any more questions.*" As He appears before us asking these questions of the Pharisees, we are struck with His *wisdom.* He does not ask, What think ye of me? though He was the true Messiah; but "What think ye of the Christ? whose son is He to be?" He detaches the question from His own claims and the claims of any other, and throws it into its broadest shape. The idea is simply this: What is your opinion of the Messiah that you are looking for? Let me hear it. There was no question, as put in this form, more adapted to stir within those men, who were the theological authorities of the day, earnest and impartial inquiries into the subject of the Messiahship. A question of more suggestive force I cannot imagine to have been addressed to them. They professed to believe in a Messiah, and to know all about Him; here, then, is a query suited to stir and sound all their information on the point. Then mark the prompt, brave, frank, and candid manner in which He propounds the interrogation. He was never at a loss, He required not that premeditation which is the necessity of mortals in discussion, but at once comes to the right question, and that in the fairest spirit. He did not address it to one or two Pharisees in order to baffle them, but while they were " *all gathered together.*" He spoke to the whole assembled body of divines. He gave them all chances, if one could help the other to a suggestion; so that if a right answer came at last, He would only be too glad. His object was not to perplex, but to instruct; not logically to conquer, but spiritually to win.

Thirdly: The words give us the Messiah as *He appears in the minds of one-sided Theologians.* These Theologians of the age had an opinion concerning the Messiah, an opinion which was correct as far as it went, but it was *partial* and *one-sided.* He was to be the

" *Son of David.*" But this was not all, this was only the human and the Jewish side of His existence. The Messiah was to be the *root* as well as the offspring of David, God as well as man; the " Son of David " as an illustrious Monarch as well as a man. The Messiah was to be in one word a *Theanthropist.* David himself recognized it: " *The Lord said unto my Lord,*" &c. Now, this, the Divine side of the Messiah's existence, the Pharisees ignored, hence the appeal of Christ from their own Scriptures threw them into a mental bafflement, and it soon appeared that the Messiah of their mind was not the Messiah of their Scriptures. The man who has merely the human view of Christ has no correct view at all of Him, for He is God-man. One-sided views of Christ, alas, have ever been common among Theologians; and hence, like the Pharisees, they are often thrown into confusion, when other phases of His character are represented.

The point I shall use this passage to illustrate is *the guiltiness of the Messianic ignorance of these Theologians.*

I. THEIR IGNORANCE REFERRED TO A SUBJECT, OF ALL SUBJECTS THE MOST VITALLY IMPORTANT. There is no subject in the universe of such vital importance as that question of Christ, " *What think ye of Christ ?* " In the history of universal inquiry there is no question than can come up of such pre-eminent moment as this.

First : *It is the most important subject in itself.* Who is Christ ? David's Lord, enthroned in the most dignified position in the universe. " He is at the right hand " of THE ABSOLUTE. Christ is the *Temple* of God, and in Him dwelleth all the fulness of the Godhead bodily. Christ is the *Organ* of God :—" By Him were all things created that are in heaven, and that are in earth," &c. Christ is the *Revealer* of God—" The brightness of the Father's glory," &c. There is no subject of thought throughout the creation so great in itself as this eternal *Logos,* who was with God, and is God.

Secondly : *It is the most important subject in its relation to man.* Christ is the subject essential for man. Unless man knows this, he knows nothing, as he ought to know, concerning Providence or the Bible. Who can understand Providence apart from the mediatorial government of Christ ? What, too, is the Bible without Him ? A printed mass of incoherences—nothing more. Take Christ from the Bible, and you will take the foundation-stone from the temple, and it falls to pieces; the sun from the system, and all is chaos and death. Without a right knowledge of Him, moreover, there is no virtue, freedom, dignity, blessedness, for the human soul. A man may be saved without knowing anything about the poets, philosophers, artists, statesmen, kings, reformers of the world; but he cannot be saved without knowing something accurately about the Messiah of God. Hence Paul exclaims, " *Doubtless, and I count all things but loss,*" &c. These Pharisees, therefore, ought not to have been ignorant about such a subject as this.

II. THEIR IGNORANCE REFERRED TO A SUBJECT WHICH THEY HAD AMPLE MEANS FOR UNDERSTANDING. Three things are involved in the appeal which the Heavenly Teacher now makes to these assembled Pharisees. (1) It is implied that they, the Pharisees, knew something about the Messiah. They could not think at all upon an object of which they knew nothing. Free as thought is, it is ever limited by the known. The Pharisees did know something of the Messiah. The coming Messiah was the great idea of the Jewish people through all past ages—it had come down to these old Pharisees; it was the very substance and charm of their Scriptures. (2) It is implied that the passage quoted from the Psalm, was admitted to be prophetic. Christ assumes that the words referred to would be readily admitted by the Pharisees as prophetic of the Messiah. (3) It is implied that David spake under the influence of Divine inspiration. David ἐν πνεύματι "in spirit, saith," &c. The spirit of God in David suggested these words. The Divine spirit of prophecy was in him. Thus they had abundant opportunities of knowing Him. They had the whole Scriptures. Moses and the prophets were full of the Messiah. They might have seen Him in the first promise,—"The seed of the woman," &c. They might have seen Him in the Mosaic ritual as the sense of all the symbols, the substance of all the shadows, the spirit of all the sacrifices. They might have seen Him in all the prophecies which were fulfilled in all the phases of His wonderful life. They had more than the Old Scriptures. John the Baptist had been amongst them, and, with a voice of thunder that rang along the wilderness, pointed Him out to them as "the Lamb of God which taketh away the sin of the world." Christ, for more than three years, had been in their midst, embodying in His own history all that the Old Scriptures had symbolized or stated concerning the Messiah. There is no excuse, therefore, for their ignorance of Him; theirs was an ignorance of a deep-dyed guiltiness.

III. THEIR IGNORANCE REFERRED TO A SUBJECT ON WHICH THEY PROFESSED TO BE AUTHORITIES. A coming Messiah had been the reigning thought in the Jewish nation for centuries. It had buoyed them under many a trial; it had nerved them for many a battle. Never was it more active than now. It was like a "spirit" in all the wheels of Jewish activity at this hour. On this national question the Pharisees professed to be authorities; professed to determine who the true Messiah would be; to know all about Him, and be alone competent to guide the people in the matter. And yet they, forsooth, were "blind guides." It is sad for any class of men to be ignorant of Christ, still more sad for those to be ignorant of Him who have all the opportunities of knowing Him, but sadder still for those to be ignorant of Him who profess to teach Him.

The question which the Heavenly Teacher addressed to these Pharisees we should take up and press on each other and on ourselves. It is, of all questions, the most momentous. "*What think ye of Christ?*" You have, doubtless, entertained some opinions concerning Him; for He has been frequently brought under your attention. What are they? Search them well in the light of His history, I entreat you. "*What think ye of Christ?*" Inaccurate

thoughts concerning Him, have given His system corrupt and dele-
terious forms in ecclesiastic institutions and theological systems.
" *What think ye of Christ ?*" Erroneous thoughts concerning Him
are inimical to the growth of goodness in the soul, and fatal to the
highest interests of our being. " *What think ye of Christ ?*" Think
upon Him, brother, you must sooner or later. In the agonies of
death, in the terrors of judgment, He will force Himself upon your
thoughts. But what do you think of Him *now ?* Do you regard
Him as a mere subject for theological creed, the mere head of your
own sect Church, the Saviour of that select few to whom you belong ?
Or do you regard Him as the Christ of God, the sublimest expression, the special medium, and the mightiest demonstration, of God's
unbounded love to a depraved world ? Merciful heaven, grant us
true thoughts concerning Thy last and crowning gift to our lost and
fallen race.

Matthew 23:1-12

" Moses' Seat,"—Christ's Judgment of the Men who occupied it

We have already examined several of the discourses which Christ
addressed *to* the Scribes and Pharisees. The paragraph before us is
part of an address which He delivered *concerning* them. He speaks
now, to " *His disciples and the multitude,*" words to expose the
hypocrisy and wickedness of the religious authorities of their age
and country. He takes off the mask from these arrogant pretenders,
and holds up to the public eye their real character in all their moral
loathsomeness. We will just present a brief outline of the four
remarkable things which are contained in the passage now under
notice.

In these words we have—
I. WORTHLESS MEN ALLOWED TO HOLD MOST INFLUENTIAL POSITIONS.
The description which Christ gives of the Scribes and Pharisees,
even in this chapter, and the woes He fulminates against them,
apart from other considerations, are sufficient to show, that amongst
all the corrupt sons of Adam, they were the most corrupt. They
were indeed, " *the children of the devil.*" Notwithstanding this, they
are allowed to occupy the most influential position in the state. They
" *sit in Moses' seat.*" * They were there as the recognised interpreters and administrators of the Divine law as given by Moses. Moses

* The probability is, that the seat of Moses does not here refer to the political,
but to the religious authority of Moses. The allusion is probably to the *pulpit* set
up in the synagogues (Nehemiah viii. 4, 9), for the declaring and interpreting the
law to the people. Those who occupied this pulpit in the synagogue were said
to " sit in Moses' seat," inasmuch as their work there was the exposition and
enforcement of the tenets of the Mosaic economy. The Scribes and Pharisees
assumed this position.

was the divine law-giver; these men professed faithfully to expound, and righteously to enforce, the laws of Moses. What higher position could men sustain in this world? Is it not extraordinary that such men should be allowed to hold such high offices? Antecedently, one might have inferred that heaven would allow none but the purest in heart to have occupied such influential positions; that the places of eminent power should evermore be kept for men of eminent piety. It is not so, however, in the history of mankind. Some of the worst men have been allowed to officiate on thrones, at altars, and in pulpits. This remarkable fact teaches two things:—

First: *The wonderful forbearance of God to men on this earth;* and Secondly: *The moral inevitableness of future retribution.* Under the government of a righteous God, such a state of things cannot, will not, must not, continue. There is a day of reckoning to come, when the eternal justice of the universe will put the degraded character in a degraded situation, and the reverse.

In these words, we have another remarkable thing:—

II. RELIGIOUS TEACHERS ACTING IN DIRECT OPPOSITION TO THE DOCTRINES THEY INCULCATED. Christ describes them here as *cruel, ostentatious,* and *vain.* They were *cruel.* "*They bind,*" says Christ, "*heavy burdens and grievous to be borne, and lay them on men's shoulders; but they themselves will not move them with one of their fingers.*" The "heavy burdens" were those worthless traditions and ceremonies which they insisted upon as of equal importance with moral precepts. They made the nation groan under the yoke of their ritualities; nor had they any mercy for the men they thus afflicted;—they heard their groans without a touch of sympathy; they would not help them "with one of their fingers." Sin had eaten out of them all the genial sympathies of their nature. They were *ostentatious.* "All their works they do for to be seen of men; they make broad their phylacteries." These phylacteries were scrolls of parchment, worn on the forehead and left arm; on them were inscribed certain passages of the law,—taken from Exodus xii. 1-10; Deut. ii. 4-9; xi. 13-21. Great sanctity was attached to these phylacteries; and they were regarded as amulets or charms to keep away evil spirits. Their ostentation was seen in making these phylacteries broad and conspicuous, as badges of their greater sanctity. They also "enlarged the borders of their garments." In Numbers xv. 38, 39, we learn that God ordained that the children of Abraham should have borders or fringes on their garments. These Pharisees had them considerably extended for the sake of show; they flaunted them before the people, to impress them with their superior sacredness. They were *vain.* "They love the uppermost rooms (*i.e.* the highest couches) at feasts, and the chief seats in the synagogues, and greetings in the markets, and to be called of men, Rabbi, Rabbi." They loved these things. "It is not," says Matthew Henry, "possessing the uppermost rooms, nor sitting in the chief seats, that is condemned (some one must be uppermost), but *loving* them; for men to value such a little piece of ceremony as sitting highest, going highest, going first, taking the wall, or the better hand, and to value themselves upon it, to seek it, and to feel resentment if they have it not; what is that but making an idol of ourselves, and then falling down worshipping?—the worst kind of idolatry. It is bad any-where,—but especially in the synagogues." What this thoughtful expositor says about these "uppermost places," &c., is equally true of "the greetings in the markets and cities." If we are *morally* respectable, there is no harm with being pleased at a respectful "greeting" from others, even in the markets, the most public places; and if we have distinguished ourselves by meritorious attainments, there is no harm in being pleased with the recognition of this by others. The evil is "in *loving* these things," living for them, and seeking our heaven in them. This these Pharisees did. Such is the conduct of these religious teachers, as delineated by the infallible artist. Now this conduct was in direct opposition to the doctrine of Moses which they professed to teach. The genius of the old Scrip-tures which they professed to interpret, inculcated *mercy*, not *cruelty; meekness*, not *ostentation; humility*, not *vanity* and *pride.* Here, then, is something remarkable; men acting in opposition to their teaching. Men are made to be governed by their ideas; their conduct should be the effect and exponent of their creed; and where the creed is *really* believed, and not merely nominally held, this is ever the case. These Pharisees did not believe what they taught, they were hypocrites. The teachers, whose conduct contravenes the doctrines they teach, have no living faith in their doctrines; they are dead formalities, religious charlatans are they all.

In these words we have another remarkable thing:—

III. ATTENTION TO THE DOCTRINE OF CORRUPT MEN DIVINELY EN-JOINED. Christ says, "*All therefore, whatsoever they bid you observe, that observe and do; but do not ye after their works: for they say, and do not.*" It seems somewhat strange that Christ should command His disciples and the multitude to attend to the teaching of such corrupt men; but He does so. The "all" here, however, must be taken with considerable limitation. It can only mean, "all that they say in accordance with the principles of Moses." In this very chapter, from 16–20, He denounces some of their teachings as the utterance of blind ignorance and preposterous folly. In the xv. chapter also, He denounces their traditions and ceremonies; and elsewhere He commends His true followers, because "they listen not to murderers and hirelings." The "all," therefore, refers to the true things. Or the language might be taken in a comparative sense, and the idea be:—as to these Scribes and Pharisees, rather attend to what they say than what they do;—let your conduct be shaped by their doctrines rather than by their doings. Anyhow, the fact that Christ should encourage attention to their teaching suggests two things :—

First : *The importance of truth to man, come from what source it may.* Man's great want is truth; and truth is truth whether it come from the corruptest devil or purest divine. It suggests :

Secondly : *The magnanimity of Jesus as a teacher.* Instead of endeavouring to turn away the attention of the people from their recognised teachers, He seems to encourage them to give a discriminating heed to their doctrines. No impostor would have done this ; no fanatic would have done this : scarcely, indeed, would any human teacher have done this. Envy, jealousy, or desire for self-fame, would probably have influenced any mere man, as a teacher, to act otherwise.

In these words we have yet another remarkable thing :

IV. The essential incompatibility both of lordship and servility with true greatness. "*Be not ye called Rabbi, for one is your Master, even Christ ; and all ye are brethren. And call no man your father upon the earth : for one is your Father, which is in heaven. Neither be ye called master : for one is your Master, even Christ.*" This haughty title "Rabbi," was introduced into the Jewish school under a threefold form : "Rab," the lowest degree of honour ; "Rabbi," a higher gradation ; and "Rabboni," the greatest dignity of all. These ambitious men coveted these appellations. Christ's prohibition, you perceive, is against two things, though opposed to each other, yet still related—and often found in the same individual —the *haughty* spirit that would domineer over others, and would play the little lord, and the *servile* spirit, that would basely cringe to the dictate of assumed superiority. In a sense, indeed, even in the Church, through the constitutional inequalities in mental organization and diversity of attainments, there must be lords and lieges, masters and servants. The greater brain, heart, being, and character, will always be lord and master of the inferior in the circle. This is right ; and it is not against this that our Saviour speaks. It is not against intellectual or moral, but *official*, lordship He speaks :—the pride of the office. The true lord, the man endowed with lordly attributes, never has the *haughty* spirit which Christ prohibits ; would not have the lordly office, spurns the very name : the true "Rabbi" laughs at the title. Christ's prohibition, however, against *servility*, is as strong as against lordly assumption. He not only says, "be not called masters," but, "*call no man master !*" Ye men, even of feeblest intellect in the Church, cherish the spirit of religious independence ; acknowledge no human authority in matters of religion ; scorn the assumption of Primates and Popes. "*One is your Master, even Christ.*" Many ecclesiastical hierarchies look miserably tawdry in the light of these wonderful words of Christ. Their greatness is but theatrical ; brilliant in the gaslight of conventional thought, but only tinselled finery in the day-blaze of gospel intelligence.

But our proposition is, that both this *haughty* and *servile* spirit in the Church are essentially incompatible with true moral greatness. Christ intimates that two things are essential to greatness. First : *Religious allegiance to one Master.* "One is your Master," &c. No authority is to be acknowledged but that of Christ ; but the haughty spirit thinks of his own authority, and the servile spirit bows to the dictates of pretenders. There cannot be greatness in either. Secondly: *Self-sacrificing service.* "He that is greatest among you shall be your servant. And whosoever shall exalt himself shall be abased; and he that humbleth himself shall be exalted." It is clear that both the *lordling* and the *hireling* in religion are miserably selfish, and therefore cannot be great according to the Divine idea. The lower the spirit falls in loving prostration before the Infinitely Great and Good, the higher Heaven exalts it: the greater the divine servant, the greater the soul. The path of true greatness is not that over which the Cæsars in proud daring rode; but that over which, with humble mien and world-wide love, the Howards pursued their self-denying course. Its mission is to minister, not to master; to give, not to govern. Its sceptre is love, not force; its throne is in the heart, and its empire over souls.

Matthew 23:13-33

The Sins of Men and the Woes of Christ

There is a courage more than human in the attitude which Christ now assumes before the religious authorities of His age. He confronts them with the majesty of a righteous judge, and the daring of an invincible reformer. He designates them by names the most withering to their pride, yet the most just to their character. He calls them *hypocrites, blind guides, fools, vipers.* He takes off their masks and makes bare their character. He hurls at them, as in a series of thunderbolts, the terrible woes which their conduct deserved.

It is noteworthy that the Woes of Christ here are levelled, not merely against the Pharisaic character as a whole, but against the evil habits of which it was composed. This suggests the idea *that there is a woe to every sin.* As these sins did not die out with the Pharisees, but have come down to us, and reign with the men of this age, the Woes are still falling from the lips of Christ. Wherever there is the moral evil there must be the Woe; they are indissolubly united. God Himself will not sunder them. To give a practical application to this section of heavenly truth, we draw from it the following observations:—

I. Antagonism to Christianity is an evil under the dark woe of Christ. "*Woe unto you, Scribes and Pharisees, hypocrites! for ye shut up the kingdom of heaven against men: for ye neither go in yourselves, neither suffer ye them that are entering to go in.*" The meaning of this is, that they were not only so opposed to the heavenly system of which Christ was the founder—the gospel—as to refuse entering it themselves, but they used all their influence to prevent others from doing so. They would not accept Christ as the Messiah. They hated His name; they rejected His doctrines;

they struggled with indignation against His rising influence; they used all the powers at their command to keep the public away from Him who was the Saviour of the world. This was a terrible iniquity, and it has a terrible Woe. But is not this evil common in Christendom, and even rampant in our England? What teeming crowds there are around us, who not only reject Christianity themselves, but who use their influence to keep others away from the truth as it is in Jesus! To such this Woe attaches as truly and as justly as to the old Pharisee. It hangs over them as a thunder-cloud. It follows them wherever they go : it darkens and spreads every day, and will break at last upon their existence with all the horrors of an unending retribution. *"If he that despised Moses' law died without mercy under two or three witnesses : of how much sorer punishment,"* &c. Shall not eternal justice link for ever one of its tremendous Woes to this the greatest crime that humanity can perpetrate ?

II. Avarice, working under the garb of piety is under the dark woe of Christ. *"Woe unto you, Scribes and Pharisees, hypocrites! for ye devour widows' houses, and for a pretence make long prayers : therefore ye shall receive the greater damnation."* Mark their cruel avarice! they devoured widows' houses. "This," as Bengel says, "the most atrocious species, is put for the whole class of rapacious actions." If the circumstances of one class of persons more than another should keep avarice at bay, and repel its greedy touch, it would be that of the *widow*. Poor woman! her house, however well furnished with comforts or even the elegancies of life, is a desolate place to her. The companion of her heart, and the protector of her rights, is gone. There is no sunshine in those rooms of hers ; there is a gloom in every chamber; a deep shadow rests on her very being, which seems to darken as she descends graveward herself. One might have supposed that the most voracious and cold-blooded avarice would keep away at least from *such* a scene. But the avarice of these Pharisees entered these homes, preyed upon the frailties of the frail, the sorrows of the sorrowful, and rifled them of the very means of existence. *" They devoured widows' houses."* But what makes the matter worse, this was done under the garb of religion ; *pietistically* done. *" For a pretence they made long prayers."* They were great prayer makers; they prayed sometimes nine times a day, and prayed lengthily too. Take care of men who talk much of prayer and love to make long ones. The spirit of true prayer, like love and every deep emotion, recoils from parade, and seeks solitude rather than society, silence rather than speech. *" Let thy words be few,"* said Solomon. "Make not much babbling when thou prayest," said the son of Sirach. " Use not vain repetitions," said the Son of God Himself, "for your Father knoweth what things ye have need of, before ye ask Him." Their prayer was mere acting, nothing more. To use the language of an old commentator—" While they seemed to soar heavenward upon the wings of prayer, their eye, like the kite's, was all the while upon their prey and the earth, some widow's house or other that lay convenient for them." The evil here denounced is nothing less than pietistic robbery, religious plunder; social frauds and oppressions practised under the costume of a high sanctity. But was this evil confined to the Pharisees? No! This also has run down through all succeeding ages, and is even amongst the men of our own times. How much money have the priests of Rome extorted from the *widow* and the fatherless, by promising the recovery of their dead from purgatory, and the absolution of their own sins! Protestantism too, has done too much in this way. How much money in this country is annually raised to support the functionaries of religion and secretaries of institutions from a mere "pretence!" Avarice, devilish in its very nature, is never more devilish than when it works through religious and benevolent institutions. The evil, then, that our Saviour denounced, is here. It did not die out with the Pharisees of Judea; it is working amongst us now in a thousand forms of "pretence." Shall not this evil have a *Woe?* Eternal Justice says yes, and Christ as a heavenly messenger, attached a terrible one to it. It shall receive the *greater* " damnation." There are degrees in damnation, and the damnation attached to this evil is a greater one. Avarice in any secular form is bad, and insures damnation; but avarice under the forms of affected sanctity. is worse; especially when directed against the " widow " and the fatherless, and will receive " greater damnation."

III. PROSELYTING SECTARIAN ZEAL IS UNDER THE DARK WOE OF CHRIST. The expression "*compass sea and land*" is a proverbial phrase, signifying that they left no effort untried to gain proselytes to Pharisaism,* which they succeeded in obtaining from heathenism, whom they made worse than they were before: "the proselyte was twofold more the child of hell." The heathen might have been bad before, but he was worse now, inasmuch as he had been induced by hypocrites to become a hypocrite. The zeal of these Pharisees in proselyting was an evil. The spirit of it was the sectarianism of a miserable sect. There is an essential difference between sectarian zeal and godly zeal; the one is selfish and mean, the other is self-denying and magnanimous. Godly zeal is a generous and a noble passion; it is zeal, not for human systems, but for Divine truths; not for the letter of a doctrine, but for its spirit; it is a zeal for the progress of the true and the just, the honourable and the lovely, throughout the world, and which rejoices in them wherever they are found; it is a zeal which enables a man's heart to see and love the good everywhere. Sectarian zeal is kindled and fed by the few peculiar opinions that distinguish its own class. These opinions, whether they refer to doctrine or ritual, are supreme in the mind of the sectarian; "his

---

* There were two kinds of proselytes. First, the proselytes of righteousness, *i.e.* complete, who embraced the Jewish religion in its full extent, and shared in all the rites and privileges of Jews themselves. Second, the proselytes of the gate ; foreigners who lived among the Jews, who were not circumcised, yet conformed to some of the Jewish laws and customs; they were admitted into the outer division of the temple, called the court of the Gentiles. The Talmudists speak against proselytes, as injurious to the purity of their religion.

principles " (as he calls them), " his church," " his denomination," are everything to him. There is no good outside his little pale; the men that join his church are converted; all else, at the best, are in a doubtful state. He vaunts his denominationalism; he lives and revels in it. All this is pure selfishness. It is the glorifying of our own little opinions; the idolizing of our own notions. It is associated with *meanness* too. A meaner class of men know I none than those who live in their religious sect; their general sympathies (if they ever had any) are gone; the charity that thinketh no evil of others has expired. The man is lost in his little creed; all who agree not with him he will either openly denounce, or, what is worse, meanly insinuate, as heretics. To thunder damnation on all outside of his system, is to him the delight of his heart and the most *unctuous* display of his gospel. But sect zeal is not only an evil in itself, but in its results as well; the men these Pharisees converted to their views became worse. The Hellenistic Jews, for such they were, were the most bitter in their antagonism to Christianity;—like all converts to a new faith that has but little truth in it, their bigotry became most fiery and intolerable. How furiously they opposed the apostles (Acts xiii. 45; xiv. 2–19, xvii. 5; xviii. 6)! Are men ever made better by joining a sect from sectarian consideration? Never! always worse. To this sectarian zeal which the Pharisees displayed, and which is as rampant now, Christ attached a Woe: and well He might;—it is an accursed thing. Like a canker, it eats the roots of all that is generous and noble in human nature. It is the spirit of that intolerance and persecution that has reigned in the church throughout all ages. It is a foul misrepresentation of that religion which consisteth not in circumcision nor uncircumcision, but in a divine spirit. "Not in meat nor drink, but in righteousness, and peace, and joy in the Holy Ghost." Woe to it! we feebly, but with all the might of our being, echo this *Woe* of Christ against this accursed thing.

IV. EXALTING THE HUMAN IN THE PLACE OF THE DIVINE IS AN EVIL UNDER THE DARK WOE OF CHRIST. "*Woe unto you, ye blind guides, which say, Whosoever shall swear by the temple, it is nothing.*" The spirit of the conduct exposed in these six verses seems to me *the exalting of the human at the expense of the divine;* making "the gold" and "the gift," which men had brought to the temple, something more sacred and divine than the temple itself, and the God whose dwelling-place it was. Christ denounces them as "blind guides and fools" in this respect, and condescends to expose their folly. "*Whether is greater, the gold (that is the gold deposited in the treasury), or the temple that sanctifieth the gold ; the gift, or the altar that sanctifieth the gift ?*" Christ does not sanction oaths. In His sermon on the mount He had prohibited them in the most emphatic and authoritative manner. He merely takes these men on their own ground in order to denounce their conduct; and at the same time He takes an opportunity to crush their futile distinctions, and to show that the validity of an oath rested not upon the thing from which it was taken, whether *gift, altar, gold, temple, or heaven;* but upon its tacit

reference to God Himself, who " *dwelleth* " in the temple, and who
" *sitteth upon the throne."* Why did these men exalt the gold and
gift above the temple and the altar? A miserable avarice was
their motive. They did so in order to encourage the people
to bring their gold to the temple and their gifts to the altar.
Setting the human above the divine, and that from sordid considerations, was the evil which Christ here denounced in these old
Pharisees. Was this evil confined to these men or to their times
and country? Alas! no. This also has descended and planted
itself wherever the footstops of men are found. It is rife even in
Christian lands. There is too much of the human at the expense of
the divine in all our churches; there is often more of man than God
in our liturgies and our sermons. The *Woe* of Christ rests upon this
evil wherever it exists.

V. THE ELEVATION OF THE RITUAL AT THE EXPENSE OF THE MORAL IS
AN EVIL UNDER THE DARK WOE OF CHRIST. " *Woe unto you, Scribes and
Pharisees, hypocrites! for ye pay tithe of mint and anise and cummin,
and have omitted the weightier matters of the law, judgment, mercy,
and faith: these ought ye to have done, and not to leave the other
undone. Ye blind guides, which strain at a gnat, and swallow a
camel."* These men, from a ceremonious zeal, did more than pay
the common tithes for the Levites, the poor, and the service at the
temple, as commanded by the law. (Num. xviii. 20-24; Deut.
xiv. 22-29.) They rendered a tenth part even of their smaller
herbs. The mint, the anise, and the cummin, were those smaller
aromatic herbs, which they offered with the most rigid exactitude.
Christ does not condemn them for doing this; on the contrary, He
appears to commend them. Their sin was that in doing this they
neglected the great moral things of the law—" judgment, mercy,
and faith." They were punctilious about ritualities, but careless
concerning the everlasting principles of morality and religion. Thus
they strained at a gnat, or rather out a gnat, and swallowed a
camel. Here the smallest insect and the greatest animal are employed to give strength to the antithesis. They would shrink from
keeping back the smallest portion of a tithe, even to the fraction of
a herb; yet they would devour widows' houses, and trample every
principle of justice, truth, and charity, in the dust. This is the evil
against which Christ hurled His *Woe.* Nor is this evil extinct; it
is also with us, the men of this age. How many are there amongst
us who attend with the greatest exactness to all the formalities of
religion, who shrink with a pious dread from a deviation from the
ordinary church service; but who amongst the poor are hardhearted,
in their business over-reaching, in their family tyrannic? They are
alive to the letter of duty, but dead to the spirit. With the lip they
will chant the responses and sing the anthems of their church; but
they have no heart to "do justice, love mercy, and walk humbly
with their God." What is a church prayer to an act of self-sacrificing benevolence? What is a gnat to a camel? Wherever this evil
exists, there is the Woe of Christ.

VI. ATTENTION TO THE OUTWARD APPEARANCE, TO THE NEGLECT OF THE HEART, IS AN EVIL UNDER THE DARK WOE OF CHRIST. " *Woe unto you Scribes and Pharisees, hypocrites! for ye make clean the outside of the cup and of the platter, but within they are full of extortion and excess,*" &c. The difference between their external deportment and internal character is here strikingly hit off by a double comparison,—a comparison between a domestic vessel internally filthy, but externally clean : a sepulchre externally white, but internally filled with the corruptions of death. So thoroughly did their outward behaviour to men and God conceal and misrepresent the loathsome depravity of their hearts. The power of man to falsify the state of his heart by his outward conduct is remarkable ;—he can appear to be what he is not. The most corrupt can so thoroughly counterfeit goodness, that they pass undetected through the shrewdest society to the end of their life. In proportion to the vileness of the heart is the force of the temptation to this hypocrisy. Were a bad man to leave his heart thoroughly uncovered in his daily life, corrupt as society is, it would shun him with horror, and his existence would scarcely be tolerated. Was this evil, this hypocrisy, confined to the Pharisees ? By no means; it has ever been one of the most common sins of mankind. Bad men everywhere counterfeit goodness, and seek to pass for what they are not. A corrupt man is a living impostor; his whole life is a deception, a hollow sham. This hypocritical acting Christ denounces as a " blind " policy, and it is so ; for the inside of the cup and platter—that is the important part—if it be filthy, might poison the life-blood, and terminate the existence of the user. A thousand times better let the outside be filthy, bad though that would be, and the inside clean, than for the inside to be defiled and the outside pure. Blind policy, too, because the " whited " sepulchre must one day be thrown open, and expose its contents to the sun. Justly, then, does the Heavenly Teacher fling His terrible *Woe* against this abominable hypocrisy.

VII. AFFECTED HONOUR FOR DEPARTED WORTH, TO THE NEGLECT OF THE LIVING, IS AN EVIL UNDER THE DARK WOE OF CHRIST. " *Woe unto you, Scribes and Pharisees, hypocrites! because ye build the tombs of the prophets,*" &c. It was customary, both among the Jews and Gentiles, to show their reverence for the dead by building or beautifying their tombs. These Scribes and Pharisees were careful to do this in relation to the graves of the martyred prophets. There was no harm in this ; reverence for departed worth and greatness is seemly and right; but such reverence they in truth had not. This, like all other virtues, they feigned. They had no vital sympathy with the spirit of these martyred prophets; on the contrary, their dispositions, purposes, and lives, were in hostility to the moral soul of these departed worthies. That moral soul or spirit was living amongst them now, even in a higher form than it appeared in any of the old patriarchs or prophets ; it looked at them, spoke to them, wrought before them, in the sublime life of Jesus of Nazareth. Yet nothing did they loathe and hate so much; their hearts flamed with a fiendish indignation as they beheld it;—they could not bear the sight of it. Their respect, therefore, for departed worth was also a pretence,—for living worth they hated and despised; and Christ tells them hey were witnesses unto themselves; their own *consciences testified it*, that they were the "children of them which killed the prophets." Is not this a common as well as a grievous evil? Is it not common for men to rear monuments to departed worth, to emblazon their virtues in history, and celebrate them in song: to parade their worth in their speeches and conversation, and yet display a practical dislike to the spirit of their heroes as it lives and works around them?* Against this evil also Christ directs His *Woe.*

Brothers, do not think that these terrible *Woes,* which seem to roll in successive thunders in the Divine paragraph which has now engaged our attention, had an exclusive reference to the old Scribes and Pharisees. They peal through all successive times, and are levelled against every man who is guilty of the evils which mark the history of these Jewish hypocrites. Art thou in spirit and life antagonistic to Christianity, refusing to enter the kingdom of heaven thyself, and preventing others from doing so? There is *Woe* for thee. Open thine ears, hear it, and take the warning. Art thou under the cloak of religion, carrying out thy avaricious desires, and trading upon the credulity of the superstitious, like those Pharisees who "devoured widows' houses"? Then there is a *Woe* for thee. Hear it, and reform. Art thou exalting the human above the divine in religion—putting man in the place of God? Then there is a *Woe* for thee. Hear it, and renounce thy practical idolatry. Art thou attending to the mere letter of duty, tithing even the "mint," the "anise," and the "cummin," in external circumstances, and wholly disregarding the weightier moral matters of the law? Then there is a *Woe* for thee. Open thy ears to it, and learn in time that "neither circumcision nor uncircumcision availeth anything," but a new creature in Christ. Art thou attending merely to thine external deportment, and neglecting the state of thy heart, robing thyself in the costume of goodness, whilst thou thyself art corrupt in soul, cleansing the outside of the cup and platter, while the inside is poisoned with putrescent filth? Then there is a *Woe* for thee. Hear it, and dart the cry to heaven, "Create in me a clean heart, O God, and renew a right spirit within me." Art thou feigning an honour for departed worth, whilst thou art neglecting, or perhaps maligning, the true and the good men around thee? Then there is a *Woe* for thee. Hear it, and link thyself at once to living worth, and honour "the saints that are in the earth, and the excellent that are now about thee." *Every moral evil drags after it a Divine Woe.*

* See Hypocritical Tomb Building, "Homilist," Vol. iv., Second Series, p. 503.

Matthew 23:34-39

The Advantages, Crimes, and Doom of Jerusalem

So numerous are the thoughts that start from this wonderful paragraph, that we feel a difficulty to group them into an order and a compactness, suitable at once for our thinking readers, and our very limited space. Most of the points may, perhaps, find a development under the three following observations :—

I. THAT THE SPIRITUALLY USEFUL MEN OF EVERY AGE ARE THE SPECIAL GIFTS OF CHRIST. *" Behold, I send unto you prophets, and wise men, and Scribes."* These appellations which designated the spiritually useful men of the Jewish dispensation, are here employed to represent the disciples, evangelists, apostles, and other holy ministers, that were to come into action under the dispensation of Christ. By one or other of these titles, every true and useful man may be denominated. " I send them to you," says Christ. Yes, all such men are *sent* by Christ. They are fountains of life which He opens up in the desert : they are stars which He kindles in the dark heavens of human history. He endows them with all their qualifications for spiritual usefulness, intellectual and moral. Every good man is a messenger from Christ, breathing Christ's spirit, and delivering Christ's commission. Two thoughts are suggested in relation to the mission of these men :—

First : *Christ sometimes sends them to scenes where their predecessors have been grievously persecuted.* He promised to send them now to Jerusalem, whose corrupt population had for ages maltreated the righteous messengers of Heaven, and martyred many a prophet of the Lord. How forbearing is His mercy ! How persevering His redemptive love !

Secondly : *Christ sometimes sends them to scenes where He knows they also will meet with similar ill-treatment.* *" Some of them ye shall kill and crucify, and some of them shall ye scourge in your synagogues."* Very literally were these predictions fulfilled in the first era of gospel history. " The Acts of the Apostles" abound with illustrations. Stephen was stoned; James was killed with the sword; some of the apostles were imprisoned, scourged, driven " from city to city ;" and tradition informs us that at least four of the twelve apostles were nailed to the cross. Christ foresaw all this. To His omniscient eye all the sufferings that His messengers would meet with in Jerusalem and elsewhere, in that age and all future times, stood as clear as in the light of day. There is no *unkindness in this ;* for He always gives them strength according to their day, and causes them to glory in their tribulation. He has ever enabled them to sing in prisons, and to shout in raptures amid the agonies of martyrdom ; and thus by their suffering He has furnished the world with the highest demonstrations of the power, the divinity, and blessedness, of His truth.

II. That the persecution of the men whom Christ thus gives
to the world is one of the greatest crimes. " *That upon you
may come all the righteous blood shed upon the earth,*" &c.   In
2 Chronicles xxiv. 20-21, we have these words : " And the Spirit of
God came upon Zechariah the son of Jehoiada the priest, which
stood above the people, and said unto them, Thus saith God, Why
transgress ye the commandments of the Lord, that ye cannot
prosper ? Because ye have forsaken the Lord, He hath also forsaken
you. And they conspired against him, and stoned him with stones,
at the commandment of the king, in the court of the house of the
Lord." Zechariah, here spoken of as stoned in "the house of the
Lord," is probably the Zacharias whom Christ here mentions. The
fact that in one place he is spoken of as the son of Jehoiada, and in
the other as the son of Barachias, can be explained by the circumstance that the Jews frequently had two names ; thus Matthew is
called Levi ; Lebbeus—Thaddeus ; and Simon—Cephas.   It may
be therefore that Jehoiada and Barachias were the names of the
same individual, and that individual the father of Zacharias.   The
position in which the martyrdom took place, " between the temple
and the altar," agrees with the account given in the Book of
Chronicles, and confirms therefore the supposition that the cases are
identical.   Why Christ should take the period of martyrdom from
Abel to this Zechariah, a period of about 3,000 years, and make no
reference to the martyrdoms perpetrated from the time of Zechariah
to the time when He was now speaking, a period of about 800 years,
it is not possible to determine.*   Some think that the martyrdom of Zechariah is mentioned in order to pre-intimate the horrid
murder of a just and good man by that name, which, according to
Josephus, took place in the temple a short time previous to its
destruction by the Romans.   Three things strike us in this extraordinary language of Christ :—

First : *The transmission of guilt from generation to generation.*
Christ asserts that the blood of all the prophets from the foundation
of the world would be required of this generation.   He held the
people to whom He spoke as in some sense accountable for all the
martyrdoms from Abel down to that hour. That children under the
government of God are made to bear the iniquities of their fathers,
is not only clearly taught in the Scriptures, but also in the *every-day
life of mankind.*   Elsewhere, we have endeavoured to show that this
hereditary principle in God's government of humanity is in harmony
with justice and beneficence.†

Secondly : *The accumulation of guilt as generations multiply.* The
spirit of crime not only descends from sire to son, but heightens its
moral enormity in its downward course.   The heinousness of a
crime greatly depends upon the moral advantages possessed by the

* Zacharias may be mentioned, as he was the last prophet slain by the whole
nation (i.e., by the king and people) ; and his appeal for vengeance is distinctly
recorded in 2 Chron. xxiv. 22.
† See " Homilist," Vol. ii., New Series, p. 277.

perpetrator. Or guilt is proportioned to our privileges. Inasmuch, therefore, as the existing generation enjoys the experience of its predecessors, its sins must have an enormity peculiar to itself. Martyrdom in the age in which our Saviour lived was a more accursed thing than martyrdom in any preceding period. Sin is sin in whatever age committed ; but sin becomes a darker and a more damnable thing as the experience of mankind augments. " Had I not come and spoken to them," said Christ, " they would not have known sin."

Thirdly : *The terrible culmination of sin in one generation.* "Verily I say unto you, all these things shall come upon this generation." The Heavenly Teacher seemed to look upon His age as the great reservoir into which all the crimes of the persecutors of all past ages, like so many streams, had flown ; or, as a great harvest field, in which all the iniquities of all past times had ripened, and now awaited the scythe of Eternal Justice. Jerusalem had truly " filled up the measure of its iniquities." Josephus, one of their countrymen, an opposer of the Gospel, bears important, because impartial, testimony to their abandoned condition. He says that they had carefully imitated, and even exceeded, all the deeds of their ancestors. Though, at the time Jesus spoke, His predictions must have seemed highly improbable, yet that generation had not all passed off the stage, before all the vials of wrath were poured out upon their doomed city and country.

III. THAT THIS, ONE OF THE GREATEST CRIMES OF A PEOPLE, EXPOSED THEM TO ULTIMATE RUIN. " *O Jerusalem, Jerusalem!* " &c. What a wail is this ! What mysterious depths of sympathy it faintly echoes ! Never did such a wail go forth on the atmosphere of our earth, or on the universe before. It is more than the wail of a patriot over the destruction of his country : more than the wail of a philanthropist over the physical ruin of his race. It is the wail of an infinitely loving Saviour over the doom of lost souls. This wail has floated down the centuries, and rings in our hearts at this moment. Christ now *abandons* Jerusalem. The words suggest three things expressive of the misery involved in this abandonment :—

First : *What the doomed people might have been with Christ.* " A hen," a very humble creature, He here condescends to employ, to represent what He would have been towards the men of Jerusalem. " *How often would I have gathered thy children together, even as a hen gathereth her chickens,*" &c. A threefold blessing is expressed in this humble but striking figure. (1) *Central unity.* They might have all been united together under the wings of Almighty love. (2) *Complete satisfaction.* How warm and happy are the young ones under the glowing wing of their feathered parent ! It is a *natural* heat and happiness they experience. Nothing more do they want, for nothing higher do they crave. It would have been so with the men of Jerusalem, had they accepted Christ's overtures ;— they would have had all that could make their *whole* natures blessed.

He has a "healing under His wings." (Malachi iv. 2.) (3) *Safe keeping.* That wing is a protection : it guards from the cold blasts of air and the ferocious birds of prey. "I give," says Christ, "unto my sheep eternal life, neither shall any man pluck them out of my hand."

Secondly : *What the doomed man must be without Christ.* "Behold your house is unto you left desolate." The ruin of Jerusalem was just at hand; the Roman eagle was on its wing thitherward. *The house* of all its houses—the temple—would soon be *desolate.* Jerusalem would soon be in ruins ;—"not one stone would be left upon another;" the lofty city would "lie low, even to the ground." The parent's wings withdrawn, and the young ones scattered, exposed to the withering blast and the foul destroyer. A terrible picture this of all men without Christ! Such men are without *unity,* without *comfort,* and without *safety.* "For I say unto you, Ye shall not see me henceforth, till ye shall say, Blessed is He that cometh in the name of the Lord." His presence as a Saviour they would no more have amongst them until they reached that moral state of mind which would induce them to hail His appearance amongst them and say, "Blessed is He," etc. Tremendous judgments must fall on them before this, and after the sufferings of ages, the Jewish people seem still far remote from such a state as this.

Thirdly : *What the doomed men must ascribe to themselves in all their misery.* The whole ruin was brought upon themselves. "*I would ; but ye would not.*" Self-loathing, self-crimination, self-denunciation! How would these add to their misery. They, in truth, destroyed themselves. Say not that the sinner has no *Will,* no power of moral action; he ruins himself; and by a *Will* so powerful as overcomes all the influences of nature, all the means of redemptive grace, all the pleadings of the Redeeming God Himself.

Matthew 24:1-51

Analogy between the Two Great Days of Judgment

In this chapter and the succeeding one we have pre-delineated Two Great Days of Judgment. The one, which was to transpire in the destruction of Jerusalem and the utter abolition of the Old Hebrew Commonwealth; and the other, which was to take place at the end of the world, the termination of man's probationary career, and the irrevocable settlement of the destinies of the human race. One Day of Judgment was local, and the other is universal; the one has dawned and closed, and is a matter of history; the other still looms with a dark and terrible significance in the future. So uniform throughout all ages are the principles on which God conducts the moral government of this world, that the events of one age are prophecies and types of what will occur in after-ages—occur for ever, so long as that form of government exists. Hence the predictions of Christ contained in this chapter of the destruction of Jerusalem so closely resembles what, in the next chapter and elsewhere, we are told will take place on the *final* Day of Judgment, that much of the language seems as applicable to the one event as to the other. Perhaps there is no better method of doing justice to this chapter, and at the same turning it to a right practical account, than by tracing the analogy subsisting between these Two Great Days of Judgment. We discover, at least, eight points of resemblance. *In both there is the abolition of religious dispensations;—in both the doomed things are not properly regarded even by Christ's disciples;—in both the foretokening circumstances are divinely delineated;—in both the attendant events are terribly appalling;—in both the interests of the good are divinely contemplated;—in both there are advents of the Son of Man; —in both there is a development of an eternal determination;—in both there is obscurity as to the specific time of occurrence;—in both there is the utmost demand for watchfulness on the part of humanity.*

I. In both there is the abolition of religious dispensations. Christ does two things:—

First: *He withdraws from the temple.* "And Jesus went out, and departed from the temple." The temple was the national scene and magnificent symbol of that religious dispensation under which humanity has been living for ages. The temple had stood as a divine lamp burning in the centre of the world through the dark night of revolving centuries: but its end has come:—Jesus now *"departed from it."* As He withdrew the Shekinah went out, and the inner sanctuary was left in blackness. The spirit fled, and it stood only as a mouldering carcass. Three days after this, its sacred veil was rent in twain, and the Holy of Holies exposed to the wanton gaze of a sin-besotted and a sin-maddened populace. Millions through distant times had worshipped within its sacred precincts; but all worship there was now over:—the last prayer had been offered, and the last psalm chanted. Christ Himself had often visited it; there He had prayed, and taught, and blessed, hundreds of His countrymen; but He now turns from it for ever, and the first step of His therefrom tolls its death knell. Of what service is a temple when its Deity is gone? Of what service is a lamp when its light is quenched?

Secondly: *He foretells its utter destruction.* "Jesus said unto them, See ye not these things? verily I say unto you, There shall not be left here *one stone upon another, that shall not be thrown down.*" At the hour when Christ uttered this prediction, few things in the history of the world seemed less likely to transpire. The massive structure was firm enough to stand the storms of many an age. What people existing at this time would be likely to destroy such an edifice? Would the Jew? No thought more revolting to his nature. Would the Roman? Rome and Judea at this time were on tolerably friendly terms. Besides, should Rome lay siege to the city, would it not spare, according to its custom, such a magnificent building, as a splendid trophy of its victorious arms ? Yet scarcely had forty years passed away before the prophecy of Christ was literally fulfilled. In A.D. 73, the Roman armies, under the command of Titus, besieged the holy city, and the work of bloodshed on that memorable occasion forms one of the most horrid and soul-harrowing chapters in human history. Titus, however, in the midst of the direful tragedy, was anxious to spare that glorious old temple ; but all his efforts for the purpose were vain. Even the Jews themselves, in the depth of their desperation, set fire to it; and one of the Roman soldiers, contrary to the wish of his general, threw a burning firebrand in through one of its windows, and thus consummated the catastrophe. The temple was destroyed, we are told by Josephus, even contrary alike to the will of the Roman general, and Cæsar himself. A short time after, we are informed that one of the Roman generals, left in command at Jerusalem, ploughed up the temple and the places about it, and thus fulfilled the whole prophecy, that " Zion should be as a ploughed field."

> " Proud Cæsar's ploughshare o'er her ruins driven,
> Fulfils at length the tardy doom of Heaven ;
> The wrathful vial's drops at length are poured
> On the rebellious race that crucified the Lord."

Thus the words of Christ were accomplished to the letter; and we have in the judgment that befel Jerusalem, the utter abolition of that temple, the divine scene and symbol of the Jewish dispensation. It is true that the Jew adhered to Judaism after this, and with a strange and sad delusion adheres to it now. But Judaism, as a system, charged with divine virtue and authority, departed with the fall of Jerusalem. In this respect Judaism was like the Brazen Serpent. That Brazen Serpent had a divine healing virtue, so long as Heaven intended it to stand upon the pole before the eye of the serpent-bitten Israelites. After it had served this purpose, it was nothing but " nehushtan"—brass. Though for ages afterwards the Hebrews continued to regard it with superstitious reverence, it was nothing but "brass." So with Judaism, up to this period it was filled with divine virtue; but whatever the modern Jew may think, it has been nothing but "brass" ever since.

It will thus be in the last great Day of Judgment, another religious dispensation,—the Christian one,—will come to an end. As Judaism departed with the destruction of Jerusalem, Christianity will depart with the dawn of the *last* judgment. The mediatorial economy, under which we in these last ages live, with its overtures of divine pardon, and regenerating spirit, and soul-cleansing influences, is not to endure for ever. It is not an everlasting temple. The time hastens on when not one stone of it shall be left upon another, that shall not be thrown down. On the final Day of Judgment Christ will deliver up this remedial system to

God the Father; and "*then shall the Son also Himself be subject unto Him that put all things under Him, that God may be all in all.*" After this no more sin will be pardoned, no more characters changed, no more souls saved. All things pertaining to the destinies of man will be fixed, unalterably, and for ever.

II. IN BOTH THE DOOMED THINGS ARE NOT PROPERLY REGARDED EVEN BY CHRIST'S DISCIPLES. His disciples came to Him to show Him the building of the temple. Mark, in referring to the same event, speaks of one of His disciples, who came to Him, and said, "*Master, see what manner of stones and what buildings are here.*" Luke, in recording the same incident, is more full and explicit, and says, "*And as some spake of the temple, how it was adorned with goodly stones, and gifts,*" Christ said, "*As for these things which ye behold, the days will come, in the which there shall not be left one stone upon another, that shall not be thrown down.*" It would seem from this that the disciples were evidently on this occasion charmed with the magnificence of the building.—"What manner of stones, what buildings are here!" An outburst of admiration this; the stones were indeed beautiful. That sacred building was constructed of prodigious blocks of white marble, some of which seem to have been upwards of thirty feet long, eighteen broad, and sixteen thick. How surprisingly beautiful it must have looked, as it stood up there upon Moriah's historic brow, glistening in the sunbeams, embosomed by the green mountains, and looking down with a sacred majesty upon the bustling city! Who wonders at their admiration? Yet there is a saddening thought connected with it, and the thought was this, it was a *doomed* thing. They did not view it in the light in which Christ viewed it; He gazed at it with a saddened eye. "*As for these things,*" He said, "which ye behold, the days will come, in the which there shall not be left one stone upon another, that shall not be thrown down." He looked at it as the gorgeous shadow of a glorious substance that was gone,—ay, and that gorgeous shadow itself, soon to be swept away by the stern justice of the universe. As if He had said "As for these things, they are scarcely worthy your admiration; they need not delight you so; their presence makes me sad. Once they had a grand spiritual significance, and a glorious spiritual function; but now they stand before me as an unmeaning and useless pile of stones, doomed very soon to be shivered to pieces. To me that temple looks as the closing scene of a wonderful past, as a token of a rapidly darkening present, as the prophecy of a tremendous future."

Now this state of mind which the disciples had in relation to the temple, Christians too generally have now in relation to those things which will be destroyed in the Day of Judgment. In both cases there is an *admiration of doomed things*. Are Christian men now ever found admiring worldly wealth and its appendages, the splendid mansion, the fine estate, and the magnificent equipage? Too much so, I fear. But "as for these things," like the old temple, they are *doomed*. They will be borne away as dust before the first blast of the Final Day. Are Christian men found inordinately admiring the productions of art? Does the breathing marble, the glowing canvas, or music's magic touch, wake their admiration? Often so. But, "as for these things," like the old temple, they are *doomed;*—before the rising sun of the Final Day they will vanish as a cloud, and be seen no more. Are Christian men found delighting in certain conventional systems of religion, glorying in their own church and creed? It is so, distressingly so, to all truly Catholic souls. But, "as for these things," also like the old temple, they are *doomed.* "Whether there be prophecies they shall fail; whether there be tongues they shall cease; and whether there be knowledge, it shall vanish away." All mere human systems in the Final Judgment will be lost as rushlights in the blaze of day. Set not your heart upon *doomed* things; and yet what beneath these heavens is not *doomed?* "As for these things," what are they? Shadows and sounds. The eternal voice of truth says, "all flesh is grass," etc.

III. In both the fore-tokening circumstances are divinely delineated :—*The portending signs are here delineated by Christ.* "And as He sat upon the mount of Olives, the disciples came unto Him privately, saying, Tell us when shall these things be? and what shall be the sign of Thy coming and of the end of the world?" The end of the world means the end of the Jewish dispensation, or age. The signs which were to precede this terrible event are :—

First :—*The abounding of religious impostors.* "Many shall come in my name, saying, I am Christ; and shall deceive many." (Ver. 5.) And again, "Many false prophets shall rise and shall deceive many." (Ver. 11.) And again, "There shall arise false Christs, and false prophets, and shall show great signs and wonders; insomuch that, if it were possible, they shall deceive the very elect." (Ver. 24). Luke, in his history of the Acts of the Apostles, tells us of Simon Magus, who was called "the great power of God;" also of Theudas and Judas of Galilee, who drew away hundreds by their delusions; also of an Egyptian, who led out into the wilderness "four thousand men who were murdered." And the great Jewish historian tells us, that in the reign of Claudius, who died about the year 54, "The land was overrun with magicians, seducers, and impostors, who drew the people after them in multitudes, into solitudes and deserts, to see the signs and miracles which they promised to show by the power of God." Thus history proves that this predicted sign of the sad catastrophe was realized to the very letter.

Another sign would be :—

Secondly : *Wars of unusual enormity.* "And ye shall hear of wars and rumours of wars; see that ye be not troubled: for all these things must come to pass, but the end is not yet; for nation shall rise against nation, and kingdom against kingdom." Six years after the death of Christ, Caligula, the Roman Emperor, that arch-demon in human form, commanded his statue to be erected in the temple of Jerusalem; the Jews resisted the desecration, and a war would have at once ensued had not the emperor died. Soon, however, the horrors of war broke forth, and human blood flowed as rivers through the Roman empire. In one year and a half, four Roman Emperors, Nero, Galba, Otho, and Vitellius, suffered violent deaths; the empire was thrown into tremendous commotions, and its provinces filled with wars and rumours of wars. The war-fiend ran riot in Palestine, Syria, and Egypt, and thousands were slain in massacres most horrible. Josephus, in several chapters of his second book, presents the most soul-rending facts in fulfilment of this prediction of Christ.*

Another sign would be:—

Thirdly: *Terrible physical calamities.* (Ver. 7.) "Famines, pestilences, and earthquakes." The former are generally the inevitable results of war; they are fruits that fall on the nations from that hellish tree. According to the prediction of the prophet Agabus (Acts xi. 27, 28), there reigned a great dearth throughout all the world. "In the days of Claudius Cæsar," Josephus tells us, "a few years previous to the destruction of Jerusalem, 'famines and pestilences' prevailed, not only through Palestine, but through various parts of the Roman Empire." He records a pestilence which raged among the Jews A.D. 40, and caused them to remove to Seleucia. And Tacitus mentioned the terrible one which raged throughout Italy about twenty years afterwards. Tremendous "earthquakes," too, prevailed. The Roman historian tells us that the Laodicea, Colosse, Hierapolis, and Pompeii were overthrown in the reign of Nero.†

Another sign would be:—

Fourthly: *Grievous religious persecution.* "Then shall they deliver you up to be afflicted, and ye shall be hated of all nations for My name's sake" (ver. 9). The Acts of the Apostles abound with facts which fulfil this sad prediction. Paul, at first, was among the greatest persecutors (Acts viii., ix.). Peter and John were imprisoned, afterwards Paul himself, and Silas. The sufferings inflicted on Paul for Christ's sake were various, and sometimes torturing in the extreme. Stephen was stoned, James was killed, and it is believed that most of the disciples of our Lord were put to death. All nations were against them; Greece and Rome alike hated the name of Christian.

Another sign would be:—

Fifthly: *Apostasy from the Christian faith.* "And then shall many be offended, and shall betray one another, and shall hate one another, and because iniquity shall abound, the love of many shall wax cold" (ver. 10, 12). John, in his first epistle, records the fact here predicted. "They went out from us, but they were not of us; for if they had been of us, they would no doubt have continued

---

* "Testimony of Jesus," by Charles Timins.

† See Antiq., Lib. xx., chap. 2; Antiq., Book xviii., chaps. 8, 9. Tacitus, Lib. xvii., 13; xii., 43; xiv., 27; l., 22.

with us : but they went out, that they might be made manifest that they were not all of us." Tacitus, in his description of the persecution under Nero, has a remark concerning the Christians which shows how many of them *betrayed one another.* " At first," he says, " several were seized who confessed, and then were convicted and executed."

Another sign would be :—

Sixthly : *The universal diffusion of the Gospel.* " And this Gospel of the kingdom shall be preached in all the world, for a witness unto all nations ; and then shall the end come."—The end of the Jewish state and polity. We learn from the records of secular history, as well as from the statements of the sacred writers, that before the close of the forty years which elapsed between the death of Christ and the destruction of Jerusalem, the Gospel had been preached throughout the whole Roman empire. Churches were planted in Asia, Africa, and Europe. Paul declares it was preached to " every creature under heaven," and that the faith of the Romans " was spoken of throughout the whole world." The very persecutions, by scattering the Christians through all parts of the world, conduced to this.

The next and last sign depicted here would be :—

Seventhly : *The foul desecration of the holy place.* " When ye therefore shall see the abomination of desolation (or the desolating abominations), spoken of by Daniel the prophet, stand in the holy place." The reference is here to the Roman armies. They were an abomination to the Jews. Their standards and ensigns had idolatrous images of their gods and emperors sculptured upon them, and therefore were to the last degree offensive to the Israelites. Josephus informs us that, when the city was taken, the Romans brought their idols into the temple, placed them over the eastern gate, and sacrificed to them there. This was the last sign. When the disciples saw the Roman armies all encamped around the temple, they might be sure that the hour of Jerusalem's doom had come,—that the Divine thunderbolt was about to fall. The awful tragedy is now on the eve of consummation; in truth, all is now virtually over. The temple—

"Is now no more,
Nor ever shall be to the end of time,
The temple of Jerusalem."

Thus are delineated by Christ in answer to His disciples, the *signs* which were to precede the fall of Jerusalem, and the consequent abolition of the Hebrew commonwealth.

Now, He, who gave His disciples at this time a sketch of the " signs " that should foretoken the Day of Judgment on their country, and the *end* of the Jewish world, has also given us an outline of some of the signs which shall precede that Great Last Day of Judgment, that is to fall upon our world. We are not going to endeavour to make out an analogy between the signs themselves that precede these two Great Days of Judgment ; although, per-

haps, it might be accomplished without even the charge of fanciful-
ness in interpretation. All the analogy that we intimate here is in
the *fact that both have pre-delineated signs.* Looking at the great
outlines which inspiration has given concerning the future of
humanity, we discover at least two things that will take place before
the Great Day of Judgment: *A universal millennium.* The Bible, in
terms the most explicit, and in imagery of every description of loveliness and sublimity, assures us that there is a period to dawn on this
sin-corrupted and sin-condemned world when knowledge shall be
universal—when righteousness shall reign the world over; when
the Eternal Will shall be done on earth as it is done in heaven.
Far distant is this period, but it must come before the Last Judgment. *A general resurrection* is the other event that must occur
before the Final Day. All that are in their graves must hear the
voice of the Son of Man, and come forth. When the dead arise
then dawns the Judgment Day;—the day to which all other days
are tending, and in which all other days shall end. The day—

"That never more shall close."

IV. IN BOTH THE ATTENDANT EVENTS ARE TERRIBLY APPALLING.
There are several verses, interspersed through different parts of this
chapter, which give a terrible picture of the appalling events that
would attend the destruction of Jerusalem. (See verses 17–22;
also verses 28–30.) It is here intimated *that the amount of human
suffering on that dread occasion will be inexpressibly great :*—"Woe unto
them that are with child, to them that give suck in those days,"
&c. And again, "there shall be great tribulation, such as was not
until that time." And again, "then shall all the tribes of the earth
mourn." "*Great tribulation!*" Have you read the account which
Josephus has given? He shows us that the siege of Jerusalem
furnishes the bloodiest page in the long history of human misery.
He tells us that if all the miseries of men from the creation were
compared with those of that day, they would *dwindle* into insignificance. We are told that three million Jews were shut up in the
city; and that the bloody work continued from April till September.
The cause of such a vast number of people assembling in the city
on that occasion, Josephus tells us, was the Passover. "They
came," says he, "up from all the country to the feast of unleavened
bread, and were in a sudden shut up by an army." Five hundred,
every day, were, by the command of Titus, crucified on the walls of
the city. The multitude of executions was so great that room was
wanting for the crosses, and crosses for the bodies. Famine, too,
slew its thousands every day. The historian tells us of one mother
snatching her son, who was a child sucking at her breast, and
exclaiming, "O thou miserable infant, for whom shall I preserve
thee in this war, this famine, and this sedition?" and she slew her
infant, and roasted it for food! Well might our Saviour exclaim,
"Woe unto them that are with child, and to them that give suck in
those days." In allusion to this, too, He observes, "Blessed are the

barren, and the wombs that never bare, and the paps which never gave suck." It was the thought of this that touched Him as He saw mothers lining the road on the way to the cross. "Daughters of Jerusalem, weep not for me." It is said that when the Roman general beheld the vast number of bodies outside the city, he was so horrified that he called God to witness that it was not his doing. We are told that upwards of one million perished in the siege by famine and pestilence, and famine and sword. Human bodies lay in heaps in all directions. Human blood ran down the streets in rivers; and decomposing corpses loaded the atmosphere with pestilence. Truly it was a terrible day of judgment for this guilty nation. The life of virtue had left that nation: it was now a moral carcass; and the Roman army, like a ravenous eagle, was fastened on its heart. "Wheresoever the carcass is, there will the eagles be gathered together." Wherever there is moral death, the eagles of retribution must inevitably come. *It is also intimated that most terrible appearances would attend that event.* "Immediately after the tribulation of those days shall the sun be darkened, and the moon not give her light." This, it is true, may be regarded only as strong figurative language, to represent the startling blackness of that dark hour of sorrow. Still there is reason to believe that there were extraordinary appearances in the heavens on this occasion. Tacitus speaks of prodigies in nature at this period. He says that "forms of chariots and troops of soldiers were seen moving in the clouds." And Josephus says, that "a great storm with lightning, terrible thunderings, and earthquakes, occurred at the commencement of the war." *

Now, on the Great Final Day of Judgment, the attendant circumstances will be similarly terrible. Indeed, perhaps, the most terrible things which occurred in the destruction of Jerusalem are only faint shadows of what will occur at the end of the world. We read, that "on that day the earth shall move to and fro like a drunkard, and shall be removed like a cottage." We read, that "all the host of heaven shall be dissolved and the heavens be rolled together as a scroll." We read, that "the heavens shall pass away with a great noise, and the elements melt with fervent heat; the earth and the works that are therein shall be burned up." We read, that "the heavens will depart as a scroll when it is rolled together, and every mountain and island be removed from the place." What imagination can picture the overwhelming prodigies connected with this day? Tremendous earthquakes may rive the globe from the equator to the poles, causing its islands and its continents to heave, and plunge, and whirl like frail vessels in Atlantic storms :—

> "Whilst withering from the vaults of night
> The stars will pale their feeble light."

V. IN BOTH THE INTERESTS OF THE GOOD ARE DIVINELY CONTEMPLATED. *Christ gives His disciples time for escape.* He tells them of the

* See "The Testimony of Jesus," p. 197.

danger forty years before it comes. *He gives directions for their safety.* He points them to a place of refuge. "Flee unto the mountains." He urges on them the utmost promptitude when the danger came. "Let him that is in the housetop not come down and take anything out of his house." The idea is that when the danger came, if it came when they were on the house-top, they were not even to wait to enter a room. He warns them to be on their guard against false prophets and false Christs. He urges them to endure unto the end, that they may be saved; and He declares that for their sake the terrible period of suffering shall be shortened; "For the elect's sake those days shall be shortened." All this shows how thoroughly He contemplated the interests of His disciples. In Luke's report of Christ's address to His disciples at this time, His interest in them is set forth even more powerfully and more vividly than it is here. He says, "*They shall lay their hands on you, and persecute you,*" &c. It is here evidently taught that most of them would be preserved in safety amid the dread perils of that awful catastrophe, and that even of the few "who should be put to death" in the sanguinary riotings of that hour, not a particle of their being or interest either should be destroyed; "*There shall not an hair of your head perish.*" Though a good man die he loses not a fraction, not even "a hair," essential either to his being or well-being. However far separated, too, they may be, He will gather them together unto a holy fellowship with Himself, and with each other. "He shall send His angels with a great sound of a trumpet, and they shall gather together His elect from the four winds, from one end of heaven to the other." By "angels" here, perhaps, we are only to understand those messengers of His gospel and His judgment, who would, as with a great sound of a trumpet, warn His disciples of their peril, and summon them to the appointed scenes of safety.

Amid the transactions of the Last Great Day of Judgment, the interests of the good are equally guaranteed by Heaven. Amidst the fires and floods of earthly affliction, He is with them as their support and their guide; their death is "precious in His sight; He will redeem their soul from the power of the grave." "And this is the Father's will which hath sent me," said Christ, "that of all which He hath given me I should lose nothing, but raise it up again in the last day." Through all the trials of this life, and the overwhelming terrors of the Last Judgment, they are kept by the power of God through faith unto eternal salvation.

VI. IN BOTH THERE ARE ADVENTS OF THE SON OF GOD. The Bible, it seems to me, refers to *four* advents of the Son of God. His advent at His birth. At His incarnation He came into the world; "He came unto His own;" "He came to seek and save the lost." His advent in His Spiritual influence. "I will not leave you comfortless, I will come unto you." "Lo, I am with you always, even unto the end of the world." "Behold, I stand at the door and knock, if any man hear my voice, I will come in unto him." He came thus on the day of Pentecost; and comes now by His Spirit to every man. His advent in Providential agency. " Be ye therefore ready, for in such an hour as ye think not the Son of Man cometh." We live under the government of Christ, and He may be said to come to us in every event of our history. His advent in the Final Judgment. "When the Son of Man shall come in His glory, and all the holy angels with Him." "Behold the Lord cometh with ten thousand of His saints to execute judgment," &c.

Now it is in His providential agency that He is spoken of as coming in this chapter. He came now by His providence to break up the Jewish commonwealth, and to inflict upon that people a just judgment for its long ages of accumulated crimes. "For as the lightning cometh out of the east and shineth even unto the west, so also shall be the coming of the Son of Man." And again, "Then shall appear the sign of the Son of Man in heaven; and then shall all the tribes of the earth mourn, and they shall see the Son of Man coming in the clouds of heaven with power and great glory." *They shall see the Son of Man coming.* It would appear as clear, to the Jewish nation, that Christ, whom they crucified, was in this stupendous judgment, as if He stood before them in person; their consciences would see the Son of Man in everything about them, vivid and all-pervading as the lightning that flashes from east to west, filling the horizon with a strange and startling glare ;—overwhelmingly oppressive, as the black, sulphurous clouds, that roll in strange thunders over them. They would see Him coming in those clouds; and truly in those clouds He was. "He maketh the clouds His chariot, and rideth upon the wings of the wind." Now, on the Final Day of Judgment, Christ is represented coming as we have already stated. "The Lord Himself shall descend from heaven with a shout, with the voice of an archangel," &c. "Behold He cometh with clouds, and every eye shall see Him," &c.,

VII. IN BOTH THERE IS THE DEVELOPMENT OF AN ETERNAL DETERMINATION. "*Now learn a parable of the fig-tree; when his branch is yet tender, and putteth forth leaves, ye know that summer is nigh,*" &c. Two thoughts are suggested in relation to the development of the eternal decree in relation to the destruction of Jerusalem. First: *It was gradual.* "Learn a parable," &c. Seated as Christ now was on the Mount of Olives, fig-trees lay thick around Him; and, according to His wont, He borrows from them an illustration of the progressive advancement of divine retribution towards the Hebrew people. As certain as the leaf that now appeared on the fig-trees indicated the approach of summer, so would the events which Christ had delineated, indicate the approach of Jerusalem's dreadful doom. Heaven's plan of judgment, as well as mercy, is *gradual.* Its upas does not overspread the guilty nation at once, with its branches clustered with curses and its shadows distilling death : but gradually, from the tiniest seed, it proceeds to grow, through many a sinful age. Its storm does not burst at once upon the world, but comes by slow degrees. From a little cloud, the size of a man's hand, appearing first upon great nature's vault, it extends and blackens, until it mantles the earth as in a starless midnight, and breaks in storms of vengeance on the guilty head. The other thought that is suggested in relation to the eternal decree is :— Secondly : *That it is inevitable.* " Heaven and earth shall pass away," &c. There was no possibility of the Jews now avoiding this threatened judgment. The strength of their fortifications, their overwhelming numbers, and their desperate earnestness in resistance, might have led one to suppose that it were impossible even for heroic Rome, with all her mighty battalions, to have destroyed it. Josephus, who records the event, thinking of its improbability, declares it was *fate that decreed its destination.* And even Titus, the Roman general, as he, flushed with conquests, surveyed the desolations he had wrought in its destruction, felt bound to ascribe the work to the decrees of heaven. " We have certainly had God for our assistant in this war, and it was no other than God that ejected the Jews out of their fortifications ; for what could the hands of men, or any machines, do towards overthrowing these ?" Yes, nothing shall stand before the Eternal decree. " Heaven and earth shall pass away," &c. Heaven and earth seem well established. Their forms look as fresh as ever ; their forces act as vigorously as ever ; and they move in their pathway as regularly as ever. Yet, firm as they are, they shall pass away sooner than God's word shall fail. *It is unphilosophic to plead the order of nature against the fulfilment of the Divine word.* God can break the order of nature, but He cannot break His word ; it is " impossible for God to lie." God has broken the order of nature as in the case of miracles ; but He has never broken His word.*

" Not earth stands firmer than Thy word,
Nor stars so nobly shine."

The Last Great Day of Judgment will also be the development of an eternal determination. " *It is appointed unto men once to die, and after death the judgment.*" Again, " *He hath appointed the day in which he will judge the world in righteousness.*" That determination is being *gradually* worked out now. All things are tending to it as to a common centre. All things suggest it ; every day the events of human life thicken which testify and predict it. The great field of humanity is gradually ripening for this harvest. That determination, too, is *inevitable.* It can no more be avoided than could of old the downfall of Jerusalem. It must come, though all the generations of men from the beginning should unite to oppose it ; it must come, though all the created universe should rise against it. It must come. As to-night, the sun of our to-morrow is on its way to our horizon, and none can keep it back or arrest for one moment its progress ; so the great orb that shall light up the Last Judgment is on its march. It may be as distant from us as the most distant comet, yet still it is on its way, and will one day flood these heavens with supernatural brightness. " Heaven and earth shall pass away," &c.

* See " Homilist," Vol. iii., New Series, p. 207.

VIII. IN BOTH THERE IS THE UTMOST DEMAND FOR WATCHFULNESS ON THE PART OF HUMANITY. " *Watch, therefore, for ye know not at what hour the Lord doth come.*" There are four reasons suggested in the paragraph for the utmost watchfulness on the part of the disciples. First : *The uncertainty as to the specific period of its occurrence.* " But of that day and hour knoweth no man, not even the angels in heaven, but my Father only." And again, " In such an hour as ye think not, the Son of man cometh." The exact time was known only to God ; even the angels in heaven, the highest created intelligences, knew not the hour. It is not for us " to know the times or the seasons which the Father hath put into His own power." A veil conceals the future from all finite visions. Presumptuous men ofttimes seek to penetrate it ; but it is *impenetrable.* Providence, in its revolutions, is constantly exposing the ignorance and reproving the presumption of those prophet-mongers, who profess to decipher the chronology of future events. It is wise and kind of Heaven to keep from us the exact hour of our doom ;—the concealment is both adapted and intended to stimulate us to a constant watchfulness. Another reason for watchfulness, suggested here is :—Secondly : *The unprepared condition in which many would be found.* Three instances Christ refers to here of unpreparedness. *The careless Antediluvians.* " But as the days of Noe were, so shall also the coming of the Son of Man be," &c. Whilst that storm was gathering, which was to drown the world, these Antediluvians were " eating, drinking, marrying," &c. They were regardless of the Divine threatening, and pursued their wonted course of sensual revelry and joy. Another instance is " Two (men—the word is masculine) shall be in the field, the one taken, the other left." " Two women shall be grinding at the mill, one shall be taken and the other left." Had these labourers been prepared, the four might have been saved ; whereas only two were rescued from the grasp of the destroyer. The other instance is that of *rioting domestics.* He speaks of those servants who, regardless of the coming of their master, began to eat and drink with the drunken. (Ver. 49.) In this state their master came. These references of Christ were intended to impress the disciples with the fact that, notwithstanding the warnings which had from time to time been addressed to the Jewish nation, their doom would meet them unprepared, and take them by surprise. Another reason for watchfulness suggested here is :—Thirdly : *The interest committed to their charge.* " Who then is a faithful and wise servant, whom his lord hath made ruler over his household, to give them meat in due season ?" With how much was the Jewish nation entrusted ! They had an ancestry illustrious in divine faith, noble purposes, and heroic deeds. They had their schools of prophets, and their gradations of priests, their gorgeous temple, and their majestic system of worship. They were entrusted with the oracles of heaven. The sublime privileges they held in trust bound them to watchfulness. Another reason for watchfulness suggested here is :—Fourthly ; *The blessing and the cursing depending*

on the state in which the event would find them. How glorious the
state of the prepared! "Blessed is that servant whom his lord
when he cometh shall find so doing. Verily I say unto you, that
he shall name him ruler over all his goods." He shall be blessed
with the royal dominion. "All things are yours," says the apostle,
"whether Paul or Cephas," &c. "Know ye not that the saints
shall rule the world?" On the other hand, how wretched the
state here depicted of the unprepared! Vengeance overtakes him
by surprise. "The lord of that servant shall come in a day when
he looketh not for him," &c. The vengeance shall be most torturing.* "He shall cut him asunder." The vengeance shall be to
the last decree excruciating. "He shall have his portion with
hypocrites." "There shall be weeping and gnashing of teeth."

Such are the reasons with which Christ urges watchfulness, in
view of the approaching destruction of Jerusalem. And do not
these reasons apply to us in relation to the Final Day of Judgment?
How concealed is our future from us! We know not when the Son
of Man may come; therefore we shall be on our guard. In what
an unprepared state will many be when He appears! Let their
condition, therefore, warn us of the danger. How great is the trust
committed to our charge; and what solemn issues depend upon the
state in which death and the judgment will find us. "Seeing that
ye look for such things, be diligent, that ye may be found of him in
peace, without spot, and blameless." Let it be ours to ascertain the
divine will, and follow it out whithersoever it may conduct us.

> "Whate'er its form, whate'er its flow,
> While life is lent to man below,
> One duty stands confest;—
> To watch incessant, firm of mind,
> And watch, where'er the post's assigned,
> And leave to God the rest."

Matthew 25:1-13

The Ten Virgins; or, Preparation for Retribution

The scenery of this parable is an oriental marriage. Such marriages are generally conducted in the night, and are often associated
with ceremonies of great pomp and splendour. The profusion of
lamps on the occasion throws a great brilliancy both over the procession and over the bridal banquet. Modern travellers assure us
that the customs alluded to here are prevalent in the East to this

---

* Though the punishment of dichotomy was inflicted by Jews and heathens, the
word is doubtless used here in a metaphorical sense; "shall sever, separate him"
from the rest of the servants, as is explained by the clause which follows. The
extreme punishment of M. xiii. 49, 50, Rev. xix. 20, is meant.

day. The Bridegroom, accompanied by his friends, goes to the house of the bride, and from thence conducts her with all the displays of a hearty joyousness to his own home. From her father's dwelling the bride is accompanied by her youthful acquaintances and friends, whilst "virgins" are appointed to meet her, at some convenient place, in order to join the procession, and enter with the whole of the bridal party into the marriage feast. On their arrival the door is closed to exclude strangers and all unwelcome guests. It sometimes happens that the procession is detained beyond the appointed hour, and that the "virgins" consequently who wait on the way have to exercise considerable patience. Such was the case in that marriage scene which the Heavenly Teacher had now in His eye. Ten of the waiting virgins, exhausted with the excitement and fatigues connected with their joyous anticipations, and the appointed hour to which they looked with such rapturous solicitude having passed, fell asleep. "While the bridegroom tarried, they all slumbered and slept." At length, however, they were aroused from their slumbers with the cry, "Behold, the bridegroom cometh; go ye out to meet him." They all "Arose and trimmed their lamps." And now it was discovered that five of them had acted foolishly, in not providing a sufficiency of oil. While they were seeking oil, the jubilant procession passed, approached the festive house, entered it, and the door was closed, and they were hopelessly excluded. Such is the ground-work of the parable. Those fanciful and spiritualizing interpreters of God's Book, who regard themselves with being specially versed in the secrets of Heaven, have, of course, given a mystic meaning to all the minor parts of this parable; but it requires very little ingenuity to do so, and that ingenuity will be thus employed in proportion to the vanity and the ignorance of the expositor. The one great subject of this wonderful picture, the one master idea of this grand parable is this :—*Man's need of preparedness for the retribution that is coming.*

To illustrate this idea, the parable suggests :—

I. That there is a certain retributive crisis awaiting the human family. It is here symbolized by the coming of the "Bridegroom." Whether the period referred to here points specially to the destruction of Jerusalem, which the Heavenly Teacher had depicted in the preceding chapter, or to the departure of man from this world by death, or to the great and final day of the world's judgment, as referred to in the latter part of this chapter, is of no practical moment in our discussion ; inasmuch as each event was an event *of retribution.* This period of retribution dawns upon *all men at death.* Here our destiny admits of modification; we can change almost the very orbits of our being,—*at death* our destiny is fixed unalterably and for ever. This retribution dawns on *some men before death.* It is too obvious to those who look upon society with the earnest eye of moral reformers and Christian philanthropists, that in the case of not a few, the character and destiny of some men are irrevocably fixed, even here, *prior* to their dissolution. They have so often resisted spiritual impressions, so often broken solemn resolutions, so often sinned against the dictates of reason and conscience, and run such lengths in the grossest sensuality, profligacy, and rebellion, that they have gone beyond the reach of the remedial influences of the gospel. There are those in that state described by the apostle, "as past feeling;" they are like the men of Jerusalem in the days of Christ; though still living, "the things that belong to their peace are hid from their eyes." Their day of probation had gone down, though the sun of life was still shining upon them.

Now concerning this *retributive* crisis, whenever or however it may dawn, whether before or after death, two thoughts are suggested by the parable:—

First: *That the minds of all have some reference to it.* The foolish virgins as well as the wise anticipated the return of the bridegroom, made some preparations for him, and up to a time awaited for him. They all, "wise and foolish," *went forth to meet the bridegroom.* The consciences of all men under all forms of religion, in all parts of the world, and throughout all ages, point to a period when justice shall take the government of mankind. Human souls, the world over and ages through, point to a day for righteously balancing the accounts of humanity, and to an everlasting heaven for compensating suffering virtue, and a quenchless hell for punishing successful vice.

Secondly: *That the minds of none are certain as to the exact arrival of the period.* The "bridegroom tarried;" he was longer than was expected. Retribution, in all the forms in which it comes to man, comes unawares. No man knows the exact time when probation ceases and when retribution begins. It is not known with regard to *the world at large.* When will the Day of Judgment dawn? Who can tell the day, or month, or year? Nay, who can tell the century or millennium? "Of that day and hour knoweth no man, not even the angels of heaven." Nor does he know it in relation to *himself individually.* He knows not the hour when his own dissolution shall take place, the decisive hour which settles his character and destiny for ever. Or should it occur before his death by the withdrawal of the Divine Spirit from him, he does not know the hour or the minute when God shall say to him, "My spirit shall no longer strive with thee." Do I complain that Heaven has thrown a veil of uncertainty over the dawn of this period? By no means. Would I have the exact hour pointed out with unmistakable precision? Not for the universe. I recognise the wisdom of Infinite Love in spreading a thick haze of uncertainty over our future life.

II. THAT FOR THIS RETRIBUTIVE CRISIS A PREPARATION IS NECESSARY. The preparation for these virgins in order to qualify them to join this bridal procession was "*lamps trimmed and burning.*" Two things will show the nature and necessity of man's preparation for the retributive period that awaits him:—

First: *Retribution is the execution of the sentence of condemnation.* No truth is taught with greater explicitness, and urged with greater frequency and force, in the Scriptures than this, that man, as a sinner, is under Divine condemnation—"He that believeth not is condemned already,"—condemned to *all the miseries that naturally and justly spring out from the sins and depravities of his nature.* When retribution comes, the sentence of condemnation is executed; all these miseries, like long pent up waters, rush upon the sinner, overwhelming him in agony. The preparation needed, therefore, is the removal of his condemnation, the annulment of this sentence. Thank God! this can be obtained through faith in the mediation of Christ. "There is therefore no condemnation to them that are in Christ Jesus."

Secondly: *Retribution is the consummation of the moral malady.* Man, as a sinner, is not only exposed to condemnation, but he is the subject of a spiritual malady. Sin has deranged his spiritual powers, and poisoned the very blood of his moral being. When retribution meets him in this condition, that disease ends in death; —the death of all hope, of all mercy, all friendship, and all blessedness; the death of everything able to make life worth having. Preparation consists in the forgiveness of sins and the spiritual removal of our moral maladies. And this is secured only by a vital and practical faith in Him, who came to "redeem us from all iniquity, and purify unto Himself a peculiar people zealous of good works."

III. THAT OF THOSE WHO ARE ENGAGED IN MAKING THIS PREPARATION SOME WILL FAIL. Observe, *all make some kind of preparation.* We find these "ten virgins" engaged in making preparations. They were all occupied with the same event, they all had the same object, they all made efforts to join the procession and to get admitted to the bridal banquet. Perhaps the vast majority of the human race are engaged in some kind of preparation for this event. Religious men of all religions have the retributive future in view, and are making some kind of provision for the same. All nominal Christians, of course, are professedly so engaged. The millions that attend the churches and chapels of Christendom are avowedly so employed. It would be a libel on the race to say that men generally neglected *all* preparations for this future. We conceive that there are but few men to be found whose minds are enlightened to any moral extent, who do not put forth some efforts, at least, with a view of reaching some propitious future. The voluminous history of our world records no trials endured, no dangers braved, no battles fought, no sacrifice made, half so great as those that have been in connexion with efforts to prepare for the great eternity. The five foolish virgins made a kind of preparation as well as the five wise.

But *whilst all prepare, some fail.* Five of these "virgins" failed; their failure was their not having oil sufficient for their lamps; they had a little oil,—oil which glowed and flickered until midnight, —the time it was most needed,—then it went out, and all was dark. Up to this time, to all human appearance, they were as well off as the other five; they had gone forth with as much agility in their mission, and displayed perhaps as much enthusiasm. Their lamps, mayhap, were as beautiful as those of the wise, and at the outset shone as brightly. They fell asleep, it is true, in waiting, but so did the others :—"they all slumbered and slept." The difference was, the wise were provided with *sufficient* oil for the emergency, while the unwise were not. During the probationary period of life *there is some amount of good in men.* When all goodness is gone out of a man, retribution begins. *Insufficient oil is the fault.* Frequently did Christ in His teaching point out the danger of a failure in spiritual attainment. He speaks of a failure sometimes under the figure of a defective soil,—a soil too stony, too superficial, or too crowded with weeds and thorns ; on another occasion, under the figure of a man intruding into the marriage feast without the garment. On one occasion especially, without figure, He showed wherein the failure consisted, in His answer to the young lawyer who came seeking eternal life, "One thing lackest thou yet." What was the lacking thing ? *Self-sacrificing love.* That is the only exhaustless oil that will keep the lamp burning. The religion of mere interest is an oil that will soon exhaust itself. So is the religion of custom, and so is that of mere sentiment. Without charity, without love, whatever else we may have, we are nothing. "He that loveth not, knoweth not God ; for God is love." "Love is the fulfilling of the law."

IV. THAT THE CONDITION OF THOSE WHO FAIL IN THE PREPARATION WILL BE LAMENTABLY DISTRESSING. Three great evils fall upon these unwise virgins :—First: *Their labour was lost.* All the preparations they had made went for nothing; the lamps which they had purchased ; the oil which they had borne with them from their homes ; the cold dark hours in which they had been watching—all went for nothing. So with those who will ultimately fail in their religion :—the books they have read, the services they have attended, the prayers they have offered, are lost. Insufficiency of moral goodness neutralizes all our efforts for happiness. All they did was merely to build a house upon the sand, which the first gust of the tempestuous Day of Judgment would sweep away. Secondly: *Their opportunity was lost.* When they found their "lamps gone out," earnestly did they apply to the other virgins ; but their reply was, "Go ye rather to them that sell, and buy for yourselves." The most holy characters have no holiness to spare ; they have only just enough for themselves. "If the righteous scarcely be saved, where shall the ungodly and the sinner appear ?" No creatures, however kind and holy they may be, can help us in that retributive day, if we are found deficient in spiritual goodness. And while they were in search of oil elsewhere, seeking perhaps at the right source, the Bridegroom came, and it was too late. "Ye shall seek me early, and ye shall not find me." Now the sacred oil may be had without money and without price : but an hour will dawn in the history of all ungodly men, when no prayers, no strugglings, can obtain a drop. "*Many will say unto me in that day, Lord, Lord,*"

&c. Thirdly : *Their hope was lost.* " And they that were ready went in, and the door was shut." The door was shut, *enclosing* a joyous fellowship, a brilliant scene, a circle in rapturous delight. (Rev. iv. 11, 12; vii. 13, 17.) The door was shut; not only to enclose all who had been privileged to enter, but to *shut out* all who had failed to gain admission.

Brothers, the time hastens on when the door of remedial mercy will be shut upon the sinner—shut ! never, never more to be opened ! That door which now for many a century has been opened to receive whosoever, from east or west, from north or south, would enter;— that door which is wide enough to admit all, the publicans and the harlots, the heartless murderer, the profane blasphemer, and the beastly sensualist; that door which received Aaron after his idolatry, and Moses after his homicide, David after his adultery and his murder, and Peter after his threefold denial of the Son of God. Terrible moment will the closing of this door be. Solemn moment was that when the great Judge shut the door of the ark upon Noah and his family. All within from that moment were secure; neither the surging waters nor the roaring hurricanes could harm after this; nor could any efforts of the excluded millions after this, however skilful and combined and mighty, be of any avail;—their destruction was inevitable. But far more solemn, far more terrible, will be the closing of the door of mercy on this last day. That door as it closes, methinks, will vibrate on the heart-strings of the universe with unutterable horror.

> " Late, late, so late ! and dark the night and chill ;
> Late, late, so late ! but we can enter still.
> Too late, too late ! ye cannot enter now.

> " No light had we : for that we do repent ;
> And learning this the bridegroom will relent.
> Too late, too late ! ye cannot enter now.

> " No light : so late ! and dark and chill the night ;
> O let us in, that we may find the light.
> Too late, too late ! ye cannot enter now.

> " Have we not heard the bridegroom is so sweet ?
> O let us in, tho' late, to kiss his feet ;
> No, no, too late ! ye cannot enter now."—*Tennyson.*

Matthew 25:14-30

The Talents

This parable leads us to look at all human talents in two aspects —as *variously distributed,* and as *variously employed.*

I. As VARIOUSLY DISTRIBUTED. Some had " five," some "two," some "one." In relation to this distribution, the following facts should be observed and pondered : First : *That the talents of all were the free gifts of the master.* He " delivered them his goods; " —*His* goods, mark ! " And unto one he gave five talents," &c. He *gave ;* — " gave " unsolicited, uninfluenced by any extraneous agency or circumstance, but of His own absolute sovereignty and good pleasure. This being the case, the man of the greatest talent has no cause for self-boasting, and the man with the least need have no self-reproach. Secondly : That the talents of all were *given in trust.* The Giver still *retained* a *claim* upon them. The receiver did not become the absolute proprietor, but merely the steward or trustee,—nothing more. That man is a *responsible agent* is clear ; he has all the conditions of responsibility ; his own consciousness attests his responsibility ; and the Bible most unequivocally teaches it. Thirdly : That the talents of all were *given to be employed.* They were not to be wrapped in a napkin. As the man who borrows money on interest is responsible to the owner for the interest as really as for the principal, so we are as responsible to God for the *use* we make of our power as for the power itself. Men of intellect, men of wealth, you are responsible for all the good you *can do,* for all the useful *possibilities* of your existence. The man of *one* talent was as much bound to employ his one talent as the man of five to employ his five. " Every man according to his several ability." He does not expect the feeble to do the work of the strong.

The parable leads us to look at human talents,—

II. As VARIOUSLY EMPLOYED. Variety of distribution must be resolved into the sovereignty of God, variety of employment into the sovereignty of man. First : *Here is a right employment and its reward.* The man with the "five " and the man also with the "two " increased their power twofold. Man, out of the materials his Maker has given him, can make himself greater;—he can supply his power, and become seraph-like. Yes, and he can make himself lesser too. Whilst one man may rise to an angel, another may sink to a grub. This is going on amongst us now. "Unto him that hath shall be given." But look at the *reward* of the right employment ! " His lord said unto him, Well done, thou good and faithful servant," &c. The man who rightly uses his power (1) Receives a divine commendation—" Well done !" What rapturous music there is in this " well done,"—conscience echoes it. (2) Receives a divine empire. " I will make thee ruler over many things." A good man gets a blessed kingship—his authority increases with every noble thought and true deed. (3) Receives a divine joy. " Enter into the joy of thy Lord." Participate in the same kind of joy which He has—the joy of benevolence, &c. Secondly : *Here is a wrong employment, and its punishment.* " Then he which had received the one talent," &c. Two evils which are generally found to attach themselves to souls of the feebler mould are expressed by this one-talented man, and thereby furnishes another proof of the agreement of Scripture with real nature. (1) *Timidity.* "I was afraid." Weak-minded men are always pleading fear as an excuse for neglecting duty. (2) *Suspicion.* "Thou art an hard man." He suspected his master of cruelty. Little men are always suspicious. The wrong employment, mark! was not destroying it, not even abusing it. He kept it safely; he hid it; preserved it; and gave it back. His crime was in the non-employment of it. But mark his *punishment.* Here is (1) Divine denunciation. "Thou wicked and slothful servant," &c. (2) Divine deprivation. "Take therefore the talent from him," &c. (3) Divine destruction. "Cast ye the unprofitable servant," &c.

Matthew 25:31-46

The Day of Judgment

There is much of the parabolical in the description which the Heavenly Teacher here gives of that momentous period which is to determine the destiny of the race for ever. The truths here are richly robed in poetic drapery, and the work of a truthful expositor is to dismantle those truths, and present them in the most intelligible forms to the men of his age. Those who disregard the figurative forms in which, for example, the final day of doom is represented in the Bible, will figure to themselves a kind of Old Bailey scene. It is Heaven's plan to reveal to man the unknown by the known, the spiritual by the material, the things of eternity by the things of time; and hence the day of judgment is set forth under the figure of the ancient courts of judicature, such as the Sanhedrim, which in general features agree with all the modern courts of the civilized world. There is the judge on his throne; there is the prisoner arraigned; there is the investigation carried on through books and documents: and there is justice administered. Now, there is quite sufficient correspondence between the courts of human justice and the judicial transactions of God at the last day, to render the former a suitable medium through which to convey to man certain important impressions of the latter. For example, there are three things in which all the trials in human courts of justice agree with the great trial of the last day. First: *In the human and the divine there is the bringing of the judge and the accused into conscious contact.* Secondly: *There is the final settlement of the question of guiltiness or non-guiltiness, according to recognised law.* Thirdly: *There is the administration of an award, to which the accused is compelled to submit.* These three things you have in every trial amongst men, and these three things you have in the last great judgment of God.

The sublimely grand and solemn representations of the final scene of retribution contained in the text, teach us the following general truths: That the whole race will have a conscious contact with Christ as their Judge; and that the whole race will be finally separated by Christ as their Judge.

I. THAT AT THAT PERIOD THE WHOLE RACE WILL HAVE A CONSCIOUS CONTACT WITH CHRIST AS THEIR JUDGE. First: *They will witness His glory as their Judge.* "When the Son of Man shall come in His glory, and all the holy angels with Him, then shall He sit upon the throne of His glory." A throne is the highest symbol of earthly glory, and hence Christ is here represented as appearing on it. St. John, in his vision of the final advent of Christ, represents Him as coming on a great white throne. "Great!" it is the fountain of all authority,—that to which all intelligent creatures are amenable. "White!" the centre of unsullied purity—incorruptible justice. He not only comes on a throne, but with all His holy angels;—"angels!" the firstborn of God, the morning stars of creation — beings that excel in strength, whose intelligence is immense, whose love for God and His universe glows with a quenchless ardour, and whose speed is as the lightning. These are His attendants—all the holy angels. Who can count their number? They are the bright stars that crowd in innumerable constellations every firmament that spans every globe and system throughout immensity. Christ is here represented as coming on His throne with all His holy angels, in order to give us the impression of the glory in which all nations will see Him in the last day. Other passages of Scripture give us the same idea. "Enoch, the seventh from Adam, prophesied, saying, Behold, the Lord cometh with ten thousand of His saints," &c. And Paul says, "The Lord himself shall descend from heaven with a shout, with the voice of an archangel, and with a trump," &c. Now the passage gives us to understand that "all nations"—the whole human race—shall see Him in His glory. Angels see Him in this glory now—He is on the throne—and so do the redeemed spirits; and they fall down in adoring reverence and worship before Him. A few good men, too, in all ages on this earth, have had such a view of Him. "Isaiah saw the Lord sitting upon a throne, high and lifted up, and His train filled the temple." (Isa. vi. 1-4.) Daniel beheld in vision "till the thrones were cast down, and the Ancient of days did sit," &c. (Dan. vii. 9-13.) The three disciples on the Mount of Transfiguration had also a vision of His glory; so had John in Patmos; and so have all those in every age to whom He has come in the all-conquering and reigning power of His truth. But those who on earth have had such visions of Him have been miserably few,—scarcely one to a thousand even in the most Christian age. To the millions in every age He has appeared as a root out of a dry ground, without any form or comeliness whatever. But in this final and judicial period of the world's history, "all nations" shall see His glory. All the men that ever have been, that are, or that ever will be, will see Him in the overwhelming glory of His character, as the judge of all mankind. "Every eye shall see Him."

> "Every eye shall then behold Him
> Clad with majesty complete."

As the Great Sun of Righteousness, He will pour His burning rays upon the eyeball of every human soul. All nations shall see Him, ay, and see everything through Him ;—see themselves, see the past, see the present, and see the future, through Him, as we see nature through the light of heaven.

Secondly: *They will confront Him as their Judge.* "And before Him shall be gathered all nations." All nations are now before Him, and ever have been. He sees them ; He sustains them ; He speaks to them by His providence and His word ; but the nations are *not conscious* of His presence. "He is in the world, and the world knows Him not." It is true that some in all ages have had a *conscious* contact with Him. Enoch walked with Him; Moses endured as seeing Him who is invisible; David set the Lord always before him ; Paul felt that the Lord stood by him in all his trials. In fact, the truly good in all ages have been enabled to say, "Truly our fellowship is with the Father, and with His Son Jesus Christ." But the nations, the great bulk of the race, have never had this *conscious contact.* Millions have denied His very existence, and millions more have lived in utter indifference to His existence and His claims; but now "all nations" are brought into *conscious* contact with Him. The blaspheming atheist, the cruel idolater, the degraded savage, the foul apostate, and the hardened worldling will feel His presence more intensely than Isaiah did when he fell down and cried "Woe is me, woe is me ;" than Peter did when he said, "Depart from me," &c.; than John at Patmos when he fell at His feet as dead. The deadest soul that ever lived will feel Him more intensely than the most delicate hand can feel the scorching flame. He will indeed be as a fire burning around their souls, flaming down into the deepest secrets of their nature, and making their past lives manifest unto themselves.

The passage teaches :—

II. THAT AT THAT PERIOD THE WHOLE RACE WILL BE FINALLY SEPARATED BY CHRIST AS THEIR JUDGE. "He shall separate them one from another, as a shepherd divideth his sheep from the goats," &c.

First : *The greatness of the separation.* The language of Christ teaches us that the separation between the righteous and the wicked is as great (1) As that between honour and degradation. "The one on the right hand, the other on the left." The allusion here is, perhaps, to the Sanhedrim, by which the acquitted was put on the right hand and the condemned on the left. The right hand of the Eternal Judge is a position of the highest honour, that on the left of profoundest degradation. The separation is as great (2) As that between banishment from God and fellowship with Him. To the one, the loving and tender word, "Come!" is addressed ; to the other, the terrible word "Depart." What is it to be banished from the Infinite Father of love ? &c. The separation is as great (3) As that between a blessed state and a cursed one. The righteous are blessed. "Blessed of my Father," says Christ—blessed with all the blessings in Christ Jesus;—the wicked are cursed. Christ does not say "Cursed of my Father." When men are cursed, they curse themselves; when men are blessed, they are blessed of the Father. The separation is as great (4) As that between the scene of devils and the kingdom of God. To the good He says, "Inherit the kingdom prepared for you." From eternity God prepared heaven for the good. The wicked are sent to the scene prepared for the devil and his angels. It is noteworthy here that whilst Christ says He blesses the good, and has prepared a heaven for them, He does not curse the wicked, and prepare hell for them. Nay! He distinctly says that a place has been prepared for the devil and his angels. The separation is as great (5) As that between everlasting misery and everlasting blessedness. "These shall go away into everlasting punishment," &c. The same word in the original is translated in one case "everlasting," and in the other "eternal;" and if the happiness is to be endless, the misery must also be endless. Such is the separation. Up to this time the tares and the wheat have grown together; the sheep and the goats have lived together; the good and bad have mingled and wrought together in the ordinary affairs of human life; and now such a mixture is ended—an everlasting separation takes place.

Secondly : *The law of the separation.* This separation takes place, not as the result of caprice or arbitrary power, but according to a settled principle in the government of God. What is that ? *A true practical benevolence.* Why were those invited on the right hand ? What is the reason the great Arbiter assigns ? Hear it: "I was an hungered, and ye gave me meat," &c. This is the principle that determines our destiny. The man who does not live here a life of godly benevolence, can never in the nature of the case be admitted into heaven. Without this, there is no conformity to God. "God is love." "He that loveth not, knoweth not God." Without this, there is no fitness for heaven. All in heaven is love. Without this, there is no possibility of happiness. Practical benevolence is heaven, practical selfishness is hell. The words suggest two things in relation to this principle. First : *That the gradations of society afford ample scope for its operation.* Christ speaks of the "least." The least in relation to secular possession, intellectual power, life-experience, and true religion ; and therefore all who in higher degree possess these things have ample scope for their benevolence. Secondly : *That the relation of Christ to society presents the strongest motive for its operation.* He represents Himself as brother to the poorest of the poor. To "the least of these my brethren," &c. He is brother to the hungry, the naked, the sick, the imprisoned, the stranger.

Here is the practical way to show your love to Christ. We have not now the opportunity of ministering to Christ's physical necessities, as Mary and Martha did of old; but we can by rendering assistance to the poor and distressed of the human family. What you do for " the least" He regards as done to Him. He regards a cup of cold water given to the poorest of His disciples as given to Him. " Is not this the fast that I have chosen," &c. (Isa. lviii. 6, 7.) " Pure religion" is to visit the fatherless and widows in their affliction. (Jas. i. 27; Deut. xv. 7–11.) " Bear ye one another's burdens, and so fulfil the law of Christ." (Gal. vi. 2.) " Whosoever shall give you a cup of cold water." (Mark ix. 41.) " He that hath pity on the poor lendeth to the Lord." (Prov. xix. 17.)

These observations of ours on the Day of Judgment seem to justify the conclusion that the dread crisis has virtually dawned upon us even *now*. The all-testing separating principle that determines the unalterable destiny of men—*Practical benevolence*—is now enforced upon every hearer of the Gospel. Those who adopt it as the spirit and sovereign of their life are *now being separated* from the selfish millions. Christ, as the world-Judge, is now enthroned on the Gospel, enforcing this principle; and before His presence the human race are constantly being separated wider and wider apart. The practically benevolent are every day rising to honour on the "right hand;" are being "blessed of the Father;" approaching nearer and nearer to Christ; are inheriting the felicities of the " kingdom prepared for them;" whilst the practically selfish are perpetually sinking into deeper degradation on the "left hand;" departing farther from God as the source of all goodness, being more cursed, not by the Father, but by their own wickedness, and sinking deeper into those scenes of moral corruption and misery, which are prepared not for them, but for the "devil and his angels." " There is a great gulf fixed,"—a gulf ever-widening between the selfish and the benevolent now. It is true that there is an hour to every man in this Day of Judgment,—the hour of death, for example, when every man will be more *intensely conscious* of his moral condition, and when no man will be able to *alter* his moral position. Now the millions of the ungodly are non-conscious of their moral position before Christ as their Judge, and now, too, there is a possibility of all, good and bad, altering their moral position ; each of the two great division smay change their relative situations, pass the gulf to the other side. The good may become bad, and the bad good. But in the period of the Judgment Day, to which our text refers, the moral consciousness of all will be intensified, and the moral condition of all irrevocably fixed.

Matthew 26:1-13

" Alabaster Box of Ointment "— Genuine Excellence

That the interesting and significant incident recorded here is the same as that recorded in Mark xiv. 3-9, and John xii. 2-8, scarcely admits of any rational doubt. It is true that one biographer mentions a circumstance or two which another omits; but the fact is *substantially* the same in all. All agree as to the scene; —it was in Bethany, a little village near Jerusalem, on the Mount of Olives. Jesus had visited this village just before; He comforted the weeping sisters of Lazarus, and raised their brother from the grave. They all agree as to the conduct of the woman ;—all speak of her as pouring on His head a " box of precious ointment." All agree, too, in the censures pronounced upon her conduct by the disciples ; and all agree too, in the account of the noble defence which Christ made against their unjustifiable attack upon her. Matthew and Mark agree as to the name of the person in whose house the scene occurred ;—" Simon the leper." This man had probably been previously cured of his leprosy by the Saviour, and he was now called a leper, to remind him of the benefit he had received ; as Matthew calls himself a publican for the same reason. This Simon the leper, out of gratitude for the wonderful cure, now prepares a feast for Jesus. But whilst Matthew and Mark agree in giving the name of the master of the house, John does more ; he states a fact or two which they omit. John tells us who the woman was that now anointed Jesus, and wiped His feet with her hair ;—it " was Mary, the sister of Martha and Lazarus." He tells us, too, that Lazarus himself was there who had been raised from the dead, and that Martha served at the table ; and that Judas Iscariot was there, and that he was Simon's son, and that he it was that found fault with the woman. Thus in circumstantials one Evangelist seems to supplement the deficiencies of the other ; but their main fact is substantially the same. We take this narrative to illustrate GENUINE EXCELLENCE ; and here we have genuine excellence in four aspects : *Devotionally employed, Unjustly censured, Divinely vindicated, and Immortally honoured.*

I. HERE WE HAVE GENUINE EXCELLENCE DEVOTIONALLY EMPLOYED. "There came unto Him a woman having an alabaster box of very precious ointment, and poured it on His head as He sat at meat." John says, " she wiped His feet with her hair." Mark and John mention that the ointment was " spikenard." The plant from which it is made, we are told, grows in India, and its aroma is so strong that the air around is perfumed when the roots are crushed or bruised. It was " very costly." The three hundred pence mentioned here amounts to about ten pounds. At oriental feasts it was customary to pour such perfumes on the head of friends. The

Psalmist, in allusion to this custom, employs it to express the blessedness of friendship with God, "I have anointed my head with oil," &c. Now this act of Mary expresses the highest devotion of soul. The *value* of the ointment only expressed the *depth* of her love. Observe the *freeness* of her devotion. There was no formal law requiring her to do it; the other guests did it not. She was not urged by any outward force to this act. Her devotions were thoroughly spontaneous. Her soul went forth as freely as that aroma from the box which now filled the house. True worship is ever free. Her devotion was *generous*. This ointment, perhaps, was the most valuable thing she had in the way of worldly wealth; yet this she freely gives. Piety is essentially generous; it is self-immolating love. Covetous piety is a contradiction. You may as well talk about fiery ice as covetous piety. As soon may snow retain its character in the burning furnace, as covetousness remain in a soul filled with supreme love to Christ. It is the essence of true love to sacrifice *all* to its object. Her devotion was *open*. It was in the presence of all the guests; and some of these guests were cold and calculating, and had perhaps but little sympathy. Nicodemus and Joseph, though they loved Christ, yet were ashamed to avow it publicly; but this woman boldly avowed her attachment before the whole assembly. Strong love is bold and defiant. "Perfect love casteth out fear." There is no reason to be ashamed of Christ. Let the Chinese be ashamed of Confucius; let the Jews be ashamed of Moses; let the Calvinists be ashamed of Calvin; but never let us be ashamed of Christ. Here then is a development of devotion demanding our imitation,—a devotion *free, self-surrendering, and demonstrative.*

II. HERE WE HAVE GENUINE EXCELLENCE UNJUSTLY CENSURED. " *But when His disciples saw it, they had indignation, saying, To what purpose is this waste?*" John tells us who the disciple was that had indignation and murmured against her; it was Judas Iscariot, Simon's son, who should betray Him. And he tells us also why it was that he did thus censure the woman; "He had the bag, and was a thief, and bare what was put therein." Observe two things here,—

First: *False estimate of property.* Why was this waste? Worldly men would of course agree with the idea of Judas, that money laid out in the cherishing or expression of mere devotional sentiment is "waste." Ay, and thousands of nominal Christians would agree with him, too, in this. Yet, is such an estimate of property true? Which is the *wasted* money? The money that is laid out in magnificent houses, gorgeous apparel, and sumptuous fare, or that which is laid out in the cultivation and development of *the moral sentiments* of the soul? Assuming that man is an accountable and undying spirit, the "waste" is in the former case. At death we leave the world with all our possessions, but we bear with us our sentiments, and our sentiments will rule our destiny. Whatever in sculpture, painting, poesy, music, or any other branch of art, assists to quicken and rightly unfold the religious sentiments of our nature, you cannot "waste" money upon; it is valuable at any price. There is no "waste" in anything that helps the soul. This precious ointment helped the woman to throw out her spirit in sentiments of loving and adoring worship. How much freer and nobler she felt afterwards. Observe,—

Secondly: *A hypocritical benevolence.* "For this ointment might have been sold for much, and given to the poor." Here is covetousness cloaking itself in charity; lucre speaking the language of love. Did Judas care for the poor? Not he. He cared only for his own aggrandizement, and he was ready to sell the Son of God Himself for this. We have a great deal of this kind of cant in the world at this present day. There are those who say, when they see Christians adorning in any truly artistic way the house in which they meet to worship the one true and living God, or laying out money to improve their psalmody, Why this "waste?" "Why not give it to the poor?" Far am I from any wish to underrate the duty to help the poor. Indeed, I have no faith in that man's piety who does not "consider the poor." James says, "Pure and undefiled religion before the Father is to visit the widow and fatherless," &c. But I say that when the claims of the poor are thus pleaded, they are only pleaded as an excuse for not contributing towards the devotional helps of the soul. The men, I believe, who are the most ready to give to the promotion of true ideas and sentiments in connection with worship, are ever most willing to help the distressed.

III. HERE WE HAVE GENUINE EXCELLENCE DIVINELY VINDICATED. "*When Jesus understood it, He said unto them, Why trouble ye the woman? for she hath wrought a good work upon me,*" &c. His vindication shows two things,—

First: *That their interference was wrong.* "Let her alone: why trouble ye her?" They had no right to interfere in this matter, and she was responsible to no being on earth. No man has a right to interfere with another on account of his religious services. No man, no priest, no kiug, should ever be permitted to come between the soul and God. "Let her alone."

Secondly: *That her devotion was right.* (1) It was right in *principle.* "She hath wrought a good work upon me." It was not the value of the ointment, nor its delicious aroma, that made the work *good* in the estimation of Christ; it was the love of the heart, of which it was the expression and sign. (2) It was right in *extent.* "She hath done what she could." Capacity is the measure of obligation. (3) It was right in *season.* "Against the day of my burying hath she kept this." She did now what Joseph did after His death—a woman has more forecast than man—anointed His body. Thus Christ vindicates her piety.

IV. HAVE WE HAVE GENUINE EXCELLENCE IMMORTALLY HONOURED. "*Verily I say unto you, Wheresoever this gospel shall be preached in the whole world, there shall also this,*" &c. How is she to be honoured? Not by dedicating a church to her name, or by keeping an annual feast in honour of her memory. No! but by chronicling her name in the most wonderful history—the history of Christ: a history the most glorious in its facts; the most momentous in its interests. "Into it angels desire to look." A history the most universal in its destiny;—it must spread over the globe;—a history most lasting in its duration. In this history her name is enrolled. "The righteous shall be had in everlasting remembrance." The pyramids shall moulder to the dust; monuments of brass, and granite, and marble, raised to the memory of the world's great men, shall decay; but the monument here raised to this woman's excellence will stand for ever. This subject,—

First: Furnishes a reproof to *worldly utilitarianism.* The *useful* is what the worldly tribes of mankind are ever reaching after. But what is their "useful?" Whatever tends to promote the material interests of the world; a man's services to his family, employers, or his country, are estimated by the wealth they produce. Whatever in labour, or capital, is wisely laid out for this end, is useful; all else is little more than "waste." The most breathing images of sculpture and painting, the most soul-entrancing strains of music, the most wonderful creations of poetry, the deepest thoughts of philosophy, the grandest peals of eloquence, all these are little else than waste," unless they result in some material profit. He who in the use of his property and faculties lets the whole of his soul out to flow in pure sentiment, as this woman let out all the ointment from the box, to float in the room where Christ was, would be regarded as an idle visionary who *wasted* his powers. Yet the constitution of the soul, and the teaching of Christ, show that such labour is the most wise and valuably productive. And,—

Secondly: An argument for *heartiness in religion.* This woman threw her whole soul into her devotions. She did not pour forth a part of the precious ointment, she broke the box open, and poured forth all. There is nothing half and half in worship, it must be thorough, or it is worthless. Godliness is the entire surrender of self—the *whole* soul going forth in supreme devotion to the Holy and the Loving One.

Matthew 26:14-16

Judas; or, Truth sold for Money

The transaction here recorded is generally regarded as one of unprecedented enormity. Judas, by common consent, is put in the front of the greatest sinners of the race. A worldly Church is horror-stricken at the memory of his deeds, and a sleepy pulpit wakes into eloquent strains of indignation whenever it approaches his character. For the crime of Judas we have no word of apology, no palliating sentence to offer; but the question which forces itself on our mind is, Are we really justified in regarding that man as standing alone in the history of crimes, as being a sinner more than all the rest? May it not be that, instead of being an isolated exception, he is the type of a large, if not the largest, class of men? Such a question as this is easily determined by ascertaining in what does the *peculiarity* of this man's crime consist. Is it in the originating principle, or the accidental manifestation?—in the *form* or in the *spirit?* If it be in the latter—if the principles that prompted him were *perfectly unique* in their turpitude—then let him be taken from all classes, and exposed as a singular phenomenon to draw forth the supreme execration of the race; but if the *peculiarity* be merely in *form*, such conduct in relation to him is unwarrantable, for reason and the Bible show that "as a man thinketh in his heart, so is he." In the light of divine ethics there is many a robber who has never deprived another of a fraction of property; many a murderer who has never inflicted the slightest injury upon the person of any one; many a heinous sinner who is clothed in all the sanctity of conventional morality and religion. It is not the working of my hand, not the utterance of my tongue, not the movements of my body, that constitute my character, but the controlling volitions and habits of my soul.

The question therefore returns : Is the peculiarity of the crime of Judas in *form* or *spirit*, or both? It is a fact that the form was *unique.* There was but *one* Christ to betray, and that *one* Christ was betrayed but *once;* and Judas did that one act. The outward act, therefore, was *peculiar;* he did that which no other man ever did before, which very few in his own day had the opportunity of doing, and which no one from that day to this has had the chance of repeating.

The *singularity* of the act may be traced to the *singularity* of the opportunity, and not to the singularity of the disposition that prompted it. Had the *opportunities* which Judas possessed been common to the race, his sin would not have been of such notoriety. What was his *prompting principle?*

First : *It was not a divine influence.* Because the sin of this man was foretold, and was a step in the development of Christianity, some have referred his conduct to a supernatural impulse. Perish the blasphemous thought! The *essential purity of the divine nature*, and the *subsequent contrition of Judas*, forbid the idea.

Secondly : *It was not a sense of public duty.* He was not of those who saw in Christ's character and teaching that which would imperil the interests of his country, and who was, therefore, inspired by a sense of social justice to help in handing Him over to the authorities. His declaration, when his sleeping conscience awoke, that he had betrayed "innocent blood" forbids this idea.

Thirdly : *It was not from any malicious feeling towards Christ.* There is not a single instance in his history of dislike to Christ. The probability is, that he admired and respected Him, and his dying words show that he had no malicious intention in this act.

What, then, is the spirit of this man's crime ? Avarice—love of money—was the prompting impulse. "WHAT WILL YE GIVE ME ?" In this question you have the man's soul, and the full explanation of his conduct. Alas! there is nothing *peculiar* in this. He therefore does not stand alone; he is the type of the largest class of every age. If in the great scenes of future retribution men will be classified according to the moral principles that governed them, none, I fear, will find themselves associated with a larger number of kindred souls than the dark betrayer of the Son of God. The question to which I now invite your attention is, What must a man *have* and *do*, in order to commit this sin of Judas, namely : *sell truth for money ?* In reply to this we observe,—

I. THAT HE MUST HAVE TRUTH AT HIS DISPOSAL. Judas at this time in no sense had Christ at his disposal; he had the *power* to betray Him. He knew Him, knew where He was, and could put Him into the hands of His enemies. Very few had this opportunity. Now a man must *have* the truth, have the knowledge of it, before he can sell it. There are multitudes who have no truth, no knowledge of moral principles ; they act from impulse or custom. *They know nothing of principles*, and they cannot, therefore, sell them. They cannot act the part of Judas, for how can they sell what they have not ? In reply to the question we observe,—

II. THAT HE MUST HAVE A TEMPTING OFFER. Judas had a tempting offer ; something was presented which he valued *more* than anything else, and he yielded. The "thirty pieces of silver" were a powerful appeal to his avarice. A man may have a knowledge of truth, and even value it, and not be able to sell it, because he cannot get anything for it. He has no temptation to sacrifice his principles. Indeed, it may so happen that he gets his living by them. He may have the spirit of Judas, and yet not sell for the want of a *tempting* offer. *The virtue in any is but vice sleeping.*

In reply to the question, we discover,—

III. THAT HE MUST DELIBERATELY ACCEPT THE OFFER. The act of Judas was deliberate. "They covenanted with him." He was not forced to it. Taking Judas as the type of all who sell truth for money, we may observe,—

First : *That men may sell truth for money, who have no dislike to it.* There is no reason to believe that Judas disliked Christ, but he liked money more. There are some who love principles in the abstract, and plead eloquently for them, but who will sell them for money.

Secondly : *That men may sell truth for money, although they feel themselves under an obligation to it.* Christ had conferred signal favours on Judas, and he must have felt His kindness. Many men will sacrifice certain principles for "filthy lucre," which they know have conferred the most signal blessings upon them and their country.

Thirdly : *That men may sell truth for money who have no intention of doing any injury to truth.* Judas, it is probable, did not intend any injury to Christ at this moment. Indeed, the probability is, that he thought it would hasten His triumph, and bring Him to the universal empire. Hence the agony of his surprise when he "saw that He was condemned." Men sacrifice principles for gain, who have no intention of injuring the holy cause of truth.

Truly, Judas is a REPRESENTATIVE. Many who denounce him, as the King of Israel denounced of old the characters drawn by the hand of Nathan, may find in his life a portraiture of their own. Our world abounds with men who, like Judas, are selling truth for money. I see in Judas the image of the man who not only opposes a righteous principle from mercenary motives, but who keeps back, or perverts, or hesitates to work out honestly, a principle, from fear of worldly loss. Let us learn to put a higher estimate upon principle than property, so that we may sell property for principle, and not principle for property. This is the true merchandise of life. What is property to principle, brother? Property may give us mansions as our homes, and put at our command not only the comforts but the luxuries of life; but principle alone can give *capacity* for enjoying them. Worldly pleasures soon lose their zest where there are no right principles in the soul. Property may raise to social eminence, but principle alone can raise in the scale of being, and give power to intellect, purity to the affections, and peace to conscience. Property is uncertain, we cannot hold it; if it does not take wing and flee from us, we must from it. But principle will remain amidst the flight of years, the wreck of the body, and the dissolution of all the ties that connect us with the world. It will spread a halo over the dying couch, and, like the ark of old, go down to the Jordan, divide its cold waves, and secure for us a safe and triumphant passage through. "The world passeth away, and the lust thereof; but he that doeth the will of God abideth for ever."

Matthew 26:17-30

The Passover giving way to the Lord's Supper

This passage brings two things under our attention:—*An old Jewish festival which is to be binding no more; and a new Christian festival which is to be binding to the end of time.*

I. AN OLD JEWISH FESTIVAL WHICH IS TO BE BINDING NO MORE. The Jewish festival which is here celebrated, was that of the Passover, one of the most significant and joyous of Jewish rites, and which has been called "the birthday feast of the chosen people." It was a feast to commemorate the deliverance of the children of Israel from Egyptian bondage, and from the sword of the destroying angel. The angel of Divine justice had been sent from the throne of the Eternal Majesty, to smite all the first-born in Egypt; and to sweep them away from the face of the earth. To the seed of Abraham, however, a means of deliverance was given, and you know wherein it consisted. Each head of a family was ordered to take a male lamb out of his flock, kill it, sprinkle its blood on the door-posts, and then quietly and confidentially remain in his dwelling. "And the blood," said the Lord, "shall be to you for a token upon the houses where you are; and when I see the blood, I will pass over you, and the plague shall not be upon you to destroy, when I smite the land of Egypt." This was the oldest Jewish institution. It was before the Aaronic priesthood, and antecedent to all Levitical ritualism;—it had been celebrated annually for fifteen hundred years. During the whole of that time it continued a *binding* ordinance upon the descendants of Abraham. But this is the *last* night of its authorized celebration;—this night was the closing scene of Judaism. The knell of all that was *binding* in its ordinances was rung in this upper room. Several things occurred in the celebration of the passover on this night of a most significant character, mentioned by some other of the Evangelists, but which Matthew has omitted. Elsewhere we are informed, that it was on this occasion that the strife arose among the disciples as to who should be accounted the greatest, which Christ decided by laying down the principle, *that true greatness consists in true service.* It was on this occasion that Christ laid aside His garments, took a towel, and girded Himself, poured water into a basin, and began to wash the disciples' feet, and to wipe them with the towel wherewith He was girded. And it was on this occasion, too, that He commanded those of His disciples who had a purse and scrip, to take them, and he that had no sword to sell his garment and buy one, thus preparing them for the perils which they were soon to meet. But we must confine ourselves to the circumstances connected with the passover celebrated this night, which Matthew *here* records; and these circumstances we may regard as furnishing us with a twofold revelation;—a revelation of Christ, and a revelation of man.

First: *We have here a revelation of Christ.* There are several things here taught concerning Christ. We learn (1) *His respect for religious institutions.* The question of the disciples, "Where wilt Thou that we prepare for Thee to eat the passover?" takes it for granted that they expected that Christ would attend to this rite. He had been circumcised and baptized, He attended the synagogue and the temple services, and probably neglected none of the Divine institutions of the Mosaic religion. "He fulfilled all righteousness." He honoured religious institutions, and in this "He left us an example that we should follow in His steps." We learn (2) *His knowledge of human affairs.* "Go into the city to such a man," &c. Another Evangelist tells us that He said, "Go ye into the city, and there shall meet you a man bearing a pitcher of water;" and that he should "show them a large upper room, furnished and prepared;" and the disciples "found as He had said unto them." All this indicates His acquaintance with human affairs. Christ knows everything about our houses; all our domestic circumstances and customs are ever naked to His eye. We learn (3) *His right to the possessions of man.* "The Master saith, My time is at hand; I will keep the passover at thy house with My disciples." The language is analogous to that which He used on another occasion, when He said concerning the ass, "The Master hath need of it;"—language which implies a sovereign right to man's property. All we have belongs to Him, and we should hold everything ready for His service. Whatever He calls for we should give,—houses, lands, friends, even life itself. We learn (4) *His command over His disciples.* "Go, make ready." This preparation consisted in engaging a guest-chamber, obtaining the articles of food—wine, bread, and herbs—preparing the paschal lamb, by having it killed and dressed by the priests of the temple—and afterwards roasting it themselves. Luke tells us it was Peter and John who were the disciples sent to do this; and this they did at once in obedience to the command of Christ. He said, "Go," and they went; asking no questions, mooting no difficulties. They loved Him, and they kept His commandments. "The disciples did as Jesus had appointed them, and they made ready the passover." We learn (5) *His acquaintance with the hearts of men.* "He said unto them, Verily I say unto you, one of you shall betray me." Nothing, perhaps, seemed more improbable to all the disciples save Judas, than this. No one could have suspected it but Judas, and he, no doubt, kept it a profound secret,—would not whisper it to any one. Yet Christ knew it. He read the dark heart of the betrayer, and knew his treacherous thoughts. He knows not only what is about man, but what is *in* him. We learn (6) *His understanding of the Divine purpose.* "The Son of man goeth as it is written," &c. He not only knows the thoughts of men, but the purposes of Heaven. Christ is the only being that ever appeared upon earth who thoroughly knew the plan of God. He said, "O righteous Father, the world hath not known thee," &c. He said, "No one knoweth the Father but the Son." No one in heaven or in earth is able to open the book of the Divine decrees but Jesus Christ. In the erection of a magnificent edifice there is generally a functionary who comes between the chief architect and the various grades of workers who toil in their several departments of labour; —a superintendent of the works. This man knows the plan of the architect, carries a draft of it in his hand, and makes each agent contribute his proper part towards its realization. A position somewhat analogous to this, Christ holds in the creation. He has the plan of the great Architect in His hand, and sees that every creature in the universe shall contribute its part towards its consummation. Such is the revelation which the circumstances narrated in this passage, give us of Christ.

Secondly: *We have here a revelation of man.* The words reveal (1) *The self-ignorance even of the best men.* "They began every one of them to say, Lord, is it I?" The very question which they here address to Christ indicates that they were by no means certain as to their capabilities for such a dark deed as this. And who, amongst the best of us, can tell what elements of depravity there may be slumbering in the heart, which, if roused to action by temptation, would prompt the commission of terrible crimes? Our self-ignorance requires that we should always be on our guard. "Who can understand his errors?" "Cleanse Thou us from secret faults, O God." The words reveal (2) *The subserviency of man's wickedness to the Divine purpose.* Judas goeth to betray Christ; goeth to commit one of the darkest crimes that have ever been perpetrated. Yet in going he contributes his part to the fulfilment of an eternal purpose. Peter brings out this truth in his address to the assembled thousands on the day of Pentecost, "Him being delivered by the determinate counsel," &c. Men may violate the precepts of heaven, they cannot frustrate its purposes. "He maketh the wrath of man to praise Him." What they intend for evil shall turn out for good. The words reveal (3) *The enormity of human wickedness, though overruled for good.* "Woe to that man," &c. Evil is evil—however it may subserve the good of the universe. Crimes lose none of their turpitude because kind heaven makes them useful. Though the crucifixion of Christ will prove the greatest blessing to the creation, the crime loses none of its enormity by the countless and ever-multiplying benefits it confers. Though Judas did a service to the creation, "Woe" to him. By the very act he places himself in a position which renders his existence an intolerable curse;—"Good were it for that man if he had never been born." This expression shows that the curse he brought upon himself was endless; for if, after the suffering of ages in the future, he would be restored to holiness and blessedness, it could not be said of him, it would "be good for him if he had never been born." * Can you conceive of a position more tremendously awful than this—the position of a man of whom it may be predicated—"good for that man if he had never been born?"— good had he never opened his eyes upon the universe? &c.† Another Evangelist tells us that, "after this, Judas went out; and it was night." Ah! it was night in more senses than one. Though in nature it was night,—the moon, perhaps, shone brightly; the darkness of the night was in his own soul. The words reveal (4) *The impious hardihood of which a sinner may be capable.* "Judas, which betrayed him, answered and said,—Master, is it I?" Did Judas ask this question for information, think you? He had already committed the act. It was for disguise. What effrontery is this! To stand before the disciples, before the searching eye of his Master, and ask, "Is it I?" when he had already wrought the horrid deed. Into what depths of wickedness a man, who has once taken a wrong step, is liable to fall!

* See page 326.
† According to a version of this text which we have seen, the sense is thus expressed: "It would have been good for him (the traitor) if this man (the Son of Man) had not been born." If this version is correct, the general idea is, that man, by sin, may make, so far as he is concerned, the greatest blessing the greatest curse.

So much for the revealing circumstances connected with the celebration of this Passover, whose *binding* character was now terminated for ever. We now proceed to notice :—

II. A NEW CHRISTIAN FESTIVAL WHICH IS TO BE BINDING TO THE END OF TIME. In connexion with this we have five things :—*A new application of old elements.—The symbolic appropriation of these elements.— The absolving virtue of this act.—The heavenly reference of this scene. —The profound religiousness of the whole.*

FIRST : *Here we have a new application of bread and wine.* "As they were eating, Jesus took bread, and blessed it, and brake it, and gave it to the disciples, and said, Take, eat ;" etc. The passover being over, Christ, instead of retiring from the table, continued, and commenced a new ceremony. Two of the elements on the table which had been employed in the passover,—" bread and wine," He takes and employs for the purpose of representing His own sacrificed existence, here expressed " by body and blood." This bread and wine, therefore, which had for so many ages been associated with the paschal Lamb, are to stand now as representatives and remembrances of His wonderful death. Why Christ took from the table of the passover the bread and wine for this purpose, rather than the flesh of the lamb and the bitter herbs, is a question which we may speculate upon, but cannot possibly determine. Perhaps, as the one is of all substances the most strengthening to the body, and the other the most animating to the spirits, they are employed to show the necessity of Christ's *self-sacrifice*, to strengthen and animate the soul. What food and drink are to the body, Christ's death is to the soul,—the necessary element of existence. This bread and wine, therefore, stand as the memorial of that self-sacrificing love which was exemplified in the crucifixion of Jesus Christ. " As often," said Paul, " as ye eat this bread, and drink this cup, ye do show the Lord's death." These elements are only representative memorials, nothing more. The doctrine of transubstantiation springs from confounding rhetoric with logic, metaphor with fact. The verb *to be* is often used in the Scriptures in the sense of *to signify*. Thus in Pharoah's dream (Gen. xli. 26), the seven good kine are said to be the seven years, and the seven good ears are seven years ; meaning of course that they signify years ; thus in Daniel vii. 24, in Daniel's vision, the ten horns are said to be ten kings. Thus in Matthew xiii. 38, it is said, " the field is the world ;" meaning that the field represents the world. Thus in 1 Cor. x. 4, Paul says, " that rock was Christ," meaning that that rock represented Christ. According to this rule, Christ says, " This bread is My body, this cup is My blood."

Secondly : *Here we have the symbolic appropriation of these elements.* He took the bread, "and said, Take, eat ; this is My body," and the cup, and said, " Drink ye all of it." Why are they to *eat* the bread and *drink* the wine ? Not because there is any mystic virtue in the elements, nor because they are suited to strengthen the body, but because the act symbolized the important duty of appropriating to ourselves that *self-sacrificing spirit* of which the physical crucifixion of Christ was but the expression and the effect. The spiritual meaning of these words may be thus expressed,—Take My self-sacrificing spirit into you, let your soul feed on it as your body would on bread, drink it into you as you would drink this wine. This is the sublime reality of the service; the material act is but the form. His self-sacrificing spirit is the water of life which He is to give, which if we drink, we shall thirst no more ; the bread of life which came down from heaven, which if a man eat he shall never die. To have this is to be made conformable unto His death, is to have His life manifest in our mortal bodies. " Whoso eateth My flesh, and drinketh My blood, hath eternal life;"—that is, whoso appropriates *the moral spirit* of My being hath eternal life.

Thirdly : *Here we have the absolving virtue of this act.* " And He took the cup, and gave thanks, and gave it to them, saying, Drink ye all of it; for this is My blood of the New Testament, which is shed for many for the remission of sins." The New Testament means the Gospel dispensation in contradistinction to the Mosaic one. The Mosaic one was sealed with blood, sprinkled by Moses upon the people ; the Gospel dispensation was to be sealed with the blood of Christ. This blood was not only the New Testament blood, but blood shed for "many,"—for all,—Jews and Gentiles ; and shed for all, for the *remission of sins.* It is through this self-sacrificing love of Christ, symbolized by the blood, that the remission of sins becomes possible, and it is only as this self-sacrificing love of Christ is drunk in by us, appropriated by us, that the remission of our sins is obtained. There is sufficient virtue in Christ's sacrifice to obtain pardon for the world, but unless that principle of sacrifice is taken in by us, acted upon by us, our sins will never be pardoned.

Fourthly : *Here we have a heavenly reference from this scene.* " But I say unto you, I will not drink henceforth of this fruit of the vine, until that day when I drink it new with you in My Father's kingdom." Christ refers here to the fellowship which they shall have with Him in heaven; and He does this in order to comfort and console them under the trials with which they are soon to be visited. It is supposed by some that just at this point in the ceremony, Christ commenced those counsels, consolations, and prayers, which commence with the beginning of the 14th chapter of John, and run to the end of the 17th. " Let not your heart be troubled," etc. Every holy circle on earth has a reference to the fellowship in heaven, is a foretaste and a pledge of the social enjoyments of the blest.

Fifthly : *Here we have a profound religiousness in the whole.* The ceremony began and ended with worship. Christ "blessed " the bread; "and when they had sung an hymn they went out into the Mount of Olives." We should like to know distinctly the hymn they sung on this occasion. Those that were sung at the conclusion of the passover were generally selected from Psalm cxv. to cxviii. inclusive, and sometimes cxxvi. to cxxxvii. From this subject we learn four things :—

(1.) *The social genius of our religion.* There are no less than *three* social scenes in the passage that has engaged our attention : There is the passover, that was social, and Christ joined in the celebration of that; there is the Lord's Supper, and this was social, and Christ joined in the celebration of that; and then there is the grand festival in our Father's kingdom above, and Christ will join in the celebration of that. "I will drink it with you in My Father's kingdom." What a magnificent fellowship that will be! "They shall come from the east and west," etc. Christ's religion brings souls together, blends spirit with spirit, and heart with heart.

(2.) *The central theme of our religion.* What is that? Some great ceremony? or some great doctrine? or some great ecclesiastical system? No, but Christ. "This do in remembrance of Me."

(3.) *The vital element of our religion.* What is that? The *self-sacrificing* love of Christ. This is His "body and blood"—His moral life. On this must we feed.

(4.) *The standing ritual of our religion.* What is it? The partaking of this bread and wine in remembrance of Christ.

Matthew 26:31-35

Significant Contrasts between Christ and His Disciples

The last Supper was now over, the parting hymn had just been sung, and Christ and His disciples had adjourned to the Mount of Olives : the same spot, it is supposed, that David retired to in his distress, weeping, as with uncovered head and bare feet, he climbed its quiet brow. (2 Sam. xv. 30.) On His way to this memorable spot, amid the solitudes of nature and the hush of night, He spoke to His accompanying disciples the words before us. They bring great contrasts under our attention;—a contrast between *His knowledge* and *their ignorance, His power* and *their weakness, His constancy* and *their inconstancy.* We have here :—

I. HIS KNOWLEDGE AND THEIR IGNORANCE. These words reveal :— First : *His knowledge.* He here shows His thorough acquaintance with three things :—(1) *With His approaching trials.* "All ye shall be offended because of Me this night." Christ knew well all that was coming upon Him that night. He not only saw all the clouds that would blacken His heavens, but knew every peal of thunder, every flash of lightning, and every drop of rain, they would send down upon His spirit that night. His agonizing trials came not on Him by surprise or accident; all was foreknown and forearranged. The very prospect of all our life-trials would crush us long before they came; but Christ had that sublime magnanimity that enabled

Him to look at them in all their enormity in the distance, approach them without a faltering step, enter them with a spirit of unconquerable loyalty to Heaven, and pass through them with the moral energy of a God. He was acquainted (2) *With the desertion of His disciples.* He foresaw their dispersion. He expressed this by quoting an old prophecy. (Zech. xiii. 7.) "I will smite the shepherd, and the sheep of the flock shall be scattered abroad." When the leader is seized, his followers will fly. "They all forsook Him and fled." He was acquainted (3) *With His resurrection from the dead* "But after I am risen again, I will go before you into Galilee." Both His knowledge and His purpose stretched beyond His death; He knew that He should die, knew that He should be buried, knew that He should rise, knew that He should meet them after His resurrection. He speaks of all with most unquestioned certainty. He was acquainted (4) *With the particular denial of Peter.* After the warning that He had given His disciples as to their dispersion, Peter on his part protests against the possibility of his committing such an offence. "Though all men shall be offended," &c. In reply to this statement, Christ assures him that, "that very night before the cock crew he would deny Him thrice." Another Evangelist tells us that on this occasion Christ said to Peter, "Simon, Simon, behold Satan hath desired to have you, that he may sift you as wheat: but I have prayed for thee, that thy faith fail not: and when thou art converted, strengthen thy brethren."

Such a prevision of future events, such a pre-telling of things that actually occurred, as indicated even in these few verses, are sufficient to demonstrate to our conviction that the sufferer of Gethsemane is the Messiah of God. But in contrast with His knowledge, here we have:—Secondly: *Their ignorance.* They did not know themselves. Peter seemed to think it impossible for him to deny Christ, although he was informed of it. The idea seemed as repugnant to him as death itself. "*Though I should die with thee, yet will I not deny thee.*" The other disciples seemed to be equally ignorant of themselves :— "*Likewise also said all the disciples.*" They are religious men, good I presume in the main, but they deny to themselves even the power of doing that, which in the course of an hour or two, one and all would be guilty of doing. In the best of men there may sleep certain elements of depravity, which, if roused by powerful temptation, would prompt them to actions, the very thought of which a few minutes before would make them shudder. "Who can understand his errors?" "Let him that thinketh he standeth take heed lest he fall."

> " Beware of Peter's word,
> Nor confidently say,
> I never will deny Thee, Lord,
> But, Grant I never may."—COWPER.

II. His POWER AND THEIR WEAKNESS. First: *His power.* His power is seen here, not only in His reference to the mysterious horrors that awaited Him, but to His anticipated victory after death.

" *After I am risen again.*" He felt Himself even now superior to death,—felt that He had a power to break His chains and tread His sceptre to dust. His resurrection from the dead implied the possession of a power superior to the power of death. Death is a mighty power; it has conquered all past generations, is conquering the present, and men of all future times shall turn to dust at the bidding of the King of Terrors. But Christ's power is stronger than this. It is a power to "abolish death." His power is superior to that of nature. Old nature is powerful. Her storms and cataracts, her heaving oceans, revolving planets and changing seasons, all impress us with her power; but nature cannot raise the dead,— never of all the millions of the dead has nature raised one to life,— never will do so. But Christ here indicates a power to overcome death. "I am risen again!" Blessed be Heaven for the revelation of a power superior to death, sin, and nature, a power to raise the dead. Here we have :—Secondly : *Their weakness.* They were too weak to stand faithfully by Him in His trials. In a few minutes they would all be so frightened, so alarmed, that they would "all be scattered abroad and leave Him alone,"—to tread the winepress of agony alone. Here is weakness,—weakness of faith, gratitude, love, and every right sentiment. Our only strength is in Christ. "May His strength be perfect in our weakness."

III. His CONSTANCY AND THEIR INCONSTANCY. First: *His constancy.* "I will go before you into Galilee." Blessed words these. As if He had said, "After I have passed through the agonizing horrors that await me, after I am risen from the dead, after you have deserted and denied me, I will yet remember you; I will go before you into Galilee, I will go there to meet you, to satisfy you with the fact of my resurrection, to establish your faith, to comfort your hearts, and to direct you to duty." How constant is Christ in His love for His disciples. "The mountains shall depart," &c. Secondly: *Their inconstancy.* "They forsook Him after all His kindness to them." What mercy He had shown them! With what truths He had feasted their spirits! With what high hopes He had fired their natures! Into what high spiritual enjoyments had He lifted their souls! After, too, all the warnings and the promises which He here so earnestly addresses to them, in order to caution them against the danger of such a sin, and to encourage them in a faithful attachment to Him; after all this they desert Him. Ah! how inconstant are the best of men as compared with Christ! We are reeds that bow to every breeze :—He is the rock which the storms of ages affect not. Shifting clouds are we, ruled by passing currents :—The eternal Son is He, pursuing His majestic path from generation to generation without a deviation or a pause.

Matthew 26:36-46

Christ in Gethsemane; the Manward and Godward direction of the Soul in Sorrow

The public life of Christ has ended now ; He bids the world adieu, and retires. For upwards of three years He was seen performing stupendous miracles, and heard proclaiming transcendent truths, in the great theatre of public life. All eyes were on Him, all minds were occupied with stirring thoughts, which He, by His wondrous deeds and more wonderful doctrines, had waked up; but now He withdraws into a little garden at the foot of the Mount of Olives, a short distance to the south of the holy city. There, amidst the quiet trees, overshadowed by the silent hills, with the pale beams of the full moon falling coldly on His brow, He retires to solitary anguish and to private prayer. Mysterious are the sufferings which come upon Him in this quiet retreat : it is " the hour of darkness " in His soul. Awful were the spiritual convulsions and battlings of this hour ! What interests depended on it ? God knows, and coming ages will reveal. The agonies He now endured were *mental*. The mind, by its abstractions, creations, and anticipations, has the power to raise itself above the *consciousness* of physical pain. Hence the martyr has sang joyously at the stake. But what can sustain a wounded spirit ? There is no faculty to bear us above mental anguish. Man can flee from it no more than from himself ; it surrounds his being like the circumambient air which he must breathe or die ; and these mental sufferings of Christ were the sufferings of *innocence*. The burnings of envy and revenge, the distractions of avarice, the disappointments of ambition, the recollection of past misdoings, the warrings of passion and principle, and the pangs of remorse, which make up the *mental* sufferings of the *guilty* could not have been the ingredients in His cup of woe, and yet His soul was " exceeding sorrowful." The passage before us gives us such a vision of our Saviour's conduct under His deep suffering, as cannot fail to interest and instruct the thoughtful. Let us attend to it.

I. THE MANWARD DIRECTION OF THE SOUL IN SORROW. Urged by the *social* instincts of His nature, Jesus sought the presence and sympathy of His friends in this dark hour of sorrow. " And He took with Him Peter and the two sons of Zebedee," &c. Having human nature with all its sympathetic instincts, He wished His friends to stand by Him in the dreadful crisis. If they could speak no cheering words, their very presence would serve to relieve the dreariness of the scene. *He, like all men, looked manward for help.* This is natural, this is right. Man is made to help man, is bound to help man. God frequently helps man through man. To look, therefore, to man for help, is not wrong in itself. In Christ's appeal to man for help now, we discover three things in relation to man as a helper.

First: *The great frailty of man as a helper.* "And He cometh unto the disciples, and findeth them *asleep*," &c. They had spent the whole evening with Him at the passover, and now they were physically exhausted, and could not watch. Our nature can bear but little; its energies are soon overtasked, and we are left without power to help our dearest friends. We discover,—

Secondly: *The necessary qualifications for man as a helper.* "Watch and pray," &c. *Watch*—Act the sentinel, look about you, observe the perils that threaten and the foes that surround; and *Pray*—look above you, ever realize your dependence upon God for guidance, protection, and support. Without watching and devout prayer, man will never be able to render true service to his fellow-man. We discover,—

Thirdly: *The proper consideration due to man as a helper.* "The spirit indeed is willing, but the flesh is weak." Where help is sought, and not rendered through physical infirmity, let us ever accept the *will for the deed.* Christ did so, and thus He ever acts. The spirit is everything.

II. THE GODWARD DIRECTION OF THE SOUL IN SORROW. Christ had, as all have, *religious* instincts, as well as social, and hence He looked to God as well as to man. "He went a little farther, and fell on His face, and prayed, saying, O my Father, if it be possible," &c. There are three things in Christ's appeal to Heaven which characterises all true prayer. First: *A definite object.* What did Jesus seek? "Let this cup pass from me." What was in that dreadful cup? It was something before which His holy nature recoiled with inexpressible horror. THE ATONEMENT was in that cup; it contained the true panacea for diseased souls. All true prayer has ever a definite object. Another thing in Christ's appeal which ever characterises true prayer is, Secondly: *A true spirit.* "O my Father." It was an *earnest* spirit. Three times did He fall down and pray. It was a *submissive* spirit. "If this cup may not pass away from me except I drink it, Thy will be done." "THY WILL BE DONE"—it was a *filial spirit*—"my Father." This is the true inspiration of prayer. There is yet another thing in Christ's appeal which ever characterises true prayer, and that is, Thirdly: *A strengthening influence.* Luke states that "an angel appeared unto Him from heaven, strengthening Him." After His prayer, all the terrific excitement seemed to pass away; the inner storm subsided, the clouds broke, and the sun shone; a halcyon calmness came over Him, and His soul rose to an energy equal to His fate. He rose from His devotions with a new power, went to His drowsy disciples, and said, "Rise, let us be going," and began His way, with a firm and majestic step, to the cross.

A Gethsemane is before us all: into scenes of deep sorrow and trial all must soon pass. The dark hour of death awaits us, and the bitter cup must be drunk. Our social nature may then urge us to look manward. Let us not expect too much, even from our dearest and holiest friends; however willing their spirit, their "flesh is weak." Their disposition to help may be strong, but their capacity is ever feeble. May we turn Godward—look to the everlasting hills for help. Up those benign heavens there is ONE whose eye sees through the darkest night, whose heart feels for all, and whose arm is mighty to save. May He befriend us then, and graciously commission some kind and ministering angel to descend and give us strength equal to our day.

Matthew 26:47-56

Judas in Gethsemane; The World, the Church, and the Redeemer

Christ was now in Gethsemane. It was the evening preceding the day of His crucifixion. In order to turn this narrative to a practical account, we shall regard it as revealing *The Wickedness of the World, the Infirmity of the Church, and the Greatness of the Redeemer.*

I. THE WICKEDNESS OF THE WORLD. We shall take Judas, "the great multitude" which followed him, and the chief priests and elders under whose authority they were acting, as illustrating the world of corrupt humanity. Taking it in this light, we discover certain elements of depravity which have prevailed in all ages, which still prevail, and which are the curse of the race. What are they? It is well to know them, that we may be on our guard. Here is *Recklessness.* The Jewish Sanhedrim had no political right whatever to arrest any one for the purpose of inflicting a capital punishment. That right resided with Rome alone. (John xviii. 31.) It required a warrant from Pilate to authorize the attempt which was now made. Hence, in this assault upon the Son of God, urged on by the impetuosity of their hatred of Christ, they recklessly defied the Roman power. It is the characteristic of wickedness to make men *reckless.* They make a bold adventure, which may or may not *temporally* succeed, but which ultimately must terminate in their ruin. Here is *Venality.* "The great multitude with swords and staves," &c. What had they against Christ? Nothing. Why then did they go forth? They had *sold* themselves. They seem to have had no personal enmity towards Christ, for in His appeal to them He says, "I sat daily with you in the temple, and you laid no hands upon Me." As if He had said, "Why are ye armed against Me now? What has wrought this change in your feelings?" They had become the miserable *hirelings* of the chief priest. For some sordid considerations they lent themselves to this infernal enterprise. Wicked men act thus now.

In commerce, politics, and religion, they can be bribed. Money can still purchase, not only the limbs, but the genius and the soul, of a wicked man for any work. Here is *Cowardice.* Why the consultation of all those seventy Jewish senators ?—Why this " armed multitude," to take the poor Galilean ? How cowardly for so *many* to lend themselves to attack *one!* The philosophy of their cowardice was this :—they had a misgiving as to the rectitude of their operations. A guilty " conscience makes cowards of us all." Wickedness is necessarily cowardly. It cannot be truly brave and heroic. It may vaunt and bluster and brandish destructive instruments, but this is not courage. Here is *Avarice.* " Now he that betrayed Him." Why did he do so ? Not because he had any ill-will towards Christ, but because he *loved money.* " What will ye give me ? " said he to the chief priests. They gave him thirty pieces of silver ; and for that he gave himself to this deed, which has attached eternal infamy to his name. The *form* of Judas' sin was peculiar— there was only one Christ to betray—but the spirit of it is common. It was this :—a stronger love for pelf than for principle, for trade than for truth. He sold truth for money ; and who does not see this done here every day ? Here is *Craftiness.* " Now he that betrayed Him gave them a *sign,* saying, Whomsoever I shall kiss," &c. The whole was preconcerted. The sign was a kiss—the symbol of good feeling and affection ; and this sign they employ undoubtedly to throw their intended victim off His guard. This is the very spirit of the devil, and the spirit which everywhere " worketh in the children of disobedience." What craft you have about you here in this age ! There is a species of freemasonry in every department of the world. Signs are employed by the cunning everywhere to delude and victimise the uninitiated. Here is *Hypocrisy.* " And forthwith he came to Jesus, and said, Hail, Master," &c. He knew the spot where Jesus often met His disciples. (John xviii. 22.) He had often, perhaps, been with Him there. By this salutation and kiss he would have Christ to regard him as coming before His enemies to point out the danger, and to separate from Him with sorrow. What foul hypocrisy is here ! kissing in order to kill, saluting in order to slay ! The world is full of this ;—men are in masquerade. " Every man walketh in a vain show." Wickedness is necessarily hypocritical. A wicked man does not show himself as he really is. Here is *Profanity.* " Then came they, and laid hands on Jesus, and took Him." What daring impiety is here in thus rudely assailing the Holy Lamb of God and the Prince of Life ! The world has no reverence for sacred things ; it treats with profanity the most awful sanctities of being.

Here then is the mirror of the corrupt world :—not only of the world as it was in the days of Christ, and in Judea, but as it is in our days, and here on this Island. The elements of evil, which we see reflected here, are the moral demons which possess the world,— demons which must be exorcised before the race can advance to its true destiny.

This narrative reveals :—

II. THE INFIRMITY OF THE CHURCH. We take Peter and the other disciples here, who *"forsook Him* (Christ) *and fled,"* as representatives of the Church. Peter, although he was about perpetrating a great wrong, yet on the whole, was a true man, and a disciple of Christ. We discover here three infirmities,—

First : *Unreasoning impulse.* Impulse is good. It is noble to see a man with strong emotional forces. They are as steam to the engine, as wind to the sails of the ship. A man of weak impulses will never do much. Peter had noble impulses, but they too often became his masters. Impulses should never be our guides. They should always be under the control of reason. Reason should guide them, as the charioteer guides his fiery steeds. Had Peter's emotional nature been under the right control of reason on this occasion, he never would have used the sword. Had he reasoned before acting, he would have seen the utter ineffectiveness of this attempt. The idea of the *one* sword of *one* man (and he evidently *no soldier,* or he would not have missed his mark in his attack), being sufficient to drive back an armed multitude of drilled Roman ruffians ! It was the height of absurdity. Or, had he, moreover, thought upon the Almighty power of his Master, for whose defence he now wielded the sword, he would not have committed the irrational act. Like all men carried away by passion, he had forgotten the past,—memory was submerged by the billows of feeling. Had not this been so, would he not have remembered how Christ hushed the storm on the Galilean lake, when he and the other disciples were imperilled in the little skiff !

This unreasoning impulse has always been too general in the Church. It is the cause of that fanaticism which lives on excitement, is impatient of thought, disregardful of adaptations, and derogatory to Christianity.

Secondly : *Carnal dependence.* Peter trusted to physical force to defend him, instead of to moral suasion, and to Christ. Physical force cannot defend a man. The most it can do is to defend his body, which is his mere wrappage. The weakness of the Church in all times has been the dependence which it has exercised on mere carnal resources. It has invoked the arm of civil authority to its support. Its weapons have been carnal. It has sought the patronage of the rich, and struggled for magnificent endowments, instead of relying upon the power of its Divine principles, and the providence of its Lord.

Thirdly : *Inconstant service.* This is seen in the fact, that " all the disciples forsook Him and fled "—forsook Him at the time when their presence and their sympathy were most desirable, and most needed. They were unequal to the occasion. This, too, alas, is the characteristic of the Church on earth—the want of steadfastness, and of invincible perseverance in duty. At one time it appears earnest and determined, at another irresolute and cold ; at one time it sweeps along like a river just fed by copious showers, at another it sleeps like a stagnant lake with scarcely a ripple on its surface. It is not "steadfast, unmovable, always abounding in the work of the Lord."

Here, then, is a mirror of the Church—and the Church is confessedly the highest type of humanity on earth—and yet how imperfect! How much there is in it to deplore, and to reform! This narrative reveals,—

III. THE GREATNESS OF THE REDEEMER. It is refreshing and delightful to turn away from the *wickedness* of the world, and even the *infirmity* of the Church, to One in whom we can not only find no fault, but who has everything about Him to inspire our highest admiration, enlist our unwavering confidence, and satisfy our loftiest aspirations;—One higher than even our highest ideal. The greatness of Christ appears,—

First: *In His address to Judas.* "Friend, wherefore art thou come?" &c. (John xviii. 3, 4.) The word "friend" does not convey the idea of attachment which we connect with it now, but simply the idea of acquaintance. It was a mere word of recognition. In this address to Judas there is no indication of anger or excitement of any kind, but a mere dignified recognition. There is a majesty of calmness about it—which must have gone to the heart of the betrayer. It was Christ's *last* word to Judas, and he has never forgotten it, nor will he ever forget it. That word "friend," after the lapse of eighteen centuries, peals more loudly than thunder in his ear. Alas, Judas! The greatness of Christ appears,—

Secondly: *In His address to Peter.* In this address we discover *His authority.*—"Put up thy sword." This is the word of an imperial Master. We discover *His prescience:* "All they that take the sword," &c. The constitution of human nature shows this to be a universal truth, and the history of the world demonstrates it. The sword can never put down the sword. Anger generates anger, violence begets violence, war begets war, and so long as mind is mind this must be so. Christ knew this, and He here emphatically declares it. In this address we discover, moreover, *His unbounded resources.*—"Thinkest thou that I cannot now pray to my Father," &c.* Christ felt that the spiritual universe was on His side, that the teeming troops of the invisible world were at His command, and that with one breath of prayer He could bring the whole to His assistance. We discover again *His heavenly loyalty:* "How then shall the Scriptures be fulfilled?" He came to do the will of the Father, and to that will He gave Himself, daring to suffer and to die. The greatness of Christ appears,—

Thirdly: *In His address to the armed mob.* "Are ye come out as against a thief?" How sublime! One lonely sufferer standing up calmly before His ruthless and bloodthirsty assailants, all armed with deadly implements, and addressing them thus: "I sat daily with you in the temple!" The effect of this majestic calmness, John informs us, was to strike the ruffians to the ground. I see no

* See "Homilist," vol. vii., p. 289.

miracle in this ; it was the natural effect of a grand manifestation of moral truth and right upon the guilty consciences of men who felt they were engaged in a mission of hellish wickedness. This is the power to conquer, the only power worthy of our nature ; the only power that can achieve truly honourable conquests : yet, alas ! a power in which the world, through its gross animalism, believes not as yet.

Friend and reader, look well into the meaning of this narrative, and see, in the reflected rays of truth, things as they really are. You must live in association either with the world, the Church, or Christ. There is no other alternative. These exhaust the departments of the moral world in which you have your being. Will you make your home in the world, where such elements of *wickedness* abound ? The idea is revolting. Will you even in the Church, where there is still so much moral imperfection ? This would be unworthy of your nature, and hazardous to your highest interests. There is no section of the Church so holy as to authorize a man to settle down in it *as his home*. Thank God, Christ is here ; make Him your guide, companion, and the dwelling-place of your soul. May you be " found in Him ! "

Matthew 26:57-68

Christ before Caiaphas : a Contrast between the Seeming and the Real

A comparison of the various accounts given by the narrators of Christ's trial, shows us, as we have elsewhere indicated,* that He was first brought before Annas (John xviii. 12). Though Annas, it is true, was not in office now, and had, perhaps, no legal power to deal with the matter, he was an old man of considerable influence in the Jewish Senate. He had been high-priest himself for many years : no less than five of his own sons had filled the same elevated office ; and even Caiaphas himself, who was now the high-priest, was his son-in-law, so that his influence in the councils of the nation, on this account, must have been, we imagine, unprecedentedly great. To get the sanction of such a man to their endeavours to convict Christ, would, of course, be of great advantage to their infernal cause. Hence Christ was brought before him first. The order seemed to have been as follows :—From Gethsemane Christ was taken before Annas (John xviii. 24) ; from Annas He was sent bound to Caiaphas ; from the hall of Caiaphas He was taken to the hall of the Sanhedrim ; from the hall of the Sanhedrim He was taken to Pilate ; from Pilate He was taken to Herod ; and from Herod back again to Pilate, where their horrid endeavours were consummated.

* See " Homilist," vol. iv., Second Series, p. 169.

The scene before us is Christ in the hall of Caiaphas, and in this scene we have revealed *a most distressing contrast between the seeming and the real.*

I. HERE ARE SEEMING JUDGES, BUT REAL CRIMINALS. In the hall of Caiaphas were assembled the great authorities of the Jewish nation, "*the chief priests, and elders, and all the council.*" These men were the recognised officers of justice, and justice in its highest forms,—justice not only between man and man, but between man and God. The high-priest, who professed to stand in the place of God, to be His representative upon the earth, was president of this assembly of the judges. No body of men on earth ever professed a profounder deference to justice than these men. Justice to them *seemed* to be everything: they spoke her dialect; they wore her insignia; they quoted her laws; yet under all this seeming righteousness what have we? Disrobe these judges of their pretensions, and what do you see? Iniquity in its most putrescent forms. What do you find them doing even in this hall? In the name of justice they perpetrate four great enormities.

First: *They assembled in their judicial capacity for the purpose of putting an untried man to death.* What did the Court assemble for now in this hall? To receive a charge made against the prisoner? To listen attentively to the evidence adduced in its support, and to weigh it well in the scale of justice? Did the judges come hither as impartial men, siding in heart with no party, determined to search the case to its very foundation, in order that justice might be done? No! With a flagrant outragement upon the spirit of justice, they assembled with their minds made up, they came not to judge, but to *murder;* their object was "*to put Him to death.*"

Another enormity which they now perpetrated was,—

Secondly: *To give the appearance of justice to their endeavours, they procured false witnesses.* "*They sought false witness against Jesus to put Him to death.*" They had already determined the sentence in their own minds. His death was the point they had resolved to reach, but they wished to accomplish their desire in harmony, as much as possible, with the forms of law. Hence they sought witnesses,—*false* ones, because they knew that no true ones could be got. It seems that there was a little difficulty at first in procuring even false ones, whose testimony would be of any service. They "*found none,*"—that is, they found none whose evidence was of any worth to their cause. Mark says, that "*their witnesses agreed not together*" (Mark xiv. 56). The Jewish law, which they professed to administer, required two witnesses to convict a man (Deut. xix. 15), and it was a difficult thing to find two who would agree exactly in their testimony. A false man's statements seldom, if ever, agree with themselves, still less likely are they to agree with the statements of others. Hence, "*though many false witnesses came,*" they found none at first who agreed. Such is the corrupt state of society, that there is not much difficulty in finding false witnesses. Venal instruments of falsehood are found in all districts of social life. At length, however, two came whose testimony agreed; and what did they say? *"This fellow said, I am able to destroy the temple of God, and to build it in three days."* We find in John ii. 19-21, that He did use words something like these, but His reference was not to the temple at Jerusalem, as they would have it, but to the temple of His own body. The false witnesses were true, perhaps, in their declaration that they heard Him utter such words, but they were false in the application which they gave them. Whilst the procurement of such witnesses brands these conventional judges with eternal infamy, it lends a strong testimony to the sublime purity of our Saviour's life. Even false witnesses, in that false age, could not be found, though tempting the bribe held out to them, to attest aught unfavourable to His pretensions.

Another enormity perpetrated was,—

Thirdly: *Without a particle of evidence they condemned as blasphemy, the declaration which they extorted from Christ.* Feeling, in all likelihood, that the testimony of these witnesses did not sufficiently agree, even with the *forms of law*, Caiaphas turns from them to Christ, and to Him makes a solemn appeal. *"And the high-priest arose, and said unto him, Answerest thou nothing? what is it which these witness against thee?"* To this appeal Christ made no reply. In a manner more solemn and authoritative, the high-priest again appeals to Christ: *"I adjure thee by the living God, that thou tell us whether thou be the Christ, the Son of God."* The meaning of which expression seems to me to be this, "I demand of Thee, upon Thine oath, by the living God, that Thou tell us whether Thou art the Messiah or not." This was the usual form of administering an oath, and when the oath was thus sworn, it was called the oath of adjuration (Num. v. 19-21; Joshua vii. 19). Christ replies to this, and in language of awful grandeur, avows His Messiahship. *"Jesus said unto Him, Thou hast said;"* or, according to Mark xiv. 62, "*I am: and ye shall see the Son of Man sitting on the right hand of power,*" &c. The high-priest at once construed this wonderful declaration into a charge of blasphemy. *"Then the high-priest rent his clothes, saying, He has spoken blasphemy."* He rent his clothes* to symbolize a horror and a grief at the awful impiety contained in the declaration of Jesus. *Blasphemy* was the crime which he professed to find in Christ's language, and at which he professed to be so terribly shocked. Blasphemy, it is true, is a great moral crime, and under the law of Moses a capital crime; but Christ was not guilty of it; it was not found either in His language, or His life.

Another enormity perpetrated now, in this hall, was,—

Fourthly: *Upon this unfounded charge of blasphemy, they pronounced Him guilty of death, and treated Him with the utmost cruelty.*

* The customs of the East tolerate more violent expressions of feeling than are usual amongst us. Explicit prohibitions were made in the Mosaic Law (Lev. x. 6, xxi. 10), that the priests should not rend their garments on funeral occasions. Frequent allusions are found, both in the classics and the Scriptures, to this singular usage (Gen. xxxvii. 29-34; 2 Kings xvii. 37, xix. 1; Job. i. 20; Acts xiv. 14).

"*What further need have we of witnesses ? behold, now ye have heard His blasphemy.*" Further need of witnesses ! Thou hypocrite, Thou needest no witness at all ! Thy mind was made up long before any witness had appeared—long before this night. Thou hast only been calling in falsehood to help thee with the murder; the whole transactions of this hour have been a solemn mockery of justice, an outrage on truth, and an insult to humanity. "*What think ye ?*" said Caiaphas to his corrupt colleagues. "*They answered and said, He is guilty of death.*" Very right; He is guilty of death if He is a *blasphemer* (Lev. xxiv. 11–16). As such, forthwith they began to treat Him; they spit at Him, they buffeted Him, and others smote Him with the palms of their hands. Here is the *utmost contempt* : "*they spit in His face.*" This was a mark of the greatest derision and abhorrence (Num. xii. 14; Deut. v. 29). Here is *cruelty* : they "*buffeted and smote*" Him. Mark says, "*that they began to cover His face;*" Luke adds, "*that they blindfolded Him.*" "With the palms of their hands they smote Him." Here is *ridicule* : "*Prophecy unto us, thou Christ, who is he that smote Thee ?*" This was a taunting challenge of His divinity. "*Many other things,*" Luke tells us, "*blasphemously spoke they against· Him.*" On this occasion they were, in truth, the blasphemers,—not He. How easily could He have displayed His divinity at this moment. By His glance He could have scathed them into ashes. But He maintained a majestic silence under all these cruelties, insults, and indignities.

What a revelation is here, then, of the moral character of these judges of the land. If such outrages on truth, morality, and religion, were practised by the chief tribunal of the country, the first court of the nation, how deeply immersed in the lowest depth of depravity must have been the whole of Jewish society at this hour; for the character of a government is evermore the product and reflection of the people. No wonder that the Son of God rolled in peals of awful thunder His denunciations against this apostate race who thus affronted Heaven with their hypocrisy. The "measure of their iniquities" was fast filling up; the whole nation had become, morally, a rotten carcass; and the Roman eagle—Heaven's messenger of justice—already scented the prey, was spreading its wings for Jerusalem, and would soon pounce down and fasten its talons upon the putrescent mass.

Such, then, is the revelation which the passage gives us of *these seeming judges, but real criminals*. But we have in the narrative just the opposite of this.

II. A SEEMING CRIMINAL, BUT A REAL JUDGE. Who is the *seeming* criminal ? Jesus of Nazareth ! How wan and sad He seems ! No friend stands by Him; all His disciples have forsaken Him and fled. He is in the hands of heartless ruffians, and at the mercy of rulers who thirst for His blood. He has just been brought up from Gethsemane, and the dark shadow of a mysterious sadness hangs over Him. He looks as the very "Man of Sorrows, and acquainted with grief." Such is the *appearance* of this criminal, but in *reality* this prisoner at the bar is the great Judge of the world. He is only conventionally at the bar ; morally, He is seated on the incorruptible bench of justice, and His conventional judges are the vile culprits.

Even in this court, at this hour, though appearing as a prisoner, His moral majesty radiates in splendour. Observe two things :—

First : *His majestic silence.* " Answerest thou nothing ? " said the high-priest to Christ. *" But Jesus held His peace."* There is a silence which is often more eloquent than speech, means more than any words, and speaks ten times more powerfully to the heart. Such, for example, is the silence when the heart is too full for utterance, and the organs of speech are choked by the whelming tide of emotion. The sight of a great man so shaken, and quivering with feeling, that the tongue can give no voice to what the heart feels, is of all human rhetoric the most potent. Such, also, is the silence of a wise man challenged to speak by those whom he feels unworthy of his words. The man who can stand and listen to the language of stolid ignorance, venomous bigotry, and personal insult, addressed to him in an offensive spirit, and offers no reply, exerts a far greater power upon the minds of his assailants than he could by words, however forceful. His silence reflects a moral majesty, before which the heart of his assailants will scarcely fail to cower. Such was the silence which Christ now maintained in this hall. He knew the utter futility of their charges. He understood their malignant spirit. He knew the truth they wanted not, and that to reason with men of their animus, would only be to cast pearls before swine. " If I tell you, ye will not believe," said He. Sublime magnanimity I see in this silence of Jesus. In His bright consciousness of truth, all their false allegations against Him melted away as the mists from the mountains in the summer sun. His divine soul looked calmly down upon the dark and wretched spirits in that hall, as the queen of the night looks peacefully upon our earth amid the rolling clouds and howling winds of nature in a passing storm. His silence showed His majesty.

We have here also :—

Secondly : *His sublime speech.* " Hereafter shall ye see the Son of Man sitting on the right hand of power, and coming in the clouds of heaven." In His language He makes no reply to their charges. He condescends to no personal explanations ; He offers no remark upon the demon spirit they were exhibiting. He only speaks a few words, but in these words He Himself appears in all His divine grandeur. We have seen sometimes in nature a strong breeze sweeping away from the face of the sun a dark mass of cloud that had wrapped it in concealment, and darkened the whole earth with its shadows. These words of Christ were something like that breeze ; they scattered the dark clouds of ignorance and error that had concealed His divinity, and made Him flash for a moment as the Sun of Righteousness upon these guilty people. *" Henceforth,"* etc. " From hence shall ye see," etc. The expression is not to be limited to the final appearing of Christ to judgment, but refers to the whole state of His exaltation,—an exaltation that was to commence at His ascension to heaven, and continue through interminable ages. Observe (1) *They would see the sublime dignity of His position.* He tells them that they shall see Him "*sitting on the right hand of power,*"—an expression indicating the highest exaltation and authority. As if He had said to them, "You are now on the visible throne : you are on the judgment seat, and I appear as a prisoner before you. 'Nevertheless I say unto you,' it is only in *appearance,* and for the *hour ;* very soon the scene will be changed, and you will see Me on the right hand of power, enthroned in majesty and might, as the judge of all mankind." Observe (2) *They will see the sublime dignity of His procedure.* They would see Him "*coming in the clouds of heaven.*" They would see Him coming not only in the destruction of Jerusalem and the ruin of their own commonwealth—as they undoubtedly would—nor merely in the dispensation of His spirit on the Day of Pentecost, nor merely in the last Great Day of Judgment; but they would one day, when their consciences would be thoroughly smitten with the conviction of their sins, either here or in the terrible hereafter, see Him coming in every event of their history. Ay, and in the history of this world they would see Him "coming" upon all the clouds that darken its horizon. A convicted conscience sees Him as the Light of all new eras, as the Morning Star of an ever-brightening future. In the history of hell He will appear in all the dark clouds of thought, foreboding, and emotion, that roll over reprobate souls.

In what a grand attitude does Christ appear now, in making this declaration ! What a picture ! A prisoner in appearance, standing before the great authorities of the country, all of whom thirsted for His blood, and He looking calmly at them, with eyes peering not only into their eyeballs but into their very hearts, and there saying, "I say unto you, Hereafter shall ye see the Son of Man sitting on the right hand of power, and coming in the clouds of heaven."

Brother, learn from this not to confound the *seeming with the real.* "Things are not what they seem." Verily the moral world is upside down. Sinners, not saints, now sit on thrones and judge the earth. Learn to unmask men and things, and judge all by the light of His great thoughts who is now sitting on the "right hand of God."

Matthew 26:69-75

The Fall and Rise of Peter

This incident, big with thrilling sentiment, has a connection with verse 58, in which we are informed that Peter "followed Him (Christ) afar off unto the high-priest's palace, and went in, and sat with the servants, to see the end." In his appearance there, there was almost as great a contrast between the "seeming and the real,"* as there was between the judges on the bench and the prisoner at the bar. Peter, sitting down with the servants, disguised his real character ; his inner nature pulsated with warmest sympathy for Christ, yet he would have all around to believe that he was either an indifferent spectator, or perhaps one of His avowed enemies. It is said that he sat without in the "palace" on this occasion. By the palace or hall is meant the opening square of the dwelling, the court which eastern houses had in the centre. An oriental house is usually built around a quadrangular interior court, into which there is a passage, sometimes arched, through the front part of the house, closed next to the street by a heavy folding gate, with a smaller wicket for single persons, kept by a porter, usually male, sometimes female. In this court Peter was now in company with those of Christ's enemies who were the miserable hirelings of the Jewish council. It was perhaps a cold, damp night, and a fire was kindled for their comfort. The room in which Christ and His judges were assembled, and in which the proceedings of a mock justice were going on, must have been close to this court, for Jesus seems to have heard all that was going on around the fire. (Luke xxii. 61.) Peter's first denial seems to have taken place in the middle of the court, on his being questioned by the female porter. After that he makes his way into the passage leading into the street, which is called "the porch," where he is again questioned by "another maid." Luke writes "another," whom Peter addresses as a man. John, in relating the event, speaks of several who questioned, and charged him on this occasion. (John xviii. 17, 25, 26.) So that both a certain maid and a certain man might have engaged in the allegation, and there is therefore no contradiction between Matthew and Luke. The third denial, which took place an hour afterwards, found Peter within the court, within the reach of Christ's eye. So much for the *scene* in which Peter's fall and rise took place.

Let us notice :—

I. PETER'S FALL. In illustrating this sad event in the history of this distinguished apostle, we may offer three remarks :—

First : *It is very intelligible.* The change in the man's history is no miracle. He was not hurled down from the pinnacle of faithful discipleship by forces over which he had no control, or by a shock which would outrage the laws of his nature. We can trace the process and mark every step he took in the downward course. There are at least four steps clearly observable, and these steps stride the whole distance of the fall. (1) *Self-sufficiency.* His confidence in his own power to do the true thing was amazing ; he felt that he could follow Christ anywhere, he avowed himself ready to lay down his life for His sake. (John xiii. 37.) When warned of this very sin, he declared that though all men denied Christ he would not ;

* See Section CXI., p. 509.

he seemed to have been so confident of his own power, that he attempted single-handedly to crush the enemies of Christ in the garden; self-confidence had almost grown into a passion in him; he felt that he was a great man, and could do almost anything. This state of mind is always the first step downwards. Presumption often ends in ruin. "Pride goeth before destruction, and a haughty spirit before a fall." A humble practical dependence upon God is the great upholding power of the soul. Another step we discover, is:—(2) *Partial knowledge.* He had not duly considered the sacrificial work of Christ. Frequently had his Master told him that He was going to lay down His life for the sheep, that His mission was a mission of mediatorial suffering. Peter seemed to have ignored all this aspect of His teaching; His mind seemed to have been taken up more with His character, as one who was to effect a temporal deliverance of His country, and establish a material empire in the world. Hence, when the sufferings of Christ began to accumulate, and the approach of a terrible death became more obvious, instead of calmly meeting the whole as a realization of his faith, he became agitated with surprise, and fear, and awful solicitude. Partial knowledge is always dangerous; one-sided views of truth are often perilous in their character. Men often fall into the dark hell of the Pharisee, the bigot, and the persecutor, through this. Another step we discover is:—(3) *Spiritual negligence.* He had been guilty of a sad neglect of duty in Gethsemane : his Master asked him to watch with Him; but he fell asleep. Had he kept watch, had his eyes marked the writhings of the agonized frame, and his ears caught the mysterious groans of his Master, he might have got such an inspiration as to the divinity of the tragedy as would have held him in faithful loyalty to the closing scene : but he lost the advantage of that wonderful power by his negligence. The same neglect he also displayed from the garden up to the palace of Caiaphas. Had he walked step by step with Jesus, close by His side, interchanged looks and words with Him, he might have had an infusion of moral power that would have kept him true and made him a hero in the strife. But he followed "afar off;" he was away from the Divine air that encircled Christ, and he breathed the atmosphere of men inspired with the very spirit of hell. Spiritual negligence is a downward step. Once omit a duty, and you receive a downward impulse. Moral remissness makes for ruin. Another step we discover is:— (4) *Fear of man.* Peter had no dislike to Christ, no desire to injure Him, but the contrary. Perhaps had he believed that his avowal would have rescued Him from His enemies, that avowal he would have made; he felt that all was over with Christ now, that His death was inevitable, and that if he acknowledged his connexion with Him, his doom also would be sealed; and hence, to save himself from the danger, he commits the sin of denial.

Secondly : *It is very heinous.* (1) *The denial succeeded great advantages.* What privileges Peter had enjoyed! What signal favours Christ had bestowed upon him! He had lifted him to the ecstasies of the transfiguration. He had forewarned him, too, of the very crime which he here commits. (2) *His denial occurred after his deprecation of the possibility of it.* "Though I should die with Thee, yet will I not deny Thee." (3) *His denial was thrice repeated.* The first denial was made to a damsel who came unto him. This damsel was probably the portress who kept the door: she observed Peter there in the centre of the courtyard, in company with the ruffians who crowded round the fire on that cold raw morning; she walked up to him, holding perhaps a lantern in his face, and said, "Thou also wast with Jesus of Nazareth." But he denied before them all, saying, "I know not what thou sayest;" as if he had said, "I do not understand thy meaning." After this he seems to have left his place, and wended his step towards the gate, struck with alarm, and hoping, it may be, to pass the porch and leave the scene unobserved. But there at the porch he met another maid, who said unto them that were there, "This fellow was also with Jesus of Nazareth." This charge seems to have been repeated by others : several, it would seem, gathered around him at this point, and charged him with having been with Jesus. But he not only persists in the denial, but repeats it with greater emphasis, adding profanity to the utterance. Finding that he could not escape, he went back to the fire, and after a while (Luke says "about the space of an hour"), there came unto him others who said, " Surely thou also art one of them; for thy speech bewrayeth thee." " The pronunciation of the people of Galilee was uncouth and indistinct, hence they were not allowed to read aloud in the Jewish synagogue."—(Lange.) Notwithstanding the number and the positiveness of those who now charged him to his face with having been with Christ, he persists in the denial. He began to curse and to swear, saying, " I know not the man." (4) *His denial was thrice repeated, each time with an increase of wickedness.* The first denial was a kind of ambiguous evasion. " I know not what thou sayest "—a pretended ignorance of the whole matter. The next is a distinct denial, breathing the rising spirit of profanity and contempt. He denied it with an oath, "I know not the man." "The *man*"— there is a sneer of contempt in his utterance. In the next his temper is gone, passion is rampant, reason and conscience are lost amidst the raging of excitement, and he begins to curse and to swear. Peter was an old sailor, and perhaps, like most mariners, in early life, had been in the habit of using profane language; and now the spirit of goodness having left him for an hour as it were, the old sailor, with all his boisterous roughness, and wild dashing profanity, comes up, and there is nothing but swagger and swearing.

Such is Peter's fall; and it was indeed a fall. He had reached a lofty altitude in spiritual experience; he received the very keys of the kingdom, to unlock the treasures of heavenly mercy, and here we find him in the hell of falsehood and profanity. Some men who concern themselves a great deal about *"falling from grace,"* need have no personal anxiety on the question. They have never been raised; they cannot fall, for they are low enough already.

II. PETER'S RISE. There is no more miracle in his rise than in his fall. He is not lifted back to his old state in a moment, irrespectively of all means. We think we can trace the pathway. We mark four stages.

First: *Here is an incidental occurrence.* "Immediately the cock crew"—crew while he was in the height of his impious rage. It would seem from Mark that the cock had crowed once before this. This was the second time. It was three o'clock in the morning, and the notes of the bird fell like a thunder-clap on the conscience of Peter. This incident arrested his downward course, struck conviction into his nature, and brought reason again into action. Incidents the most simple are the ministers of God, ministers which often arrest the careless, guide the perplexed, soothe the sorrowing, and bless the true. God can give the most microscopic object in nature an arrow to pierce the soul, the weakest sound a voice that shall rouse the conscience into fury.

Secondly: *Here is an action of memory.* "And Peter remembered the words of Jesus." The echo of this bird of the morning brought, as with a flash, the words of Christ to his memory, and on these words he dwelt in thought. Mark says, *"when he thought thereon he wept."** A providential incident is powerful to a man only as it awakens thought, and powerful to him for good only as the thought is engaged on the right subject. Thought is the rudder by which man turns the vessel of his being towards the haven of purity and peace.

Thirdly: *Here is a divine manifestation.* Luke tells us, *"the Lord turned and looked upon Peter."* What a look was that! †

Fourthly: *Here is a repentant effect.* "He went out and wept bitterly." He went out from the companionship of ruffians and the scene of bigotry and injustice—he went out from the circle where he had been tempted to a course of wickedness whose memory now struck him with horror and alarm—he went out into the solitudes of nature, under the quiet vault of night, to weep his tears at the foot of Justice, and to breathe his sighs into the ear of Mercy—he went out to unburden himself of that load of guilt which he had contracted, and to consecrate his being once more to the will of his Master. He wept bitterly, and his tears were—

> "Like blessed showers,
> Which leave the skies they come from,
> Bright and holy."

---

* "Homilist," Second Series, vol. ii., p. 109.
† See "Homilist," Second Series, vol. ii., p. 109.

Matthew 27:3-5 *

Judas; or, Aspects of a Guilty Conscience

The history of Judas teaches us three things. First: *The power of one sinful feeling to counteract the influences of the best society.* Judas was "one of the twelve." For nearly three years he associated with the pure, loving-hearted John, the ardent and honest Peter, the truthful and upright James. Above all, with Jesus. What doctrines and prayers he heard! What dispositions and deeds he witnessed! But notwithstanding this all went for nothing with him. Like showers on rocks and sands. Why was this? The corrupt feeling of *avarice* was within, and this perverted all. It rotted all the good seeds that were thrown into him. Secondly: *The power of man to conceal his sinful feelings from others.* When Jesus, at the Last Supper said, "One of you shall betray me," each began to say, "Lord, is it I?" They did not know who. We know not what is going on in the breast of others. Each is a world to himself. Thirdly: *The power of conscience to inflict merited punishment.* This is seen in the text.

Here you have a guilty conscience in four aspects:—

I. WAKING INTO ANGUISH AT THE ACCESSION OF NEW LIGHT. "When he *saw* that He was condemned, repented himself." First: *The nature of the anguish which he now experienced.* He "*repented himself.*" Who shall estimate the misery represented by these words? This anguish was not the fear of punishment. He knew that he had done a popular act, and that his countrymen, perhaps, would make him a hero for ridding them of such a public disturber as Christ. It was the *essential wrongness*, not the *personal consequences*, of the act that pained him now. It is self-crimination, self-loathing, self-reprobation. "A wounded spirit who can bear?" Secondly: *The accession of the new light which produced it.* "When he saw that He was condemned." He did not expect this result, when he perpetrated the deed. He had no unkind feeling, perhaps, towards Christ. Probably he thought his act would bring on the crisis in His history, which he, in common with the other disciples, anticipated—His ascension to universal empire. But, when "he saw" the opposite result, then his conscience bounded into fury. Let heaven cast *new* light upon the sinner's deeds, and then conscience will start. This new light must come.

II. INEFFECTUALLY STRUGGLING TO OBTAIN RELIEF. He makes two useless efforts. First: *Restitution in a wrong spirit.* "*He brought again the thirty pieces of silver*," &c. To his avaricious nature they were once very valuable, but now he felt they were curses. Conscience reverses our estimates. These silver pieces now seemed red

---

* The first two verses of the chapter belong to the next section but one, and will be there noticed.

with blood and hot with fire. He could not retain them. But the restitution was in a wrong *spirit*; it was from a *selfish* desire for relief, and not from a *self-sacrificing* desire to make satisfaction for the injury. He makes—Secondly : *Confession to the wrong party.* To the chief priests and elders—not to God—he says, "I have sinned," &c. The confession I take as a powerful testimony to two things. (1) *To the moral freedom of human nature.* Logically, we debate as to whether internal impulses and external circumstances do not coerce men, destroy their liberty of action, and make them slaves. An awakened conscience despises such logic, and makes short work with it. It impels the man to say with all the emphasis of his nature—"*I have sinned,*" I am the author of the act; not my propensities or circumstances, but I. This confession is a powerful testimony ;—(2) *To the moral purity of Christ's life.* "Innocent blood." I can see a good reason why Christ elected such a man as Judas to be one of His disciples. He, being admitted into the inner circle of our Saviour's social life, in common with other disciples, had every opportunity of judging of His real character; and now, therefore, his testimony to the purity of His life is far more powerful than the testimony of any other could possibly be. Far more so, for example, than Pilate's—Pilate only saw the outward, Judas the inward.

III. HEARTLESSLY REPULSED BY GUILTY ASSOCIATES. "*What is that to us ? See thou to that.*" "The ungodly," says Bengel, "though associating in the commission of a crime, desert their associates when it has been accomplished." The godly, though not taking part in the crime, endeavour, after its commission, to save the sinner's soul. I submit three remarks on the conduct of these men. First : *It was cruel.* They were the tempters : they offered the bribe; and in doing so, no doubt, they were genial and bland. Secondly : *It was unavoidable.* They had guilty consciences as well as Judas, and in this very matter too. Perhaps their consciences began to trouble them a little now. The guilty *cannot*, if they would, comfort the guilty. Thirdly : *It was representative.* It was a specimen of conduct that must ever take place under similar circumstances. It is so in hell. Every appeal of the tempted to his tempter will meet with the response, "*What is that to us ? See thou to that.*" The infidel to his disciples, the debauchee to his victims, &c. The heartless response of every seducer in hell, to the agonizing entreaties of his victim is, "WHAT IS THAT TO US ? SEE THOU TO THAT." Your bland tempters must become your tormenting devils.

IV. PLUNGING INTO ETERNITY IN DESPERATION. He "*went and hanged himself.*" Two things here—First : *The intolerableness of his existence.* Life itself became an unbearable burden. Secondly : *The irrationality of his existence.* Conscience threw reason off its balance. If he had reasoned a moment he would have known that suicide could not destroy *existence, conscience, sin, or misery ;* but, on the other hand, would make all these more terribly real.

From this subject we infer—(1) *That there is a moral government over man in this world.* A guilty conscience proves this. (2) *That compunction is not conversion.* (3) *That a guilty conscience must find either hell or pardon.*

Matthew 27:6-10

The History of a Property

Few subjects are more worthy of an historic treatment than that of human property. To take the secular property which any man holds, and expound the way in which it has been acquired, how it is employed, the influence it exerts upon its possessor, and its general bearings, would be to reveal many principles both in human nature and in the divine government of great interest and importance.

The history of wars, philosophies, scientific discoveries, and religions, which abounds does not and cannot present exactly those phases of truth which are developed in the history of a man's worldly fortune. The passage before us presents, as the prominent subject, the property of Judas; and its history may be fairly taken as the history of the property of thousands in every age and land.

I. WE SEE IT HERE DESCENDING AS THE LEGACY OF CRIME. "*And the chief priests took the silver pieces.*" (1) The silver pieces were once the property of Judas. They were in his hands, and at first, no doubt, he rejoiced in them as his own. (2) He acquired this property by wickedness. It was his reward for betraying the Son of God. "*What will ye give me?*" This was his avaricious question. He sacrificed principle for property—his Lord for lucre. (3) The wickedness with which he acquired this property stung him into an intolerable remorse. Under the accusations of his conscience, his existence became unbearable, and he destroyed himself. (4) This property falls into the hands of the very men from whom he obtained it at first. He desired it, he obtained it, it ruined him, he dies, and he leaves it behind him, as the legacy of a tremendous crime. How many fortunes held by the men of this age are the legacies of crime!

II. WE SEE IT HERE INHERITED AS A SOURCE OF ANXIETY. These silver pieces, coming into the hands of the chief priests, filled them with strange solicitude; they knew not what to do with them. (1) Their consciences would not allow them to retain them for their own personal use. They felt that they had used this money as a bribe to tempt Judas to a tremendous crime, and that it had come back to them red-hot with avenging justice. Bad as they were, their consciences were not utterly steeled. (2) Their religion would not allow them to devote it to the Temple. "It is not lawful for to put them into the treasury, for it is the price of blood." The treasury was the chest in the court of the women, for receiving the offerings of worshippers. These technical and hypocritical religionists found the law against putting such money as this into the treasury of the Temple in Deut. xxiii. 18.

Thus this money gave them great anxiety : something, they felt, must be done with it, but what ? that was the question ; they could not keep it. Money is often a troublesome possession.

III. WE SEE IT HERE EMPLOYED AS AN EXPIATORY GIFT. "And they took counsel, and bought with them the potter's field, to bury strangers in." This field was near Jerusalem, and had been used for making earthenware. We are not told the size; the probability is that it was of but little value. They bought it as a cemetery for such persons as died at Jerusalem and did not belong to it. Perhaps the Ξένοι, for whom the field was purchased, were foreign Jews who attended the festivals. " In the time of Jerome the poorest outcasts were buried there."—(Webster and Wilkinson.)

That there was no real *charity* in this act is clear from the fact that Providence brands the field with a name that shall stand for ages as a memorial of their crime. " Wherefore that field was called the field of blood unto this day."

No, they bought this "old exhausted clay-pit," not from any humane sentiment or generous impulse, but to atone, if possible, their consciences. How much money in all ages has been contributed to the cause of religion and philanthropy with the sole view of expiation !

IV. WE SEE IT HERE OVERRULED AS THE INSTRUMENT OF PROVIDENCE. There is a Providence over all, originating the good and subordinating the evil. Hence the act of these wicked men in purchasing the field fulfilled an old prophecy. "Then was fulfilled that which was spoken by Jeremy the prophet, saying, And they took the thirty pieces of silver, the price of Him that was valued, whom they of the children of Israel did value ; and gave them for the potter's field, as the Lord appointed me." This is a quotation, not from Jeremiah, but from Zech. xi. 12, 13. The exact language is not given, but the application of the idea is made. The reason why Jeremiah is given instead of Zechariah is a question which has received very different explanations. The most satisfactory seems to be this, that Jeremiah standing first in the Rabbinical order of prophets, gave a title to the whole series.*

Wicked men, however uncontrolled in their wickedness, are always made the instruments in working out the Divine arrangements.

Matthew 27:1, 2, 11-25

Christ at Pilate's Tribunal

The first two verses of this chapter inform us as to the time and manner in which Christ was brought before Pilate, also concerning

---

* See Wilkinson and Webster's Greek Testament. Also Bengel.

the persons who were engaged in the iniquitous undertaking, and the malignant object they had in view. The words are, in the first two verses,—" *When the morning was come, all the chief priests and elders of the people took counsel against Jesus to put Him to death. And when they had bound Him, they led Him away, and delivered Him to Pontius Pilate the Governor.*"* It was in the "morning" that followed the dark night in Gethsemane, and opened the dread day of the crucifixion. The Paschal supper, His arrest in the garden, His appearance before Annas, Caiaphas, and the Sanhedrim, all took place in the *night*, whose reign was now giving way before the grey beams of a wonderful morning. The grand object of the chief priests and elders in bringing Him to Pilate, was to get Him *put to death*. This fell purpose had grown into a raging passion in the bosom of these technical religionists. But why did they bring Him to Pilate? Why did they not commit the murder themselves? They had not the legal power to do so. The Jews had no power to put any man to death. This power belonged entirely to the Roman authority. Pilate, the Roman Procurator, had, in Jerusalem, jurisdiction in cases of capital crime, and hence, before his bar they brought Christ. Tacitus the Roman historian, in his annals, refers to the trial of Christ before Pontius Pilate; his words are, "Christus, the founder of that name [that is of the Christians], was put to death as a criminal by the Procurator, Pontius Pilate, in the reign of Tiberius." †

Now, it was here, before Pilate, that He received His *condemnation* to death. The following is the sentence said to have been rendered by Pontius Pilate, acting Governor of Lower Galilee, stating that Jesus of Nazareth shall suffer death on the cross. "In the year seventeen, of the empire Tiberius Cæsar, and the 25th day of March, the city of holy Jerusalem, Anna and Caiaphas being priests, sacrificators, of the people of God, Pontius Pilate, Governor of Lower Galilee, sitting on the presidential chair of the Prætory, condemns Jesus of Nazareth to die on the cross, between two thieves—the great and notorious evidence of the people, saying :—(1) Jesus is a seducer. (2) He is seditious. (3) He is an enemy of the law. (4) He calls Himself falsely the Son of God. (5) He calls Himself falsely the King of Israel. (6) He entered into the temple, followed by a multitude, bearing palm branches in their hands. Order the first centurion, Quillus Cornelius, to lead Him to the place of execution. Forbid to any person whomsoever, either poor or rich, to oppose the death of Jesus. The witnesses that signed the condemnation of Jesus are, viz.: I. Daniel Robani, a Pharisee. II. Joannas Rorobable. III. Raphdel Robani. IV. Capet, a citizen. Jesus shall go out of the City of Jerusalem by the gate of Struenus." ‡

* See Homily on the Imprisonment of Christ, New Series, vol. iv., p. 169.
† Annales, xv. 44.
‡ The above sentence is engraved on a copper plate : on one side are written these words :—"A similar plate is sent to each tribe!" It was found in an

Now, perhaps, we cannot better use the record which Matthew here gives of the condemnation of Christ by Pilate, than by developing those suggestions which it affords, not only to demonstrate Christ's innocency of the particular charge brought against Him, but also the general purity of His character. We shall discover, if I mistake not, in the circumstances that transpired, and the conduct that was developed by the different parties in this last trial of Christ, what will satisfy the common sense of every man : that the circumstances of His condemnation are amongst the strongest proofs of His móral purity. His condemnation in Pilate's court is a commendation of His character to the confidence, the reverence, and the admiration, of humanity.

We discover five things in this last trial of Christ as here recorded, which will glorify the accused, and condemn the accuser. Consider :—

I. THE NATURE OF THE ACCUSATION. What was the charge bróught against Him now before Pilate ? The question which Pilate addresses to Him, "*Art thou the King of the Jews ?*" suggests that the charge was a POLITICAL one; and Luke supplies the omission of Matthew, and gives us a distinct statement of their accusation. Luke's words are, "And they began to accuse Him, saying, we found this fellow perverting the nation, and forbidding to give tribute to Cæsar, saying that He himself is Christ, a King." This is the charge, and its spuriousness is most transparent. First : *The suddenness with which it is framed, renders it most suspicious.* It was not mentioned an hour or two before when He stood before Caiaphas and the Sanhedrim. There was no word mentioned before them of insurrectionary aims and kingly pretensions of Christ. The charge there was a religious one : it was blasphemy, not political rebellion. The reason for such a charge here so suddenly, was merely to get their *mortal* malignity carried into effect; they knew that the charge of blasphemy before Pilate would amount to nothing. The Roman law tolerated religious differences, and Pilate himself had no sympathy with Jewish religionists. Hence they framed of a sudden a charge to meet the occasion. This charge came within Pilate's jurisdiction, and he had every temptation to deal with the utmost severity with those who could be proved guilty of the crime. Secondly : *The social position of Christ as He appeared before Pilate rendered the charge absurd.* He was a poor peasant, socially; He

antique vase of white marble, while excavating in the ancient city of Aquila, in the kingdom of Naples, in the year 1820, and was discovered by the Commissariats of Arts attached to the French armies. At the expedition of Naples it was found enclosed in a box of ebony, in the sacristy of Caserta. The French translation was made by the members of the Commission of Arts. The original is in the Hebrew language. The Chartrom requested earnestly that the plate might not be taken away from them. The request was granted as a reward for the sacrifice they had made in the army. M. Denon, one of the savans, caused a plate to be made of the same model, on which he had engraved the above sentence. At the sale of his collection of antiquities, &c., it was bought by Lord Howard for 2,890 francs.— JACOBUS.

never aspired to anything more. He claimed no high relations. He owned no worldly property. He knew what hunger was. He was but "a man of sorrows and acquainted with grief." Such a charge against one of such a humble condition and appearance was so preposterous that it carried with it its own refutation. Thirdly : *The loyal tenor of His whole life and teaching, added to the manifest absurdity of the charge.* He never uttered a word of disloyalty, always recognized civil authority, and taught submission to the claims of Cæsar. Thus the very accusation, rightly pondered, demonstrates His innocence. Consider :—

II. THE BEARING OF THE PRISONER. The conduct of the prisoner on this trying occasion, instead of developing one symptom of guilt, radiates in every point with innocence. Observe two things, *His speech* and *His silence*. First : *His speech.* In answer to Pilate's question, "Art thou the King of the Jews?" He says, "*Thou sayest;*" which means, *It is so.* John informs us, that on this occasion Jesus made a fuller declaration of Himself. In answer to Pilate's question, He said, "My kingdom is not of this world : if my kingdom were of this world, then would my servants fight; that I should not be delivered to the Jews : but now is my kingdom not from hence." And again, He says, "To this end was I born, and for this cause came I into the world—that I should bear witness unto the truth. Every one that is of the truth heareth my voice." In this language we have an *affirmation* and a *denial*. He affirms that He has a kingdom, and that He has servants; but He denies that His kingdom is of this world. His kingdom is over the thoughts, emotions, purposes, souls of men. His kingdom is won, not by material forces, but by spiritual truths. The true king is he that governs souls. All other kingdoms are bubbles compared with His. Observe :—Secondly : *His silence.* When the chief priests and elders accused Him in the court, it is said, "that He answered nothing." Pilate observed this silence,—and appeals to Him,—"Hearest thou not how many things they witness against thee?" Jesus retains His silence. "*He answered him never a word.*" At this "the governor marvelled greatly." And well he might. Silence, in such exciting circumstances, where there was so much to provoke torrents of speech. Silence to the appeals of the civil magnates of His age, who held His earthly destiny in their hand, was indeed a marvellous thing; "*As a sheep before her shearers was dumb, so He opened not His mouth.*" "*When He was reviled, He reviled not again, when He suffered, threatened not, but committed it to Him who judgeth righteously.*"

Do not both the speech and the silence of the Prisoner, in these terribly trying circumstances, attest His more than earthly innocence and goodness ? His conception of the moral kingdom, was grand. The claiming of such an empire before a tyrant judge, was sublimely magnanimous; and His dignified silence, amid such mighty provocatives to speech, demonstrated a self-control and a consciousness of rectitude more than human. Consider :—

III. THE CHARACTER OF HIS ACCUSERS. Who were His accusers? They were two classes—"the chief priests and elders, and the people." Let us ask the character of each of these. Are they truth-loving, trustworthy men? First: *What are these chief priests and elders? Are they to be believed?* If we look at them merely as they appear on this occasion, as men whose moral natures were rotten to the core, we shall discover that they are men destitute of any attribute to awaken confidence. The first verse of the chapter shows that they were inspired with a *deadly malice.* They thirsted for His life, like beasts of prey. In John's narrative (John xviii. 28), we have an account of their odious sanctimoniousness. They would not enter the judgment-hall themselves, *lest they should be defiled.* Such sanctimoniousness, as fears the defilement of places, is one of the worst symptoms of a rotten nature. The greater the outer sanctity, the more foul the fiend within. In the passage before us, it is said, that Pilate himself knew *"that the chief priests had delivered Him from envy."* Where *envy* reigns, virtue has no lodgment. Can such people as these be credited? From the nature of these technical religionists, all generous impulses had oozed away; all sentiments of truth and justice had died out. Secondly: *What are these people, that are inside of the judgment-hall, sent inside for, by the hypocritical chief priests and elders, who were too holy to enter?* Are they trustworthy? No; they were the mere tools of the religious rulers. The clamouring multitude in the hall, crying out for Barabbas, demanding the crucifixion of Christ, imprecating His blood to rest on them and on their children, "the chief priests and elders persuaded." This multitude belonged to that intellectual rabble, which, alas! makes up the larger portion of every generation, that follow the demagogue, applaud the charlatan, and sell themselves to their superiors, to work the foulest deeds. The populace in every age have preferred Barabbas to Christ. Such men as these cannot be trusted; they are fawning sycophants to their superiors, and heartless tyrants to those below them, who oppose their wishes, excite their ire, and fall into their power. Heaven deliver any country from the sway of a democracy, unconverted and unenlightened. Those who aspire to popularity, and labour to become the idols of the crowd, are not only to be censured for their vanity, but pitied for their folly; those who cheer them on the stage to-day, will hiss them off to-morrow.

IV. THE STRANGE MESSAGE OF PILATE'S WIFE. *"When he was sat down on the judgment-seat, his wife sent unto him, saying, Have thou nothing to do with that just man; for I have suffered many things this day, in a dream, because of Him."* It would seem that it was only in the reign of Tiberius, that the governors of provinces had been permitted to take their wives with them. Matthew's incidental notice, therefore, of Pilate's wife being now at Jerusalem, is a striking proof of the veracity of the evangelist. She, being in Jerusalem with her husband, having her mind occupied all the day with thoughts about Christ—thoughts which filled and agitated the whole city on that occasion—on her retiring to sleep in the shadows of the night, those thoughts were, in some strange and startling forms, reproduced in her dreams. The vision she had in the dream-world was of Him whom her husband had, at his tribunal, assured her was a "just man;" and deeply in her sleep did she feel distressed on account of the wicked and heartless treatment He was receiving; "I have suffered many things," &c. This was no ordinary dream —this dream of bitter agony. Had it been a mere common vision of the dream-hour, is it likely that this Roman wife would have sent a dissuasive message to her husband, when seated on the judgment seat? It was something supernatural,—an apparition from the invisible,—a messenger from the all-Righteous Eternity.* Her dream, I have no doubt, embodied the moral judgment of Jerusalem and the neighbourhood, concerning the character of Christ. All men in their consciences must have pronounced Jesus, "that just man." Here, then, in this court, where Christ was condemned, is another striking testimony to the rectitude of His character. Consider:—

V. THE CONDUCT OF PILATE THROUGHOUT THE TRIAL. At the outset, Pilate's conscience seemed satisfied as to Christ's innocence. Hence the efforts which he made to rid himself of the responsibility of condemning Him. (1) He sought to hand Jesus over to the Jewish court. When the chief priests and elders brought Christ to him, at once he said, "Take ye Him, and judge Him according to your law." (John xviii. 31.) As if he had said, "I shrink from the responsibility of the work you are imposing upon me." (2) After having put certain questions to Christ, he leaves the court, and goes forth to those chief priests and elders who are too holy to enter the hall, and declares, "*I find no fault in this man.*" (3) Having been driven by the clamour of Christ's accusers, to ascend again the judgment seat—and put questions to Christ, the moment a reference was made to Galilee in their charge, he seized on the idea of sending Him to Herod for trial. "*And as soon as he knew that he belonged unto Herod's jurisdiction, he sent him to Herod, who himself also was at Jerusalem at that time.*" (Luke xxiii. 6, 7.) (4) When He was sent back from Herod, to him again for trial, "Pilate, when he had called together the chief priests, and the rulers, and the people, said unto them, Ye have brought this man unto me, as one that perverteth the people: and, behold, I, having examined Him before you, have found no fault in this man touching those things whereof ye accuse Him: no, nor yet Herod: for I sent you to him; and, lo, nothing worthy of death has been done by Him. I will, therefore, chastise Him, and release Him." (Luke xxiii. 13-16.) (5) Discovering that there was no chance of satisfying the accusers in this way, he suggests that he shall use his prerogative, as a judge, and release Christ as a prisoner. "At that feast,"—that is, the feast of the Passover, which was now being celebrated at Jerusalem.— "The governor was wont to release unto them, a prisoner, whom they would." It was a custom that, on that season, one prisoner should be released; "of necessity, he must release one unto them

* See "Homilist," vol. i., p. 154.

at the feast." There are two prisoners now,—Christ and Barabbas; the people must choose which. He hopes that Christ will be chosen, —and thus his conscience will be, in some measure, set at rest—and his responsibility somewhat removed. But the multitude, the miserable tools of the ˙priests, like moral maniacs, choose Barabbas, the notorious robber. (6) Christ being thus left with him, as a prisoner, with whom he was bound, by public clamour, to deal,—he tries another expedient, in order to deliver his conscience. He appeals to their better feelings, *"What shall I do, then, with Jesus, which is called Christ?"* As if he had said, "You will not require me to be severe with Him—to inflict any great punishment on Him—since you see I find no fault in Him; consult your reason and your conscience,—and let me know what I shall do." In reply to this, they all cried out, "Let Him be crucified." Pilate, as if shocked for a moment with this iniquitous demand, interposed, and said, "What evil hath He done?" But they cried out the more, saying, "Let Him be crucified." (7) When every effort failed, and, contrary to the protests of his conscience, he pronounced the sentence, and delivered Him up to be crucified; *"He took water, and washed his hands before the multitude, saying, I am innocent of the blood of this just person."* Wretched man! Thou hast sacrificed justice to popularity, and now seekest by an empty ceremony to appease thine outraged conscience. Oh, Pilate, the waters of a thousand Atlantics cannot wash out that stain of guilt, which thou hast now contracted! I do not wonder that, after this moral enormity, thine existence on this green earth became intolerable; and that thou, like Judas, becamest thine own executioner. Thus, the whole conduct of Pilate in the court, on this last trial, was the strongest attestation to the moral rectitude of Christ; and thus, indeed, as we have seen, all the incidents connected with His last trial and His condemnation to death, confirm the language that "He did no sin; neither was guile found in His mouth."

Matthew 27:26-33

Christ on His way to Calvary

In our last section our attention was occupied with Christ at Pilate's tribunal, and in connexion with that trial we discovered five things which demonstrated that the condemnation which He there received placed beyond all question the fact that He was not only innocent of the charges brought against Him, but that He was a being of the most exalted holiness of character. In the brief period of His history which elapsed between His condemnation by Pilate and His arrival at Calvary, as recorded in these verses, there are several things that are noteworthy and suggestive.

We have here,—

I. PILATE DELIVERING HIM OVER TO CRUCIFIXION. "*Then released he Barabbas unto them: and when he had scourged Jesus, he delivered Him to be crucified.*" According to Carpenter, the probable order of events was the following:—"Pilate, after washing his hands, yields to the Jews, releases Barabbas to them, and, in their presence, has Jesus scourged for crucifixion. Jesus is then taken within the fortress and mocked by the Roman soldiers. Pilate brings Him within the Prætorium. He then brings Him forth, formally condemns Him, and delivers Him to be crucified." Pilate has done his work—has performed his last part in this hellish tragedy. He stands before us as the example of a man perpetrating three enormous evils.

First: *Sinning against the dictates of his own conscience.* Some men sin *without* convictions. What they do wrong, they do ignorantly. Some sin *with* their convictions. Such are the crimes of conscientious persecutors; such was the crime of Saul in persecuting the Church. He thought he was doing God's service. But here is a man, this Pilate, sinning *against* his convictions. Every effort of his in the piece has been a fearful battle against his own conscience. Miserable man! His was a desperate struggle against the divinity within him,—a divinity which can only be put down temporarily, and put down to rise as the merciless tormentor of its assailant. He who by a crime prostrates his conscience, will soon have it up as the avenging Nemesis of Eternal Justice. This Pilate stands before us as the example of a man,—

Secondly: *Sacrificing truth for popularity.* "He, willing to content the people, gave sentence that it should be as they required." The people's will, not his own conscience, was his rule; the people's favour, not the Eternal, was his god. The voice of an infuriated rabble told more mightily on him than the Divine voice of duty. In this he was a type of a class of public men who abound in all ages, who love the praise of men more than the praise of God,—men who court public sentiment, flow with the stream, and flatter public vanity, in order to be the idols of the hour. The men now, who sacrifice a truth because it is unpopular, and give out those forms and shapes of thought which the populace will welcome, commit in spirit the very crime of Pilate, who delivered up Christ to be crucified, and released Barabbas to liberty. This Pilate stands before us as the example of a man,—

Thirdly: *Having committed a crime, and growing reckless in evil* With immense difficulties, we have seen, he was brought to pronounce the condemnation; but having so far broken through all moral restraints as to commit that fearful enormity, he seems ready for the moment to plunge into any other iniquity. Hence we are told, that, immediately after the sentence, he "*scourged Jesus.*" "The cruelty of this infliction may be conceived of, when it remembered that the thongs were usually filled with pieces of le iron, or bone, to cause a great laceration of the flesh, and that the poor sufferer was obliged to receive the blows upon the naked back in a stooping posture. The ancient scourging appears to have very much resembled the modern knout of Russia. The law of Moses forbade more than forty stripes, but the Romans were subject to no such merciful restriction. The punishment sometimes occasioned death, and appears to have weakened Jesus, in conjunction with other causes, so, that he was unable to carry his cross, and died in four hours upon the fatal tree. Scourging always preceded cruci-fixion as well as other executions, and added greatly to its pains, on account of the pressure of the torn and bleeding back against the frame of the cross, and the general inflammation of the system." That the man, who, in his conscience, considered Christ innocent, and who, with the utmost difficulty, was forced to condemn Him, should now give himself up to this infernal torture of Christ's body, reveals an awful fact in the history of sin, namely, that one crime so prepares for another, that at last the soul riots and revels in enor-mities. As the taste of blood maddens the beast of prey with the spirit of destruction, the commission of sin rouses the depravity of the soul to crimes of deeper dye. Sin is as when " one letteth out water." Once open for the pent-up waters an aperture, however small, and soon the whole will roll itself through with ever-increas-ing force and flow.

We have here,—

II. THE PEOPLE RECEIVING THE OBJECT OF THEIR CHOICE. "*Then released he Barabbas unto them.*" Who was Barabbas ? Another Evangelist tells us that he was a robber, "who, for a certain sedition made in the city, and for murder, lay bound with them that had made insurrection with him." From this we infer that he was notorious amongst those bloody insurgents, the chief amongst the men of plunder, rebellion, and murder. This was the man the people selected; they were unanimous in their vote, they cried out " all at once," and that repeatedly, "*Away with this man, and release unto us Barabbas.*" You can see in this choice of the people two things, which, alas ! you can see in all subsequent ages—the un-popularity of right, and the popularity of wrong.

First: *The unpopularity of right.* "Away with this man," said they. Why away with *this* man ? Because he was the embodiment of right, and the exponent of principles which clashed with the pre-judices, the passions, the interests, and the habits of the age. Truth in its majestic all-sidedness has never been popular. It acts on the public conscience as strong daylight on the diseased eye, and the people shrink from it and " love darkness." Were a man of the same humble condition and aspect as Christ to appear in this age to us—the men in this island—to live as Christ lived, and preach out the great things which Christ preached, denouncing the Scribes and Pharisees of the hour, the thundering invectives against wrong on all hands, regardless of men's prejudices, interests, frowns, or smiles, would not the " away with Him" reverberate from one end of Britain to the other ? Right has ever been unpopular, and still is.

Secondly : *The popularity of wrong.* These people would not only not have the right, but would have the wrong; and not only would crucify Christ, but would release Barabbas. Barabbas, the representative of fraud and violence, they elected in preference to Christ, the representative of purity and peace. Who have ever been the popular idols? Not the men who exhibit most of the spirit of Him who would not cause " His voice to be heard in the street, break the bruised reed, or quench the smoking flax; " but the men of dashing swagger, unscrupulous daring, and unbounded pretensions. The people's heroes have always borne a greater resemblance to Barabbas than Christ. The fact is, the world is corrupt, and the corrupt world can only love its own. There is no honour in being the people's idol. The people always deify their own attributes. Verily, woe unto the man when all the people speak well of him. Since ʾthe people voted incarnate virtue to death, and incarnate wickedness to freedom, one has no confidence in their suffrage; their voice to one's ear is anything but the voice of God. Their praise is but the breath of depravity, which, however fragrant for the moment, is essentially noxious:—

> " Who grasped at earthly fame, grasped wind—nay, worse,
> A serpent grasped, that through his hand slid smoothly,
> And was gone, but left a sting behind, which
> Wrought him endless pain."—POLLOK.

We have here,—

III. THE SOLDIERS' TREATMENT OF CHRIST. " *Then the soldiers of the Governor took Jesus into the common hall, and gathered unto Him the whole band of soldiers,*" &c. The scourging by ruffians, under the direction of Pilate, being over—with blood flowing from every pore, a thrill of agony on every nerve, the whole frame quivering with torture—Christ is subjected to other indignities by fresh hands. He is taken to the common hall, the Governor's palace or house, by the soldiers. This was a magnificent edifice built by Herod the Great. Here He is at their mercy. The Jews cannot enter this place; they are too holy for it. Contact with the soldiers would defile them for the Passover, forsooth. The soldiers, therefore, have it all their own way. " The whole band," or cohort in the Roman army, numbering, perhaps, from four to six hundred men, are assembled around the sufferer, not to heal His wounds or to alleviate His anguish, but to aggravate the agony. These men, trained to deeds of infamy and blood, the miserable hirelings of wickedness, revelled in their fiendish work. The whole genius of wickedness seems to blaze out in their conduct, as from the fires of the accursed world. We may learn from their conduct here (1), *that the genius of wickedness is malignant.* These men could have had no personal reason for disliking Christ; He had never, perhaps, come into direct contact with *their* prejudices or interests, and one might therefore have expected that when He was handed over to them ¡. bleeding agony, that their hearts would have been touched with kindness and sympathy. But no; wickedness is essentially malignant. Sin is malevolence, and the destiny of its victims is the torment of each other. The head of the great family of the wicked, both in hell and on the earth, is like "a roaring lion, walking about, seeking whom he may devour." We may learn from their conduct here (2), *that the genius of wickedness is venal.* These miserable soldiers sold themselves to such work. They were the base minions of their masters. What they did they did to please their "governor," and would have done anything for hire. Like all wicked men—heartless tyrants to those beneath them, but fawning sycophants to those above. The great father of all such crawls as a serpent. Moreover, we may learn from their conduct here (3), *that the genius of wickedness is scoffing.* Their work now consisted, in a great measure, of mockeries and taunts and sneers. In mockery they put on Him "a scarlet robe." Mark says it was "purple." Probably some old cast-off general's coat which they found, and threw around Him in derision. The "purple" here does not designate colour, but badge. It was the royal hue. In mockery they "*plaited Him a crown of thorns and put it on His head;*" they wove a chaplet of thorns, and, in derision, placed it on His brow, as well to torture as to insult Him. In mockery they put "a reed in His right hand," which bore a ridiculous contrast to that strong staff of gold and ivory which kings were wont to wield as a sceptre. In mockery they "*bowed the knee before Him,*" playing off the farce of loyalty in order to show the contempt which they had for His kingly pretensions. In mockery they cried, "*Hail, King of the Jews!*" Scorn is ever an attribute of wickedness. Jeers and gibes, sneers and ridicule, directed against sacred things, are the ritualism of devil-worship. He who sits in the seat of the scorner, sits by the threshold of hell. Having done all this, "*they spit upon Him, took the reed and smote Him on the head,*" &c. Then they "*led Him away to crucify Him.*" It is remarkable that during the whole of this treatment Christ offered no resistance and uttered no words. Sublimely passive is He. "As a sheep before her shearers is dumb, so He openeth not His mouth." He who with the glance of His eye could have scathed them into ashes, appears as a lamb in the jaws of a wolf, as a dove in the claws of a vulture.

Here we have :—

IV. Simon compelled to bear His cross. "*And as they came out, they found a man of Cyrene, Simon by name; him they compelled to bear His cross.*" As they came out of the city—for the execution of criminals was commonly outside the gates. Who was this Simon? Mark and Luke speak of him as a man coming out of the country. Mark adds, that he was the father of Alexander and Rufus. Cyrene is in Africa, lying west of Egypt, on the Mediterranean Sea, belonging to Lybia. It was a great resort for the Jews, because they there enjoyed peculiar immunities and privileges. Probably he had come up to Jerusalem to attend the Passover. He seems to have been a stranger, and, to human appearance, casually met with on this occasion. He was compelled to bear the cross now, not from pity for Christ. Christ's bleeding and lacerated frame had lost its strength, and the burden of the cross He could not carry farther.

It would seem from John xix. 17, that He had borne it for some distance, but He gave way under His weakness and His wounds. That cross must be borne to the place of execution, and they compelled this stranger to bear it. Nor did Simon bear it from pity; he was "compelled" to do so. The instrument of torture he bore by compulsion. Pity! Christ met with no pity from these hardened ruffians; the fires of wickedness had burnt out the kinder sentiment of their natures.

Here we have :—

V. THE MISDIRECTED COMPASSION OF THE WOMEN. This is not recorded in Matthew's narrative before us; but it occurred during Christ's journey to Calvary, as the other evangelists testify. "*And there followed Him a great company of people, and of women, which also bewailed and lamented Him. But Jesus, turning unto them, said, Daughters of Jerusalem, weep not for me, but weep for yourselves, and for your children. For, behold, the days are coming in the which they shall say, Blessed are the barren, and the wombs that never bare, and the paps which never gave suck. Then shall they begin to say to the mountains, Fall on us; and to the hills, Cover us. For if they do these things in a green tree, what shall be done in a dry?*" As we have elsewhere remarked on this passage, we need offer no comment here.*

Matthew 27:33-56

Christ on the Cross

We have traced the history of Christ up to this point. The review of His trial forces certain lessons on us of such universal importance as to require a distinct statement of them before we proceed to contemplate the awful tragedy of the crucifixion.

First : *That priestism is an immense power in the world.* It was the hierarchal force that not only moved the Jewish people, but Pilate and his soldiers, to the enormities which they inflicted upon Christ. Priestism has ever been, and still is, one of the mightiest powers in the world; it throbs through the hearts of generations in some form or other. The *rationale* of this force may be found in three things. (1) *The strength of the religious element in human nature.* The religious spirit is the very sap and substance of human nature; excite it, and you excite the entire man. (2) *The universally felt need of mediation in religion.* Account for it how you like, the general feeling of mankind in relation to God is that they must not approach Him *directly;* they can only appear before Him through the mediation of those whom they consider to stand higher with Him than themselves. This is a fact, and we have its solution in the Gospel. (3) *The universal ignorance of man in relation to the*

* See " Homilist," vol. ii., p. 123; also vol. v., p. 398.

nature of true religion. The general idea is, that religion is a thing of ceremonial observances, rather than of spiritual sentiments—a something that might be done for us by others, rather than a life obligation, to be discharged only by personal conduct. In these things we have something of the philosophy of priestly power.

Another lesson which the review forces on us is :—

Secondly : *That religious zeal is no valid evidence of genuine religion.* The whole excitement connected with the trial of Christ was religious. Zeal for what was considered orthodox in thought and practice towards God, was the fire that flamed in the great council of the nation, and heated the spirit of the ignorant populace. What is called religious zeal, is frequently nothing more than a zeal for our own small theological notions, or the advancement of our own little sect. The Scribes and Pharisees were zealous ; "They compassed sea and land to make one proselyte."

Another lesson forced on our attention is :—

Thirdly : *That corrupt spirits are often the most vigorous in their attention to formalities.* How punctilious were the chief priests and elders in the formalities of the trial. The court must be properly convened, the prisoner must attend, the charge must be brought, witnesses must be there to give their evidence ; the whole procedure must be in thorough keeping with the letter of Jewish trials. Iniquity spoke the dialect of right ; wickedness robed itself in the garb of justice. This had become the fixed character of these religionists : "they made clean the outside of the platter," &c. Their corrupt spirits lived in holy words and sacred forms. As a rule, perhaps, the basest spirits are ever the most rigid in their attentions to forms of virtue.

Another lesson forced on our attention is :—

Fourthly : *That civil authority is a dangerous power for religious officials to wield.* Though the Sanhedrim, a priestly body, had not the civil power at this time to inflict capital punishment, its power in every other respect was immense ; it was the civil position they occupied that gave them that power to excite the people to demand the crucifixion of Christ. The true priest will never seek civil authority. The authority he aspires to is moral : the authority of truth and goodness. This is the kingdom that Christ came to establish, the kingdom in which all true men reign.

Another lesson forced upon our attention is :—

Fifthly : *That the prosecution of wrong is not always easy work.* Immense difficulties the Scribes and Pharisees had ; they often met and deliberated. Various stratagems they projected, according to the emergencies of the hour. Often were they foiled, and it was only after many a failure that they succeeded. So with Pilate. What difficulties beset his path ! What agonizing battles he fought, now against the force of public sentiment, and now against the force of his conscience, before he proceeded in pronouncing the condemnation ! "Verily, the way of transgressors is hard." The transgressor sets his face against his own conscience, the moral constitution of the world, the holy universe, and the great God.

His successes are only seeming, casual, and temporary; his failure is real, necessary, and eternal.

We must now proceed to the crucifixion. At the outset we must notice its *scene* and *mode*. In verse 33, the place is called Golgotha, a Hebrew or Syriac word, meaning a "skull." Whether it was so called because its shape resembled that of a skull, or because it contained the skulls of malefactors who had been executed, is a question which has not yet been satisfactorily determined, and is of no practical moment. In Luke it is called Calvary, which in the Latin also means "skull." There is also difficulty in determining the exact spot. Dr. Lange and others maintain that this Golgotha is the site of the Church of the Holy Sepulchre, now in possession of the Mahommedans, and about the key of which England was mad enough, a few years ago, to unite with France in a bloody war against Russia. As to the *mode* of the crucifixion, it was that which combined the greatest agony with the greatest disgrace. To use the language of another, the manner of crucifixion was briefly this: "The sentenced man was stripped of all his clothing, saving a strip about the loins, and then severely whipped, so that he sometimes died under this; smarting and exhausted, he was compelled, as soon as possible, to bear his cross to the spot. Four soldiers of the Prætorian guard, under the superintendence of a centurion, were the common executioners. These drove each a nail into the hand or foot of the man, sometimes before and sometimes after the cross had been set up in its place in the ground. Resting on the small seat which was fixed about the middle of the cross, the person could be nailed to it after it was set up. It was a slow and severe death, not exceeded in physical suffering, perhaps, by any method of torture. It was also the most ignominious punishment: 'For it is written, Cursed is every one that hangeth on a tree.' Robbers and slaves were generally doomed to this kind of death. Hence *the offence of the cross.* Hence the wonder of Christ's humiliation: 'EVEN THE DEATH OF THE CROSS.' A person generally lived on the cross till the third, fourth, or fifth day; the nails poisoning and inflaming the whole system, and through the nerves among which they were driven, making the pain indeed EXCRUCIATING; a term which is derived from the word *crux*, a cross. With the Jews it was not lawful that a malefactor's body should hang on the cross over night. (Deut. xxi. 23.) Hence the soldier tried with the spear to see if He was yet dead, else they would break His bones to hasten His decease." The whole of these verses lead us to look at Christ upon the cross in four aspects:—*As the victim of wickedness; as the exemplar of religion; as the deserted of heaven; and as the power of God.*

I. CHRIST UPON THE CROSS APPEARS AS THE VICTIM OF WICKEDNESS. We see:—

First: *Wickedness here fastening Him upon the cross.* It had secured His condemnation, and thus outraged every sentiment of justice; it had scourged and insulted Him in the hall of Pilate, and it had compelled Him to bear on His lacerated frame the cross, from the hall of judgment to Golgotha, the scene of execution. It now fastens Him on that cross, drives the rugged nails through His hands and feet, and suspends Him there in unknown torture. This seems the masterpiece of wickedness. Christ seems powerless before its force. He hangs there in excruciating agony as the helpless prey of human vultures. Their ruthless talons are fastened on the tenderest nerves of His heart and being. He seems to be in the red-hot iron grasp of wickedness. The fiendish thousands of His age closed about Him like wild beasts. "Many bulls have compassed me about, strong bulls of Bashan have beset me round." For six thousand years wickedness had been growing. It had wrought deeds of impiety and crime that had wrung the ages with agony, and often roused the justice of the universe to roll her fiery thunderbolts of retribution through the world. But now it had grown to full maturity; it stands around this cross in such gigantic proportions as had never been seen before; it works an enormity before which the mightiest of its past exploits dwindle into insignificance, and pale into dimness. *It crucifies the Lord of life and glory.*

Secondly : *We see wickedness here tormenting Him while on the cross.* It is said that Socrates spent his last hours in quiet. No one was suffered to disturb the tranquillity of his philosophic soul; weeping friends and loving disciples were with him to buoy him up with their kind words and loving looks; even his executioner was touched into compassion, and wept when he gave the fatal cup of hemlock into his hand. But Christ is not allowed to die even with the agonies of the cross, great as they were; His enemies, even until His last breath, endeavour to heighten His tortures by acts and words of heartless cruelty and blasphemous insults. The two great divisions of world—the Gentiles and Jews—united in their endeavour to aggravate His sufferings.

First, observe the *conduct of the Gentiles.* How did they act while He was dying ? (1) "*They gave Him vinegar to drink mingled with gall.*" Mark calls the drink "wine mingled with myrrh."* It would seem that the Romans were accustomed to give their criminals in their mortal sufferings some stupefying drink. This does not seem the kind of draught which was now presented to Christ; His was mingled with gall, having a quality to heighten rather than deaden the anguish. (2) "*They parted His garments, casting lots,*" &c. It would seem that the soldiers who acted as executioners, were entitled to the garments of the deceased. "They made four parts," says John, "to every soldier a part, and for His coat they cast lots." They stripped Him, and gambled for His garments. "That it might be fulfilled," &c. Even supposing this verse is not an interpolation, the language must not be understood as meaning that these soldiers divided His garments, in order to fulfil a prophecy, but only that an old passage of Scripture received illustration by that act. (3) "*Sitting down, they watched Him there.*" This, we think, means more than an official duty—guard-

* See Davidson, p. 361.

ing Him to prevent a rescue ; it means a feasting of their eyes upon His tortures. Like those who now attend executions, they had a morbid pleasure in witnessing such a tragedy. (4) " *They set over His head His accusation, written,* THIS IS JESUS THE KING OF THE JEWS." Other evangelists inform us that Pilate wrote this superscription, and that it was written in letters of Hebrew, Greek, and Latin. And John informs us that the chief priests found fault with it at first, and said, "Write not, The King of the Jews, but that He said, I am King of the Jews. Pilate answered, *What I have written I have written.*" Pilate had already ruined himself by gratifying their wishes, and perhaps his conscience told him so ; and with an irritation he said now, "What I have written I have written ;" I will concede no more. Though it was the accusation of which He was condemned before Pilate, it was utterly groundless. Christ disavowed all political objects, and declared His kingdom was not of this world. (5) " *Then were there two thieves crucified with Him, one on the right hand, and another on the left.*" Two robbers or highwaymen, with which Judea then abounded, were selected as His companions in suffering. Thus, "He was numbered with the transgressors."

Such is the wicked treatment of the *Gentiles*, during His sufferings on the cross. Let us now turn and observe :—

Thirdly : *The conduct of the Jews.* We shall find that the malignity which the Jews displayed during His sufferings was far more intense and turbulent than that displayed by the Gentiles. (1) Look at the Jewish populace on this occasion. " *They that passed by reviled Him, wagging their heads, and saying, Thou that destroyest the temple, and buildest it in three days, save Thyself. If Thou be the Son of God, come down from the cross.*" They reviled Him, literally blasphemed, moving their heads in gestures of ridicule and insult. They challenged Him to come down from the cross. Little did these miserable mockers imagine that within three days He would rebuild the temple which they were now destroying. Easily might He have come down that moment from the cross, and, with a breath of His lips, swept them into endless perdition. But He forebore. (2) Look at the Jewish officials on this occasion. They were the instigators of the whole ; the infernal fires of their malice had kindled up those wild flames of passion that now burst forth from the thousands around the cross. " *Likewise also the chief priests mocking Him, with the scribes and elders, said, He saved others ; Himself He cannot save. If He be the King of Israel, let Him now come down from the cross, and we will believe Him. He trusted in God ; let Him deliver Him now, if He will have Him : for He said, I am the Son of God.*" Their language involves an affirmation and a denial. *The affirmation is sublimely true, and it condemns them.* It is true that He saved others. He went about doing good. His whole life was restorative. This being true, why should they treat Him thus ? Where is the justice, where is the humanity, aye, where is even the simple propriety of putting a social benefactor to death, and treating Him thus ? *The denial is gloriously true, and it condemns them.* In the divinest sense He could not save Himself. Physically, of course, He could have delivered Himself, "come down from the cross," and overwhelmed His enemies with destruction. But morally He could not, and His moral weakness here is His glory. He could not, because He had undertaken to die, and He could not break His word. He could not, because the salvation of the world depended upon His death. The greatest man on earth is the man who *cannot* be unkind, who cannot téll a falsehood, who cannot do a dishonourable act, or be guilty of a mean, selfish deed. The glory of the omnipotent God is, that "He *cannot* lie." These men, therefore, should have honoured, yea, have adored the weakness which they acknowledged. Their very confession condemns their conduct. (3) Look at His companions in suffering on this occasion. "*The thieves also that were crucified with Him cast the same in His teeth.*" Though Matthew and Mark speak of the thieves, Luke distinctly states that only one of the malefactors reviled Christ, and records the penitence and the prayer of the other. The supposition—which is a very natural one, and one adopted by Chrysostom, Jerome, and others— that at first both reviled Christ, that afterwards one of them repented, and that Luke's language refers to a period subsequent to that alluded to by Matthew and Mark, removes the discrepancy.

Thus, then, one of the aspects in which Christ appears to us now upon the cross, is that of a victim of wickedness. He is beset with fiendish spirits, and He seems helpless in the hands of His enemies.

Having contemplated Christ upon the cross *as the victim of wickedness*, we proceed, according to our plan, to consider Him:

II. As THE EXEMPLAR OF RELIGION. It is the account which the other evangelists give of Him upon the cross, that exhibits Him to us in this interesting aspect. They give what Matthew here omits: His prayer for His enemies, His direction to John to take care of His mother, and the committing of His spirit into the hands of the everlasting Father. So that on the cross He displays three features of character, demanding the imitation of the world—the highest love for enemies—the highest filial affection—and the highest confidence in the Eternal.

First: *Here on the cross He exhibits the highest love for enemies.* "Father, forgive them, for they know not what they do." (Luke xxiii. 34.) This prayer, in all probability, was offered at the time when the executioners were in the act of driving the iron into the tender nerves and tendons of the feet and palms of the hand. The expression, "they know not what they do," inclines us to the thought that the prayer was especially for those Roman ruffians who were officially engaged in the crucifixion, and who had not the opportunity the Jews had of ascertaining His Messiahship. The doctrines contained in this prayer are—*that sin, though committed in ignorance, requires forgiveness—that forgiveness is evermore the prerogative of God the Father—that the exercise of this prerogative is secured through the intercession of Christ—that this intercession is available for the chief of sinners—and that the religion of Jesus is essentially antagonistic to the spirit of retaliation and revenge.* If ever revenge could be justified, it would be now. If ever language of vindictive denunciation could be warranted by circumstances, it would be now. But, for the men who there nailed Him on the cross, and drove the most excruciating agony into every nerve of His being, He has no feeling but that of compassion. He is on the cross ; crowds rage in malignity around Him, and seek in every way to aggravate His tortures.

> " Still from His lips no curse has come,
> His lofty eye has looked no doom ;
> No earthquake burst, no angel brand,
> Crush the black, blaspheming hand.
> What says those lips, by anguish riven ?
> ' God, be my murderers forgiven.' "

This is the new spirit, the new commandment that He brought into the world—this love for enemies. The religious philosophers and moralists of the old world, in their highest elevations, never reached such a thought as this. In truth, both in Greece and Rome, revenge was impersonated as a deity for men to worship and adore. Cicero, foremost and brightest amongst the moral sages, in one of the most benign and pacific of his mental moods, formulated this rule : " Hurt no man unless first provoked by injury." But this is contemptibly low when compared with the teaching and spirit of Christ ; it breathes resentment, and therefore is foreign to the sublime morality which Christ inculcated upon the mountain, and the spirit which, in His prayer, He breathed upon the cross. This spirit of love for enemies is the very essence of ethical Christianity, the epitome of the Gospel.

Secondly : *Here on the cross He exhibits the highest filial affection.* " When Jesus therefore saw His mother, and the disciple standing by, whom He loved, He saith unto His mother, Woman, behold thy son ! Then saith He to the disciple, Behold thy mother." Elsewhere we have noticed the heroic love, the parental affection, the filial sympathy, and the obedient discipleship implied in these words.* Christ, in the midst of His agonies, was mindful of His mother : " Behold thy son ! " As if He had said, " I am leaving the world, but John will be a son to thee." Such words must have been as a gleam of unearthly sunshine to Mary, relieving the blackness and calming the fury of the tempest that was beating on her soul. Here on the cross, then, the world has the highest practical exemplification of the fifth commandment in the decalogue : " Honour thy father and thy mother." Though uttered in a dying whisper, it speaks to the heart of the world with an impressiveness a thousand times more powerful than that which announced it amidst the thunders, the lightnings, and the earthquakes of Sinai. Filial affection is essentially associated with genuine religion. He that loveth not his earthly parents whom he hath seen, loveth not the Eternal Father whom no man hath seen. The earthly affection is an essential stage to the heavenly. It is a flame in the heart which lights the soul up to the Infinite Father. Where it is not,

---

* See " Homilist," vol. i., p. 191, new series.

every spark of virtue is extinguished, and the spirit is a benighted orphan without God in the world. Genuine filial affection towards earthly parents, are like the flames we kindle here below; they live by struggling upwards, and throw light upon the regions that are above.

Thirdly: *Here on the cross He exhibits the highest confidence in the Eternal.* "And when Jesus had cried with a loud voice, He said, Father, into Thy hands I commend my spirit: and having said thus, He gave up the Ghost." (Luke xxiii. 46.) What unbounded confidence in God do these words express! Confidence in His *presence.* He feels that God is near Him—in immediate contact with Him—so close that He could put His spirit at once into His hands. Confidence in His *power.* He feels that He has that Almighty capacity necessary to guide, to guard, and bless His immortal spirit through all the future of its wondrous history. Confidence in His *love.* His trust in His fatherly affection is as strong as His trust in Almighty power. Hence He yields Himself into His hands. In His death He makes the Eternal the TRUSTEE of that which is of infinitely more value than worlds and systems—Himself. Such confidence as this in God is the characteristic of the highest piety, and the philosophy of an easy death. Piety is the self-dedication to God, not in death only, but in life as well; and when this is done in life, there will be a calm and triumphant death. Stephen felt this, and said, "Lord Jesus, receive my spirit." A life of dedication to God is the only guarantee of a happy death. It is our life which shapes our death, gives a character to our last hour, weaves the moral drapery around our dying couch. "Mark the perfect man, and behold the upright, for the end of that man is peace."

Here, then, on the cross, amidst the inexpressible anguish of His last hours, we see Him exemplifying piety in its highest forms. His moral goodness encircles Him with radiance. Like the rainbow, it spans the clouds of the departing tempest. Let us learn our lessons of piety, not from the conduct of professors, or the *credenda* of sects, but from the cross of Christ. Oh, to be made conformable to the spirit of His death, to catch the moral genius of His dying hours!

We proceed now to look upon Him, according to our plan, as :—

III. THE DESERTED OF HEAVEN. About the ninth hour Jesus cried with a loud voice, saying, "*Eli, Eli, lama sabacthani.*" This expression, *Eli, Eli, lama sabacthani,* is Hebrew in Matthew. Mark has it in Syro-Chaldaic; a dialect which was supposed to have been used by our Saviour and His contemporaries. The expression is, undoubtedly, an ejaculation wrung from Him by the intense sufferings of the moment. It was the cry of dissolving nature. There is a depth of sentiment about this utterance which we cannot fathom. It is said of Luther, when he pondered on this enigmatical utterance, that he continued for a long time without food, sat wide awake, and as motionless as a corpse, in his chair; and when at last he rose from the depths of his cogitations, as from the shaft of a mysterious mine, he broke into an exclamation, "God forsaken of

God: who can understand it?" Though it has depths which our poor intellect cannot reach, we may be benefited by inquiring, with devout humility, into its meaning. The language can only be taken in one of two senses—either as expressing a *fact* or a *feeling*. A *fact* in relation to God, or a *feeling* in relation to Christ. In other words, it must be considered either that God had actually deserted Him, or that Christ merely had the *feeling* that He had done so. The question, therefore, for us to determine is, which is the more probable supposition.

Can we accept the former? Are there any just grounds for believing that the Eternal Father did now so change, either in feeling or conduct, towards His Son, as to warrant the idea of desertion? Did anger now take the place of love in the Divine heart? Did a dark frown of indignation take, for a moment, the place of a Father's smile? Did He, who before declared, " This is my beloved Son, in whom I am well pleased "—now, for a moment, feel, " This is my abhorrent Son, in whom I am displeased "? We confess an utter inability to accept such an idea as this, however popular it may be in some theologies. To us it seems in the last degree repugnant to the character of Him who is immutable in love, and who has pledged Himself never to forsake those who trust in Him; repugnant moreover to the distinct declaration of Christ, " *Therefore doth my Father love me, because I lay down my life.*" (John x. 17.) Christ felt that His giving His life in agony for humanity was rather a reason for Divine love than otherwise.

We are, therefore, left to the acceptance of the other idea, namely, that this cry expresses a feeling of desertion in Christ's mind. Our idea is, that, amidst the dying agonies of the moment, He felt as if the God of infinite love had left Him. Let it not be imagined, that, because it might be only a feeling in the mind of Christ, and not a fact in the Divine conduct, that it is not a terrible reality. So far as the subject is concerned, it is desertion in its most overwhelming force. The fact, unless it be felt, is powerless. Supposing that God in reality forsakes a man, and that man does not feel the fact, the desertion is nothing to him. On the contrary, supposing that no such desertion takes place on God's part, yet, if a man deeply feel it, it is to him the most terrible of realities. Christ, then, we may suppose, had the feeling in its mightiest force. It was only, of course, as a man that He suffered; and, as a man, the anguish of this moment might cloud His consciousness of nearness to Infinite love. It was, moreover, to Him, the hour of darkness at this moment. Satan was at the height of his power, and his huge and hideous proportions, as he passed before the eye of Christ's spirit, would intercept the rays of Divine love, and throw a dark and chilly shadow upon His heart. The feeling seems only to have been momentary; it was just as if hell rolled between Him and the heavens—an eclipse for the time of His moral sun.

Accepting this, then, as the more likely interpretation, the utterance suggests three observations in relation to Christ at this moment: *That His sufferings were associated with the feeling of distance from*

God ; that His feeling of distance from God was associated with a ter-rible amazement ; and that His terrible amazement was associated with confidence in the Divine character.

1. THAT HIS SUFFERINGS WERE ASSOCIATED WITH THE FEELING OF DISTANCE FROM GOD. We make two remarks :—

First: *That it was natural under the circumstances.* There is a something in great suffering to superinduce this feeling in the mind. From the constitution of the soul, we instinctively conclude, that, where the God of infinite love is, there is happiness, and only hap-piness. Unsophisticated reason says, "In Thy presence is fulness of joy." Where the sun is, there is light. Where love is, there is blessedness; and the converse of this—where there is overwhelming suffering, God is absent. Thus Job felt in his trials, and he ex-claimed, "O that I knew where I might find Him !" Thus David felt, "My God, my God, why hast Thou forsaken me ?" And thus the old prophets felt in trial, "Verily Thou art a God that hidest Thyself." Hence, too, souls in anguish involuntarily cry out for God's presence. The feeling, therefore, of Divine desertion in suffering is somewhat natural ; and being natural, is not wrong in itself. An involuntary feeling which agrees not with eternal reali-ties, if it be not cherished, is not wrong. Another remark which we make concerning this feeling is :—

Secondly : *It is ever an element of anguish.* What greater misery can be imagined than a consciousness of being forsaken of God ? Saul felt this ; and in the dark cave of Endor, trembling before a wicked enchantress, he cried, "I am sore distressed, for God hath departed from me, and answereth me no more, neither by prophets nor by dreams." This feeling is the hell of the lost. Conscious banishment from God is perdition. Christ was now permitted to have this feeling, and in this feeling there was a mysterious hell.

2. THAT HIS FEELING OF DISTANCE FROM GOD WAS ASSOCIATED WITH A TERRIBLE AMAZEMENT. "*Why hast Thou forsaken me.*" His faith is tried, His reason seems to stagger. Surprises rush on Him like a wild tempest. His faculties seem baffled with sore astonishment. *Why ?* "It cannot be that I have offended Thee. I came into the world to do Thy will ; and it has been my study and delight to this hour. I am about finishing the work which Thou gavest me to do. I am unconscious of the slightest deviation from Thy will. It has been my meat and my drink to do what Thou hast commanded. Why, then, hast Thou forsaken me ? Surely Thou art not change-able in Thy affections. Thy love is as immutable as Thyself. What can be the reason of this awful desertion ? My disciples forsook me and fled. I knew their weakness, and understood their conduct. But why dost *Thou* forsake me, and leave me in this utter solitude of inexpressible anguish ?" Here, then, the Holy Sufferer seems to have been tried in His reason : the desertion He felt was something most unaccountable and perplexing ; violently clashing, it may be, with His clearest and most established ideas of His Father's wisdom and His Father's love. In His wonderful life, He had not, perhaps, any other trial of His reason equal in mental agony to this. We do

not often find Him thus interrogating Heaven on account of its
mysteries. As a man, of course, He had His intellectual trials, but
His loving and loyal heart would supply such a solution as would
allay distress. Had He not, however, been thus tried in some
measure, He would not have been " in all points tempted like as we
are ;" for we, His poor disciples, are constantly tried in our reason
with questions touching the character of the Eternal, and the procedure of His providence.

3. His TERRIBLE AMAZEMENT WAS ASSOCIATED WITH UNSHAKEN CON-
FIDENCE IN GOD. The felt mystery of His Father's conduct did not
destroy His confidence in His character ; He continues lovingly to
look to Him as His God : " *My God, my God.*" " On other occasions," says Bengel, " He was accustomed to say ' Father ;' now
He says ' My God,' as being in a degree estranged. Yet He does
so twice, and adds, ' My ' with confidence, patience, and self-resig-
nation." There is a lesson for us here. However much our rational
faculties may be confounded by the mysteries of the Divine dealing,
let us never lose confidence in the wisdom and the love of God.
Let us feel, that, although He often seems to hide Himself from us,
and move in ways inscrutable to our poor understanding, that all
His movements are prompted by infinite love, and directed by
unerring intelligence. Let us trust Him where we cannot trace
Him, and feel with Job, " Though He slay me, yet will I trust in
Him." Though He might permit us to be overwhelmed with suffer-
ing, confounded in intellect, and agonized in heart, let us feel that
He is still our God, and in our deepest hour of distress call out,
" My God, my God ! "

We proceed now to look upon Christ as He is suspended upon
the cross, in the other and final aspect in which this history presents
Him.

IV. As THE POWER OF GOD. Though nailed to the cross, and
apparently at the mercy of His malignant foes, He yet exerts a
power altogether supernatural and manifestly Divine. On the
cross He displays a power at once over the *material system* and the
spiritual world.

First : *He displays a power over the material system.* The effects
of His power in this department are seen upon the sun, the earth,
the temple, the bodies of the dead. (1) " *Now from the sixth hour
there was darkness over all the land unto the ninth hour,*" *i.e.*, from
twelve A.M, till three P.M. The forms of expression, " over all the
land," ἐπὶ πᾶσαν τὴν γῆν (Matt.) ; " over the whole land," ἐφ᾽ ὅλην
τὴν γῆν (Mark and Luke)—do not determine how far the darkness
extended. Whether the darkness extended literally over the whole
earth or not, we pass by as a question of no importance. Obviously
it wrapped Jerusalem and its neighbourhood in a mysterious gloom.
There is no accounting for it on natural principles. There is no
known law of nature that can explain it. An eclipse of the sun it
was not, for it was at the time of the passover, and that was at full
moon, when an eclipse is impossible ; besides, a total eclipse can
never last longer than a quarter of an hour, and this darkness held

its rayless empire for three long hours. It was produced, undoubtedly, by the direct *fiat* of Omnipotence, and symbolized some terrible things to the spiritual world. (2) " *The veil of the temple was rent in twain from the top to the bottom.*" There were two veils, one before the holy and one before the most holy place. (Exod. xxvi. 31–36.) This veil symbolized that the way into the holiest of all was not yet made manifest. It excluded all from that sacred spot, and none dared enter save the high-priest, and he only once a year, on the great day of atonement, and then never without the blood of atonement in his hand, which he sprinkled upon and before the mercy-seat seven times (Lev. xvi. 14). That thick veil remained for ages, impressing man with the awfulness and difficulty of approaching the Most High. But now that veil was rent from "top to bottom." Rent, not by human hand, or any secondary cause, but by the will of Him who now, by His death, opened up to universal man a way of free access to God. (3) " *The earth did quake and the rocks rent.*" A great earthquake is said by the Latin writers to have occurred about this time, but it cannot with certainty be identified with the one in the text. With His dying eyes He looked upon the earth and it trembled; with His thoughts He touched the mountains and they smoked. Extraordinary rents and fissures are observed in the rocks near this spot. There they stand in ghastly attitude, as witnesses to attest the terrible fact. (4) " *And the graves were opened, and many bodies of the saints which slept arose, and came out of the graves after His resurrection, and went into the holy city, and appeared unto many.*" This was a grand symbol of the fact that His death had to do with departed as well as existing humanity, and that He swallowed up death in victory. Elsewhere we have referred to these subjects, and we need not enlarge further upon them here.* Such, then, is the power which we see the dying Jesus exert upon the realm of dead matter.

Secondly : *He displays a power over the spiritual world.* This is seen in five things :—First : *In the salvation He vouchsafed to the dying penitent.* There hangs the dying thief. The aggravated sins of a whole life press on his soul with a weight heavy enough to sink him in the lowest hell. He is about sinking into the black profundities of despair. A Divine power, however, touches his soul into penitence and faith, and with his last breath he cries to Jesus for salvation, " Lord, remember me." And what is the result ? That dying One showed Himself mighty to save. He rolled the crushing burden of guilt from the man's conscience. He renovated the man's corrupt nature. He pardoned his sins and cleansed his spirit. He plucked him, as a brand, from the burning. He saved him to an everlasting paradise. " To-day shalt thou be with me in paradise." Here is power, the highest kind of power in the universe, the power to save ruined souls involved in the greatest guilt, and in the last moment of their mortal existence. Christ is indeed the power of God for this purpose. His power is seen :—Secondly : *In*

---

* See " Homilist," vol. ii., page 129.

the authority which He exemplified over the celestial region. This comes out in the wonderful response He gave to the cry of the dying thief, " To-day shalt thou be with me in paradise" (Luke xxiii. 43). By general consent the word paradise here refers to the celestial world—and Christ's words imply a commanding power over that world, a power to go into it Himself, and a power to take others thither. His power extends to all the realms of being that lie beyond the sphere and ken of mortals. Though dying, He felt that the universe was His, and that in person He would soon be exalted above all heavens.* His power is seen:—Thirdly : *In the change which He wrought in the mind of the centurion.* The centurion was the commander of the Roman soldiers who attended at the place of execution. Luke represents him as saying, " *Certainly this was a righteous man.*" As this Roman commander was undoubtedly a polytheist, his exclamation must be regarded, not only as a declaration that Christ was no impostor, but as also indicating a thorough change in his own mind. He passed from Paganism to Christianity ; he reached the conviction of the Messiahship of Jesus. " Truly this was the Son of God." It is worthy of note, that Judas who betrayed Him, Pilate who condemned Him, and now the Roman soldier who superintended His crucifixion, all attest His innocency. The darkened heavens, the quaking earth, the riven rocks, the opening graves, the mysterious reverberations and throes of an earth mantled in sackcloth, were, perhaps, the means to work this conviction into the heart of the centurion. But Christ's power was at once the cause and efficiency of these tremendous means. His power is seen:—Fourthly : *In attracting to Himself His true disciples.* " And many women were there, beholding afar off, which followed Jesus from Galilee, ministering unto Him : and which was Mary Magdalene, and Mary the mother of James and Joses, and the mother of Zebedee's children." These women were His disciples ; they had ministered to Him during His missionary tours in Galilee (Luke viii. 1, 3). They accompanied Him from Galilee, and ministered to His wants on His final journey from Galilee to Jerusalem, and now they stood around His cross. He was the magnet of their souls. He held them there as the sun holds the planets. He here displays a power, therefore, to bind spirits to Himself ; the power of an unearthly excellence and of an unconquerable love— the moral power of God. This power He exerts now in heaven. He is in the midst of the throne, and binds the hierarchies of heaven and the true Church of Christ to Himself. His power is seen :— Fifthly : *In the effect it produced on the consciences of sinners.* " And all the people that came together to that sight, beholding the things that were done, smote their breasts, and returned " (Luke xxiii. 48). " They smote their breasts : " a brief but graphic description of the mingled grief, remorse, and terror which convulsed the souls of those who were spectators of this awful drama. This is only a specimen of that power which His cross has ever exerted to rouse

* For a full development of the truths suggested by the cry of the penitent thief and the response of Christ, see vol. ii., p. 2, new series, 132.

the guilty consciences and break the hard hearts of sinners. The same effect has been produced in all subsequent ages, wherever He has been faithfully exhibited to the spiritual eyes of men as crucified for sinners. It is cheering to believe that scarcely a Sabbath closes during which there have not been thousands who, at the sight of Christ upon the cross, have smote their "breasts" with deep contrition for their sins, and "returned" to their homes to dedicate themselves to the will and service of Heaven.

Thus we have viewed Christ upon the cross in four aspects: as the Victim of Wickedness, as the Exemplar of Religion, as the Deserted of Heaven, and as the Power of God. Our vision is too dim to see a thousandth part of what there is to be seen, and what one day will be discovered in this wonderful scene; and even our limited views are given in forms the most sketchy, in order to suggest to others things we have failed to see. Let us keep our eyes upon this scene. It is the scene for us; the scene we want. Let the cross ever be the most commanding object in our mental horizon. From it may we draw our doctrines of theology and our code of duty! Under its living radiance may we live and labour; there may we die, and rise to the retributions of eternity!

> " The cross ! it takes our guilt away;
>   It holds the fainting spirit up;
> It cheers with hope the gloomy day,
>   And sweetens every bitter cup.
> It makes the coward spirit brave,
>   And nerves the feeble arm for fight ;
> It takes the terror from the grave,
>   And gilds the bed of death with light.
> The balm of life, the cure of woe,
>   The measure and the pledge of love,
> The sinner's refuge here below,
>   The angel's theme in heaven above."

Matthew 27:57-61

The Burial of Christ : a Display of a Threefold Power

From the various references in the evangelical record to Joseph of Arimathea and Nicodemus, we gather that they were both men of *worldly wealth* and *social influence*. Both were members of the great council of the nation; sustained a good moral reputation; and also felt a considerable interest in the history of Jesus Christ.* They now met at the cross, in order to pay their tribute of affection, which, hitherto, they had been too timid to avow.

* In the third chapter of John, we find Nicodemus as an inquirer; and in the seventh, timidly siding in the council with Christ, saying, " Doth our law judge any man before it hear him, and know what he doeth ? " In relation to Joseph, Mark tells us, that he was an " honourable counsellor, who waited for the kingdom ; " pronounces him " a good man and just," and tells us, that " he had not consented to the deed of them " who sentenced Jesus to death.

The incident illustrates a *threefold force*, to which all *good* men are subject in this life.

I. HERE IS THE POWER OF THE WORLD. What prevented these men from *declaring*, up to this moment, that attachment to Christ, which they unquestionably felt? The WORLD. There were here, perhaps, three elements of *worldly* power that influenced them in the matter.

First: *Wealth*. It would seem that the Jews resolved, that, whosoever confessed that Jesus was the Christ, should be cast out of the synagogue, and be entirely excommunicated. Excommunication, amongst the Jews, involved the sacrifice of *civil* rights and privileges as well as religious. The rich man, in those days, who followed Christ, would lose his wealth. The home of comfort and luxury would have to be exchanged for a state of penury and want. Decision for Christ was always a question in those days between principle and property—conscience and cash. Hence, Christ frequently told His hearers that if they followed Him, they would have to sacrifice their worldly all. Neither Joseph nor Nicodemus had sufficient moral strength to sacrifice their worldly possessions for Christ.

Secondly: *Popularity*. They were in elevated positions; members of the Sanhedrim; looked up to and honoured by the populace. The desire of power, and the love of social approbation, which belong to us all, would be strengthened in them by their exalted office. Now, if they had followed Christ, all this popularity would have gone at once; they would be execrated, instead of praised; "for of the people, there was none with Him." This popularity they had not moral strength enough to sacrifice; "they loved the praise of men more than the praise of God."

Thirdly: *Caste*. They were members of a certain class—the highest class in Jewish society. The whole class not only stood aloof from Christ, but cherished and displayed the most malignant hostility towards Him. Class-feelings are always powerful. Because none of "the rulers believed on Him," these men were too weak to come out on His side.

Such are the elements of worldly power, which, probably, acted on these men, and prevented them from avowing publicly their attachment to the Son of God. Ah! and such elements are at work now, and though not so strong as in the days of those men, yet strong enough to keep millions away from Christ.

II. HERE IS THE POWER OF THE CROSS. What was it that now brought forth these timid men?—brought them forth to Pilate to beg the body of Him, to whom, when alive, they were afraid to avow their attachment? It was the cross. There was something about His death that roused them to manly energy. There were two *wonders* connected with His death which would tend to produce this effect.

First: *The material*. The rending of the veil, the riving of the rocks, the quaking of the earth, the darkening of the sun at high noon, the rising of the dead, the mysterious quiverings of nature at every point as if struck with mortal anguish; these wonders must have produced a deep impression upon the most sceptic spectator, but much deeper upon those in whose hearts there "lurked a latent love."

Secondly : *The moral.* To a reflective mind, these wonders are far more impressive. See the *moral majesty* of Him who dies between two malefactors, and amidst the furious rage of a maddened populace. *His reply to the prayer of the dying thief; the interest He displayed in His mother; the prayers He presented for His murderers; the surrender of His spirit to God; the deep, calm, and unconquerable love that He displayed.* In all these there was "a still small voice," a soul-penetrating one. All whose spiritual ear could catch the sound, must have said, "Truly this was the Son of God." These men, undoubtedly, felt the power of all this; and as they now handled the mangled, lifeless frame, many a tear, we may suppose, of self-reproach fell as they thought of their past unfaithful and unmanly conduct. Thus, the power of the cross overcame in them the power of the world; and this *cross* is the power, and the only power, by which we can overcome the power of the world. "God forbid that I should glory, save in the cross of our Lord Jesus Christ."

III. HERE IS THE POWER OF PROVIDENCE. Upwards of seven hundred years before this, it was predicted that "*His grave was appointed with the wicked; but with the rich man was His tomb.*" Up to this moment, nothing seemed more unlikely than that He should have a tomb with the rich. It seemed clear that His body would be thrown with those of the other malefactors into the valley of Gehenna, or into some such execrable place. But now, at the last moment, this old prophecy meets its fulfilment. These men are the agents; they act freely, separately, and probably without the slightest knowledge of the prediction; and yet they act out the predestined plan of God. *Here is the power of God over all events and actions.* This should teach us,—

First : *That the world is not in human hands.* There is a Divine power over us. "Him, being delivered by the determinate counsel and foreknowledge of God, ye have taken."

Secondly : *That the cross is the great organ of Divine power.* It was through the cross these men were now drawn to their work. This is the "Arm of the Lord revealed."

Thirdly : *That Divine purposes, however long delayed, will one day be realized.* Ages may transpire—but God does not forget His word. All opposition to His counsels is fruitless. "Why do the heathen rage?"

Matthew 27:62-66; 28:1-10

The Resurrection of Christ; or, the Vicissitudes of Truth

There are three aspects in which the resurrection of Christ is generally and properly looked upon:—First: *As a confirmation of the truth of Christianity.* Assuming the resurrection of Christ to be a fact—and you must strike a deadly blow at all history not to regard it as such—it is a most incontrovertible argument for Christianity. It shows beyond all question, that Jesus was, what the old prophets had represented Him to be, and what He too had represented Himself to be—associated with omnipotent energy. The apostle tells us that He was "declared to be the Son of God with power, by the resurrection from the dead." It is also looked upon, Secondly: *As a pattern and pledge of the resurrection of the good.* "Now is Christ risen from the dead, and become the first-fruits of them that slept." "The sheaf of the first-fruits," which, under the law of Moses, the people brought unto the priest to "wave before the Lord," was at once a sample and security of the whole crops yet in the fields to be gathered in. As He rose we shall rise, and our vile bodies shall be made like unto His glorious body. It is, moreover, looked upon, Thirdly: *As a symbol of man's true spiritual elevation.* "If ye, then, be risen with Christ, seek those things which are above, where Christ sitteth at the right hand of God." In the true spiritual culture of humanity there is a "crucifixion," a "burial," and a "resurrection." But whilst these are interesting and instructive aspects, in which the resurrection of Christ is generally looked upon, we intend at present to turn it to another account which, although uncommon, is obviously legitimate, and will, we trust, be profitable. We shall regard Christ's burial and resurrection as representing *the vicissitudes* of truth.

I. HERE WE HAVE TRUTH SUPPRESSED BY WICKED MEN. "Command, therefore, that the sepulchre be made sure." Why were they so anxious on this subject? Not because (1) He was an alien—for He was a Jew; not because (2) on account of His miracles—these were liked; not because (3) of any wrong in His moral character—for they could find no fault in Him; nor because (4) there was anything peculiarly repulsive in his bodily person. *It was because of the truths* that He represented—the truths that flowed from His lips, and were embodied in His acts. Had His body been the organ and advocate of their views, they would have hailed it to their homes, and pressed it to their bosoms. This hatred and dread of Him arose from the *truths* He represented. When we speak, therefore, of their endeavour to keep Him in the grave as the *suppression of truth*, we are not trifling with Scripture—we are not using the language of accommodation,—we are designating the very spirit of the act. Their command to "make sure" the sepulchre, may be translated, Keep *down the truth;* gag intellect—thought—conscience—speech.

Why were these priests and Pharisees so anxious to suppress the truths that Jesus represented?

First: *Because they clashed with their prejudices, pride, and interests.* They had a prejudice that the Messiah would be a great man in the *worldly* sense, the wealthiest in worldly possession, the mightiest in worldly rule, the most triumphant in worldly victories, the most magnificent in worldly pageantry, greater than any of their Solomons or Cæsars, who would make Jerusalem the Rome of the world. They sustained a religious position of influence which flattered their pride,—they were the religious leaders and idols of the people; and they drew revenues which sustained them in affluence and luxury by imposing upon the superstitious credulity of an ignorant populace.

Now, the truths of Jesus struck at once at their *prejudice, pride, and interest.* He taught, that He, the poor Galilean, was the true Messiah—this struck their *prejudice;* that true greatness was not in elevated positions, nor in gilded externalisms; but in great thoughts, noble purposes, and Divine aspirations—this struck at their *pride;* He taught, that piety was a thing entirely between the individual man and his God, and that worship required no particular temple, ceremony, or office—and this struck at their *interests.* These three things have always sought to bury truth; they have always been, and still are, active to make " sure its sepulchre." Certain professions, trades, institutions, and churches, like these priests and Pharisees, can only hope to flourish, or even stand, as they make " *sure the sepulchre* "of buried truth.

Secondly : *Because they had no confidence in their own principles.* Had they been quite sure that He was an impostor, and not the true Messiah—that what He taught was erroneous, and that they were thoroughly right in doctrine and practice, would they have been anxious about making " sure the sepulchre "? No ! they would have been perfectly indifferent. But the fact was, they had more faith in Him than themselves. The man of true faith is never found amongst your little, nervous, fussy, talkative religionists, who are ever anxiously hounding out heresies. " He that believeth shall not make haste." True faith has always a dignified calmness and perfect self-possession. It is not over-anxious about making " sure the sepulchre " of that which it does not believe in. It says, rather, " He that has a dream, let him tell it."

II. HERE WE HAVE TRUTH EMANCIPATED BY THE GREAT GOD. " In the end of the Sabbath, as it began to dawn towards the first day of the week, came Mary Magdelene and the other Mary to see the sepulchre, and behold there was an earthquake ; for the angel of the Lord descended from heaven, and came and rolled away the stone from the door of the sepulchre " (1–4). The extraordinary incident recorded in these verses we may regard as suited to illustrate two things :—

First : *The short-sightedness and helplessness of the opponents of truth.* We may suppose that these priests and Pharisees, and all the religious functionaries of Jerusalem, were not a little delighted on the Sabbath-day that Christ was in the grave. The thought that He who had been exciting the country for three years in a way unfavourable to them, was now in the grave, that the sepulchre was sealed, and made sure, and that sixteen brave Roman soldiers were guarding it, was not a little gratifying to them. Many a congratulation, we may suppose, was exchanged that day by these men, as they met in the streets, or in the Temple. All would now hope that the religious mind of the country would settle down into its wonted quietude, and that things would go on as usual. Little did they imagine that the efforts they employed to suppress this obnoxious thing, would so swell the tide of its influence, as to carry the mind of the world with it. No stones, nor seals, nor craft, nor soldiery, nor legislation, will succeed in permanently keeping down the truth.
It illustrates:—

Secondly: *The tremendous phenomena which are sometimes connected with the emancipation of truth.* Here were the " earthquake," and the " angel," and the Roman soldiers " falling as dead men." There was buried truth raised on Sinai of old, and what a convulsion ! How Moses and the people trembled ! There was buried truth raised by Hezekiah, when he found the book of the law ; and how it struck with terror the young king and his people ! There was buried truth raised by Peter on the day of Pentecost, and thousands felt the shock of a moral earthquake. There was buried truth raised by Luther, and all Europe was convulsed. There will be buried truth raised in the final judgment, and how appalling will be the effects ! indeed, it is ever so, *individually* as well as socially, that the rising of a buried moral truth is attended with much that is terrible. What are all the terrors of conviction for sin, but the bursting into life and power of long-buried truths ? These Roman soldiers, who now fell as dead, had, I have no doubt, like men of their degraded class, often boasted of their courage and feats of bloody daring, but they were too cowardly to stand erect before the moral Majesty of risen truth.

It illustrates :—

Thirdly : *The certain and punctual fulfilment of the Divine word.* It was predicted that He should rise on the "third day," and the third day He rose. God has promised that truth shall " spring from the earth," and it will. How much of Divine truth is buried here—buried under stones of ignorance, sensuality, superstition, and worldliness ! But it shall rise. Yes ! neither the craft of priests nor the force of governments shall keep it down ; its myriad graves shall send forth their dead.

III. HERE WE HAVE TRUTH SOUGHT, DISCOVERED, AND PROCLAIMED, BY TRUE DISCIPLES.

First: *Here you have truth sought.* "Early in the morning came Mary Magdalene and the other Mary to see the sepulchre." (1) They sought Jesus with *loving* hearts, to do Him homage. The real *truth-seeker* is always inspired, in his search, by love for the object sought. (2) They were *supernaturally* directed in their search ; "And the angel answered and said unto the woman," &c. (verses 5, 6, 7).

Secondly: *Here you have truth discovered* (v. 9). How full of worship are the discoverers !

Thirdly : *Here you have truth proclaimed.* Having found Christ, they were commanded " to go into Galilee," &c. (v. 10).

Matthew 28:11-15

The Resurrection of Christ : an Argument for the fact drawn from the Explanation of Enemies

Dr. Arnold has said, in relation to the resurrection of Christ, " I have been used for many years to study the history of other times, and to examine and weigh the evidences of those who have written about them; and I know of no one fact in the history of mankind which is proved by better and fuller evidence of every sort to the mind of a fair inquirer, than the great sign that God has given us, that Christ died and rose again from the dead." The proof of the Redeemer's resurrection the third day, it is granted, rests entirely upon the accounts furnished us in the New Testament. The genuineness and credibility, therefore, of Gospel narratives must of course be assumed in the argument. The assertion of Spinoza and his disciples, that the resurrection of Christ was an event that took place not in the material but in the moral world, and that the evangelical narrative is only a material representation of a spiritual fact, has long since been exploded as one of the greatest extravagances of sceptical philosophies.

Arguments for the fact drawn from the Gospel records are of two kinds, the *one from the conduct of Christ's friends, and the other from that of His enemies.* That from the former is perhaps the most convincing, and is consequently the most frequently employed. There are different ways of stating it. Our statement of it would include two general propositions :—

First: *That the apostles had the most powerful faith in the fact.* They were soon convinced by His appearance to them, and having been once convinced, they *never* after seemed to have had any doubt on the question. The powerfulness of their faith will be seen when the following things are considered: (1) They were unanimous in their declaration of it, a few days after, on the very spot on which it occurred, and that to men who were prepared to do anything to conceal the fact. Had the apostles waited some months before they began its proclamation, and had they gone to a distance to do so, and confined their declaration to those who sympathized with them, there would not, of course, have been such evidence as to the powerfulness of their conviction on the point. But they declare the fact at once, standing as it were upon the very margin of the empty sepulchre, and to thousands who had every opportunity of being satisfied as to the truth or the falseness of their statement. (2) In their unanimous declaration of it, they acted in direct opposition to their previous beliefs and to their worldly interests. Had their prejudices been in favour of His resurrection, one might have accounted, in some measure, for their readiness to believe in it, apart from the power of the evidence. But what was the fact? They did not expect His resurrection; when He died they thought it was all over. Hence we find that when Mary Magdalene and the other women first conveyed the information of His resurrection to the apostles, " *their words seemed to them as idle tales* " (Luke xxiv. 11). Hence, too, when Peter and John had actually looked into the sepulchre, and saw the linen clothes lying, and no Jesus there, it is said, after that, " *That they knew not the Scripture, that He must rise again from the dead* " (John xx. 9). And hence, also, Thomas would not believe in His resurrection until he had himself handled the very marks of the wounds of Christ. How *powerful*, therefore, must have been the evidence to have given them at once so strong a faith in an event so directly opposed to all their preconceived notions. But the declaration of this fact was not only contrary to their prejudices, but to all their worldly interests. By this very act they set themselves in direct hostility to the authorities of their country and the spirit of their age, and thus exposed themselves to the greatest privations, to persecutions, and to death itself. (3) They, by their declaration of the fact, induced thousands of the very enemies of Christ to believe in it, and that close to the time and near to the very spot on which it occurred. Peter, standing up on the Day of Pentecost, with the sepulchre of Christ almost under his eye, and the scene of Christ's crucifixion fresh in the memory of all, declared before assembled thousands His resurrection from the dead, and thousands believed it, were pierced with its moral meaning, and were converted to the unpopular faith. And thus it went on, until in the course of a few years we find tens of thousands of Jews, as well as Gentiles, believing in it with a faith by which they were prepared to suffer even death itself, and that in its most horrid forms. How can this fact be accounted for? What was the power by which these few poor illiterate disciples induced such thousands to believe in the fact? Had they been men of the loftiest genius, of the strongest powers of argument, and the most commanding gifts of oratory; had they, by education, become masters of logic, and invested with the most persuasive charms of eloquence, would they by all this have succeeded in converting such numbers to such an unpopular creed, if in that creed they had anything like doubt? Certainly not. The philosophy of their success is this,—the power of their own faith, and the power which every man has of convincing others of facts which he intelligently and earnestly believes himself. All these remarks go to show the truth of our proposition, that the apostles had the most powerful faith in the fact of Christ's resurrection. The other proposition which the statement of our argument would include, is,—

Secondly: *That the apostles had every opportunity for thoroughly satisfying themselves on the point.* It might be said that our first proposition asserting the power of their faith amounts not to much, unless it can be shown that they had sufficient opportunities of thoroughly understanding the evidence. A man may get a strong faith of a thing from a misrepresentation or a mistake. What opportunities, therefore, had these apostles for knowing that Jesus had risen from the dead? Their opportunities were abundant. Christ appeared and lived amongst them for forty days after His resurrection. No less than ten different times did He appear to them in different numbers and in different circumstances.* Once there were even five hundred present. He spoke to them long discourses, He ate with them, He allowed them to handle Him, and by " many infallible proofs" He worked the fact of His resurrection into their consciousness as the most undebatable of all truths.

* There are outlines of discourses on all these appearances in the second and third volumes of the " Homilist," second series.

Such is a very *brief outline* of one form of the argument that may be drawn from the conduct of His friends. An eloquent writer, in summing up such an argument as this, sketches a number of extravagant suppositions that must be advanced if the resurrection of Christ is denied. " It must be supposed that men who have been imposed on in the most odious and cruel manner in the world, hazarded their dearest enjoyments for the glory of an impostor. It must be supposed that ignorant and illiterate men, who had neither reputation, fortune, nor eloquence, possessed the art of fascinating the eyes of all the Church. It must be supposed either that five hundred persons were deprived of their senses at a time, or that they were all deceived in the plainest matters of fact; or that multitudes of false witnesses had found out the secret of never contradicting themselves or one another, and of being always uniform in their testimony. It must be supposed that the most expert courts of judicature could not find out a shadow of contradiction in a palpable imposture. It must be supposed that the apostles, sensible men in other cases, chose precisely those places and those times which were most unfavourable to their views. It must be supposed that millions madly suffered imprisonments, tortures, and crucifixions, to spread an illusion. It must be supposed that ten thousand miracles were wrought in favour of falsehood, or all these facts must be denied; and then it must be supposed that the apostles were idiots; that the enemies of Christianity were idiots; and that all the primitive Christians were idiots."

But our text and our purpose leads us to examine more particularly *the argument drawn from the conduct of His enemies;* and I shall confine myself to the conduct of the men who are exposed in the verses I have read. We find here, that when the Roman soldiers who had been appointed to watch the sepulchre of Christ appeared before the chief priests, informing them that Christ had left His grave, they at once assembled together to consider as to the best way of so accounting for Christ's absence from the grave, as to enable them to deny the fact of His resurrection. After their united, and we may be sure, earnest deliberation, the expedient they adopted was this,—to bribe the soldiers with large sums of money to report that the disciples came by night and stole Him away while they slept. Now there are *three impossibilities* developed in this narrative, which I think go a great way to show the *impossibility of denying the resurrection of Christ from the dead.*

I. It was impossible for these enemies to deny that Christ had, by some means or other, left the grave. *This fact, observe, is taken for granted in their conduct recorded in these verses.* If it could have been denied, of course the " watch " would not have returned with the report to the chief priests. If He had been still in His grave, there would be no reason for their appearance. That the grave was empty, they knew they could not deny. The disciples had looked into the empty tomb, and spread the report which was, perhaps, widely circulated before these soldiers left the sepulchre. We read only of " some of the watch " who came to the chief priests; perhaps the other portion of the soldiers were so astounded at the fact, and, it may be, so convinced with its divinity, as to regard any attempt of the Jewish council to deny it as both futile and wicked, and therefore they would not appear with their comrades. Nor did one of the members of the council intimate a doubt as to the fact. They agreed that Jesus, who had been buried by Joseph, one of their number, in his own grave, and whose burial had been witnessed by Nicodemus, another of their own number, was not in the sepulchre; there was nothing there but the grave-clothes in which He had been folded. That the grave, in which, perhaps, they themselves had seen Christ put on the Friday, with a large stone upon it sealed with a Roman seal, was now empty, they could not deny. It was one of those facts which are so thoroughly palpable as to admit not of the slightest doubt; and hence they proceeded at once, not with any attempt to deny it, but simply to invent such an explanation of it as would enable them to deny that He Himself had risen from the dead.

II. IT WAS IMPOSSIBLE FOR THEM TO GIVE ANY OTHER EXPLANA-TION THAN THAT WHICH THEY NOW INVENTED. *Their grand object was to deny that He rose Himself from the dead; and how could they explain His absence from the grave in any other way than they did?* If He did not rise Himself, He must have been raised by men; and if by men, the men must either have been His enemies or His friends. It could not be entertained for a moment that His enemies stole Him away, for the enemy had every motive, and employed every power to secure Him in His grave. The very day after His burial, we read that "the chief priests and Pharisees came together to Pilate, saying, Sir, we remember that that deceiver said while He was yet alive, After three days I will rise again; command there-fore that the sepulchre be made sure until the third day, lest His disciples come by night and steal Him away, and say unto the people, He is risen from the dead: so the last error shall be worse than the first." To this Pilate replied, "Ye have a watch: go your way, make it as sure as you can; so they went and made the sepulchre sure, sealing the stone, and setting a watch." Here, then, you have the great council of the Jewish nation expressing the *strongest anxiety* to keep Him in His sepulchre, and securing the Roman power to make the most effective efforts to prevent Him from being taken away. They were, therefore, shut up to the ex-planation which they gave, namely, that "*the disciples stole Him away.*" They had to explain His absence from the grave in such a way as would enable them to deny His resurrection; and this they could not do by saying that His enemies had taken Him away, for their wishes and whole conduct had notoriously proved the con-trary. *The explanation they gave, therefore, was the only one they could give.*

III. IT WAS IMPOSSIBLE FOR THIS, THE ONLY EXPLANATION THEY COULD GIVE, TO BE CREDITED. First: *It is in the last degree impro-bable that the disciples could have stolen Him away even if they had attempted it.* Who could suppose that the frail and timorous disciples, of whom the boldest—Peter—had not the courage before a servant-girl, to acknowledge Christ, and all of whom, when Christ was taken in the garden of Gethsemane, were struck with fear, and "fled!" Who can suppose that such persons would dare, not only the whole Jewish council, but the power of Rome? Who could suppose that they would attempt to break the Roman seal, to defy and overcome the Roman soldiers who were there sworn to guard that awful place? If they did it, they must have done it either by bribing the soldiers, or overcoming them. Poor men! they had nothing wherewith to bribe the soldiers, and as to overcoming them by force, the idea is absurd. Even one minute's contest with them at such a time, when the moon was full, and the vicinity crowded with men who had come up to keep the Passover, would scarcely have failed to have roused the neighbourhood, and thus led to their detection,—and their detection would have ended in their ruin. Who, therefore, can believe for a moment that the disciples ever made the attempt?

Secondly: *It is in the last degree improbable that all the Roman watch were asleep.* The short time the soldiers had to watch, renders their sleeping improbable. There were four watches in the course of the night; each watch, therefore, would only be for two or three hours at a time. If there was only one man at a time, the chances are that that one would not have slept;—but there were many. No doubt, Pilate, to satisfy the fears of the Jewish council, sent a large number there on duty. How absurd to suppose that all slept when the hours of duty were so short! Add to all this the terrible penalty the Roman soldier would subject himself to, if found sleeping on duty. Were he found sleeping on duty, death would have been the result.

Thirdly: *It is in the last degree improbable that the Jewish council would have voted large sums of money merely to have reported a truth.* "They gave large money* unto the soldiers, saying, Say ye, His disciples came by night and stole Him away while we slept." "Say ye!" "Why even tell them to *say* it? If it is true, they *will* say it fast enough to satisfy the social communicativeness of their nature, as well as to please their master. But still more, why *pay* them to say it? The communication of such an event is a pleasant thing, its own reward, and money is not required as a motive. The money proves the falsehood, the bribe exposes the imposture. Men may require a bribe to suppress truth, but not to declare it. Truth has an instinct that struggles evermore for utterance.

Fourthly: *It is in the last degree improbable that on the assumption the soldiers slept they could know what transpired.* If they slept, how were they to know what had happened? This explanation of these chief priests and elders, I submit, carries with it its own condemnation. It is a falsehood which I have no doubt took a great deal of

---

* ἀργύρια ἱκανά. Like the French "assez," enough to satisfy the soldiers, so as to secure their acquiescence. ἱκανός generally means "sufficient," "competent," here in quantity or value; in dignity or moral worth, Matt. iii. 11; in ability, efficiency, power, 2 Cor. iii. 5, 6; 2 Tim. ii. 2.

thought and discussion in its fabrication, but which carries with it at the same time its own contradiction.

Now, when it is remembered that this Jewish council comprised some seventy or more men ; that some of these men were sharp lawyers, and others possessing all the craftiness of a mercenary and narrow-minded priesthood ; and that after deliberation, this is the only explanation they could furnish for the absence of Christ from His grave; we feel that their preposterous explanation is, in itself, a sufficient proof that Christ " *rose from the dead according to the Scriptures.*"

In looking at the whole argument we are ready to exclaim with the apostle, " If Christ is not risen from the dead, our faith is vain : " in fact, faith in everything is vain. Our faith in historic statement is vain ; if this fact is without foundation, there is no fact in history *that can be sustained.* Our faith in moral character is vain. If we cannot believe in such a character as that presented of Christ in the evangelical record, where can we find a character to trust in ? Yet, if He rose not from the dead He was an impostor. Our faith in common sense is vain. To account for His absence from the grave in the way in which the enemies have done, involves a violation of the dictates of our rational nature. Our faith in Christianity is vain. If He has not risen from the dead the whole system falls to pieces, as a building whose foundation has given way. Our faith in the future improvement of our world and in a future life is vain. We are the miserable victims of deception. We have been all our life building houses on the sand.

But, thank God, He " has risen from the dead." He has risen, and thus demonstrated the divinity of His power, and the sufficiency of His atonemont. He has risen, and thus fulfilled the predictions of the old prophets, and verified the old Scriptures. He has risen, and thus given a reality and grandeur to that character of His, which His biographers have sketched. He has risen, and thus laid the firm ground of hope for our acceptance with Heaven, for the general resurrection of the dead, and for life everlasting.

> " Up, and away !—
>   Thy Saviour's gone before ;
> Why dost thou stay,
>   Dull soul ? Behold the door
> Is open, and His precept bids thee rise,
> Whose power hath vanquished all thine enemies."
>
> GEO. HERBERT.

Matthew 28:16-20

Christ's Appearance to His Disciples at Galilee

The appearance of Christ recorded in these verses is by far the most *public* of any that took place. It is generally supposed that, besides the eleven mentioned by Matthew, there were also the five hundred referred to by Paul. This formed a large assembly of spectators, who met according to Christ's own appointment on some lonely mountain in Galilee. Whether it was on the Mount of Transfiguration, or on the brow of some other Galilean hill, is scarcely worth speculation. It was, we may rest assured, on one of those commanding scenes of nature's solitude, where, under the eye of day, He could best display His resurrection body to the assembled hundreds.

Three remarks are suggested in relation to this great meeting:—

I. ALL WHO NOW MEET HIM DO SO IN OBEDIENCE TO HIS APPOINTMENT. In the preceding verses (7–10) we are told that as the women, who at the sepulchre had been spoken to by an angel, and commanded to go and tell Christ's disciples that He would be seen of them in Galilee, Christ Himself met them on the way, and said to them, " *Go tell my brethren that they go into Galilee, and there shall they see me.*" In accordance with this command, this meeting now takes place; the women discharge their message to the disciples; the disciples assembled, and Christ, true to His promise, was there. His meeting them thus by appointment serves two important services,— First: *It served to give them the best opportunity of satisfying themselves as to the reality of His resurrection.* He did not rush on them unexpectedly, take them by surprise, and carry away their judgment by a sudden flood of wonder and astonishment. They came prepared: they had hours, probably days, to think about the wonderful meeting. We may suppose that the subject revolved in their minds in all its conceivable aspects. These five hundred, therefore, ascended that mountain, not as wild fanatics, but as men of calm and deliberate thought. Secondly: *It served to demonstrate the fidelity of Christ's word, and the conscious rectitude of His character.* He promised to be there, and there He was. If His promise specified the hour or minute of meeting, He to the hour or minute was there. Christ ever keeps His word. "Heaven and earth shall pass away," etc. But His conscious rectitude is evinced here as well as, fidelity. Had He been an impostor, would He have acted thus? Would He have invited hundreds of men to meet Him out in open day? Impostors never act thus. Nothing but conscious rectitude could have challenged this publicity.

II. ALL WHO NOW MEET HIM EXPERIENCE NOT THE SAME KIND OF FEELING. Some " *worshipped,*" and some " *doubted.*" "And when they saw Him they worshipped, but some doubted." Most probably the great body of them worshipped;—felt their spirits borne aloft with the sentiments of gratitude, reverence, and adoration. They felt, perhaps, as Peter felt on the Mount of Transfiguration;— " Lord, it is good to be here." But some " *doubted.*" A few who had a little more of dry logic than Divine life in them, were not, it would seem, perfectly satisfied on the subject of His resurrection. They had doubts. There are three classes of doubters. There are the *innocent* doubters;—a class of nervous, moody, hypochondriacal persons, who are almost too weak to believe in anything. Their intellects grasp nothing; they see nothing distinctly; they live in a kind of mental fog. There are *virtuous* doubters. Men who hold back their credence till more evidence come; men who would believe, but cannot, until they get more proof,—which proof they earnestly and sincerely seek. These are honest doubters; to this class the disciple Thomas belonged. Then there are *wicked* doubters. Men who, because they hate the truth presented, reject all evidence, and eagerly seize every idea or circumstance that will lend a sanction to their unbelief. To which of these classes of doubters this assembly belonged, we cannot exactly say. It is not likely, however, that any of the latter class were there. The statement here that some "worshipped and some doubted," shows two things :—First : *The transparent honesty of this biographer of Christ.* Had it been Matthew's object to write up a character, to invest his subject with the attributes of an all-commanding hero, he would not have said concerning any of those who met Christ after His resurrection, "Some doubted." He would have said that *all* "worshipped,"— that they were all enthusiastic in their admiration, &c. Secondly : *The freedom of thought allowed to those who were the witnesses of Christ's resurrection.* Had all in that large meeting felt exactly the same, had their idea and impression of Christ been thoroughly identical, the thing would have been so unusual and unnatural that we might have concluded that they were under some magic spell or supernatural enchantment. But the fact that some "worshipped" and some "doubted," shows that every mind in the vast assembly was free. Christ allows men liberty of thought in relation to Himself; and this being the case, some men will doubt, though He stand before their naked eye, sends His voice into their ear, and breathes His divine Spirit all around them.

III. ALL WHO NOW MEET HIM RECEIVE THE SAME EVANGELIZING COMMISSION. "Go ye therefore and preach to all nations, baptizing them," &c. Observe,—First : *The authority on which the commission is founded.* It is on the authority of Him on whom all power is conferred, "All power is given to me," &c. From which expression we learn that Christ's power is *universal* and *delegated.* Observe,— Secondly : *The work which this commission requires.* The work here seems to include two things : (1) *Bringing those who are out of the system into it.* "Teach all nations." The word "teach" here is not a translation of the same Greek word as that translated "teaching" in the next verse.—Μαθητεύσατε. The sense of this word is, *make disciples,* proselytise them, bring them over to my religion ; and in this work the same ceremony which has ever been employed in proselyting men from heathenism to Judaism, is to be employed, namely, baptism. "Baptizing them." Proselytes to the Jewish religion were baptized, infants as well as adults. Christ here as in the Passover turns an old ceremony to a new account. All that is said about the *mode* of administering this rite is alone that which is of any importance ;—it is profoundly *religious.* The subjects are to be received into this Divine system of truth in "the name of the Father," who is the author of it; "the Son," who is the substance of it; and "the Spirit," who is the effective applier of it to the hearts of men. The glory of this old initiatory rite is, that it is *symbolic* of the two great truths which enter into the very essence of Christianity; namely, that human nature is so morally corrupt, even in its infant stages, that it requires the application of an extraneous influence to meeten it for the kingdom of God. The work here includes (2) *An indoctrinating of those who are brought into it, into a practical observance of its holy truths.* "Teaching them to *observe* all things whatsoever I have commanded." The *initiatory* work having been done, this is the work to be pursued. The proselyte having been brought in, is to be *practically* taught. For a specimen of the things which Christ commanded, see Matthew v., and John xv. Διδάσκοντες,—teaching, is the word generally employed to designate the work both of Christ and His apostles, in their endeavours to instruct and edify the minds of men. And this is the work we have now to do for men whe theoretically and by profession attach themselves to the Christian religion. Indeed, the former part of the work but seldom comes within the province of men here in England; for most are nominal Christians. Missionaries are pre-eminently our modern proselytizers. Our work here now, is to *teach men to observe the commands of Christ;*—to stimulate them, "to deny ungodliness and worldly lusts." As ye have received Christ Jesus the Lord, so walk ye in Him.

Two facts lend their support to this twofold division of evangelizing labour which we have thus indicated. (1) *That multitudes in the New Testament are represented as being disciples of Christ who were not vitally united to Him.* And, (2) *Thousands were baptized by John, and thousands more by the disciples of Christ, who had no faith in Jesus Christ.*

Thirdly: *The extent which this commission comprehends.* "All nations." It is not to be confined to the Jewish people. The Gospel is to be limited by no religious, politic, or geographic, boundary. It is race-wide in its provisions and aims. "All nations." Are there any nations where there are not children? If not, where is your authority for excluding children from baptism? Observe,—

Fourthly: *The promise with which this commission is associated.* "Lo, I am with you alway, even unto the end." I am with you:— not my system of truth merely, not my influence merely; exerted either by my truths or my servants: but *I* Myself am with *you*. Not merely in your corporate capacity, but with you individually. "*Alway.*" Not now and then merely; but through all the periods of your existence, unto "the end of the world;" not merely the end of the Jewish age but the end of all ages. Here is the sublime encouragement. It is a promise not made to ecclesiastics, but to disciples, not to prelates and popes, but to Christian men, even in the humblest capacity. Brothers! let us take heart and pursue our labours. We are ignorant, we are weak, and we are dying; but we have wisdom, power, and eternal life ever at our side.